IGNATIAN PEDAGOGY

Classic and Contemporary Texts on Jesuit Education from St. Ignatius to Today

Commissioned by
the Secretariat for Education
of the Society of Jesus

Edited by
José Mesa, S.J.,
Secretary for Education of the Society of Jesus

LOYOLA PRESS.
A JESUIT MINISTRY
Chicago

LOYOLA PRESS.
A JESUIT MINISTRY

3441 N. Ashland Avenue
Chicago, Illinois 60657
(800) 621-1008
www.loyolapress.com

Print
ISBN-13: 978-0-8294-4595-4
ISBN-10: 0-8294-4595-1

PDF
ISBN-13: 978-0-8294-4596-1
ISBN-10: 0-8294-4596-X

Library of Congress Control Number: 2017943738

Printed in the United States of America.

17 18 19 20 21 22 23 Tshore 10 9 8 7 6 5 4 3 2 1

Contents

INTRODUCTION

In February 1556, just a few months before the death of Saint Ignatius, Fr. Pedro Ribadeneyra, S.J., commissioned by Saint Ignatius himself, wrote the following words to King Philip II of Spain: "All the goodness in Christianity and of the whole world depends on the proper education of the youths." With these words Ribadeneyra exemplifies the belief among early Jesuits of the apostolic importance of schooling. His words also clearly illustrate the difference between the first companions who had founded the Society with the idea of serving God and the Church through preaching and mobility and the emerging reality of founding and staffing schools.

Many Jesuits will become schoolmasters, and the government of the Society will be busy making decisions about where to open new schools, how to teach, and what to teach. Ignatius himself dedicated a lot of effort to this newfound ministry. Chapters of the *Constitutions* are dedicated to the education of externs, and some of the most prominent early Jesuits such as Nadal, Polanco, Canisius, Lainez, Borja, and Ribadeneyra greatly shaped the way education was conceived in the Society.

Over the years, General Congregations and Fathers General have often stressed the importance and centrality of education to Jesuit ministry. They have also provided guidelines to deal with new contexts while maintaining the apostolic relevance of this ministry.

Today, universities and secondary/pre-secondary schools are still a central part of what the Society does. Moreover, in the cultural imagination of our time, the Jesuits are mainly known by their educational institutions, even though we are involved in many other apostolic ministries such us refugee services, parishes, retreat houses, social centers, missions, spiritual direction, astronomic observatories, and so on.

The present book aims to accomplish three interrelated goals:

1. Provide basic texts about Jesuit education so that the reader can trace the development, importance, and meaning of Jesuit education from the foundation of the Society of Jesus to our present times.

2. Emphasize that the tradition of Jesuit education is a living tradition which has evolved to respond to new contexts. This book wants to bear witness to the creative fidelity that invites Jesuit schools to stay in continuous discernment and renewal as they seek the best way to achieve their apostolic mission. That mission and the mission of the Society of Jesus today is "the call to serve faith, promote justice, and dialogue with culture and other religions in the light of the apostolic mandate to establish right relationships with God, with one another, and with creation." (GC 35, D.3, No. 12)

3. Assist in the formation of secondary school teachers, university professors, and school administrators interested in being part of the Jesuit tradition of education.

I have decided to include mostly official texts with an international reach such as the *Constitutions*, General Congregations, letters from Fathers General, and addresses given at international meetings. In addition to official texts, I have included the works of a few particular Jesuits whose influence in Jesuit education has been long recognized. These writers include Nadal, Ribadeneyra, Polanco, and Ledesma. I have also included a few articles from prominent scholars, including John W. O'Malley and Gabriel Codina, to clarify historical, cultural, philosophical, and pedagogical contexts.

I strove to preserve the original texts as much as possible. Thus, the reader will encounter various anachronisms in the spelling, language, and grammar, especially in the earliest monographs included in this book. Each paragraph has been numbered to help in navigating the texts; these numbers are bold and are followed by a slash (/), for example, **1/, 2/**, etc. If the original text also included numbered paragraphs, I retained this numbering as well to help the reader locate the text in the source material. If sections from the original texts were omitted, such omissions are clearly demarcated. References to omitted sections have been removed to avoid confusion. Finally, I preserved the formatting of endnotes to match the format used in the original text.

The book is addressed not only to Jesuit educators but to all educators who feel inspired by the spirituality and vision of Ignatius and their impact on education. Educators will find inspiring texts and ways to understand the educational tradition initiated by Ignatius of Loyola and the first Jesuits which continues developing today in the context of new challenges and opportunities.

I also want to thank Fr. John Padberg, S.J., who has provided very valuable feedback and insights for this present textbook.

José A. Mesa, S.J.
Secretary for Education
Society of Jesus
Rome

Visiting Professor
School of Education
Loyola University
Chicago

PART I: THE BEGINNINGS OF JESUIT EDUCATION (1540–1572)

The First Jesuits: The Schools

John W. O'Malley, S.J., Chapter 6 in *The First Jesuits*.

1/   ON 10 AUGUST 1560, Polanco wrote in Laínez's name a letter to all superiors that revealed an immensely significant development in the way the ministries of the Society had come to be conceived by that date. He said that "generally speaking, there are [in the Society] two ways of helping our neighbors: one in the colleges through the education of youth in letters, learning, and Christian life, and the second in every place to help every kind of person through sermons, confessions, and the other means that accord with our customary way of proceeding." The letter thus explicitly recognized that the schools were by that date understood not simply as one ministry among many, but as a super-category equivalent to that into which all the other *consueta ministeria* fell.

2/   For that super-category Polanco made his crucial point: "Every Jesuit must bear his part of the burden of the schools"—"portar parte del peso delle schuole."[1] He duly qualified this generalization, but the whole orientation of the letter manifested the practical priority that the schools had assumed among the ministries. Since approximately 1551 the Jesuits had begun to open schools at the rate of about four or five per year and were on the way to opening many more. In roughly the first decade of their history, the Jesuits in effect had no schools. This is the major difference that distinguished that decade from all that followed.

3/   We know a great deal about the origins of Jesuit commitment to form schooling and the context in which it took place.[2] Not all questions have been answered, but the essential framework is clear. What is still surprising, however, is how easily the first Jesuits glided into a decision of this magnitude and how little account they seem to have taken of its manifold impact upon them. The sources never fully satisfy on this issue.

4/   Once the Jesuits undertook this ministry, they did not falter. This was true of Ignatius himself, whose previous history as a "pilgrim" and chief architect of the *Formula* indicated a quite different orientation. Nonetheless, as Polanco observed in 1551 upon the prospect of opening a school in Bologna, "The idea pleased Ignatius, who was always very much inclined toward the idea of educating youth in letters and matters of the spirit":[3] In pursuit of this program, Ignatius relegated to a lesser status the "professed houses," one of his favorite ideas and main safeguards for the kind of poverty that was to mark the Society. As Polanco wrote to Borja in 1555, just a year before Ignatius's death, "Our father's intention is that, especially in these initial stages, the colleges must multiply rather than the houses."[4]

5/   In other words, Ignatius was willing to make immense adjustments to accommodate this new ministry and to deal with the many problems and frustrations it entailed. He did not see the schools as incompatible with his original vision or with the Compagnia in which it resulted. Both the vision and the Compagnia had from the beginning, in fact, a plasticity that encouraged moving beyond a rigid interpretation of the *Formula*. Moreover, he and the original companions, graduates of the University of Paris, had always seen learning as related to the piety they embodied and wished to inculcate in others. They saw it as even more intrinsically related to their particular "way of proceeding" in ministry and, hence, essential for those who would later join the Society to engage in its ministries. These are the essential elements that allowed them to move gradually along a path that led in 1548 to the great turning point, the opening of the school in Messina.

TOWARD MESSINA AND BEYOND

6/   Shortly after Laínez and Favre arrived in Rome with Ignatius in 1537, they lectured on theology at the University of Rome at the request of Paul III. In 1542–43 Favre lectured on the Psalms at the University of Mainz, and in 1543–44 Jay filled the chair of theology at Ingolstadt left vacant by the death of Johannes Eck.[5] In 1545 Ignatius agreed that Rodrigues should become tutor to the son of John III of Portugal.[6]

7/   The bull *Licet debitum* of 1547 granted permission for the general to depute members of the Society to teach theology and all other disciplines "anywhere," a permission difficult to obtain at the time.[7] In 1549

Ignatius responded to negotiations originating with Duke Wilhelm IV of Bavaria and assigned three Jesuits to teach theology at the University of Ingolstadt—Jay, Salmerón, and Canisius. He arranged through Cardinals Marcello Cervini and Giammaria del Monte for them to stand for a doctoral examination at the University of Bologna, which they passed in early October. Shortly after the Jesuits arrived in Ingolstadt, Canisius was elected dean of the theological faculty, then rector, and in 1551–52, vice-chancellor. But by February of that last year they had all received new assignments and moved elsewhere.[8]

8/   It was not occasional assignments like these, however, that primarily grounded Jesuit engagement with formal education, but the *Formula*'s provision that the Jesuits establish colleges near universities where future members of the order might be trained. The idea possibly originated with Laínez, with discussion centering on how to fund the institutions in a way that accorded with the poverty the Jesuits professed.[9] Even before September 1540, the companions resolved the problem by allowing these "colleges"—unlike the other houses of the Society, which were to live off alms—to be endowed and thus have a fixed income.

9/   Although classes were taught at the colleges of the University of Paris, with which the companions were familiar, the colleges for future Jesuits that they foresaw in 1539–41 would be simple domiciles, without any instruction—"no estudios ni lectiones en la Compañia."[10] The Jesuit college, which would have no formal relationship to the university, would provide lodging for the scholastics, who would take all their classes at the university or at its other colleges. The first scholastics were sent, in accordance with the predilection of the companions, to the University of Paris, where the house faltered for lack of funding and ran into further difficulties in 1542 when the outbreak of war meant that all subjects of the emperor had to leave Paris. Those Jesuits went to Louvain.

10/   By 1544 there were seven such colleges—at the universities of Paris, Louvain, Cologne, Padua, Alcalá, Valencia, and Coimbra. Except for the last, they were all small and financially unstable. Under the generous auspices of King John III of Portugal, however, the college at Coimbra opened in 1542 with twelve scholastics. By 1546 it had almost a hundred and within a year was fully endowed—the only one of the seven that measured up to the original plan. The basic obstacle to funding was persuading benefactors to contribute to an institution reserved exclusively for Jesuits, a group of men untested and practically unknown.

11/   Jay wrote to Salmerón from Germany in early 1545 about precisely this difficulty. Surely nothing, he believed, could be expected from the German bishops, whose own clergy badly needed such resources. Jay, convinced of the necessity of a reformed system for the training of the diocesan clergy in Germany, was an early, insistent, and lonely spokesman for the idea with German bishops, as he showed during the first period of the Council of Trent.[11] His shock at the condition of the German clergy even led him to propose in the letter to Salmerón that the Society found or staff some colleges in Germany for their future training. He prefaced his idea with the important disclaimer that he was of this opinion even though he knew that "our vocation is not ordered to undertaking professorships or 'ordinary' lectureships in the universities."[12] No immediate action was taken on his proposal.

12/   The idea that members of the Society might do some formal teaching on a restricted basis and in extraordinary circumstances, however, continued to surface. Since 1543 a few Jesuits had been teaching reading, writing, grammar, and catechism at a kind of "seminary" in Goa for about six hundred male students between ten and twenty years of age, and they were soon on their way to taking full responsibility for the institution, which they did in 1548. In 1545, moreover, Ignatius consulted Laínez about the possibility of having Jesuits give some instruction in the colleges to other Jesuits, somewhat like the pattern in the colleges at Paris.

13/   The issue arose out of the situation at Padua, where Polanco and some other Jesuits were enrolled. Although Polanco found the teachers and the lectures good, he believed that they had to be supplemented if one wished to make fast progress, as he had learned to do while studying philosophy at Paris.[13] Ignatius decided that under such circumstances lectures, repetitions, drills, and similar exercises could be conducted by Jesuits for other Jesuits. This was an important departure from an earlier decision, but also a key moment in the Jesuits' growing awareness that the *modus parisiensis* had something distinctive to offer to Italian schools.

14/   Meanwhile the duke of Gandía, Francisco de Borja, who had overseen the founding of the Jesuit college at the University of Valencia, had by late 1544 petitioned Paul III to assign certain ecclesiastical revenues to a Jesuit college in Gandía itself. But the college at Gandía was special in two ways: first, there was no university at Gandía, which meant that the Jesuits would give all the instruction; second, the duke wanted other students to be educated there along with the Jesuits—in fact, his principal aim was the education of the sons of his Morisco subjects.[14] Ignatius, always partial to the duke's suggestions, agreed, and in 1546 Jesuits began to teach "publicly"— that is, to students who were not Jesuits. Soon thereafter Paul III granted this exceedingly modest institution the status of *Studium generale,* which meant it was a university.[15]

15/   Jerónimo Doménech was meanwhile laboring in Sicily, where he found "such an immense ignorance in the clergy that you would not believe it unless you saw it." Aware of what had happened in Gandía, he told Ignatius that Leonor Osorio was eager for the Jesuits to found a college.[16] After some maneuvering, her husband, the viceroy, saw to it that not he but the officials of the city of Messina formally ask Ignatius on 19 December 1547 to send five Jesuit scholastics to study there and five teachers for classes in theology, cases of conscience, "arts," rhetoric, and grammar—"all disciplines," as Nadal said, "except law and medicine."[17] The officials promised they would supply food, clothing, and lodging for the Jesuits according to their need, so that the instruction could be given free of charge.

16/   By March 1548, Ignatius had not only complied with the petition but had chosen the ten Jesuits—four priests and six scholastics. He selected some of the best talent available to him in Rome, but also seemed concerned to make the group as international as possible—the priests, for instance, were Nadal, Canisius, Andre des Freux, and Cornelius Wischaven. He allowed them to elect their superior, Nadal. Never before had a group of this size been gathered and "sent" for any ministry. Never before had so much talent been concentrated on a single undertaking. Ignatius obviously pinned high hopes on the venture. The solemnity of the enterprise was underscored by an audience with Paul III, who encouraged the Jesuits to combat the errors of the Lutherans.

17/   For Ignatius the arrangement solved the problem of how to fund the education of younger members of the Society, but what further motivated him at this point is not clear. For the founders in Messina, the training of their sons in "good letters" was of course the paramount consideration. Almost from the moment the school opened its doors their priority prevailed. Both parties had heavy stakes in seeing the venture succeed. The energies of the young Jesuits, however, got directed to teaching other students rather than to their own education.

18/   These factors, plus the palpable success of the undertaking from the very beginning, distinguished the college of Messina from its predecessors in Goa and Gandía.[18] Nadal's enthusiasm was contagious, and, although relatively few of his letters from this period survive, they must have helped convince Ignatius and others to move with bold, even precipitous speed along a path where previously they had taken only a few tentative steps.[19]

19/   Within months after the Collegio di San Nicolo opened in Messina in 1548, the thirty members of the senate of Palermo petitioned Ignatius to establish a similar college in their city. In this petition they were warmly supported, as we have come to expect, by the viceroy, who wrote to both Ignatius and Paul III about it, and especially by his wife, who had a large inheritance assigned to it as an endowment. On 1 June 1549, Ignatius responded positively to the senators, designated Laínez and Doménech to attend to the immediate details, and soon selected eleven Jesuits from five different nations to begin the school. On 25 November Pedro de Ribadeneira, a twenty-two-year-old scholastic, inaugurated the academic year in an assembly of municipal and regional dignitaries with a typical humanistic oration in praise of study. The Jesuits had chosen for the school a building they found admirably suited to their purposes, leading Father Paolo d'Achille to affirm that better classrooms were not to be found even in Paris.[20]

20/   Word reached distant Cologne about what was happening at Gandía, Messina, and Palermo, and on 4 October 1549 Leonard Kessel, the rector of the college, wrote to Ignatius registering his surprise but also his enthusiasm. "If it has come to the point that the brethren have begun to teach publicly," he had the highest hopes for it as a way of "gaining all youth to Christ."[21] A college for students who were not Jesuits was in fact not opened in Cologne until 1557,[22] but at the very time Kessel wrote, Ignatius was already at work establishing colleges in Naples, Venice, and possibly elsewhere.[23] By the next year the offer of financial support by the duke of Gandía helped make possible on 22 February 1551 the opening under modest circumstances of the Collegio Romano. Over its door hung the inscription "School of Grammar, Humanities, and Christian Doctrine, Free"—"Schola di Grammatica, d'Humanità e Dottrina Christiana, gratis."

21/   Enthusiasm for the colleges had within a few short years seized the Jesuit leadership in Rome. On 1 December 1551, Polanco on commission from Ignatius wrote a brief letter to Simao Rodrigues, then provincial of Portugal, encouraging him to open schools like those operating in Italy.[24] On that same date he wrote two other letters, even more important. The first, addressed to Antonio de Araoz, the provincial of Spain, similarly encouraged the opening of schools.[25] Polanco also reviewed some examples to show how they might be funded—by the city, as happened in Messina and Palermo; by some prince, as in Ferrara and Florence by their respective dukes, or as in Vienna by King Ferdinand; by some private individual, as in Venice and Padua by the prior of the Trinity, Andrea Lippomano; by a group of individuals, as in Naples, Bologna, and elsewhere.[26]

22/   Aside from the different sources of funding, the very number of colleges opened or about to open between 1548 and 1551, of which this is not a complete listing, is an astounding revelation. Polanco's letter to Araoz is especially important, however, for other reasons. It succinctly described, for instance, how the curriculum was to be built up from the base of classes in grammar and what discipline and religious practice were expected of the students. It concluded with a list of fifteen goals the Society hoped to achieve through the schools.

23/   The second letter, addressed to all members of the Society, outlined the religious program for both Jesuit students and others.[27] The Jesuits were not to be sent to the colleges to study unless they were firm in their vocation; they should assist at mass every day, set aside time for prayer and examination of conscience daily, receive the sacraments of confession and Communion every week, and attend sermons and catechism class every Sunday and feast day. They should also help in preaching and other ministries in the college. The program for the other students was simpler, but it moved along the same lines. Polanco began it with the statement: "First of all, we accept for classes and literary studies everybody, poor and rich, free of charge and for charity's sake, without accepting any remuneration."

24/   Both documents obliquely but clearly reveal a new understanding of the broader pastoral potential of the colleges. Until about 1550 the theory prevailed that the *consueta ministeria* of the *Formula* would not be exercised in and from the colleges but would be reserved to the other houses. The experience of Messina defeated this theory when it was seen how successful a base for such ministries the colleges in their new form could be.

25/   This meant, among other things, that even when the scholastics were sent to the colleges to continue their own studies they were expected to teach and help with the other ministries. In most of the colleges, because of their small size, this last expectation almost immediately overwhelmed the first, so that Jesuit scholastics in fact studied only in colleges with a large faculty and student body. They studied, therefore, alongside their lay peers. In this way, as well as others, their training was radically different from what eventuated for the diocesan clergy in most of the seminaries inspired by the legislation of the Council of Trent.[28]

26/   The colleges became the principal centers for all Jesuit ministry, which helps explain why Ignatius's interest in the "professed houses" waned, despite the role he assigned them in the Constitutions. As time went on, he was reluctant to accept a college unless a church was attached.[29] In other words, although Polanco's letter of 10 August 1560 divided the ministries of the Society into the two categories of the schools and the *consueta ministeria,* these categories were not in practice so distinct as the letter suggested.

27/   By the time Ignatius died, the Society operated thirty-five or more colleges, depending on one's definition of "college." Nineteen of these were in Italy, with negotiations for others under way in distant places.[30] By 1565 the Jesuits had thirty colleges in Italy alone and had just opened two in Poland, at Braniewo and Pułtusk. During the early years the number of students in the schools varied considerably. In 1556 enrollment ranged from a mere 60 in Venice to 800 in Billom and 900 in Coimbra. That same year there were 120 in Bologna, 160 in Naples, 170 in Perugia, 280 in Palermo, and 300 in Córdoba. In Vienna there were over 320, some of whose parents were "alienated from the Catholic faith," as was also true in Modena.[31] Enrollment tended to be larger in schools outside Italy, except for the Collegio Romano.

28/   Protestant students were expected to follow the religious program, but concessions were made. In Prague, for instance, the Jesuits admitted Lutheran and Hussite boys along with Catholic without distinction *(promiscue)* and even accepted them as boarders. The Lutherans were exempted from reciting the Litany of the Saints. Hussite parents successfully insisted that Jesuits not speak to their sons about faith and exempt them from receiving Communion, but they agreed to the hearing of mass and in some instances even to confession. The Jesuits confiscated and burned any heretical books the boys had and then gave them others as compensation.[32]

29/   They immediately saw, therefore, that the schools could in certain localities be instruments for winning young converts from Protestantism and for likewise influencing their parents. In those same localities, the schools could and would be powerful instruments for confirming wavering

Catholics and, more important, for building the future through an articulate laity and clergy. When in 1554 Canisius inquired of Ignatius how the Society might best help Germany, he replied, "colleges."[33]

30/   Nonetheless, despite the commission from Paul III for Messina, the Jesuits did not in the first instance undertake the colleges with an apologetic, much less a polemical, purpose. The original impulse came from the need to provide a certain amount of training for their own members, along with the need to devise a formula that would assure adequate funding for such a venture.

31/   But even as Messina was being founded, other motives were already strong and becoming stronger. As Polanco's letter to Araoz demonstrates, the Jesuits soon became convinced that lay peers would derive from a program of study and devout practices the same benefits they hoped for their own members, a persuasion perfectly in accord with their "way of proceeding" from the beginning. Within a few years after 1548, most of the institutions in which this persuasion found incarnation were operated by Jesuits exclusively for the education of lay persons. They saw this work as a ministry and clearly designated it as such.[34] Moreover, at least some of them realized that, although there were vague antecedents, they were undertaking something that had never before been done by any religious order.[35]

32/   The Constitutions described the schools as a "work of charity."[36] By using that term, they suggested that it was a form of the traditional spiritual and corporal works of mercy—among the former of which was "instructing the ignorant." The extent to which the Jesuits consciously made such a connection is not clear, but the designation "work of charity" indicated the motivation they believed impelled them. It was an alternative formulation of their favorite description of their ministries, "the help of souls."

THE FAITH IN EDUCATION

33/   Ignatius related in his *Autobiography* that after his return from Palestine in 1524 he felt inclined to study for some time in order to "help souls" better. The belief in a relationship between learning and effective ministry that underlay this decision was traditional. Nonetheless, Ignatius was born into an age in which arguments for that relationship and, indeed, for an intrinsic relationship between education and an upright life had been propounded with new insistence and from a new viewpoint ever since Petrarch, "the Father of humanism," first made them popular in the mid-fourteenth century. That a relationship existed between "good literature" and virtue was a propelling assumption of the humanist movement.

34/   Although by no means unrelated to educational traditions of the Middle Ages, that assumption challenged many medieval notions about texts, curriculum, and related matters, especially as those notions had since the twelfth century found expression in the universities. In their criticism of university (or "scholastic") education, the humanists were especially vociferous about its failure to relate learning to a life of virtue and public service.

35/   The institutional embodiment of the humanists' educational concerns were the primary/secondary schools inspired by their ideals that began in Italy in the fifteenth century and then gradually spread to other parts of Europe. These institutions originated one of the great revolutions in education in the Western World, a revolution whose enduring influence was evident in the curriculum of Greek and Roman authors at the center of "the best" secondary education until well into the twentieth century.

36/   We are well informed about the size and shape of these schools in sixteenth-century France, whence the Jesuits derived many elements of their pedagogy, and in Italy, where they founded their first schools and became dedicated to the venture.[37] In all cities of Italy were to be found schools of two types—the "Vernacular School," which imparted practical skills in reading, writing, and calculation needed for business or a trade; and the "Latin School," which operated more or less according to the principles propounded by the humanists.

37/   The Latin Schools, no matter how many there might be in a town or city, often consisted of a single schoolmaster, with perhaps an assistant hired by the municipality, by a confraternity, or by a group of parents. In many instances the schoolmaster simply "freelanced." He might be a layman or a priest, and he often gave instruction in his home. However elaborate or modest these schools might be in any given locality, they were established institutions in Italy by the time the Jesuits opened their collegio in Messina. Despite their Latin curriculum, some of them may have been relatively innocent of the high claims humanists were making for this style of education.

38/   Did the Jesuits make the same claims? At the urging of Ignatius, Pedro de Ribadeneira wrote to Philip II of Spain on 14 February 1556 to explain why the Society was so deeply committed to its colleges. One sentence jumps from the page: "All the well-being of Christianity and of the whole world depends on the proper education of youth."[38] It was a humanistic commonplace. Ribadeneira's claim is noteworthy, therefore, not for originality but for indicating that the faith in the formative powers of good literature promulgated by the humanist movement found powerful echo in the Society. That faith motivated Jesuits, and they used it to motivate others.

39/   However, the origins of the colleges for members of the Society and even for others cannot be precisely identified with that faith. The origins were more pragmatic and traditional for both these groups. They were thus basically in accord with the values of the social classes from which the first Jesuits mostly came—classes for whom literary and professional training was indispensable for maintaining their status. Furthermore, the academic program initiated at Messina included theology and cases of conscience, which were not disciplines in a strictly humanist curriculum. The former discipline was in fact taught only in universities, which therefore demanded a more elaborate institution than the Latin School and by definition implied one friendly toward scholastic—that is, university-style—theology.

40/   Nonetheless, at Messina and in the schools that followed, the typically humanistic disciplines such as grammar and rhetoric and the cultivation of Latin, Greek, and, in many places, Hebrew became the most popular part of the curriculum—or its only part. The teaching of these disciplines and languages was by the mid-sixteenth century inseparable from some belief in the formative power of the educational program of which they were the most distinctive expression. The Jesuit program was a species within the genus, and it increasingly subscribed to the educational faith enunciated so forcefully by Ribadeneira.

41/   The propaganda that in the Renaissance extolled the power of education to form or reform the mores of individuals and entire societies doubtless exceeded the reality and did not always correlate with the plodding and pedestrian methods of instruction in the classrooms.[39] Nonetheless, inflated though the claims sometimes were, they were not utterly unfounded, and they possessed a certain self-fulfilling dynamism. In any case, the Jesuits by and large came to subscribe to them. The claims provided an expansive aim for their educational undertakings as well as a lens through which to view what they actually accomplished.

42/   The Jesuits were not of a disposition, however, to be swept along in the enthusiasm without more palpable and pragmatic reasons, especially for the study by Jesuits themselves of the *cosas de humanidad.* Shortly after Polanco was first appointed secretary in 1547, he wrote a letter to Laínez precisely on this subject in order to dispel Laínez's misgivings.[40] The reasons he adduced favoring such study were used by humanists, but they were not ones that made the broadest claims. The study of *humanidad,* said Polanco, helps in the understanding of Scripture, is a traditional propaedeutic to philosophy, provides a pedagogically sound entrance into other subjects, enables a person to express his thoughts better, fosters the skills in communication that Jesuit ministries require, and develops the facility in different languages that the international character of the Society demands.

43/   Some of these arguments would be valid for lay students of *humanidad* while others would not, but the Jesuits, like the humanists, saw the civic and social applications for their students of the "humane" disciplines. When they opened their school in Tivoli in 1550, they did so for the "utility of the city"—"ad civitatis utilitatem."[41] When they urged the bishop of

Murcia in 1555 to establish a college, they said it would be of great benefit to the "republic" by producing good priests, good civic officials, and good citizens of every status.[42] This was of course standard humanist talk, but its employment by the Jesuits indicates the breadth that marked their desire to "help souls." As with their other *opera caritatis,* their ministry of education had civic and societal dimensions that carried the Jesuits beyond the evangelical models that principally inspired them.

44/   When Polanco indicated in 1552 for Valencia that colleges were powerful instruments "for the reform of cities," he adduced an article of faith.[43] The faith derived not from a confessional stance but from a broad consensus among the learned elite of Europe about the power of education. On the one hand, the faith assumed standards formulated by that elite, but on the other, the standards could not be imposed without the assent of the parents because of the voluntary character of enrollment in the schools. If the Jesuits were ultimately interested in using their schools to exercise "social control," as has been passionately argued by some critics, they were in that regard far from unique among their contemporaries.[44]

45/   The Jesuits' ideals were socially conservative. It never occurred to them that they should make concerted efforts to break down traditional roles and class structures. As we have already seen, they depended for the endowment of their schools on the wealthy and powerful. They opened their schools, however, to all who were qualified and who would abide by their rules. They were to be "for everybody, poor and rich," Ignatius enjoined upon the Jesuits in Perugia in 1552—"per tutti quanti, poveri et ricchi."[45] Polanco told the Jesuits at Ingolstadt in 1556 to accept "every kind of person"—"ogni sorte di persone"—in order to "animate and console them."[46]

46/   With a notable exception or two, the Jesuit schools during the period I am considering did not favor the sons of the rich over other students. While they generally had a mix of social classes, some catered especially to the poor, even the rural poor. Nadal in 1561 described the college at Monreale, outside Palermo, as "small, uncomfortable, without a church and without endowment . . . From neighboring hamlets come some four hundred students, mostly of the humble poor *[pauperculi]*."[47] Although not social revolutionaries, the Jesuits in theory and practice supported improvement of status through education.

47/   Their decision to adopt the humanist rather than the vernacular curriculum, however, directed their schools toward the classes of society for whom that curriculum had particular appeal.[48] Moreover, in 1551 Ignatius decided for the Collegio Romano that boys had to attain the basic skills in reading and writing before they were admitted because he believed the Society did not have the manpower to expend on such instruction; later that year he made the rule general.[49] The Constitutions, which were being composed at about the same time, stated more mildly that Jesuits did not "ordinarily" teach those skills.[50] Many exceptions therefore continued to be made, but wherever the provision was enforced it tended to exclude from Jesuit schools boys from the lower social classes, who had little opportunity otherwise to learn the skills prerequisite to admission. The Jesuits' determination to minister to all members of society regardless of rank had to do battle, therefore, with the dynamism intrinsic to the humanist program as such and with the repercussions of not teaching the so-called ABC's.[51]

48/   The Jesuits adopted the humanistic program for a number of reasons, but especially because, like their contemporaries, they believed that humanistic studies formed upright character, *pietas*. Although different in many ways from the *Christianitas* that the Jesuits wanted to instill by their teaching of catechism, *pietas* correlated with it in that the truths learned were expected to have an impact on the pupil's behavior and outlook. In this regard their schools correlated with that earlier inspiration.

49/   When in 1552 Nadal asserted the primacy of *pietas* in the educational system the Jesuits were undertaking, he spoke for them all—"Omnia vero selecte ita ordinanda, ut in studiis primum locum pietas obtineat."[52] He merely echoed one of the most prevalent sentiments of his day.[53] Moreover, the Jesuits took for granted that learning and literacy were goods in and of themselves, and they felt at home in promoting them.

50/   The motivation behind the Jesuits' decision to undertake formal schooling as one of their ministries cannot, therefore, be reduced to a simplistic formula, as Polanco's list of the fifteen benefits conferred by the schools indicates.[54] The list is relevant as much for what it did not mention as for what it did. Polanco divided it into three parts—benefits for the Society, for the students, and for the locality:

51/   *For the Society*

1. Jesuits learn best by teaching others.
2. They profit from the discipline, perseverance, and diligence that teaching requires.
3. They improve their preaching and other skills needed in ministry.
4. Although Jesuits should not try to persuade anybody to enter the Society, especially not young boys, their good example and other factors will, nonetheless, help gain "laborers in the vineyard."

52/   *For the students*

5. They will make progress in learning.
6. The poor, who could not possibly pay for teachers, much less for private tutors, will be able to do the same.
7. Students will be helped in spiritual matters by learning Christian Doctrine and hearing sermons and exhortations.
8. They will make progress in purity of conscience and every virtue through monthly confession and the instilling of good habits.
9. They will draw much merit and profit from their studies by learning to direct them to the service of God.

53/   *For the locality*

10. Parents will be relieved of the financial burden of educating their sons.
11. They will be able to satisfy their consciences of their obligation to educate their children.
12. The people of the area will be helped by the Jesuits' preaching and administration of the sacraments.
13. Parents will be influenced by the positive example of their children to live as good Christians.

14. Jesuits will encourage and help in the establishment of hospitals, houses of convertidas, and similar institutions.

15. Those who are now only students will grow up to be pastors, civic officials, administrators of justice, and will fill other important posts to everybody's profit and advantage.

54/   The practical viewpoint that underlays this list seems poles apart from Ribadeneira's grandiloquent claims to Philip II, and it better captured what originally steered the Jesuits toward this form of ministry and later sustained them in it. The list betrays no preoccupation with orthodoxy, and it does not mention "reform." It expects of the colleges only benefits they might realistically be hoped to deliver. It is straightforward in its recognition of the advantages they will procure for the Society itself.

55/   The Jesuits were moved in this direction by other considerations. The advantages of labors sustained with the same group of people over a long period of time, instead of the pastoral blitz, came to be noted and commended in the Constitutions, and they balanced the emphasis on mobility.[55] Like so many educators, Jesuits also came to believe that the values they espoused could be communicated more easily and effectively to the young not yet corrupted by other influences.[56]

56/   From the beginning, the Jesuits produced for their schools a huge amount of documentation. Almost all this material dealt with curriculum, textbooks, pedagogical principles and techniques, and the role of religious practices such as mass and confession. Influential as an early codification of such materials was the letter to Polanco from Annibal du Coudret, 14 July 1551, which described in detail the program at Messina.[57] Documentation like this occasionally expressed in aphoristic fashion the ideal and goal toward which such great energy and effort were being expended—for example, the hope of instilling a "learned piety" *(docta pietas)* or producing "good citizens," but going little further. In other words, despite the Jesuits' great faith in education, they did not elaborate a philosophy of education in the ordinary sense of that term, probably because the humanists had already done it for them.[58]

57/   Among the exceptions to that generalization, however, was the *Ratio studendi,* written at the Collegio Romano in 1564 by the Spanish professor of philosophy Benito Pereira.[59] Pereira began with the important statement that the goal of study was knowledge of the truth, which is the perfection of the human mind. He recalled that Aristotle said that, although it was fine to be a friend of Socrates and Plato, it was more important to be a friend of the truth. This meant that one sometimes had not only to disagree with others but, if truth demanded it, to change and retract one's own opinions.

58/   He continued with other reflections that went beyond techniques on what made for effective teaching and effective learning and described how both body and mind were to be disposed for study. He provided rules for literary criticism. He took for granted that the goal of schools was to cultivate the intellectual talents of the individual and to bring them to the highest point of perfection. There were three such talents—intelligence, memory, and judgment. All were necessary, but what was most valued in a mature person was good judgment; education should concentrate its efforts in the cultivation of that faculty. Pereira here captured something central to the Jesuits' educational endeavors. Under the influence of Quintilian and other theorists, the Jesuits looked more to formation of mind and character, to *Bildung,* than to the acquisition of ever more information or the advancement of the disciplines.[60]

59/   Pereira's *Ratio* is a synthesis of classical, medieval, and Renaissance ideas on education. Not therefore original, it is important in the Jesuit context because it rose above details of curriculum and pedagogical technique without claiming education to be the panacea for all the ills of church and society. Pereira ended with a section on "topics" or "commonplaces" for speaking and writing, which climaxed with typically humanist considerations about "human dignity." That theme accorded with the benign relationship between nature and grace that the Jesuits espoused and, hence, fitted in a generic way with the positive view of human nature that, at least in theory, undergirded Jesuit enthusiasm for education in the humanistic mode.[61] The last words of the treatise were typical of such an appreciation:

"Because of the excellence and almost divine quality of their virtues and deeds, many men were in bygone days honored with not only the highest human but even divine honors, and *by* the ancients were numbered among the gods."

TRANSCENDING THE MODUS PARISIENSIS

60/   The Constitutions indicated two basic kinds of educational institutions that the Society might operate.[62] The first was the college, in which "humane letters, languages, and Christian Doctrine," as well as possibly "cases of conscience," formed the curriculum.[63] The second was the university, where the higher disciplines would also be taught—logic, metaphysics, ethics, the sciences, mathematics, and theology.[64] Excluded from universities operated by the Society were, under normal circumstances, the faculties of law and medicine.[65] In this Fourth Part of the Constitutions, directives were given on the order of teaching the disciplines, the techniques for teaching them, the *texts* to be used, the degrees to be conferred, the moral and spiritual values to be inculcated, and the duties to be fulfilled *by* the officials in charge of the institution.

61/   One of the earliest sources for these provisions was a long document composed about 1552 by Nadal, fresh from his experience in Messina, but with his *eyes* on the greater potential of the Collegio Romano. *De studii generalis dispositione et ordine* was among the first of his many important writings dealing with the general topic.[66] The detail and sophistication of *De dispositione* could have come only from somebody like Nadal, who had broad experience of educational institutions across Europe—the universities of Alcalá, Paris, Avignon, Majorca, and the Jesuit experiment at Messina.

62/   The Constitutions and other prescriptive documents including the *De dispositione* can be deceiving, however, when they suggest that many or most of the schools that the Jesuits operated contained all the disciplines they describe. Few of the schools during this period taught anything more than the "lower disciplines," which meant three years of "grammar," another of *humanitas* (poetry, history), and another of "rhetoric," that is, classical oratory. The best of them, like Messina, were *trilingue* in that besides Latin and Greek they also taught Hebrew. (In Italy the Jesuit curriculum differed most notably from earlier Italian practice in that it elevated Greek to a secure place in the syllabus.)[67]

63/   The students entered at about ten years of age for an approximately six-year program. These "colleges" thus resembled most immediately the American high school, but to the degree they prepared students for the professional schools the university incorporated, they also corresponded to American undergraduate colleges.

64/   In these early days the outstanding example of a school that did more than teach the "lower disciplines" was the Collegio Romano, which within a few years of its inception taught the full curriculum described in the Constitutions and was, in effect, a "university."[68] This meant, however, that it also taught the "lower disciplines." The two stages beyond "humane letters" taught at the Collegio Romano, the future Gregorian University, were "arts" or "philosophy"—logic, metaphysics, ethics, mathematics, and physics, according to the texts of Aristotle for the most part—and, finally, theology, considered the apex of the curriculum.[69]

65/   As has often been pointed out, the model for this pyramid culminating in theology was the University of Paris that the architects of the Jesuit system knew so well.[70] The pyramidal structure was only one element, however, in the complex reality of the *modus parisiensis* that the Jesuits introduced into their schools in Italy and thence exported, as modified by their Italian experience, to their schools elsewhere in the world. Their early persuasion of how much it differed from the *modus italicus* and their belief in its superiority gave them a sense of cultural mission in propagating it. In many parts of Europe the difference was a major factor in making their schools distinctive and attractive.

66/   In 1553, just two years after the opening of the Collegio Romano, Polanco wrote to all Jesuit superiors about the hopes the Society entertained for the new institution.[71] Among them was that "it be academically

distinguished for having professors who are not only erudite but also diligent pedagogues, who will introduce into the college the style of academic
exercises used at the University of Paris. This will be a marvelous help to
Italy, in whose schools two things are notably lacking—a well-ordered program of lectures and exercises to assure the assimilation of the materials.
Diligent students, we therefore hope, will achieve more with us in a short
time than elsewhere in a long time; and perhaps other schools will improve,
inspired by our example."

67/   In describing the Italian system Polanco drew on his experience at
the University of Padua, but he and other Jesuits applied the same criticism
also to primary and secondary education in Italy: it was not sufficiently
structured according to the age and competence of the students, and it did
not make sufficient use of drill and other ways of actively engaging the
students to assure assimilation of information and skills.

68/   The *modus parisiensis* was, as the Jesuits saw it, the polar opposite
of much of what they found in Italian schools and schoolmasters. It was
based on an exacting program of lectures, complemented by a full array of
drills, repetitions, and *disputations—exercitia,* or *exercitationes*—in which
the student demonstrated mastery of the materials. Students at all levels
were divided into classes according to a set plan of progression from mastery of one skill or author to mastery of the next. Examinations determined
who was ready to move to the next class. A "class" represented a unit of
work to be mastered, not a period of time. Hence, brighter boys could move
through the curriculum more quickly than others. If the classes were large,
students were divided into groups of ten under a more accomplished peer
(the *decurio),* who drilled them and reported to the teacher on their progress
or lack of it.[72]

69/   These principles and techniques, though applied to "humane letters,"
developed at Paris as part of the scholastic tradition, with its great penchant
for order, system, and "disputation."[73] The *modus parisiensis* encompassed
many things, but what it most broadly gave to the Jesuit system was an
organized plan for the progress of the student through increasingly complex

materials and a codification of pedagogical techniques designed to elicit active response from the learner.

70/   Despite the "Parisian" designation, these principles and practices had undergone significant development in the Low Countries in the fifteenth century with the Brethren of the Common Life, who themselves had been influenced by developments in France and Italy. From the Brethren, they were exported back to France—to some of the colleges at the University of Paris, including the Collège de Montaigu, where Ignatius first studied, as well as to other schools in the kingdom.[74] They were exported elsewhere, as to the humanistic school founded by Johannes Sturm in Strasbourg in 1535.[75] They were introduced into Coimbra by King John III of Portugal.[76] They had found their way to the University of Alcalá, where Ignatius, Laínez, Salmerón, Bobadilla, Nadal, Ledesma, and other early Jesuits had studied. In other words, the so-called *modus parisiensis* or elements of it were already on their way to becoming an international phenomenon by the time the Jesuits introduced them into Italy, and they had themselves encountered them even before they studied in Paris.

71/   The similarity between the Jesuit schools in Italy and Sturm's in Protestant Strasbourg led to allegations that the Jesuits borrowed their ideas from him. There is no evidence indicating that this is what happened. Even before the Jesuits thought of opening their own schools, Polanco as a student at Padua had pointed out the advantages of the *modus parisiensis*. The similarity between Sturm and the Jesuits was due to a common origin, as scholars now recognize. The similarity points, moreover, to the assumption generally shared by leaders in sixteenth-century Europe of the necessity of the "war against ignorance" for the good of religion and society. The necessity was so patent for these generations that it needed no justifying arguments.

72/   Polanco noted instances where in Italy the new methods introduced by the Jesuits positively influenced other teachers. In Palermo in 1552 one of the older schoolmasters came to the Jesuits' classes to learn firsthand the "right way to teach," by which boys made so much progress in so little time. It did not escape Polanco, however, that others preferred to remain ignorant, an oblique indication of the resentment the schoolmasters often felt toward the Jesuits, who were taking away their students.[77] After the Collegio Romano had been in operation for a few years, Polanco said that people began to regard the teaching at its rival institution, the University of Rome, as "cold and, in comparison, useless," but even there teachers began to be more diligent because of the Jesuits' example—and competition.[78]

73/   When the college opened in Vienna in 1551, the Jesuits offered a mishmash of courses, which "displeased Ignatius" when he heard of it. He made it clear that students were to lay a foundation in "humane letters," then give their attention to "philosophy," and only then move on to theology.[79] Two years later the *modus parisiensis* was seen in Vienna as distinctive of the instruction given by the Jesuits.[80] In Cordoba in 1554 people gave the Jesuits credit for introducing the "new" practice of frequent written and oral exercises.[81]

74/   There were other features in the colleges, however, that find no exact counterpart in the *modus parisiensis*. One of these was the introduction into the curriculum of classes in Christian Doctrine once a week. Although in theory theology was the discipline toward which the others pointed, it was not taught in the colleges, that is, in the secondary schools, and its place was taken in a certain sense by this much more elementary exercise. Sturm also introduced catechism into the curriculum, requiring more of it than did the Jesuits.[82]

75/   Another difference was the widespread practice of offering classes in "cases of conscience" even in these lower schools, although who the students were and how these classes functioned is not always clear. In 1553 the colleges at Evora and Lisbon offered only the lower program in "humane letters," but "cases of conscience" were also taught.[83]

76/   Although the program of classes and academic exercises in Jesuit schools was demanding and the academic year long, there were regular and frequent holidays, and the Jesuits showed themselves in other ways sensitive to the students' need for relaxation, recreation, and sports.[84] In boarding institutions, the "prefect of health" was to provide "good meals, well seasoned, from food of good quality."[85]

77/   Some cities and communes in Europe had devised means to provide education without "direct cost" to children of their citizens, but even in these places the Jesuit schools generally accepted more students and were much cheaper for the municipality, since the Jesuits required no salaries, needing only enough money to cover food and clothing expenses. In this aspect of their venture, they were true innovators. They inaugurated in Italy and many other places the first systematic and widespread effort to provide free education for large numbers of students in a given town or city.[86] Moreover, the Jesuits granted free of charge all advanced degrees, which could cost "a small fortune at regular universities."[87] They refused to charge tuition out of the religious motives that from the beginning led them to refuse payment for any of their ministries. This stance made Jesuit schools financially attractive to parents and local governments and was a powerful factor contributing to their spread.

78/   The Jesuits installed in their schools the spiritual program whose basic elements Polanco described in his letter of 1 December 1551, summarized above. The program's precedents were the practices in the colleges at the universities of Alcalá and Paris, where they varied from college to college but included frequent or daily attendance at mass, fasts and other penances, daily participation in at least part of the liturgical Hours, daily examination of conscience, and confession and Communion at determined intervals.[88]

79/   The Jesuits employed many of the same elements, but, as we have seen, with a sense of some intrinsic cohesion among them. Moreover, they extended the program to students who continued to live at home or somewhere else outside the institution—which was the vast majority, since few of the schools at this time had provisions for boarders. This factor, plus the general tenor of Jesuit spirituality, meant that the program eliminated or mitigated some of the practices of Alcalá and Paris. The program had no counterpart in the pre-university schools run by municipalities and, for the most part, by other educators. At least in theory the program was voluntary, and the Constitutions forbade expelling students simply for not complying with it.[89]

80/   Polanco described the program at the college at Palermo the year after it was established.[90] All students went to confession every month, some every two weeks. They assisted at mass daily and heard a sermon on Sundays and feast days. In the afternoons of class days, a number of them went privately and spontaneously to the Jesuits to talk about their spiritual lives. But what was especially important, reported Polanco, was the weekly talk given by Laínez "about matters concerning them related to their progress in virtue and learning."

81/   Vespers on Sundays and feast days became standard, daily examination of conscience inculcated, and eventually in some places, students encouraged or obliged to do part of the Spiritual Exercises. Taken for granted all along was encouraging students, as far as their age allowed, to practice the works of mercy that the Jesuits favored.[91] Further extension and intensification of the program resulted from the introduction of the Marian Congregations into the schools after 1563. Like the *modus parisiensis,* those Congregations became a distinctive mark of the Jesuit schools.

82/   Gioseffo Cortesono was rector of the Collegio Germanico in Rome from 1564 until 1569. Sometime late in his term of office, he composed at the order of Borja the *Constitutiones Collegii Germanici,* another document that rose above stipulation of particulars.[92] Somewhat misnamed, it was less a juridical instrument than a reflection on broad educational issues, "based on experience." The several sections dealing with the spiritual program spoke of course of the devout practices expected of the students, but also manifested a concern for the interiorization of religious and moral values through those practices and through the guidance that the students, young Italian laymen for the most part, were to receive from the Jesuits.

83/   In the "entrance interview" for the students, for instance, the Jesuit should explain what piety *(il spirito)* consists of—liberation from the tyranny of sin, peace of conscience, friendship with God, "walking in the light," and "tasting the sweetness, joy, and contentment of things of the spirit."[93] This was another paraphrase of what the Jesuits meant by consolation.

84/   The Jesuits should encourage students to go to the sermons in the Jesuit church, but not do so in a way or to a degree that would annoy them. The students should then be encouraged to take special note of the parts of sermons that "moved their affections" and afterward to discuss them with one another. Of even more help would be the exhortations delivered in the college that were intended specifically for them—either for all of them assembled together or for special groupings among them.[94] From the Collegio Germanico at about the same time came a recommendation from Michele Laurentano to employ the older students to talk to the younger ones about the spiritual life as well as to give them examples of how to make progress.

85/   He described what seems to have been the practice, for he observed: "This method of helping the laity by means of the laity results in good success when it is done well, and they generally accomplish more than [do the] religious."[95]

86/   Concern for the spiritual well-being of students was supposed to be manifested in the classroom. The Constitutions put the matter simply: "The masters should make it their special aim, both in their lectures when occasion is offered and outside of them too, to inspire the students to the love and service of God our Lord and to a love of the virtues by which they will please God."[96]

87/   Favre related how, when he was a boy, his teacher made "Christians" out of the classical authors he was studying.[97] Official Jesuit educational documents never go quite that far, but Nadal repeatedly urged teachers to find pietas in all the authors and subjects studied and to draw out the "spiritual" meaning imbedded in the texts.[98] Polanco reported that these "little digressions," which he considered a form of devout conversation, produced great effect even with boys "much addicted to the vices of *youth.*"[99]

88/   The "humane letters" to which a spiritual interpretation was applied were the classics, and, although the Jesuits did not in principle exclude works by the Fathers of the Church, such as Augustine, Jerome, and Gregory the Great, they in fact never formed part of the curriculum.[100] Calvinist schools were at this time turning more decidedly in favor of the Bible and Christian texts.[101] The Jesuits fully appropriated, moreover, the humanists' persuasion that culture and moral responsibility were inseparably connected.[102]

89/   Jesuit educational documents spoke of the spiritual well-being of students without regard for the religious controversies of the age, but in their correspondence the Jesuits sometimes betrayed that they saw sound spirituality as a bulwark against the "errors of the times," subscribing to the traditional view that immorality was the hotbed and prerequisite for heresy. This view surfaced of course more often concerning northern Europe, but was not unknown elsewhere. Luis Gonçalves da Câmara, a leader in the more rigorous party in the Portuguese province, wrote to Nadal from Lisbon, for instance, on 29 May 1561: "I desire that our schools concern themselves especially with the virtues necessary for this kingdom and in particular [work] against the vices . . . for they seem to open the door and provide the disposition that allows heresy to enter."[103]

90/   Classes and the program of religious practices formed the backbone of the Jesuit schools, but also important from the beginning were the plays and academic celebrations in which students displayed their talents and skills to a wider public. At Paris and elsewhere the early Jesuits had learned that such events were part of the *exercitium* required of students by good pedagogy and, hence, an integral part of their education.[104] The Jesuits brought memories of such "spectacles" with them into Italy, where some of these events, like orations in the universities to open the academic year, had long been practiced. The Jesuits were conscious, however, whence they derived their model, for they opened the academic year at Ferrara in 1552 with Latin poems and orations recited by the students in a program "celebrated in the Parisian style."[105] From their experience they saw the enthusiasm thus engendered especially in younger students, and they set about exploiting it as an aid for appropriating skills learned in the classroom.[106] These events were also effective advertisements for the school and won public support for it.

91/   In Florence that same year for the same occasion, three Jesuits delivered panegyrics on the virtues, on the Latin language, and on the relationship between them—a significant but traditional theme.[107] The academic year opened at the Collegio Romano in 1553, just two years after it was founded, with disputations on philosophy, theology, and rhetoric, which were attended by a number of "cardinals, bishops, and other men of great authority."[108] Two years later public celebrations lasted for eight days—three days devoted to theology and the rest to "arts" (logic, ethics, physics, mathematics, metaphysics) and to "humane letters."[109]

92/   The awarding of doctoral degrees at the Collegio Romano quickly emulated ceremonies in other universities, as we see from Polanco's descriptions for 6 February and 2 May 1556, and for one celebrated *valde solemniter* on 1 September 1557, at which Nadal presided.[110] But "recitals" were interspersed throughout the academic calendar both in Rome and in the humbler *collegia*. At Bologna in 1555, for example, a student, age eleven, delivered a Latin oration on "The Boy Jesus" at the opening of the year, another did the same at Christmas on "The Birth of Christ," and others at Pentecost on "Christ's Ascension," on "The Descent of the Holy Spirit," and similar topics.[111]

93/   Students were sometimes sent to other locations to demonstrate their accomplishments. In 1556 the bishop of Genoa expressed to the Jesuits a desire to hear an oration on "Good Government." On Pentecost Sunday in the cathedral after a long liturgy a twelve-year-old student delivered an oration on the subject written by a Jesuit teacher. He was such a success, Polanco reported, that Andrea Doria, the great admiral and political master of Genoa, summoned the boy to repeat it for him privately.[112] A few weeks later the bishop invited two more boys to deliver orations after vespers on the feast of Corpus Christi.[113]

94/   Within the schools, orations like these were combined with other exercises, even with catechism, as Polanco reported—again for Genoa that same year:

> People came eagerly to an event where the students recited Christian Doctrine and interspersed the recitation with the delivery of Latin orations they had written, which aroused great admiration in the audience because it was something not done in other schools. The chance to deliver their orations engenders enthusiasm in the boys and is also an incitement to the parents to send them to school. The rector afterward praised the "orators," who had performed so well, and explained the necessity of actual practice "of the rules of the art of oratory they had studied."[114]

95/   Orations and poetry were employed in all the schools for celebratory occasions, and in the larger ones philosophical and theological disputations according to the standard scholastic style were also used. In some schools more elaborate forms like "dialogues," where verses set to music were sung between the "acts," began to appear.[115] At Bologna in 1556 during the Christmas season, the students appeared in a *sacra representatio,* a kind of pageant portraying the birth of Christ and the arrival of the Magi, and at Easter in another, accompanied by verses, portraying Christ's deposition from the cross.[116] Italians were quite familiar with the genre, for their confraternities had been producing such pageants for many generations.[117] From these *rappresentazioni* it was but a short step to full-fledged drama.

96/   There are numerous studies of Jesuit theater, including a detailed, multivolume work on it in German-speaking lands from 1554 until almost the end of the seventeenth century, as well as a two-volume repertoire into the eighteenth.[118] In general these studies do not pay sufficient attention to music and dance (including ballet), usually an integral part of the performance that with the passing of time became ever more cultivated and important.[119] They show, in any case, that the significance of theater in all its aspects for Jesuit colleges can hardly be overestimated. Again, the Jesuits did not invent the "school drama," but they cultivated it to an especially high degree over a long period of time in a vast network of schools almost around the globe. They were involved in it within a few years after they opened the school in Messina.

97/   One of the first plays of which there is clear record was *Jephthah Sacrificing His Daughter,* written by the Jesuit scholastic José de Acosta and produced at Medina del Campo in 1555. The play was well received—all the more so, Polanco tells us, because Acosta was born and raised in Medina.[120]

98/   The next year Acosta wrote and produced two more, one of which was *Joseph Sold into Egypt.*[121] From a family of New Christians, Acosta was fifteen years old when *Jephthah* was produced and had already been a member of the Society for three years. He went on to a brilliant career in Spain and Peru as administrator and writer. His best-known and most celebrated work was *Historia natural y moral de las Indias* (1590).[122]

99/   In 1556 a "comedy" entitled *On Good Morals* was produced at the school in Syracuse. Word about it spread and some leading citizens from a nearby town asked the rector to let the students present it there. The rector denied the request on the grounds that plays were produced in the schools "to encourage love of literature in the students, not as spectacles for the public."[123] This opinion did not prevail. By the 1560s elements of such productions were given in the vernacular to accommodate the wider audience,[124] and occasionally entire plays were produced in the vernacular.[125] In Munich in 1561, two years after the college was founded, the play was first performed for the general public and then for the duke and his court. Two years later in Innsbruck the first performance was in the Rathaus, the second in the imperial court before the emperor and empress.[126]

100/   When Robert Claysson wrote back to Rome in 1558 about the plays, eclogues, academies, and similar events in the college at Billom, the first Jesuit school in France, he interpreted their purposes broadly and positively by affirming that their spiritual impact was the equivalent of a good sermon.[127] Most Jesuits shared his enthusiasm, but not all. That same year a Jesuit in Bologna complained that the boys spent their time on nothing else but getting ready for the play and that it was improper for members of religious orders to sponsor such events; in fact, children ridiculed the Jesuits in the streets with the cry "Here come the comedy priests!"—*"Ecco li preti delle comedie!"*[128]

101/ Other Jesuits, including the ever-vigilant Juan Ramirez, complained that the plays were too costly to produce and caused scandal.[129] In the Collegio Germanico in 1570 a brawl broke out between the students and the actors from the Collegio Romano. Weapons were brandished. The incident led the general, Borja, to remove the rector from office and to expel one of the students, "the author of the sedition."[130]

102/ From about 1560, Jesuit authorities imposed on the plays a number of regulations, which were inconsistently enforced and sometimes reversed; on rare occasions they discouraged plays altogether, but in general enthusiasm for them was high. Two or even three plays per year were regularly produced in some schools during the sixteenth century.[131]

103/ The Jesuits wrote their own plays and produced those written by other ancients and contemporaries. In Vienna, for instance, an adaptation of Terence's *Adelphi* was produced in 1556 and 1566, and an adaptation of Plautus's *Aulularis* in 1565.[132] Under Nadal's aegis, in 1557 the students at the Collegio Romano produced Terence's *Heautontimorumenos*. Twenty-five plays written between 1556 and 1572 by the Spanish Jesuit Pedro Acevedo still survive.[133] At Messina, Stefano Tucci wrote and produced in 1562 *Nabuchodonosor* (Nebuchadnezzar) when he was a scholastic only twenty-one years old; he followed in successive years with *Goliath* and *Judith*.[134] At Como about the same time students acted in *The Rebels* by the Dutch neo-Latin playwright Georgius Macropedius (1486–1558).[135] In 1555 *Acolastus* by the Dutch humanist Gnaphaeus was produced at the colleges in Cordoba and Lisbon.[136] *Euripus: Tragedia Christiana* by the Franciscan Levin Brecht was especially popular in German schools.[137]

Seemingly peculiar to Cologne were overtly polemical pieces, with Luther, Calvin, and the Devil among the principal characters.[138]

104/ These are but samples of a phenomenon that within a year or two of the inception of a given school became a staple of its educational program. The aesthetic limitations of "school drama" are well known, but to put them into perspective we need to recall that Lope de Vega, Calderon, Andreas Gryphius, Jacob Bidermann, Corneille, and Moliere received their first training in theater in Jesuit schools.

JESUIT EDUCATION

105/ Despite problems, sometimes severe, the Jesuit schools enjoyed success in most localities even during these early years, and they soon assumed the preeminent place among the ministries of the Society that Polanco attributed to them in 1560. Some reasons for their success should by now be clear. The Jesuits at times founded schools where there were none before. More often they simply offered something that seemed better than its alternatives. As was often true of them in other endeavors, the Jesuits created relatively few of the components of their educational program, but they put those parts together in a way and on a scale that had never been done before.[139] It was the combination, not any single feature, that distinguished the education offered in the Jesuit schools from what was offered elsewhere.

106/ The Jesuits produced an immense amount of documentation concerning their educational enterprise as they moved toward the definitive edition of *ratio studiorum* in 1599. The very quantity of their writings makes it difficult to find the forest amidst the trees. The Jesuits themselves often could not find it. The documents tend, moreover, to jumble together features that today would be neatly sorted out into charters, job descriptions, "mission statements," "profiles of the ideal graduate," class schedules, curricula, pedagogical techniques, and syllabuses.

107/ Nonetheless, at least ten characteristics can be identified as contributing to the Jesuits' initial success and to a new, international educational style. First, the schools charged no tuition. Second, at least in principle they welcomed students from every social class. Third, especially the schools of "humane letters" conformed to the emerging consensus of the age in curriculum, the importance of character formation, and similar matters. The disciplinary regulations by and large conformed to the same consensus. Fourth, the Jesuits postulated compatibility between an education in "humane letters" on the one hand and in Aristotelian philosophy/science and Thomistic theology on the other, a compatibility vaguely adumbrated in the "Rules for Thinking with the Church" in the *Exercises*.[140]

108/ Fifth, from the *modus parisiensis* they implemented division into classes (each with its own teacher), ordered progression from class to class according to clear curricular goals, and similar provisions. Sixth, again from the "Parisian Mode" they borrowed the insistence on active appropriation of both ideas and skills—*exercitium*—that consisted not only in written compositions and oral repetitions in the classroom, but also in plays, disputations, and other "spectacles" open to the public.

109/ Seventh, they sponsored a clear, coherent, and basically simple religious program, adaptable to students of different ages and backgrounds—a program that in principle sought to move the student beyond pious practices to an inner appropriation of ethical and religious values. Eighth, through their Marian Congregations they gave further articulation to their religious program by adopting and adapting one of the most popular institutions of the day, the confraternity.

110/ Ninth, they were on the way to creating an international network of schools, the largest by far under a single aegis the world had ever seen, in which information was effectively shared about what worked and what did not. Their normative documents with their sometimes obsessively detailed stipulations pushed them toward conformity, especially once the *Ratio* was published in 1599, but the Jesuits could never forget the necessity of accommodation to times, places, and circumstances.

111/   Finally, most difficult to calculate, the "teaching under the teaching" was different coming from this special group of men. The Jesuits were on the whole better educated and motivated than most pre-university schoolmasters almost anywhere in Europe. Further, they tried to influence their students more by their example than by their words. They repeatedly inculcated in one another the importance of loving their students, of knowing them as individuals, of enjoying a respectful *familiaritas* with them.[141] Whenever these ideals were achieved, they were crucially important in contributing to a school's success. Failure to achieve them would perhaps be even more telling.

112/   The blend of these features resulted in an educational program that in some parts of Europe appeared as a notable improvement on practices already in operation, in other parts as a stunning innovation. It resulted in a program that in its totality transcended the designation *modus parisiensis*. An inversion of terminology began to take place, as the Jesuits now occasionally used *modus italicus* to indicate the style of *their* schools in Italy, which they in turn wanted to introduce into Paris.[142] "Our way of proceeding" had developed its educational component.

FAILURES, FRUSTRATIONS, AND CRISIS

113/   "The Society is being ruined by taking on so many schools." That was the frank judgment of Cortesono at the end of the period I am considering. He gave his reasons: the schools were such a burden that the Jesuit scholastics were sent to teach in them at the price of curtailing their own studies; in order to ensure a supply of teachers, the Jesuits accepted unsuitable candidates into the Society; for the same reason they tolerated within their midst even rogues *(discoli);* this was leading to a loss of the Society's true spirit; the financial problems of the schools would lead to the adoption of choir (with benefices), and so forth. He further judged that although the Society undertook the teaching of letters to form youth in Christian piety, experience showed little evidence of the success of such formation, except with boarders. His remedy in this apologia for the Collegio Germanico was to curtail drastically the number of schools, so that each province have no more than two or three, and whenever possible to turn them into boarding schools—like the Germanico, of which he was the rector.[143]

114/ Plausible as Cortesono's charges may have been, they did not exhaust the list of questions and problems. In almost every conceivable way the Society was unprepared to open in rapid-fire fashion as many schools as it had in the first years after Messina, which by 1553 had led to a crisis in personnel that became almost endemic. There were too few Jesuits for the number of schools, as well as for other commitments. Many among those few performed badly in the classroom, either because they did not know the subject or because they were incompetent pedagogues. Practically none were ready by training and temperament to assume the administrative duties these institutions required.

115/ These were the almost desperate sentiments of Miguel de Torres, provincial of Portugal, conveyed to Ignatius in 1553 and then repeated to Laínez eleven years later.[144] As provincial of Andalusia, he in 1555 estimated that among those who were in charge of schools in that area no more than two had the talent requisite for the job.[145] Similar sentiments were expressed by others elsewhere in the Society and justified by the facts.[146] Although Jesuit headquarters in Rome heard about how well things sometimes were going, complaints also poured in.

116/ A common complaint from students and their parents was that the Jesuits changed teachers too often, and almost as often replaced them with less competent ones.[147] Foreigners sometimes had only a rudimentary grasp of the local language and spoke Latin with accents to which the natives were unaccustomed—a sensitive issue in Italy.[148] The manpower situation was exacerbated by the necessity of supplying teachers for distant places. In 1561, for instance, Nadal searched the Iberian peninsula for six qualified Jesuits to be sent to India—a rector for Goa, three teachers of Latin, a teacher of philosophy *(las artes),* and a teacher of theology.[149] Moreover, Jesuits in the schools sometimes had to be reminded that their primary responsibility was to their students, not to adults who came to them for confession or counsel.[150]

117/   The difficulties in opening new schools were so overwhelming that some Jesuits simply abandoned their vocation to the Society, and Polanco warned as early as 1553 that "experience teaches" that only the "most proven and constant" should be sent into these situations, a warning with scant possibility of being heeded.[151] Some of those sent occasioned disturbance of the peace *(perturbationes)* in their communities, and sending them elsewhere did not solve the problem.[152]

118/   Older Jesuits began to complain that the scholastics sent to the colleges, especially from the highly touted Collegio Romano, knew their Terence better than their Aquinas. The scholastics had become accustomed to niceties in food and clothing, showed favoritism in dealing with students, had little interest in teaching, were "arid in things of the spirit" and dreamed of the "honor of a chair." In a word, "The colleges are being ruined by the disorder they cause, and every year one must begin again to repair the damage done by the end of the previous year."[153] In his letter of 10 August 1560, Polanco required that all Jesuits do their part in "bearing the burden of the schools," but not all Jesuits were equal to the task.

119/   What about the students? From many schools came enthusiastic reports about the progress the students made in studies and virtue and about the hope they inspired for the future.[154] Although the Jesuits were proud of their triumphs, they were also pragmatic observers and frank communicators to each other of what succeeded or failed. When they reported success, as they often did, they must be taken more or less at their word. The same assumption applies for failures. Some schools reported intractable problems with discipline. A scholastic at Ferrara in 1556 could handle classes of no more than nine or ten students, but another sometimes had only two or three. That year enrollment in the school seriously declined, and occasionally no students showed up for some of the classes. Polanco conceded that part of the reason was the poor quality of instruction, but added that the youth of Ferrara was less disciplined *(liberior)* than the Jesuits had hoped.[155]

120/ In Florence the "insolence" of some students caused ongoing problems for the Jesuits.[156] As early as 1548 Nadal laid down the rule in Messina that students could not enter the school buildings bearing arms. This was a somewhat standard regulation for educational institutions of the day, but the Jesuits kept repeating it for their schools.[157] The boys at Gubbio were tough—"unmanageable and like beasts, who have been known to kill each other."[158] Especially when there were boarders, as in the Germanico, the Jesuits had suspicions, seemingly not ungrounded, about the sexual mores of the students, and they feared that, unless something was done, "our schools will end up like the others in Italy." Some Jesuits thought, rather, that too much surveillance in this regard was making matters worse.[159]

121/ Although the Jesuits did not particularly favor schools that accepted boarders, they had undertaken some, especially in northern Europe. They did so to protect the boys from a Protestant environment. Within a few years of opening, the college at Vienna had 6 boarders.[160] By 1562 the college at Tournai, for instance, had 125 boarders and 120 day students; the college at Cologne, 51 boarders and 444 others.

122/ A composite list of problems consistently arising in such institutions, which has an almost timeless quality to it, went somewhat as follows: Jesuits talked with students about things concerning the school that students had no right to know; the students complained about the quantity and quality of the food; prefects were so overburdened as to lose all privacy, and by their frequent contact with the students, lost their respect; the boys invented cruel nicknames for their teachers and prefects and united against them; students had a lingo of their own in which they communicated to frustrate those in charge of them.

123/ How to discipline unruly students was no less a problem for the Jesuits than it has been for educators through the ages. The Jesuits were repeatedly admonished to do so gently, sparingly, by word rather than deed, to prefer rewarding good behavior to punishing bad. Like their contemporaries, however, they believed that physical punishment was sometimes required, at least for the younger boys. When in Messina in 1557 they experimented with abolishing corporal punishment, the boys' parents objected, and the Jesuits had to reinstitute it.[161]

124/ But who was to administer the blows? According to Ignatius, the Jesuits themselves were never, under any circumstances, to do so. It would be difficult to find a single issue on which he was more adamant, unbudging, intransigent than this one, and behind which he more repeatedly threw the full weight of his authority. In the reputedly militaristic discipline of the Society of Jesus, commands issued "under holy obedience," that is, in virtue of the vow, were extraordinarily rare. But, once Ignatius realized by 1553 that he was not being heeded in the matter of physical discipline, he imposed on all Jesuit teachers in Italy precisely such an injunction, from which he would not tolerate the slightest deviation.[162] Could Jesuits at least strike students on the palms of their hands? The answer was negative.[163] Why was he so insistent on this issue? He believed that physical punishment diminished respect for the one administering it and ruptured the bond of affection between Jesuits and those they were trying to "help." His stance caused the Jesuits untold minor agonies in trying to be faithful to it.

125/ The solution Ignatius suggested was to hire a "corrector," but some schools were too poor to do so or could not find somebody at the price they were willing to pay.[164] At Venice in 1556 some "pious matrons" said they would supply funds until the position could be endowed.[165] Some schools resorted to having the older boys punish the younger—with bad results. Parents objected, and little improvement was noted in the offenders.[166] At Gubbio the outcome was utterly disastrous; the younger boys, "armed," ganged together and beat up on their oppressors.[167] The problem dragged on in the Society without satisfactory resolution, although in 1558 the First General Congregation mitigated Ignatius's prohibition by allowing the general to dispense from it "when necessary."[168]

126/ Some of the problems I have been describing are endemic to secondary schools, even if not in the aggravated degree to which they sometimes afflicted the Jesuit colleges during this period. But the schools had opened at such a hectic pace and raised so many new issues that by 1553 a systemic crisis ensued. In that year Polanco composed a document dealing with the problem of their rapid multiplication, and Ignatius set down norms for the number and competence of Jesuits required to establish a school, for its endowment, and for other necessities before the Society would accept an invitation to open a school.[169]

127/ The First General Congregation, 1558, ratified the provisions concerning the number of Jesuits needed for a school and reiterated the same interesting distribution of tasks: two or three priests for confession and ministry of Word, four or five teachers, a few others as substitutes in case of sickness and other emergencies, and two temporal coadjutors to take care of material needs. This added up to about a dozen or more, less than half of them fulltime teachers.[170] In those few teachers considerable versatility was required; Nadal himself taught Greek, Hebrew, and mathematics in the first years at Messina.

128/ Meanwhile, schools began to close—at Argenta, Gubbio, Frascati, Foligno, Montepulciano, Modena, and elsewhere, sometimes amid great bitterness. Some schools made a poor showing against already established institutions, as in Florence, and many incurred overwhelming debts.[171] In some localities the resentment of local schoolmasters raged against them, causing the Jesuits to lose students and the financial support they so desperately needed.[172] At Segovia in 1570 the citizens withdrew their financial support from the school of "humane letters" and it had to close.[173] Whereas some towns sought out the Jesuits because their schools would fill a vacuum, others resented them and considered their schools superfluous. Modena, for instance, seemed to have plenty of schoolmasters, and its citizens never warmed up to the Jesuits, partly because of their hard line against persons suspected of Lutheranism.[174] The bishop held out little hope for the college because the teachers were not Italians.[175] In France the Jesuits in general had difficulty gaining acceptance.[176]

129/ In any case, if a great strategy was operative behind decisions when and where to establish schools, it is far from apparent, except for a preference for schools in larger and more important cities.[177] Ignatius did not wait for an invitation from Duke Cosimo I to establish a school in Florence, for example, but in 1551 had Laínez try to persuade the duke that it was a good idea.[178] It is true, moreover, that in 1555 Ignatius began to show himself less inclined to open more colleges in Italy, hoping to divert some of the available manpower to places like Hungary, Transylvania, Bohemia, Poland, France, and of course Germany, with an obvious eye to the struggle in those places against heresy.[179] It is also true that Antonio Possevino a few years later formulated a strategy for Piedmont and Savoy.[180]

130/ Otherwise opportunities were seized or created without benefit of a master plan and, it seems, often without adequate consideration of what the market would bear and what Jesuit talent could sustain. In 1565, in any case, the Second General Congregation decreed a drastic slowdown in opening new schools, no matter how important they may seem, until the Society had a more adequate supply of teachers and other persons to staff them.[181]

131/ Perhaps the major remedy the Society applied to bring order out of the many problems raised by the schools and to coordinate efforts in this far-flung enterprise was, besides an avalanche of written documents, the employment of "commissaries," those representatives of the general with practically plenipotentiary powers. As we have seen, the first and most out- standing of these was Nadal, appointed by Ignatius himself for Spain and Portugal, 1553–54, and then reappointed by him and his two immediate successors. Although in that first visitation Nadal was to promulgate and explain the Constitutions and to resolve doubts about "our way of pro- ceeding" the first task listed for him was to give order and method to the schools. This task continued to engage Nadal's energies in subsequent visi- tations—to the Empire and Italy in 1555, to Spain and Portugal in 1561, to France, Belgium, and the Empire in 1562–63, and to the same regions in 1566–68. Problems persisted, but through commissaries and other means a measure of stability was achieved, and some schools that earlier foundered began to flourish.[182]

TRAINING THE CLERGY

132/ The Jesuit educational venture originated with concern for the training of younger members of the Society, whose education the first companions hoped would be at least the equivalent of their own. Those companions must themselves be numbered among the clergy that benefited from the best their age had to offer. From their observations, however, and from many other sources as well, we know that the training of the diocesan clergy followed an extraordinarily haphazard pattern across Europe.[183] Although a small percentage were well educated and devout, the seemingly vast majority were so ill-trained as to constitute a major scandal, and some were ignorant almost beyond description. It was almost inevitable that the Jesuits would be drawn into attempts to alleviate the situation.

133/ They did so before the famous decree on seminaries of the Council of Trent, 1563, and would continue to do so afterward. Although after 1563 the Jesuits were surely influenced by the Council, their most typical institution did not fall into the pattern of the "Tridentine Seminary," that is, a free-standing and programmatically integral institution reserved exclusively for the future diocesan clergy under the direct jurisdiction of the local bishop. The Jesuits' preferred instrument for the training of their own members and young diocesan clerics was a school they themselves managed, perhaps with residences attached, that was open to both of those groups and also to lay students.

134/ The best way to get a sense of their thinking in this regard is to look at three Roman institutions—the Collegio Romano, the Collegio Germanico, and the Seminario Romano. Almost immediately upon its founding, the Collegio Romano assumed a special position because Ignatius urged Jesuit superiors around Europe to send scholastics there for training, and he entertained the hope that it would be the preeminent educational institution of the Society.[184] By 1555 it had Jesuit students from Italy, Spain, Portugal, France, Flanders, Germany, Bohemia, Dalmatia, Greece, and elsewhere, housed in the Collegio apart from the *casa professa*.[185] Moved from location to location until finally settled in 1560 in the present Piazza del Collegio

Romano, it was school building and residence for both Jesuit teachers and Jesuit students.[186]

135/ From the beginning its financial status was precarious, often desperate. The endowment from Borja fell far short of expectations and need. Polanco wrote to all Jesuit superiors in 1553 telling them that the Collegio would be an "ornament for the Holy See" but until the much later pontificate of Pope Gregory XIII (1572–85) financial support for it from the popes was sporadic and paltry.[187] Begging money for the Collegio was invariably one of Nadal's assignments on his Iberian trips. When in the fall of 1555 Ignatius sent some hundred Jesuits out of Rome to other colleges in Italy, Spain, and Portugal, he did so at least partly because he was constrained by the dire financial situation. He could not afford to feed them at the Collegio.[188]

136/ Among the colleges, however, the Collegio Romano was the apple of Ignatius's eye. He tried to provide for it the best teachers, drawn from Jesuit provinces throughout Europe. His successors continued the policy, which ensured the preeminence Ignatius had desired. Francisco de Toledo, for instance, arrived in 1559 to teach logic, but moved on to teach physics, metaphysics, cases of conscience, and scholastic theology; he eventually became one of the most important Catholic theologians of his day. As early as 1561, he published *Introductio in dialecticam Aristotelis.*[189] That same year, Juan de Mariana began at age twenty-four to teach Scripture and then scholastic theology. He remained at the Collegio until 1565, and many years later published his great masterpiece, *Historia general de Espana,* and the work for which he is best known, *De rege et regis institutione,* with its famous thesis on the permissibility of regicide. Cristoph Clavius, the distinguished German mathematician and astronomer, began teaching there in 1564. Moreover, regulations, procedures, and textbooks adopted at the Collegio were held up as the norm and ideal for schools elsewhere.[190] Although other students were admitted to the Collegio Romano in great numbers, in Jesuit eyes it had a special character because of its role in educating Jesuits. Almost from the beginning, it was conceived as a center from which Jesuits would be sent on various pastoral missions and from which "new colonies" would be formed for the founding of other schools.[191]

137/ The year after the Collegio Romano opened its doors, so did its closely related institution the Collegio Germanico.[192] The idea for the school originated with Cardinal Giovanni Morone, who proposed it to Ignatius. Assisted by Cardinal Marcello Cervini, Morone soon won approval for it from Pope Julius III. Its purpose was to provide training in Rome as future diocesan priests for young men from Germany and other areas of northern Europe "infected with heresy," such as Bohemia, Poland, and Hungary.[193] In a letter in 1554 in which Ignatius tried to win financial support for the Germanico from Emperor Charles V, he argued unsuccessfully that more was to be expected for the restoration of Catholicism in the Empire from the school than from arms or even from the Council of Trent.[194] Later that year in a letter to a Spanish Jesuit, Nadal expressed his enthusiasm for young men of "northern" nations being trained there "to preach and guide souls" by their example and learning, for there was a great lack of such pastors in those regions.[195]

138/ The Germanico opened with twenty-four students, who took their classes at the Collegio Romano. In other words, the Germanico was basically a residence. The Jesuits were in charge, and some resided there, overseeing the discipline, the religious program, and the academic repetitions, disputations, and similar exercises. The rules for the students were similar to those for the Jesuit scholastics. "Protectors" of the Germanico who sent students to it were expected to provide the financing for poor youths who wanted to be priests.[196]

139/ Even an institution of this simple design faltered. Except among the Jesuits, it failed to spark enthusiasm. Neither the German bishops, the Italian cardinals, nor Popes Julius III and Paul IV provided any consistent financial aid, and by 1556 the whole financial burden fell on the Society. There were also disciplinary problems.[197]

140/ The number of German students had meanwhile fallen below even the originally modest number. The Germanico admitted only one new student in 1555, none in 1556 and 1557. In an effort to save the institution at least in principle, Laínez in 1558 allowed admission of other students as paying boarders. Most were Italians. They were not expected to be candidates for holy orders. Within a few years and after several changes of location, the expedient resulted in a great influx of these new students. They were all under fifteen years old. The costs of boarding meant that they had to come from wealthy backgrounds; indeed, some of them were from the most distinguished families of their locality—the Dorias of Genoa, the Bentivoglios and Buoncompagnis of Bologna, the Fuggers of Augsburg. Names like these confirm the good reputation the Jesuits had already achieved as educators. By 1565 the Germanico had students from many countries of Europe, including Poland, England, and Scotland, and even two from Turkey.[198]

141/ Wealthy though the students were, they of course paid no tuition to the Collegio Romano, but they had to pay for their meals and the other expenses of a boarding school.[199] They had to pay for any servants in their own employ.[200] Between 1563 and 1573 the number of students resident in the college was about two hundred, with the ratio of about one German seminarian to ten of the others.[201] This means that the Germanico had devolved during this period into an institution reserved largely for the wealthy elite.

142/ The disciplinary problems arising from this mix of nationalities and from the sometimes recalcitrant students get due attention in the abundant documentation that has survived.[202] The Germans, according to Nadal, were "disobedient and trouble-makers."[203] The Italian *putti* were often bad when they first arrived, but the Jesuits saw them change for the better with time.[204] However, they often resented the Jesuit scholastics who were sent there to help with the discipline of the house and other matters.[205]

143/ Despite problems and the reservations about the enterprise entertained by some Jesuits, Polanco painted an optimistic picture in his circular letter to the Society in 1565, emphasizing how fond the students had grown of their collegio.[206] About 1567, Cortesono, who was the rector and ought to have been better informed, went so far as to suggest the abandonment of the institution as it was originally conceived, because "Germany is not so much in need as before."[207] By 1570 Laurentano, soon to be rector himself, vigorously supported the direction the Germanico had taken: "Just as the ecclesiastical seminaries are ordered for the reform of the clergy, so does this college serve for the reform of the lay nobility . . . The Society does not have a better means to help the nobility and great lords and magistrates of our times."[208] Two years later, on the eve of the transfer of the non-German boarders to the Seminario, he argued the same position.[209]

144/ The original purpose of the Germanico was thus largely thwarted during this period, and some Jesuits did not see great urgency in its recovery. Other counsels prevailed. When Pope Gregory XIII gave moral support to the original purpose and backed it up with substantial financing, the non-German boarders were moved out in 1573. Bishops of the Empire had meanwhile begun to send students in greater numbers. From this time forward the Germanico became an important instrument in the restoration of Catholicism in many parts of Germany through the pastors and especially the theologians and future bishops it trained. Jesuit universities elsewhere often followed the same pattern of having colleges for diocesan clergy attached to them. The Germanico also served as a model for the establishment of papal seminaries in Germany in the 1570s and 1580s.[210]

145/ The Germanico and its parent institution, the Collegio Romano, were the first institutions of international scope established in Rome for the training of future Catholic clergy. After 1573, the Germanico became the model for other national colleges of clerical students attached to the Collegio Romano that would become characteristic of the city.[211] These two colleges were the first and decisive steps in a process that eventually turned Rome into the center for training clergy that it has remained to this day.

146/ In 1564 Pope Pius IV founded the Seminario Romano for the archdiocese of Rome in conformity with the Tridentine decree of the previous year.[212] Although he was at the time annoyed with the Jesuits, he confided its direction to them, an action that set off widespread resentment in the Roman clergy against the Society, not least because the pope truced them to support the new institution. In that context Bishop Ascanio Cesarini proclaimed that he could not bear having Roman youth taught by Germans and Spaniards—that is, heretics and Jews! Nonetheless, in February 1565, after the death of Laínez the previous month, the Seminario opened its doors to some eighty students.[213]

147/   The Seminary was basically a residence for the Germanico. The students took classes at the Collegio Romano, up to but not including courses in theology. The Jesuits found the students extremely difficult to handle and complained that, unlike at the Germanico and other schools fully under the aegis of the Society, they had no control over admissions and dismissals. In 1568 the Roman province of the Jesuits decided to ask Pope Pius V to relieve the Society of the Seminario and give it to others, but to no avail.[214]

148/   Sometime around 1570 the Jesuit rector and his assistant wrote reports that made the seminarians sound like outlaws. Although they came from the lowest rungs of Roman society, they were nonetheless filled with an overweening pride. They were liars, cheats, ingrates, utterly untrustworthy, corruptors of the few good among them, devoid of any pastoral or religious motivation, intent only upon gaining fat benefices with no pastoral duties attached. They called the seminary a "prison" and the Jesuits "spies and hypocrites," their "jailers and executioners." In the rector's opinion, the Germanico was in comparison "a paradise."[215]

149/   Through many vicissitudes the Jesuits continued in their role at the Seminario until the Society was suppressed in the late eighteenth century. At least in the sixteenth century they were disinclined toward undertaking other institutions of this type. In 1565 the Second General Congregation, which was convoked to elect a successor to Laínez, took up the issue formally and decreed that the Society not assume responsibility for "episcopal seminaries about which the Council of Trent decreed," even if the bishops were willing to commit their full governance to the Society. The Congregation allowed the general to make exceptions, but only under certain stringent conditions.[216] Why this reluctance?

150/   The furor and ill will aroused by their acceptance of the Seminario Romano surely made an impact on the Jesuits gathered for the Congregation, and an even more complicated imbroglio in Milan surrounding the new seminary sponsored by Carlo Borromeo had to increase their misgivings.[217] But there were deeper reasons. Even when assurances to the contrary were given them, the Jesuits worried about losing in such institutions their independence to act as they saw fit. They may have feared implication in matters proper to diocesan officials. In any case, in 1568 Borja, now general, stated that the "statutes prescribed for seminaries by the Council of Trent" made them incompatible with the Jesuit Institute.[218]

151/   Even more fundamentally, the Jesuits believed that their own colleges were already "true and excellent seminaries," as Polanco wrote to Nadal from Trent on 6 July 1563, an idea allowed by the Tridentine decree.[219] As early as 1553, Ignatius agreed as part of the statutes to accept as students at the college of Compostela four candidates for ordination from that archbishopric and eight from other bishoprics of Galicia.[220] More generally, the Jesuits prided themselves on the number of the students in their colleges who decided to become priests or enter religious orders. When in 1550 Ignatius described to Ercole d'Este, duke of Ferrara, the college he wanted to establish there as "a seminary, from which will come regularly new laborers in the vineyard of the Lord," he surely meant to include such students in that description.[221]

152/   The colleges were in fact far superior in both their academic and religious programs to the diocesan seminaries that eventuated from the legislation of Trent. Concerned though the Jesuits were with the proper training of the diocesan clergy, they much preferred to promote it through their own institutions.[222]

153/   The model Jesuits envisaged for the education of the diocesan clergy even after Trent, therefore, was an adapted form of the late-medieval practice of special residences for the clergy, which might also contain lay students, located in the vicinity of an educational institution like a university and attached to it. At the Jesuit university at Pont-à-Mousson in the early seventeenth century, for instance, there were three "seminaries" for students from three different dioceses, as well as several convents for students from other religious orders.[223]

154/   There was another way, however, in which Jesuits contributed to the training of the diocesan clergy in several parts of the world. Building on the early pattern of the temporary teaching assignments of Laínez and Favre at the University of Rome and of Jay, Salmerón, and Canisius at Ingolstadt, Jesuits began to accept more long-term assignments to teach especially philosophy and theology in universities not under the aegis of the Society. Only priests or candidates for ordination studied theology at universities, and many students of philosophy were drawn from that same group.

155/   At Ingolstadt beginning in 1556, for instance, the number of Jesuits teaching theology, small though it was, equaled or surpassed the number of others. From 1560 until 1575 three Jesuits taught theology at the University of Cologne. In Trier as early as 1561 Jesuits had in effect taken over the faculties of philosophy and theology and were soon on the way to doing the same at Mainz. The pattern continued into the seventeenth century. The number of Jesuits thus engaged was relatively modest, but their influence through their students, who often became teachers themselves, was significant.[224]

156/   As we have seen, the Jesuits inserted into the formal university program courses on cases of conscience—courses that had a direct bearing on pastoral practice. Their insistence on the study of rhetoric, on the "Tones," and on similar exercises to help develop preaching skills broke, on the one hand, a pattern of university training that ignored such skills and, on the other, a pattern of apprenticeship training that lacked the means to communicate them effectively. In codifying these developments among Catholics, the Jesuits were pioneers.

THE IMPACT OF THE SCHOOLS

157/ The Jesuits opened a new era for formal education in Roman Catholicism. The Society was the first religious order to undertake systematically, as a primary and self-standing ministry, the operation of full-fledged schools for any students, lay or clerical, who chose to come to them. It marked a decided break with earlier patterns of relationship between the church and educational institutions.[225]

158/ Over the course of the next two centuries, the Society established its remarkable network of more than eight hundred educational institutions, primarily in Latin Europe and Latin America, but also in other parts of the world, a truly unique phenomenon in the history of education that ended with the suppression of the order in 1773. When the Jesuits were restored by Pope Pius VII in 1814, they resumed the task. Moreover, since the latter part of the sixteenth century their example encouraged many other religious orders of men and women to do the same, down to the present century.

159/ Jesuit schools greatly influenced religion and culture in many areas of the world, but the very immensity of the Jesuit educational enterprise and the complexity of the questions it raises practically preclude a comprehensive assessment. We must be content with studies limited to specific territories, chronologies, and issues—and thence draw larger, highly qualified conclusions.[226]

160/ A somewhat more tractable problem . . . is the impact the schools had on the Society of Jesus itself. The Jesuit Constitutions stipulated that "the first characteristic of our Institute" was for the members to be free to travel to various parts of the world.[227] The foundational model for this characteristic was the itinerant preachers of the Gospel described in the New Testament. Although the evangelical model was dominant in the early years, it was of course not the only one, for stable residences were foreseen from the beginning. Nonetheless, that model now had to be further tempered by the reality of being resident schoolmasters. The tension between the continuing insistence on the necessity of mobility and the long-term commitment required by the schools would remain throughout Jesuit history.

161/ Even in the early years the schools were comparatively large and complex institutions that required the best talent for their management and faculty. Their governance and the officials needed for it became a special focus of attention and legislation. The Jesuit communities attached to them grew to considerable size, and this development hastened and conditioned the usual sociological repercussions of transition from an informal situation to something larger and more regularized. The fact that most members of the Society would be housed in the endowed institutions that were the schools changed an important aspect of the vow of poverty described in the Constitutions. Moreover, the Jesuits became property owners on a large scale, for their schools with their classrooms, observatories, theaters, and courtyards were often huge establishments, to which were attached a Jesuit residence and church.

162/ While in many ways the schools enhanced the other ministries, which so often used them as a base, they also absorbed manpower and talent to an extraordinary degree. This meant that an increasing amount of Jesuit energy would be spent on adolescent boys. Those boys were often, but by no means exclusively, drawn from the middle and upper classes of society, and the Jesuit schools to some extent drew the other ministries along with them in that direction. From these classes of society, moreover, the Jesuits would tend to attract their own new members. The Jesuits never lost their concern for the poor and "outcast," and some would expend great energies on them. But with the passage of years it was indirect assistance through the Marian Congregations and other confraternities they inspired that became increasingly important.

163/ Until the Collegio Romano opened in 1551, the Jesuits intended that their own members would be taught by university teachers who were not Jesuits. After that date they began to take for granted, though the

Constitutions suggest otherwise, that Jesuits would be trained by other Jesuits in schools run by Jesuits. This change helped forge a clearer sense of identity for the members of the Society, but it also meant a more closed intellectual atmosphere.

164/ Perhaps the most important change the schools wrought within the Society, however, was the new kind and degree of its members' engagement with culture beyond the traditionally clerical subjects of philosophy and theology. The earliest Jesuits from the beginning wanted their recruits to have a first-rate education, but with the schools came the obligation to train their members to teach what they had learned, and therefore to appropriate it in a more profound way. Moreover, much of what they taught related only indirectly to the Christian religion as such.

165/ The *Constitutions* of the Dominicans from the thirteenth century stipulated that student-members of the order were not to read books by pagans or learn any "secular sciences" except by dispensation: "let these student-members and all others read only books of theology."[228] The Dominican *Constitutions* allowed exceptions, which subsequent General Chapters authorized, but the stipulation continued to be observed and to have effect into the sixteenth century and beyond.[229] The history of the first six or seven years of the Jesuits did not preclude a similar route for them, especially given the conservative turn taken in Catholic circles at about that time. However, by force of their vocation as teachers of the humanities and of "natural philosophy," that is, the physical sciences, the Jesuits had to move in precisely the opposite direction.

166/ Ignatius foresaw Jesuits writing books on ministry and in refutation of "the heretics," which they did, but many of the first books that Jesuits produced were textbooks on grammar, rhetoric, and the Latin and Greek classics—subjects that almost every Jesuit taught at some point in his career. *De arte rhetorica* by Cipriano Soares, first published in 1562, ran through more than two hundred editions into the nineteenth century.[230]

167/ Jesuits taught mathematics, astronomy, physics, and other sciences, wrote on these subjects, ran observatories and laboratories, and attained renown in these fields.[231] The schools also brought theater with them, and with theater came dance and music, so that the early misgivings about music were challenged from another direction and gradually overcome. In some places they brought training in fencing and horsemanship. The large buildings that Jesuit schools required led members of the Society into a new relationship with architects and architecture. The schools, though run under Jesuit auspices, were institutions of civic import that gave the Jesuits an access to civic life that their churches alone could never provide.

168/ Thus began an engagement with secular culture, modest enough at first, that became a hallmark of the order and an integral part of its self-definition, not present at the beginning. That engagement was not occasional or incidental, but systemic. It became interwoven with the very fabric of the Jesuits' understanding of their ministry, of their "way of proceeding." Their religious mission remained basic to them, but, especially as a result of the schools, they also began to see themselves as having a cultural mission.

169/ A basic premise of the humanist tradition in the Renaissance was that religious and moral inspiration could be found even in pagan authors. The Jesuits subscribed to that premise, which generically correlated with the tendency in Thomistic theology to find as much harmony as possible between "nature and grace," also a theme of the Jesuit Constitutions. Although the Jesuits were not uncritical in their engagement with secular culture, they tended in general to be welcoming of it.

170/ When the Jesuits first embarked on their educational venture about a decade after their founding, they could not have foreseen its impact on them. They treated the schools as if they were one more—although an especially important—ministry added to an already long list. They did not grasp that this ministry had an intrinsic dynamism that would change the organization undertaking it.

1   *Monumenta paedagogica Societatis Jesu (M Paed.),* 2nd ed. rev., (Rome, 1965–86), 3:305–306.
2   For the general background, see R R. Bolger, *The Classical Heritage and Its Beneficiaries: From the Carolingian Age to the End of the Renaissance* (New York: Harper and Row, 1964); Paul F. Grendler, *Schooling in Renaissance Italy: Literacy and Learning, 1300–1600* (Baltimore and London: The Johns Hopkins University Press, 1989), especially pp. 363–381; Gerald Strauss, *Luther's House of Learning: Indoctrination of the Young in the German Reformation* (Baltimore and London: The Johns Hopkins University Press, 1978); Anthony Grafton and Lisa Jardine, *From Humanism to the Humanities: Education and the Liberal Arts in Fifteenth- and Sixteenth-Century Europe* (Cambridge, Mass.: Harvard University Press, 1986); George Huppert, *Public Schools in Renaissance France* (Urbana and Chicago: University of Illinois Press, 1984); Marie-Madeleine Compère, *Du collège au lycée (1500–1850): Généalogie de l'enseignement secondaire français* (Paris: Editions Gallimard, 1985), and the bibliographical review edited by Grendler, "Education in the Renaissance and Reformation," *Renaissance Quarterly,* 43 (1990), 774–824. On the Jesuits, see especially Allan P. Farrell, *The Jesuit Code of Liberal Education: Development and Scope of the Ratio Studiorum* (Milwaukee: Bruce Publishing Company, 1938); George E. Ganss, *Saint Ignatius' Idea of a Jesuit University (Milwaukee: Marquette University Press, 1954); Ladislaus Lukács, "De origine collegiorum externorum deque controversiis circa eorum paupertatem obortis," Archivum Historicum Societatis Iesu (AHSI), 29 (1960), 189–245; 30 (1961), 1–89; John W. Donohue, Jesuit Education: An Essay on the Foundation of Its Idea (New York: Fordham University Press, 1963); Mabel Lundberg, Jesuitische Anthropologie und Erziehungslehre in der Frühzeit des Ordens (ca. 1540– ca. 1650) (Uppsala: Almquist & Wiksells, 1966); Gabriel Codina Mir, Aux sources de la pédagogie des jésuites: Le "Modus parisiensis" (Rome: Institutum Historicum Societatis Jesu, 1968); François de Dainville, L'education des jesuites (XVIe-XVIIIe siècles), ed. Marie-Madeleine Compère (Paris: Les éditions de minuit, 1978); Karl Hengst, Jesuiten an Universitäten und Jesuitenuniversitäten: Zur Geschichte der Universitäten in der Oberdeutschen und Rheinischen Provinz der Gesellschaft Jesu im Zeitalter der konfessionellen Auseinandersetzung (Paderborn: Ferdinand Schöningh, 1981); Gian Paolo Brizzi, ed., La "Ratio studiorum": Modelli culturali e pratiche educative dei Gesuiti in Italia tra Cinque e Seicento (Rome: Bulzoni Editore, 1981); Aldo Scaglione, The Liberal Arts and the Jesuit College System (Amsterdam and Philadelphia: John Benjamins Publishing Company, 1986).*
3   Juan Alfonso de Polanco, *Vita Ignatii Loiolae et rerum Societatis Jesu historica [Chronicon] (Chron.),* (Madrid, 1894–98), 2:195.
4   *Monumenta Ignatiana. Sancti Ignatti de Loyola Societatis Jesu fundatoris epistolae et instructions (MI Epp.),* (Madrid, 1903–11), 9:83.
5   See Hengst, *Jesuiten,* pp. 80–86.
6   *Chron.,* 1:156–157.
7   *Institutum Societatis Jesu,* 2 vols. (Prague: Typis Universitatis Carolo-Ferdinandeae, 1757), 1:18.
8   *Chron.,* 1:410. See Hengst, *Jesuiten,* pp. 86–90.
9   *Fontes narrative de S. Ignacio de Loyola et de Societatis Jesu initiis (FN),* (Rome, 1943–1965), 1:610. See Antonio M. de Aldama, The Constitutions of the Society of Jesus: An Introductory Commentary on the *Constitutions,* trans. Aloysius J. Owen (St. Louis: The Institute of Jesuit Sources, 1989), p. 147, n29.
10 See Lukács, "De origine," (1960), 197–199.
11 See James A. O'Donohoe, Tridentine Seminary Legislation: Its Sources and Formation (Louvain: Publications Universitaires de Louvain, 1957), pp. 35–37, 64–73.
12 *Epistolae PP. Paschasii Broëti, Claudii Jagi, Joannis Codurii et Simonis Rodericii (M Broët),* (Madrid, 1903), pp. 286–291.
13 See Angelo Martini, "Gli studi teologici di Giovanni de Polanco alle origini della legislazione scolastica della Compagnia di Gesù," *AHSI,* 21 (1952), p. 272.
14 See Francisco de Borja de Medina, "La Compañía de Jesús y la minoría morisca (1545–1614)," *AHSI,* 57 (1988), 3–136, especially 32–38.
15 *M Paed.,* 1:373–375.
16 Litterae Quadrimestres ex universis praeter Indiam et Brasiliam locis in quibus aliqui de Societate Jesu versabantur Romam missae (Litt. Quadr.), (Madrid and Rome, 1894–1932), 1:51.
17 *Epistolae P. Hieronymi Nadal Societatis Jesu ab anno 1546 ad 1577 (M Nadal),* (Rome, 1962), 2:3. See also *FN,* 3:746–753.

[18] See Dennis Edmond Pate, "Jerónimo Nadal and the Early Development of the Society of Jesus, 1545–1573" (Ph.D. diss., University of California, Los Angeles, 1980), pp. 53–136, and Mario Scaduto, "Le origini dell'Università di Messina: A proposito del quarto centenario," *AHSI*, 17 (1948), 102–159.

[19] *M Nadal*, 1:53–63.

[20] *Chron.*, 1:385.

[21] Litt. Quadr., 1:172.

[22] See Hengst, *Jesuiten*, pp. 99–109.

[23] *Chron.*, 1:390, 404–405.

[24] MI Epp., 4:11–12.

[25] *MI Epp.*, 4:5–9.

[26] See Miguel Batllori, Cultura e Finanze: Studi sulla storia dei Gesuiti da S. Ignazio al Vaticano II (Rome: Edizioni di Storia e Letteratura, 1983), especially pp. 121–138.

[27] *MI Epp.*, 4:9–11.

[28] See, for instance, Thomas Deutscher, "Seminaries and the Education of Novarese Priests, 1593–1627," The Journal of Ecclesiastical History, 32 (1981), 303–319, and "The Growth of the Secular Clergy and the Development of Educational Institutions in the Diocese of Novara (1563–1772)," ibid., 40 (1989), 381–397.

[29] *M Paed.*, 1:606; Nadal, Scholia, p. 384.

[30] *Chron.*, 5:550. Lukács gives the number as forty-six, "De origine," (1960), p. 241. Scaglione gives thirty-three for 1556, *Liberal Arts,* p. 61.

[31] See Lukács, "De origine," (1960), 242–243; *Chron.*, 2:460; 6:340–341.

[32] Polanci Complementa. Epistolae et commentaria P. Joannis Alphonsi de Polanco (*P Co.*), (Madrid 1916–1917), 2:657; *Chron.*, 6:373–374, 379–380.

[33] See Lukács, "De origine," (1960), 234–235.

[34] *M Nadal*, 5:462, 832.

[35] *M Paed.*, 2:872.

[36] The *Constitutions* of the Society of Jesus (Const.), #440, 451.

[37] See Huppert, Public Schools; Grendler, Schooling in Italy; Codina Mir, *Aux sources*; Scaglione, Liberal Arts.

[38] *M Paed.*, 1:475.

[39] See Grafton and Jardine, *From Humanism*, pp. 1–28.

[40] *MI Epp.*, 1:519–526. See Mario Fois, "La giustificazione cristiana degli studi umanistici da parte di Ignazio di Loyola e le sue conseguenze nei gesuiti posteriori," in *Ignacio de Loyola y su tiempo*, ed. Juan Plazaola (Bilbao: Ediciones Mensajero, 1992), pp. 405–440.

[41] *Chron.*, 2:19.

[42] *Chron.*, 5:535·

[43] *Chron.*, 2:651.

[44] See Gian-Mario Anselmi, "Per un' archeologia della Ratio: Dalla 'pedogagia' al 'governo,'" in Brizzi, *"Ratio studiorum,"* pp. 11–42.

[45] *MI Epp.*, 12:310.

[46] *M Paed.*, 1:485.

[47] *M Nadal*, 271.

[48] On these two types of schools in Renaissance Italy, see Grendler, *Schooling in Italy*, pp. 111–329.

[49] *M Paed.*, 1:89–90, 284–285, 526; *MI Epp.*, 3:722–724.

[50] *Const.*, #451.

[51] See Scaglione, Liberal Arts; Grendler, *Schooling in Italy*, pp. 381–399; Gian Paolo Brizzi, La formazione della classe dirigente nel Sei-Settecento: I seminaria nobilium nell'Italia centro-settentrionale (Bologna: Il Mulino, 1976); Gian Paolo Brizzi, Alessandro D'Alessandro, and Alessandra del Fonte, *Università, Principe, Gesuiti: La politica farnesiana dell'istruzione a Parma e Piacenza (1545–1622)* (Rome: Bulzoni Editore, 1980).

[52] *M Paed.*, 1:136; *M Nadal*, 5:462, 832.

[53] Scaglione, *Liberal Arts*, p. 43.

[54] *MI Epp.*, 4:7–9.

[55] *Const.*, #623g.

[56] Nadal, *Pláticas*, p. 132.

[57] *M Paed.*, 1:93–106.

[58] See Donohue, *Jesuit Education*, pp. 125–136, and Strauss, *Luther's House of Learning*, pp. 48–70.

[59] *M Paed.*, 2:670–685.
[60] See, for example, Scaglione, *Liberal Arts*, p. 57.
[61] See Lundberg, *Jesuitische Anthropologie.*
[62] See de Aldama, *Constitutions,* pp. 139–187.
[63] *Const.,* #394, 392–439.
[64] *Const.,* #446–451, 440–509.
[65] *Const.,* #452.
[66] *M Paed.,* 1:133–163.
[67] See Grendler, *Schooling in Italy,* p. 379.
[68] See Ricardo García Villoslada, *Storia del Collegio Romano dal suo inizio (1551) alla soppressione della Compagnia di Gesù (1773)* (Rome: Pontificia Università Gregoriana, 1954).
[69] *Const.,* #446.
[70] See Codina Mir, *Aux sources,* pp. 282–288.
[71] *M Paed.,* 1:425–426.
[72] See Farrell, *Jesuit Code,* pp. 119–121, and Scaglione, *Liberal Arts,* pp. 13–14.
[73] See Codina Mir, *Aux sources,* pp. 109–131.
[74] See Huppert, Public Schools, pp. 47–60, and James K. Farge, "The University of Paris in the Time of Ignatius of Loyola," in *Ignacio y su tiempo,* pp. 221–243, especially pp. 230–231. See also Scaglione, *Liberal Arts,* for correctives to Codina Mir, *Aux sources.*
[75] See Anton Schindling, *Humanistische Hochschule und freie Reichsstadt: Gymnasium und Akademie in Strassburg, 1538–1621* (Wiesbaden: Franz Steiner Verlag, 1977).
[76] *M Paed.,* 1:599–602.
[77] *Chron.,* 2:544.
[78] *M Paed.,* 1:458.
[79] *Chron.,* 2:270.
[80] *Chron.,* 3:241.
[81] *Chron.,* 4:445.
[82] See Codina Mir, *Aux sources,* pp. 220–221.
[83] *M Nadal,* 2:8.
[84] See Scaglione, *Liberal Arts,* pp. 92–93, and Jacqueline Lacotte, "La notion de jeu dans la pédagogie des jésuites," *Revue des Sciences Humaines,* no. 158 (June 1975), 251–268.
[85] *M Paed.,* 2:910.
[86] See Grendler, *Schooling in Italy,* p. 365.
[87] See Scaglione, *Liberal Arts,* pp. 68–69.
[88] See Codina Mir, *Aux sources,* pp. 141–147.
[89] *Const.,* #482.
[90] *Chron.,* 2:37.
[91] *Chron.,* 2:223–224.
[92] *M Paed.,* 2:864–934.
[93] *M Paed.,* 2:877.
[94] *M Paed.,* 2:911.
[95] *M Paed.,* 2:949.
[96] *Const.,* #486.
[97] *B. Petri Fabri primi sacerdotis e Societate Jesu Epistolae, memorial et processus (M Fabri),* (Madrid, 1914) p. 491.
[98] *M Paed.,* 1:158; 2:29, 95; *M Nadal,* 4:490; Nadal, Scholia, p. 383.
[99] *Chron.,* 2:242–243.
[100] See Codina Mir, *Aux sources,* p. 306.
[101] See Scaglione, *Liberal Arts,* pp. 48–49.
[102] See, for example, Charles Trinkaus, "Themes for a Renaissance Anthropology," in *The Scope of Renaissance Humanism* (Ann Arbor: The University of Michigan Press,1983), pp. 364–403.
[103] *M Nadal,* 1:473.
[104] See Codina Mir, *Aux sources,* pp. 128–130.
[105] *Chron.,* 2:501.
[106] *Chron.,* 6:164.
[107] *Chron.,* 2:514.
[108] *Chron.,* 3:8. See Villoslada, *Collegio Romano,* p. 29.
[109] *M Nadal,* 1:271.
[110] *P Co.,* 2:582, 584, 605.

[111] *Chron.*, 5:120–121.

[112] *Chron.*, 6:163–164.

[113] *Chron.*, 6:164.

[114] *Chron.*, 6:163.

[115] *P Co.*, 1:267–268; 2:582.

[116] *Chron.*, 6:179.

[117] See, for example, Nerida Newbigin, "The Word Made Flesh: The *Rappresentazioni* of Mysteries and Miracles in Fifteenth-Century Florence" in *Christianity and the Renaissance: Image and Religious Imagination in the Quattrocento,* ed. Timothy Verdon and John Henderson (Syracuse: Syracuse University Press, 1990), pp. 361–375; Cyrilla Barr, "Music and Spectacle in Confraternity Drama of Fifteenth-Century Florence" ibid., pp. 376–401; Paola Ventrone, "Thoughts on Florentine Fifteenth-Century Religious Spectacle" ibid., pp. 405–412; Konrad Eisenbichler, ed., *Crossing the Boundaries: Christian Piety and the Arts in Italian Medieval and Renaissance Confraternities* (Kalamazoo: Medieval Institute Publications, 1991), pp. 11–107, 237–262.

[118] Jean-Marie Valentin, *Le théâtre des jésuites dans les pays de langue allemande* (1554–1680), 3 vols. (Bern: Peter Lang, 1978), and *Le théâtre des jésuites dans les pays de langue allemande: Répertoire chronologique des pièces représentées et des documents conservés* (1555–1773), 2 vols. (Stuttgart: A. Hiersemann, 1983–84). See also "Gegenreformation und Literatur: Das Jesuitendrama im Dienste der religiösen und moralischen Erziehung," *Historisches Jahrbuch*, 100 (1980), 240–256; Ruprecht Wimmer, *Jesuitentheater, Didactik und Fest: Das Exemplum des ägyptischen Joseph auf den deutschen Bühnen der Gesellschaft Jesu* (Frankfurt am Main: Vittorio Klostermann, 1982); Géza Staud, "Les décors du théâtre des jésuites à Sopron (Hongrie)," *AHSI*, 46 (1977), 277–298; Jan Okon, "Sul teatro dei Gesuiti nell'antica Polonia: Dopo i primi volumi di una pubblicazione fondamentale," ibid., 51 (1982), 319–328; L. E. Roux, "Cent ans d'expérience théâtrale dans les collèges de la Compagnie de Jésus en Espagne," in *Dramaturge et société: Rapports entre l'oeuvre théâtrale, son interprétation et son public au XVIe et XVIIe siècles,* ed. Jean Jacquot, 2 vols. (Paris: Centre national de la recherche scientifique, 1968), 2:479–523; Florencio Segura, "El teatro en los colegios de los jesuitas," *Miscellanea Comillas*, 43 (1985), 299–327; for France, see de Dainville, *L'education des jésuites*, pp. 473–517. A comprehensive study in English, reliable but outdated, is William H. McCabe, *An Introduction to the Jesuit Theater: A Posthumous Work,* ed. Louis J. Oldani (St. Louis: The Institute of Jesuit Sources, 1983). See as well Michael C. Halbig, *The Jesuit Theater of Jacob Masen: Three Plays in Translation with an Introduction* (Bern: Peter Lang, 1987); Joseph Simons, *Jesuit Theater Englished: Five Tragedies of Joseph Simons,* ed. Louis J. Oldani and Philip C. Fisher (St. Louis: The Institute of Jesuit Sources, 1989), and especially Nigel Griffin, *Jesuit School Drama: A Checklist of Critical Literature* (London: Grant & Cutler, 1976), and the supplement under the same title, 1986. For comparisons, see Edith Weber, "Le théâtre humaniste protestant à participation musicale et le théâtre jésuite: Influences, convergences, divergences," in *Les jésuites parmi les hommes aux XVIe et XVIIe siècles: Actes du Colloque de Clermont-Ferrand (avril 1985),* ed. G. and G. Demerson, B. Dompnier, and A. Regond (Clermont-Ferrand: Association des Publications de la Faculté des Lettres et Sciences Humaines, 1987), pp. 445–460, and Marguerite Soulié, "Le théâtre et la Bible au XVIe siècle," in *Le temps des Réformes et la Bible,* ed. Guy Bedouelle and Bernard Roussel (Bible de tous les temps, 5) (Paris: Beauchesne, 1989), pp. 635–658.

[119] See, however, Raymond Lebègue, "Les ballets des jésuites," *Revue des cours et conférences,* 37 (1935–36), 127–139, 209–222, 321–330, and Judith Rock, "Terpsichore at Louis Le Grand: Baroque Dance on a Jesuit Stage in Paris" (Ph.D. diss., Graduate Theological Union, Berkeley, 1988).

[120] *Chron.*, 5:421–422.

[121] *Chron.*, 6:567.

[122] See *Obras de P. José de Acosta de la Compañía de Jesús: Estudio preliminar y edición,* ed. Francisco Mateos (Madrid: Ediciones Atlas, 1954).

[123] *Chron.*, 6:303.

[124] See Segura, "El teatro," pp. 326–327; Bernhard Duhr, *Geschichte der Jesuiten in den Ländern deutscher Zunge im XVI. Jahrhundert* (Freiburg: Herdersche Verlagshandlung, 1907), p. 337.

[125] See Villoslada, *Collegio Romano*, p. 77. For examples from a later period, see Staud, "Les décors à Sopron," pp. 279–282.

[126] See Duhr, Geschichte der *Jesuiten,* pp. 339, 342.

[127] *M Paed.*, 3:269–271.

[128] *M Paed.*, 3:267–268.

[129] *M Paed.*, 3:390–392, 439–440.

[130] *P Co.*, 2:710. See Villoslada, *Collegio Romano*, pp. 76–77.

[131] See Valentin, *Le théâtre: Répertoire*, 1:1–48.

[132] Ibid., 1:1–7.

[133] See Melveena McKendrick, *Theatre in Spain, 1490–1700* (Cambridge: Cambridge University Press, 1989), p. 52.

[134] See Scaduto, *Laínez*, 2:358.

[135] Ibid., 2:432.

[136] See Segura, "El teatro," p. 324.

[137] See Duhr, *Geschichte der Jesuiten*, pp. 331–332, 337, 339, 340.

[138] Ibid., pp. 337–338.

[139] See Donohue, *Jesuit Education*, pp. 39–40.

[140] The Spiritual Exercises of Ignatius of Loyola (*SpEx*), critically edited in *Monumenta Ignatiana. Exercitia spiritualia S. Ignatii de Loyola et eorum directoria* (Madrid, 1903–1911), #363. See Marc Fumaroli, "Definition et description: Scholastique et rhetorique chez les jésuites des XVIe et XVIIe siècles," *Travaux de linguistique et de litterature*, 18 (1980), 37–48.

[141] *Chron.*, 4:507; 5:563; *M Paed.*, 2:883, 946.

[142] *Chron.*, 3:294.

[143] *M Paed.*, 2:870–871.

[144] *Chron.*, 3:391; *M Paed.*, 3:362–365.

[145] *Chron.*, 5:528.

[146] *Chron.*, p58. See, for example, A. Lynn Martin, *The Jesuit Mind: The Mentality of an Elite in Early Modern France* (Ithaca: Cornell University Press, 1988), pp. 53–57.

[147] *Chron.*, 4:58, 100–101; *M Paed.*, 3:342, 374–375.

[148] *Chron.*, 2:524; 4:100.

[149] *M Nadal*, 1:367.

[150] *Chron.*, 3:60.

[151] *Chron.*, 3:47.

[152] *Chron.*, 3:161.

[153] *M Paed.*, 3:341–342, 373–375, 377–382, 443–444.

[154] *M Paed.*, 3:261–262.

[155] *Chron.*, 6:196, 199–200.

[156] *Chron.*, 5:101.

[157] *M Paed.*, 1:21, 200, 637; 3:32.

[158] *Chron.*, 3:28.

[159] *M Paed.*, 2:977, 993.

[160] See Duhr, *Geschichte der Jesuiten*, pp. 295–296.

[161] See Pietro Tacchi Venturi, *Storia della Compagnia di Gesù in Italia*, 2 vols. in 4 (Rome: Edizioni la Civiltà Cattolica, 1938–51), 2/2:356.

[162] *Chron.*, 3:23–24; *M Paed.*, 1:423–424; *Const.*, #397, 488, 489.

[163] *Chron.*, 4:204.

[164] *Chron.*, 6:178–179, 226; *M Paed.*, 1:464, 591.

[165] *Chron.*, 6:226.

[166] *Chron.*, 4:62; 5:140; *M Paed.*, 1:591.

[167] *Chron.*, 3:28; *M Paed.*, 1:553.

[168] *Institutum*, 1:464.

[169] *M Paed.*, 1:446–449; Lukács, "De origine," (1960), 238–241. See also Miguel Batllori, "Su la fondazione del collegio di Sassari: 1562. Nel IV centenario della Università turritana," *AHSI*, 31 (1962), 360–377; Jan Korewa, "Les débuts de la Compagnie de Jésus en Pologne, 1549–1564," ibid., 34 (1965), 3–35; John Patrick Donnelly, "The Jesuits at Padua: Growth, Suppression, Attempts at Restoration, 1552–1606" ibid., 51 (1982), 45–79.

[170] *Institutum*, 1:469–470.

[171] *P Co.*, 2:680, 704; *M Nadal*, 2:7. See Scaduto, *Laínez*, 2:440–449, 462.

[172] *Chron.*, 2:459, 480–481; 4:148–150; 5:161.

[173] *P Co.*, 2:715.

[174] *Chron.*, 4:99–103; 5:151.

[175] *Chron.*, 5:146–149. See Susanna Peyronel Rambaldi, *Speranze e crisi nel Cinquecento*

modenese: Tensioni religiose e vita cittadina ai tempi di Giovanni Morone (Milan: Franco Angeli, 1979).

[176] *P Co.*, 2:637–638; Scaglione, *Liberal Arts*, pp. 55–56, 111–133.

[177] *Const.*, #622e. See, for example, Marc Venard, "Y-a-t-il un stratégie scholaire des jésuites en France au XVIe siècle?" in *L'université de Pont-á-Mousson et les problèmes de son temps* (Nancy: Université de Nancy, 1974), pp. 67–85.

[178] See Tacchi Venturi, Storia, 2/2:420–433.

[179] *Chron.*, 5:11.

[180] See Mario Scaduto, "Le missioni di A. Possevino in Piemonte: Propaganda Calvinistica e restaurazione cattolica, 1560–1563," *AHSI*, 28 (1959), 51–191.

[181] *Institutum,* 1:489.

[182] See Farrell, *Jesuit Code*, pp. 187–216.

[183] See, for example, Deutscher, "Seminaries," and "Growth of Clergy"; Maurilio Guasco, "La formazione del clero: I seminarii;" in *Storia d'Italia: Annali 9*, ed. Giorgio Chittolini and Giovanni Miccoli (Turin: Giulio Einaudi, 1986), especially pp. 634–658, and Guerrino Pellicia, *La preparazione ed ammissione dei chierici ai santi ordini nella Roma del secolo XVI* (Rome: Pia Societa San Paolo, 1946).

[184] *MI Epp.,* 4:684–690.

[185] *Chron.*, 5:24–25.

[186] See Villoslada, *Collegio Romano*, pp. 49–55.

[187] *MI Epp.,* 4:685.

[188] *MI Epp.,* 9:638–640; 10:60–61, 167. See Pate, "Nadal," pp. 178–180.

[189] See Justo Fernandez Alonso, "El Cardenal Francisco de Toledo, S.J., y su fundación en Santa María la Mayor," *Anthologica Annua*, 37 (1990), 363–379.

[190] See Lukács, "De origine," (1960), 230–231.

[191] *MI Epp.,* 4:687; *Chron.*, 2:166.

[192] See O'Donohoe, Tridentine Seminary Legislation, pp. 71–87, and Peter Schmidt, *Das Collegium Germanicum in Rom und die Germaniker: Zur Funktion eines romischen Ausländerseminars (1552–1914)* (Tübingen: Max Niemeyer Verlag, 1984).

[193] *MI Epp.,* 4:172–173, 185–186, 349–350.

[194] *MI Epp.,* 6:229–233.

[195] *M Nadal,* 1:271–272.

[196] *M Paed.,* 1:106–129.

[197] FN, 1:673–674, 690.

[198] *P Co.*, 1:569.

[199] *Chron.*, 6:15.

[200] *M Paed.,* 2:926.

[201] See Scaduto, *Laínez*, 2:325–333.

[202] *M Paed.,* 2:799–1004.

[203] *P Co.*, 2:622.

[204] *P Co.*, 1:215, 476–477.

[205] *M Paed.,* 2:801.

[206] *P Co.*, 1:568–570.

[207] *M Paed.,* 2:927.

[208] *M Paed.,* 2:935.

[209] *M Paed.,* 2:994–1004.

[210] See László Lukács, "Die Gründung des wiener päpstlichen Seminars und der Nuntius Giovanni Delfino (1573–1577)," *AHSI*, 23 (1954), 35–75, and "Die nordischen päpstlichen Seminarien und P. Possevino (1577–1587)," ibid., 24 (1955), 33–94.

[211] See Schmidt, *Collegium Germanicum*, pp. 1–4.

[212] See O'Donohoe, *Tridentine Seminary Legislation*, and "The Seminary Legislation of the Council of Trent," in *Il Concilio di Trento e la riforma tridentina*, 2 vols. (Rome: Herder, 1965), 1:157–172; Mario Scaduto, "Seminari e collegi: In margine al centinario tridentino," Civiltá Cattolica, 115/2 (1964), 343–352; 115/3 (1964), 18–28. On tlie origins and early years of the Seminario, see Pelliccia, *Preparazione ed ammissione*, pp. 257–303, and Pio Paschini, "Le origini del Seminario Romano," in *Cinquecento romano e riforma cattolica: Scritti raccolti in occasione dell'ottantesimo compleanno dell'autore* (Rome: Lateranum, 1958), pp. 1–32.

[213] *P Co.*, 2:637; *M Paed.*, 3:356–357. See Scaduto, *Laínez*, 1:435–441.

[214] *M Paed.,* 3:16–17, 23–24.

[215]*M Paed.*, 2:1011–1028.

[216]*Institutum*, 1:491–492; *M Paed.*, 3:9–10.

[217]See Scaduto, *Laínez*, 1:442–457, and "Scuola e cultura a Milano nell'età borromaica," in *San Carlo e il suo tempo*, 2 vols. (Rome: Edizioni di Storia e Letteratura, 1986), 2:963–994.

[218]*M Paed.*, 3:16–17, n9.

[219]*M Paed.*, 3:343.

[220]*M Paed.*, 1:436.

[221]MI Epp., 3:56.

[222]See, for example, Scaduto, "Seminari e collegi," and Arno Seifert, *Weltlicher Staat und Kirchenreform: Die Seminarpolitik Bayerns im* 16. Jahrhundert (Münster: Aschendorffsche Verlagsbuchhandlung, 1978).

[223]See Joseph M. O'Keefe, "The Pedagogy of Persuasion: Jesuit Education at Pont-à-Mousson" (S.T.L. thesis, Weston School of Theology, Cambridge, Mass., 1989), p. 61. See also Lukács, "Die nordischen Seminarien."

[224]See Hengst, *Jesuiten*, pp. 98–127.

[225]See Grendler, *Schooling in Italy,* especially pp. 363–381.

[226]Especially notable is Marc Fumaroli, *L'âge de l' eloquence: Rhétorique et "res litteraria" de la Renaissance au seuil de l'epoque classique* (Geneva: Droz, 1980). As an example of a specific issue, see Bernabé Bartolomé Martínez, "Las librerías e imprentas de los jesuitas (1540–1767): Una aportación notable a la cultura española," *Hispania Sacra*, 40 (1988), 315–388.

[227]*Const.*, #626. See also #82, 92, 304. 308, 603, 605.

[228]See A. H. Thomas, *De oudste Constituties van de Dominicanen* (Louvain: Leuvense Universitaire Uitgaven, 1965), p. 361.

[229]See Rivka Feldhay, "Knowledge and Salvation in Jesuit Culture," *Science in Context*, 1 (1987), 195–213.

[230]See Lawrence J. Flynn, "The De Arte Rhetorica of Cyprian Soarez, S.J.," *The Quarterly Journal of Speech*, 42 (1956), 365–374, and "Sources and Influence of Soarez' De Arte Rhetorica," ibid., 43 (1957), 257–265.

[231]See, for example, Feldhay, "Knowledge and Salvation"; William A. Wallace, *Galileo and His Sources: The Heritage of the Collegio Romano in Galileo's Science* (Princeton: Princeton University Press, 1984); Steven J. Harris, "Transposing the Merton Thesis: Apostolic Spirituality and the Establishment of the Jesuit Scientific Tradition," *Science in Context,* 3 (1989), 29–65; Joseph MacDonnell, *Jesuit Geometers* (St. Louis: The Institute of Jesuit Sources, 1989).

Constitutions, Part IV

Excerpts from Part IV of *The Constitutions of the Society of Jesus and Their Complementary Norms.* Edited by John W. Padberg, S.J.

Chapter 7 [392–399]
The Schools Maintained in the Colleges of the Society

1/ [392] 1. To take care that in our colleges not only our own scholastics may be helped in learning, but also those from outside in both learning and good habits of conduct, where schools [open to the public] can be conveniently had, they should be established at least in humane letters /A/, and in more advanced subjects in accordance with the conditions found in the regions where the colleges are situated /B/, looking always to the greater service of God our Lord.

2/ [393] *A. It will belong to the general to decide where it will be opportune to have such schools.*

3/ [394] *B. The situation of the Society should also be taken into account. However, our intention would be that humane letters, languages, and Christian doctrine should ordinarily be taught in the colleges; if necessary, lectures on cases of conscience should be given. If persons are available for preaching and hearing confessions, this should be done, without entering upon higher branches of knowledge. For learning these, students who have studied humane letters should be sent from the colleges to the Society's universities.*

4/ [395] 2. In these schools measures should be taken that the extern students are well instructed in matters of Christian doctrine, go to confession every month if possible, attend the sermons, and, in sum, acquire along with their letters the habits of conduct worthy of a Christian. Since there must be great variety in individual cases, according to circumstances of places and persons, the treatment here will descend no further into particulars, except to state that there should be rules covering everything that is necessary in each college /C/. The only recommendation made here is that {suitable correction should not be lacking /D/ in the case of externs for whom it is necessary, and that this should not be given by the hand of any member of the Society}.

5/   [396] C. {From the rules of the *Roman College*, the part which is suitable to the other colleges can be adapted to them}.

6/   [397] D. *For this purpose there should be a corrector where this is possible. Where it is not, there ought to be some method of administering punishment, either through one of the students or in some other suitable way.*

7/   [398] 3. Since it is so proper to our profession not to accept any temporal remuneration for the spiritual ministries in which we employ ourselves according to our Institute to aid our fellow men, it is not fitting for us to accept for a college any endowment with **an attached obligation of supplying** a preacher or a confessor or **a lecturer on theology** /E/. For, although the reason of equity and gratitude moves us to give more careful service in those ministrations proper to our Institute in those colleges which have been founded with greater liberality and devotion, there ought nevertheless to be no entering into obligations or agreements which impair the sincerity of our manner of proceeding, which is to give freely what we have freely received [Matt. 10:8]. However, for the sustenance of those who serve the common good of the colleges or who study for the sake of it, the endowment which the charity of the founders is wont to assign for the divine glory is accepted.

8/   [399] E. *When the superior general or the Society accepts the charge of a university, the fact that an obligation arises to give the ordinary lectures of the university will not be against the intention of this constitution, even if lectures on theology are included in them.*

Chapter 9 [415–418]
Removal from Studies

9/   [415] 1. Some /A/ are removed from the colleges for the reasons stated in Part II and in the manner explained there [209–30], so that others in their place may make better progress in the service of God our Lord, since the same reason holds true for removing from the colleges as from the houses.

10/   [416] *A. {Others are removed after seven years, namely, those who were admitted to the colleges for that length of time without a fixed resolution to enter the Society, as has been said /338/. But a dispensation could be given in regard to this period of seven years, by prolonging it when such students give much good example in such a way that much service of God is expected from them, or when they are useful to the college}.*

11/   [417] 2. Sometimes, too, they will be removed because a different place is useful for their better progress in spirit or in learning or because it is useful for the universal good of the Society, **as is the case when someone is removed from one college where he has studied arts to lecture on them in another before he studies theology,** and similarly for other purposes of greater service of God our Lord.

12/   [418] 3. The usual manner of removal from a college where all the subjects are studied will be after a person has finished his studies, namely, after he has completed the course in arts and studied theology for four years. Near the end of this period the rector ought to furnish the general or provincial with a report on the man's competence, and then to follow the order given him for the glory of God our Lord.

Chapter 10 [419–439]
The Government of the Colleges

13/ [419] 1. In accordance with the bulls of the Apostolic See, the Professed Society will hold the superintendency over the colleges. For since it may not seek any gain from the fixed revenues nor employ them for itself, it may be expected in the long run to proceed with greater disinterestedness and a more spiritual attitude in regard to what ought to be provided in the colleges for the greater service of God our Lord and for the good government of the colleges.

14/ [420] 2. Except for what pertains to the Constitutions, and to suppression or alienation of such colleges, all the authority, administration, and in general the execution of this superintendency will be vested in the superior general. He, keeping his mind fixed on the end of the colleges and of the entire Society, will see best what is expedient in them.

15/ [421] 3. Therefore the general, by himself or through another to whom he delegates his authority in this matter, {**will appoint one of the coadjutors**} in the Society as the rector who is to have the principal charge. This rector will give account of his charge to the provincial or to whomever the general designates. The general will likewise have power to remove the rector, or to change him from this charge, as seems better to him in our Lord.

[422] (This section has been omitted.)

16/ [423] 4. Care should be taken that the rector be a man of great example, edification, and mortification of all his evil inclinations, and especially a man of proven obedience and humility. He ought likewise to be discreet, fit for governing, experienced both in matters of business and of the spiritual life. He should know how to blend severity with kindness at the proper times. He should be solicitous, stalwart under work, a man of learning, and finally, one in whom the higher superiors can confide and to whom they can with security delegate their authority. For the greater this delegated authority will be, the better will the colleges be governed to the greater divine glory.

17/   [424] 5. The function of the rector will be first of all to sustain the whole college by his prayer and holy desires, and then to see that the Constitutions are observed */B/.* He should watch over all his subjects with great care, and guard them against difficulties from within or without the house by forestalling the difficulties or remedying them if they have occurred, in a way conducive to the good of the individuals and to that of all. He should strive to promote their progress in virtues and learning, and care for their health and for the temporal goods both stable and movable */C/.* He should appoint officials discreetly, observe how they proceed, and retain them in office or change them as he judges appropriate in the Lord. In general he ought to see to it that what has been stated about the colleges in the preceding chapters is observed.

18/   He should fully maintain the subordination he ought to keep not only toward the superior general but also to the provincial superior, informing and having recourse to him in the matters of greater moment and following his directions since he is his superior, as it is right that those in his own college should act toward him. These ought to hold him in great respect and reverence as one who holds the place of Christ our Lord, leaving to him with true obedience the free disposal of themselves and their affairs, not keeping anything closed to him */D/,* not even their own conscience. Rather, as has been stated in the Examen [93–97], they should manifest their conscience to him at fixed times, and more frequently when there is reason, without showing any repugnance or any manifestations of contrary opinion, so that by union of opinion and will and by proper submission they may be better preserved and make greater progress in the divine service.

19/   [425] *B. Thus, just as it will pertain to the rector to see that the* Constitutions *are observed in their entirety, so it will be his to grant exemptions from them with authority from his own superiors (when he judges that such would be the intention of the one who enacted them, in particular case* *according to occurrences and necessities and while keeping his attention fixed on the greater common good).*

20/ [426] C. *This statement includes appropriate care to retain friendships and to render adversaries benevolent.*

21/ [427] D. *Anything closed means a door, cabinet, and the like.*

22/ [428] 6. For the good government of the house, the rector ought to appoint not merely as many officials as are necessary, but also such as are as well fitted as possible for their office. He should give each one the rules of what he ought to do and take care that no one interferes in the business of another. Furthermore, just as he ought to have help given to them when they need it, so when time is left over he ought to see to it that they employ it fruitfully in the service of God our Lord.

[429]–[433] (These sections have been omitted.)

23/ [434] 8. The rector should see that all in the college observe complete obedience towards each official in his own office, and the officials towards the minister and to the rector himself, in accordance with his directions to them. In general, those who have charge of others who must obey them ought to give the latter an example by the obedience they themselves observe towards their own superiors, as persons holding for them the place of Christ our Lord.

24/ [435] 9. A regular order of time for study, prayer, Mass, lectures, eating and sleeping, and so on, will be helpful for everything. Thus a signal will be given at designated times //. When it is heard, all should go immediately, leaving even a letter they have begun. When these hours ought to be changed because of the seasons or other unusual reasons, the rector or the one in charge should consider the matter, and what he orders should be observed.

25/ [436] 1. *The signal will be given by a bell* which will be sounded for retiring for sleep, for taking meals, and so forth.

[437]–[439] (These sections have been omitted.)

Chapter 11 [440–445]
The Acceptance of the Universities

26/   [440] 1. The same considerations of charity by which colleges are accepted, in which public classes are held for the improvement in learning and in living both of our own members and even more of those outside the Society, can extend also to accepting charge of universities in which these benefits may be spread more universally, both through the subjects which are taught and the numbers of persons who attend and the degrees which are conferred so that the recipients may teach with authority elsewhere what they have learned well in these universities for the glory of God our Lord.

27/   [441] 2. However, to decide under what conditions and obligations /A/ and in what places universities should be accepted will be left to the judgment of the one who has the universal care of the Society. After he has heard the opinion of his assistants and of the others of whose counsel he may wish to avail himself, he will have the power to decide by himself upon the acceptance. {**But once such universities have been accepted, he cannot suppress them without the general congregation**}.

28/   [442] A. *When the founder desires that the Society should have to provide a certain number of lecturers, or to undertake some other obligations, it should be noted that if these obligations are accepted because this is deemed to be a lasting aid to the Society in achieving its ends for the service of God our Lord, there ought to be no failure to fulfill them. Conversely, more than what is obligatory in this regard (especially if this could be interpreted as inducing a new obligation) should not readily be done without the general's consent. Neither ought the general to be lenient in such a matter; rather, consulting his assistants he should take care that he does not burden the Society. If he makes a concession on some point, it should be made clear that no obligation is assumed but that what is added is something voluntary.*

29/   [443] 3. However, since the Society's religious tranquility and spiritual occupations preclude the distraction and other detriments entailed in holding the office of judge in civil or criminal affairs there should be no acceptance of such jurisdiction, which the Society would be required to exercise either by itself or through others who depend upon it. However, for what properly pertains to the well-being of the university, it is desirable that in regard to the students the ordinary civil or ecclesiastical ministry of justice should carry out the will of the rector of the university when he has expressed it in regard to punishing the students /B/; and that this ministry should in general give its support in matters pertaining to the studies, especially when such matters have been recommended to it by the rector /C/.

30/ [444] *B. If a student has been so unruly or scandalous that it would be proper to expel him not only from the classes but also from the city, or to put him into prison, it would be a matter properly pertaining to the well-being of the university for the ordinary ministers of justice to be informed and take immediate action. For this and similar matters it would be wise to have the authorization in writing from the ruler or supreme power. Similarly, the recommendation from the rector in favor of a student ought to carry weight with the ministers of justice toward preventing the students from being oppressed.*

31/ [445] *C. Since exemption from ordinary magistrates cannot serve as a means to attract a large number of students, efforts should be made to compensate for this through other concessions and privileges.*

Chapter 12 [446–452]
The Subjects Which Should Be Taught in the Universities of the Society

32/   [446] 1. Since the end of the Society and of its studies is to aid our fellow men to the knowledge and love of God and to the salvation of their souls, and since the subject of theology is the means most suited to this end, in the universities of the Society the principal emphasis ought to be placed upon it. Accordingly, there should be diligent treatment by excellent professors of what pertains to scholastic doctrine and Sacred Scripture, as also to that part of positive theology which is conducive to the aforementioned end, without entering into the part of canon law directed toward court trials.

33/   [447] 2. Moreover, since both the learning of theology and the use of it require (especially in these times) knowledge of humane letters */A/* and of the Latin, Greek, and Hebrew languages, there should be capable professors of these languages, and that in sufficient number. Furthermore, there may also be teachers of other languages such as Chaldaic, Arabic, and Indian where these are necessary or useful for the end stated, taking into account the diversities of place and the reasons for teaching them */B/.*

34/   [448] *A. Under the heading of* humane letters *is understood, in addition to grammar, what pertains to rhetoric, poetry, and history.*

35/   [449] *B. When a plan is being worked out in a college or university to prepare persons to go among the Moors or Turks, Arabic or Chaldaic would be expedient; and Indian would be proper for those about to go among the Indians; and the same holds true for similar reasons in regard to other languages which could have greater utility in other regions.*

36/   [450] 3. Likewise, since the arts or natural sciences dispose the intellectual powers for theology, and are useful for the perfect understanding and use of it, and also by their own nature help toward the same ends, they should be treated with fitting diligence and by learned professors. In all this the honor and glory of God our Lord should be sincerely sought */C/.*

37/   [451] *C. Logic, physics, metaphysics, and moral philosophy should be treated, and also mathematics, with the moderation appropriate to secure the end which is being sought.*

38/   *To teach how to read and write would also be a work of charity if the Society had enough members to be able to attend to everything. But because of the lack of members these elementary subjects are not ordinarily taught.*

39/   [452] 4. The study of medicine and laws, being more remote from our Institute, will not be treated in the universities of the Society, or at least the Society will not undertake this teaching through its own members.

Chapter 13 [453–463]
The Method and Order of Treating the Aforementioned Subject Matters

40/   [453] 1. To provide such proper treatment of both the lower subjects and of theology, there should be a suitable arrangement and order both for the morning and the afternoon.

41/   [454] 2. And although the order and hours which are spent in these studies may vary according to the regions and seasons, there should be such conformity that in every region that is done which is there judged to be most conducive to greater progress in learning /A/.

42/   [455] *A. Concerning the hours of the lectures, their order, and their method, and concerning the exercises both in compositions (which ought to be corrected by the teachers) and in disputations within all the faculties, and in delivering orations and reading verses in public—all this will be treated in detail in a separate treatise [approved by the general]. This present constitution refers the reader to it, with the remark that it ought to be adapted to places, times, and persons, even though it would be desirable to reach that order as far as this is possible.*

43/   [456] 3. Furthermore, there should be not only public lectures but also different masters according to the capacity and number of the students /B/. These masters should take an interest in the progress of each one of their students, require them to give an account of their lessons /C/, and make them hold repetitions /D/. They should also have the students of humane letters get practice in regularly speaking Latin, writing compositions [in a good style], and delivering well what they have composed. They should make them, and much more those studying the higher subjects, engage in disputations often. Days and hours should be designated for this; and in these disputations the students should debate not only with the members of their own class, but those who are somewhat lower down should dispute about matters they understand with students who are more advanced, and conversely those who are more advanced should debate with those lower down by coming down to subjects which these latter are studying. The professors too ought to hold disputations with one another. All should preserve the proper modesty, and there should be someone to preside, cut off the debate, and give the doctrinal solution.

44/   [457] *B. Ordinarily, there will be three teachers in three different classes of grammar, another who is to lecture on humanities, and another on rhetoric. In the class of these last two groups there will be lectures on the Greek and Hebrew languages, and on any other if it is to be learned. Thus there will always be five classes. If there should be so much to do in one of them that a single teacher does not suffice, an assistant should be given to him. If the number of students makes it impossible for one teacher to attend to them even with assistants, the class can be divided into two sections so that there are two fifth classes or two fourth classes; and all the teachers, if possible, should be members of the Society, although in case of necessity there may be others. If the small number or the quality of the students is such that so many classes or teachers are not required, discretion will be used in everything to adjust the number by assigning those who suffice and no more.*

45/   [458] *C. Whether in addition to the ordinary masters who have special care of the students there ought to be someone or several who in the capacity of public lecturers are to give lectures on philosophy or mathematics or some other subject with greater solemnity than the ordinary lecturers, prudence will decide, in accordance with the places and persons involved, looking always to the greater edification and the greater service of God our Lord.*

46/   [459] *D. There will be repetitions not merely of the last lesson, but also of those of the week and of a longer time when it is judged that this ought to be the case.*

47/   [460] 4. Likewise, it will always be the function of the rector to see to it himself or through the chancellor that the newcomers are examined and placed in those classes and with those teachers that are suitable for them. Furthermore, it is left to his discretion (after he has heard the counsel of those deputed for this purpose) to decide whether they ought to be retained longer in the same class or to advance into another. So too in regard to the study of the languages other than Latin, he is to determine whether it should precede the arts and theology or follow them, and how long each should study these languages. The same holds true for the other higher subjects. According to the difference of abilities, ages, and other circumstances that must be considered, it will be the rector's function to investigate to what extent each student should begin these subjects or continue in them, although it is better for those who have the age and ability to advance and distinguish themselves in all these areas for the glory of God our Lord */E/.*

48/   [461] *E. It can happen that because of someone's age or capacity Latin, together with as much of the other subjects as is required to hear confessions and deal with his neighbor, suffices for him. Such might be certain persons who have a curacy of souls and are not capable of great learning. Likewise, others may advance farther in the sciences, although it will be up to the superior to decide to what extent some subjects should be dropped and others taken up. After he has explained this to the students from outside the Society and if they still desire to proceed differently, they should not be coerced.*

49/   [462] 5. Just as steady application is necessary in the work of studying, so also is some relaxation. The proper amount and the times of this relaxation will be left to the prudent consideration of the rector to determine, according to the circumstances of persons and places */F/.*

50/   [463] *F. At least one day during the week should be given to rest from dinner on. On the other points the rector should consult with the provincial about the order to be observed in regard to the vacations or ordinary interruptions of the studies.*

Chapter 14 [464–470]
The Books to Be Lectured On

51/   [464] 1. In general, as was stated in the treatise on the colleges [358], those books will be lectured on which in each subject have been deemed to contain more solid and safe doctrine; books which are suspect, or whose authors are suspect, will not be treated */A/.* But in each university these should be individually designated.

52/   In theology there should be lectures on the Old and New Testaments and on the scholastic doctrine of St. Thomas */B/;* and in positive theology those authors should be selected who are more suitable for our end */C/.*

53/   [465] *A. Even though the book be without suspicion of bad doctrine, when its author is suspect it is not expedient that it be lectured on. For through the book affection is acquired for the author; and part of the credence given to him in what he says well could be given to him later in what he says badly. Furthermore, it is rare that some poison is not mixed into what comes forth from a heart full of it.*

54/   [466] *B. The Master of the Sentences will also be lectured on. But if in time it seems that the students will draw more help from another author, as would be the case through the writing of a compendium or book of scholastic theology that seems better adapted to these times of ours, it will be permitted to make this book the subject of the lectures, after much consultation and study of the matter by the persons deemed most suitable in the whole Society and with the superior general's approval. In regard to the other subjects and humane letters too, if some books written in the Society are adopted as being more useful than those commonly used, this will be done after much consideration, with our objective of greater universal good always kept in view.*

55/   [467] *C. For example, in connection with some section of canon law, the councils, and so on.*

56/   [468] 2. In regard to the books of humane letters in Latin or Greek, in the universities as well as in the colleges, lecturing to the adolescents on any book which contains matters harmful to good habits of conduct should be avoided, as far as possible, unless the books are previously expurgated of the indecent matters and words /D/.

57/   [469] *D. If some books, such as Terence, cannot be expurgated at all, it is better that they should not be lectured on, in order that the nature of the contents may not injure the purity of the minds.*

58/   [470] 3. In logic, natural and moral philosophy, and metaphysics, the doctrine of Aristotle should be followed, as also in the other liberal arts. In regard to the commentaries, both on these authors and on those treating humanities, a selection should be made. Those which the students ought to see should be designated, and also those which the masters ought to follow by preference in the doctrine they teach. In everything which the rector ordains, he should proceed in conformity with what is judged throughout the whole Society to be more suitable to the glory of God our Lord.

Chapter 15 [471–480]
The Terms and Degrees

59/   [471] 1. In the study of humane letters and the languages no definite period of time for their completion can be established, because of the difference in abilities and knowledge of those who attend the lectures, and because of many other reasons which permit no other prescription of time save that which the prudent consideration of the rector or chancellor will dictate for each student /A/.

60/   [472] *A. In the case of beginners of good ability, one should see whether a single semester in each of the four lower classes would be enough, and two semesters in the highest class spent in studying rhetoric and the languages. However, no definite rule can be given.*

61/   [473] 2. In the arts, it will be necessary to arrange the terms during which the natural sciences are to be lectured upon. It seems that less than three years would be insufficient for them /B/. Another half year will remain for the student to review, perform his academic acts, and take the master's degree in the case of those who are to receive degrees. In this way the whole curriculum enabling a student to become a master of arts will last three years and a half. Each year with the help of God one such cycle of treatises will begin and another will come to its end /C/.

62/   [474] *B. If someone has attended the lectures on some part of the arts elsewhere, this can be taken into account. But ordinarily, in order to be graduated one must have studied for the three years mentioned. This holds true also for the four years of theology, in regard to being admitted to the acts and receiving a degree in it.*

63/   [475] *C. If because of insufficient personnel or for other reasons facilities for that arrangement are lacking, the best that will be possible should be done, with the approval of the general or at feast of the provincial.*

64/   [476] 3. The curriculum in theology will be one of six years. In the first four years all the matter which must be lectured on will be expounded.

In the remaining two, in addition to the reviewing, the acts customary for a doctorate will be performed by those who are to receive it.

65/   Ordinarily, the cycle of the curriculum will be begun every fourth year, and the books to be lectured on distributed so that a student can enter the curriculum at the start of any one of the four years /D/ and, by attending the lectures on the rest of the four-year curriculum and the next one up to that point, will have heard the lectures of the entire curriculum within four years.

66/   [477] *D. If in a* college *or* university *of the Society the situation is such that it appears better to begin the cycle of subjects every two years, or somewhat later than every four, with the consent of the general or of the provincial that which is found to be more suitable may be done.*

67/   [478] 4. In the matter of the degrees, both of master of arts and of doctor of theology, three things should be observed. First, no one, whether a member of the Society or an extern, should be promoted to a degree unless he has been carefully and publicly examined /E/ by persons deputed for this office, which they should perform well, and unless he has been found fit to lecture in that faculty. Second, the door to ambition should be closed by giving no fixed places to those who receive degrees; rather, they should "anticipate one another with honor" [Rom. 12:10], observing no distinction of places. Third, just as the Society teaches altogether gratis, so should it confer the degrees completely free, and only a very small expenditure, even if it is voluntary, should be allowed to the extern students, so that the custom may not come to have the force of law and no excess in this matter may creep in with time /F/. The rector should also take care not to permit any of the teachers or other members of the Society to accept money or gifts, either for themselves or for the college, from any person for anything he has done to help him. For according to our Institute, our reward should be only Christ our Lord who is "our reward exceedingly great" [Gen. 15:1].

68/   [479] *E. If it appears, for sufficiently weighty reasons, that someone ought not to be examined publicly, with the permission of the general or* *provincial that may be done which the rector judges will be for the greater glory of God our Lord.*

69/   [480]   F. *Thus, banquets should not be permitted, nor other celebrations which are costly and not useful for our end. Neither should there be any conferring of caps or gloves or any other object.*

Chapter 16 [481–489]
What Pertains to Good Moral Habits

70/   [481] 1. Very special care should be taken that those who come to the universities of the Society to obtain knowledge should acquire along with it good and Christian moral habits. It will help much toward this if all go to confession at least once every month, hear Mass every day and a sermon every feast day when one is given. The teachers will take care of this, each one with his own students /A/.

71/   [482] *A. When this can be done easily, students should be obliged to what has been said about confession, Mass, the sermon, Christian doctrine, and declamation. The others should be persuaded gently and not be forced to it nor expelled from the classes for not complying, provided that dissoluteness or scandal to others is not observed in them.*

72/   [483] 2. Furthermore, on some day of the week Christian doctrine should be taught in the college. Care should be taken to make the young boys learn and recite it; also, that all, even the older ones, should know it, if possible.

[484]–[485] (These sections have been omitted.)

73/   [486] 4. In the classes no cursing, nor injurious words or deeds, nor anything immoral, nor anything indecent or dissolute should be allowed on the part of the externs who come to classes from elsewhere. The masters should make it their special aim, both in their lectures when occasion is offered and outside of them too, to inspire the students to the love and service of God our Lord, and to a love of the virtues by which they will please him. They should urge the students to direct all their studies to this end. To recall this to their minds, before the lesson begins, one of them should recite a short prayer which is ordered for this purpose, while the master and students stand attentive and have their heads uncovered /C/.

74/   [487] *C. The prayer should be recited in a manner which furthers edification and devotion, or else it should not be said, but the teacher should uncover his head, make the sign of the cross, and begin.*

75/   [488] 5. For those who are derelict either in proper diligence in their studies or in what pertains to good moral habits, and for whom kind words and admonitions alone are not sufficient, there should be a corrector from outside the Society. He should keep in fear and should punish those who need chastisement and are fit for it. When neither words nor the corrector avail and some student is seen to be incorrigible and a scandal to others, it is better to dismiss him from the classes rather than to keep him where he himself is not progressing and others are receiving harm /D/. This decision will be left to the rector of the university, so that everything may proceed in a manner conducive to the glory and service of God our Lord.

76/   [489] *D. If a case should arise in which dismissal from the classes is not enough to remedy the scandal, the rector will take care to provide what is more suitable. However, as far as possible he ought to proceed in a spirit of leniency and to maintain peace and charity with all.*

Chapter 17 [490–503]
The Officials or Administrators of the University

77/   [490] 1. The complete charge, that is, the supervision and government of the university, will belong to the rector /A/. He may be the same person who governs the principal college of the Society and should have the qualities that have been mentioned in his regard [423], so that he may be able to perform satisfactorily the office entrusted to him of directing the whole university in learning and habits of conduct. The task of selecting him will be vested in the general or in someone else to whom he entrusts it, such as the provincial or a visitor; but the confirmation of the appointment will always belong to the general. The rector will have four consultors or assistants who in general can aid him in matters pertaining to his office and with whom he discusses the matters of importance /B/.

78/   [491] *A. However, the rector will not change the principal lecturers, nor officials such as the chancellor, without informing the provincial, or the general if he is nearer (unless the higher superior has entrusted the matter to the rector). The rector ought to keep the higher superior informed about all things.*

79/   [492] *B. One of these consultors can be a collateral associate if this seems necessary to the superior general. If the personnel is not sufficient to have so many officials, the best that will be possible should be done.*

80/   [493] 2. There will also be a chancellor, a person distinguished for learning and great zeal who is able to judge wisely in the matters which will be entrusted to him. It is his duty to act as general representative of the rector in carefully organizing the studies, in directing the disputations in the public acts, and in judging the competence of those to be admitted to the acts and degrees. He himself will confer the degrees.

[494]–[500] (These sections have been omitted.)

81/   [501] The university will be divided into these three faculties. In each one of them there will be a dean and two others assigned as deputies, chosen from among those who better understand the affairs of that faculty;

these, when called into consultation by the rector, can tell him what they think would be advantageous for the welfare of their faculty. When they perceive something of this kind while conferring among themselves, they should inform the rector even without being consulted.

82/   [502] 6. In regard to the matters pertaining to one faculty alone the rector will consult, in addition to the chancellor and his assistants, the dean and the deputies of the faculty involved. In what pertains to all the faculties, the deans and deputies of all of them should be consulted /H/. If it seems wise to the rector, he may also consult others from within and without the Society, in order that by learning the opinions of all he may the better decide upon what is expedient.

83/   [503] *H. Although the decision will not depend upon their votes, it is proper that they be consulted and heard. The rector should take fitting account of the opinion of those who are more cognizant. However, if all have an opinion contrary to his, he should not go against them all without consulting the provincial about the matter.*

Letters and Instructions, 1 December 1551

Juan de Polanco, S.J., *Monumenta Ignatiana. Sancti Ignatti de Loyola Societatis Jesu fundatoris epistolae et instuctiones, 4:7–9.*

Editor's Introduction: Juan de Polanco (1517–1576) served as secretary of the Society of Jesus under St. Ignatius and two subsequent Generals. His influence in the early Society is immense. According to Polanco, the schools provide many benefits: for the Jesuits (1–4), for the students (5–9), and for the local communities (10–15).

1/   (. . .) So far, I have talked about the means; I will now focus on the usefulness for the Society, for the foreign listeners, and for the town or province where the school is located, that from my experience can be found in this type of schools, even though it can be linked to what has been said.

2/   And regarding our community, firstly, the ones who read help each other and learn a lot by teaching the rest and end up being more determined and in control of their knowledge.

3/   2nd. Those in our community who listen to them can take advantage of the care and continuity and diligence with which the teachers carry out their jobs.

4/   3rd. Not only do they take advantage of the humanities, but also in preaching and teaching the Christian doctrine, and they practice the means which they will use later on to help others, and they feel the joy of observing the fruit that the Lord Our God allows them to see.

5/   4th. Even though there is no one who can persuade the scholars, especially the servant boys that join the Society, setting a good example and conversation and with the Latin declamations read on Sundays on the virtues they are interested and many can be gained for our Lord's vineyard. And this usefulness will serve the Society itself.

6/   For the outsiders who come to listen and get help, there are the following ones:

7/   The 5th. The ones where the studies are taught thoroughly, placing special care in their learning of all the lessons and arguments and compositions, and so they experience a great improvement in their studies.

8/   6th. That the poor, who do not have means to pay for the ordinary teachers, and even less for the domestic instructors, found here for free the knowledge they would barely achieve by working very hard.

9/   7th. That regarding spiritual matters they get help; learning the Christian doctrine and understanding what in the sermons and customary exhortations is convenient for their eternal health.

10/   8th. In the plurality of the conscience they take advantage—and consequently are in full virtue—of the monthly confessions, and care is taken to make sure they are honest in their words and virtuous throughout their entire lives.

11/   The 9th. That they will get much greater merit and results from their studies by trying to direct them to the divine service from the moment they start learning, as they have been instructed. For those coming from the region or province where these schools are located there are also the following amenities.

12/   The 10th. Regarding time: relieving their parents from certain expenses since their children have teachers who teach them humanities and virtues.

13/   11th. That they can have a clear conscience in the doctrine of their children; and the ones who could hardly find someone to trust—even if they assume the expenses of doing so—will certainly find them in these schools.

14/   12th. That they have, outside the humanities, someone in the schools and monasteries who preaches to the people and who helps them with the sacraments with great results (as it has been proved).

15/   13th. That their families and themselves turn to spiritual things after their children's example, and they get used to going to confession more often and to living atoned lives.

16/   14th. They found locals through us who encourage them and help them in religious works like hospitals, houses for converts and the like, among which there is also a place for charity for our people.

17/   15th. That those who are currently only students will eventually leave school to follow different paths: some preaching and taking care of the souls, some governing the land and administrating justice, and some will find other jobs. Lastly, since adults grow from the children, a just institution and doctrine throughout their life will be advantageous to many others, spreading the fruit more and more every day.

18/   I could further discuss it but this is enough to state what is felt here about this kind of school.

Letter to King Philip II of Spain, 14 February 1556

Petrus de Ribadeneyra, S.J., *Monumenta paedagogica Societatis Jesu,*
1:475–476.

Editor's Introduction: Petrus de Ribadeneyra (1526–1611) was a young
Jesuit when St. Ignatius was Superior General of the Society of Jesus.
Ignatius trusted him greatly, as demonstrated by this letter to King Philip II
of Spain. The letter reflects the conviction among the first Jesuits that the
ministry of education was central and vital for them and for the common
good. Ribadeneyra expresses the humanistic conviction that the road for
good character and good societies requires education.

1/ [1] Our Father Professor Ignatius ordered me—after having kissed
the hands of Your Majesty on his behalf and on behalf of our Society—to
show Your Majesty the wish Our Lord God has granted us: to believe in
the use of the little volume that He communicated to us for His glory and
help for the souls at Your Majesty's service. I state that, being our Society's
institution such as it is, that those who live in it not only have to have the
growth of their own souls in mind but also that of others'[1], each of them,
according to the talent that God has granted them; their salvation must
be assured, be they loyal or infidels or heretics; and given that the light of
wisdom is necessary to instruct and teach a village, it is necessary to build
schools and offer financial help (since learning cannot take place comfortably without first covering these basic needs). And of those who enter our
school and are not good with their studies, after being trained in the things
of perfection let them be indoctrinated with the sciences necessary in order
to help the souls[2].

2/ [2] It is also known that it is very difficult for those who are already
aged in sin to renew themselves and to take off their bad habits, to wear
fresh and new clothes and offer themselves before God. All the goodness
in Christianity and of the whole world depends on the proper education of
the youths, who—since they are as soft as butter in their childhood—are
more easily imprinted with any kind of teaching, for which there is a great

lack of virtuosos and learned teachers who bring together example and doctrine; our same Society, with the professional commitment that it has been granted by Christ Our Lord, has knelt to include this role which is less honorable but no less profitable of the institution of the boys and young men, and therefore, among the other offices we exercise, in this, not the least important one, of having schools and colleges in which not just yours but others are taught, free of charge, along with the virtues and things necessary for a good Christian, all the principal sciences, from the rudiments and rules of grammar to the higher faculties, to the greater or lesser comfort that exists in different schools, which have been founded for this end all around Spain, Portugal, Italy and Germany[3]. These schools have been received so well, with so much willingness and gratitude by the villages in which they have been founded, and having such proof of it and it being so advantageous for all—as we can infer from the event and the expansion and spread that Our Lord has conferred on this work from the moment it began only a few years ago, as if it were from his own hand.

3/   [3] Therefore, as Father Professor Ignatius has seen the universal benefit that has arisen in these places from this way of teaching, and on the one hand considering how profitable and necessary they would be for these states, the pain and havoc that is beginning to be wreaked by heresies with new and monstrous types of sects and mistakes, as Your Majesty is certainly more than aware of, and of the heretical parents who never fail to raise their children in their heresies and mistakes; and on the other hand seeing that Our Lord God has deigned to call many people of virtue and studies in this nation to our Society's institute, as well as other youths of good wits and hopes, who in a few years' time could become loyal instruments of your glory in these states. It would seem like we were not accomplishing all the matters related to the good health of our souls and service to Your Majesty, if at the very least there was no demonstration of our wish to serve Your Majesty, and with works we did not offer all our minimal Society to your perpetual service in all areas, and especially for these, as they are most in need for help and relief.

---

[1] Cf. Exam. gen. c. 1 n. 2, in MI Const. III 2.

[2] Cf. Const. P. IV Prooem. A, in MI Const. III 100–1 et Lukács S.I., De origine collegiorum *AHSI* 29 (1960) 191–4 (5–8).

[3] Elenchum collegiorum usque ad annum 1556 diversis in locis erectorum vide sis *ib.* 242–3 (56–7).

Spiritual Sermons, 1561

Jerónimo Nadal, S.J., *Pláticas Espirituales del P. Jerónimo Nadal en Coimbra,* 88, 91, 125, 130–131, 161–163.

Editor's Introduction: Jerónimo Nadal (1507–1580) was one of the most influential Jesuits of the nascent Society of Jesus. He was also the first rector of the first Jesuit school in the world at Messina, Italy (1548). Nadal not only helped shape the Society of Jesus in general but also certainly played a very important role in embracing the ministry of education as central to the mission of the Society. In the following excerpt you can appreciate Nadal's view on education.

6TH SERMON

1/ [14] There are two or three types of schools. The first one was to study ourselves, without reading. Then, other schools aimed at reading, and this partly or totally, *scilicet*[i], with reading Latin and Arts and Theology, etc. There are other schools aimed at the general studies such as in Gandia[ii], which is a school linked to the University and under its privilege, as it is in Evora[iii].

7TH EXHORTATION

2/ [1] The parts of the Society were listed, dividing people, jobs, and places. Now we will discourse about each part with God's grace, beginning with a list. There are novices, scholars, coadjutors, the professed; *similarly* General, Commissioner, Principal, etc. Houses for professed, for novices, schools, pilgrimages. All of the aforementioned are needed for our purposes.

[2] (This section has been omitted.)

3/ [3] And the houses are arranged accordingly: no learning in the probationary one, but virtue and prayer and devotion; in those where there is learning, it is always linked to virtue (otherwise, one must turn back to probation); which, even though humanities are good, *subserviant tamen* *spiritui,* as stated by Father Ignatius, who wished that we would always teach them devotion[iv]; this is the [*Fol 30 v*] most important.

11TH EXHORTATION

4/   [5] However, brethren, seek not to obtain any (even though this may be) *scientia* that does not represent *sapientia* for you, be sure you combine it with devotion, even in grammar; for *scientia inflat, caritasas vero aedificat*[v] *et qui addit scientiam, addit laborem*[vi]. It is therefore important to have a good foundation in virtue and not only to occupy oneself with the speculative nature of the sciences but also the practice[vii] to help other souls as according to our institution, and to present oneself before them having obtained—or at least having tried to obtain, as judged by the almighty— humility, patience, mortification, prayer and its use; if you take the studies as proof and an exercise which, carried out by obedience, aimed at our goal, then not only will it not weaken but increase all the virtues which, in truth, will mean that all of this exercise *attingit finem.*

12TH EXHORTATION

5/   [1] We will end today, with divine grace, with the matter of scholars, leaving many details, just as with others, because of the lack of time. And what follows will serve as a beginning. The first point will be about teachers, which began 15[viii] years ago in our Society, before the Constitutions. And one of the reasons to start teaching was, among others, so that our community could be accomplished in its studies, and also because we could have schools that were ideal and sufficient for the service to the Lord[ix].

6/   [2] The aforementioned teachers have the reputation of scholars but to a higher degree. And when speaking about those who read Theology and Philosophy and Latin, they are considered to be on a higher scholarly level because, already being erudite in what they teach, they have a greater advantage and superiority in their reading studies and should attempt to help many others, and *religiose* with our goal: that they do not hesitate but that they act with the right intentions and that sometimes with good judgment they set a good example, which is the best skill of those who read Theology. Luckily, they can, together with the studies, make their disciples grow in virtue and good habits, and each teacher knowingly attends to growth and proficiency in their studies, as this is one of the main reasons for the Society to have Teachers[x].

7/   [3] *Item,* The Teacher has a very similar job to that of the professed. As the professed is fully committed to the well-being of their neighbors, they are in charge of the good manners that they inculcate since they work with boys or youth. The teachers should be aware that all the [*Page 52v*] dispositions we listed as necessary for the students are also necessary for them, as they are, although in greater degree.

8/   [4] And they must strive to not be weak in their enthusiasm, but should fully trust that the Lord will help them teach others, that they are carrying out an angel's task; that, likewise they are in charge of enlightening our understanding, they are in charge of enlightening our knowledge to better understand things. And they should strive to purely observe obedience and to dress in accordance with the principles of the science they work with, as long as they do not clutter their religion.

9/   [5] And with this they will grow to be able to read better, even if they lack time or study. And if eventually[xi] they have a natural feebleness, tell the Superior, and the Superior will provide for it, and you should never think to the[xii]contrary. And if it is impossible to provide for it, the need itself will provide for it just as a sickness manifests itself.

15TH SERMON

[1]–[15] (These sections have been omitted.)

10/   [16] There are also schools; and these, in which there are only students, like the one above, or in which readings are also carried out, like the school down in Coimbra[xiii]; which did not exist at the beginning. But then our Father commanded for them to exist so that from an early age[xiv] we might teach a sound doctrine and morality to many, and so place them in a position where God works with them to follow the true Christian path and they are encouraged towards perfecting it; and so some win, but hopefully we are not the origin of their determination, even though we help them approach God, which gives it grace.

11/ [17] And this was of great relevance, for the harm done to children by bad men of bad discipline and habits. It was also relevant for those who would complete the studies, and in this became proficient, so they could *libere* be sent by the Pope against other heretics and important things of relevance and of great service to our Lord, to the credit of their achievements in their studies. And thus we will reach the goal of our institute of helping souls as much as we can.

12/ [18] There are also schools with University, such that different degrees can be undertaken there, like in Gandia, Mesina, Cordoba, and Evora, even though the ones in Mesina and Cordoba have yet to be finished. Also in Rome; however, not *simpliciter* but *aequivalenter*, since only our community can graduate there; but I believe the grace has been reached to allow everyone to graduate there. And this was applied to the schools, so people became affectionate towards us and we acquired authority with them, and so we can take them, since those who enter the universities[xv] are distinguished and notable and others rely on them, and they can teach others well and excel in their studies.

13/ [19] There are also houses of the professed, where studying does not take place but the studies are put into practice[xvi]; in which Our Lord God greatly increases knowledge, since it is always useful to study to carry out their ministry properly and is granted God's special grace. In this house all matters related to the Society will be dealt with and from it people who carry standards with the Cross with different missions will leave for many locations; and these missions are a very major part of the Society. Thus with them we can state that the whole world is our home, because we must— through our missions and those of the Pope and of our superiors—search everywhere for all souls so that they do not get lost.

14/   We trust *[Fol. 66v]* in God, since He has given us the schools as a means towards this end; he will grant us abundant grace to reach him and will make sure that in all the homes hosts for this; and He will ensure that everything is in accordance with our vocation and our institution, for the greater glory of His Divine Majesty.

---

[i]   n—Aside: o· en parte . . . scilicet.
[ii]   8—On this foundation in Gandia cf. MHSI, Ignat., Epist., I, 697. 698. 419. 420.
[iii]   9—Soon after Nadal would take off to go over the Statutes of the University with the Cardinal Infante in Lisbon; cf. Ephemerides: N. II, 77.
[iv]   2—Constit. p. 4, c. 4, n, 2; c, 6, n. 1, 2; p. 10, n.2
[v]   4—1 Cor. 8:1
[vi]   5—Eccles. 1:18
[vii]   b—Ms. sermon.
[viii]   1—In 1546 Father Andrés de Oviedo decided to start an Arts course in the school in Gandia, which was attended not only by the scholars in the Society but also by any other lay person who wished to attend the lectures. Francisco Onfroy was in charge of the course, proficient in Philosophy. Cf. MHSI, Epist. mixtae I, 315; ASTRAIN, Historia de la Compañía I, 275.
[ix]   2—In a statement, December 1, 1551, this was said about the utility of schools, by the same Society: "Firstly, the ones who read help each other and learn a lot by teaching the rest and end up being more determined and in control of their knowledge. . . . 4th Even though there is no one who can persuade the scholars, especially the servant boys that join the Society, setting a good example and conversation and with the Latin declamations read on Sundays on the virtues they are interested and many can be gained for our Lord's vineyard". MHSI, Ignat., Epist., IV, 7.
[x]   a—Aside: Teachers.
[xi]   b—Ms. ansí.
[xii]   c—Ms. el.
[xiii]   15—It is known that the Society had two schools in Coimbra. One was the School of Jesus, in the beneficial upper part; and the other in the College of Arts, which was part of the University of Coimbra. Cf. POLANCO, Vita Ignatii Loyolae et rerum Societatis Iesu historia VI, 710; F. RODRIGUES, S.I., História da Compañía de Jesus na Assistência de Portugal, t. I, vol 1,304–327, 405–430; 2°, 336–400.
[xiv]   d—Aside: from that point.
[xv]   e—Aside: to read at Universities.
[xvi]   f—Ms. sermon. Please refer to reference m in the first sermon.

Constitution or Arrangement and Order of the Seven Classes of Grammar, Humanities, and Rhetoric

Diego Ledesma, S.J., *Monumenta paedagogica Societatis Jesu, 2:528–529.*

Editor's Introduction: Diego Ledesma (1524–1575) was the Prefect of Studies at the Roman College. During his tenure he put together a plan of studies to guide teachers in the new model of education. This work would be the base of the *Ratio Borgiana*, an early precursor to the *Ratio Studiorum* of 1599. This chapter captures well the final goals of a Jesuit education at that time. It is a text that Fr. Peter-Hans Kolvenbach (1920–2016) will use to explain Jesuit education during his tenure as the Superior General of the Society.

FIRST BOOK: ON LANGUAGE LEARNING: PLAN AND INSTRUCTIONS

CHAPTER 1—ON LITERARY SCHOOLS AND THEIR DIVERSITY

1/   Literary schools are of paramount importance in a truly Christian republic and in the Church of Christ for the human race, as well as for the many comforts in this life and also towards a right management of public affairs and laws, and also for the embellishment, splendor and perfection of the rational beauty. Mainly, [these schools are necessary] for the faith in God and for our religion—for its teaching, defense and spreading—and, lastly, [they are necessary] for men to be guided towards their final goals more comfortably and easily. However, before that, the goals have to be identified and classified and the differences between them stated.

The Education of Youth

Monumenta paedagogica Societatis Jesu, 3:402n15

"The education of the youth is the renewal of the world."

Fr. Juan Bonifacio, S.J., is considered the author of this phrase that encapsulates the conviction of the early Jesuits of the importance of the educational ministry to renew society. It connects them to the broader humanistic movement by which Jesuit Education was so much inspired. It became the favorite catchphrase to explain the conviction and goal of Jesuit education before the suppression of the Society.

—José Mesa, S.J., editor

PART II: THE RATIO STUDIORUM (1599)

"Our Way of Proceeding" in Education: The *Ratio Studiorum*

Gabriel Codina, S.J., 1999. *Educatio S.J.* 1:1–15.

1/   The object of this presentation, directed above all to those who are involved in the educational apostolate of the Society, is to introduce the history and the contents of the *Ratio,* in view of the interest awakened on the occasion of the 400th anniversary of the publication of this document. For the historical section, we rely upon the exhaustive investigations of Lázló Lukács, S.J., published in *Monumenta Paedagogica Societatis Iesu,* and upon our work on the origins of Jesuit pedagogy.

1. THE ORIGINS OF THE *RATIO*

A Little History

2/   Four centuries ago, on the 8th of January, 1599, to be exact, Giacomo Domenichi, Secretary of the Society, promulgated by mandate of General Claudio Acquaviva and sent to all the provinces the document entitled *Ratio atque Institutio Studiorum Societatis Iesu,* or "Plan of Studies of the Society of Jesus." This was the first document on pedagogy approved by the General of the Society for all the educational establishments of the Order. This was the birth certificate for the famous "Jesuit educational system," which evolved with such consistency and sense of unity throughout the world until the suppression of the Society in 1773.

3/   The *Ratio* did not arise by spontaneous generation. Ignatius of Loyola had already treated the subject of studies in Part IV of the Constitutions, where we find a series of principles and norms for the universities, schools and educational establishments of the Society. But Ignatius did not descend into many details. One of his principles was to always adapt to the concrete reality: "adjustment may be introduced according to place, time and persons" (*Const.* S.J., 455). For this reason, the *Constitutions* defer to a more detailed "separate document" on this topic to follow later.

4/   The treatise which Ignatius announced, and which the recently established schools were demanding insistently, did not arrive until some 40 years after his death. Nevertheless, already during the life of Ignatius sprung up various *Ratio* and instructions for studies, since, following the principle of adaptation, Ignatius left the rectors of the schools free to prepare their own plans of studies, while awaiting the promulgation of the announced common norms. Even as early as 1541 we find a profusion of such documents—*Charters of Colleges, Constitutions of the College of Padua, Industriae, Constitutions of Colleges*—all these even before the publication of the *Constitutions* of the Society. Ignatius took these into consideration in the preparation of Part IV of the Constitutions. These documents refer mostly to the studies of the Jesuits themselves, and not directly to those for non-Jesuit students.

The First Plan of Studies: the College of Messina (1548)

5/   The documents which most influenced the preparation of the *Ratio* were those of the first establishments for "extern" (i.e., non-Jesuit) students, principally the College of Messina (1548). It was in Messina that the educational work of the Society with non-Jesuit students began; although it is certain that a little bit earlier, in the early days of the University of Gandía and in the college which was confided to them in Goa, the Jesuits had already entered into the education of externs. Messina is considered to be the first college and the "prototype" of the subsequent colleges of the Society, because of the importance of the experience which began there and the influence which the plan of studies of Messina had upon all subsequent norms of the Society which refer to studies.

6/   The author of this plan of studies—*The Constitutions of the College of Messina*—was the Majorcan Jerome Nadal (1507–1580). The document of Messina spread like fire through the first colleges of the Society and came close to becoming "the" plan of studies for the entire Society. Ignatius himself in 1550 considered the possibility of approving the *Constitutions* of Messina, extending them to all the schools of the Society.

7/   The plan of studies of Messina did not become the *Ratio* for the whole Order, but it had an extraordinary influence on the preparation of the *Ratio* of 1599. The channel for this was the Roman College, founded by Ignatius in 1551, where this plan of studies of Messina was adopted. Due to its importance and location, the Roman College was destined to develop in its turn into the undisputed model for all the schools of the Society, and the center for the irradiation of Jesuit pedagogy in all the world. In 1558, two years after the death of Ignatius, was published the *Ratio Studiorum Collegii Romani,* or the "Plan of Studies of the Roman College" which was to serve as the model for the rest of the schools of the Society. The Roman College, where the most eminent humanists, theologians, philosophers, and the best corps of professors of the Society were concentrated, became the "mother" and seed-bed for all the other schools, and a true pedagogical laboratory for the entire Order. It was there that the *Ratio* was born.

The Precursor of the *Ratio:* Jerome Nadal

8/   Jerome Nadal was the man who contributed first and most to establish the pedagogy in the Society. Nadal was also a key figure in the diffusion of this pedagogy throughout the schools. Named Commissioner by Ignatius of Loyola for Spain and Portugal (1553), Nadal established order in the schools of these countries, which had not had a well-defined program. The watchword was to follow the *"modus docendi"* of Messina and the Roman College. Shortly after his return to Rome (1554), he was named Vicar General of all the Society, the right arm of Ignatius for the governance of the order. In the following year (1555), he was designated Commissioner General to promulgate the *Constitutions* of the Society in Italy, Austria, and other regions. Jerome Nadal took advantage of his role and his journeys to spread the "way of teaching" proper to the Society. Sent again to Germany in 1562, he drew up the following year the *Ordo Studiorum Germanicus,* which is an adaptation for Germany of the program of the Roman College. In 1564, we find him again in Rome, as superintendent of the Roman College, working on a new plan of studies.

9/   Jerome Nadal can rightly be considered the founder of Jesuit pedagogy, since he laid the foundations upon which the entire scholarly edifice of the Society of Jesus was to rise. Nadal is more responsible than anyone else for the establishment of the network of schools of the early Society, which little by little acquired a common face. The profusion of rules and instructions which he went about leaving in all parts would serve later as the basis for the definitive *Ratio*.

The Source of Jesuit Pedagogy: the Method of Paris

10/   What did Nadal use to write the first plan of studies for the Society? He certainly did not invent it, but rather took it from somewhere else. Nadal himself recognizes its origins. The method which is followed in Messina is "the method of Paris" *(modus parisiensis)*, "because it is among all the most exact and the most useful." It is necessary to go back a few years to understand the importance which the University of Paris had in all of the pedagogy of the Society since its beginnings. Ignatius narrates in his autobiography that, after having made his studies in Alcala and Salamanca in a most disorganized way, "he decided to go to Paris to study" *(Autobiography,* 71). Alone and on foot he made his way to Paris, where he arrived on a cold day in February 1528. "And he went to study humanities at Montaigu . . . He studied with children *following the order and method of Paris"* (*Aut.* 73).

11/   It must not be forgotten that the first Jesuits all studied and were recruited by Ignatius at the University of Paris. From its very beginnings, the Society of Jesus bears the stamp of Paris. The Bull of approval of the Society emphasized the fact that the companions were "masters of arts and graduates of the University of Paris." All of them kept very good memories of the University, which they considered always as the *alma mater* of the Society. Ignatius especially was very grateful to the University in which he had finally been able to finish his studies, at no less than 43 years of age. When his brother asked his advice about where to send his son Millán Loyola to study, Ignatius did not hesitate one moment: Paris. "He will make more progress here in four years than in any other, that I know of, in six." It is not strange, therefore, that in the moment in which the Society decided to opt for a concrete pedagogical method, it decided in favor of "the manner called of Paris, where the Society first studied and knows the manner which is followed there."

12/ If it were necessary to summarize in a few words the principle characteristics of the manner of Paris, we would describe them as follows:
- good order in the studies, arranged in a systematic and progressive form
- separation and gradation in the studies of the subject matter
- settled duration of courses and examinations for the mastery of each of them
- insistence on the necessity of establishing good foundations before going ahead
- the division of students into classes, according to their levels of knowledge
- abundance and frequency of exercises, with great activity on the part of the students
- the use of emulation
- strict discipline and regimentation of student life
- study of the liberal arts with a humanistic and Renaissance content with a Christian inspiration
- insistence upon joining virtue with letters

13/ Some of these elements may seem obvious to us today. But they were not so obvious in their time, when the Jesuits thought that the manner of Paris was so appropriate and advantageous. Many of these points from *the manner of Paris* are similar to various methodological aspects that we find in the Spiritual Exercises of St. Ignatius, especially in the *Annotations*. St. Ignatius did not study in Paris in vain.

Jesuits and Protestants: a Strange Similarity

14/ But the Jesuits were not the only ones who had studied in Paris. Within the same classrooms and, in some cases, in the same schools

frequented by the Jesuits, passed more or less in the same years, person-
alities such as Calvin, Johannes Sturm, André de Gouveia, and numerous
other humanists caught up in the cause of the Reformation. They also were
becoming familiarized with the manner of Paris. It is therefore not strange
that when the Reformers who had studied in Paris began to open their own
schools, their establishments also bore the mark of Paris. The programs
of the Protestant schools of Bordeaux, Strassbourg, Geneva, Nîmes, and
Lausanne, which were opened a bit before Messina, present a strange similarity with the program of the latter school. And the same may be said of
the other later Jesuit schools, created according to the model of Messina and
the Roman College.

15/   To this should be added the fact that both the Jesuits and the
Reformers, in and outside of Paris, experienced in diverse ways the influence of the *Devotio Moderna,* a spiritual current which originated in the
Low Countries with Gerard Groote (14th century) and was spread by the
fraternity of the Brothers of the Common Life, who themselves created
an entire network of schools in the Low Countries and in Germany. The
spiritual and pedagogical movement of the Brothers also had an important
impact in Paris, above all through the College of Montaigu, where Ignatius
studied. In reality, many of the pedagogical elements of the *manner of Paris*
come from the Brothers. The schools founded by the reformer Melanchton
in Germany find themselves also within the Renaissance humanism of the
Brothers. This is another reason that explains many concrete similarities
between the pedagogies of the Jesuits and the Protestants.

16/   For years this resemblance fed the controversy as to whether it was
the Jesuits who had plagiarized the Protestants, or vice versa. Today it is
clear that it is not precisely a matter of plagiarism. Jesuits and Protestants
were drinking from the same sources, which were the *manner of Paris* and
the current of the Brothers of the Common Life. This explains the family resemblance.

17/   Nevertheless, neither the Jesuits nor the Protestants had a monop-
oly on the *manner of Paris,* since other schools, lay and communal, took

their inspiration from Paris. But there is no doubt that the most consistent adaptations of the *manner of Paris* were those made, each separately, by the Jesuits and the Protestants. And that the systematization made by the Jesuits, especially through the *Ratio,* was unquestionably the most successful and the one which was most widespread.

18/ The originality of the Jesuits was not so much in the elements which they included in the plan of studies—many of which coincide with those of the Protestants—but rather in the manner in which they used these same elements to construct a new educational project, of worldwide scope. In conclusion, the originality of the *Ratio* is not in its mere literality, but in the inspiration which animates it, which is the same spirit which molds the *Constitutions* of the Society of Jesus, and the conception of the world, of the human being, and of God which are presented by the Spiritual Exercises of Ignatius of Loyola.

2. THE DIFFERENT VERSIONS OF THE *RATIO*

The *Ratio "Borgiana"* (1565–1572)

19/ The elaboration of the definitive *Ratio* of 1599 was a very laborious process. Diego Laínez, the successor of Ignatius as General of the Society, did not forget the promise of Ignatius to provide the schools with certain norms, and entrusted the preparation of the work to the Roman College. He himself compiled several rules for extern students (1561), which were much appreciated in their time. It seems that it was Laínez who gave to Ignatius the idea of having schools for externs. A multitude of rules and instructions date from this epoch. During four years a commission worked on the compilation of certain norms, which were sent to the provinces in 1569, already during the generalate of St. Francis Borgia. This is the first *Ratio* strictly speaking, known as the *Ratio Studiorum Borgiana,* and was published in several stages. The defect of this *Ratio* was that it said *what* should be done in the schools, but did not say *how*.

20/ The *Ratio Borgiana* treated the study of the humanities, but omitted references to the studies of philosophy and theology. One of the problems which occurred since the beginning in the redaction of the different versions of the *Ratio* was precisely that of determining the doctrine that the Society should uphold in its schools, especially regarding theology. Should liberty of opinion be allowed, so that the professors might express their own points of view more freely? Or should the theological opinions to be held be spelled out? The question was not a negligible one. On it would depend whether the schools of the Society would teach a uniform doctrine or if liberty of instruction would be allowed. The topic bristled with difficulties, especially in the context of the diffusion of the doctrines of Luther. The controversy lasted for years and made the redaction of the *Ratio* difficult. Four hundred years ago, the problem of how to combine orthodoxy and the security of doctrine, on the one hand, with freedom of opinion, on the other, was already in place. Themes such as justification, predestination, or the philosophy of Averroes were then of burning relevance.

The *Ratio* of 1586

21/   Time passed and the provinces were demanding a definitive version of the *Ratio,* which would settle once and for all the question of freedom of opinion. The new General, Claudio Acquaviva, made the theme a high priority of his administration. Again the question was whether it would be good to compile a list of propositions which were to be prescribed or prohibited, and whether it would be good that the Society wedded as the only doctrine the teachings of St. Thomas Aquinas. Old Alfonso Salmerón, one of the first companions of Ignatius, wisely opined that it would be better not to restrict themselves to one particular doctrine, not even that of St. Thomas Aquinas, because of the difficulties which could derive from this.

22/   In 1583, Acquaviva named a commission of six experts from diverse nations to work in Rome on the redaction of the *Ratio.* The good fathers compiled no less than 597 propositions relative to the doctrine which the Society should follow. The professors of the Roman College rejected them, and—with good sense—reduced them to 130. Eventually, in April of 1586, Acquaviva promulgated the *Ratio,* generally considered as the "first" version of the *Ratio,* although in reality the Borgian version had proceeded it, as we have said. The text did not pretend to be a definitive version, but only a provisional working document, an "intermediate" text, to be sent to the provinces to be examined for six months, and so that observations could be sent to Rome. This explains why very few copies were printed and why the General, once the final version was promulgated in 1599, instructed that any remaining copies of this earlier edition be burned.

23/   The *Ratio* of 1586 consists of two parts. The first refers to the "Selection of Opinions" which are to be held in the Society's teaching. The second is the "Practice and Order of Studies" and refers to the order in which the studies should follow, from theology and philosophy to the humanities. This second part does not contain juridical rules or didactic norms, but rather a series of rather general considerations regarding diverse themes of a scholarly nature, and are therefore not as practical as their title suggests.

24/   The response of the provinces to the document was negative, particularly regarding the way that the "Selection of Opinions" was compiled. It was evident that the first part of the document was very restrictive, and that the second part was very vague. The general opinion was the document should be completely redone, both the speculative and the practical parts. Besides this, the document had aroused the attention of the Spanish Inquisition, which confiscated all the copies. The question ended up in the Holy Office in Rome, from which it left free of all suspicion.

The *Ratio* of 1591

25/   After the ill fortune of the *Ratio* of 1586, the process repeated itself. After receiving the remarks of the provinces at the end of the same year, a commission of three fathers began to prepare a new document. The theme of the "Selection of Opinions" was prepared by Stefano Tucci. At the end of 1589 he had already completed a new version, which the General had sent to the Pope for approval—to be on the safe side. In 1591, the "Practical Part Regarding the Studies" was also ready.

26/   In the end, the *Ratio* was sent to the provinces in the fall of 1591, but with a noteworthy peculiarity. Only the "Practical Part Regarding the Studies" was included in the published version. The "Selection of Opinions" was sent out a year later, in 1592, as a simple manuscript, in a separate treatment entitled "Speculative Part," very much reduced and with directives which were more general. Evidently, the purpose was to avoid new conflicts with the Spanish Inquisition.

27/   The portions regarding studies had been completely transformed, with a series of precise rules for the authorities, for those responsible for the different disciplines, and for the students. In an appendix were added particular norms for the individual provinces, and an example of the development *(praelectio)* for a humanities program.

28/   The part of the new *Ratio* of 1591 which referred to students was sent to the provinces on an experimental basis, for a period of three years. The speculative part, in contrast, was promulgated as obligatory and definitive. Very few copies of this *Ratio* were printed as well, which, as was the custom, succumbed to the pyromaniacal tendencies of the epoch, once the final version was published in 1599.

29/   The *Ratio* of 1591 was a much more elaborate and convincing document. This does not mean that all the provinces embraced it with too much enthusiasm, either the speculative part or the practical. The speculative section did not gain the assent of all, and the practical was too long and repetitive. At once, observations began to arrive in Rome. Complaints rained down from Spain, Belgium, Austria, Germany, Poland, even from Italy. The provinces complained that, in spite of everything, the particular situation of each country had not been sufficiently taken into account. It was felt that a document on this matter, applicable to the whole Society, was impractical.

30/   In 1593 General Congregation V convened. One of its first decisions was to name a commission for the revision of the *Ratio,* presided over by Roberto Bellarmino, then Rector of the Roman College. Surprisingly, the

Congregation was very decisive in the question of the liberty of opinions, which had dragged on for years: the Society should just follow the doctrine of St. Thomas Aquinas. After years of work by commissions, consultations, discussions, lists and more lists of obligatory and free propositions, the question was settled in a brief decree. As to the practical part regarding studies, the Congregation reflected the great diversity which existed in the provinces. The Congregation had to recognize the wisdom of St. Ignatius in the *Constitutions*, that accommodation be made to place and time and persons.

The Definitive *Ratio:* 1599

31/ The *Ratio* of 1591 was still on an experimental basis. Yet, it seemed that the process of elaboration and re-elaboration of documents and more documents was finally reaching its end. After General Congregation V, Acquaviva entrusted to a commission of three Italian fathers the definitive revision of the document, from the entire arsenal of rules, norms, resolutions, suggestions, opinions, and observations accumulated over such a long period of time. The work of the commission lasted three years (1595–1598).

32/ Finally, the definitive document was made public. It was the first days of the year 1599. The speculative part had been omitted, but a catalogue was added of the doctrine which the professors of theology and Sacred Scripture were to follow. The appendix referring to the particular norms for the provinces was also omitted, a matter which was referred to the discretion of the General. A few other rules were also added. The work had been completed.

33/ The first edition was printed in Naples in 1599. A multitude of other editions followed. The text approved and promulgated by General Acquaviva was slightly retouched by General Congregation VII (1616), and remained in effect without any change for 174 years, until the suppression of the Society (1773). The "treatise" which Ignatius had announced in the Constitutions to give *"order and method"* to the studies of the Society, had a long and laborious gestation. But it had finally seen the light of day.

The Men of the *Ratio*

34/   The *Ratio* of 1599 and the versions which preceded it were not the work of any one person, not even of a commission, but rather the result of a collective work in which many teams and individual persons participated, many of them unknown, throughout the entire second half of the 16th century. For half a century, from the first *Constitutions of the College of Messina* in 1548, passing through the *Ratio Borgiana* of 1565, through to the *Ratio* of 1586 and 1591, a multitude of theologians, philosophers, humanists, and other experts took part in the construction of the plan of studies of the Society of Jesus, finally published in 1599. Claudio Acquaviva, whose name is associated with the *Ratio,* was the one who, beginning in 1581, urged on the last steps of the process, widened consultation and experimentation, sped up the redaction, and finally promulgated the definitive version.

35/   The true authorship of the *Ratio* corresponds to a few Jesuits of the first generation, contemporaries of Ignatius, and a larger group of Jesuits of the second generation. We recognize the names of several of these co-authors. We will point out only those who, in our judgment, played a more important role.

36/   Among the oldest documents which serve as a basis for the *Ratio* are those composed by Juan de Polanco, the secretary of Ignatius, which were used by the founder in the preparation of the Constitutions. Next comes Jerome Nadal, whose educational program in Messina marked the starting point in the entire process of the construction of the *Ratio* itself. Among those who worked with Nadal in the plan of studies in Messina and put it into practice, we must mention the humanists André des Freux (Frusius), Isidoro Bellini, Hannibal du Coudret (Codrettus), all former students in Paris, besides Peter Canisius, Cornelius Wischaven, and Benedetto Palmio. As regards the rules for students, Diego Laínez made an important contribution.

37/   Among the theologians who most influenced the *Ratio,* Diego de Ledesma, the first prefect of the Roman College and confidant of Francis

Borgia, was the most celebrated and the one who was most responsible for the theological orientation of the successive revisions. His position on the question of liberty of opinion in the teaching of theology was one of the strictest. Ledesma was not known particularly for his humanistic spirit, so we should be grateful that the humanistic part of Borgia's *Ratio* took into account the opinion of a good humanist such as Pedro Perpinyà. A role of the first order in the later versions of the *Ratio* was played by the renowned humanist Stefano Tucci, the worthy successor of Ledesma as regards theological orthodoxy. In considering the question of liberty of opinion, Acquaviva also consulted Roberto Bellarmino, Alfonso Salmerón, and Juan Maldonado, all of these with a more open mindset and whose opinions held great weight.

38/ The six experts named by Acquaviva for the revision of the *Ratio* in 1586 were Juan Azor (Spain), Gaspar Gornçalves (Portugal), James Tyry (Tirius, Scotland), Petrus Buys (Busaeus, Flanders), Antoine Guise (Belgium), and Stefano Tucci (Italy). The three fathers appointed for the revision of the *Ratio* of 1591 were Stefano Tucci, Juan Azor, and Gaspar Gornçalvez. Finally, the team for the revision of the *Ratio* of 1599 was comprised of the Italians Jeronimo Brunelli, Filippo Rinaldi, and probably Orazio Torsellini.

39/ But if it were necessary to mention one collective author of the *Ratio,* no doubt this distinction would go to the Roman College, in recognition of the leading role which it played both in the theoretical systematization and the concrete practice.

3. THE CONTENTS OF THE *RATIO*

The Rules

40/ "A comprehensive program for our course of studies" are the first words of the letter of Secretary Domenichi, promulgating the *Ratio*. Next, and without much of a preface, follows a succession of rules for the different persons responsible and the other actors in the educational process, one after another. In all there are 30 rules, with a total of not less than 467 articles. Everything related to educational life is regulated to the smallest detail: the governance of the schools, the selection of the professors, the admission of the students, the programs of studies, the authors and texts, the methodology, scholastic and extra-curricular activities, religious formation, discipline, rewards and punishments, time schedules, vacations . . .

41/   A simple reading of the *Ratio* may be deceptive for someone who is searching in it for grand pedagogical principles. Much of its contents seem today picturesque and anachronistic. Taken out of their context, they lend themselves to humorous commentaries and can be subjected to a superficial critique. The *Ratio* has been criticized for its lack of a general vision of education, or for the absence of a "declaration of principles" but in order to pass judgment upon it, one must be aware of the spirit with which it was written.

42/   It must not be forgotten that the *Ratio* is, in a sense, a prolongation of *Part IV of the Constitutions of the Society of Jesus*. It is the famous "separate document" promised there by Ignatius. It is within this perspective that the document should be read and understood, in the framework of the Constitutions and in the light of the Exercises of Ignatius of Loyola. The Jesuits to whom it was directed, had before their eyes this frame of reference and did not need to be reminded of it. They were not asking for a pedagogical treatise, but rather practical orientations for their concrete work. The *Ratio* is not a theoretical treatise, but an eminently practical manual, which describes our way of proceeding in education. To read the *Ratio* without this perspective is to fall into the illusion that it is only a tedious scholastic rule book, with an unending stream of details, minutia, and exhausting repetition. Nevertheless, although much of the practical detail is out of fashion today, much of its contents continues to be valid.

The "Pedagogy of the Jesuits" in the *Ratio*

43/   It would be out of place to pretend to offer a complete picture of the *Ratio*. We will limit ourselves simply to tracing roughly some of the most characteristic elements of the "pedagogy of the Jesuits," as it is reflected in the *Ratio*.

44/   The highest authority is that of the Provincial, to whom corresponds the ultimate responsibility for all that pertains to education. "It is the principal ministry of the Society of Jesus to educate youth in every branch of knowledge that is in keeping with its Institute" (*Rules of the Provincial*, 1). Under the Provincial, leading the school is the Rector, assisted by a Prefect of Higher Studies—for the studies of philosophy and theology—and a Prefect of Lower Studies—for the classes of rhetoric, humanities, and grammar. The Rector is without exception nominated by the General, according to the Constitutions. In this, the Society distanced itself from the prevailing norms of that era, especially in the universities of Italian style, where the Rector was elected.

45/   Next is considered the faculty, composed entirely of Jesuits. Nevertheless, the document insists curiously on the necessity that the professors be carefully selected and well formed. Nothing strange, if one recalls that the "boom" of schools and the scarcity of capable personnel had forced the Society to make due with young professors. The constant switching of Jesuit schoolmasters and their lack of preparation had occasioned numerous complaints by families and ruined the reputation of not a few schools. The theme of the formation of the Jesuits in the face of the escalating demands of the schools is not far removed from the overall problematic of the number of the professed and non-professed in the Order. A controversy arose in parallel regarding the poverty of the schools, and whether or not the schools were the specific ministry of the Society and in conformity with the mind of the founder.

46/   Certain requirements needed to be followed for the admission of the students, including an examination to know the extent of their previous studies and to place the student in the corresponding class. The division of students into classes and the progression in the studies to the extent that the exams were passed is a characteristic norm. There are "noble" students who are given "the choicer seats" (in class each student has his fixed seat). But there is no discrimination according to social class in the admission process: "he must not, however, refuse anyone admission because of poverty or inferior social status" (*Rules of the Prefect of Lower Studies*, 9). The Jesuit schools should be endowed with a foundation or be able to count on fixed incomes sufficient to make them accessible to all. At the door of the recently inaugurated Roman College (1551), a sign declared that instruction was given "gratis."

47/   The course of studies began with three years of grammar (low, middle, high) one year of humanities, and one of rhetoric. But the time which each student would remain in a course could vary, according to his own pace. According to the Constitutions, reading and writing was ordinarily not taught (*Constitutions,* 451). This also explains why for centuries the Society did not become involved in elementary education.

48/   Classical studies, based upon the Greco-Latin culture predominant in the Renaissance, were the basis of the curriculum. Latin, Greek, and even Hebrew were the languages to be gradually acquired. A mastery of Latin was imperative and generalized, to the point that the students were denounced and punished when they had failed to speak in it at the appointed times. The use of the vernacular language was in large part repressed to favor the mastery of Latin. A curious selection of the best authors guaranteed the quality of the classical formation, more the ancient than the modern authors. In Latin, Cicero, Caesar, Salustius, Titus Livius, Virgil (excluding the *Eclogues* and the loves of Dido and Aeneas in the *Aeneid*), and Horatius (selected odes) were the preferred authors. Much care was given to "expurgate" the authors to omit all obscenity. For years, already during the life of Ignatius, the propriety of studying the good pagan authors (or the works of Christians of suspect doctrines, such as Erasmus) was debated. The Solomonic solution was to make use of them "as of the spoils of Egypt."

49/   The goal of a humanistic formation was the classical man, well-balanced and fully developed in all his faculties, inspired along the lines of the Greco-Latin authors, enhanced by the Christian dimension as well. In a very famous expression, to reach perfect eloquence "eloquentia perfecta" (*Rules of the Teacher of Rhetoric*, 1), which meant not only being able to speak, to write, and to communicate one's own ideas with facility and elegance, but also having the capacity to reason, to feel, to express oneself, and to act, harmonizing virtue with learning. In a word, the integral formation and style of life along the lines of what today we would call "human excellence." In philosophy and theology, the question of "proficiency" *(mediocritas)* and the qualities or talents required to go on to higher studies and to possible responsibilities of governance were a theme of discussion in the Society for centuries.

50/ After rhetoric followed three years of philosophy and four of theology. In philosophy, Aristotle was the prescribed author, as was St. Thomas in theology. After the long debate about the doctrine which the Society ought to defend in its teaching, the *Ratio* did not enter into further detail. St. Thomas was the author who ought to be followed by obligation to such an extent that those who were little fond of him had to withdraw from their teaching posts. But St. Thomas did not have to be followed slavishly to the point of never deviating from his doctrine: "The members of the Society therefore should not be more strictly bound to him than the Thomists themselves." (*Rules of the Professor of Scholastic Theology*, 2) Interestingly the students of theology were permitted to depart from the opinions of their teachers and to defend their own in public acts, on condition that they were well founded—and did not depart from the teaching of St. Thomas: of course! (*Rules for Those Reviewing Theology in Private Study,* 10)

51/ A technique specific to the lower classes is the praelectio which consists of a specific way of expounding the text of an author. The professor begins with a brief summary or synthetic presentation of the topic, and continues by breaking up and analyzing the entire contexts of the text, explaining and commenting upon it from all angles: words, phrases, its correct translation, grammatical rules, style, images, background and form, historical context, characters, significance, etc. The *praelectio* forced the students to become accustomed to not merely passing superficially over the texts, or stopping at the surface, but rather to penetrating deeply into the work and to growing in maturity in their judgment and in their personality.

52/ The timetables were intense: two to two and a half hours in the morning and as much in the afternoon, not counting the time dedicated to study and scholastic exercises. The vacations were neither less than one month nor more than two in the higher studies, and were reduced by half this for the lower courses, down to only a week for the poor students in the lowest grades. Besides Sunday, there was one other weekly day of rest, either Wednesday or Thursday: Thursday prevailed in the century-old tradition of the Society. Saturdays were days dedicated to repetitions of the lectures of the week, to the recitation of the catechism, and to scholastic debates.

53/ Frequent and abundant exercise is one of the characteristics of the pedagogy of the *Ratio*. The activities carried out in class had a group character to them, with intense interaction among the students. The types of exercises were extremely varied: writing, descriptions, imitation of authors, compositions in prose and in verse, transcriptions from prose to verse and vice versa, translations, recitations, declamations, discourses, repetitions, vocabulary drills, *disputationes* or a type of scholastic debate with arguments pro and con, written examinations, oral examinations, public functions . . . These are some of the activities which kept the students active at every moment, with continuous demands upon their intelligence, memory, imagination, and feelings. Practice and usage were more important than the rules. It was most definitely a pedagogy eminently active and interactive.

54/ Other extra-curricular activities rounded out the day. Among them, the Academies. These came to be like study clubs, formed by selected students, who would meet on Sundays or holidays to practice and cultivate their hobbies delving deeper into topics related to their studies. Theatrical presentations, greatly cared for from the very beginning—the famous Jesuit theater—had also a place in the *Ratio*. It is specified, however, that tragedies and comedies be given rarely, in Latin, about pious themes, and without any female costumes or characters. In this case the practice also went far beyond the law, and soon became highly developed.

55/ Emulation was another typical element of Jesuit pedagogy, reaching almost mythical proportions by the way it was interpreted. In the lower classes, each student had a peer *(aemulus)* for mutual stimulation in the scholastic exercises, specially correcting each other's homework and going over the repetitions of the lessons. Each class was divided into two groups. Each one had its own officers, who took the names of the Roman magistrates (emperors, consuls, tribunes . . .) The groups competed among themselves and the student leaders in each group occupied the first seats. Every one or two months the officers were rotated.

56/   One particular exercise was the *concertatio,* or a contest in which the rivals responded to certain questions, or the two groups competed among themselves, or else an individual would challenge another who was in a higher rank to snatch the rank from him. The objective is "so that honorable rivalry which is a powerful incentive to studies may be fostered" (*Common Rules for the Teachers of the Lower Classes,* 31). It is an echo of the "holy rivalry" of which St. Ignatius also spoke (*Constitutions,* 383).

57/   Within this pattern, rewards and punishments also play a role and were the object of special rules. In each class, the students were divided into *decuriae* or groups of ten. Within each of these there was a decurion, a type of professor's assistant, whose duty was to take the memory lesson of his fellow students. In each class there was also someone in charge of discipline, known as the chief decurion (censor, praetor), who had the privilege of imposing punishments upon his companions, interceding for them, and reporting the faults committed in the presence or the absence of the professor. When warnings did not suffice, sanctions followed. However, no professor could apply corporal punishments, otherwise common at that time; neither were they allowed to insult or humiliate a student. The Jesuits would turn them over to the secular authorities: an external corrector, not a Jesuit, especially paid, who had the exclusive responsibility for applying sanctions. But the *Ratio* wisely notes that "faithful observance will be better served by the hope of honor and rewards and the fear of disgrace than by corporal punishment" (*Common Rules for the Teachers of the Lower Classes,* 39).

58/   Attention to the person reveals itself throughout the *Ratio,* although the expression "cura personalis" or other similar terms do not formally appear in the *Ratio* in any particular place. The *Ratio* not only asks the professor to pray for his students and meet with them in private sessions, but, significantly, it also recommends: "he must not regard anyone with contempt, but assist the efforts of the poor as much as those of the rich. He should seek the advancement of each and every one of his charges" (*Common Rules for the Teachers of the Lower Classes*, 50).

59/   A special rule gives norms for prizes, which were conferred once a year. Written contexts were held in the diverse disciplines, in which the students participated anonymously. A panel judged the works and announced the names of the winners, who were awarded prizes with all solemnity.

60/   As can be supposed, attention to the teaching of Christian doctrine and religious formation, as well as the practices of piety, occupy pride of place in the *Ratio*. Daily Mass, prayer, the examination of conscience in the evenings, the frequent reception of the sacraments, devotion to the Our Lady, weekly exhortations to the students, pious lectures, sermons on feast days and various devotions mark the entire *Ratio*. Each class begins with a brief prayer given by a student, which the professor and students listen to on their knees. The teachers are advised to have private colloquies with the students in order to impress upon them the virtues. One of the means most recommended are the Marian Sodalities, which are to be established in each school, for the students who aspire to a deeper spiritual life. Being a member of a congregation is a prerequisite for taking part in an academy.

61/   In summary, joining piety and letters is the result hoped for in the students. The study of liberal arts in a Jesuit school had no other goal than the service and the love of God and others.

Our Way of Proceeding in Education

62/   We are not going to pronounce a critical judgment on the *Ratio* of 1599, its undeniable successes and its deficiencies. Numerous historians and pedagogues have already done that. Nothing can replace the direct consultation and study of the rich literature which exists on the matter to form one's own idea of what the *Ratio* was and what it meant in the history of education and of the Society.

63/   We would argue simply that the *Ratio,* with its positive and negative aspects, and with the qualities and defects of the Jesuits who put it into practice, allowed for the organization of an educational system and the implantation of a pedagogical practice which perhaps has never been duplicated in world history. Whatever may be one's judgment of the *Ratio* and the pedagogy of the Jesuits, it is undeniable that both have made their mark in the history of culture and education.

64/   For Jesuits and for those who are committed to the educational mission of the Society, the *Ratio* has another special feature: that of being a concrete historical expression, applied to the field of education, of what Ignatius of Loyola called our way of proceeding.

4. FOUR CENTURIES LATER

A Failed Attempt: The *Ratio* of 1832

65/   Suppressed in 1773, the Society, once restored in 1814, immediately resumed its educational labors. It first seemed obvious that the schools would return to the famous *Ratio Studiorum.* But, since the French Revolution, the world was no longer the same. The birth of the modern states implied radically distinct tactics in the educational field. This was especially true in the states formed according to the Napoleonic model, which promoted the state school and assumed control of education. To think of a uniform plan of studies, commonly acceptable in all countries, was thereafter an illusion.

66/   General Congregation XX, the first of the restored Society (1820) decreed "the adaptation of the *Ratio Studiorum* to our times." An attempt was made to revise the *Ratio* to conform to the national educational systems. General Jan Roothaan strongly supported drafting a new *Ratio,* which appeared in 1832. Sent to the provinces, it suffered even a worse fate than its predecessors of the 16th century: more than ever, it was impossible to prepare a document which would be universally valid for the entire Society.

The Jesuits ran the risk of pursuing their own plan of studies, in parallel with the secular legislation in effect, and without official recognition. Besides, the contents were obsolete. Continuing teaching according to the classical ideas of Renaissance humanism, in a world in which the scientific disciplines, the national languages, and modern authors were gaining ever more importance, was to go against the current of history.

67/   The *Ratio* of 1832 was stillborn. In 1906, General Congregation XXV declined to impose a common *Ratio* for all the schools of the Society, given the variety of secular legislation in effect. In practice, it was left to the provincials to see how to apply the *Ratio*. The same Congregation had to admit that the study of non-classical authors "is not contrary to our Institute." This one declaration speaks for itself of the change which had occurred.

68/   Realistically, the Catholic school was given way to state pressure. In order to ensure recognition by the state, Jesuit schools in Europe were gradually accommodating their programs and methods to the requirements of the ministries of education. In other countries, such as the United States, in which one enjoyed more liberty and there was not the same pressure from the State, the schools were shaping their own model of a Catholic and Jesuit school, inserted into the surrounding culture. Several of the schools were distancing themselves from the mythical *Ratio,* of which only external symbolic elements remained. Sometimes the old terminology was used, such as classes of *grammar, poetry, rhetoric, humanities*, but the words were losing their original meaning. The Jesuit educational system seemed to have been installed in as many different models as countries. What still gave a unity was not a common document, but rather a spirit.

From the *Ratio* to the Characteristics

69/   Let us make a jump in history. The memory of the last few years is too fresh in our minds to need repeating. Since the excitement of the Council and the institutional crisis of the 60s and 70s, which particularly affected the education, the Society entered in a new path. The apostolic works of the Society, among them education, entered a process of profound revision, in order to accommodate itself to the new formulation of the mission expressed by the General Congregation XXXII (1975).

70/ The need to give a sense of unity to the educational apostolate was felt in all parts, not by means of a new pedagogical code, but by the adherence to certain common principles and ways of doing things. Thus was born in 1986 the *Characteristics of Education of the Society of Jesus*. Fruit of the work of many teams and consultations much more agile than those of four centuries ago, the *Characteristics* do not pretend to be a new *Ratio*, but rather seek to give a common vision and a sense of purpose to education in the Society. In 1993 was published *Ignatian Pedagogy: A Practical Approach*, which offers a model for the application of the *Characteristics* to the concrete terrain of the classroom, by means of a practical pedagogy inspired by the Exercises.

71/ The merit of the *Characteristics*—which is only a working instrument—consists in having given a sense of unity to education in the Society, not through a plan of common studies, but by springing from the fundamental Ignatian inspiration. This inspiration was without doubt latent in the *Ratio*. But perhaps never as much as today has it become clear that the raison d'être of education in the Society is rooted in the vision of Ignatius, and in the mission of the Society, in the framework of a four-century-old spiritual and pedagogical inheritance.

72/ Once again, the Society is trying to be faithful to the wise principle of adaptation "to places, times, and persons." And, under the inspiration of Ignatius, it is attempting to serve the Lord and to help souls in the field of education, according to our way of proceeding.

RATIO STUDIORUM—TABLE OF CONTENTS
Rules of the Provincial

Rules of the Rector

Rules of the Prefect of Studies Common Rules of Professors of the Higher Faculties

Rules of the Professor of Sacred Scripture

Rules of the Professor of Hebrew

Rules of the Professor of Scholastic Theology

Rules of the Professor of Cases of Conscience

Rules of the Professor of Philosophy

Rules of the Professor of Moral Philosophy

Rules of the Professor of Mathematics

Rules of the Prefect of Lower Studies

Rules for Written Examinations

Laws for Prizes

Common Rules for the Teachers of the Lower Classes

Rules of the Teacher of Rhetoric

Rules of the Teacher of Humanities

Rules of the Teacher of Highest Grammar Class

Rules of the Teacher of Middle Grammar Class

Rules of the Teacher of Lowest Grammar Class

Rules of the Scholastics of the Society

Instruction for Those Engaged in the Two-Year Review of Theology

Rules for the Teacher's Assistant or Beadle

Rules for Extern Students

Rules of the Academy

Rules of the Moderator of the Academy

Rules of the Academy of Theologians and Philosophers

Rules of the Moderator of the Academy of Theologians and Philosophers

Rules of the Academy of Students of Rhetoric and Humanities

Rules of the Academy of Students of the Grammar Classes

Catalogue of some questions from St. Thomas' "Prima"

CURA PERSONALIS

"CURA PERSONALIS" The expression *"cura personalis"* (attention or care to the person) does not come from Ignatius nor does it appear in the earliest writings of the Society. It seems to be the modern equivalent of an attitude which certainly is very characteristic of Ignatius and the Society:

"prudence suited to places and persons," "the circumstances of the persons," "the diversity of persons and natures," etc.

We find it (for the first time?) in the *Instruction* of General Vladimir Ledóchowski on the Universities and Colleges of the American Assistancy (August 15, 1934): *"Personalis alumnorum cura"* (*Art.* 7,2) and in the *Instruction* revised by General John Baptist Janssens (September 27, 1948). This explains how the subject of the *"cura personalis"* began to spread throughout the English-speaking world.

The *Ratio Studiorum* of 1599: A Basic Overview

John O'Malley, S.J.

1/   The *Ratio Studiorum* is the "plan of studies" for Jesuit schools, published in 1599 by the then Father General, Claudio Acquaviva. In 1583, Acquaviva called to Rome six Jesuits from different parts of Europe and gave them the task of bringing order out of the educational documents circulating in the Society. In 1586 this committee sent a "plan" to Jesuit institutions and asked for comments on it. Five years later the revised text, based on reactions to the first, was again sent out for comments and experimentation. The result was the definitive text of 1599. It is an educational document of critical importance for the subsequent history of the Jesuits and in the broader culture as well, where it was both admired and denounced.

2/   In constructing the *Ratio*, the committee understandably took as its two building blocks the two educational institutions that dominated the educational scene in the late sixteenth century—the university and the humanistic college. It took these institutions as normative and conjoined them in the *Ratio*, which envisaged an institution where the student moved from the "lower disciplines" of the college to culmination in the "higher disciplines" of the university subjects of philosophy and theology.

3/   The *Ratio* is essentially a compilation of best practices in school administration and, especially, in pedagogy as developed by Jesuit institutions in the previous decades. These best practices are codified in the *Ratio* as a series of rules for the different officials of the schools and for the teachers of the standard subjects of the curriculum. As the rules prescribe best practices, they also became job descriptions. The *Ratio* begins, for instance, with "Rules for the Provincial" and "Rules for the Rector [president]." It contains "Rules for the Teacher of Sacred Scripture," "Rules for the Teacher of Rhetoric," and so forth.

The *Ratio* aims, therefore, to be a practical instrument for effective pedagogy and administration. It is at the same time an instrument of quality control for the Society of Jesus. The quality of an institution could now be measured by the strictness with which the rules were followed.

4/   Best practices were exercised on a body of texts taught in the universities and colleges of the day. The *Ratio* accepted those texts as a given. They were, with a few exceptions such as Aquinas's *Summa Theologiae*, texts from classical antiquity. The *Ratio* assumes the normative quality of these texts, and it takes them for granted as perennially valid and irreplaceable.

5/   If that is what the *Ratio* is, what is it not? It is not a theoretical treatise. It is not a philosophy of education. It is not a document that is in any way explicit about the deeper values of Jesuit education or spirituality. Indeed, it can sometimes sound superficially moralistic. What must be kept in mind is that the *Ratio* assumed its program would be carried out in an atmosphere in which certain values were taken for granted and therefore did not need articulation. With the passage of time, however, corporate memory faded, and those values needed to be made explicit.

6/   Because the *Ratio* provides rules for those who teach the lower disciplines, it was applicable to all the schools operated by the Society of Jesus because every school taught those disciplines. As a full-fledged "plan of studies," however, it was applicable only to the relatively few schools in the system that were universities or their equivalent. By the middle of the seventeenth century in Italy, for instance, the ratio of colleges to schools who taught the full program of the *Ratio* was 20 to 1.

7/   This often-overlooked character of the *Ratio* is indicated by the high priority it gives to philosophy and theology. As mentioned, they were subjects taught in universities. That was especially true for theology, which was a strictly professional discipline like law and medicine. It was, therefore, restricted to clerics, just as medicine was restricted to students who wanted a degree in medicine. In that regard we need to be aware that at the time of the *Ratio* and for some time thereafter, most priests did not study theology—at least not theology as a university discipline. Only those relatively few clerics who wanted to be or, as with the Jesuits, were expected to be professional theologians studied in a theological faculty. In other words, the "student pool" for theology was small.

8/   Theology remained restricted to clerics until the latter half of the twentieth century. Put into perspective, therefore, we can say that the *Ratio*, when viewed in its entirety, was a "plan of studies" principally or almost exclusively for Jesuits in training. It was in no way a plan expected to be implemented in its fullness in all the schools the Society operated.

9/   The colleges took boys at about eight or ten years of age, and they kept them for some six or eight more years. The curriculum was fundamentally the lower disciplines, that is, literary classics of Greece and Rome—Demosthenes, Sophocles, Cicero, Virgil, and the others. The "extracurricular" but essential components of the education of the colleges were catechism classes, regular sermons and attendance at Mass, and participation in other religious exercises.

10/   The program of the colleges was essentially that laid out by Renaissance humanists such as Pier Paolo Vergerio the Elder, other Italians, and most especially Erasmus. These humanists, who drew their ideas from Cicero, Quintilian, and other classical writers, elaborated a sophisticated justification for their program, which was in essence a philosophy of education.

11/   According to that philosophy, the program was geared to preparing students for active and positive participation in the affairs of their community by teaching them how to speak and write persuasively and by fostering in them an upright character. This was a radically student-centered philosophy based on the premise that the study of "good literature" would, if properly taught, inspire students to achieve their best selves. The humanists managed to persuade Europeans that nobody was truly educated who was not educated according to their system.

12/   The Jesuits were among those they convinced. They saw their schools as producing, in the words of Polanco, Saint Ignatius's brilliant executive secretary, "pastors, civic officials, administrators of justice, and will fill other important posts to everybody's profit and advantage" (*The First Jesuits* [Boston: Harvard University Press, 1995], 213). Ignatius himself typically promoted the colleges as founded "for the good of the city," *ad civitatis utilitatem.*

13/ The humanist program was complete in itself and was not as such preparatory for university studies. In other words, the colleges were not "prep schools." Although in their curriculum they evince characteristics of secondary schools today, they were not secondary in that they looked to completion in a tertiary institution. When a young man left a Jesuit college in his late teens, he was considered fully educated and ready to take his place in the world. Of course, if he wanted to enter one of the three standard professions—law, medicine, or theology—he would then, and only then, go on to a university. Relatively few took that option

14/ However, because the *Ratio* includes the lower disciplines and moves from them to university studies, it creates the impression today that those disciplines were indeed considered nothing more than "prep" for the higher disciplines. Although that was somewhat true for the Jesuit students, it was certainly not true for the young laymen who were the vast majority of the students in the colleges—or, in most of them, the only students.

15/ Of course, reality is always more complicated than any plan. Some Jesuit colleges were more ambitious than others and introduced at least some courses in philosophy. The most popular were those in "natural philosophy," the seedbed of modern science. Such courses included mathematics, optics, and astronomy, based upon classics such as Ptolemy, Euclid, and especially Aristotle. No college, however, taught theology.

16/ Until relatively recently, the term *Jesuit universities* must be used with considerable caution, as Paul Grendler makes clear in his work *The Jesuits and Italian Universities 1548–1773*. There was a wide variety of arrangements in different settings where Jesuits taught the higher disciplines. Nonetheless, wherever the Jesuits had a foothold in such institutions, the institutions were special, though not unique, in that they included a program in the lower disciplines, as mentioned earlier. They were also special in that the Jesuits did not teach the other two subjects that were included in the standard curriculum of the university: law and medicine. This restriction was principally due to the fact that Jesuits themselves were not normally trained in these disciplines and, hence, not qualified to teach them. Sometimes Jesuits got around this anomaly by staffing the philosophy and theology faculties of universities operated by others.

17/   Although the *Ratio* provides no philosophy of education, we can safely assume that the Jesuits who compiled it were thoroughly conversant with the educational philosophy that underlay the lower disciplines. Therefore, they felt no need to express it, nor would an expression of it be pertinent to the purpose of the *Ratio* itself. The higher disciplines had no equivalently articulated philosophy. The implicit justification for including these disciplines in the *Ratio* was that they were the typical clerical subjects, even though philosophy had a broader clientele.

18/   The style of education proposed in the *Ratio* is radically text-based. It inculcates the reading, hearing, and study of texts. As text-based, the *Ratio* is also authority-based. It assumes that education consists essentially in appropriating and reflecting upon past knowledge and past wisdom. It makes no provision, therefore, for experienced-based or experiment-based education as we understand those terms. It makes no provision for what we today call the production of knowledge.

19/   As text-based, the *Ratio* makes no provision for the arts, but it does inculcate active learning on the part of the student by insisting that the student perform in various ways. Nonetheless, it restricts the number of dramas a school might mount on an annual basis, and it thus gives a distorted view of the education as actually practiced in the colleges, where productions of various kinds—theater, dance, and concerts—came to be considered hallmarks of Jesuit schools.

20/   With the passage of time the *Ratio* assumed a sacrosanct character and began to labor under the assumption that it had said all that ever needed to be said. It became impervious to serious revision, a development aided by the fact that the *Ratio* itself did not provide for further adaptation. Basic to the *Ratio* was the principle that "one curriculum fits all," and it admits nothing resembling an "elective." The authors of the *Ratio* would have been horrified by the prospect of students constructing their own programs.

21/   Within a few decades of the publication of the *Ratio*, however, certain developments were taking place in the world of culture that had serious consequences for the *Ratio's* program. Those developments became ever more important with the passage of time. The first was the development of vernacular literatures. Despite the merits of Sophocles and Virgil, it became increasingly difficult to exclude contemporary writers from the curriculum on the basis of the clear superiority of the classics from the past. This problem became more acute as Latin gradually ceased being the language of scholarship and international communication.

22/   Many Jesuits were, of course, keenly aware of the problem, especially as the "quarrel between the ancients and the moderns" became more heated in general culture, and they did their best to make room for modern literature. Nonetheless, the classics of antiquity continued to dominate the curriculum.

23/   The second development was experimental science and the subsequent demotion of the ancients, particularly Aristotle, as definitive in natural philosophy. Once again, many Jesuits were sensitive to these developments, and some were fully abreast of them. Their interest and accomplishments were reflected in the curriculum of the schools. In the latter half of the eighteenth century the Jesuits produced Roger Boscovich (1711–1787), who had such an international reputation as a natural philosopher as to be elected to the Royal Society of London and the American Philosophical Society. Boscovich taught for a time at the Jesuit College of Nobles in Milan, where French and German played an important role in the curriculum and where an up-to-date program in natural philosophy was operative.

24/   Beginning with Descartes came new approaches to other branches of philosophy. Nonetheless, as late as 1730 the 16th General Congregation— and then again in 1751 at the 17th General Congregation—prescribed that the Society's teachers adhere to Aristotle not only in metaphysics and logic but in physics as well, as set down in the *Ratio*. Although in any vibrant institution there is always a certain discrepancy between normative documents and actual practice, in the Society the discrepancy had in this instance become acute and undermined the authority of the normative document.

25/   The third development was the decline in prestige of virtually all universities in the seventeenth and eighteenth centuries. They were looked upon as bastions of conservative thinking, impervious to new ideas. The Jesuit faculties were no exception to this criticism. New institutions that provided specialized, often highly practical training in subjects sometimes related to traditional university curriculum began to spring up in competition. Among them, for instance, were specialized schools of surgery (The Hague, 1637; Paris, 1724), engineering (Moscow, 1712), Oriental languages (Naples, 1732), and commerce (Hamburg, 1768).

26/   Just as important was the rise of more informal institutions such as the Royal Society and the American Philosophical Society, where men of letters and men of science gathered to discuss their ideas and to compare notes on their experiments. It was to such organizations, not to the universities, that the brightest thinkers belonged. This convergence of the learned led to important discoveries and generated a body of important literature that advanced the state of learning. Jesuits were only rarely elected to such societies—Boscovich was a notable exception—which meant that the Jesuits stood outside these vibrant institutions.

27/   The final development came in the nineteenth century, when German universities revived and redefined the purpose of the institution. In so doing, they created what we know as the research university. No longer was the transmission of information sufficient as the goal of the institution. It now had to foster original research so as to produce new knowledge. This goal was utterly foreign to the *Ratio*, as it was to the institutions that it had taken as its models.

28/   Moreover, as universities revived in the nineteenth century, they no longer restricted their program to philosophy, theology, law, and medicine. They took on schools of agriculture, schools of commerce, even schools of nursing, and they thereby took on institutions that earlier functioned apart from the universities and in competition with them. In this way, too, the university scene changed radically from the model in the *Ratio*. Jesuit schools, though sometimes still called colleges, adapted as best they could to the new developments and began to incorporate into themselves these other "schools."

29/   By the middle of the twentieth century, therefore, it had become devastatingly clear to Jesuit educators that the *Ratio Studiorum* of 1599 could no longer function as a practical instrument for their schools and that its revision in 1832 under Father General Jan Roothaan did not change the situation. The revision continued to embody a program operative in the sixteenth century that had been surpassed and rendered irrelevant on almost every level. Jesuit educators had to strike out on their own.

30/   Where does that leave us? The *Ratio* is a document from long ago that does not translate into the present; vain are the efforts to make it do so! Nonetheless, as a classic in the history of Western education it can be studied with profit, even if it does nothing more than put our own situation into clearer light by providing a striking contrast to it. But the *Ratio* does more than that. There are things to learn from it that are pertinent today.

31/   Not least among them is the high priority the *Ratio* gives to pedagogy. Educators today are obsessed with curriculum—how many curriculum-revision committees have we all served on!—but pay little attention to how the subjects in the curriculum are taught. In that regard the *Ratio* is the polar opposite. Certainly, in Jesuit schools, pedagogy means more than techniques for efficient appropriation of learning. It means, more profoundly, techniques to show the pertinence of the material for one's life and for the well-being of the world at large. This is a value of capital importance.

32/   Basic to the lower disciplines in the *Ratio* was rhetoric, the art of saying what one means and meaning what one says. This is not a goal or value that has lost its crucial importance with the passage of time. The current international revival of scholars' interest in "Jesuit rhetoric" is proof positive that this value, so central to the *Ratio*, is as important for educators today as it ever was.

33/   Literature may not be able to inspire moral excellence, but it certainly can show the complexity of life and of human motivation and thus, if properly taught, help students reflect on the tangle of emotions and impulses in which they find themselves and their peers caught. They can thus develop a sensitivity to human and humane values and be less likely to divide the world into good guys and bad guys, a step in creating a more livable world.

34/   Finally, character formation was the ultimate objective of the lower disciplines, but it was meant to be operative all the way through the program. No one is under the delusion that formal schooling of any kind provides a sure recipe for furthering the process. However, Jesuit schools have taken it on today with a force perhaps as great as it ever was, with a focus on producing men and women for others—men and women intent on improving the common weal, that is, *ad civitatis utilitatem*. St. Ignatius and the creators of the *Ratio Studiorum* would be pleased with a development so much in accord with what they hoped to accomplish through the schools of the Society.

John W. O'Malley

Ratio Studiorum, 1599

The Ratio Studiorum: *The Official Plan for Jesuit Education.*
Translated by Claude Pavur, S.J.

[H22] Rules for the Prefect of Lower Studies

1/   [242] *Final goal*

1. He should realize that he has been chosen for this: to devote his every effort and all his attention to helping the rector direct and administer our classes so that those who are attending them progress in the moral integrity of their lives, no less than in humanistic studies.

2/   [243] *Subordination to the general prefect*

2. He should consult only the rector in matters that pertain to moral discipline in our classes, but in those that pertain to studies, he should consult the general prefect of studies. He should not deviate from what they have prescribed. He should neither abrogate any established custom nor introduce a new one.

3/   [244] *Who should approve the declamations*

3. He should see to it that whatever will be publicly declaimed by the students of rhetoric and the lower classes, at home and elsewhere, will be turned in to the prefect for inspection.[138] But emblems and poems that are collected for public display on some of the most important days of celebration should all be read by two that the rector will appoint,[139] and the best ones should be selected.

4/   [245] *Observe and help the teachers*

4. He should keep in his possession a copy of the rules for the teachers and students of the lower classes and attentively see to it that they are followed as well as his own rules are. He should help and guide the teachers themselves, and he should take special care that nothing diminishes their esteem or authority in the eyes of others, but especially in the eyes of the students.

5/   [246] *A single approach in teaching*

5. He should give particular care to ensuring that new teachers consistently keep their predecessors' manner of teaching and other customs (though nothing foreign to our overall plan), to keep non-Jesuits from criticizing the frequent change of teachers.

6/   [247]   *Visiting the classes*

6. At least every fifteen days he should attend a class given by each teacher. He should note whether they are giving due time and attention to Christian doctrine, whether they are making satisfactory progress in both finishing and reviewing their assignment, and finally whether they are conducting themselves honorably and commendably in all matters with the students.

7/   [248]   *Feast days and changes in schedule*

7. In due time, he should notice and point out to the teachers both the feast days and the vacation days, whether common to all provinces or proper to his own, especially ones occurring during the week, and the hours at which classes have to start and end in each season of the year. The same holds for when the students have to be dismissed for public prayers and other things of that nature, or when they have to be told or forbidden to do something out of the ordinary.

8/   [249]   *Five grades of classes*

8. He should take care that the grades that make up the lower classes, namely, rhetoric, humanities, and the three grammar classes, are not in any way mixed; so that if some class, on account of a large enrollment, is ever split into two at the instruction of the provincial, each should retain the same grade. And if ever additional levels are organized in a single class, they should correspond to those grades that will be described in the rules for professors.

9/   [250]   *Division of grammar into three books*

9. To better and more easily keep this distinction, all the rules of Emmanuel ought to be divided into three books; each of them should be proper to each of the classes. The first book for the lowest class will include the first book of Emmanuel, and a brief introduction to syntax drawn from the

second.[140] The second book for the middle class will include the second book of Emmanuel from the syntax of the eight parts of speech up to constructio figurata, with the addition of the easier appendices.[141] The third book for the highest class will cover the appendices of the second kind from the second book and from the constructio figurata up to the end, and the third book, which is about the measurement of syllables.[142] A division similar to this one in three parts corresponding to the three classes would have to be made also by those provinces that follow a method other than the Roman one.

10/   [251] *The split arrangement for the lowest class*
10. The teacher will usually finish each class's book in the first semester; in the second, he will review it from the beginning. But since the lowest class's book is larger than can be completely taught and reviewed in one year, it is therefore divided into two parts. And certainly it would help not to admit boys unless they have been well instructed in the first part, so that the second part can be explained to everyone and reviewed, just as in the other classes. But where this is not possible, this lowest class ought to be divided into two levels. The book's first part should be taught to one and its second should be taught to the other, usually in the first semester. But in the second semester, each should be reviewed from the beginning. Wherever the class is split, since there are two levels in it, one teacher can teach the lower level, and a second the higher one.

11/   [252] *The usefulness of review*
11. This review is useful in two ways: First, what is more frequently repeated will be more deeply retained. Second, if any have outstanding intellectual talent, they will complete the course more quickly than the rest, since they can advance to a higher level each semester.

12/   [253] *The college of five classes*
12. So where there are five classes, each grade should be kept separate "in the way in which they have been" described in the rules for teachers.[143] And there should never be more than one level allowed in any of them, with the exception of the lowest.

13/   [254] *Of four*

13. Where there are four classes, either rhetoric should be removed, and the four remaining ones should differ not at all from those that we have just mentioned; or, preferably, the highest should be rhetoric, and it should decidedly keep to the grade described in the rules for the professor of rhetoric; the second should be the humanities class, and likewise, it should keep to the grade stated in the rules for the professor; the third should be divided into two levels, of which the upper should correspond to the highest grammar class, and the lower to the middle one; finally the fourth will correspond to the lowest class. It can be split into two levels, as is stated in its rules. If only the higher level is allowed, the third should contain only one grade, and it should be the highest class of grammar; but the fourth should contain two, and it should be the middle and the lowest.

14/   [255] *Of three*

14. Where there are three classes, the two lower ones should keep the grade just prescribed for the final two in the college of four classes. But the highest should either be straight humanities, or it should be divided into two levels, of which the higher corresponds to rhetoric, and the lower to humanities. But in any case the higher level should not be introduced unless the rector has been consulted, when there is a good number of students who are capable of that level. And this should be done in such a way that the teacher does not skimp on any of the attention and care that the lower level should get.

15/   [256] *Of two*

15. Where there are two classes, the lower one should have two levels. Of these, one should correspond to the highest level of the lowest class, and the other to the intermediate class. Likewise, the upper one should have two, of which one should correspond to the highest grammar class, and the other to the humanities class.

16/   [257] *Review of the assigned war in the classes of two levels*

16. Also in these classes where there is a splitting in the levels, there will be for each level the same review of the year's work that was mentioned in number [10]. And in fact where it would be possible, each would have its

own part taught in the first semester and repeated in the second. Over the course of the two years, the students in the same class would get as far as they would have gotten in two classes that consisted of one level each. But where this seems too difficult, it will require additional time.

17/ [258] *What is common, what is distinctive in the same situation*
17. In order for this to be achieved in these classes in which there are two levels, everything except for the grammar lesson will be common to everyone. Most important, the lesson on Cicero will be common,[144] so that easier things are demanded of the lower level, more difficult ones of the upper. Then a single theme can also be given, so that the upper level takes it all, the lower only the first or the last part, which has been modified to fit the rules that have been explained to them. Finally, everyone can usually join in the exercises and competitions. Therefore, since only the grammar lesson is distinct, either on every other day in each level, or in a period divided between the two levels, each level will have its own material presented or reviewed every day.

18/ [259] *New students*
18. To the extent that it is possible, he should register no one not brought in by his parents or guardians, or not known to him, or about whom he cannot easily be fully informed by others that he already knows. But he should exclude no one on the grounds that he is poor or not of noble blood.

19/ [260] *Their examination*
19. He should examine the new arrivals this way: He should ask what studies they have worked on and how far they have gotten. Then he should propose a certain topic and tell them to write something on their own. Likewise, he should require a few rules of the subjects that they have studied. He should propose some short sentences for them to translate into Latin, or, if necessary, to interpret from some writer.

20/ [261] *Admission*
20. He should admit those whom he finds to be properly trained and of good character and nature. He should inform them of the rules for our

students, so that they might understand what is expected of them. He should register their names, surnames, countries of origin, ages, parents or guardians, and whether any student is familiar with their homes. He should mark down the day and the year in which each was admitted. Finally he should place each one in that class and with that teacher who is right for him, in such a way that he can seem worthy of a higher one rather than unworthy of his own.

21/   [262] *Who should not be admitted*
21. He should usually not admit into the lowest class youths who are too old or, unless they are quite suitable, little boys who are too immature even if they were sent only to be properly trained.

22/   [263] *Promotion*
22. A general and formal promotion ought to be made once a year after the annual vacations. Nevertheless, if any are far superior, and it seems that they would make more progress in a higher class than in their own (which he should realize by examining the record book and by asking the teachers), they should not by any means be held back, but they should move to the higher class at any time of the year, after an examination. And yet, such an advancement from the first class to humanities hardly appears likely on account of the prosody that is taught in the second semester, as does an advancement from humanities to rhetoric on account of the general overview of Cyprian.[145]

23/   [264] *There should be a written examination*
23. For the examination, all the classes should write a prose composition once, or, if it is necessary, a second time, but the highest class of grammar and the humanities class should write once also in poetry and, if it seems good, once in Greek, after an interval of some days.

24/   [265] *The regulations for the examination should be read out*
24. About two or three days before the examination, he should have the teachers announce that there will be composition for the examination. And

he should have the regulations for the examination compositions (attached to the end of these rules) read out in each of the classes.

25/   [266] *The prefect should supervise*

25. The prefect himself, or another person whom he assigns to take his place, should supervise those who are writing. On the day set for taking the examination, after giving the signal, this person should give a theme, a brief one rather than a long one.[146]

26/   [267] *Compositions to be turned in to the examiners*

26. He should keep the compositions in his possession, bundled in alphabetical order. And if nothing prevents it, he should divide them up among the examiners so that, if they wish, they can read them and mark the mistakes in the margin.

27/   [268] *Examiners*

27. There should be three [oral] examiners. Typically, one will be the prefect himself; the rector, along with the prefect, will appoint two others, not teachers if possible, who are quite experienced in literary studies. The decision will rest on the weight of the votes made by these three. Where there is a very large number, nothing prevents the arranging of two or more three-member examination boards.

28/   [269] *Number of those to be examined*

28. A group of three or even more should be summoned to the examination from the classes, especially the lower ones. And from then on, the same number should be sent up by the teacher, keeping alphabetical order or some order that is more convenient.

29/   [270] *The record books should be examined*

29. The examiners should first of all read through the teacher's record book and review the marks noted in it for each one, when the student is coming to take the examination. They should compare them, if necessary, with earlier record books from the same year, so that the progress that each one has made or is going to make might be more readily apparent.

30/   [271] *The structure of the examination*

30. This will be the structure of the examination: First, each should read out, if it seems good, part of his own composition. Then he should be told to correct his errors, and to give an account of them, indicating the rule that was broken. Later, something in the vernacular should be proposed to the grammar students for translation into Latin on the spot;[147] and everyone should be asked about the rules and the material taught in each class. Finally, the examiners should require a brief commentary, if necessary, on some passage from the books taught in class.

31/   [272] *When they should vote*

31. After the examination of each set of three, when the examiners' judgments are still fresh, there should be a vote on the examinees, taking into account the composition, the grade submitted by the teacher, and the way the examination went.

32/   [273] *About doubtful cases*

32. To settle doubtful cases, the prefect should call for their daily work at intervals. He should have a discussion with those examiners so that, if it seems right, they should have them take another written and oral examination. Moreover, in cases of doubt, they ought to take account of their age, the time they have spent in that particular class, their talent, and their diligence.

33/   [274] *The judgments ought to be kept quite confidential*

33. When an examination is over at last, the decision on each person should be kept quite confidential, except that each teacher will have to be shown his own record book before it is publicly announced.

34/   [275] *The incompetent*

34. If anyone is plainly incompetent to advance to the next level, there should be no place for an intercessor. If anyone is just barely competent but nevertheless, on account of his age, the time spent in the same class, or another reason, it seems right to advance him, then, unless something prevents it, this should happen on the condition that if his effort fails to

satisfy the teacher, he will be sent back to a lower class and an account of his performance not kept in the record book. Finally, if any are so ineffective that it is not fitting that they be advanced, and no good result would be expected in their own classes, it should be arranged with the rector that they do not keep their place in the school, after their parents or guardians have very courteously been given notice.

35/   [276] *Public announcement*

35. The list of those who are to be advanced should be publicly read out, either to each of the classes separately or in the hall at the same time to everyone. If any stand out far beyond the rest, they should be named first, to honor them. For the rest the order of the alphabet or the level of learning will be followed.

36/   [277] *List of books*

36. Before the formal reopening of studies, he should in good time bring to the rector's attention the matter of drawing up the list of books that are going to be taught that year in our classes, so that the general prefect and the teachers might participate in this matter. In the same way, there should be a decision on whether perhaps any books or authors should be changed that year.

37/   [278] *Supply of books*

37. He should ensure that the public booksellers are engaged early on so there is no shortfall in the supply of books that we (both the Jesuits and non-Jesuits) either use from day to day, or are going to use in the coming year.

38/   [279] *Assignment of places*

38. At the beginning of any year he should assign each of the students his own bench and bench partner, either directly or through the teachers. He should do this both for the day students and for the boarders through their directors (unless perhaps somewhere the order of seating is determined by the level of instruction). Of course, he should assign the better seats to those of noble families; but to Jesuits and to other religious likewise, if they

are present, he should assign seating separate from that of the non-Jesuits. And he should fully expect that no great change will be made without his knowledge.

39/   [280] *Time for private study*

39. It is a matter of very great importance that the prefect, through the teachers or through other prefects of those colleges, so structure the schedule not only for Jesuit students but also for the day students and boarders, and if nothing prevents it for outsiders as well, that they might manage their private study time well.

40/   [281] *No exemption*

40. Except for a serious reason, he should give no one an exemption, especially an extended one, from learning poetry, even Greek poetry.

41/   [282] *Monthly declamations*

41. He should see to it that the monthly declamations that are held by the rhetoricians publicly in the hall are graced not only by the assembly of rhetoricians and humanities students but also by that of the upper grammar classes. And therefore the teachers should be reminded that each should invite his own students. No Jesuits should be allowed to be absent without obtaining permission from the rector.

42/   [283] *Class disputations*

42. He should consider when, according to what form, and where the classes ought to convene to dispute among themselves. And he should not only prescribe ahead of time the structure of the disputation, but also, while the debate is going on, he himself should be present and take constant care that all things are managed productively, temperately, and peacefully. In the same way, he should attend the declamations or classes of the rhetoricians and humanities students that are usually held in the school.

43/   [284] *Academies*

43. He should make an effort to have the literary exercises take a firm hold. If the rector approves, academies should be organized, not only for the classes in rhetoric and the humanities, but also for those in grammar.

In these academies, on set days and according to the particular regulations that are included at the end of this book, there should be a rotating presentation of lessons, disputations, and other activities that are characteristic of a good student.

44/   [285] *Public prizes*

44. Early on, he should remind the superior about giving out awards and about holding a declamation or perhaps a dialogue on that occasion. In the distribution of the awards, the regulations that are placed at the end of these rules must be followed, and they ought to be formally read out in each of the classes before the writing.

45/   [286] *Private ones*

45. He should also see to it that, in addition to the public prizes, the teachers, each in his own class, also spur the students on with private little prizes or some sign of victory, which the rector of the college will supply. This should happen when, from time to time, they seem to have merited them either by overcoming an opponent, or by reviewing all of some book, or by reciting it by heart, or by doing some such noteworthy thing.

46/   [287] *Censor or praetor*

46. He should appoint in each class his own public censor, according to local custom, or if the name of censor is not so appealing, a chief decurion, or a praetor.[148] This person should be honored with some privilege, so that he is respected among his fellow students. With the teacher's approval, he will have the right to release his classmates from lighter punishments. He should notice if anyone is either wandering away from his classmates in the courtyard before the signal is given or going into classes that are not his own, or leaving his own class, or his own place. He should also report to the prefect the ones absent each day; if anyone who is not a student has come into the class; and finally, if any mischief occurs in class whether the teacher is present or not.

47/   [288] *Disciplinarian*

47. On account of those who fall short sometimes in their diligence and sometimes in those things that pertain to good character, and with whom kind words and exhortations alone are not enough, a disciplinarian who does not belong to the Society should be appointed. When one is not available, a way to punish them should be devised, administered either through one of the students themselves or by some suitable method. But they should not be whipped in class for some transgression having to do with their home life, except rarely and for a substantial reason.

48/   [289] *Those who refuse correction*

48. The ones who refuse to take a whipping either should be compelled, if this can be done safely, or if it ever becomes unseemly, as it certainly does with the bigger students, forbidden to enter our school. But still the rector must be apprised of the matter. The same should also be the case with those who are frequently absent from class.

49/   [290] *Those who should be removed from class*

49. When neither words nor the disciplinarian's office is sufficient, and someone is not expected to improve, and he seems to be a hindrance to the others, it is better to remove him from classes than to keep him where he himself is getting little help and harming others. But this judgment will be left to the rector, so that everything might proceed, as it should, for the glory and the service of God.

50/   [291] *Those that must be punished more severely*

50. If some incident occurs where expulsion would not be a sufficient remedy for an offense committed, he should report it to the rector, so that he might see what might be a fitting alternative arrangement. And yet, as far as it can be, the matter ought to be handled in a spirit of gentleness, preserving peace and charity with everyone.

51/   [292] *Easy readmission to classes should be available to no one*

51. Without the rector being advised beforehand, readmission to our classes should be unavailable to any of those who have either been expelled once or

have left on their own initiative without a good reason. It will be up to the rector to decide what solution is the best.

52/   [293] *The quiet of the courtyard*
52. He should tolerate no weapons, no idle pursuits, no shoving or shouting in the courtyard or in the classes, even the higher ones. He should allow no swearing in them, or verbal or physical injuries, or anything vile or licentious. If any such thing occurs, he should restore order immediately. And he should take it up with the rector, if there is anything that in any way disturbs the quiet of the courtyard.

53/   [294] *Make rounds of the courtyard and the classes*
53. Not only should he constantly be present in the courtyard, or in a room that looks out onto the courtyard, during the entire time for classes, but he should also occasionally make rounds of the classes before the signal to enter has been given. And he should always be on hand at the door of the courtyard when everyone is leaving.

54/   [295] *Church and Masses*
54. He should make sure that the classes enter and leave the church without noise. And they should never attend Mass unless there is some teacher present, or even several of them. They should all attend every day not only devoutly but also seated in good order and by their rank in class.

55/   [296] *Confession*
55. On the days and hours set for hearing students' confessions, he should see that the confessors are there on time. He himself should repeatedly enter the church during that time. And he should see to it that the boys are behaving calmly and devoutly.

56/   [297] *Students not to be called out of class*
56. Especially when lessons are underway, not even the prefect himself should call students from their classes, except sparingly. If any others fail to follow this policy, he should fully inform the rector.

57/   [298] *Do not make use of student labor*

57. At no time should he make use of student labor, either for writing or for any other thing, or allow others to make use of it.

58/   [299] *Make a set of the rules available*

58. The common rules for all non-Jesuit students ought to be openly posted in a place where they can be read publicly, and in every class besides. And usually at the beginning of each month they ought to be read out in the rhetoric classes and in the other lower ones.

59/   [300] *Assuming the role of the general prefect*

59. Where there is not going to be a prefect for higher studies, he himself, with the approval of the rector should take charge of reviewing those things that are openly declaimed and of distributing books to Jesuit students, with the rector's full awareness.

---

[138] Declamations: formal speeches, often displaying attention to rhetorical devices.

[139] Emblems: this use of the word *emblem* is now obsolete. It refers to "a drawing or picture expressing a moral fable or allegory; a fable or allegory such as might be expressed pictorially" (OED). For the early history of emblems, see Daniel Russell, "Alciati's Emblems in Renaissance France," 534f. For the distinctive Jesuit contributions to this genre, see Peter M. Daly and G. Richard Dimler, S.J. *The Jesuit Series.*

[140] Emmanuel:[Emmanuel's *Grammar*—ed.] The syntax of the eight parts of speech. Emmanuel gives the eight parts of speech as "*nomen, pronomen, verbum, participium, praepositio, adverbium, interjectio, and conjunction*" (Emmanuel, *De institutione grammatica,* 104). The first page of the second book of his grammar carries the title *De octo partium orationis constructione,* and it explains that syntax in Greek or *constructio* in Latin means "the right arrangement of the parts of speech with one another" (ibid., 224).

[141] *[C]onstructio figurata:* this phrase denotes artful variation on the expected patterns of speech, new "twists" of phrases that may appear to be errors but should not be classified as such (ibid., 384 f.). [T]he appendices: these are short sections added at the ends of sections to expand upon the grammatical principles just given.

[142] [M]easurement of syllables: knowing the "quantity" or "length" of syllables is important for correct pronunciation and for the scansion (and hence for the composition and appreciation) of classical Latin and Greek poetry and rhythmical speech. It plays some part in distinguishing otherwise ambiguous words (e.g., *hic* means "here" if the vowel is long, "this" if short).

[143] Grade: *gradus* (Latin for "step") indicates the stage of learning, a particular segment of the entire course of education. Many classes at the same grade level can exist in a school, but they would all be unified by a conscious adherence to an explicit statement of the grade's goal, by the particular contents presented in each class, by the particular methods and practices outlined in the *Ratio,* and by the shared schedules for the year and for the daily order.

[144] Cicero was the most celebrated ancient Roman orator and philosophical writer (106–43 B.C.). In addition to his speeches and philosophical treatises, he left behind a substantial collection of letters and several works on rhetoric.

[145] Cyprian: Cypriano Soarez or Cipriano Suarez or Cypriano Soario (1524–93), author of *De arte rhetorica libri tres* (Venice, 1569).

[146] Theme: the Latin word *argumentum* means the gist or summary sketch of a composition. It can be expressed in a single phrase like "the onset of winter," but more frequently, in the Ratio it seems to refer to a short, prepared paragraph dictated to students who will creatively elaborate the topic. Sometimes *argumentum* is translated as "summary of the content" or as "subject."

[147] [S]omething in the vernacular: *vernaculum aliquid*. The vernacular language is sometimes also called the *patrius sermo* or the *sermo vulgi*.

[148] *Censor, praetor, decurion:* terms taken from ancient Roman civil and military administration.

[H24] Regulations for Prizes

60/ [312] *The number of awards*

1. Eight awards should be offered in rhetoric: two for Latin prose, two for poetry; two for Greek prose, the same number for Greek poetry. In the humanities class and in the first grammar class, six should be offered in like manner but keeping to the same arrangement, leaving aside, of course, Greek poetry, which is generally not practiced before rhetoric. Next, four awards should be offered in all the other lower classes, also leaving aside Latin poetry. In addition in each of the classes, one or two who recite Christian doctrine best of all should be given an award. Still, where the number of students is very high or low, more or fewer awards can be given, provided that the place of Latin prose is always given the greater emphasis.

61/ [313] *Days for writing*

2. The writing competition should be divided up into separate days in such a way that one day is given to Latin prose and another to the writing of verses, and likewise two other days to Greek prose and poetry.

62/ [314] *Set hours*

3. Everybody should assemble, each in his own class, on the days and at the hours assigned for writing.

63/ [315] *Leaving and talking is forbidden*

4. After the summary of the composition's content has been given, no one should leave his class before the writing is finished and turned in; and no one should speak with anyone else, inside or outside the school. If, however, someone has to leave, then after permission has been granted, the topic and whatever he has written should be left with the one who is in charge of the class at that time.

64/ [316] *How the time should be extended*

5. If anyone requests a longer period to complete the assignment more carefully, he should stay as long as he wishes, provided that he does not set foot outside the class, or extend the time beyond sunset.

65/   [317] *The composition should be marked with a sign*

6. When he wishes to leave, each one should turn in his own composition, carefully written out, to the school prefect, or to another person whom the prefect has put in his place, adding some sign that he prefers, but without a name; likewise, he should turn in to the same person another page on which the same sign has been set, along with his name and surname, carefully folded so that the name cannot be seen.

66/   [318] *They should be kept safe*

7. The prefect of each school should keep constant and faithful guard over all of these papers, and he should not unfold the papers containing the names before the decision has been made.

67/   [319] *Judges*

8. Three judges who are both learned and respected should be chosen. One of them can be from outside if local custom requires it. They should not know to which person each of the compositions belongs. When they have read through all the compositions and carefully examined the contents, these judges should declare by a plurality of votes all the winners by level, and also one or two in each category out of those who came very close to the winners.

68/   [320] *The criteria for the decision*

9. In the decision, the composition that has the better structure should be preferred over all the rest, even though they have written the most. If there are any whose writing is equally good in that particular genre and style, then the longer composition should be preferred to the shorter one. If in this respect they are equal as well, the winner should be the one whose spelling is better. If they tie in spelling and in the other categories, the prize should be awarded to the one whose penmanship is more elegant. If they tie in all respects, then the prize should be divided or doubled, or taken by lot. If anyone does better than the rest in all the writing categories, he should also get the awards in all the categories.

69/   [321] *The names to be disclosed*

10. After arriving at a decision, the prefect, together with the rector and the general prefect, should open up the papers on which the names of the competitors have been written in connection with their signs. He should carefully examine the names of the winners on the basis of the signs so that he does not make a mistake. And he should announce what he has learned to no one except for the teachers.

70/   [322] *Ceremonies for awarding the prizes*

11. Then on the appointed day, with as much ceremony and in the presence of as large an assembly as possible, the names of the winners should be announced publicly, and their prizes should be given out in a dignified way to each of them as they proceed to center stage. If anyone is not present, he should lose his prize, even if he has every right to it, unless he has gotten permission from the prefect for good reasons that are approved by the rector.

71/   [323] *Distribution*

12. The announcer will call each winner forward usually in this way: "What a happy and favorable occasion it is for Literature, and for all the students of our school, that (NAME) has merited and won the first, second, third, etc. prize for Latin prose composition, for Greek composition, for Latin poetry, for Greek, etc." Then he should hand the prize to the winner, usually with some very short poem especially appropriate to the achievement which if it can be conveniently managed, should be repeated at that very moment by singers. At the end, the announcer should add any who came very close, and to these something can also be given as a prize.

72/   [324] *Penalty for cheating*

13. If anyone is guilty of an infraction of these regulations or engages in any cheating, no account should be taken of his composition.

[H25] Rules Common to All the Professors of the Lower Classes

73/   [325] *Final goal*

1. The teacher should train the youths who are entrusted to the Society's education in such a way that, along with letters, they also and above all interiorize the moral behavior worthy of a Christian. However, his special attention, both in the lessons whenever the occasion arises and apart from them, should be directed at preparing their impressionable young minds for the devoted service and love of God and the virtues by which we ought to please him. But he should take special note of those things that follow.

74/   [326] *Prayer before the lesson*

2. Before the beginning of class, someone should say a brief prayer composed for this purpose. The teacher and all the students will listen attentively, kneeling down with their heads uncovered. Before the beginning of the lesson, the teacher should bless himself with the sign of the cross, head uncovered, and begin.

75/   [327] *Mass and sermon*

3. He should see to it that they are all present at the Mass and at the sermon—at Mass every day, but at the sermon on feast days. Beyond this, he should send them to the sermon at least twice a week in Lent or even take them, according to the local custom.

76/   [328] *Christian doctrine*

4. Especially in grammar classes, or in others as well if necessary, Christian doctrine should be learned by heart and recited from memory on Friday or Saturday, unless perhaps in some places it would seem good for it to be recited even more frequently, by new students as well.

77/   [329] *Exhortation*

5. On Friday or Saturday, for half an hour, he should give a devout exhortation or a doctrinal lesson. However, he should most especially exhort them to pray to God every day, and particularly to pray daily the rosary or the office of the Blessed Virgin,[150] to make an examination of conscience at

evening, to receive the sacraments of penance and Communion frequently and properly, to avoid bad habits, to hate vices, and finally to cultivate the habits worthy of a Christian person.

78/   [330] Spiritual *conversations*
6. In private conversations as well, he will impress on them the same things pertaining to devotion, but he will do this in such a way that he does not appear to be enticing anyone to our form of religious life. But if he does notice anything along this line, he should send the person off to his confessor.

79/   [331] *Litanies and devotion to the Blessed Virgin*
7. He should have the litanies of the Blessed Virgin recited in his class on Saturday around evening,[151] or if it is in keeping with the custom, he should take them into the church to hear them with the rest. And he should diligently encourage his students to cultivate a devotion to the Virgin and also to their guardian angels.[152]

80/   [332] *Spiritual reading*
8. He should enthusiastically recommend spiritual reading, especially about the lives of the saints. And on the other hand, he should not only for his own part refrain from teaching to the young those writers that are not wholesome and avoid altogether those in whom there is anything that can be damaging to good morals, but he should also discourage students as much as he possibly can from reading them even outside of class.

81/   [333] *Confession*
9. He should make sure that no one misses confession each month. However he will tell them to turn in to the confessors their own names, surnames, and classes, written down on a piece of paper, so that when later reviewing the slips he might know which ones have missed it.

82/   [334] *He ought to pray for the students*
10. He should pray often to God for his own students, and he should edify them by the examples of his own religious life.

83/   [335] *Obey the prefect*

11. He will obey the prefect of these studies in what pertains to the academic work and to class discipline. Without consulting with the prefect, he will not admit any student into class or dismiss him, nor will he take up any book to teach, nor will he give anyone an exemption from the common class exercises.

84/   [336] *The grade of each class*

12. Every class should keep to its own particular grade.[153] Both rhetoric and humanities will be treated separately, but there ought to be three grammar classes, which should bring to completion a certain kind of course of study in this subject. Accordingly, all the rules of Emmanuel should be divided into three parts. Of these, each part should be proper to each of the classes, but in such a way that each class reviews what was taught in the class immediately preceding it, just as the rules for each teacher will indicate.

---

[150] Rosary: a structured set of prayers said while the person praying meditates on particular events of the Christian story of salvation, often measured off by the use of a string of beads, under the spiritual patronage of Mary. The Latin word for rosary here is *corona*. [D]evotion to the Virgin: for example, the Office of the Blessed Virgin, which is "A liturgical devotion to the Blessed Virgin, in imitation of, and in addition to, the Divine Office." See *CathEncy,* s.vv. "Little Office of Our Lady."

[151] Litanies: "[a] litany is a well-known and much-appreciated form of responsive petition, used in public liturgical services, and in private devotions, for common necessities the Church, or in calamities—to implore God's aid or to appease His just wrath" (*CathEncy*, s.v. "Litany").

[152] Guardian angels: the spiritual beings who are given the special care of individuals.

[153] See 12/ n143 for an explanation of "grade."

[H27] Rules for the Professor of Humanities

85/   [395] *Grade*

1. The grade of this class consists in the preparing of the ground, as it were, for eloquence, after the students have passed beyond the stage of grammatical study. This preparation happens in a threefold way: by an understanding of the language, by some scholarly learning, and by getting a summary notion of the rules pertaining to rhetoric. For the knowledge of the language, which consists especially in propriety and abundance of expression, the daily lessons should be devoted to teaching Cicero alone of the orators, usually through those books that contain his moral philosophy; Caesar, Sallust, Livy, Curtius, from the historians, and any others like these; from the poets, especially Virgil, setting aside the *Eclogues* and the fourth book of the *Aeneid;* in addition, select odes of Horace, and likewise, elegies, epigrams, and other poems of famous ancient poets, provided that they have been expurgated of everything indecent and offensive. Scholarly learning should be employed moderately, so that now and then it stimulates the mental powers and refreshes them without impeding the learning of the language. The brief summary overview of the rules of rhetoric from Cyprian will of course be given in the second semester. At that time, Cicero's philosophy being set aside, some of the easier speeches, like the *Pro lege Manilia, Pro Archia, Pro Marcello,* and the others delivered to Caesar can be taken. The part of the Greek language that is properly called syntax pertains to this class. In addition, care should be taken that the students attain a passable understanding of the writers and an ability to write something in Greek.

86/   [396] *Schedule*

2. This will be the schedule: In the first hour in the morning, Marcus Tullius and prosody should be recited from memory to the decurion.[163] The teacher should correct the written work that has been picked up by the decurions, meanwhile giving the students various exercises to do (on this, see rule 4 below). At the very end of the hour, several students should recite in front of the class, and the teacher should review the decurions' marks. In

the second hour of the morning, the last lesson should be reviewed briefly, and a new one should be taught for half an hour or for a little more. Right away the students should be asked to repeat it, and, if there is any time left, they should compete with each other on it. In the final half hour, at the beginning of the first semester, a historian and prosody should be taken on alternate days; but when prosody is finished, a historian should be covered every day. Then in the second semester, Cyprian's *Rhetoric* should be taken every day, sometimes taught, sometimes reviewed, or there should be disputation. In the first afternoon hour, a poet and a Greek author should be recited from memory; while the teacher checks over the marks of the decurions and corrects the written work, either what was assigned in the morning, or what is left of the homework. At the very end, a theme should be dictated. The following hour and a half should be split equally between a poet, sometimes in review, sometimes in explanatory presentation, and Greek, sometimes a lesson and sometimes a composition. On the break day, in the first hour, what was taught on the preceding break day should be recited from memory, and the remaining compositions should be corrected as usual. In the second hour, there should be something from the epigrams or odes or elegies or something from Cyprian's third book on tropes, on figures, and especially on oratorical rhythm and measures, so that they get accustomed to them at the beginning of the year; or some *chria* or preparatory exercise should be taught and gone over again;[164] or lastly there should be a competition. On Saturday, in the first hour of the morning, the lessons of the entire week should be recited from memory in front of the group, and they should be gone over again in the second hour. In the final half hour, either a declamation or a lesson should be given by one of the students, or they should go to hear the rhetoricians, or there should be a competition. After the midday meal, in the first half hour, a poet and the catechism lesson should be given back from memory,[165] while the teacher reviews the marks of the decurions and the written assignments, if there are any left over from the week. The following hour and a half should be split equally in the same manner between reviewing a poet or in the explanation of some short poem and the testing of students on it, and Greek. The last half hour will be given to teaching catechism to the students or giving them a devout exhortation, unless this was done Friday. If it was, then the half hour will usually be given to whatever had been displaced by the catechism study at that time.

87/   [397] *Method of correcting the composition*
3. In the correction of the composition, he should point out if anything is lacking in propriety or elegance or measure; if a literary passage assigned for imitation is not quite correctly expressed; if there is any mistake in spelling or anything else. He should tell them to express the same thing in different ways, so that they might acquire a great abundance of expressions from this exercise.

88/   [398] *Exercises during the correction*
4. There will be exercises while he is correcting the written work, for example, selecting phrases from the lessons, varying them in several ways, putting in order a scrambled sentence from Cicero, composing verses, transposing a poem from one genre into another, imitating some literary passage, writing Greek, and other things of the same kind.

89/   [399] *Lesson*
5. To the extent that the teaching of the passage demands it, the lesson should sometimes be sprinkled lightly with ornaments of scholarly learning. The teacher should put the whole focus of his efforts on making comments on the Latin language and on the sense and the root meanings of words, which he should glean from approved authors, especially from the ancients; on the use and variety of expressions, and on the imitation of the author. And he should not think it out of place that from time to time he cite some expression in the vernacular, either if it is especially helpful for getting the meaning or if it has some other noteworthy feature. However, when he teaches a prose composition, he should examine the rules of the art. At the very end he can, if it seems good, translate everything into the vernacular, but as elegantly as possible.

90/   [400] *Summary of the composition's content*

6. The summary of the composition's content should be dictated. Of course, in the first semester, it should be done word for word, usually in the form of a letter, and in the vernacular. Often it will help to compose it in such a way that the whole thing is taken here and there from the lessons already taught. Usually once a week they should write their compositions without any outside help, after some type of letter has been taught, and after the relevant letters of Cicero or Pliny have been referenced.[166] Then in the second semester, their wit should be sparked: after the proposal of an easy and broad subject, they should compose *chriae* at first, then *proemia,* narratives, and embellishments.[167] The teacher should dictate the subject of a poem in Latin with a considerable variety of expression. The same method will be used for the Greek theme as for the Latin prose, except that it is usually to be taken right from the author, and the way the syntax works should be pointed out in advance.

91/   [401] *Competition*

7. Competition or exercise will find a place sometimes in the correction of errors that one rival has caught in the other's composition; sometimes in presenting what they practiced in the first hour; sometimes in reciting from memory or varying phrases given by the teacher; sometimes in giving back or applying the rules for letter writing and rhetoric; sometimes in determining the quantity of syllables, citing from memory a rule or example from a poet; and in searching out some particular quality or root meaning of a word; sometimes in explaining the meaning of some passage of a Greek or Latin author; sometimes in conjugating the more difficult and irregular Greek verbs; and in other activities of this kind, at the teacher's discretion.

92/   [402] *Prosody and rhetoric*

8. Prosody will be covered quickly, by sticking only to those things that the students seem to need more, and by practice more than by explanation. Likewise, it is not so much the words of Cyprian's Rhetoric as his rules that should be concisely clarified, with examples added from the same book and, if the material supports it, from the daily lessons.

93/   [403] *Greek lesson*

9. In the Greek lesson, the grammar and an author will be taught on alternate days. After briefly running through the grammatical material that had been covered in the first class, he should treat the syntax and the way the accents are used. In the first semester, one of the easier prose writers will be chosen, like some speeches of Isocrates and of Saints Chrysostom and Basil, or selections from the letters of Plato and Synesius, or something chosen from Plutarch. In the second semester, some poem will be taught, for example, from Phocylides, Theognis, Saint Gregory Nazianzen, Synesius, and the like. The teaching, in accordance with this class's grade, should promote language comprehension rather than scholarly learning. However, as the year comes to an end, the system of Greek syllables can be given together with an author, on alternating days. From time to time, they can also rearrange scrambled poems into poetic meters.

94/   [404] *Poems should be posted*

10. The choicest poems composed by the students should be posted on the walls of the class, usually every other month, to enhance some particularly special day, or to announce the officers formally, or on some other occasion. And certainly, in accordance with local custom, there should also be some briefer bits of prose, like inscriptions, such as for shields, churches, tombs, gardens, statues; like descriptions, such as for a city, a port, an army; like narratives, such as deeds performed by some saint; finally, like paradoxes. Pictures should sometimes be added, only with the rector's permission, ones that correspond to an emblem or to a subject that has been proposed.

---

[163] Marcus Tullius: Cicero. See the note on §258 above.

[164] *Chria:* a little story ending with a point or a witty saying. Preparatory exercise: *progymnasma* in Greek (plural: *progymnasmata*).

[165] Catechism lesson: catechisms are "summaries of Christian doctrine for the instruction of the people" (*CathEncy,* s.vv. "Roman Catechism"). They are frequently structured in question-and-answer form.

[166] Pliny: Pliny the Younger (Gaius Plinius Caecilius Secundus, A.O. 61/62–113?) held a number of political offices under Domitian, Nerva, and Trajan and was the author of letters (*Epistulae*), published in ten books.

[167] 167—*Proemia:* introductions.

PART III: THE RESTORATION (1814–1910)

The Society of Jesus Suppressed

John W. Padberg, S.J., 2014. *Conversations on
Jesuit Higher Education* 45:2–4

1/   On the early evening of August 16, 1773, a papal functionary along with a small group of soldiers came to the Jesuit Curia in Rome. They summoned Father General Lorenzo Ricci and his assistants and presented to Ricci a document entitled "Dominus ac Redemptor" ("Our Lord and Redeemer") from Pope Clement XIV. In it, in the words of the document itself, the pope said that "in the fullness of apostolic power we put our existence and suppress the Society of Jesus; we do away with and abrogate each and every one of its offices, ministries, works, houses, schools, colleges . . . in whatsoever land they exist . . . as well as its statutes, usages, customs, decrees and Constitutions, and we declare perpetually abolished and entirely extinguished all authority of the superior general and of provincial superiors and visitors and any and all superiors in the afore-mentioned Society. . . ." Some days later Father Ricci and his assistants were imprisoned in Castel Sant'Angelo. After two years of strict confinement there deprived of enough food, heat, and light, Ricci died a papal prisoner on November 25, 1775. Thus did the supposedly universal suppression of the Society of Jesus take place.

2/   But the piecemeal extinction of the Society had begun previously over a period of 14 years before 1773. For decades the Society had been the bête-noir of several quite hostile groups. They included, first, the Jansenists in their rigorist interpretation of Christian life and, on the other hand, many so-called "philosophes," the deistic or materialistic thinkers of the 18th century French Enlightenment who saw the Jesuits as defenders of an obscurantist church. Second, there were national governments intent on their supremacy in church-state relationships. Third, there were some powerful enemies in Rome who opposed a variety of Jesuit theological opinions and pastoral practices in Europe and Jesuit attempts in foreign mission lands to present the faith in a way consonant with the social and cultural concepts and structures of the peoples of those lands.

3/   The destruction began in 1759 in Portugal, where the government had been determined to bend the Church to its will. For years its leader, Pombal, had waged an unremitting pamphlet war of slander against the Jesuits, seen as defenders of the papacy. Finally, they were packed into ships and unceremoniously dumped on the territory of the Papal States. From the missions in Brazil they were shipped back, many of them to rot in Lisbon dungeons for years.

4/   In France in 1762 the ardently Gallican Parisian Parlement, which had been for almost 200 years anti-Jesuit, decreed the dissolution of the Society of Jesus there. As its decree went on page after page, the Society was guilty, among other crimes, of "simony, blasphemy, sacrilege, magic, witchcraft, astrology, idolatry, superstition, immodesty, theft, parricide, homicide, suicide, and regicide . . . blaspheming the Blessed Virgin Mary . . . destructive of the divinity of Jesus Christ . . . teaching men to live as beasts and Christians to live as pagans." If so, the Jesuits were certainly busy.

5/   In 1767 in Spain, King Charles III, influenced especially by his regalist government ministers to fear the Jesuits, banished them from Spain and all of its possessions, including most of Latin America. Within three days, in Spain itself in March-April 1767, 2,700 Jesuits were forced out onto the roads to its port cities thence to be shipped and dumped on the Papal States.

6/   On February 2, 1769, Pope Clement XIII, a staunch defender of the Society of Jesus through all those years, died. After a conclave of several months, with the governments of Spain, France, and Portugal alternately threatening and bribing the participants, finally Cardinal Lorenzo Ganganelli was elected as Pope Clement XIV. Then began four years of incessant harassment and bullying of the pope by the Spanish and French ambassadors to the Holy See. The threats went so far as to include hints of schism if he did not suppress the Society universally. Unable to stand up to the pressure of the Bourbon courts, Clement finally did so.

7/   The apostolic works of the Society of Jesus around the world were destroyed. Their schools (more than 700 of them) were closed. Their libraries were either confiscated or trashed. Their churches were turned over to others. Their overseas missions were ruined. More than 22,000 Jesuits were no longer such. In most circumstances individual ex-Jesuits had to make their own way with the exception of the work of one young Spaniard, Joseph Pignatelli. Over the long, long years of suppression he effectively kept united, at least in mutual support, a great portion of the Spanish former Jesuits.

8/   For the suppression to take effect canonically, "Dominus ac Redemptor" had to be promulgated by the bishop of each diocese in which a Jesuit community was located. This circumstance kept a remnant alive in one place, Russia, contrary to the expectations of everyone, because the document was not promulgated there.

9/   Now onto the stage of this drama came an act with a whole new cast of characters. It included two popes, both favorable to the Jesuits but constrained by the intransigence of Spain and France, an ambitious archbishop, a puzzled superior, a supposedly amused king, and, most importantly, a ruler who tolerated no opposition. It was a serious drama with touches of what was almost comedy.

10/   To start with the popes, Pius VI had been elected after Clement XIV died in 1774. He reigned until 1799, one of the longest papacies and one in its last ten years burdened with the antireligious events of the French Revolution. He and his successor, Pius VII, pope from 1800 to 1823, were each for some time imprisoned by the revolutionaries and Napoleon. Pius VII wanted to restore the Society, but in the turmoil of the time he could not do so.

11/   The archbishop was Stanislaw Siestrzeńcewicz, a convert to Catholicism, auxiliary bishop of Vilna and soon to be elevated to a much higher post.

12/   The puzzled superior was Fr. Stanislaw Czerniewicz, designated vice-provincial of the Jesuits in the part of Poland that Catherine had taken in the first partition of the country, apportioned to Prussia, Austria, and Russia in 1772, one year before the suppression of the Society.

13/   Most importantly, the person who brooked no opposition, who set all these characters into interaction, was Catherine the Great, Empress of Russia, who willed the suppressed Society into continued existence in her recently acquired former Polish lands.

14/   When the first partition of Poland took place in 1772, Russia acquired territory that had a large Catholic population of about 900,000 and also 201 Jesuits in a variety of residences and schools, 18 communities in all. Catherine wanted to maintain the good will of her new Catholic subjects and to maintain the Jesuits schools, which were by far the best in all her lands. Typical of Catherine, she had decided to organize, on her own, the Roman Catholic Church in Russia. So, in December 1772, she decreed that a Latin diocese for the whole country be set up at Mogilev. She named Siestrzeńcewicz as bishop. All of this she did without the least consultation with Rome. The land was hers, she was the ruler, and her decisions were law.

15/   Frederick the Great of Prussia also kept the Jesuits in existence but only for a few years. To him is attributed the remark that while the Society of Jesus was destroyed by "their Most Catholic, Most Christian, and Most Faithful Majesties" [of Spain, France and Portugal], it was preserved by "his Most Heretical Majesty" and "her Most Schismatical Majesty."

16/   When "Dominus ac Redemptor" arrived in Russia in September 1773, Catherine simply ordered that it be considered nonexistent. She forbade its promulgation; she made this quite clear to the bishop; she informed the Jesuits that she was going to maintain and keep them protected in her lands. Hence the dilemma: What were those Jesuits supposed to do? They knew of the existence of the brief of suppression. They knew Catherine's public position, and they knew better than to contradict it. They also knew of conflicting opinions in canon law on what they ought to do.

17/   To the forefront now come Czerniewicz as vice-provincial of the "Jesuit" communities now under Russian rule. After the papal suppression he turned out to be the only Jesuit major superior left in the world. When Pius VI succeeded Clement XIV in 1774, Czerniewicz wrote to him through one of the pope's official secretaries and asked for a sign of what his intentions were for these "Jesuits." The reply in Latin came with infinite diplomatic finesse on January 13, 1776: "Precum taurum exitus, ut auguro et exoptas, felix." ("The result of your prayers as I foresee and as you ardently desire, will be a happy one.") With that enigmatically favorable reply, the Jesuits in the Russian territory had to be content for the moment. But as one sympathetic observer in Rome remarked, "Intelligenti pauca" ("A few words to the wise are sufficient"). The pope could do no more because he had the Portuguese, Spanish, and French monarchs still adamantly opposed to any existence of the Society. Meanwhile Bishop Siestrzeńcewicz had ordained to the priesthood a group of these former Jesuit scholastics "because of parish needs."

18/   Then between 1780 and 1783 three events assured the existence and growth of this remnant. A Jesuit novitiate opened; a vicar general was elected; and the pope gave verbal but nonetheless explicit approval of who these men were and what they were doing, at least in Russia. Already in 1779 Catherine had agreed to such a novitiate. Then she agreed that the Jesuits in Russia could call a general congregation to elect a superior. In 1782 it chose Czerniewicz. Catherine finally sent an envoy to Rome to regularize her arrangements for all Latin Rite Catholics in Russia, to approve the Jesuit novitiate, and indirectly to approve the election of Czerniewicz. The pope could not at all give the last approval formally in writing, but publicly in the presence of witnesses three times he repeated "Approbo" ("I approve.") So just ten years after the universal suppression, the Jesuits in Russia now had a definitive sign that they were still in existence, if only there. More importantly, as the news got out, it inspired more former Jesuits to join their Jesuit brethren there. But at the same time, "Dominus ac Redemptor" was still canonically in effect and the Society of Jesus was still universally suppressed. But was it? If one had put this whole scenario in the form of a novel or a screenplay today and attempted to market it for publication as a book or production as a movie, it would undoubtedly have been turned down for a total lack of verisimilitude. These events simply could not have happened. But they did.

19/ And then, with the French Revolution, kings were swept away, armies marched, regimes changed. In Western Europe two groups formed, pledging to enter the Society if restored. By 1793 one of the now chastened rulers, the Duke of Parma, asked for Jesuits from Russia. In 1801 Pius VII recognized in writing the canonical correctness of the Society centered in Russia. By 1803 provinces dependent on that group were established elsewhere. In 1805 five U.S. members of the Old Society reentered the group. In Russia itself, over the years four vicars-general, successors to Czerniewicz, were elected, and the Society and its works expanded and flourished. With the defeat of Napoleon, the pope returned to Rome from exile and imprisonment.

20/ On the morning of August 7, 1814, Pope Pius VII celebrated mass at the Gesù in Rome. Then he came to the Jesuit Curia next door and in the document "Sollicitudo omnium ecclesiarum" ("Care for all the churches") and "despite. . .'Dominus ac Redemptor,' the effects of which we expressly abrogate" he put an end to the Suppression and restored universally the Society of Jesus.

21/ But the Restoration is another story, almost as improbable in its details as is the story of the Suppression itself.

The Beginnings of the New Society

Miguel Coll, S.J., 2014. Yearbook of the Society of Jesus: 65–68

1/ "After having implored with fervid prayers the divine help, having heard the opinions and advice of many of our Venerable Brothers, Cardinals of the Holy Roman Church, with certainty and with full Apostolic authority, we have decided to ordain and establish, with this Our Constitution, which must remain in effect in perpetuity, that all the concessions and all the faculties given by Us solely for the Russian Empire and the Reign of the Two Sicilies [regarding the Society], We now intend to extend . . . to Our entire Ecclesiastical State and to all other States . . ."

2/ On August 7, 1814, Pius VII reconstituted universally the Society of Jesus (Bull Sollicitudo omnium ecclesiarum), thereby abrogating the Brief Dominus ac Redemptor of Clement XIV (July 21, 1773). This began a new stage in the life of the Ignatian Order, characterized by a reawakening of its own traditions and by a remarkable apostolic vigor.

3/ The reestablishment of the Society is a subject much less studied than the suppression. The stereotypical Jesuit of the 1800s has generated prejudices to the point of obscuring an evenhanded historical understanding. It is a difficult subject not only because of its complexity, but also due to its polemic nature.

4/ The reestablishment poses several questions: 1. When does it end? 2. What were the differences between the Jesuits of the 1800s and their predecessors? 3. Is there continuity in the Society before and after the suppression? 4. Is it just to apply to the post-suppression Jesuits the adjective "conservative" in any case?

5/ Pius VII, through the Brief *Catholicae fidei* (March 7, 1801) officially recognized the Society of Russia (with around two hundred members) where it was protected by Catherine II. The Brief gave origin in the following decade to a wave of requests on the part of individual groups coming from Europe and the United States to obtain affiliation with the Russian group.

The Pope approved several requests coming from Switzerland, Belgium, Holland, and England.

6/ Three factors hastened the overturning of the Clementine Brief: 1. The rupture of the unity in the House of the Bourbons regarding the Jesuits: Duke Ferdinand of Parma annulled the decree of expulsion and called for the return of the Jesuits to his State, asking Catherine II for a group of the Jesuits in Russia (1793). On July 30th, 1804, Pius VII extended the concession found in *Catholicae fidei* to the Kingdom of the Two Sicilies (Brief *Peralias*). Ferdinand IV, struck by the events of the French Revolution, asked the Pope to permit the return of the Jesuits to Naples. 2. The gradual change of Pius VI from cautious approval to an explicit desire to reestablish the Society, although he died without having been able to make any official declaration. 3. The resolve of Pius VII who, returning to Rome, decided the universal restoration of the Order to assure the religious reconstruction required after the revolution.

THE BULL OF RECONSTITUTION: RELEVANT ASPECTS AND CONSEQUENCES

7/ A) The bull refers to the extension of the privileges that the Apostolic See had granted to Russia and to the Kingdom of the Two Sicilies, to "Our Ecclesiastical State and to all the other States and governments."

8/ B) It possesses a universal and prescriptive value.

9/ C) It pointed the Jesuits towards instructing the youth in the Catholic religion and instructing it in good habits within the colleges and seminaries. There is no allusion at all to the *Spiritual Exercises*.

As to the consequences:

10/ A) The Superior General, Taddeo Brzozowski, and his deputies obtain the faculty "to be able to admit and associate freely and licitly . . . all those who ask to be admitted . . . to the Society of Jesus who . . . conform their way of living to the prescriptions in the Rule of St. Ignatius of Loyola approved and confirmed by the Apostolic Constitution of Paul III."

11/   B) The Society may direct seminaries and colleges and practice their individual ministries with the permission of the bishops.

12/   C) The Jesuits are taken by the Pope under his immediate protection. The Pontiff reserves to himself and to his successors the right to take any steps he will think best "to consolidate, provide for and purify the Society if this would ever be necessary."

13/   Faithful to the *Formula of the Institute* and to the *Constitutions*, the Society faced its mission with great fervor, impulse and apostolic zeal. Still, it took up its work officially overly conditioned by the politics of restoration inspired by the Congress of Vienna. Since then the Society has been inevitably associated with anti-liberal reaction. The absolutist princes made use of them to secure the stability and the permanence of the old order, creating thereby a link that would never be forgiven by the liberal bourgeoisie, whose reform agenda will make the neutralization of the Jesuits a prime objective.

THE CONSOLIDATION AND THE EXPANSION OF THE SOCIETY OF JESUS (1814–1853)

The Generalate of Luigi Fortis (1820–1829)

14/   The Russian government rejected the insistent request of Fr. General Taddeo Brzozowski to get to Rome, and he remained there until his death (1820). The 20th General Congregation elected Luigi Fortis as his successor. There were three fundamental problems at that point: maintaining the spiritual and juridical character of the Institute, the formation of its members, and the efficiency of the apostolate of the colleges. Fortis dedicated himself to this wide-ranging program of reconstitution not without experiencing certain difficulties, in particular the disagreement between the diverse sectors, especially in Italy, regarding the equilibrium between the former traditions and the new circumstances.

15/ In 1824 Leo XII restored to the Society the Roman College and the Church of St. Ignatius and gave it the direction of the German College and that of the Nobles. Two years later the pontiff confirmed the privileges and added others (Bull *Plura inter*). The greatest success of Fortis was surely his giving to the future generations of Jesuits a Society secure in its historical continuity. In 1820 there were around 1,300 Jesuits, and in 1829 there were already 2,100.

The Generalate of Jan Roothaan (1829–1853)

16/ On July 9, 1829, the 21st General Congregation elected the Dutchman Jan Roothaan, who, during his 24 years of generalate exerted a decisive influence on the development of the reestablished Society. We recall some of the principle aspects of this period.

17/ 1. The Society extended geographically (it arrived in the Americas, Asia, Africa, and Australia) and grew to 5,209 members, of whom 19% were overseas.

18/ 2. Roothaan wrote six exhortations to the entire Society. The most important were *De amore Scoietatis et Instituti nostri* ("On love of the Society and of our Institute," July 7, 1830), *De Missionum exterarum desiderio excitando et fovendo* ("On promoting and supporting the desire for the external Missions," December 3, 1833), and *De spiritualium Exercitiorum S.P.N. studio et usu* ("On the study and use of the Spiritual Exercises of St. Ignatius," December 27, 1834).

19/ 3. Besides the letters, the most important document was the new version of the *Ratio Studiorum* of 1832 (that is, the collection of rules which direct the pedagogical and scholastic activity of the Society of Jesus), which included the history of the Church and canon law in the theological curriculum. In the course of the philosophical studies, the role of mathematics, physics, and chemistry was emphasized. The humanistic studies were enriched by geography and history, while greater importance was given to the vernacular languages.

20/   4. The Dutch general gave the Spiritual Exercises a central position in the formation and the life of the Jesuits. Roothaan published the *versio litteralis* and the *vulgate* (1835) and promoted the Popular Missions and the Apostolate of Prayer founded by Fr. Gautrelet. He dedicated his strengths particularly to the overseas missions; seminaries were founded in China, Albania, India, Syria, and on the island of Reunion.

21/   5. There is also one curious aspect. The frequency of contacts of Gregory XVI (1831–1846) with the Superior General inspired the people of Rome, it would seem for the first time, to give the nickname of black pope to the Superior General of the Jesuits. It is known nevertheless that the Pope rarely asked his opinion; on the contrary, it seems that he merely wanted to be informed punctually on matters by the trustworthy Fr. Roothaan.

REFLECTIONS: THE SOCIETY OF JESUS IN THE 1800S

22/   The pretext of Pius VII to reestablish the Society of Jesus signified the overturning of the Brief of suppression promulgated by Clement XIV 41 years earlier. The reestablishment had been a long and difficult process. Nevertheless the adversities were illuminated by the flowering of vocations. During the period of Fr. Roothaan the characteristic identities of the Institute were consolidated and have endured in practice up until the Second Vatican Council.

23/   We have asked ourselves about the continuity of the Society before the suppression and after the reestablishment, that is, if the numerous Jesuits who entered with the reestablishment recognized themselves in their older predecessors. This is the question: was it possible that such a high number of vocations would persevere without putting at risk the tradition of the Society that had been interrupted by a generational gap of four decades? The most common answer is that the reestablished Society became more "conservative" than the previous one. It is said that it assumed a life style which was more "conventual," that, combined with the apologetic stands imposed by the historical circumstances, it had betrayed its foundational charism.

24/   We note that the discontinuity hypothesis, although legitimate up to a certain point, can become deceiving. To hold that the reestablished Society resembled a "conventual" type of congregation requires a clarification, if not a demonstration. It needs to be pointed out that accentuation of the spiritual and "community" life does not belong only to the 1800s. The insistence on the order of religious life in the Society is found already from the times of Fr. Mercurian (1573–80) to whom is owed the *Summary of the Constitutions*, the rules on ministries, the observance (inherited) of the hour of prayer prescribed also for the professed, the norms of the organization of houses and the *Ordo domus probationis*.

25/   What happens in the reestablished Society is not simple nor can it be reduced to simplifications. We believe rather that, in the 1800s, the structural tension inherent in the Institute from its foundation emphasized certain particular aspects. Making use of a visual example, it is as if the new Society was the same image but now painted using different colors and shadings, chosen by the artist to bring out new details in an image that was already well known. These new "colors" were the apostolic zeal, the spiritual fervor, ultramontanism, the valuing laced on the virtues, as well as a disciplinary conception of obedience.

26/   All this being said, being tied to the legendary past history of the Institute, it was inevitable that the Jesuits would assume a rather unique presence in society. Their recognized anti-liberalism and the protection on the part of the well-to-do sectors of society made them targets of much criticism, although at the same time they gave rise to meritorious projects of social assistance.

27/   The question of the continuity or discontinuity of the restored Society with the previous one is a theme which remains open to historical research and that deserves to be studied in greater depth. It must be recognized that, in spite of the efforts of the absolutist forces, it was not possible to turn the clock back. The world of the nineteenth century was irrevocably changed on the political, social, as well as cultural levels. The Society, which without desiring it, was a reflection of the era of absolutism, did not escape the changes imposed by historical circumstances.

28/   It is certain that there have been several transformations in the Society in response to the requirements of a world in evolution. Perhaps the most delicate point is the change produced in the principle of the gratuity of the ministries. Although the Jesuits continued to live an austere life, their colleges were no longer free. The scholastic expenses had to be assumed by the families of the students. The professed houses were not able to survive because of political upheavals.

29/   The world in which the Society arose in the 1600s evolved after three centuries into the world of capitalism and secular liberalism. The defensive attitude that the Jesuits of the restored Society were compelled to adopt and the necessary adaptation to the new economic requirements probably eroded their independence and credibility in a society which was growing ever more pragmatic. We still assert with assurance that the apostolic vigor of the Society of Jesus goes beyond any calculation.

30/   The extremely numerous vocations of the Society which arose after 1814 were marked by a strong apostolic zeal and a great human religious generosity; this fact makes it impossible to seriously sustain that such an overabundance of vocations was a mere expression of the conservative spirit of the Church and the Society of the 1800s. How can we question the fidelity of such heroic men to the spirit of Saint Ignatius and their continuity with the Jesuits of 1773?

Cover Letter for the *Ratio Studiorum* of 1832

Jan Roothaan, General Superior of the Society of Jesus,
"To Provincial Superiors, Rectors of Colleges, Prefects of Studies,
and Teachers." Translated by Claude Pavur, S.J.

Editor's Introduction: Fr. Jan Roothaan (1785–1853) was elected as the 21st Superior General of the Society of Jesus during General Congregation 21 in 1829. Throughout his more than twenty years as General, he was in charge of reestablishing the Society after the Restoration of 1814. This letter of Fr. Roothaan is particularly interesting in understanding how the restored Society felt about the *Ratio Studiorum* of 1599; it also reveals their view of their historical context (pessimistic and yearning for the good old times, for the most part). Fr. Roothaan recognized the importance of the apostolate of Jesuit education, and he worked tirelessly for its success. In this letter he recognizes the need to adapt the *Ratio Studiorum* of 1599 to the new signs of the times. However, Fr. Roothaan's efforts to have a new *Ratio Studiorum* are not successful, and the Society will struggle for the next hundred years to situate the *Ratio* in the changing landscape of Jesuit education.

1/ In the first general Congregation after the restoration of the Society, the provinces petitioned for, and subsequent experience has all the more demonstrated the great necessity of, updating the plan for our studies. This task has been attended to on the authority of the last Congregation, and it has finally found its way to completion. I set the results before you, Reverend Fathers, to be realized in such a way that if anything detrimental is discovered in its employment, it can be remedied; and if any likely improvement might be made, it can be added in its own good time.

2/ I called to Rome, as you know, several Fathers chosen from different provinces. They had brought along with them points noted and commented upon in the *Ratio Studiorum*. After devoting long effort and careful attention to the comparison of these items with one another, they finally proposed what the Fathers Assistant and I have examined and carefully analyzed. At last I offer this to you to be tested by experience and practice, so that then, corrected anew where there is need, or expanded, they might obtain the universal force and sanction of law. Whatever else it was, it was certainly a weighty undertaking, one in which nothing could have been done nonchalantly or precipitately. But neither was it a matter of having to fashion a new order of studies (as I pointed out in the letter to the provinces that called for fathers to be deputed to draw up what was necessary for this work). Rather, it was a matter of adjusting the very same venerable text to our times, so that people might realize with what great reverence this undertaking had to be handled, and how nothing was to be changed offhandedly or rashly in that work that had been composed by the very best men after a long process of gathering a great body of advice, well tested by the successful experience of almost two centuries, and often recommended by the praise even of the very enemies of the Society.

3/   What, then? Of all the many innovations introduced into the education of young people over the last fifty years and more, could they all possibly be approved and adopted in our schools? New methods, new forms devised day after day, new arrangements of content and sequences in treating the disciplines, often in fact even conflicting and contradicting one another—how could these be able to become a norm for our studies? Rather what right-thinking person would not deplore so many innovations that have born such bitter fruits for Church and Society?

4/   That in the more advanced classes or in the treatment of the more serious studies there is nothing really solid though there is much with a superficial appeal; that there is a disordered abundance of exuberant erudition and too little precise reasoning; that the disciplines, if you except physics and mathematics, have not made genuine progress but hover in almost utter confusion so that often you can hardly tell where the truth stands— all well-meaning people everywhere groan over these realities. From the abandonment and disregard of the study of rigorous logic and dialectic, errors worked their way even into the minds of quite educated people, and (by some unfathomable fate or fortune) the following propositions are celebrated as certain truths and praised to the skies: that nothing can be precisely and accurately said, and that no account should be taken of definition or distinction. And so, after the philosophical disciplines have been lightly sampled, young people go forth furnished with no weapons against the sophistries of the innovators, which they do not even know how to distinguish from solid arguments. Hence their minds are ensnared and captivated by all manner of errors (even ones so completely absurd that, if it did not involve the most important issues, they would deserve laughter rather than refutation)—but they have no way to unmask and demonstrate their falsity.

5/   About secondary schooling what should I say? Every effort has been made that the boys learn as much as possible, but that they learn it in as short a time as possible and with the least possible effort. All well and good! But if the boys barely taste so many different disciplines without truly digesting them, that variety may indeed lead them to think that they know a great deal and someday to swell the mob of the half-educated that undermines the learned disciplines just as much as society, if anything else— and yet they know nothing truly and solidly. *A bit of everything; nothing fully.* So, covering the humanities in a short time at a very impressionable age, even with their talent still undeveloped, they proceed to the most serious study of philosophy and the higher disciplines, from which they take almost no real profit, and by their enjoyment of greater freedom, they are swept headlong along on the wrong way as captives, soon to be teachers, to be sure, but (to put it quite mildly) not fully mature.

6/   The devising of ever easier methods, if it has any advantage, certainly has the disadvantage (not at all a small one) that what first is attained without effort also is only most tenuously rooted in the mind, and what is quickly acquired is quickly forgotten. Then, there is a far more serious loss in the education of children, although perhaps many people do not pay it much attention: the important capacity gained by becoming accustomed at a very young age to serious intellectual endeavor and to enduring the work as they experience some pressure on themselves. All wise persons throughout history have realized how valuable this habit is, from youth on into every period of life, in mastering wicked emotional impulses and exercising self-control. The Holy Spirit teaches the same lesson where he says: "It is good for a person to bear the yoke from the time of his own youth" [Lamentations 3:27].

7/   These manifold innovations and harmful procedures, therefore, especially insofar as they damage Church and society, are such that we cannot adopt them at all unless we would like to clearly deviate from the end for the sake of which the Society involves itself in the labors of education: that end is not at all limited to literary training alone but has especially as its goal the Christian education of youth. Without that, the unhappy experience of many years has proven that any abundance of scholarship and learning whatsoever brings more loss than advantage to society.

8/   But although it is not fitting that we should permit these new methods nor right that we should do so insofar as they run counter to the Society's Institute and aim, and although we could not even satisfy these lovers of innovations even if it were quite allowable or useful to do so, since many of them demand things as inconsistent and contradictory among themselves as with what is traditional; nevertheless, in some things that do not touch on the substance of a solid education, the necessity of the times compels us to diverge from the practice of our Fathers. In this case, serving that necessity is not only not wrong but even quite fully compatible with the manner of our Institute for the greater glory of God.

9/   And indeed in taking up higher studies, how many points that once were not even controversial but that are now being sharply attacked in the unreasonableness of the times need to be established with secure arguments so that the very foundations of the truth are not overturned! And again, how many things that once were also elaborated at great length more to exercise ingenuity than to establish the truth should now be more profitably omitted, so that there may be time for more necessary matters, to confirm those teachings, I say, on which everything depends, and so that there might be in the light of truth an analysis and refutation of what ill-intentioned or wicked people have devised to raise doubts about even the most certain and most obvious matters!

10/   A better age might have been allowed and those who seek no harm are allowed to indulge their talent and to dwell at length on less useful questions; but now certainly we have a greater obligation to attend to what is necessary, even all the more so because the course of studies is circumscribed almost everywhere within narrower limits. For that disadvantage we ourselves can indeed hope to provide a remedy, but we can hardly dare to expect it—and maybe not even hardly!

11/   The same necessity now demands that more time than before be given to physics and to mathematics. The Society has never thought that these studies are foreign to our Institute, nor is it permissible for us now to neglect what has become so important in our times, and without which the Society's educational institutions can in no way defend their own honor or answer people's expectations. Even if many have abused these disciplines to the detriment of most holy religion, that is no reason at all for us to abandon them; in fact, that is the very reason why it is necessary for Ours to devote themselves more zealously especially under this title [of religion] so as to be able to snatch from our enemies the weapons that they abuse to impugn the truth and use them rightly to defend it. For truth is everywhere self-consistent and in all the disciplines it always stands out as one and the same. It cannot happen that what is true in physics or in mathematics ever contradicts the truth of a higher order, provided that fictions capriciously and rashly affirmed are not thrust in in place of what is true and undoubted. Exposing and shattering this very artifice of the wicked is most worthy of a Christian and religious physicist and mathematician.

12/   Finally, in the plan for secondary schooling, we had to provide both that some time be scheduled for learning certain accessory subjects and that careful attention be given especially to the vernacular language and literature, but in such a way that the study of Greek and Latin language and literature always remains safe and secure. These are even now, as they once were, the leading sources of solid learning and good literature and examples of most perfect beauty. If they were better kept before our eyes and hearts, there would not appear day after day from so many clever people compositions that are quite strange and singular not less in form and style of expression than in ideas and opinions. These are indeed popular objects of amazement and stupor; nevertheless, all those who are wise and interested in true beauty painfully deplore them as glaring indications of an eloquence which has been disfigured along with our morals in these times.

13/   All this effort to adapt the plan of studies has therefore been poured into serving the needs of our times, but in such a way that there might be as little as possible a departure from the solid and correct training of the young.

14/   Now it remains, Reverend Fathers, that you enthusiastically and diligently put into practice what we have prepared and present to you here. It may be that some of the provisions are for now merely temporary until under the guidance of practice and experience we see what might perhaps be changed, what added, what removed. Nevertheless, if we only half-heartedly put these things into play because they are not yet thoroughly defined and established, we would never be able to render a reliable judgment about their outcome. So I strongly recommend that superiors urge the execution of the plan. And in every college, some persons should be appointed to observe the outcome and to note any difficulty that may arise or possible improvement that may be made, and the provincials should submit to us their observations, after considering and evaluating them with their consultors.

15/   And since the new opinions springing up day after day, especially in the philosophical disciplines, rightly ought to sharpen our vigilance, I judge that we must press for what the first Congregation of the restored Society instructed should be done, namely, that the provincials should prepare for my approval a list of opinions that it would not be useful for Ours to teach.

16/   And so let us devote ourselves to the great service of educating the younger generation, energetically and each according to his own grade and office. For since it is one of the chief ministries of our Society, for the sake of which (among other things) Pius VII of blessed memory wanted the Society restored, and rulers and peoples especially sought the same, let us consider, I ask you, how much we should take it to heart, so that we may answer the expectation of Church and society, and commend our work to Almighty God, which is the most important thing: him I have not ceased begging for the happy outcome of this great work, offering many thousands of masses drawn from the treasury of the Society; nor, furthermore, will I cease begging, and I desire that you be fellow suppliants with me before the Lord in this same undertaking.

Rome, July 25, 1832[1]

---

[1] Translated by Claude Pavur, S.J., June 2, 2014, with the generous assistance of Dr. Clarence Miller and Fr. John Padberg, S.J. This text has been taken from pages 228 to 233 in G.M. Pachtler, S.J., *Ratio Studiorum et Institutiones Scholasticae Societatis Jesu per Germaniam olim vigentes collectae concinnatae dilucidatae*. Edited by Karl Kehrbach. Tomus 2. *Ratio studiorum* ann. 1586, 1599, 1832. *Monumenta Germaniae paedagogica* 5. Berlin: A. Hofmann & Comp., 1887.

General Congregation 20, 1820

For Matters of Greater Moment: The First Thirty Jesuit General Congregations: A Brief History and a Translation of the Decrees. Edited by John W. Padberg, S.J., et al.

Editor's Introduction: The following four chapters present excerpts from General Congregations after the Restoration—covering the years 1820 to 1906—dealing with education. These texts bear witness to the discernment about the meaning and place of the *Ratio* within its new historical context. Finally, in 1906, General Congregation 25 decrees that a new edition of the *Ratio Studiorum* "should not be attempted" since the times do not allow it.

Decree 10

1/ The provinces have requested that our *Ratio studiorum* be adapted to meet the needs of our times. In granting this petition, the congregation decreed that Reverend Father General should delegate to certain chosen members of the Society the charge of reviewing the *Ratio studiorum;* then with his assistants he should examine the revision and prescribe that, once he has approved it, all the provinces of the Society should observe it, allowing, however, the provinces a reasonable amount of time to send observations to Rome that could be of service in improving and enhancing the *Ratio.*

2/ In the meantime, however, the congregation prescribed that in order to introduce some degree of uniformity at least in individual provinces, the provincials should set down certain provisional regulations from which the professors may not deviate, and that the provincials should propose for Father General's approval a list of opinions that Ours should not teach or hold and also a list of authors who should not be lectured upon in our schools.

General Congregation 21, 1829

For Matters of Greater Moment: The First Thirty Jesuit General Congregations: A Brief History and a Translation of the Decrees.
Edited by John W. Padberg, S.J., et al.

Decree 15

1/ A postulate made by nearly all the provinces came to the floor: According to decree 10 of the last congregation, the *Ratio studiorum* should be accommodated to the needs of our times as soon as possible. On this subject, before the congregation took any action, Our Reverend Father, anticipating the intent of the congregation, declared that he fully recognized how much the very circumstances of the times themselves demanded what the whole Society was calling for, and that he had a sure and fixed resolve to apply himself to this task at the earliest possible moment. But he warned that this was not a matter that could be either treated superficially or completed in a short time; indeed, he had personally decided that in this matter he would establish nothing definite possessing the force of law that experience had not actually proved effective in the provinces. The congregation gratefully received these and other statements to the same effect and gave its hearty approval.

General Congregation 22, 1853

For Matters of Greater Moment: The First Thirty Jesuit General Congregations: A Brief History and a Translation of the Decrees.
Edited by John W. Padberg, S.J., et al.

Decree 38

1/   The judgment of the commission fathers was read concerning the postulates dealing with the entirety of the *Ratio studiorum*. In summary it was as follows:

2/   1. Consideration should first be given to all the reports assembled to date and such other reports (if there are more) as are to be sent from individual provinces, and advice should be sought to profit from the knowledge and experience of men adept in every branch of learning; then the *Ratio studiorum* should be revised under the care of Reverend Father General.

3/   2. After the work has been completed, this revised and improved *Ratio studiorum* is to be prescribed for observance by all the provinces.

4/   3. Supposing that the items which are substantials in this *Ratio studiorum* are everywhere kept in force, the provincials retain the authority (which they have by reason of rule 39 of the provincial and rule 15 of the professor of lower classes) to prescribe special applications demanded either by differences in regions or the evil conditions of the times.

5/   The congregation approved individually these three headings of the opinion of the commission.

General Congregation 25, 1906

For Matters of Greater Moment: The First Thirty Jesuit General Congregations: A Brief History and a Translation of the Decrees.
Edited by John W. Padberg, S.J., et al.

Decree 12

1/   1. Some provinces made the request for a new edition of the *Ratio studiorum,* as applied to lower studies. The general congregation feels that in these times of ours, characterized by such variety and instability in legislation concerning schools and the subject matter taught there, this should not be attempted. But in order the more surely to avert the undesirable consequences that are feared, it strongly recommends the study of the sound pedagogy whose principles are carefully explained by our holy father in Part 4 of the Constitutions, are developed in the *Ratio studiorum,* and are clearly explained by more than a few writers of the Society.

2/   2. Still, since it must be admitted that not even the new *Ratio studiorum* of Father Roothaan can be followed satisfactorily today and because other difficulties and needs exist in the various provinces, the provincial superiors, after listening to their consultors and their most experienced teachers, should develop an ordinance on lower studies each for his own province, and should do the same for any areas whose conditions are fairly similar; and then they should submit this work to Our Father for approval.

3/   3. In the development of these ordinances, consideration ought to be given, as is right, particularly to that goal which the Society sets for itself in its colleges, namely, not only to help develop all the faculties of our students by an appropriate method but also, and especially, to lead them toward faith, piety, and good morals, to accustom them to discipline, and to teach them to act out of virtue. Therefore, before all else, administrators must take care that as far as possible priests are assigned to teach Christian doctrine and suitable time is allotted for it. Also, Marian congregations [sodalities] should be properly inaugurated, fostered, and well directed. For teaching the other disciplines, if at times extern teachers must be used, only men of proven faith and virtue are to be accepted. Those provincials deserve much praise who, despite any and all difficulties, take care to provide with degrees as many of our teachers as are needed and useful for the instruction of our students, so that they are rarely or never compelled to seek the help of externs. Still, special precautions are always to be taken that because of these studies the religious spirit of Ours suffers no harm and that Ours duly complete our own studies.

4/   4. Lastly, all must preserve, as far as possible and in whatever subject matter is being treated, that method which is proper to the Society and recommended by the *Ratio studiorum*.

PART IV: EARLY CONTEMPORARY TEXTS
(1967–1993)

Ignatian Pedagogy

Gabriel Codina, S.J. In *Diccionario de Espiritualidad Ignaciana*
[*Dictionary of Ignatian Spirituality*]. 2:1426–1430.

1/ *1. Ignatian Pedagogy and Jesuit Pedagogy.* "Ignatian pedagogy" does not correspond exactly to "Jesuit pedagogy." Applied to pedagogy, the term "Jesuit" does specifically refer to the syllabus and methodology systematized by the Society of Jesus since the middle of the 16th century and which is set out in the *Ratio studiorum* (1599); "Ignatian" is related to the spirituality of Ignatius as is especially reflected in the Exercises. "Jesuit" in the pedagogical field refers to the Society of Jesus and implies that the Society has an ultimate institutional responsibility as well as an identification with its "mission"; Ignatian embraces the spiritual side of the life and work of Ignatius, his "vision." Ignatian and Jesuit are not correlated in the same way. In terms of the Jesuit, the Ignatian inspiration is implied; however, the Ignatian does not always imply a link to the Society. On the educational map, hundreds of institutions project an Ignatian face more than a Jesuit one, therefore demonstrating that an Ignatian orientation can be achieved without necessarily referring to the Society.

2/ The *Ratio studiorum* constituted a true system, the first of its kind with a worldwide nature, a model of the so-called Jesuit pedagogy. With the blooming of the modern states and new laws in education, nowadays it would be hard to talk about a Jesuit pedagogy or pedagogic school in the style of Montessori or Dewey. Many elements of Jesuit pedagogy are no longer unique to the Jesuits but have become the heritage of a universal pedagogy. Meanwhile, the Jesuits have had to incorporate elements from other pedagogical trends into their practice.

3/ Despite this, it is still possible to talk about "Ignatian pedagogy" (IP). Despite its points in common with other pedagogies, what makes IP different is Ignatius's particular vision or conception of God, the human being, and the world. Some of the elements which are considered characteristic of IP—excellence, care for the person—are not, because they can also be found in the "common market" of education. What cannot be found in the market is the Ignatian inspiration which confers a specific stamp on these and other elements. It is not the singular character of each feature but the peculiar combination of a whole series of characteristics that infuses IP with its own specificity: it is the inspiration that springs from the Exercises, from Part IV in the Constitutions, and from the life of Ignatius. IP could be described as "our way of proceeding" in education.

4/   *2. The* Pedagogy *of the* Exercises. Without pretending to state that all the features of IP stem from the Exercises, some of the principles of the *Exercises* and their methodology should be considered since they have certainly contributed to shaping it.

5/   Ignatius let God educate him, and He treated him "like a school teacher treats a child, by teaching him" [*Autobiography (Au)* 27]. The educator—as the person who "gives us the Exercises"—is only a discreet facilitator who helps the student create an experience in order to seek out and identify the meaning of their life and to act accordingly. Nobody can create this experience without the help of someone else. This axiom serves both for the transmission of knowledge and for the learning of how to choose, act, and live. Everyone should seize this experience according to their own personality. Adapting to each person and respecting their differences will be a basic principle in this pedagogy. A person's development and maturity do not relate to the realm of knowledge ("For it is not much knowledge . . ." [*Spiritual Exercises, (Ex), 2*]) but to the realm of personal experience. The constant exercise, the use of active methods, systematic advancement, and personal support elicit a personal response in the student, the spirit of initiative, the will to outdo oneself ("what is more" [*Ex.* 23]); all of it will depend on their objectives ("what I desire" [*Ex.* 76]). The final term will be decision-making and action. Within a broader perspective, Ignatius in the *Exercises*—and the educator in IP—bring a person to place themselves in the center of the universe ("the other things on the face of the earth" [*Ex.* 23]), to make them aware of their responsibility in the history of good and evil in the face of God's plan. This personal experience is by no means individualist but rather in solidarity with others, integrated into the human community and the Church.

6/ Ignatius's references to the "Three Powers" have been highlighted as well as the use of creative and imaginative mental faculties through meditation, contemplation, and application of the senses. The same is true of the psychological framework of "to go through the exercises better" (Additional Directions [*Ex.* 73–82]), of the preparation of the prayer ("preludes," "points"), of the variety of techniques and means that are utilized, of careful examination at the end of the process. All of it has a clear impact on the pedagogical terrain.

7/ Just as in the *Exercises*, IP helps people free themselves from everything that conditions them ("inordinate attachments" [*Ex* 1]) in order to be able to make the right decisions with complete freedom, involving not only the brain but also the heart and the person. Discipline is combined with freedom, structure, and flexibility, order and method are adapted to the circumstances of "places and times and persons" [*Constitutions (Co)* 455]. This characteristic is what allows IP to accommodate eternally new situations.

8/ Some researchers in education have not hesitated in discovering a whole new underlying theory of learning in the Exercises. This theory would include, among other things, the use of the brain hemispheres, multiple intelligences, and the use of various learning styles. The *Exercises* are not a pedagogical treatise, but they certainly constitute an educational experience in their own right and contain elements of certain educational practices. In a spontaneous and intuitive way—more than a systematic and deliberated one—Ignatius had the genius to lay the foundations that have shaped IP in the *Exercises*.

9/ *3. Characteristics of the Ignatian Pedagogy.* In 1980, the Society of Jesus created a commission (ICAJE) that was aimed at carrying out a large enquiry and research on the distinctive features of IP. This resulted in the publication of *Características de la Educación de la Compañía de Jesús [The Characteristics of a Jesuit Education]* (1986). Even though the document primarily refers to the Society's education, it reflects the Ignatian signature better than the Jesuit one. The document bases the general aspects of IP on Ignatius's spiritual vision. These aspects are gathered together under nine main topics, which we will present shortly. Finally, a number of characteristics of IP derive from each of these topics.

10/   *3.1. God, Key to Understanding Reality.* IP affirms the radical goodness of the world, filled with God's greatness. Its aim is to achieve the most complete development possible of all the talents each person has been gifted within the human community. This orientation involves quality intellectual training in all of the artistic, scientific, and technological disciplines. IP promotes the critical use of communication as well as the imagination, creativity, and emotional nature of each student. Its religious and spiritual dimension leads to knowledge of God in the world and understanding of the meaning of life.

11/   *3.2. Each Human Being Gives God a Free and Personal Response.* The IP syllabus is based on personal attention to each student more than on the program of studies and adapts to each individual personality. IP stimulates the growth of freedom, personal reflection, active participation, creativity, the process of learning to learn, an opening to growth throughout one's life.

12/   *3.3. Starting from Reality.* The methodology used is essentially inductive: starting from reality, not from the principles of reality. An optimistic conception of the world and reality cannot hide the existence of sin—both in the person and in the world—and the need for conversion. IP is value-oriented, stimulates knowledge linked to the moral context, self-discipline, and optimistic acceptance of oneself; at the same time, it endeavors to identify and fight the roots and effects of evil. It promotes mutual respect, believes that people and structures can and should change, and it is committed to transformation.

13/   *3.4. Jesus Christ, Focus and Model for Human Life.* No matter what the students' beliefs, IP suggests Christ as a model for human life. For Christians, this means love and worship of God. Pastoral attention, prayer, and the celebration of faith are essential components of school life. Everyone should feel supported through the discovery of their vocation and their response to the personal call of God. Within this framework, the practice of the Exercises is encouraged.

14/ *3.5. Committed to Christ through Works.* Following Christ, the man who serves others, IP prepares students for a commitment to action and a life of service. Faith must do justice through just actions in the personal, familiar, business, social, political, and religious spheres. This same institution educates for faith and justice with its set of values, programs, ways of acting, and through deeds demonstrates a special concern for the poor.

15/ *3.6. Education, Apostolic Tool, and Part of the Church's Mission.* The IP promotes loyalty and service to the Church and its teachings. It stimulates reflection and the search for answers to the issues related to faith and culture and, within a Christian context, it prepares the students for an active participation in the ecclesiastic community.

16/ *3.7. Striving for Magis, the Greatest Service.* IP strives both for academic and human excellence. It proposes training of competent leaders by developing all the qualities of a person with the aim of using them to serve others, not to compete, thus helping them become agents promoting change. In their commitment to faith, students are asked to "identify" themselves, thereby showing their following of Christ.

17/ *3.8. Institutional Identity and Spirit of Collaboration.* IP strives for all the members of the community—both religious and lay—to identify themselves with the unique nature of their educational project and to contribute to the fulfillment of the Ignatian vision. The Center is led by a clear "mission statement," an exponent of its Ignatian identity. The governing boards, principals, teachers, and support staff form a team imbued with the same inspiration, each of which assumes their own responsibilities. The parents, students, and alumni loyally accept and share the identity of the center and participate and cooperate to maintain and strengthen this identity.

18/   *3.9. Discernment and Adaptation.* The decision-making process takes place based on a permanent process of discernment and adaptation based on the given circumstances. Reflection and evaluation are part of this process. IP offers opportunities for professional, personal, and spiritual training, including in Ignatian spirituality.

19/   *4. Ignatian Pedagogical Paradigm (IPP).* The *Characteristics* constitutes an open document, liable to new modifications, which should be adapted to the reality of each place. However, how should the Ignatian principles be applied to pedagogic practice in class? In 1993, the ICAJE commission published a new document: *Pedagogía Ignaciana. Un planteamiento práctico* [*Ignatian Pedagogy: A Practical View*] which presents a paradigm or pedagogic model aimed towards applying the Ignatian vision to the teaching and learning process. This paradigm does not involve the addition of a pedagogic methodology to official study plans, but instead presents a new point of view, a particular "procedure" that is compatible with other systems.

20/   The outlines of the paradigm are five steps that are in constant interaction: a) the "context" in which the student is placed and in which the process is developed; b) the "experience" that brings a cognitive, affective, and global approach to reality; c) the "reflection" that allows for a critical understanding of the deeper meaning of our experiences and prepares us for the decision-making process; d) the "action" or external manifestation of the reflection on the experience, expressed in opinions, behaviors, and coherent actions; e) the permanent "evaluation" of the whole process.

21/   The Ignatian paradigm has outlined in a few words the profile of the person we intend to teach: competent, conscious, compassionate to those in need, committed to change.

22/   In conclusion, the *Characteristics* and the *Ignatian Pedagogical Paradigm* have brought a sense of identity and unity to Ignatian-inspired institutions like no other document since the early *Ratio*. Its influence surpasses the boundaries of the Society of Jesus and it is extended to a whole

"Ignatian network" of institutions that wish to transform Ignatius's vision into a source of inspiration for their pedagogy.

BIBLIOGRAPHY

Aa.Vv., *Características de la Educación de la Compañía de Jesús,* CONEDSI, Madrid 1987; Aa.Vv., *Pedagogía Ignaciana. Un planteamiento práctico,* CONEDSI, Madrid 1993; Bartolomé, B., "Los colegios de jesuitas y la educación de la juventud", en *Historia de la acción educadora de la Iglesia en España I. Edades Antigua, Media y Moderna* (Bartolomé, B., dir.), BAC, Madrid 1995, 644–682; Costa, M., "Notas sobre las líneas fundamentales de la pedagogía de la Compañía de Jesús", *CIS* 18–20 (1987–1989); 91–121; Decloux, S., "La pédagogie jésuite et son inspiration ignatienne", *Lumen Vitae* 45 (1990) 127–140; Guerello, F./ Schiavone, P. (coords.), *La pedagogia della Compagnia di Gesù,* E.S.U.R.-Ignatianum, Messina 1992; Klein, L.F., *Actualidad de la pedagogía jesuita,* ITESO, Guadalajara 2002; Kolvenbach P.-H., "Educar en el espíritu de San Ignacio", *RyF* 236 (1997) 21–31; Lange Cruz, I., *Carisma ignaciano y mística de la educación,* UPComillas-CONEDSI, Madrid 2005; Meirose, C.E. (compil.), *Foundations,* JSEA, Washington, D.C. 1994; Metts, R.E., *Ignacio lo sabía. La pedagogía jesuita y las corrientes educativas actuales,* ITESO, Guadalajara 1997; O'Malley, J.W., *Los primeros Jesuitas,* M-ST, Bilbao-Santander 1995, 249–298; Osowski, C.I./ Bergamo Becker, L. (orgs.), *Visão inaciana da educação, Desafios hoje,* UNISINOS, São Leopoldo 1997; Revuelta, M., *Los colegios de jesuitas y su tradición educativa, 1868–1906,* UPComillas, Madrid 1998.

General Congregation 31, 1967

*Jesuit Life & Mission Today: The Decrees & Accompanying Documents
of the 31st–35th General Congregations of the Society of Jesus.*
Edited by John W. Padberg, S.J.

Editor's Introduction: General Congregation 31 constituted an important turning point for Jesuit education. It not only elected Fr. Pedro Arrupe as Superior General of the Society but also called the Society of Jesus to respond to the call of renewal of the Second Vatican Council. The Congregation began a time of renewal felt throughout the whole Society and which we are still part of. The Congregation also called for the renewal of Jesuit education according to the new times, and it will create the Secretariat for Education of the Society to foster "the whole work of Education."

Decree 28

THE APOSTOLATE OF EDUCATION

I. Introduction

1/   1. Throughout the world today, whether in the advanced or in the evolving nations, there is clear recognition of the importance of education for the formation of society and particularly for the initiating of youth into a human way of life and fellowship. Nothing is more esteemed by political leaders than this education of the citizenry, for without it no nation or state can develop or progress and meet the national and international responsibilities imposed by the needs of this age.

2/   2. The Church has, therefore, reflected upon "the paramount importance of education in the life of man, and its ever-mounting influence on the social progress of this era"[1] and once again affirmed its own role in the development and extension of education. To fulfill this function the Church wishes to employ all appropriate means. Yet it recognizes that schools are educational agencies of "special importance,"[2] for in these institutions Christian teachers are to promote the renewal of the Church and maintain and intensify her beneficent and salutary presence in the contemporary and, particularly, the intellectual world.[3]

3/   3. In our day we are witnessing everywhere the rapid emergence of new social forms and the society of the future. When new ideas are so widely sown it is not hard to discern the birth of new patterns of thought and action in the modern world. The promoters of these new ideas, especially when they work out of centers of higher culture and research, are exercising a mounting influence upon the whole of social culture through highly effective modern means of popularization. But since this influence inclines ever more toward an atheistic and agnostic ideology and makes itself felt particularly in educational centers, the presence of Christians in those centers is of the highest moment if the Church is indeed to make an opportune contribution to the society of the future by forming and educating its mind to reverence for God and in the fullness of Christ.

4/   4. For many centuries the Society of Jesus, in accordance with its Institute, has diligently exercised its teaching function almost uninterruptedly throughout the world. Now, impelled and inspired by the Second Vatican Council, the Society, through its 31st General Congregation, wishes to confirm the high regard it has for this apostolate of education and earnestly to exhort its members that they maintain unflaggingly their esteem for this significant apostolate.

5/   There are some members of the Society, however, who think that our educational institutions in certain parts of the world have become practically useless and should therefore be given up. There are others who recognize the continued effectiveness of these institutions but believe that there are other ministries in which we would perhaps be even more effective. Hence they conclude that it is necessary, or at least appropriate, to leave the work of formal education to laymen or to religious whose institutes dedicate them exclusively to this apostolate. This Congregation judges that there is no uniform solution for this very real and pressing problem. The solution it requires will necessarily vary according to differences of circumstances. Therefore, it must be determined by superiors, with the aid of their brethren and according to the norms for the choice of ministries as applied to the needs of each province or region.

6/   The intention of this present decree, however, is, in the first place, that the Society may think with the Church concerning the paramount importance and effectiveness of the educational apostolate, particularly in our times. Secondly, it is intended that our schools be outstanding not so much for number and size as for teaching, for the quality of the instruction, and the service rendered to the people of God. Thirdly, we should be receptive toward new forms of this apostolate, particularly adapted to the present age, and we should energetically investigate or fashion these new forms either in our own schools or elsewhere. Finally, for those laymen who generously spend themselves with us in this apostolate, the way should be opened to a wider collaboration with us, whether this be in teaching, administration, or on the board of directors itself.

7/   5. It is evident that we can exercise the apostolate of education in various ways either in our own institutions or by collaborating with others. There is an extensive variety today whether one is speaking of colleges and universities, or vocational schools, or the so-called normal schools for the training of teachers. Which forms of the apostolate of education the Society should take up is a matter for superiors to decide according to the norms for the selection of ministries. But in making this selection, we should consider the new means of social communication, particularly radio and television. For these are highly effective instruments for new kinds of educational organization and pedagogy since they extend to the widest possible audience and reach those who would otherwise be deprived of schooling. Besides, they are very much in line with the present day "culture of the image."

8/   The Society should have its own educational institutions where resources and circumstances permit and a greater service of God and the Church can be thereby expected. For these schools constitute at least one effective instrument for the promotion of our educational purpose, i.e., the synthesizing of faith and culture. Through these schools a firmer and more lasting social presence in the community is achieved, both because they are a corporate effort and because through them the students' families are influenced. Thus the school becomes an apostolic center within the community.

9/   If, indeed, there is question of closing schools or of handing them over to others, superiors are to work out the best way of doing this in consultation with the local Ordinary and with the approbation of Father General.

II. Decree

10/   6. Let Jesuits have a high regard for the apostolate of education as one of the primary ministries of the Society, commended in a special way by the Church in our time. For the transmission of human culture and its integration in Christ significantly contribute to realization of the goal set by our Lord "that God may be all in all things."[4]

11/   7. This apostolate aims to provide a service of love for mankind redeemed by Christ. On the one hand, it aims so to educate believers as to make them not only cultured but, in both private and public lives, men who are authentically Christian and able and willing to work for the modern apostolate.

12/   On the other hand, it aims to provide non-Christians with a humanistic formation directed towards the welfare of their own nation and, at the same time, to conduct them by degrees to the knowledge and love of God or at least to the acceptance of moral, and even religious values.[5]

13/   8. Let the provincials see to it that the apostolate of education, along with other ministries, be really and continually adapted to the circumstances of men, time, and place, making use in this of the advice both of experts and of the committee on the choice of ministries. Let the provincials also see to it that really competent men are prepared in education.

14/   9. In collaboration with the bishops, other religious, and their fellow citizens, let Jesuits be alert to correlate the Society's activity with the complex of pastoral and educational work in the whole region or nation. Since, moreover, dialogue in this pluralistic world is both possible and desirable, let them also willingly cooperate with other organizations, even if these do not depend either on the Church or the Society. Let Jesuits therefore keep in mind the special importance of collaborating with those international organizations which promote education, especially in the less developed countries.

15/   10. *a*) Let students be selected, as far as possible, of whom we can expect a greater progress and a greater influence on society, no matter to what social class they belong.

16/   *b*) In order that this criterion of selection may be equitably applied, Jesuits should firmly advance the claims of distributive justice, so that public aid will provide parents with the real liberty of choosing schools for their children according to their conscience.[6]

17/   *c*) However, until such rights have been vindicated, the Society, in accordance with its Constitutions[7] and traditional practice, must make it easy for talented young people, particularly in the emerging nations, to attend our schools. Therefore, let all Jesuits try to obtain public or private endowments, with the help of our alumni, or of those who are bound to the Society through special friendship or apostolic zeal.[8]

18/   11. Our educational institutions should be established only when and where they show promise of contributing significantly to the welfare of the Church, and can be furnished besides with an adequate supply of competent Jesuits without harm to the training or studies of our own members.[9] Let superiors inquire whether it is more suitable to open or to retain schools of our own or whether it would be better in some circumstances to teach in public schools, or in schools directed by others.

19/   12. *a*) The first care of Jesuits should be that Christian students acquire that knowledge and character which are worthy of Christians, along with the letters and sciences. To this end, it will help very much if, in addition to the suitable amount of time given to the teaching of Christian doctrine and religion according to modern methods, Jesuits also offer to the students a good example of hard work and dedication as well as of religious life.[10]

20/   *b*) We should try in a special way to imbue our students with the true charity of Christ, according to the social doctrine of the Church. Let them learn to honor and be grateful to laboring men; let them learn to hunger and thirst for that justice which aims to provide all men with an adequate recompense for new work, that the distribution of wealth be more equitable, that the sharing of spiritual goods be fuller and more universal.[11]

21/   *c*) Let youth be progressively formed to liturgical and personal prayer. As they come to be more mature, exercises of piety should be proposed to them rather than imposed.

22/   *d*) Selected spiritual and apostolic activities which will really be an efficacious means of character formation, for example the sodalities, should be properly established and directed and esteemed by us all. For they serve to introduce and educate our students in apostolic activities step by step.

23/   *e*) Special importance should be attributed to the spiritual direction of students. For this is an effective way of nourishing a person's sense of responsibility both for the ordering of his spiritual life and for the choosing of an adult vocation in accordance with the divine will. In addition, every effort should be made for a fresh increase of priestly and religious vocations so as to help the Church in its present needs.

24/   *f*) Regarding non-Christian students, care must be taken throughout the whole course of studies and especially in ethics courses that men be formed who are endowed with a sound moral judgment and solid virtues. Therefore in their training, the first rank of importance must be given to the formation of a true and right moral conscience, and at the same time of a firm will to act according to it. For in this way they will be best prepared to have a saving effect on family life and society, and in addition to serve their country and to obtain the reward of eternal life.

25/   13. *a*) Let Jesuits remember that the task of teaching is not restricted to some hours nor only to some persons.[12] Let all give a witness of religious and apostolic life; let all be convinced that the common task is more important than individual success; and let them try continually to renew themselves in spirit and understanding. To this end, superiors should favor research, experiments, the discovery of new methods of teaching, and see to it that the members have libraries, audio-visual aids, conferences by experts, possibilities of attending meetings, and other helps.

26/   *b*) Scholastics and younger brothers who are sent to the colleges should be watched over with special care by superiors and spiritual fathers.[13] They should remember that regency is established for their own growth, and so that their virtue may develop, their character be trained, their gifts manifested, and they themselves may make progress in studies. But the real assistance they provide for the work of education should also be considered, and so they should share in the common responsibility for and the discussion of plans concerning the school, according to its statutes.

27/   14. For its part, the Society should help those many children of the Church who are being educated in non-Catholic schools. Superiors should be mindful of the Church's solicitude in this matter. In their concern for the spiritual formation of all youth, superiors should attentively and willingly listen to bishops who ask for the collaboration of the Society in this ministry, especially in directing Catholic centers for students, in the office of chaplains, and also in teaching in non-Catholic schools.[14]

28/   15. *a*) Young people who travel abroad for their education, as often happens nowadays, should be attentively helped. This is especially important in the case of those, whether Catholic or not, who are outstanding and can be expected to become leaders when they return to their own country.[15]

29/   *b*) We should maintain a relationship with our former students, the products of our whole educational effort, so that they may take their place in society in a Christian and apostolic way and help one another in their respective tasks. The bond which they have with the Society ought to become closer as time goes on so that their influence assists its work.[16]

30/   16. Elementary schools may be founded and directed where it is necessary. For they are very important and not contrary to our Institute. Nonetheless they should not be accepted without a real and great need, lest on account of the lack of men a greater good would be hindered. Where they are accepted, so far as possible our priests should have only the teaching of religion.[17]

31/   17. It is during the period of secondary education that many young people (twelve to eighteen years old) either synthesize religion and culture in themselves or fail to do so and are strongly oriented towards good or away from it. Hence, having weighed the objections often made nowadays against secondary schools by those who would rather restrict themselves to pastoral ministries, the Society again asserts that the teaching of youth according to the principles of our Institute, even in the so-called profane disciplines, is entirely conformed to our vocation and to our sacerdotal character. Indeed, it is the ministry to which the Society owes most of its growth.[18]

32/   18. Secondary schools, be they old ones retained or new ones founded, should improve continually. They should be educationally effective as well as centers of culture and faith, for lay cooperators and the families of students and alumni. Thereby they will help the whole community of the region. Let Jesuits also foster to a closer cooperation with the parents of students, upon whom the primary responsibility of education rests.[19]

33/   19. *a*) Each province should have its own *ordinationes* for secondary schools, in harmony with its own needs.[20]

34/   *b*) As far as subject matter is concerned, the education of our students should be in conformity with the genuine cultural tradition of each nation or region, in so-called classical literature, or modern literature, or in science.

35/   *c*) Moreover, other schools, such as technical and agricultural schools may well be opened where need or great utility suggest it.[21]

36/   20. *a*) Subjects should be so taught that the mind of the young is not overwhelmed with a multiplicity of details, and that all their powers may be suitably developed and they may be prepared for higher studies. In addition, our students should be helped so that they can make progress by themselves, and so that there may grow in them firmness of mind, uprightness of judgment and sensibility, aesthetic sense, a capacity to express themselves, orally and in writing, a sense of community and of civil and social duty, and depth of understanding.[22]

37/   *b*) Regarding the method of teaching, let there be kept in all fields, as far as is possible, the proper method of the Society which is commended in the *Ratio Studiorum*. Therefore let all be familiar with those principles of sound pedagogy which are set down by our holy founder in the Constitutions, Part IV, developed in the *Ratio Studiorum*, and clearly explained by many writers of the Society.[23]

38/   21. After they have consulted Father General, provincials should decide in light of the circumstances of persons and place, whether daily Mass should be obligatory in our residential secondary schools.[24]

39/   22. So-called apostolic schools can be kept and established where, all things considered, they seem to be for the greater glory of God. What is said primarily concerning secondary schools is to be applied also to them.[25]

40/   23. Coeducation in secondary schools is not to be allowed except with the approval of Father General.[26]

41/   24. *a*) On account of the ever-growing importance of universities and institutions of higher learning for the formation of the whole human community, we must see to it that the Society and its priests are present to this work. Let there be, therefore, an ever-greater number of professors prepared for such institutions, whether directed by the Society or by others. These professors should be able not only to teach advanced courses, but also to contribute to scholarly progress by their own research and that of their talented students whom they have trained.[27]

42/   *b*) Among the faculties belonging to our institutions of higher education, theology and philosophy should especially have their proper place to whatever extent they contribute, in various places, to the greater service of God.[28]

43/   *c*) The prohibition in the Constitutions, according to which that part of canon law which serves for contesting suits is not to be touched by Jesuits, is to be thus understood: "unless the general judges that something else is good."[29]

44/   25. The education of priests, as a work of the highest value, is to be considered one of the chief ministries of the Society. Therefore, the seminarians who attend our universities are to be watched over with special attention, and directors and teachers chosen from among our best men are to be assigned to those clerical seminaries whose direction is accepted by the Society.[30] But if there is question of diocesan seminaries, a definite contract shall be made with the bishop and approved by the Holy See.[31]

45/   26. Not only youth but adults are to be educated, both for the advancement of their professional lives and for the efforts which make their conjugal, family, and social life more human and Christian, and develop a better understanding of the faith.[32]

46/   27. *a*) According to the mind of the Second Vatican Council, a close collaboration with the laity is recommended. On the one hand, we can give them help in their formation by schools, conferences, spiritual exercises and other suitable works, and by our friendly dealing with them and the testimony of our life. On the other hand, let Jesuits consider the importance for the Society itself of such collaboration with lay people, who will always be the natural interpreters for us of the modern world, and so will always give us effective help in this apostolate. Therefore, we should consider handing over to them the roles they are prepared to assume in the work of education, whether these be in teaching, in academic and business administration, or even on the board of directors.[33]

47/   *b*) It will also be advantageous to consider whether it would not be helpful to establish in some of our institutions of higher education a board of trustees which is composed partly of Jesuits and partly of lay people; the responsibility both of ownership and of direction shall pertain to this board.

48/   28. Men of our time are very interested in new and more adequate intercommunication, by which international union and progress are fostered. Therefore Jesuits should be concerned to promote among their students and alumni and other members of the social community those efforts and means which can lead to a greater and more efficacious collaboration among nations.

49/   29. Prefects or directors of education should be named who will help the provincials in directing the whole effort of education; they can be so united that the whole Society can enjoy the benefits of the studies and the experiments which are being carried on in various regions of the world.

50/   30. In each province or region there should be a permanent committee of experts who will help superiors in this apostolate, drawing up and continually adapting regulations concerning our schools, in harmony with each one's needs.[34]

51/   31. To help Father General in fostering the whole work of education, a secretariat of education should be established. Its task will be to collect and distribute information about the apostolate of education carried on by Jesuits and also to promote alumni associations and periodic conventions.

52/   32. Decree 141 of the *Collection of Decrees* is abrogated.

---

[1]   *(Gravissimum Educationis) Declaration of Christian Education. (*GE) introduction.

[2]   GE 5.

[3]   GE conclusion.

[4]   GE introduction: *Collectio Decretorum Congregationum Generalium Societatis Iesu (CollDecr)* 131 [141].

[5] *CollDecr* 136 §I. [141].

[6] Cf. GE 6.

[7] *Constitutiones Societatis Iesu (Cons)* IV. 15. 4 [478].

[8] *CollDecr* [143].

[9] *CollDecr* 133.

[10] *CollDecr* 136 § 1.

[11] Cf. Fr. Janssens. *Acta Romana Societatis Iesu (ActRSJ)* 11 (1949) 720–21; John XXIII, *Mater et Magistra, passim;* GS 29.

[12] *CollDecr* 142.

[13] *CollDecr* 145.

[14] Cf. GE 7. 10.

[15] *CollDecr* [418].

[16] *CollDecr* [144].

[17] *CollDecr* 132.

[18] *CollDecr* 131.

[19] Cf. GE 3.

[20] *CollDecr* 139.

[21] *CollDecr* 140 § 1.

[22] *CollDecr* 140 § 2.

[23] *CollDecr* 140 § 3.

[24] *CollDecr* [316].

[25] *CollDecr* 135.

[26] *CollDecr* [314].

[27] *CollDecr* [417].

[28] *CollDecr* 137 § 1.

[29] *CollDecr* 137 § 2.

[30] OT 5; *CollDecr* 134.

[31] *CollDecr* 134; ES I,30 § 1.

[32] Cf. GE introduction, 9.

[33] Cf. decree 33 (relationship of the society to the laity).

[34] *CollDecr* 139, [142].

Decree 29

Scholarly Work and Research

53/   1. *a*) Jesuits should have a high regard for scholarly activity, especially scientific research properly so called, and they are to view this as one of the most necessary works of the Society. It is a very effective apostolate, entirely in accord with the age-old tradition of the Society from its earliest times.[1] It is a generous response to recommendations that the popes have often repeated, especially during the past hundred years.[2] It is most suited to the needs of the men of our times and an excellent means for opening up and carrying on dialogue with them, including nonbelievers, for establishing confidence in the Church and for elaborating and teaching a synthesis of faith and life.

54/   *b*) All of this applies first of all to the sacred sciences and those connected with them, which have the first claim on the scholarly potential of the Society. It applies also to those sciences which are called positive, both those which look to man and society and the mathematical-natural sciences, as well as the technical sciences proceeding from them, which profoundly affect the mentality of our times.

55/   2. Those Jesuits, therefore, who are assigned to this work by superiors are to give themselves entirely and with a strong and self-denying spirit to this work, which, in one way or another, makes demands upon the whole man. They are to be on guard against the illusion that they will serve God better in other occupations which can seem more pastoral, and they are to offer their whole life as a holocaust to God. At the same time they should do this in such a way that they do not lose touch with the other apostolic activities of the Society. Finally they are to strive earnestly to show themselves truly religious and priestly men. They should remember that in undertaking this work, they are enlisted in the cause of Christian truth and are serving the people of God either by showing forth the presence of the Church among the men of the scientific community or by enriching the understanding of revelation itself through the progress of human knowledge.

56/   3. Provincials, for their part, must not be deterred by the demands of other works of the province from applying to this work in the sciences, definitively and in good time, men whom they find inclined and in the judgment of experts truly suited, yet well proven in the spiritual life. Once assigned to this work, they are not to be taken away from it without grave reason, especially when they have finished their studies, even post-doctoral work, and have begun to produce. Since many of the positive sciences often require youthfulness for their study if one is to become really outstanding in them, provincials are not to hesitate to propose suitable changes in the ordinary course of study to Father General, as need may dictate, according to the Decree on the Training of Scholastics Especially in Studies. Priests who are applied to these studies are to be mindful that the more advanced they are in any science the more careful they should be that their knowledge of theology is broad and sound, in order that they may be able to exercise their scientific apostolate with greater authority and profit.

57/   4. Superiors, especially higher superiors, are to take care that those applied to work in the sciences give themselves primarily to the work of research, study, and writing, and that the necessary leisure and helps are provided for this work. They are to acknowledge that scholars have "a lawful freedom of inquiry and thought and the freedom to express their minds humbly and courageously about those matters in which they enjoy competence."[3] Superiors are to permit them to join national and international professional organizations and to attend their meetings when it seems expedient. Finally they are to encourage Jesuits to work not only in our own centers but also in public universities and scientific institutions according to the various opportunities and necessities of the region. In this way they will cooperate more closely with laymen in penetrating the whole human culture with the Christian spirit and better ordering the world to God, its ultimate end.

58/   5. Small periodic meetings of Jesuits who are expert in the different sciences, especially those closely related, are recommended to provincials. These should promote interdisciplinary communication from time to time and, after careful study of the condition of the scientific apostolate in each region, procure among themselves greater collaboration of all who are working in the sciences. They should also help superiors with their advice in planning, coordinating, preparing, promoting, and also abandoning scientific works, in such a way that the effort expended in this apostolate may be directed more efficiently to its end.

---

¹ *Ordination on Training Mathematics Teachers,* by Father Robert Bellarmine, promulgated in 1593 by the authority of Father Claudius Aquaviva. (Archivum Romanum Societatis Iesu, *Epp. NN.* 113, fol. 184); *Ordination of Father Carafa of Aug. 17,1647 to the Province of Austria* (Bernhard Dühr, *Geschichte der Jesuiten in den Ländern deutscher Zunge in der ersten Hälfte der XVII Jahrhundert* [1913] II, 556); *Discourse of Father Christopher Clavius* ("De modo et via quo Societas Iesu ad maiorem Dei honorem, et animarum profectum augere hominum de se opinionem, omnemque Haereticorum in litteris aestimationem, qua illi multum nituntur, convellere brevissime et facillime possit"), in Archivum Romanum Societatis Iesu, Hist. Saec. 5c. fol. 185–87; etc.

² Cf., e.g., Leo XII, *Quod Divina Sapientia* (1824); Leo XIII, Motu Proprio *Ut Mysticam Sponsam* (March 14, 1891); Pius XI, Allocution in honor of the twenty-fifth anniversary of the Pontifical Biblical Institute *(ActRSJ* 7, 648–51); Pius XI, Allocution at the inauguration of the new Vatican Observatory at Castel Gandolfo *(ActRSJ* 8, 84–86); etc.

³ GS 62.

Promotion of Justice and Education for Justice, 1973

Pedro Arrupe, S.J.

Editor's Introduction: In 1965, Pedro Arrupe (1907–1991) was elected the 28th Superior General of the Society of Jesus by General Congregation 31. He served as General until 1983. Fr. Arrupe is an inspiring leader who presided over the renewal of the Society within the spirit of Vatican II. The two discourses included in this book—*Promotion of Justice and Education for Justice* (1973) and *Our Secondary Schools: Today and Tomorrow* (1980)—are his two most influential addresses dealing with education. *Promotion of Justice and Education for Justice*—also known as the "Men for Others" address—was his keynote speech at the European Alumni Congress. This discourse was highly controversial at that time because it questioned the work of the schools for the mission of **a faith that does justice** and encouraged them to understand their goal as preparing **men and women for others** (an expression that has become the motto of Jesuit education today). In *Our Secondary Schools: Today and Tomorrow*, Fr. Arrupe highlights the importance of the apostolate of secondary education for the Society and reflects on the path of renewal needed today.

CONTENTS

A. Starting Point: The Teaching and the Significance of the 1971 Synod

   a) The church's attitude of listening in the Synod

   b) The document's introduction: an attitude of listening and the result

   c) The document's central part: an attitude of listening and the result

B. An Attitude of Reconciliation and Complementary Theses

   a) Tensions in the Church

   b) Overcoming the alternatives that exclude one another

   c) Six pairs of complementary theses

C. Development of the complementary theses

   a) Effective justice for people and a religious attitude toward God

   b) Love of God and love of other persons

   c) Christian love (charity) and justice

   d) Personal conversion and reform of structures

   e) Salvation and liberation in this life and in the other

   f) The Christian ethos and its technological and ideological mediations

II. MEN AND WOMEN FOR OTHERS: PERMANENT FORMATION AND EDUCATION FOR JUSTICE

A. Men and Women for Others: Justification and Meaning of the Phrase

   a) Preliminary considerations

   b) The dehumanization of egotism

   c) The humanization of love

B. Agents and Promoters of Change

   a) General attitudes for promoting change

   b) Building the future

C. The "Spiritual" Person

   a) The infusion of love

   b) Discernment of spirits

CONCLUSION

PREFACE

1/   The Tenth European Congress of Jesuit Alumni was coming to an end. On the afternoon of August 1, 1973, the closing session was solemnly convened. Conclusions were approved, new officers were elected, some statements were formulated, and some discourses were delivered. Then Fr. Arrupe, with his usual energy and enthusiasm (or perhaps even more), gave the following conference.

2/   Limitations of time did not permit him to read the whole text, but the Acts of the Congress later published it as written. Here you have it.

3/   The contents of this dissertation had broad resonance. Some people were angry, and among alumni associations it gave rise to resignations, which were few but notorious. At the same time, the discourse was well received by wide sectors of public opinion and since then has been the object of study and laudatory commentaries.

4/   When part of the Spanish press of the time published severe criticisms of the discourse that included scurrilous attacks on Fr. Arrupe, Cardinal Villot, Vatican Secretary of State, wrote a letter to Fr. Pedro Arrupe, General of the Society of Jesus on September 30 of that year, thanking him in the name of His Holiness for the text of the conference that he had addressed to the Jesuit alumni in Valencia. He also expressed "[the Holy Father's] satisfaction with the incisive way in which you, basing yourself on the Gospel message and on the perennial teaching of the Church's Magisterium, have urged your listeners to practice and bear witness to Christian charity and justice, principally through interior reform and overcoming of personal and social self-centeredness."

5/   The complete text of the discourse was published in "Iglesia y justicia. Actas del X Congreso de la Confederación Europea de Asociaciones de Antiguos Alumnos de Jesuitas." Valencia, Spain, 29 July–1 August 1973, pp. 92–118.

A Little Bit of History about "Men for Others" English Translation

6/   Fr. Pedro Arrupe, General of the Society of Jesus, presented his influential address: *The Promotion of Justice and the Formation in the Alumni Associations* during the Congress of The European Jesuit Alumni at Valencia, Spain (July 29–August 1, 1973). This address is commonly referred to as *Men for Others* and it has become a classic text for understanding contemporary Jesuit Education, especially the central role of the promotion of justice that we assign to Jesuit Education today. However, surprisingly, Fr. Arrupe's text has not been translated into English yet. Many English readers may be bewildered why the text has never been translated, but it is actually simple to explain why this is the case.

7/   Fr. Arrupe spoke Spanish during his speech. The Spanish text and a French translation were published by the Confederation of the European Alumni. However, as the Secretariat for Education explains: "Since English is not one of the official languages of the Confederation, those who would like to read the entire book must select either the Spanish or French version" (*Nuntii Pedagogici*, No. 2, October 15, 1973, Rome, p. 12).

8/   So what is the text that the English-speaking people have known so far as Arrupe's *Men for Others* discourse? Again, the Secretariat for Education responds: "The Original text of Father General's address and his responses to the students are available in Spanish and French while an English condensation of the address will soon be ready." (*Nuntii Pedagogici*, No. 2, October 15, 1973, Rome, p. 12).

9/   This English condensation was published by the Secretariat with the title *Men for Others* with *Education for Social Justice and Social Action Today* as subtitle. The Secretariat asked Fr. Horacio de la Costa, who was from the Philippines Province and at that time General Assistant to Fr. Arrupe, to prepare this edition. Fr. de la Costa wrote the introduction and "has also edited and condensed the text of the Valencia address for the English readers" ("Foreword," *Men for Others, Education for Social Justice and Social*

Action, International Secretariat of Jesuit Education, Roma, p. 3). This text, which is clearly not a translation of the original but a condensation and edition of it, is what English readers know as Fr. Arrupe's address at the Congress in Valencia. This text certainly reflects the main ideas and style of the original, but it is much shorter than the original and it cannot be considered a proper translation. Since many of the publications today do not tell the whole story, the English readers have assumed they are reading what Fr. Arrupe said. As with edition or condensation, some of the ideas of the original discourse are subject to the interpretation and emphasis of the editor.

10/   A final clarification: there are two versions of Arrupe's original discourse. First, there is the longer written version that was published in the proceedings of the Congress. Arrupe could not read the full discourse he had written because of time constraints, so he actually presented a shorter version to the participants of the Congress. That is the second version. The longer version in Spanish was published in *Iglesia y Justicia. Actas del X Congreso de la Confederación Europea de Asociaciones de AA.* (AA. de Jesuitas, Valencia, España, 1973). Also the longer verson may be found in Arrupe, P. *Hombres para los demás*, second edition. (Asociación de antiguos Alumnos de Caspe y Sarriá, Barcelona, 1983). The shorter version in Spanish was published in "Información SJ, No. 27 (Septiembre-octubre 1973) 230–238, Madrid."

16 June 2014
José Mesa S.J.
Secretary for Education
Rome

INTRODUCTION

A. Presentation of the Theme

a) Education for justice

11/   The theme of "education for justice" has in recent years become one of the Church's major concerns. It received special attention at the recent Synod of Bishops, whose main theme was "Justice in the World." The Church has acquired a new awareness of how Christians' action on behalf of justice and liberation from all oppressive situations—and consequently their participation in the transformation of this world—now form a constitutive part of the mission which the Lord Jesus has entrusted to her.[1] This new consciousness impels the Church to educate (or better to re-educate) herself, her children, and all men and women by methods that teach us to "live our lives in the global context and according to the evangelical principles of personal and social morality as they are expressed in living Christian witness."[2]

b) Men and women for others

12/   Our educational goal and objective is to form men and women who live not for themselves but for God and for his Christ, who died and rose for us. "Men and women for others" are persons who cannot conceive of love of God without love of neighbor. Theirs is an efficacious love that has justice as its first requirement; for them justice is the sure guarantee that our love of God is not a farce or perhaps a pharisaical guise to conceal our selfishness. All the scriptures make us aware of this intimate relation between love of God and efficacious love of others. Listen simply to these verses of Saint John: "Those who say, 'I love God,' and hate their brothers and sisters are liars, for those who do not love a brother or sister whom they have seen cannot love God whom they have not seen." "How does God's love abide in anyone who has the world's goods and sees a brother or sister in need and yet refuses help? Little children, let us love, not in word or speech, but in truth and in action."[3]

c) Obstacles

13/   This educational task of forming men and women who truly live for others is confronted with tremendous obstacles. The Synod itself warns us of this and makes us aware that in most of the world the orientation of the present educational system (including schools and mass media) is moving in precisely the opposite direction. Instead of producing men and women with social consciousness, "they encourage a narrow *individualism.*" Instead of viewing education as preparation for service, they produce "*a mentality that exalts possession of things*" and that reduces schools and universities to being the training grounds for learning how to obtain promotions, earn money, and rise above others, sometimes through exploitation. Finally, and perhaps most seriously, the established social order (or disorder) has such great influence on educational institutions and the mass media that these, instead of creating "new men and women," merely reproduce "people as they are," the "people that the established order desires; that is, people in its own image and likeness," incapable of bringing about any true transformation of reality.⁴

B. Our Initial Attitude

14/   After this preamble, you will understand that it is not at all easy for a General of the Society of Jesus to speak to alumni of Jesuit schools, that is, to the men and women who have been educated by us. As I will say in a moment, I take up this theme with a firm attitude of confidence and with an optimistic spirit. I believe that the family atmosphere that envelops us here will awaken a profound wisdom among us and also allow us to speak with complete sincerity.

a) Humility: we are not educated

15/   Feeling buoyed by this confidence, I want to respond in all sincerity to a question that for some time has been floating in the air and has no doubt been asked by more than one of you. Have we educated you for justice? Are you educated for justice? Let me try to answer. If we use the term "justice" and the phrase "education for justice" in the profound sense in which the Church uses those terms today, then I think that we Jesuits in all humility have to give a negative response: we have not educated you for justice in the way that God requires of us in these days. And I believe I can also ask you to be humble enough to respond likewise: no, you are not educated for justice, and you must still supplement the education you have already received. There is a very profound sense in which we must all be in a process of permanent education.

16/   What is more, even though real advances have been made in some places, I would not dare to say that even today we are educating for justice the students presently in our schools or the other persons whom we influence in our various apostolic activities. I think I can assure you, nevertheless, that for some time now the Society has been quite concerned in this regard and that our concern has already shown some fruits. Indeed, we have experienced much incomprehension and even some persecution as a result of our efforts.

b) Confidence: the probing spirit proper to the Society

17/   As I just told you, recognizing our past and present limitations does not prevent us from treating the theme before us with confidence and optimism. And our confidence and optimism are based on the following: despite our historical limitations and deficiencies, I believe that the Society has transmitted to you something of the very essence of the Ignatian spirit, and I believe you have preserved this spirit well, just as the Society has. We have preserved something that allows us to renew ourselves continually, namely, the spirit of continual searching for the will of God and a keen spiritual sensibility for discerning the ways in which God wants Christianity to be lived at the different stages of history.

18/   It has been said with some truth that the Society of Jesus—and even more the spirituality of the Exercises—offers very few concrete details for defining a Jesuit or, correspondingly, a person who has been educated by Jesuits. There is no fixed and permanent image available. In saying that, I don't mean to say that the person who emerges from the *Exercises* is amorphous, colorless, and featureless. Quite the contrary. The *Exercises* are a method for making concrete decisions according to the will of God; they are a method for choosing among various alternatives. Nevertheless, the *Exercises* of themselves do not limit us or confine us to any particular alternative; rather, they open us completely to the horizon of manifold alternatives so that the One who marks our path is God himself in his tremendous originality.

19/   An example taken from the Society itself will help us to understand what I mean. The Society was born before Trent and before the Catholic reaction to the Protestant Reformation had taken definitive shape. The Society was born free and ready for whatever was needed. The Society came into being at that particular moment of history without being concretely defined, except for an attitude of seeking God's will and being ready for anything. The Society sought God's will in the three places where it becomes manifest: in the Gospel, in the concrete life of the Church under the Roman Pontiff, and in what we would today call "the signs of the times." By heeding and discerning the voice of the Spirit as it was revealed through those three channels, the Society gradually found its specific path and took on particular features and characteristics. The Society of Jesus has not been a shapeless order. It has made options that have defined it quite concretely. In fact, most historians consider it to be the kind of order that is typical of Trent and the post-Tridentine period. Its basic pluralism—or what might be called its "pluralist potential"—leaves it in principle open to almost everything, but that pluralism has not left the Society lacking in functional effectiveness; rather, pluralism has been the foundation on which very clear options have been made in accord with the requirements of history.

20/   And that is precisely what the Society is doing today. As the Church moves beyond the post-Tridentine period and as new "signs of the times" emerge on the historical horizon, the Society feels itself obliged to ask about the path it is currently taking and to seek out once again, on the basis of its fundamental pluralist potential, the historical form it should take. What is essential to the Society is not the spirit of Trent but fidelity to the historical call of God, which at a certain moment in time asked it to adopt that spirit of Trent, but which today is asking it to embody the spirit of Vatican II in its life and its concrete options. If the Society wants to be faithful to itself, if it does not want to betray what is most characteristic of its spirit, then paradoxically, it must profoundly change most of the concrete forms it assumes in any particular epoch.

21/ Let us return now to you alumni and the theme of justice. If we have not failed totally in the formation we gave you, then we trust that we've transmitted to you this spirit of availability and openness to change—or in biblical language, a capacity for repentance and conversion. I believe we have taught you to listen to the living God, to read the Gospel in such a way that by its light we are able to discover ever new aspects of God's revelation. We have taught you to be attentive to the Church, in whose realm the Word of God, ever ancient and ever new, sounds with the precise tone that each age needs. That is what is important, and on that alone our confidence rests.

22/ Therefore, despite any limitations in the education we have given you, if we have succeeded in giving you this Ignatian spirit, then we have ultimately given you everything. For the important thing is not that you are former students of the Society of Jesus. In fact, I'm happy to say that I have no inclination to tell you in triumphal fashion: "We Jesuits have taught you everything. Just remember what you learned from us!" No, nothing like that. Our glory, if we have any—or better, our joy—is not in reminding you that you are our former students but in realizing that you, perhaps with the help of the training we gave you, are now, along with us, students and disciples of the Lord Jesus. As such, you are men and women who want to discern God's will for the present times. Therefore, I do not speak to you as a father but as a simple companion. We are all schoolmates seated together on the same benches, trying to hear the Lord's words

C. Proposition

23/   The purpose of my words today is only to help you to listen to God. We want to begin a dialogue in which you also take part so that among all of us we discover what the Spirit is asking of the Church today in this matter of justice and education for justice.

24/   I am going to limit myself to two series of considerations. In the first series, I want to draw on the teaching of the last Synod in order to examine in depth the very idea of justice; a concept which, thanks to the combined light of the Gospel and the signs of the times, is taking on an ever clearer profile for us. The second series of considerations will deal with the kind of person we want to form, the type of person we must become if we want to serve the evangelical ideal of justice. We are talking about spiritually renewed persons, men and women for others, moved by the Spirit that transforms the face of the earth.

I. JUSTICE

A. Starting Point: The Teaching and the Significance of the 1971 Synod

25/   The starting point for our reflection on justice will be, as we just stated, some statements of the last Synod of bishops, held at the end of 1971.

a) The church's attitude of listening in the Synod

26/   These statements are not merely a repetition of what has been taught before in the Church, nor are they simply a sort of abstract development of doctrine. Rather, they are a poignant expression of the earnest plea that God is making to the Church and to all human beings to adopt generous attitudes and to undertake effective action on behalf of those who are oppressed and suffering.

27/   The introduction to the Synod document describes for us the attitude of listening and conversion that the bishops adopted at the Synod so that God could appeal to them and show them his concrete will. Their listening was not something superficial and improvised. It involved asking questions of God and discerning the action of his Spirit in the signs of the times, so that, thus enlightened, they could reinterpret the message of salvation and detect in it nuances that previously had gone unnoticed. This is a vital process that has been spreading and developing in the Church for years now. It clearly originated in Vatican II, and its application to the problem of justice was strongly advanced by the encyclical *Populorum Progressio*. This spark was ignited at the center of Christianity but then quickly spread to the outlying parts, especially the poorest regions. The Synod is only the latest blaze generated by those flames.

28/   Let us keep in mind these dates. In 1967 Paul VI issued *Populorum Progressio*, a document to which he had already alluded during his trip to India in 1966. During the three years following the publication of the encyclical, the pope presided at various meetings of Third World bishops who came together to reflect on what God was asking of their churches in the post-conciliar period, most especially in regard to justice. Someday history will pass judgment on the tremendous importance of these meetings, which are already giving the Church a new complexion. In 1968 there was a meeting of the Latin American Church in Medellín. In 1969 there was a meeting of the African Church in Kampala. In 1970 there was a meeting of the Asian Church in Manila. As a result of these meetings, shortly before the Synod, in 1971, the pope wrote *Octogesima Adveniens*, which was far from being a final statement. In fact, it wasn't even issued in the solemn form of an encyclical but simply as a letter addressed to a cardinal. This was the pope's way of telling us that the purpose of the document was to generate dialogue and encourage people to an active part in it. This is the setting in which we should understand the Synod. The working documents given to the Synod Fathers were precisely the main texts dedicated to justice from the meetings in Medellín, Kampala, and Manila.

b) The document's introduction: an attitude of listening and the result

29/   Now that we are conscious of the full force they have, we can read some paragraphs from the introduction of the Synod document:

30/   "Gathered from the whole world, in communion with all who believe in Christ and with the entire human family, and opening our hearts to the Spirit who is the whole of creation new, we have questioned ourselves about the mission of the People of God to further justice in the world.

31/   "Scrutinizing the 'signs of the times' and seeking to detect the meaning of emerging history, . . . we have listened to the Word of God so that we might be converted to the fulfilling of the divine plan for the salvation of the world.

32/   "We have been able to perceive the serious injustices which are creating in the world a network of domination, oppression, and abuses.

33/   "At the same time we have noted an inmost stirring that is moving the world in its depths. . . . In associations of people and among peoples themselves, a new awareness is arising which is shaking them out of any fatalistic resignation and which is spurring them on to liberate themselves and to be responsible for their own destiny. People are organizing movements which express hope in a better world and a will to change whatever has become intolerable."[5]

34/   After these initial words with the questions they pose, the bishops astutely anticipate in the same introduction *the answer they believe they have heard from God.* They state that the preaching of the Gospel cannot be separated from action in favor of justice, or from participating in the transformation of the world, or from liberating people from all oppressive situations. For all of these are a constitutive part of the Gospel and of the Church's mission. But let us hear their own words: "Listening to the cry of those who suffered violence and are oppressed by unjust systems and structures, . . . we are keenly conscious that the Church's vocation is to be present in the heart of the world by proclaiming Good News to the poor, freedom to the oppressed, and joy to the afflicted. The hopes and forces which are moving at the very foundations of the world are not foreign to the dynamism of the Gospel, which through the power of the Holy Spirit frees people from personal sin and from its consequences in social life."

35/   The introduction goes on to say that our present-day history, with all its vicissitudes and tragedies, "directs us to sacred history, where God has revealed himself to us and made known to us, as it is brought progressively to realization, his plan of liberation and salvation which is once and for all fulfilled in the Paschal Mystery of Christ."

36/   The final and perhaps most important words are the following: "Action on behalf of justice and participation in the transformation of the world fully appear to us as a constitutive dimension of the preaching of the Gospel, that is, of the Church's mission for the redemption of the human race and its liberation from every oppressive situation."[6]

c) The document's central part: an attitude of listening and the result

37/   Allow me to read still another paragraph, one taken from the very heart of the document. It expresses with even greater clarity both the Church's new awareness of her mission to promote justice and the originality of this awareness, which results from the theological method of heeding the signs of the times and re-interpreting the Gospel accordingly.

38/   Listen first to these words concerning this method, which harmonizes closely with our Ignatian method: "The present situation of the world, seen in the light of faith, calls us back to the very essence of the Christian message, creating in us a deep awareness of its true meaning and its urgent demands."

39/   The document then shows the result of applying this method to the problem of justice: "The mission of preaching the Gospel requires at the present time that we dedicate ourselves to the liberation of people even in their present existence in this world."[7]

B. An Attitude of Reconciliation and Complementary Theses

40/   With the foregoing as a basis, let us now consider some factors that will help us to advance toward a Christian conception of justice and to lay a firm foundation for effective action. We can begin by speaking about the need for us to reach agreement on several theses that are sometimes presented nowadays as contrary or contradictory. Harmonizing these opposed theses will be impossible if we fail to adopt a sincere attitude of reconciliation among ourselves.

a) Tensions in the Church

41/   You are quite aware that serious tensions exist today within the bosom of the Church, and even more so within associations of Catholic inspiration. These tensions are in large part based on the different degrees to which we have assimilated and accepted the new appeals the Lord is making to us. I am not referring to persons who are holding fast to what they call traditional ways as a means of defending their personal or their group interests; such attitudes end up collaborating with oppressive political and economic structures.[8] Instead, for many people the temptation is more subtle, and, in some cases, their reluctance to change has some foundation. They fear that the new currents will diminish Christianity and reduce it to the level of simple humanism which takes no account of God, Christian love (as opposed to simple justice), grace, sin, personal conversion, or the afterlife. They fear that these will be replaced by the cold demands of justice, a strictly this-worldly humanism, the reform of structures, and the belief that God's Kingdom should come in this life.

b) Overcoming the alternatives that exclude one another

42/   As long as the opposing sides view the problem in terms of alternatives that exclude one another, there can be no solution to the problem. We will soon begin the Holy Year of Reconciliation, and even if we cannot solve this problem definitively, perhaps we can contribute to true reconciliation within the Church by trying to move beyond this dilemma of conflicting alternatives.

43/   Those who have gladly heard the new interpretations of the Spirit of the Lord and are conscious of their great novelty should not forget that they are coming from the same Spirit who has always been active in the Gospel and in the Church. Their novelty does not annul the traditional teachings of the Christian message; indeed, it reaffirms them and brings them to greater fullness. We should also be mindful that forgetfulness of this or simply insufficient explanation—especially if joined to a harsh and contemptuous attitude toward those who think differently—will understandably provoke a conservative reaction. As a result, many people who find novelty more difficult to accept will be deprived of the new lights and graces with which the Lord now wishes to enrich us.

44/   At the same time, Christians who are concerned about preserving the perennial values should also learn from today's Church that those values should be viewed not as dead realities but as living realities that are capable of producing new flowers and fruits of surprising, unexpected richness. They should also reflect that their refusal to accept sincerely and unreservedly the newness of life to which the Spirit now impels us will provoke a reaction that is also understandable: some people will abandon or treat as secondary other less known but no less important aspects of the Gospel message and of the Christian way of life.

c) Six pairs of complementary theses

45/   My purpose here is not to bring about an opportunistic harmonization of irreconcilable opposites. I am convinced that the principal Christian affirmations and attitudes relating to justice are true and correct only if they bring into profound harmony extremes which at times are presented as contradictory and conflicting. I here offer a list of the main pairings of apparent oppositions.

1. Effective justice for people and a religious attitude toward God
2. Love of God and love of others
3. Christian love (charity) and justice
4. Personal conversion and reform of structures
5. Salvation and liberation in this life and in the other
6. The Christian ethos and its technological and ideological mediations

C. Development of the complementary theses

46/   A completely satisfactory development of these affirmations would require a long treatise. I am going to limit myself to a few sketches about how to harmonize each of these oppositions.

a) Effective justice for people and a religious attitude toward God

47/   First of all, we need to overcome the apparent opposition, and even separation, between the human, historical imperative of promoting justice for people and maintaining a religious attitude toward God, an attitude that becomes concrete in the Church's mission of preaching the Gospel and bringing integral salvation to all people. Certainly the church's mission does not consist only in the promotion of justice here on earth; nevertheless, promotion of justice is a constitutive element of that mission. The God of the Bible, the God of Exodus, is the God who liberates the poor and the oppressed here in this world.[9] The Ancient Covenant, the pact between God and his chosen people, included as a basic element the practice of justice, such that a violation of the justice due to human beings implied a rupture of the Covenant with God.[10] We can even claim that in the beginnings of the history of revelation the relations of human beings with God were viewed more in terms of temporal, earthly welfare. The prophets developed that conception by adding more spiritual elements, but these in no way negated the earlier ones. The Messiah who was promised and awaited was seen as a liberator who would bring justice to the poor and the oppressed.[11]

48/   The truth is that Christ, when he came, superseded that conception and broadened the horizons of salvation, but without undoing the ancient contents. In many gospel passages Saint Matthew and Saint Luke see in Jesus the eschatological Prophet announced in Isaiah 42:1–4 and 61:1–2. Jesus received from God the mission of announcing the Good News to the poor, of liberating those who were oppressed, and of bringing about the triumph of justice. This is the context in which we should understand the meaning of the Beatitudes, which, according to the best modern exegetes, should be interpreted in their simplest, most direct sense: the poor are blessed because the Kingdom has arrived and they will no longer be poor, for their Liberator is already at hand.[12]

b) Love of God and love of other persons

49/ In the foregoing discussion of how Christ assumed and radicalized the horizontal dimension that was so evident in the Old Testament and so fused with the vertical dimension in himself, we already touched on the second complementary thesis: the identification of love of God with love of other human beings. It was Jesus himself who, without being asked, proclaimed that the second great commandment was similar to the first. He went so far as to unite them into a single commandment that summed up the Law and the Prophets. Consequently, the sole criterion to be used in the Final Judgment, according to the teaching of Jesus, will be love for other persons, because "Whatever you did to one of the least of these who are my sisters and brothers, you did it to me."[13] And in order for this to be the case, the person being judged does not even have to be aware of the fact that Jesus is identified with those other men and women.[14]

50/ We can express this same perspective using the words of a contemporary theologian from whom we have taken many of the ideas presented in this conference: "Our belonging to or our being excluded from the Kingdom announced by Jesus is decided by our attitude in dealing with the poor and the oppressed, those whom Isaiah 58:1–2 describes as victims of human injustice and for whom God wants to make manifest his justice. But what is truly new is that Jesus makes these despised, marginalized people his 'sisters and brothers.' He enters into personal solidarity with all those who are poor and vulnerable, with all those who suffer hunger and misery. All those who find themselves in such a situation are sisters and brothers of Christ. That is why what is done on their behalf is done for Christ himself. Those who provide genuine assistance to these 'sisters and brothers' of Jesus belong to the Kingdom; those who abandon the poor to their condition of misery exclude themselves from the Kingdom."[15] All the other writing of the New Testament—James, Paul, John—repeat with countless nuances this same doctrine about the unity that exists between love of God and love of other persons, above all the oppressed.[16]

c) Christian love (charity) and justice

51/   With this reflection we are already touching on the third of our pairs of complementary concepts. Just as love of God and love of neighbor are so fused together in our Christian conception that they are impossible to separate, so also love (charity) and justice become fused together and practically identical.

52/   A process of abstraction has led Western thought to make a drastic distinction between charitable love and justice, and this process has had a reductive and impoverishing effect on both concepts. At the present time that distinction is not so marked, but we have still not been able to overcome it completely. In recent centuries, the word "charity" (especially as applied to our neighbors) has been used principally to indicate the so-called "works of charity." Since these are considered to be supererogatory, a very problematic element is introduced into the Christian ethos.

53/   Justice, on the other hand, is taken to indicate something that is strictly obligatory. The symbol of justice is a blind figure with an impassive face; she has a balance in one hand and a sword in the other. If her image is carved in marble, that's all the better because she is perceived to have a cold heart or perhaps no heart at all. Her equanimity is not to be disturbed by any human sentiment or sympathetic feeling. We should not think, however, that that is the only ideal of justice. In the East things are very different, almost the contrary. In classical China, for example, the ideal of justice does not tend toward impersonalization; instead, it assumes the maximum personalization of relationships. A just judge is not the one who judges by applying rules that are formal, abstract, and inflexible; rather, the just judge takes the concrete situation into account and judges persons according to their concrete qualities; that is, with equity and with full knowledge of how everyone will be affected.[17] Let us note in passing that even in the West the Roman concept of justice, while maintaining its substantive character, was greatly enriched in the medieval period by the Christian notion of equity.

54/   In any case, we do not deny a certain value to the theoretical distinction between charity and justice, but we want to affirm that on the concrete, existential plane the person who does justice cannot be distinguished from the person who loves. Moreover, for Christianity *the two notions are inseparable*, each one implying the other. Let us examine this statement in more detail.

55/   First and most important is what the Synod document itself tells us: "Christian love of neighbor and justice cannot be separated. For love implies an absolute demand for justice, that is, recognition of the dignity and rights of one's neighbor."[18] How is it possible to love and to be unjust toward the person loved? Removing justice from love is to destroy its very essence. There is no such thing as love which fails to consider and recognize the beloved as a person and to respect that person's dignity, with all that that implies.

56/   The second point assumes the first: "Justice attains its intrinsic completeness only in love." Even when using the Roman notion of justice ("giving all persons what is owed to them"), Christians must affirm that what they owe all human beings, enemies included, is precisely love. The Synod gives us the reason for this: "Since every person is truly a visible image of the invisible God and a sibling of Christ, Christians find God himself in every person and therefore recognize God's absolute demand for justice and love."[19] Saint Paul confirms this teaching: "Pay to all what is due them—taxes to whom taxes are due, revenue to whom revenue is due, respect to whom respect is due, honor to whom honor is due. Owe no one anything except to love one another, for the one who loves another has fulfilled the law. . . . All the other commandments are summed up in this word, 'Love your neighbor as yourself.' . . . Therefore, love is the fulfilling of the law."[20]

57/   We have still one more step to take in this process of identification. It is impossible to conceive of Christian love that does not begin with justice and include justice as a constitutive element, but we cannot talk sensibly about Christian justice either if it is not crowned with love. Indeed, there is still more to be said because we are not talking just about human love but about love infused in us by God: no one can be just without loving with the very love that is God's gift to us. "The message of Jesus," Father Alfaro tells us, "carries the Old Testament demands regarding justice to the most profound human level, to the most radical interior dimensions of love; only sincere love of neighbor can give us the strength we need to make justice effective in the world."[21]

58/   Just as we never know whether we love God unless we love our neighbor, so also we never know whether we love our neighbor unless we do so with a love that has justice as its first fruit. I would even dare to say that the most difficult step for us to take is that step from love to justice; it is the step that is least prone to self-delusion, and it most clearly reveals whether our religious attitude is a charade or not.[22]

59/   Clearly, we are talking about justice as revealed to us in the Word of God. We understand it in the light provided by the scriptures and actively catalyzed by the signs of the times. This justice is not limited to an individualist kind of "accomplishment." Rather, it consists, first of all, in an attitude of enduring respect for all men and women, such that they are never used as instruments for the profit of others. Second, this justice demands a determined effort never to take advantage of or be cajoled into situations and mechanisms of privilege (which are correspondingly mechanisms of oppression); even by passively tolerating such situations, we make ourselves accomplices of this world's injustice, and we silently enjoy the fruits of that injustice. Third, this justice requires us to mount a counter-offensive, that is, we must resolve to dismantle the unjust structures by taking the side of the weak, the oppressed, and the marginalized.

60/ Those who practice this dynamic and this liberating type of justice will seek above all to eliminate injustice from their own lives. Such justice has nothing in common with the vindictive hatefulness of those who feel oppressed or those who are simply reacting against their oppression. The persons who practice this liberating justice will gain nothing by it in this life because they will have to forego many of the fruits of the unjust structures. Moreover, their active solidarity with the weak will bring on them the persecution of the powerful, as was the case with Christ and the prophets. It is clear that no one can make this commitment unless impelled and sustained by love for other human beings and by love (sometimes anonymous) for God. Love is at the root of true justice, and love is also its crown and the seal of its authenticity. We can express all this in still another way: justice is the modality necessarily adopted by authentic love in a world lacerated by personal and structural injustices. In this kind of world, love takes the form of an option for the marginalized and the oppressed because that is the only way to love all human beings, and that is the only way to liberate the oppressed from oppression and the oppressors from the misery of being oppressors. This perspective helps us to understand better the power for renewal that comes from Christ's personal self-identification with the little ones and those who are suffering.

d) Personal conversion and reform of structures

61/ Let us proceed now to the harmonization of the fourth pair of concepts: personal conversion and reform of structures. To do this, let me make a small detour, which we'll soon see is closely connected with what has gone before.

62/ The asceticism of Christian tradition is founded on the following basic truth: sin is not only a personal act that affects the inmost center of ourselves and makes us guilty of offending, but it extends also to what might be called the surface of our being, where it disorders our habits, our customs, our spontaneous reactions, our criteria for judgment, our ways of thinking, our will, and our imagination. At the same time, we are not the only ones who influence what we have called the surface of our personality; it is also affected by all those who have educated us and been part of our lives. We know, moreover, that we have been born with original sin and a nature that is inclined to evil—what is called "concupiscence" in theological language. Concretely, concupiscence in each of us is the combined effect of the sin of Adam and all the personal sins of history, including our own. All of them have a negative effect on our manner of being and acting.

63/   When we are converted, that is, when God works in us the marvel of justification, then our personal center turns both to God and to neighbor so that sin in the strict sense disappears from our inward being. Nevertheless, the effects of sin continue to exercise their tremendous power on the surface of our being, even though we are sometimes not even conscious of it. Those effects are also called "sin" by Saint Paul; they are objectifications or materializations of sin which remain in those who have already been justified. The Council of Trent tells us that concupiscence can be called sin, not because it is sin in the strict sense but because "it proceeds from sin and inclines toward sin."[23]

64/   As we noted above, this truth is the foundation of Christian asceticism and spirituality. Christ has come to liberate us from sin and to flood the center of our being with his grace, but that grace must display its full potency by conquering for God not only our inner being but also what we have called the surface. Such conquest is necessary in order for justification to produce even more abundant fruits through works of love for God and for other human beings. The work of Christ is not destined to remain hidden away in the secret depths of each human heart, working there a mysterious transformation which will become outwardly known only in the other life. Christ came not only to eliminate sin but also the present effects of sin in this life. To deny this would be to minimize Christian asceticism and spirituality. What is more, concupiscence is not only something that proceeds from sin; it is a materialization of sin itself, so that if it is not combated and eliminated to the fullest extent possible, then it will tend to reproduce itself in the form of personal sin. Consequently, acquiescing to concupiscence means acquiescing to sin itself (and sinning in the strict sense).

65/   Let us now try to relate all this to our effort to relate personal conversion and reform of structures. In a certain sense, these two concepts fit well with what we just said. We have already seen that it is not enough to understand personal conversion strictly in terms of the justification that is brought about in the interior depths of our personality. Such justification is only the root source (though, in the long run, also the effect) of a process of renewal and reform of the outward structures of our being, which at first remain outside our personal center but can little by little be reformed *from* that center.

66/   Naturally we struggle against concupiscence and the effects of sin, which tend to keep sin itself alive, but in doing so, need we limit our struggle only to the effects that influence us individually and affect only our own personal structure? Why not attack also the effects that influence all of us through the social structures in which we live? There is no profound theological reason not to do so. In this regard, there has been a lacuna in our traditional ascetical and spiritual teaching, and to understand why this is so we should realize that in the past people were more or less conscious that they can change themselves but not much more. Given this consciousness, which was reinforced by Christianity, people felt a moral imperative to change and to eliminate the traces of sin in themselves. It is only in very recent times that people have become aware that the world in which they live—with its structures, its organizations, its ideas, its systems, etc.—is also in large part a product of human freedom and is therefore modifiable and changeable if people truly have a mind to change it.

67/   If we grant this, then the consequences come quickly. In large part, the structures of this world are also objectivizations of sin—by structures we mean customs; laws; social, economic, and political systems; exchange relations; and in general the concrete forms of human interactions. The structures are objectified sin, that is, the fruit of historical sin, and at the same time they are the continual source of new sins. We even have the benefit of a biblical concept to designate this reality: it is the "sin of the world" in the negative sense given it by Saint John. If this concept has not been developed in theology in the same way that the concept of concupiscence has, it is because earlier times did not allow us to go beyond a purely individualist conception of sin. Now that we have developed a new consciousness, we need simply apply to the "sin of the world" the same theological concepts devised for concupiscence in order to give it a tremendous new dynamism. The "sin of the world" becomes in the social sphere what concupiscence is in the individual sphere. We could even call it "social concupiscence," which, like individual concupiscence, "proceeds from sin and inclines toward sin." Accordingly, social concupiscence should be the object of our efforts to achieve ascetical purification, in the same way that individual concupiscence is; in this way, a basis would be provided for a new spirituality, or even better, a drastic expansion of the traditional field of asceticism and spirituality.

68/   We have always been told that interior conversion is not enough; we must continually strive to improve ourselves and reclaim for God the whole of our being. Now we become aware that what we have to reclaim and reform is also the whole of our world. In other words, personal conversion cannot be separated from reform of structures. Even if the former is fundamental in the sense that all objectivization of sin proceeds from personal sins and is overcome only through personal conversion, it is also true that, once the objectivizations of sin (especially those of a more general nature) become established, they maintain such a grip on the lives of many people that personal conversion becomes almost impossible without eliminating the objectivizations themselves. It is also true that none of us can say that we have been personally converted if we still take advantage of those structures for our own benefit or if, being aware of our involvement in them, we simply acquiesce to the structures and reject the idea of eliminating them. As is the case in our individual lives, abstentionism is of no use here but is rather a form of collaborating with sin.

69/   That is why we can affirm, in accord with the Synod, that the "dyna-mism of the Gospel" frees people not only from personal sin but also "from its consequences in social life," because "action on behalf of justice and par-ticipation in the transformation of this world" are "constitutive dimensions of the preaching of the Gospel and the Church's mission."[24]

e) Salvation and liberation in this life and in the other

70/   We have perforce already arrived at the fifth of our harmonized the-ses: salvation and liberation in this life and in the other. The Synod text we just read is quite explicit, but there is another which is even more so: "The mission of preaching the Gospel dictates at the present time that we should dedicate ourselves to the liberation of people even in their present existence in this world."[25]

71/   Let us observe here that we are not being told that our this-worldly efforts will fully attain for us in this life the salvation we seek. Neither are we being told that Christian salvation consists simply in the this-worldly objec-tives for which we strive. Ultimately our hope always resides in something beyond. Moreover, as we've warned already, those who truly work on behalf of justice can hardly expect anything else in this life except persecution.

72/   Nevertheless, that does not mean, first of all, that the tension involved in achieving that this-worldly purification and liberation is not an intrinsic part of the Christian attitude, such that those who reject such tension and refuse to struggle for justice are implicitly renouncing love for their fellow human beings and consequently love for God. Second, the con-viction that the struggle for justice never ends and that our efforts are never going to be crowned with complete success in this life does not mean that they are useless or that they achieve nothing at all. Even partial successes are desired by God for they are the first fruits of the salvation brought by Jesus; they are signs of the coming of God's Kingdom; and their abid-ing aspects are anticipatory realizations, even if not complete ones, of the Kingdom that has already come and that is always mysteriously growing among us. Third, the failure experienced by those who are defeated and destroyed in their struggle against the world is only apparent, for the world inevitably pursues and tries to annihilate all those who are not of the world and those who are opposed to it. The persons who, like Christ, "go about doing good and healing everyone"[26] are precisely the ones who die on a cross. The eschatological future of their personal existences is in the hands of God for they were faithful to his Covenant established for the liberation of the poor, and they were faithful to the point of death.

f) The Christian ethos and its technological and ideological mediations

73/   I will treat this final harmonizing thesis very briefly, but it is an important one; without this thesis, this whole talk could be characterized either as ineffective "angelism" or as revolutionary "immediatism"—that is, something ultimately and absolutely futile. Everything we have presented thus far moves at the level of what we might call the "Christian ethos for justice," and it provides us the basic attitudes we need. However, passing to action, which is one of the components of that ethos, requires the mediation of technologies and even of ideologies. These are needed first of all for analysis. It is not enough simply to state in general fashion that there are injustices in the world. We must also study the concrete context of this world in order to discover the neuralgic points where sin and injustice are entrenched. Second, there is also a need for technologies, ideologies, and dynamic reform programs to demonstrate the existence of various types of injustice and to uproot them effectively from their bastions. To do that we need plans, tactics, and strategies; we need ordered hierarchies of objectives and determined time-lines; and these are almost always incompatible with the naïve demand for immediate results.

74/   It is no simple matter to harmonize the simple Christian ethos in favor of justice and the technological and ideological mediations that are required by the ethos itself. A certain tension is inevitable and beneficial. Without the mediations, the ethos is useless, but we must also remember that the ethos, if it lets itself become submerged in the complexity of the

242 Promotion of Justice and Education for Justice, 1973

mediations, runs the risk of being suffocated or deformed or hopelessly lost in the labyrinth. We must not forget that the technologies and the ideologies, as necessary as they may be, are also the joint products of what is good and what is sinful. Injustice can also infect them, no matter what sign they carry.

75/ The Christian ethos must make use of the mediations, but it must also judge them and relativize them and never allow them to become idols. The encyclical *Octogesima Adveniens* recognizes how much value there is in protest and in utopian ideals for gaining a critical perspective on ideologies and especially on the systems by which the ideologies seek to become concrete reality. "Such criticism of the established society often stimulates the future-oriented imagination not only to perceive the disregarded possibilities hidden within the present but also to direct itself towards a fresh future; it thus sustains social dynamism by the confidence it imparts to the inventive powers of the human mind and heart; and finally, if it remains open to the fullness of reality, it can respond anew to the Christian calling." We could affirm in this regard that what we have thus far called the Christian ethos in favor of justice is a utopian ideal characterized by—to continue citing *Octagesima Adveniens*—"the Spirit of the Lord, who animates a humanity renewed in Christ and continually breaks down the horizons within which human understanding likes to find security and the limits to which human activity would gladly restrict itself. There dwells within men and women a power which urges them to go beyond every system and every ideology. . . . The dynamism of Christian faith here triumphs over the narrow calculations of egoism. Animated by the power of the Spirit of Jesus Christ, the Savior of humankind, and upheld by hope, Christians involve themselves in the building up of the human city, one that is called to be peaceful, just, fraternal, and acceptable as an offering to God."[27]

76/ None of this, however, denies the need for technological and even ideological mediations. We may have a healthy reaction against the deification of particular systems and ideologies[28]—or against technology and science themselves when they become ideologies[29]—but that reaction should not make us think that we can build a better world without their help. *Octogesima Adveniens* also warns us about this danger: "The appeal to a utopia is often a convenient excuse for those who wish to escape from concrete tasks in order to take refuge in an imaginary world. To live in a hypothetical future is a facile pretext for rejecting immediate responsibilities."[30]

77/   This is all the more true insofar as Christians can look to the Church and her hierarchy for spiritual light and nourishment. However, lay people should not imagine that their pastors are always great experts; they cannot be expected to give a concrete solution to every problem which arises, no matter how complicated, nor should their mission be conceived as such.[31] As a religious and hierarchical community, the Church can provide society with what we have called the Christian ethos for justice, which involves criticism, relativization, and demythologization of particular systems and ideologies. Such an ethos works for the "defense and promotion of the dignity and fundamental rights of the human person," and a constitutive part of her mission is "to denounce instances of injustice, when the fundamental rights of people and their very salvation demand it."[32] *Octogesima Adveniens,* however, warns us that none of this is sufficient by itself. "It is not enough to recall principles, declare intentions, point to crying injustices and utter prophetic denunciations; these words will lack real weight unless they are accompanied by a livelier awareness of personal responsibility and by effective action on the part of each individual."[33]

78/   To take the step into action, we need mediations, and every Christian must decide concretely how the mediations are to be handled. "The members of the Church . . . must accept their responsibilities in this entire area. . . . In this way they testify to the power of the Holy Spirit through their service to others in those things which are decisive for the existence and the future of humanity. While in such activities they generally act on their own initiative without involving the responsibility of the ecclesiastical hierarchy, in a sense they do involve the responsibility of the Church whose members they are."[34]

II. MEN AND WOMEN FOR OTHERS: PERMANENT FORMATION AND EDUCATION FOR JUSTICE

79/   After this long dissertation on the Christian notion of justice, I would be happy if we were able to gain from it just one fruit: the conviction that we are far from completely assimilating this notion either in our spontaneous ways of thinking or in our practical activities. If we have come to this conviction, then we have taken a decisive step toward achieving the principal objective of this talk and even of this assembly.

80/   The reason why we are meeting here is to rethink the meaning and the goals of our Alumni Associations, and we believe in principle that such associations are called today to be privileged channels of ongoing formation.

81/   Today there is much talk of ongoing formation, but it is often understood in a very limited way. It is seen simply as a matter of updating our technical and professional skills so that we can keep up with the ever more challenging competition we face. Sometimes ongoing formation also includes the goal of reeducating people to live in a "totally different society" or to face the challenge of a continually changing world. This task is absolutely necessary for living in today's world, but it cannot give us all we need. From the perspective of Christian values, such reeducation is a neutral task and can even be a negative one; it all depends on the basic orientation we have given to our existence. To the extent that we orient them toward others and toward justice, there is positive value in technical and professional training and in the ability to find new meaning in the midst of change; but if we use them only for our own personal interests or for our group interests, then they are negative. In any case, the concept of ongoing formation, as used in common parlance, lacks what is most specific to all Christian formation, namely, the call to conversion. Speaking about ongoing formation in Christianity means speaking about continual conversion, and today that means speaking specifically about formation for justice.

82/   We were not joking when we began this talk by confessing that we have not really been educated for justice. Only when we become aware of this lack and make this humble confession, accompanied by a determination to change, will it make sense for us to discuss seriously the problem of our own formation. Naturally, I leave to your own deliberations the analysis of the concrete forms which this formation for justice can and should take, and I also leave to your study and judgment the choice of the organizational means for putting it into practice.

83/   Under the general motto, "men and women for others," I am going to limit myself in this second part of my talk to sketching out three series of considerations. The first will try to justify our use of this expression and explain the meaning we have given it. The second series will consider one indispensable quality that those "men and women for others" should have today if they truly want to serve others effectively: they must be agents and promoters of change. The third series will deal with another important and quite radical condition: that of being a person docile before God. "Men and women for others" should be persons who are impelled by the Holy Spirit, the Spirit whose anointing will endow them with flexibility and sensitivity in their most inward being. Thus inspired, they will be able to discern, hear, and follow the Spirit's voice, which will be made manifest to them in the works which the same Spirit accomplishes in the world, in the entire life of the Church, and in their own personal depths. All this will take place in the light of a continual rereading of the Gospel message, which will release little by little, in an unending process, the fullness of its meaning and its demands.

A. Men and Women for Others: Justification and Meaning of the Phrase

a) Preliminary considerations

84/   My first approximation will be of a philosophical nature but without any pretensions. It seems that the human person may be characterized as a "being for self," that is, a being centered on himself or herself. Simple reflection on the data of our experience provides us with evidence that a being's degree of plenitude and perfection increases in proportion to its internal capacity for self-centralization, which paradoxically coincides with the degree of its complexity. The most perfect beings are at once the most centralized and the most complex: we move from protons to atoms to simple molecules to crystals to macromolecules to viruses to protozoan cells to complex plants, which harmonize and unify millions of cells, and finally to animals, which have even greater complexity and yet also a greater centrality, giving them sensation and movement. Finally there are human beings, possessed of the radical centrality that endows them with consciousness. Thanks to their intelligence and the power they derive from it, human beings tend to dominate the world by taking control of it and orienting its activities to themselves.

85/   Nevertheless, we also know from experience that human beings can "lose their center" when they become too self-centered. Each human person is a spiritual center endowed with consciousness, intelligence, and power. But we are centers who are called to go out of ourselves, to give of ourselves, and to reach out to others in love. Love is the definitive and encompassing dimension of human beings; it is the dimension that gives all the other dimensions their meaning, their value, or their lack of value. Only the person who loves becomes fully realized as human. We are most truly persons not when we close in upon ourselves but when we open up to others. Our "knowing" and our "having," that is, our centering on ourselves and appropriating things through intelligence or power, are certainly dimensions that enrich us, but they are such only to the extent that they do not close us off to other persons but rather enhance our loving self-donation to others. When people not only increase their worldly "knowledge" or "wealth" but also place them at the service of humanity, they are carrying out the task of humanizing themselves and humanizing the world.

b) The dehumanization of egotism

86/   Frequently, however, things happen otherwise, and the centralizing movement stops within the person. When there is an accumulation of "knowledge" and "power" and "wealth" and they are used exclusively to serve oneself and are withdrawn from others, then the process becomes perverted and dehumanizing.

First of all, the accumulating process dehumanizes the direct victims of the conduct. The least that can be said of persons who do not live for others is that they contribute nothing to their sisters and brothers. The first step in the ladder is thus a sin of omission of which we are almost never conscious. This sin can take the form of simply a listless existence, or it can go further and take the form of an existence based on speculative transactions. In this group can also be placed those who participate positively in the productive process (by contributing to the growth of wealth or knowledge), but who take such advantage of their situation of privilege and power in setting the terms of contracts that those who are weaker end up with a negative balance.

87/   Let us suppose, however, that we are in a situation where there is still no type of unjust appropriation. Those persons who live for themselves alone fail to contribute anything to society, but what is more, they tend to accumulate ever greater parcels of knowledge, power, and wealth, and in so doing they displace from the centers of power great multitudes of persons, leaving them marginalized.

88/   Not only that, but selfish persons do not humanize things, for the only way that things can be humanized is by putting them at the service of others. Instead, they convert human persons into things, making them objects of exploitation and domination and appropriating to themselves part of the fruit of their labor.

89/   Second, at a more radical level, those who do not live for others dehumanize themselves. Such cases are unfortunately very common because, for such dehumanization to take place, it is not necessary to take advantage of others in reality; it is sufficient simply to desire to do so. Many persons who are victims of the indifference or the oppression of others also become tyrants over themselves (and sometimes over other persons as well) simply because they have assimilated the behavioral patterns of their oppressors. Almost all of us—especially those of us imprisoned by the subtle webs of consumer society—take an active part in this suicidal work of dehumanization.

90/   If we're honest, we'll admit that we all tend to evaluate ourselves by the same criteria that society uses to evaluate us. And modern society does not value people for what they *are* or even for what they *know,* but simply for what they *have* or what they *can obtain.* Power and wealth are the measures of value. Our spontaneous tendency, therefore, is to identify with our wealth. In the eyes of others and in our own eyes, our being and our value are measured by the wealth we possess. When this happens, wealth very quickly ceases to be a means and becomes rather an end. Human beings need very few things to live humanly, but their desires know no limits when their value is measured by wealth or by the power they possess. Even when we complain about being treated as "things," we actually make ourselves into things when we identify with our wealth. We have the conviction that we have triumphed in life, not when we have given disinterestedly to others but when we have gained a position, won a business deal, exercised influence, bought a farm, or fattened our stock portfolio.

91/   Nevertheless, something deep within us gets revealed each time we define ourselves in terms of things. We feel frustrated. In our depths we know that what we possess does not determine who we are or what we are worth. We want simply to be ourselves, but we don't dare to break the vicious circle. We strive to "have even more" or, what is worse, to "have more than others," thus making life into a senseless competition. The spiral of ambition, competitiveness, and self-destruction twists endlessly over itself, in ever wider circles that bind us with ever greater force to a dehumanized, frustrating existence. As a result, it becomes ever more necessary to increase our power and improve the efficacy of the mechanisms that produce oppression and yield profit. In this way, our dehumanization of ourselves leads directly to the dehumanization of others, which we spoke of in an earlier section.

92/   This brings us to the third dehumanizing aspect of our selfish attitudes: not only do they dehumanize ourselves and others, but they dehumanize social structures as well. This is one of the clearest examples of what I called "objectified sin" in the first part of my talk. As a result of our sins of selfishness and our dehumanizing acts, which not only exploit others but also destroy our own human integrity, sin becomes hardened and objectified into ideas, structures, and anonymous organisms that escape our direct control. Sin installs itself in the world as a titanic force that has us firmly in its grip.

c) The humanization of love

93/   How to escape from this vicious circle? It truly is a circle, because the three dehumanizing effects of unrestrained selfishness weave themselves tightly together to form a knot that is nearly impossible to untie. We are well aware that personal egotism, the sum total of all our personal attitudes of selfishness, is at the root of this whole process. But at the same time we feel that it would be useless and even suicidal to try to live lives of love and justice in a world where most other people are selfish and unjust and where injustice and selfishness have become structurally entrenched.

94/   Such lives, however, are precisely what the Christian message impels us to live; in fact, they are the essence of Christian ethics. Saint Paul wrote something that illustrates precisely what I'm trying to tell you; he stated, "Do not be overcome by evil, but overcome evil with good."[35] As we'll see, this teaching reflects the teaching of Christ about love of enemies; it is the touchstone of Christianity. We would all like to be good to others, and all of us, or at least most of us, *would* be relatively good in a good world. What is difficult is being good in a bad world, in a world where structural selfishness and the selfishness of others assault us from all sides and threaten to annihilate us. When that happens, we believe that the only possible reaction is fighting evil with evil, selfishness with selfishness, hate with hate; if possible, we would even destroy the aggressors with their own arms. But that is precisely the moment when evil conquers us most thoroughly and most deeply. Not only does it destroy us externally, but it also dehumanizes us and perverts us from within. It inoculates us with its own poison; it makes us evil. That is what Saint Paul calls being overcome with evil.

95/   Evil can be overcome only by good, hate only by love, selfishness only by generosity; all those are necessary in this concrete world in order to implant justice. In order to be just, we have to do more than simply refrain from contributing to the already gigantic reserve of injustice in the world; we must also voluntarily experience the effects of injustice, we must refuse to continue playing its game, and above all we must replace its dynamic of hatred with the dynamic of love. For that purpose, we need more than the love of the self-interested, who love only their friends and hate their enemies. That is no solution; at best, it maintains the status quo. Christian love, in contrast, is like God's love, which makes the sun rise on both the good and the evil.[36] This creative love does not love only what is lovable; it loves everything, and by the power of love makes everything that is loved lovable.

96/   In the same passage Saint Paul tells us: "Bless those who curse you; bless and do not curse them. . . . Do not repay anyone evil for evil, but take thought for what is noble in the sight of all. If it is possible, so far as it depends on you, live peacefully with all. Beloved, never avenge yourselves. . . . No, if your enemies are hungry, feed them; if they are thirsty, give them something to drink; for by doing this you will heap burning coals on their heads"[37]—those are burning coals of affection that will eventually soften their hearts and restore their humanity. We must sow love in this way, planting the seeds of love where there is no love so that one day we may harvest love. It is true that, between the sowing and the harvest, the grain of wheat may just possibly die. Only the grain that dies bears fruit. But herein lies the true victory, the victory in which there are no losers. We were saying before that when other people's hatred of us gives birth to hatred in ourselves, we are the losers; we are the ones who are overcome, even when we succeed in crushing our enemy. But when we respond to hatred with love and even give our lives if necessary, as Christ did, loving and forgiving our enemies, then most probably we are the ones who will end up infusing our love into others. That is when we most truly overcome, by achieving a complete victory in which there are no losers but only winners because our enemies have become our friends, our sisters and brothers.

97/ The great difficulty is that all this seems to us quite lovely but hopelessly ineffective. We do not have faith in love. Nevertheless, nothing is more effective than love. In fact, if we were to use this strategy of God, then the pain and suffering that human beings experience in constantly defending themselves and in futilely trying to implant a bit of justice in the world would be much less than it is. Many people, even those with high ideals and noble aims, are willing to kill for the sake of establishing justice in the world. Indeed, many are willing to die fighting for that goal. But there are very few who are willing to die simply loving. Yet it's almost never necessary to go that far. Normally it's enough just to love and put up with some of the consequences of loving. In order to drive back the realm of injustice significantly, I think it would be enough simply to reproduce a series of well-coordinated groups of valuable people whose lives are guided by the spirit I'm speaking of here, which I will try to describe more concretely in the following section.

B. Agents and Promoters of Change

98/ Let us not forget that, although the root of the kingdom of injustice is within ourselves (which is why we dedicate our best efforts to reeducating and reforming ourselves), injustice is structurally embedded in the world and functions independently of any individual. What is more, we cannot completely change ourselves if we do not change our world. Education for justice is therefore educating for change; it means forming men and women who will be effective agents for change and transformation.

99/ As we saw in the first part, what we need is a formation that enables us to analyze the situations that must be transformed in each concrete case and to elaborate efficient strategies and tactics for attaining the goals of transformation and liberation. That task obviously exceeds the objectives of this talk, although it possibly does not exceed the objectives of the Alumni Associations. I believe that you alumni, among yourselves, should undertake initiatives of this type at different levels, with diverse degrees of coordination, and with a wide latitude of pluralism.

100/ Here I will limit myself simply to indicating some very general attitudes which I believe we should form part of the tactics we develop in everything we undertake. I wish also to call attention to the need for us to stimulate a forward-looking imagination, that is, an imagination that makes us take very seriously the task of building a better future for humanity.

a) General attitudes for promoting change

101/ I'm going to enumerate just three general attitudes that will contribute effectively to change, especially when diverse groups adopt these attitudes and apply them in coordinated action.

102/ The first attitude is a firm resolve to give a much simpler tone to our individual, family, social, and collective lives by refusing to take part in the spiral of luxurious living and social competitiveness. Making drastic reductions in our festivities, our gifts, our clothing, and our accoutrements would free us from the need for certain (perhaps rather dubious) sources of income or would allow us to direct such income generously toward others. Such reductions would also serve as a symbolic gesture of tremendous social efficacy.

103/ Let me give you one very simple example. Celebrating a certain class of wedding easily costs a half-million to a million pesetas. Such extravagance is not necessary in order to attain the legitimate and deeply human satisfaction of bringing good friends together for such a moment. If we're really sincere, we'll admit that we're aiming for more than conviviality; the wedding becomes a question of social prestige, and often it's even a calculated scheme of exchanging gifts. Such costly weddings also have the disturbing social consequence of inciting social competitiveness; the people among whom we move cannot be disappointed; the next wedding has to be better still, and the money to pay for it has to be gotten in any way possible. This is just another turn in the screw of luxury and oppression, which gets twisted ever deeper into the structure of the world and becomes firmly fixed there. The decadent example spreads, and those with fewer means join the game as well, often spending money they don't have. Thus to the foolish idol of prestige are sacrificed values that are much more fulfilling and profound, such as a reasonable honeymoon, a comfortable apartment for the new couple, etc.

104/   What would happen if a group of Christians, publicly announcing their decision, were to break with the usual ways of acting? At the explicit desire of the couple, guests would be invited to a simple, truly religious ceremony in which the love between the spouses would be honored; they would both promise to support one another mutually and to form a community open to helping others and to working for great humanization of the world. Such a ceremony would be accompanied by a frugal repast with the guests and the donation of a hefty sum—the largest expense of all—to some work of human development.

105/   The example has value but only as a symbol. Such a symbol would serve no purpose at all unless it truly expressed a totally new conception of a way of life which needs to be made concrete in many other details. We must form men and women who are not enslaved to a consumer society and whose lives are not ruled by the desire to be and to appear a little better than others. Rather, their ideal should be to trail always slightly behind others in order to unscrew bit by bit the screw of luxury and competitiveness. They should be men and women who, instead of feeling compelled to buy everything that the next-door family has managed to buy, are able to do without many things that others in like circumstance do without and that most of humankind must willy-nilly do without. The ancient counsel of moralists, when they were trying to determine what level of luxury was in keeping with the Gospel, was that Christians should adopt without excess whatever was customary at each social level. But this counsel is no longer useful since it presupposed a static society that was concerned only about individual justice. Such a society could not even conceive that the very social structure which determines those different social levels was itself an incarnation of injustice. Since that is in fact the case, the only attitude that can be considered truly moral in our day is one which strives to dismantle and level out the established social pyramids. Viewing it from another perspective, we need to form truly liberated men and women who are not slaves of consumer society—men and women who, when viewing the TV advertisements and the display windows of the stores, rejoice with satisfaction in their own freedom and are able to exclaim, "What a lot of things I can do without! How free I am!"

106/ I'll be much briefer in describing the second and third fundamental attitudes.

107/ The second attitude is a firm resolve not only to refrain from sharing in any gain from clearly unjust dealings, but also to gradually reduce one's own sharing in the benefits accruing from social and economic structures that are decisively organized to favor the most powerful sectors of society. It's not a question of reducing one's expenses and even less of reducing income based on unjust structures. Rather, it is a conviction that obliges us to move against the current. Instead of trying always to shore up our position of privilege, we should rather let it decline in favor of those who are less privileged. The Alumni Associations should carry out honest and thorough analyses to determine the extent to which our most advantaged citizens (well-situated professionals, big-business owners, industrial and financial magnates, etc.) appropriate to themselves a share of the social product that is in excess of what it would be if social structures were more just. And I would ask you not to exclude yourselves too quickly from this analysis, because I am convinced that all persons of a certain social level enjoy these advantages, at least in certain ways, even if they are, at the same time, unfairly disadvantaged compared to even more affluent groups. But let us not forget that our decisive point of reference are the masses of truly poor people in our own countries and in the Third World.

108/ The third attitude is connected with the second. It may be possible for us to reduce our expenses and live a much simpler life without clashing with society's norms. It is true that our attitude may arouse displeasure, but for that very reason it does society some good. If we propose, however, to reduce our income to the extent that it derives from our participation in unjust structures, then that is not possible without transforming the structures themselves. It would then be inevitable that those who feel themselves displaced from their privileged positions, along with us, would adopt a defensive position of counterattack. Renouncing every position of influence would be too facile a solution.

109/ In certain cases, such renunciations may be appropriate, but for the most part they would only serve to hand over the entire world to those who are most avaricious. This is the basic reason why the struggle for justice is so difficult, and it also shows the need for mediations, as we've mentioned already. But here we can enlighten one another through the Alumni Associations themselves, by calling on our alumni who belong to the working class. Even though the thematic of this second part of my conference has shifted to other perspectives, we should not forget that the principal agents of transformation and change are going to be the people who are oppressed. The corollary of this is that those who are more privileged, when they take up the cause of the oppressed, will be simple collaborators who are managing the control points of the structures that need to be changed.

b) Building the future

110/ Let me offer a few more words about how you can collaborate responsibly in building the future. Ralph Lapp compares our world to "a train that is gaining speed and moving swiftly along tracks with switches that lead to unknown destinations. There is not a single scientist in the locomotive, and there may be demons at the switches. Most of society is in the caboose, looking backward."[38]

111/ The love that Christians have for their fellow human beings will inspire them to try to take control of the locomotive and guide the train toward the right destination. But that requires many things: knowledge of how the controls work, familiarity with the territory through which the train is traveling, information about the system controlling the switches, and even familiarity with the demons meddling with the switches. At the controls of the locomotive it is not enough to have persons of good will; it's not even enough to have the scientific experts mentioned in the quote. The persons we need at the controls are profound thinkers in the sense that I will explain in a minute. We might even say that we need spiritual persons there in the cabin of the locomotive, true sages who know how to exorcise the demons ruling the world.

112/ Sometimes a long detour through rough terrain may be the only way to avoid catastrophe. That's why it will be necessary to deal with the anger of the passengers at the back of the train who want to travel only through rolling countryside. Christians should never forget that they are at the service of the people who are traveling in the train. They are men and women for others, and for that very reason they must prudently but resolutely have recourse to the necessary technological and ideological mediations. And they must do so without forgetting their fundamental ethos and without converting the mediations into ends, for that would be equivalent to abandoning the locomotive and a forward-looking vision; it would be like retreating to a laboratory car in the train and being quite as isolated from the truth of reality as those traveling in the caboose.

113/ But neither can Christians be dilettantes who try to find the right track by random guesses or who let themselves be carried away by the trendiest currents or countercurrents. Following the latest trend is especially dangerous when people react, often with good reason, against some excess by moving vehemently in the opposite direction. Every form of totalitarianism has taken root in societies dominated by that type of reaction. Alvin Toffler, while rejecting the idolization of technology, is reacting against a contemporary tendency which simply rejects technology out of hand. He writes: "We should ask those who, in the name of some vague human values, preach anti-technological absurdities: what do you understand by 'human'? To turn the clock back deliberately would mean condemning billions of human beings to a state of permanent, inescapable misery, precisely at the moment in history when their liberation becomes possible. It is clear that we need more, not less, technology. At the same time, it is undoubtedly true that we often apply new technologies in stupid and selfish ways." It is for that reason that legitimate reactions against technocracy arise, but these reactions become stupid themselves if they are absolutized. Toffler states: "These protests against the ravages caused by irresponsible use of technology could crystallize pathologically into an anti-futuristic fascism in which scientists would replace the Jews in the concentration camps. Sick societies need scapegoats. As the pressure of change increases on individuals and future shock gains force, this nightmare ending appears more likely. There was a very significant slogan scrawled on a wall by the students in the Paris strike: 'Kill the technocrats!' The incipient worldwide movement for control of technology should not be allowed to fall into the hands of irresponsible technophobes, nihilists, and Rousseauian romantics."[39]

114/ This is just one example that speaks to us of the difficulty of the task before us. It makes us mindful of the sincerity, the prudence, and the profundity with which Christians should act in this sphere.

C. The "Spiritual" Person

115/ We reach the point in this talk where I want to show that only "spiritual" persons—in the sense of men or women of God who are led by the Spirit—will in the long run be able to be persons for others, persons for justice, persons capable of contributing to a true transformation of the world that will eliminate from it the structures of sin.

116/ In saying this, I do not deny that there are men and women of impeccable good will who share with genuine Christians all the qualities noted in our exposition. To the extent that this is the case, they are in our eyes the ones who are today called "anonymous Christians." They are our sisters and brothers who, in loving their fellow human beings radically and sincerely, love God and his Christ without knowing it. The only thing they need is to hear the Good News of the Gospel, which gives their faith, their hope, and their love precise expression and completion.

a) The infusion of love

117/   According to Saint John, love has its origin in God. God takes the initiative. Love does not consist in our loving God but in God's loving us.[40] By loving us, God has transformed us in turn into founts of love that have the same characteristics as God's own love, which is a self-surrendering love that bears with enmity and so overcomes it. It is love that allows itself to be killed by the injustice of this world but in dying destroys injustice, thus converting the triumph of evil into defeat. It is love which embraces the enemy with transformative love, making the one loved lovable and thus converting him into a friend. In the end, it is a love that is effective and victorious. That is the love that God has infused into us by his Spirit. If we have such love and truly love our sisters and brothers, then we have been born of God. If we reject it and do not truly love our sisters and brothers, then we reject God's love and with it the gift of his Spirit which makes us children of God and sisters and brothers of Jesus Christ.[41]

118/   In its essence, Christian faith is faith in love.[42] What is more, it is faith in victorious love and so the foundation of our hope. That is why Saint John can declare: "This is the victory that conquers the world: our faith."[43]

b) Discernment of spirits

119/   This love which is the first aspect of our life in the Spirit is without a doubt the principal one and the one that gives energy to all the rest, but it is not enough. Not only must we love, but we must love with discernment. And here is where we need to understand the second way in which a person can be "spiritual."

120/   This concrete world, from which we must dislodge the injustice imbedded in ourselves and in the structures of society, is in fact a product of the joint influence of the Holy Spirit and of sin. That is why, when striving for justice, we need the gifts of counsel and discernment; we need to be able to distinguish between diverse spirits in order to separate, in each feature of the world, what comes from God and what comes from sin. Neither simple observation nor sociological analysis of our social reality is sufficient. Some people try to identify the results of sociological analysis with the "signs of the times," but they run the risk of understanding as a work of God what is perhaps an effect of sin. Sociology provides us only the raw material on which spiritual discernment must be exercised. With the help of spiritual discernment, our task is to discover where precisely the sin of the world is located and, above all, where it is most densely concentrated. As we insert ourselves into the drama, we need also to discover the signs of the times that can instruct us about how to go about dislodging sin from its lairs.

121/ We should not dismiss the idea that the Spirit will address us directly in order to show us new paths and solutions and mark them out for us, but only those persons who possess the Spirit will be capable of hearing and understanding the Spirit adequately, wherever he may manifest himself. Saint Paul tells us that, just as no one knows "what is truly human except the human spirit that is within," "so also no one comprehends what is truly divine except the Spirit of God." But Paul then makes this tremendous statement: we have received "the Spirit that is from God so that we understand the gifts bestowed on us by God. And we speak of these things in words not taught by human wisdom but taught by the Spirit, interpreting spiritual things to those who are spiritual. Those who are unspiritual [natural, *psychikos*] do not receive the gifts of God's spirit, for they are foolishness to them, and they are unable to understand them because they are spiritually discerned. Spiritual persons discern all things, and they are themselves subject to no one else's scrutiny. 'For who has known the mind of the Lord so as to instruct him?' But we have the mind of Christ!"[44]

CONCLUSION

122/ This is the ideal human being, the person who is the goal of our educational efforts. This is the spiritual or "pneumatic" person, guided and sustained by the *Pneuma* of God, by the Holy Spirit. This is no longer *homo faber*, the clever tool-maker who at the dawn of history began to be radically differentiated from other animals and to rise toward world domination.

Nor is it simply *homo sapiens,* the species whose intelligence and wisdom raised it above the rest of creation and gave it the ability to understand and explain the universe. It isn't even *homo prometheanus,* who is conscious of sharing in the creative power of God and who is called not only to contemplate the world but to transform it. Neither is it *homo politicus,* who is fully aware of the complexity of this world and adroit in finding and tapping into the neuralgic points that determine the great transformations. Nor is it simply *homo ludens,* who is endowed with the capacity to live life to the full and to rejoice in the intrinsic beauty and value of all creatures. All these aspects of human reality, as valuable as they are in themselves, do not reach the heights of what Saint Paul calls *homo psychicus*; that is, the spiritual person in the sense of one endowed with the human spirit or psyche, the purely natural human being. Such a person does not exist concretely but is simply an ambivalent abstract possibility that, to a greater or lesser extent, is either humanized or dehumanized. Such a person can become, on the one hand, *homo lupus,* a wolf preying on other human beings, or on the other, *homo humanus, homo concors, homo philanthropus;* that is, a profoundly human and passionate lover of concord and fellow human beings.

123/ Normally, such a person will also be *homo religiosus*—open to transcendence—and, if the religious spirit is genuine, committed to the indestructible unity of love of God and love of neighbor. But such an ideal is ultimately not within our reach without the action of God, who transforms us into *homo novus,* the new human person, the new creature whose ultimate vital principle is the Holy Spirit. This is *homo spiritualis,* the person who is capable of loving even sworn enemies in this iniquitous world, and who is therefore also capable of transforming that world. And because such a person has the charism of discernment, he or she is capable of discovering and actively bonding with the deepest, most effective dynamism of history, the one that is powerfully impelling the already initiated construction of the Kingdom of God.

124/ This Spirit who makes us spiritual is also the Spirit of Christ, who makes us Christians and makes us other Christs. In this task of promoting justice, Christ is everything: our Way, our Truth, and our Life. He is par excellence the "man for others," the one who goes before us in the construction of the Kingdom of Justice; he is our model and our obligatory point of reference. His words and his life provide us the stability we need in order not to lose our way in this ever-changing world. But most importantly, Jesus is still alive, and he is the Lord of this history that is moving swiftly forward. He is seated at the right hand of the Father and continues to help his Church. Through his Spirit he sheds more light on and gives ever deeper meaning to the words that fell from his lips in former times. In this way they become new words, capable of illuminating the darkened paths of history.[45] Thus even his absence is in a way a lively presence: "It is to your advantage that I go away, for if I do not go away, the Advocate will not come to you; but if I go, I will send him to you. . . . When the Spirit of truth comes, he will guide you into all truth. . . . He will declare to you the things that are to come. He will glorify me because he will take what is mine and declare it to you."[46]

125/   Finally, Christ is also the foundation of that very Ignatian "Magis" which moves us never to put limits on our love, but rather to say "more" and "more," and to seek always the "greater glory of God," which will be realized concretely in our greater commitment to human beings and the cause of justice.

---

[1]   *Justice in the* World, Document of the 1971 Synod of Bishops, ## 6, 37.

[2]   *Justice in the World,* # 49.

[3]   1 John 4:20; 3:17–18.

[4]   *Justice in the World,* # 51.

[5]   *Justice in the World,* # 1–4.

[6]   *Justice in the World,* # 5–6.

[7]   *Justice in the World,* # 35.

[8]   Cf. Juan Alfaro, S.J., "Cristianismo y justicia," Comisión Pontificia Justicia y Paz (La justicia en el mundo, 3), PPC (Madrid, 1973), p.42. Fr. Alfaro, professor of the Gregorian University, took part in the 1971 Synod as one of the "special assistants to the Secretary."

[9]   Ibid., pp. 11–13.

[10]   Ibid., pp. 14–17.

[11]   Ibid., pp. 18–19.

[12]   Ibid., pp. 19–26.

[13]   Ibid., pp. 19–26.

[14]   Ibid., pp. 25, 37–39.

[15]   Ibid., p. 24.

[16]   Ibid., pp. 26–32.

[17] Cf. Max Weber, *The Religion of China. Confucianism and Taoism*. Free Press/Collier-MacMillan Ltd., New York/London 1964, p. 149.

[18] *Justice in the World, # 34.*

[19] *Justice in the World, # 34.*

[20] Rom 13:7–10.

[21] Alfaro. Cf. supra, pp. 24–25.

[22] Editor's note: We feel obliged to transcribe here what Pope John Paul said nearly nine years later regarding the relation between justice and love: "Christian love energizes justice, inspires it, reveals it, perfects it, makes it feasible, respects it, elevates it, surpasses it, but does not exclude it. To the contrary, Christian love presupposes justice and demands it because true love and true charity cannot exist without justice. Is not justice the minimum measure of charity?" ("To the Workers of the Solvay Co. Factory," 29 March 1982. Cf. "Ecclesia," no. 2072, 3 April 1982, p. 13. The pope worked at Solvay, in Cracow, during World War II.)

[23] Cf. Enrique Denzinger. *El magisterio de la Iglesia,* Herder. Barcelona, 1955. no. 792 (5), p.227.

[24] *Justice in the World, # 5, 6.*

[25] *Justice in the World, # 37.*

[26] Acts 10:38.

[27] Paul VI, *Octogesima Adveniens, # 37.*

[28] Ibid., ## 25–26.

[29] Ibid., ## 25–26.

[30] Ibid., # 43.

[31] *Gaudium et Spes* (Vatican II. Constitution on the Church in the Modern World), # 43.

[32] *Justice in the World, ## 36–37.*

[33] *Octogesima Adveniens, # 48.*

[34] *Justice in the World, # 38.*

[35] Rom 12:21.

[36] Matt 5:43–48.

[37] Rom 12:14–20.

[38] Alvin Toffler, *Future Shock.*

[39] Ibid.

[40] 1 John 4:10.

[41] 1 John passim.

[42] 1 John 4:16.

[43] 1 John 5:4.

[44] 1 Cor 2:11–15.

[45] John 14:26.

[46] John 16:7–15.

Our Secondary Schools:
Today and Tomorrow, 1980

Pedro Arrupe, S.J.

1/ 1. I do not intend to cover the same ground as those who will publish the proceedings of this Symposium on the *Apostolate of the Society in Secondary Education*. They will have their work cut out for them, given the wealth of experience, reflection and reports of pioneering efforts that you have exchanged during these past few days! I am not even going to enter into the two specific points which you have discussed in such great detail: lay collaboration in our schools, and education for justice.

2/ I prefer, instead, to devote the time at my disposal to some considerations of a more general character concerning the apostolate of education, and, more specifically, concerning our Jesuit secondary schools. For many years, I have been deeply convinced of the apostolic potential of our educational centers and specifically of our institutions of secondary education. And today, after hearing from you about the difficulties and the problems, as well as the possibilities offered by the new focus of this apostolate, both within and outside the institutions, my conviction about the importance of the secondary schools is stronger than ever—if that were possible!—both in themselves, and in their relationship to other forms of the Society's apostolate.

I. SECONDARY EDUCATION

3/ 2. In contradistinction to primary and university education, secondary education gives us access to the minds and hearts of great numbers of young men and women at a privileged moment of their lives. They are *already* capable of a coherent and rational assimilation of human values illuminated by Christian faith. At the same time, their personality has *not yet* acquired traits that are so set that they resist healthy formation. It is especially during the years of secondary education that the mindset of young people is systematically formed; consequently, it is the moment in which

263

they can and should achieve a harmonious synthesis of faith and modern culture. (Cf. General Congregation 31, Decree 28, no. 17.)

4/   We usually define secondary education in terms of its educational content—sometimes too closely bound up with academic programs—or else in terms of the age of the persons being educated. I would include in the category of secondary education the educational work which the Society is providing to adults in many different places: in literacy campaigns, or projects of professional or cultural improvement. This kind of work has many of the same goals (and therefore offers many of the same apostolic opportunities) that are characteristic of traditional secondary education. The adult student in such a situation approaches the teacher voluntarily, even eagerly, with a receptivity which is not generally true for his or her age level; this inspires the kind of openness to formation which we find in secondary school students.

5/   3. The Society has taken giant strides in recent years in this type of education, especially in culturally depressed countries or regions. Inspired by the direction of the last two General Congregations, the Society has initiated an imaginative use of modern mass media of communication, creating educational institutions of a new type: radio, audiovisual, correspondence courses, etc. However, the characteristics, advantages, and limitations of this type of education—and of the institutions and structures which serve it—are not the theme which I wish to develop here. Nor will we analyze now the role which they have to play in the future. We must return to this theme on another occasion and with the depth which such an important topic deserves. But I could not let the occasion pass without at least mentioning this new educational reality, which so hopefully enriches and diversifies the Society's educational apostolate. What I have to say here with explicit reference to our secondary schools, established according to the traditional model in the Society, can and should be applied in an analogous way to this new kind of educational institution.

II. THE COLLEGE, AN APOSTOLIC INSTRUMENT

6/   4. The basic idea behind all that I have to say is simply this: the secondary school is an effective apostolic instrument which the Society entrusts to a community, or to a definite group of men within a community; the purpose can only be apostolic. This commitment, of such men and for such a purpose, is an authentic act of "mission." The secondary school is the primordial means of apostolate for that community. And that community, inasmuch as it is an apostolic group of the Society, must concentrate its activity toward attaining the greatest possible apostolic results from its use of this educational instrument.

7/   Since the secondary school is an instrument, and an instrument for a specific mission whose nature is so clearly spiritual, it is evident that the instrument should achieve the purposes of God, the Principal Cause. That which joins this instrument with this principal cause is precisely the Jesuit community, to which the instrument has been entrusted. And the Jesuit community will use the instrument in order to achieve a precise goal: the spread of the Kingdom. The community which is dedicated to work in a secondary school absolutely must interiorize this outlook, and live out this conviction; the Society has given them a specific mission; and in order to accomplish the mission, it has entrusted to them this specific instrument. Any deviation from the mission, which would tend to diminish the value of its educational and apostolic finality—for example, by reducing it to a mere cultural or humanistic project which has an accidental potential for catechesis—and any kind of abusive usurpation of the instrument—for example by an inordinate attachment to it, with a consequent erosion of apostolic availability—will detract from the fundamental character both of the mission and of the instrument.

III. PRELIMINARY CRITERIA

8/   5. There are many criteria for deciding whether there should be an educational center in the first place and then for deciding what kind it should be, etc. The relative value of each criterion in different types of concrete circumstances will be conditioned and given a new meaning by many different factors. It would be a mistake to give absolute value to any one criterion, however pure it might seem to be. To take only one example, our evaluation of the value of a secondary school in a country where Catholics are in the minority, but where the country enjoys a high level of technology and cultural refinement, such as Japan, must be very different from our evaluation of a secondary school in another country, say in Europe, where there are abundant opportunities for Catholic education, or, again, the evaluation of a school in the developing world, where the cultural self-discovery of the masses is an overriding concern of the highest priority.

9/   This necessary diversity of criteria does not confer legitimacy on every institution simply because it exists; nor does it justify the excessive individualism of those who claim that "our situation is different" in order to resist any interference from outside, with no willingness to listen or to learn. Such an attitude of self-sufficiency, or even of superiority, is infantile and narcissistic, generally without objective foundation, and is contrary to the very nature of education, which is supposed to be a humanizing enterprise, fostering openness to others.

10/   There is also the opposite danger, an even more destructive result of a false sense of superiority: the intolerant dogmatism that insists on imposing on everyone one's own concept of education and of the proper kind of educational institution.

11/   6. *Any Decision Should Be the Result of Discernment* The nature of the institution, its location, the number of students, the formulation of objectives for academic quality or of the publics to be served, etc., are elements which diversify the instrument in order to adapt it to the circumstances in which it is being employed. Consequently, these elements should be arrived at by way of an Ignatian discernment in which, along with the usual criteria for the choice of ministries, account is taken of local circumstances as well as the comprehensive pastoral plan of the Province and of the local Hierarchy. In one place, the Church will need a center which offers an option of high academic quality that can compete with comparable institutions. Somewhere else, the need might be for a college geared to large numbers, as many as possible—in some cases with coeducation—in order to meet the pressing demand for schooling, or the specific needs of Christians, or in order to express an attitude of openness and invitation to an unbelieving world. In still other regions, an emergency situation—which, for St. Ignatius, can override all other criteria—might call for literacy education, or mass cultural programs through the use of radio, records, and printed works. Each of these will be a form of education in support of evangelization.

12/   The Ignatian criteria for selection of ministries are not absolutes. Before listing them in the *Constitutions*, St. Ignatius, with his customary prudence, prefaces them with the caution: *"When other considerations are equal (and this should be understood in everything that follows) . . ."* [622].

13/   7. *We Are Committed to Educate any Class of Person, without Distinction* It cannot be otherwise, because the educational apostolate (just as every other apostolate of the Society) bears the indelible Ignatian imprint of universality. To be sure, this total openness of the total educational work of the Society takes on—or should take on—individual characteristics according to local conditions. But what is never admissible is any kind of exclusiveness. Obviously, this total openness is joined to the Society's preferential option for the poor, an option which applies to every apostolate, education included. I think it is safe to say that there is no great problem in meeting the educational needs of the wealthier classes, and that there is a considerable problem—at times of tragic proportions—in meeting the educational needs of the poor. Although civil society has the prime responsibility to meet this social need, the Society feels an obligation, by reason of its vocation, to help to meet this human and spiritual need. It thus embodies the Church's right to teach in whatever way, to whatever degree is necessary. And even though the more comfortable classes have no lack of educational opportunities, there is a great need for evangelization among these people. And because instruction and education are the most efficacious means of evangelization, the Society cannot limit its educational apostolate exclusively to the poor. Moreover, looking to the long-range interests of the poor and the disadvantaged, again using Ignatian criteria, the Society should actively promote the Christian transformation of other social classes. Nor should we lose sight of the silent middle class, also a part of the People of God, and so seldom mentioned when problems are discussed in terms of the two extremes.

14/   8. *A Negative Criterion: Disavowal of Economic Discrimination* Because the secondary schools of the Society are necessarily instruments of the apostolate—and are therefore subject in principle to the radical gratuity of our ministries, and to our poverty—their availability to students cannot be conditioned by ability to pay. This statement of principle is our ideal. I know very well that the reality is necessarily very different in various countries and in various kinds of institutions. But as long as this ideal has not yet been realized, any Jesuit institution must live with the tension of striving to achieve a situation in which no capable student is refused admittance because he cannot pay. The recovery of genuine equality of opportunity and genuine freedom in the area of education is a concern that falls within the scope of our struggle for the promotion of justice.

15/   9. *A Positive Criterion: Excellence* Whatever be the other characteristics of a Jesuit secondary school, one trait should be common to all: excellence, which is to say high quality. I am obviously not referring to structures and physical plants but rather to that which specifically defines an educational center and provides the basis for its evaluation, its product: the men and women who are being formed. The excellence which we seek consists in producing men and women of right principles, personally appropriated; men and women open to the signs of the times, in tune with their cultural milieu and its problems; men and women for others. Instruction, education, evangelization: these are three levels of operation which, in different countries and in different circumstances, can have different priorities and degrees of urgency. But each one must be pursued with excellence as its goal, at least relative excellence. The true objective of a center of instruction—it would be better to say of education—is in the area of the specifically human and

Christian. And here I want to make a special point about the importance of academic excellence in our educational work in mission countries. It would be a mistake to sacrifice this—not only at the university level, but also in secondary schools—for the sake of other goals, which might be good enough in themselves and would claim priority in another type of institution, or simply in order to increase the number of students.

16/   10. *Ignatian Education* A Jesuit secondary school should be easily identifiable as such. There are many ways in which it will resemble other schools, both secular and confessional, including schools of other religious orders. But if it is an authentic Jesuit school—that is to say, if our operation of the school flows out of the strengths drawn from our own specific charism, if we emphasize our essential characteristics and our basic options—then the education which our students receive should give them a certain "Ignacianidad," if I can use such a term. I am not talking about arrogance or snobbery, still less about a superiority complex. I simply refer to the logical consequence of the fact that we live and operate out of our own charism. Our responsibility is to provide, through our schools, what we believe God and the Church ask of us.

IV. THE STUDENTS WE ARE TRYING TO FORM

17/   11. Here, I take for granted the academic and educative aspects of the school. I want to concentrate on other aspects of the integral formation that we should be giving to our students.

18/   *a. Men and Women of Service, According to the Gospel* This is the "man or woman for others" that you have heard me speak about so frequently. But here I want to rework this idea from a new viewpoint, especially for those among our students who are Christians. They must be men and women who are motivated by a genuine Gospel charity, which is the queen of the virtues. We have spoken about faith/justice so often. But it is charity which gives the force to faith and a desire for justice. Justice does not reach its interior fullness except in charity. Christian love both implies justice and extends the requirements of justice to the utmost limits by providing a motivation and a new interior force. All too frequently, we pass over this basic idea: faith must be informed by charity and faith is shown in works that are inspired by charity. And justice without charity is not evangelical. This is something we must insist on; if we are to understand our fundamental option correctly and make use of its tremendous potential, we must understand and assimilate this basic point. It can lead to a holy respect and a tolerance which will temper our impatience for justice and the service of the faith. And, especially in non-Christian countries, we must adopt this and look for ways to insert those Christian values which are also human values, which are recognized as being genuinely human.

19/   12. *b. New Persons, Transformed by the Message of Christ, Who Will Be Witnesses to His Death and Resurrection in Their Own Lives* Those who graduate from our secondary schools should have acquired, in ways proportional to their age and maturity, a way of life that is in itself a proclamation of the charity of Christ, of the faith that comes from Him and leads back to Him, and of the justice which He announced. We must make every effort to inculcate those values which are a part of our Ignatian heritage. We can even pass them on to those who do not share our faith in Christ if we translate them into ethical and human values of moral uprightness and of solidarity, which also come from God.

20/   The really crucial question is this: If the finality of our education is the creation of new persons, men and women of service, then what are the pedagogical repercussions? Because, this really is the purpose of the education that we are giving. It is a different kind of focus, at least to the extent that it gives priority to human values of service, of anti-egoism. And this has to have an influence on our pedagogical methods, our educational curriculum, our extra-curricular activities. A desire for Christian witness, service of one another, cannot thrive in an atmosphere of academic competition or where one's personal qualities are judged only by comparison to those of others. These things will thrive only in an atmosphere in which we learn how to be available, how to be of service to others. We need to rethink our educational methods in the light of these objectives: how to form the evangelical person, who looks on every other man and woman as a brother or sister. Universal brotherhood will be the foundation of one's personal, family, and social life.

21/   13. *c. Men and Women Open to Their Own Times and to the Future*
The students that we are leaving our imprint on day after day, that we are forming at a time when they are still more or less receptive, are not "finished products" that we launch out into the world. We are dealing with human beings who are in constant growth. Whether we like it or not, they will, throughout their lives, be affected by all of those forces through which they will influence the world or through which the world will influence them. The result of this struggle will determine whether they continue to live a personal life that is evangelical, a life of service, or whether they will live a kind of neutral apathy, overcome by indifference or unbelief. For this reason, perhaps even more important than the formation that we give them, is the capacity and concern to continue their own formation; this is what we must instill in them. It is important to learn, but it is much more important to learn how to learn, to desire to go on learning all through life.

22/   What I am trying to say is that our education, in its psychological aspects, must take this future into account. It must be an education which will be the seed for further personal growth; an open-ended education; an introduction to a basic thrust which will continue to be operative throughout life: continual formation.

23/   Among other things, the formation we give must take into account the kind of civilization or culture that we are living in and that our students will be called on to live in for the rest of their lives: the civilization of the image, of visualization, of the mass media transmission of information. The revolution created by the printing press at the beginning of the Renaissance is child's play compared to the revolution being produced by modern technology. Our education must take this into account. We must use it and help our students to get accustomed to it.

24/   14. *d. The Balanced Person* Perhaps I am asking for too much, after all the things I've already mentioned. And yet, this is an ideal that we must not give up. All of the values already mentioned: academic, evangelical, persons of service, of openness, of sensitivity to the present and to the future—these are not lost, but rather are mutually helped, when they are combined together in a balanced way. The ideal of our schools is not to produce little academic monsters, dehumanized and introverted. Neither is it to produce pious faithful, allergic to the world in which they live, incapable of responding to it sympathetically. Our ideal is much closer to the unsurpassed model of the Greeks, in its Christian version: balanced, serene, and constant, open to whatever is human. Technology threatens to dehumanize man, and it must be the mission of our educational centers to safeguard humanism without at the same time renouncing the use of technology.

V. THE EDUCATIONAL COMMUNITY

25/   15. This is a concept which has undergone great change. The traditional *Ratio Studiorum* of the Society, and I include the revised version of the last century, has many merits which have been recognized throughout its history. But it could do no more than reflect the restricted notion of a pedagogical community that was known at the time. The changed conditions of our own times have forced us to make generous use of the faculty foreseen in the Constitutions [457], to have collaborators who are not Jesuits. But this gives us a new responsibility: we must take whatever means are necessary to ensure that the formation given in our secondary schools continues to be a Jesuit formation, such as I have been describing.

26/   The educational community is made up of the Jesuit community, the + collaborators, the students, and their families. And also, remembering that the school is the first stage of a formation that will continue throughout life, it includes also—and must include—our former students.

27/   16. *The Jesuit Community* The mission of the Society is entrusted, in the first place, to the Jesuit community; to it is entrusted the secondary school, as the apostolic instrument through which this mission is to be carried out. The Jesuit community, therefore, must be the primary source of inspiration for the educational work, even in those cases in which lay persons have been appointed to administrative offices; for it is clear, in principle, that they must be persons who are in full harmony with the principles which guide our mission. And we must make special efforts to ensure this in the new structures in which financial responsibility, maintenance and business affairs, and even the academic administration of the school have been transferred to an association or board of which only a part is Jesuit.

28/ The Jesuits of the secondary school must be seen to be a united community, one which is authentically Jesuit and easily recognizable as such. That is to say, they should be a group of men with a clear identity, who live the true Ignatian charism, closely bound together by union of minds and hearts <u>ad intra</u>, and similarly bound, <u>ad extra</u>, by their generous participation in a common mission. The Jesuit community will examine itself regularly, evaluate its apostolic activity, and use an ongoing discernment process in order to decide which from among the available options will best accomplish their mission. This religious community will be the nucleus of the larger educational community, binding it together and giving it meaning. If the Jesuit community in the school is divided, then those who collaborate with them in the school will also be divided, and the secondary school will fulfill the dictum of St. Ignatius; if it is not united, the Society not only cannot function, but it cannot even exist (*Const.* 655).

29/ 17. The inspiration that the Jesuit community brings to the school will consist, first of all, in its specific application of the Ignatian vision to the educational apostolate. Concretely, this means that the Ignatian vision is evident in the objectives of the school, in the type of person we are trying to form, and in the selection of the means necessary to attain that end.

30/ Here I would like to add a word about the priestly activity of the Jesuits who are engaged in the educational work of our secondary schools. Teaching is surely a fully apostolic work; so is administration, or any of the other types of work necessary for the well-being of the school. Nevertheless, every Jesuit priest should also be engaged in some priestly activity in the strict sense of that term. This can be in the school or outside of it. Within the school, it could take the form of a sacramental ministry, preaching, spiritual counseling, or the pastoral direction of different kinds of groups. Outside of the school, it might mean regular or occasional help in parishes, convents, hospitals, prisons, other institutions for the needy, Christian movements, etc. Such work could be daily, on weekends, or more occasional, even limited to vacation periods. What is important is that we keep alive in ourselves our priestly identity and have other people see us in this way. To unite ourselves to Christ, to share in His priesthood, His mission of redemption and sanctification: this was the ideal that drew us to the Society, and it is the only ideal that will preserve us in it. I am slow to accept the excuse of "lack of time" as a reason for total withdrawal from specifically priestly works. Such a situation would seem rather to call for a reordering of other priorities. Experience has shown us that total withdrawal from all priestly activity, over a period of years, can lead to the loss of a sense of priestly identity. And this is especially the case when the priesthood is not exercised in the early years after ordination. From there, it is a short step to a loss of Jesuit identity. And the consequences of this second step are easy to predict.

31/   18. In the second place, the Jesuit community should be the source of inspiration and stimulation for the other components of the educational community (the lay collaborators, the students, the families, the former students) through the testimony of its life and its work. *The witness of our lives is essential.* If what we are trying to form in our students is the whole person, and not just the intellect, then we have to do this with our whole person and not just through our teaching. The students, their families, our colleagues, all have a right to see us as integrated, to see no division between what we teach, what we say, and how we live. And we have an obligation to respond to this need. We are being hypocritical if we warn our students about the consumer mentality while we live lives that are secure and comfortable. And what I said above about priestly identity applies also here: a lack of priestly identity can lead to a secularized way of life—in the bad sense of that word—and perhaps rather easily in an educational institution (though not just there, of course). Style of dress, behavior, use or abuse of property, the way we speak, etc.: all these form a part of our witness and, consequently, of our educational activity. Young people are not yet able to make mature judgments based on profound values; for them, these are often the basis for making judgments about individual Jesuits, and about the Society. We need to think about our responsibilities in this area and about the relationships all this may have to the problem of vocations.

32/   19. The witness of our lives includes also the *witness of our work.* I know that some of the men in our secondary schools are overworked; because of the reduced numbers of Jesuit personnel, some individual Jesuits have taken on unreasonable workloads. Does this sometimes lead to less excellence in our work? Could it lead to a lessening of inspiration in our mission? We are working at times that we ought to be devoting to reflection. We load ourselves with administrative details, or management that could be more easily delegated, and fail to do those things which cannot so easily be done by others.

33/   On the other hand, the opposite danger also exists in every institution, large or small. We can become immovable, untouchable, even though we are turning out work that is hardly satisfactory, work that suffers in comparison with that of other members of the educational community. We resist any change in the order of the day, any attempt at evaluation, any request that we help out with priestly or extra-curricular activities, or anything that might fall outside our "professional responsibilities." It is up to Superiors to make sure that our educational institutions do not become havens for the underemployed, the "antiquated," the immovable. Frequently, the best solution would seem to be to assign such a man to a new type of work, in which his priestly and apostolic zeal can be restimulated. Preventing this type of parasitism is especially important in secondary schools where, more than at the university level, we are engaged in forming adolescents, especially sensitive to the influence of witness. What I am saying here has nothing to do with the presence in the community of older Fathers and Brothers who continue to live in the school after a lifetime of hard work there. These men bring the example of their goodness, of their presence, their sense of tradition, a sense of being a family to the educational community.

34/   With regard to the question of the relationship between community and work, the separation of the place of residence from the place of work is, in itself, neither a necessary nor a sufficient solution. There are cases, however, where it might be a necessary first step.

35/   20. *The Lay Collaborators* Lay collaborators form a most important part of the educational community. In this regard, the Society has made great progress. I have already indicated how the *Constitutions* admit the possibility of collaboration as a substitute when there are not enough Jesuits. We are cautioned there that the contributions of the laity should not exceed certain limits. But this thinking was a reflection of the times; it was based on a concept of the role of the laity in the Church that was widely held until quite recently. Since Vatican II, the role of the laity has been reassessed; the place of lay people in the mission of the Church is now recognized explicitly. Then why not their role in the mission of the Society? This means that it is no longer the lack of Jesuits that determines the number of lay collaborators in our secondary schools, but rather the profound conviction that lay people have an invaluable contribution to make in our apostolate; they help us to extend the apostolate almost without limit. In former times, it was possible to find a community of fifty Jesuits engaged in the education of two or three hundred students—in a boarding school for instance! Let us frankly admit that this was disproportionate, and if we look to the needs of today's world, such attention would even be called unjust, or showing partiality. To maintain such a Jesuit-student ratio today would be a scandal in the Church. It is wrong to regret the passing of former days.

36/   21. Today we need multipliers, and that is what our lay collaborators are. This under one condition, naturally, and that is that we have correctly assessed their ability to be integrated into our apostolic educational mission. This means that we do not regard them as salaried employees, hired to do work under a master's supervision. They are not that! Their salaries should be adequate to relieve them of preoccupation with economics; they should be freed to dedicate themselves to full-time work, with complete dedication, without the need for an additional job. If they work with a divided spirit, they will almost out of necessity become incapable of becoming real educators and not even good teachers.

37/   But there is much more. What we truly need are not just teachers. We need responsible collaborators who share in the fullness of our mission. This is how we must accept them. And we need to learn from them; learn about the specific charism of the laity in the furthering of the work of the Church. This is the only way that their integration into the educational community can have any meaning; this is the only way in which they will become true multiplying agents.

38/   There are two things implied here. First, that they assimilate the Ignatian principles that give inspiration to our mission, and second, that they become a part of the decision-making process with positions of responsibility in which their educational potential can yield its maximum fruit.

39/   With respect to the first, it is clear that just as we ourselves needed a formation in order to assimilate and put into practice our Ignatian vision, so the lay collaborators must receive a formation from us—a formation adapted to them. Constant attention must be given to this; it must be an ongoing process, with due respect for the individual personality of each one. Even when they are not Christian, as will necessarily be the case in many countries, we can learn from them and allow them to share, according to their own capacity, in those values of our mission which are universal. However, those who are incapable of appreciating our vision of man and of gospel values are not suited for education in a secondary school run by the Society, whatever academic and teaching qualities they may have. I am not talking here about forming mini-Jesuits! What we need to form are persons who are lay, but who also resonate with Ignatian ideals. To give this type of formation requires time and money. But it is an investment which will yield great dividends for the ends that we are seeking. And we can hardly neglect necessary formation of our collaborators and at the same time expect them to share in our mission wholeheartedly!

40/   Concerning their integration into administrative positions in the school, what I have in mind is more than just a type of partnership. I assume that much! What I am talking about is offering, to those lay persons who are well prepared, not just administrative and managerial assignments, but the very highest levels of educational responsibility, and to do this with full confidence. This includes even the direction of the school (as principal or headmaster) when it is necessary or useful. We reserve to the Society only its essential role as the animator and inspirator, as I have explained already.

41/   For many of our schools, participation of competent lay people is the only way to survive, if we wish the school to be a place of Ignatian education; it is simply impossible to allocate the numbers of Jesuits that would be required. But for all of our secondary schools this collaboration with the laity (so long as they share in our mission and do not just function as hired teachers—for, ultimately, teaching by itself is not the most important element) is absolutely indispensable in our day, when the influence of the Church and of the Society needs to be multiplied.

42/   22. *The Families* We know that families have ultimate responsibility for the formation of their children. But this is just one more reason why we should also be working with the families. We should cooperate with them in the work of education, especially in those very frequent situations in which the married couples are hardly prepared to form their children. I want to give special praise to those organizations—associations, journals, formation courses—which promote the educational formation of the parents of our students, to prepare them for a more effective collaboration with the secondary school. Also, the school can and must function as a catalyst between parents and their children to bring about unity. One of the evils of our time is precisely the disintegration of the family: not just of the marriage, but also of children with respect to their parents. The school is a privileged place for a real encounter of parents with their own children; there they can come to appreciate their interests. It is important, then, that families have contact with the school, participate in its life, and cooperate in its cultural, social, extracurricular, and other activities.

43/   23. *Former Students* I have dealt with this theme many times in recent years, and I don't want to repeat myself here. I want only to reiterate one point: the ongoing formation of former students is an obligation; it is a strict responsibility which the Society cannot ignore. It is a work that only we can do, practically speaking, because it is a question of redoing the formation that we gave twenty or thirty years ago. The person that the world needs now is different from the persons we formed then! It is an immense task and well beyond our own abilities; we need to seek the help of lay people who can help to bring it about. But this, of course, assumes that we first form such lay persons! The Provincials need to provide for this by assigning to Associations of Former Students a sufficient number of Fathers who have both the aptitude and the time to devote to this work. If we do not do this, the Associations will languish, and the reeducation of our former students will not take place.

44/   24. *Present Students* The students are the center of focus, the principal component of the educational community. I have talked about them quite extensively in these pages, and there is no need to repeat what I have already said. I would only like to add one additional point: how much our students can teach us! We have to be in close contact with them. Because in dealing with our students, we can learn so much. We learn patience by encountering their impatience; we learn generosity by seeing their capacity to make sacrifice; we learn to be men for others by seeing how much they can give of themselves if only we stimulate them with the right motivation! Through these young people, we contact a civilization from which we ourselves will be excluded; in them we see the society of tomorrow; through them, we have a glimpse of the future. This is why it is impossible to educate the young from a guarded distance—living outside of their milieu, in antiseptic isolation, filled with academic dignity (and perhaps also with inferiority and timidity). This is not the way to get abundant vocations, and this is not the way to encourage young people to know the beauty of our Ignatian ideal: life in the service of Christ.

VI. THE SECONDARY SCHOOL: OPENNESS AND INTEGRATION

45/   25. You have been very clear on this point during your meetings these past few days. The secondary schools of the Society cannot remain in "splendid isolation" from the Province or from the local Church. It may well have been true in the past that some of our schools, because of their size and academic reputation, were ahead of their times and became pioneers for the city or the region, leading to a certain amount of isolation from the other schools. But this isolation, conscious or unconscious, wherever it exists, must disappear. Besides the fact that there have been profound changes in a very short time, we are the Catholic Church; we are the Society of Jesus. The secondary schools of the Society must take common cause, form a united front, with other educational institutions of the Church. They must participate in the different types of organizations which have been formed: professional, trade union, apostolic. This is especially important in those countries in which liberty of teaching, equality of opportunities, financial support, and other similar issues are hotly contested by opposing ideologies.

46/   But the more fundamental reason why our secondary schools must have this openness and ongoing contact with others is this: we need to learn, and we have an obligation to share. There are enormous advantages to be gained through collaboration of every type. It would be foolish to pretend that we have nothing to learn. It would be irresponsible to think only of ourselves in our planning without considering the need to cooperate with other secondary schools, whether religious or secular, in the areas of elective subjects, for example, or specialized studies, or in teaching standards, courses for teachers and parents, etc. This articulation of concrete needs with similar educational institutions in a local, regional, or national ecclesial setting will make us more effective apostolically and will at the same time increase and strengthen our sense of being a part of the Church.

47/   The secondary schools must also be integrated into the Province; their development must fit into the overall apostolic planning of the Province. Their relationship with other apostolic works in the Province must be fruitful. The schools are one segment of the individual unity of the "mission" of the Province, and they must be harmoniously joined to the other segments. I am not just speaking about a polite interest in the work that others are doing or in cordial fraternal relations. I mean something much more specific: real collaboration! The pastoral aspects of the educational apostolate provide secondary schools with opportunities for cooperation with other Jesuit works which can be of benefit to all. Other Jesuits, for example, can help out in the extra-curricular pastoral activities for the young people; they can help with spiritual care, the *Exercises*, Christian movements, etc. And the Jesuits in the school community can help out in the parishes and residences at the times of greatest demand. And, when distance and time permit, our scholastics and young priests still in studies could also share in this fraternal collaboration. These activities will introduce other Jesuits to the apostolic activities of their own Province, bring home to them the wide range of possibilities, and at the same time bring to light their abilities and interests. Both of these are important when the time comes for young Jesuits to receive a definitive mission.

48/   Such opening up will benefit both the Jesuit communities in the schools and also the students. It will keep Jesuit teachers in touch with the activities and needs of the Church and of the Society in other areas—and this is a valuable psychological preparation for the day when some from among them, for whatever reason, must begin a new line of work. These men will not be entering an unknown world. As I have already indicated, a certain amount of priestly activity in addition to one's primary educational work is an important means, at the personal level, for personal development of an attitude of sharing. The students will have their own horizons opened up by such contacts, by the opening up of the school. From their young years, they will become accustomed to the ecclesial and social dimensions of their lives. I wonder whether some of the hostility to Christian commitment or to social commitment, apparent in some of our former students, may not be at least partly due to the hothouse atmosphere of some of our secondary schools in the past.

49/ 26. Openness and institutional contacts should lead to <u>wide-ranging apostolic influence</u>. Each Jesuit institution is an apostolic platform. Whether it is a parish or a hospital or a prison, a radio transmitter, or a neighborhood social center, each institution is a focal point from which we Jesuits and the students we direct can develop some type of apostolate. Don't the students have need of this? But we need it ourselves! I would dare to say that we need it even more than they do. If the absence of all priestly or apostolic influence is justified by the amount of school work, and the resulting fatigue, then a discernment has to be made. Would it be better to accept, or gently impose, a reduction in the number of school tasks (even at the cost of cutting back on needed Jesuit personnel) so that there can be increased quality in the school life? In this sense, that there will be room for direct priestly activity and formation of students in the needs of the apostolate.

50/ Is it possible to do more than we are presently doing to involve parents, former students, present students, and the many good people who support activities—by making our school plants more available for night classes, literacy programs, professional courses, socials, sports activities, artistic or recreational activities—and all of this for the surrounding neighborhood? Isn't it a little scandalous (and also unjustified, in terms of sound business management) that our large school plants are in effective use, sometimes, for only eight or ten hours during the day, and scarcely two hundred days of the academic year? This is only about 20 percent of the available time, and they could be so useful for so many in so many different ways! Surely there is a place here for applying our doctrine concerning the social function of material goods!

VII. TO WHOM THESE PAGES ARE ADDRESSED

51/ 27. I want to conclude where, perhaps, I should have begun: by speaking about those to whom these pages are addressed. I am not just speaking to you, the fifteen Jesuits who have come from so many different parts of the world in order to participate in this seminar; you are not the only ones I have in mind. During these days we have had lengthy discussions, and you already know my thinking on all of these issues. I have prayed with you to Him Who is the Only Master: the Light, the Truth, the Way. I have listened to your experiences, your reflections, your preoccupations, your hopes. In your notes, and in the documentation which will be the result of your work during these days, you will find more than enough material for reflection and for inspiration concerning the future of your secondary schools.

52/   I am sure of that. And so I would say, rather paradoxically, that you are not the ones that I am really speaking to! You are not, perhaps, the ones who most need to hear all that I am saying.

53/   I am thinking, first, of the communities of Jesuits presently working in our secondary schools. These men, priests, and brothers have given themselves to a work that is very often hidden; the schedule they are subjected to—for the day and for the year—is very rigorous; often enough they are overworked. And their personal austerity is sometimes obscured by the apparent opulence of the institution they are working in. I confer on these men, once again, the mission that they have already received from the Society. I repeat, once again, that the Church and the Society of Jesus hold the educational apostolate in the very highest esteem. And I encourage them to go on doing their work with dedication and enthusiasm.

54/   And at the same time, I caution these men about the danger of inertia. It is absolutely essential that they become more aware of the changes that have taken place in the Church and in the Society, and aware also of their need to keep pace with these changes. If some of our secondary schools, at least those which have the reputation of "great old institutions," have become apostolates that are little appreciated by different groups of Jesuits, perhaps we should admit that the disenchantment of the younger, dynamic generation of Jesuits may be due in part to the failure of these institutions to adjust to the new demands of today's Society, Church, and society at large. That Jesuit community which believes that its school has no need to change has set the stage for the slow death of that school; it will only take about one generation. However painful it may be, we need to trim the tree in order to restore it to strength. Permanent formation, adaptation of structures in order to meet new conditions: these are indispensable.

55/   29. The second group that I wish to address is our younger men, or perhaps the not-so-young, whose apostolic impetuosity makes them look on our educational institutions—and perhaps the very apostolate of education itself—with distrust, with low esteem. They are quick to indiscriminately label all of our secondary schools, and especially the more "affluent" ones, as centers of power, symbols of a disregard for the poor, as countersigns to our fundamental option for the poor. Often enough, they ignore the real spirit of sacrifice that is needed to live and work in the school. I know that such a spirit is not always there; and I never stop urging the men in the schools to a greater personal and community austerity, just as there are other aspects—sometimes more important ones—that I have to insist on in other apostolates.

56/   But the apostolate of education is absolutely vital for the Church. So vital is it that educational work is the first, and often the only, work prohibited to the Church by certain political regimes. And this is enough to ensure the de-Christianization of a nation, without bloodshed, in the space of a few generations.

57/   Education is absolutely necessary. And it cannot be done on the scale, and with the excellence, that I have been referring to unless it is carried out in some type of an institution. At the beginning of these pages, I have already talked about different kinds of possibilities. I have alluded to the fact that we need to educate the total person. In a social body, we cannot limit ourselves to education of the hands or of the arms; we must also educate the head. The training of future leaders is important, and Ignatian criteria are in agreement with this. Therefore, in order to promote the necessary renovation that can only come through the introduction of new blood, I urge our scholastics to consider the apostolic value of our educational works in a realistic way, and to offer themselves—or accept cheerfully—an assignment to these works with the evangelical and priestly attitude that I have already described. Let us not fall into the injustice of reproaching our educational centers for their immobility, and then at the same time deny them the means for moving forward! The solution is both "ab intus" by encouraging those already in the schools toward a personal renewal, and "ab extra" by renewing these Jesuit communities with new recruits.

58/   30. Finally, I am thinking about Superiors, Provincials, Regional Vice-Provincials, Commissions on Ministries, and all those who do the apostolic planning for the Provinces. They must see whether the number and type of existing educational institutions is justified by the real apostolic needs of the area; they must see whether the present apostolic works are responding to those needs or whether new apostolic works should be begun. Which ones, where, with what characteristics, they must work toward a more perfect coordination of the educational apostolate with the other apostolates of the Province, and develop the entire Province apostolate in accord with the desires of the local Church. They must stimulate Rectors to the type of renewal that is needed in order to go forward. They must support the Rectors in their efforts to call the members of the educational community, especially the Jesuits, to a renewal of their academic and evangelical training. They must strengthen the faculties, as far as this lies within their power, both by the assignment of generous young men, and by the reassignment of those men who are still in the schools, but have lost their effectiveness in teaching and evangelization, to other more appropriate apostolates.

59/   31. Concretely, I suggest the necessity of preparing young Jesuits specifically for the educational apostolate. The reduced time given to Juniorate studies and to the period of regency in many Provinces has resulted, among other things, in a poorer training in the humanities and a weaker remote preparation for the educational apostolate. The Province should have a number of men who are experts in Pedagogy (with the appropriate academic degrees), a number proportionate to the number of its educational institutions. Finally, I commend the regional and national efforts that have been undertaken to promote the continuing education of personnel, both Jesuits and lay, often in conjunction with other religious and secular groups.

60/   32. I realize that, in spite of the length of this address, there is much more to be said. As a matter of fact, for each of the topics I have treated, a veritable library exists! It was not my intention to say everything, but only to recall to your minds some of the matters that I consider more urgent or important: matters that you yourselves have suggested to me. I ask you to carry back to your Provinces a message of my heartfelt encouragement and my constant concern for your fellow educators and for the work they are doing in education. The words of one of our most famous Jesuit educators remain true today: "Puerilis insitutio est renovation mundi"—the education of youth is the transformation of the world![i]

September 10, 1980

---

[i]   Juan de Bonifacio, 1538–1606; cf. *Monumenta. paedagogica Societatis Jesu.* III, 402, note 15.

The Characteristics of Jesuit Education, 1986

CONTENTS

287

2.3 Characteristic 8: Jesuit Education Encourages Life-Long Openness to Growth.

joy in learning; desire to learn

adult members open to change

SECTION 3: QUEST FOR FREEDOM

3.1 Characteristic 9: Jesuit Education Is Value-Oriented.

knowledge joined to virtue

school regulations; system of discipline

self-discipline

3.2 Characteristic 10: Jesuit Education Encourages a Realistic Knowledge, Love, and Acceptance of Self.

Christian humanism; sin and its effects

obstacles to growth

development of a critical faculty

3.3 Characteristic 11: Jesuit Education Provides a Realistic Knowledge of the World.

awareness of the social effects of sin

realization that persons and structures can change

SECTION 4: CHRIST THE MODEL OF HUMANITY

4.1 Characteristic 12: Jesuit Education Proposes Christ as the Model of Human Life.

inspiration from the life and teaching of Christ

for Christians, personal friendship with Jesus

4.2 Characteristic 13: Jesuit Education Provides Adequate Pastoral Care.

religious faith and religious commitment

the *Spiritual Exercises*

response to a personal call from God

4.3 Characteristic 14: Jesuit Education Celebrates Faith in Personal and Community Prayer, Worship, and Service.

progressive initiation to personal prayer

community worship

for Catholics, Eucharist and the Sacrament of Reconciliation

faith leads to commitment to follow Christ

SECTION 5: ACTION

5.1 Characteristic 15: Jesuit Education Is Preparation for Active Life Commitment.

5.2 Characteristic 16: Jesuit Education Serves the Faith that Does Justice.

    justice informed by charity

    action for peace

    a new type of person in a new kind of society

    justice issues in the curriculum

    school policies and programs witness to justice

    works of justice

    involvement in serious issues of our day

5.3 Characteristic 17: Jesuit Education Seeks to Form "Men and Women for Others."

    talents: gifts to be developed for the community

    stress on community values

    witness of adults in the educational community

5.4 Characteristic 18: A Jesuit Education Manifests a Particular Concern for the Poor.

    "preferential option" for the poor

    Jesuit education available to everyone

    free educational opportunity for all the poor

    the context of Jesuit education

    opportunities for contact with the poor

    reflection on the experience

SECTION 6: IN THE CHURCH

6.1 Characteristic 19: Jesuit Education Is an Apostolic Instrument in Service of the Church as It Serves Human Society.

    part of the apostolic mission of the church

    Ignatian attitude of loyalty to and service of the church

    faithful to the teachings of the church

    reflect on culture in the light of church teachings

    serve the local civil and religious community

    cooperation with other apostolic works

    active in the local community

    collaboration in ecumenical activities

6.2 Characteristic 20: Jesuit Education Prepares Students for Active Participation in the Church and the Local Community for the Service of Others.

    instruction in the basic truths of the faith

    for Catholics, knowledge of and love for the church and the sacraments

    concrete experiences of church life

    promote Christian Life Communities

SECTION 7: *MAGIS*

7.1 Characteristic 21: Jesuit Education Pursues Excellence in Its Work of Formation.

"human excellence"

excellence depends on the needs of the region

fullest possible development of individual capacities

leaders in service

excellence in faith

commitment: to do "more"

competition

7.2 Characteristic 22: Jesuit Education Witnesses to Excellence.

excellence in school climate

adult members witness to excellence

cooperation with other schools and educational agencies

SECTION 8: THE COMMUNITY

8.1 Characteristic 23: A Jesuit Education Stresses Lay-Jesuit Collaboration.

a common mission

willingness to assume responsibilities

the Jesuit attitude

8.2 Characteristic 24: A Jesuit Education Relies on a Spirit of Community.

a) Among Teaching Staff and Administrators:

people chosen to join the educational community

common sense of purpose

b) Among the Jesuit Community:

life witness

life within the community

provide knowledge and appreciation of Ignatius

hospitality

priestly activities

relations with school director

c) Among the Governing Boards:

d) Among Parents:

close cooperation with parents

understanding the school character

consistency between values promoted in the school and those promoted in the home

e) Among Students:

f) Among Former Students:

g) Among Benefactors:

INTRODUCTION

1/   (1) In September of 1980 a small international group, Jesuit and lay, came together in Rome to discuss several important issues concerning Jesuit secondary education. In many parts of the world, serious questions had been raised about the present effectiveness of Jesuit schools: Could they be instrumental in accomplishing the apostolic purposes of the Society of Jesus? Were they able to respond to the needs of the men and women in today's world? The meeting was called to examine these questions and to suggest the kinds of renewal that would enable Jesuit secondary education to continue to contribute to the creative and healing mission of the church, today and in the future.

2/   (2) During the days of discussion, it became evident that a renewed effectiveness depended in part on a clearer and more explicit understanding of the <u>distinctive nature</u> of Jesuit education. Without intending to minimize the problems, the group asserted that Jesuit schools can face a challenging future with confidence <u>if they will be true to their particularly Jesuit heritage</u>. The vision of Ignatius of Loyola, founder of the Society of Jesus, had sustained these schools for four centuries. If this spiritual vision could be sharpened and activated and then applied to education in ways adapted to the present day, it would provide the context within which other problems could be faced.

3/   (3) Father Pedro Arrupe, who was then Superior General of the Society of Jesus, reaffirmed this conclusion when he spoke at the closing session of the meeting. He said that a Jesuit school

> should be easily identifiable as such. There are many ways in which it will resemble other schools. . . . But if it is an authentic Jesuit school—that is to say if our operation of the school flows out of the strengths drawn from our own specific charism, if we <u>emphasize our essential characteristics and our basic options</u>—then the education which our students receive should give them a certain "Ignacianidad," if I can use such a term. I am not talking about arrogance or snobbery, still less about a superiority complex. I simply

refer to the logical consequence of the fact that <u>we live and operate out of our own charism</u>. Our responsibility is to provide, through our schools, what we believe God and the church ask of us.[1]

4/   (4) The delegates at the Rome meeting recommended the establishment of a permanent international group to consider questions related to secondary education, and urged that one of the first responsibilities of this group be to clarify the ways in which the vision of Ignatius continues to make Jesuit secondary education distinctive today.

5/   (5) In response to the recommendation, the International Commission on the Apostolate of Jesuit Education (ICAJE) was established; it held its first meeting in 1982. The members are Daven Day, S.J. (Australia), Vincent Duminuco, S.J. (U.S.A.), Luiz Fernando Klein, S.J. (Brazil, since 1983), Raimondo Kroth, S.J. (Brazil, until 1983), Guillermo Marshall, S.J. (Chile, until 1984), Jean-Claude Michel, S.J. (Zaïre), Gregory Naik, S.J. (India), Vicente Parra, S.J. (Spain), Pablo Sada, S.J. (Venezuela), Alberto Vasquez (Chile, since 1984), Gerard Zaat, S.J. (The Netherlands), and James Sauvé, S.J. (Rome).

6/   (6) This present document, composed by ICAJE, is the fruit of four years of meetings and worldwide consultations.

7/   (7) Any attempt to speak about Jesuit education today must take account of the profound changes which have influenced and affected this education—since the time of Ignatius, but especially during the present century. Government regulations or the influence of other outside agencies affect various aspects of school life, including the course of study and the textbooks that are used; in some countries the policies of the government or high costs threaten the very existence of private education. Students and their parents seem, in many cases, to be concerned only with the academic success that will gain entrance to university studies, or only with those programs that will help to gain employment. Jesuit schools today are often coeducational, and women have joined laymen and Jesuits as teachers and administrators. There has been a significant increase in the size of the student body in most Jesuit schools and at the same time a decline in the number of Jesuits working in those schools. In addition:

8/   a. The course of studies has been altered by modern advances in science and technology; the addition of scientific courses has resulted in less emphasis on, in some cases a certain neglect of, the humanistic studies traditionally emphasized in Jesuit education.

9/   b. Developmental psychology and the social sciences, along with advances in pedagogical theory and education itself, have shed new light on the way young people learn and mature as individuals within a community; this has influenced course content, teaching techniques, and school policies.

10/   c. In recent years, a developed theology has explicitly recognized and encouraged the apostolic role of lay people in the church; this was ratified by the Second Vatican Council, especially in its decree *On the Apostolate of the Laity*.[2] Echoing this theology, recent General Congregations of the Society of Jesus have insisted on lay-Jesuit collaboration, through a shared sense of purpose and a genuine sharing of responsibility, in schools once exclusively controlled and staffed by Jesuits.

11/   d. The Society of Jesus is committed to "the service of faith, of which the promotion of justice is an absolute requirement"[3]; it has called for a "reassessment of our traditional apostolic methods, attitudes and institutions with a view to adapting them to the needs of the times, to a world in process of rapid change."[4] In response to this commitment, the purposes and possibilities of education are being examined with renewed concern for the poor and disadvantaged. The goal of Jesuit education today is described in terms of the formation of "multiplying agents" and "men and women for others."[5]

12/   e. Students and teachers in Jesuit schools today come from a variety of distinct social groups, cultures, and religions; some are without religious faith. Many Jesuit schools have been deeply affected by the rich but challenging complexity of their educational communities.

13/ (8) These and many other developments have affected concrete details of school life and have altered fundamental school policies. But they do not alter the conviction that <u>a distinctive spirit still marks any school which can truly be called Jesuit. This distinctive spirit can be discovered through reflection on the lived experience of Ignatius, on the ways in which that lived experience was shared with others, on the ways in which Ignatius himself applied his vision to education in the *Constitutions* and in letters, and on the ways in which this vision has been developed and been applied to education in the course of history, including our present times</u>. A common spirit lies behind pedagogy, curriculum, and school life, even though these may differ greatly from those of previous centuries, and the more concrete details of school life may differ greatly from country to country.

14/ (9) "Distinctive" is not intended to suggest "unique" either in spirit or in method. The purpose is rather to describe "our way of proceeding"[6]: the inspiration, values, attitudes, and style which have traditionally characterized Jesuit education, which must be characteristic of any truly Jesuit school today wherever it is to be found, and which will remain essential as we move into the future.

15/ (10) To speak of an inspiration that has come into Jesuit schools through the Society of Jesus is in no sense an exclusion of those who are not members of this Society. Though the <u>school</u> is normally called "Jesuit," the <u>vision</u> is more properly called "Ignatian" and has never been limited to Jesuits. Ignatius was himself a layman when he experienced the call of God which he later described in the *Spiritual Exercises*, and he directed many other lay people through the same experience; throughout the last four centuries, countless lay people and members of other religious congregations have shared in and been influenced by his inspiration. Moreover, lay people have their own contribution to make based on their experience of God in family and in society and on their distinctive role in the church or in their religious culture. This contribution will enrich the spirit and enhance the effectiveness of the Jesuit school.

16/   (11) The description that follows is for Jesuits, lay people and other Religious working in Jesuit schools; it is for teachers, administrators, parents, and governing boards in these schools. All are invited to join together in making the Ignatian tradition, adapted to the present day, more effectively present in the policies and practices that determine the life of the school.

THE CHARACTERISTICS OF JESUIT EDUCATION
Introductory Notes

17/   (12) Though many of the characteristics on the following pages describe all Jesuit education, the specific focus is the basic education of the Jesuit high school, or *colegio* or *collège*. (Depending on the country, this may be only secondary education, or it may include both primary and secondary levels.) Those in other Jesuit institutions, especially universities and university colleges, are urged to adapt these characteristics to their own situations.

18/   (13) A short historical summary of the life of Ignatius and the growth of Jesuit education appears in Appendix I. Reading this summary will give those less familiar with Ignatius and early Jesuit history a better understanding of the spiritual vision on which the characteristics of Jesuit education are based.

19/   (14) In order to highlight the relationship between the characteristics of Jesuit education and the spiritual vision of Ignatius, the twenty-eight basic characteristics listed on the following pages are divided into nine sections. Each section begins with a statement from the Ignatian vision, and is followed by those characteristics that are applications of the statement to education; the individual characteristics are then described in more detail. A tenth section suggests, by way of example, some characteristics of Jesuit pedagogy.

20/   (15) The introductory statements come directly from the world-vision of Ignatius. The characteristics of Jesuit education come from reflection on that vision, applying it to education in the light of the needs of men and women today. (The Ignatian world-vision and the characteristics of

Jesuit education are listed in parallel columns in Appendix II. The notes to that Appendix suggest sources for each of the statements summarizing the Ignatian vision.)

21/   (16) Some characteristics apply to specific groups: students, former students, teachers, or parents. Others apply to the educational community as a whole; still others, concerning the policies and practices of the institution as such, apply primarily to the school administrators or the governing board.

22/   (17) These pages do not speak about the very real difficulties in the lives of all those involved in education: the resistance of students and their discipline problems, the struggle to meet a host of conflicting demands from school officials, students, parents, and others, the lack of time for reflection, the discouragement and disillusions that seem to be inherent in the work of education. Nor do they speak of the difficulties of modern life in general. This is not to ignore or minimize these problems. On the contrary, it would not be possible to speak of Jesuit education at all if it were not for the dedication of all those people, Jesuit and lay, who continue to give themselves to education in spite of frustration and failure. This document will not try to offer facile solutions to intractable problems, but it will try to provide a vision or an inspiration that can make the day-to-day struggle have greater meaning and bear greater fruit.

23/   (18) The description of Jesuit Education lies in <u>the document as a whole</u>. A partial reading can give a distorted image that seems to ignore essential traits. A commitment to the faith that does justice, to take one example, must permeate the whole of Jesuit education—even though it is not described in this document until section five.

24/   (19) Because they apply to Jesuit secondary schools throughout the world, the characteristics of Jesuit education are described in a form that is somewhat general and schematic. They need amplification and concrete application to local situations. This document, therefore, is a resource for reflection and study rather than a finished work.

25/   (20) Not all of the characteristics of Jesuit education will be present in the same measure in each individual school; in some situations a statement may represent an ideal rather than a present reality. "Circumstances of times, places, persons, and other such factors"[7] must be taken into account: the same basic spirit will be made concrete in different ways in different situations. To avoid making distinctions which depend on local circumstances and to avoid a constant repetition of the idealistic "wishes to be" or the judgmental "should be," the characteristics are written in the categoric indicative: "Jesuit education <u>is</u> . . ."

SECTION 1: GOD

26/   (21) *1. For Ignatius, God is Creator and Lord, Supreme Goodness, the one Reality that is absolute; all other reality comes from God and has value only insofar as it leads us to God.*[8] *This God is present in our lives, "laboring for us"*[9] *in all things; He can be discovered, through faith, in all natural and human events, in history as a whole, and most especially within the lived experience of each individual person.*

27/   (22) <u>Jesuit education</u>:
- is world-affirming.
- assists in the total formation of each individual within the human community.
- includes a religious dimension that permeates the entire education.
- is an apostolic instrument.
- promotes dialogue between faith and culture.

1.1 Characteristic 1: Jesuit Education Is World-Affirming.

radical goodness of the world

a sense of wonder and mystery

28/   (23) Jesuit education acknowledges God as the Author of all reality, all truth, and all knowledge. God is present and working in all of creation: in nature, in history, and in persons. Jesuit education, therefore, affirms the <u>radical goodness of the world</u> "charged with the grandeur of God,"[10] and it regards every element of creation as worthy of study and contemplation, capable of endless exploration.

29/   (24) The education in a Jesuit school tries to <u>create a sense of wonder and mystery</u> in learning about God's creation. A more complete knowledge of creation can lead to a greater knowledge of God and a greater willingness to work with God in His ongoing creation. Courses are taught in such a way that students, in humble recognition of God's presence, find joy in learning and thirst for greater and deeper knowledge.

1.2 Characteristic 2: Jesuit Education Assists in the Total Formation of Each Individual within Community.

fullest development of talents (intellectual, imaginative, creative, affective, creative, effective communication skills, physical)

the balanced person

within community

30/   (25) God is especially revealed in the mystery of the human person, "created in the image and likeness of God;"[11] Jesuit education, therefore, probes the meaning of human life and is concerned with the total formation of each student as an individual personally loved by God. The objective of Jesuit education is to assist in the fullest possible development of all of the God-given talents of each individual person as a member of the human community.

31/   (26) A thorough and sound intellectual formation includes mastery of basic humanistic and scientific disciplines through careful and sustained study that is based on competent and well-motivated teaching. This intellectual formation includes a growing ability to reason reflectively, logically, and critically.

32/   (27) While it continues to give emphasis to the traditional humanistic studies that are essential for an understanding of the human person, Jesuit education also includes a careful and critical study of technology together with the physical and social sciences.

33/   (28) In Jesuit education, particular care is given to the development of the imaginative, the affective, and the creative dimensions of each student in all courses of study. These dimensions enrich learning and prevent it from being merely intellectual. They are essential in the formation of the whole person and are a way to discover God as He reveals Himself through beauty. For these same reasons, Jesuit education includes opportunities—through course work and through extracurricular activities—for all students to come to an appreciation of literature, aesthetics, music, and the fine arts.

34/   (29) Jesuit schools of the 17th century were noted for their development of communication skills or "eloquence," achieved through an emphasis on essays, drama, speeches, debates, etc. In today's world so dominated by communications media, the development of effective communication skills is more necessary than ever before. Jesuit education, therefore, develops traditional skills in speaking and writing and also helps students to attain facility with modern instruments of communication such as film and video.

35/   (30) An awareness of the pervasive influence of mass media on the attitudes and perceptions of peoples and cultures is also important in the world of today. Therefore Jesuit education includes programs which enable students to understand and critically evaluate the influence of mass media. Through proper education, these instruments of modern life can help men and women to become more, rather than less, human.

36/   (31) Education of the whole person implies physical development in harmony with other aspects of the educational process. Jesuit education, therefore, includes a well-developed program of sports and physical education. In addition to strengthening the body, sports programs help young men and women learn to accept both success and failure graciously; they become aware of the need to cooperate with others, using the best qualities of each individual to contribute to the greater advantage of the whole group.

37/   (32) All of these distinct aspects of the educational process have one common purpose: the formation of the balanced person with a personally developed philosophy of life that includes ongoing habits of reflection. To assist in this formation, individual courses are related to one another within a well-planned educational program; every aspect of school life contributes to the total development of each individual person.[12]

38/   (33) Since the truly human is found only in relationships with others that include attitudes of respect, love, and service, Jesuit education stresses—and assists in developing—the role of each individual as a member of the human community. Students, teachers, and all members of the educational community are encouraged to build a solidarity with others that transcends race, culture, or religion. In a Jesuit school, good manners are expected; the atmosphere is one in which all can live and work together in understanding and love, with respect for all men and women as children of God.

1.3 Characteristic 3: Jesuit Education Includes a Religious Dimension that Permeates the Entire Education.

religious education

development of a faith response that resists secularism

worship of God and reverence for creation

39/   (34) Since every program in the school can be a means to discover God, all teachers share a responsibility for the religious dimension of the school. However, the integrating factor in the process of discovering God and understanding the true meaning of human life is theology as presented through religious and spiritual education. Religious and spiritual formation is integral to Jesuit education; it is not added to, or separate from, the educational process.

40/   (35) Jesuit education tries to foster the creative Spirit at work in each person, offering the opportunity for a faith response to God while at the same time recognizing that faith cannot be imposed.[13] In all classes, in the climate of the school, and most especially in formal classes in religion, every attempt is made to present the possibility of a faith response to God as something truly human and not opposed to reason, as well as to develop those values which are able to resist the secularism of modern life. A Jesuit school does everything it can to respond to the mission given to the Society of Jesus "to resist atheism vigorously with united forces."[14]

41/   (36) Every aspect of the educational process can lead, ultimately, to worship of God present and at work in creation and to reverence for creation as it mirrors God. Worship and reverence are parts of the life of the school community; they are expressed in personal prayer and in appropriate community forms of worship. The intellectual, the imaginative and affective, the creative, and the physical development of each student, along with the sense of wonder that is an aspect of every course and of the life of the school as a whole—all can help students to discover God active in history and in creation.

1.4 Characteristic 4: Jesuit Education Is an Apostolic Instrument.[15]

preparation for life

42/   (37) While it respects the integrity of academic disciplines, the concern of Jesuit education is preparation for life, which is itself a preparation for eternal life. Formation of the individual is not an abstract end; Jesuit education is also concerned with the ways in which students will make use of their formation within the human community, in the service of others "for the praise, reverence, and service of God."[16] The success of Jesuit education is measured not in terms of academic performance of students or professional competence of teachers, but rather in terms of this quality of life.

1.5 Characteristic 5: Jesuit Education Promotes Dialogue Between Faith and Culture.

43/   (38) Believing that God is active in all creation and in all human history, Jesuit education promotes dialogue between faith and culture—which includes dialogue between faith and science. This dialogue recognizes that persons as well as cultural structures are human, imperfect, and sometimes affected by sin and in need of conversion;[17] at the same time it discovers God revealing Himself in various distinct cultural ways. Jesuit education, therefore, encourages contact with and a genuine appreciation of other cultures, to be creatively critical of the contributions and deficiencies of each.

44/ (39) Jesuit education is adapted to meet the needs of the country and the culture in which the school is located;[18] this adaptation, while it encourages a "healthy patriotism," is not an unquestioning acceptance of national values. The concepts of "contact with," "genuine appreciation," and being "creatively critical" apply also to one's own culture and country. The goal is always to discover God, present and active in creation and in history.

SECTION 2: HUMAN FREEDOM

45/   (40) *2. Each man or woman is personally known and loved by God. This love invites a response which, to be authentically human, must be an expression of a radical freedom. Therefore, in order to respond to the love of God, each person is called to be:*

- *free to give of oneself, while accepting responsibility for and the consequences of one's actions: free to be faithful.*
- *free to work in faith toward that true happiness which is the purpose of life: free to labor with others in the service of the Kingdom of God for the healing of creation.*

46/   (41) Jesuit education:

- insists on individual care and concern for each person.
- emphasizes activity on the part of the student.
- encourages life-long openness to growth.

2.1 Characteristic 6: Jesuit Education Insists on Care and Concern for Each Person.

developmental stages of growth

curriculum centered on the person

personal relationships ("cura personalis")

responsibilities within the community

47/   (42) The young men and women who are students in a Jesuit school have not reached full maturity; the educational process recognizes the developmental stages of intellectual, affective, and spiritual growth and assists each student to mature gradually in all these areas. Thus, the curriculum is centered on the person rather than on the material to be covered. Each student is allowed to develop and to accomplish objectives at a pace suited to individual ability and the characteristics of his or her own personality.

48/   (43) Growth in the responsible use of freedom is facilitated by the personal relationship between student and teacher. Teachers and administrators, both Jesuit and lay, are more than academic guides. They are involved in the lives of the students, taking a personal interest in the intellectual, affective, moral, and spiritual development of every student, helping each one to develop a sense of self-worth and to become a responsible individual within the community. While they respect the privacy of students, they are ready to listen to their cares and concerns about the meaning of life, to share their joys and sorrows, to help them with personal growth and interpersonal relationships. In these and other ways, the adult members of the educational community guide students in their development of a set of values leading to life decisions that go beyond "self" that include a concern for the needs of others. They try to live in a way that offers an example to the students, and they are willing to share their own life experiences. "Cura personalis" (concern for the individual person) remains a basic characteristic of Jesuit education.[19]

49/   (44) <u>Freedom includes responsibilities within the community</u>. "Cura personalis" is not limited to the relationship between teacher and student; it affects the curriculum and the entire life of the institution. All members of the educational community are concerned with one another and learn from one another. The personal relationships among students, and also among adults—lay and Jesuit, administrators, teachers, and auxiliary staff—evidence this same care. A personal concern extends also to former students, to parents, and to the student within his or her family.

2.2 Characteristic 7: Jesuit Education Emphasizes the Activity of Students in the Learning Process.

personal study

opportunities for personal discovery

reflection

50/   (45) Growth in the maturity and independence that are necessary for growth in freedom depends on <u>active participation</u> rather than passive reception. Important steps toward this active participation include <u>personal study, opportunities for personal discovery and creativity,</u> and an attitude of

<u>reflection</u>. The task of the teacher is to help each student to become an independent learner, to assume the responsibility for his or her own education.

2.3 Characteristic 8: Jesuit Education Encourages Life-Long Openness to Growth.

joy in learning; desire to learn

adult members open to change

51/   (46) Since education is a life-long process, Jesuit education tries to instill a <u>joy in learning</u> and a <u>desire to learn</u> that will remain beyond the days in school. "Perhaps even more important than the formation we give them is the capacity and concern to continue their own formation; this is what we must instill in them. It is important to learn; but it is much more important to learn how to learn, to desire to go on learning all through life."[20]

52/   (47) Personal relationships with students will help the adult members of the educational community to be <u>open to change</u>, to <u>continue to learn</u>; thus they will be more effective in their own work. This is especially important today, given the rapid change in culture and the difficulty that adults can have in understanding and interpreting correctly the cultural pressures that affect young people.

53/   (48) Jesuit education recognizes that intellectual, affective, and spiritual growth continue throughout life; the adult members of the educational community are encouraged to continue to mature in all of these areas, and programs of ongoing formation are provided to assist in this growth.[21]

SECTION 3: QUEST FOR FREEDOM

54/   (49) *3. Because of sin, and the effects of sin, the freedom to respond to God's love is not automatic. Aided and strengthened by the redeeming love of God, we are engaged in an ongoing struggle to recognize and work against the obstacles that block freedom—including the effects of sinfulness—while developing the capacities that are necessary for the exercise of true freedom.*

55/   *a. This freedom requires a genuine knowledge, love, and acceptance of self, joined to a determination to be freed from any excessive attachment: to wealth, fame, health, power, or anything else, even life itself.*

56/   *b. True freedom also requires a realistic knowledge of the various forces present in the surrounding world and includes freedom from distorted perceptions of reality, warped values, rigid attitudes, or surrender to narrow ideologies.*

57/   *c. To work toward this true freedom, one must learn to recognize and deal with the influences that can either promote or limit freedom: the movements within one's own heart; past experiences of all types; interactions with other people; the dynamics of history, social structures, and culture.*

58/   (50) <u>Jesuit education</u>:
  * is value-oriented.
  * encourages a realistic knowledge, love, and acceptance of self.
  * provides a realistic knowledge of the world in which we live.

3.1 Characteristic 9: Jesuit Education Is Value-Oriented.

knowledge joined to virtue

school regulations; system of discipline

self-discipline

59/   (51) Jesuit education includes formation in values, in attitudes, and in an ability to evaluate criteria; that is, it includes formation of the will. Since a knowledge of good and evil and of the hierarchy of relative goods is necessary, both for the recognition of the different influences that affect freedom and for the exercise of freedom, education takes place in a moral context: <u>knowledge is joined to virtue</u>.

60/ (52) Personal development through the training of character and will, overcoming selfishness and lack of concern for others and the other effects of sinfulness, and developing the freedom that respects others and accepts responsibility, is all aided by the necessary and fair <u>regulations </u>of the school; these include a <u>fair system of discipline</u>. Of equal importance is the <u>self-discipline </u>expected of each student, manifested in intellectual rigor, persevering application to serious study, and conduct toward others that recognizes the human dignity of each individual.

61/ (53) In a Jesuit school, a framework of inquiry in which a value system is acquired through a process of wrestling with competing points of view is legitimate.

3.2 Characteristic 10: Jesuit Education Encourages a Realistic Knowledge, Love, and Acceptance of Self.

Christian humanism; sin and its effects

obstacles to growth

development of a critical faculty

62/ (54) The concern for total human development as a creature of God which is the "Christian humanism" of Jesuit education emphasizes the happiness in life that is the result of a responsible use of freedom, but it also <u>recognizes the reality of sin and its effects</u> in the life of each person. It therefore tries to encourage each student to confront this obstacle to freedom honestly, in a growing self-awareness and a growing realization that forgiveness and conversion are possible through the redemptive love and the help of God.[22]

63/ (55) The struggle to remove the obstacles to freedom and develop the capacity to exercise freedom is more than a recognition of the effects of sin; an ongoing effort to recognize all <u>obstacles to growth</u> is also essential.[23] Students are helped in their efforts to discover prejudice and limited vision on the one hand and to evaluate relative goods and competing values on the other.

64/   (56) Teachers and administrators assist students in this growth by being ready to challenge them, helping students to <u>reflect on personal experiences</u> so that they can understand their own experience of God; while they accept their gifts and develop them, they also accept limitations and overcome these as far as possible. The educational program, in bringing students into realistic contact with themselves, tries to help them recognize these various influences and to <u>develop a critical faculty</u> that goes beyond the simple recognition of true and false, good and evil.

3.3 Characteristic 11: Jesuit Education Provides a Realistic Knowledge of the World.

awareness of the social effects of sin

realization that persons and structures can change

65/   (57) A realistic knowledge of creation sees the goodness of what God has made, but includes an <u>awareness of the social effects of sin</u>: the essential incompleteness, the injustice, and the need for redemption in all people, in all cultures, in all human structures. In trying to develop the ability to reason reflectively, Jesuit education emphasizes the need to be in contact with the world as it is—that is, in need of transformation—without being blind to the essential goodness of creation.

66/   (58) Jesuit education tries to develop in students an ability to know reality and to evaluate it critically. This awareness includes a <u>realization that persons and structures can change</u>, together with a <u>commitment to work for those changes</u> in a way that will help to build more just human structures, which will provide an opportunity for the exercise of freedom joined to greater human dignity for all.[24]

SECTION 4: CHRIST THE MODEL OF HUMANITY

67/ (59) *4. The world view of Ignatius is centered on the historical person of Jesus Christ. He is the model for human life because of his total response to the Father's love in the service of others. He shares our human condition and invites us to follow him under the standard of the cross,*[25] *in loving response to the Father. He is alive in our midst and remains the Man for others in the service of God.*

68/ (60) Jesuit education:
- proposes Christ as the model of human life.
- provides adequate pastoral care.
- celebrates faith in personal and community prayer, worship, and service.

4.1 Characteristic 12: Jesuit Education Proposes Christ as the Model of Human Life.

inspiration from the life and teaching of Christ

for Christians, personal friendship with Jesus

69/ (61) Members of various faiths and cultures are a part of the educational community in Jesuit schools today; to all, whatever their beliefs, Christ is proposed as the model of human life. Everyone can draw inspiration and learn about commitment from the life and teaching of Jesus who witnesses to the love and forgiveness of God, lives in solidarity with all who suffer, and pours out his life in the service of others. Everyone can <u>imitate him</u> in an <u>emptying of self</u>, in accepting whatever difficulties or sufferings come in the pursuit of the one goal to be achieved: responding to the Father's will in the service of others.

70/ (62) Christian members of the educational community strive for <u>personal friendship</u> with Jesus, who gained forgiveness and true freedom for us through his death and resurrection and is present today and active in our history. To be "Christian" is to <u>follow</u> Christ and be like him: to share and promote his values and way of life as far as possible.[26]

4.2 Characteristic 13: Jesuit Education Provides Adequate Pastoral Care.[27]

religious faith and religious commitment

the *Spiritual Exercises*

response to a personal call from God

71/   (63) Pastoral care is a dimension of "cura personalis" that enables the seeds of <u>religious faith and religious commitment</u> to grow in each individual by enabling each one to recognize and respond to the message of divine love: seeing God at work in his or her life, in the lives of others, and in all of creation; then responding to this discovery through a commitment to service within the community. A Jesuit school makes adequate pastoral care available to all members of the educational community in order to awaken and strengthen this personal faith commitment.

72/   (64) For Christians this care is centered on Christ, present in the Christian community. Students encounter the person of Christ as friend and guide; they come to know him through Scripture, sacraments, personal and communal prayer, in play and work, in other persons; they are led to the service of others in imitation of Christ the Man for others.[28]

73/   (65) Making the *Spiritual Exercises*[29] is encouraged as a way of knowing Christ better, loving him, and following him. The *Exercises* will also help the members of the educational community understand the vision of Ignatius, which is the spirit that lies behind Jesuit education. They can be made in various ways, adapted to the time and the abilities of each person, whether adult or student.

74/   (66) The Jesuit school encourages and assists each student to respond to his or her own personal call from God, a <u>vocation</u> of service in personal and professional life—whether in marriage, religious or priestly life, or a single life.

4.3 Characteristic 14: Jesuit Education Celebrates Faith in Personal and Community Prayer, Worship, and Service.

progressive initiation to personal prayer

community worship

for Catholics, Eucharist and the Sacrament of Reconciliation

faith leads to commitment to follow Christ

75/   (67) Prayer is an expression of faith and an effective way toward establishing the personal relationship with God that leads to a commitment to serve others. Jesuit education offers a <u>progressive initiation to prayer</u>, following the example of Christ, who prayed regularly to his Father. All are encouraged to praise and thank God in prayer, to pray for one another within the school community, and to ask God's help in meeting the needs of the larger human community.

76/   (68) The faith relationship with God is communal as well as personal; the educational community in a Jesuit school is united by bonds that are more than merely human. It is a <u>community of faith</u>, and expresses this faith through appropriate religious or spiritual celebrations. For Catholics, the Eucharist is the celebration of a faith community centered on Christ. All adult members of the community are encouraged to participate in these celebrations, not only as an expression of their own faith, but also to give witness to the purposes of the school.

77/   (69) Catholic members of the educational community receive and celebrate the loving forgiveness of God in the Sacrament of Reconciliation. Depending on local circumstances, the Jesuit school prepares students (and also adults) for the reception of other sacraments.

78/   (70) The obedience of Christ to his Father's will led him to give of himself totally in the service of others; a relationship to God necessarily involves a relationship to other persons.[30] Jesuit education promotes a faith that is <u>centered on the historical person of Christ</u>, which therefore <u>leads to a commitment</u> to imitate him as the "Man for others."

SECTION 5: ACTION

79/   (71) *5. A loving and free response to God's love cannot be merely speculative or theoretical. No matter what the cost, speculative principles must lead to decisive action: "love is shown in deeds."*[31] *Ignatius asks for the total and active commitment of men and women who, "to imitate and be more actually like Christ,"*[32] *will put their ideals into practice in the real world of the family, business, social movements, political and legal structures, and religious activities.*[33]

80/   (72) Jesuit education:

- is preparation for active life commitment.
- serves the faith that does justice.
- seeks to form "men and women for others."
- manifests a particular concern for the poor.

5.1 Characteristic 15: Jesuit Education Is Preparation for Active Life Commitment.

81/   (73) "Love is shown in deeds"; the free human response of love to the redeeming love of God is shown in an active life of service. Jesuit education—in progressive stages that take into account the developmental stages of growth and without any attempt at manipulation—assists in the formation of men and women who will put their beliefs and attitudes into practice throughout their lives. "We . . . challenge you and try to inspire you to put into practice—in concrete activity—the values that you cherish, the values that you have received in your formation."[34]

5.2 Characteristic 16: Jesuit Education Serves the Faith that Does Justice.[35]

justice informed by charity

action for peace

a new type of person in a new kind of society

justice issues in the curriculum

school policies and programs witness to justice

works of justice

involvement in serious issues of our day

82/   (74) The "decisive action" called for today is the faith that does justice: "The mission of the Society of Jesus today is the service of faith, of which the promotion of justice is an absolute requirement. For reconciliation with God demands the reconciliation of people with one another."[36] This service of the faith that does justice is action in imitation of Christ; it is the justice of God, which is informed by evangelical charity: "It is charity which gives force to faith, and to the desire for justice. Justice does not reach its interior fullness except in charity. Christian love both implies justice, and extends the requirements of justice to the utmost limits, by providing a motivation and a new interior force. Justice without charity is not evangelical."[37] The Kingdom of God is a Kingdom of justice, love, and peace.[38]

83/   (75) The promotion of justice includes, as a necessary component, action for peace. More than the absence of war, the search for peace is a search for relationships of love and trust among all men and women.

84/   (76) The goal of the faith that does justice and works for peace is a new type of person in a new kind of society in which each individual has the opportunity to be fully human and each one accepts the responsibility of promoting the human development of others. The active commitment asked of the students—and practiced by former students and by the adult members of the educational community—is a free commitment to the struggle for a more human world and a community of love. For Christians, this commitment is a response to the call of Christ and is made in humble recognition that conversion is only possible with the help of God. For them, the Sacrament of Reconciliation is a necessary component of the struggle for peace and justice. But all members of the educational community, including those who do not share Christian faith, can collaborate in this work. A genuine sense of the dignity of the human person can be the starting point for working together in the promotion of justice and can become the beginning of an ecumenical dialogue which sees justice as intimately tied to faith.

85/   (77) In a Jesuit school, the focus is on <u>education</u> for justice. Adequate knowledge joined to rigorous and critical thinking will make the commitment to work for justice in adult life more effective. In addition to this necessary basic formation, education for justice in an educational context has three distinct aspects:

86/   (78) 1. <u>Justice issues are treated in the curriculum</u>. This may at times call for the addition of new courses; of greater importance is the examination of the justice dimension always present in every course taught.[39] Teachers try to become more conscious of this dimension, so that they can provide students with the intellectual, moral, and spiritual formation that will enable them to make a commitment to service—that will make them agents of change. The curriculum includes a <u>critical analysis of society</u>, adapted to the age level of the students; the outlines of a solution that is in line with Christian principles is a part of this analysis. The reference points are the Word of God, church teachings, and human science.[40]

87/   (79) 2. The <u>policies and programs</u> of a Jesuit school <u>give concrete witness to the faith that does justice</u>; they give a counter-witness to the values of the consumer society. Social analysis of the reality in which the school is located can lead to institutional self-evaluation, which may call for structural changes in school policies and practices.[41] School policy and school life encourage mutual respect; they promote the human dignity and human rights of each person, adult and young, in the educational community.

88/   (80) 3. "There is no genuine conversion to justice unless there are <u>works of justice</u>."[42] Interpersonal relationships within the school manifest a concern for both justice and charity. In preparation for life commitment, there are opportunities in Jesuit education for actual contact with the world of injustice. The analysis of society within the curriculum thus becomes reflection based on actual contact with the structural dimensions of injustice.

89/   (81) Members of the educational community are <u>aware of</u> and <u>involved in</u> the <u>serious issues of our day</u>. The educational community, and each individual in it, are conscious of the influence they can have on others; school policies are made with an awareness of possible effects on the larger community and on its social structures.

5.3 Characteristic 17: Jesuit Education Seeks to Form "Men and Women for Others."[43]

talents: gifts to be developed for the community

stress on community values

witness of adults in the educational community

90/   (82) Jesuit education helps students to realize that <u>talents are gifts to be developed</u>, not for self-satisfaction or self-gain, but rather, with the help of God, <u>for the good of the human community</u>. Students are encouraged to use their gifts in the service of others, out of a love for God:

> .   Today our prime educational objective must be to form men and women for others; men and women who will live not for themselves but for God and his Christ—for the God-man who lived and died for all the world; men and women who cannot even conceive of love of God which does not include love for the least of their neighbors; men and women completely convinced that the love of God which does not issue in justice for men and women is a farce.[44]

91/   (83) In order to promote an awareness of "others," Jesuit education <u>stresses community values</u> such as equality of opportunity for all, the principles of distributive and social justice, and the attitude of mind that sees service of others as more self-fulfilling than success or prosperity.[45]

92/   (84) The adult members of the educational community—especially those in daily contact with students—<u>manifest in their lives</u> concern for others and esteem for human dignity.[46]

5.4 Characteristic 18: A Jesuit Education Manifests a Particular Concern for the Poor.

"preferential option" for the poor

Jesuit education available to everyone

free educational opportunity for all the poor

the context of Jesuit education

opportunities for contact with the poor

reflection on the experience

93/   (85) Reflecting on the actual situation of today's world and responding to the call of Christ who had a special love and concern for the poor, the church and the Society of Jesus have made a "preferential option"[47] for the poor. This includes those without economic means, the handicapped, the marginalized and all those who are, in any sense, unable to live a life of full human dignity. In Jesuit education this option is reflected both in the students that are admitted and in the type of formation that is given.

94/   (86) Jesuit schools do not exist for any one class of students;[48] Ignatius accepted schools only when they were completely endowed so that education could be available to everyone; he insisted that special facilities for housing the poor be a part of every school foundation that he approved and that teachers give special attention to the needs of poor students. Today, although the situation differs greatly from country to country and the specific criteria for selecting students depends on "circumstances of place and persons," every Jesuit school does what it can to make Jesuit education available to everyone, including the poor and the disadvantaged.[49] Financial assistance to those in need and reduction of costs whenever possible are means toward making this possible.

95/   (87) In order for parents, especially the poor, to exercise freedom of choice in the education of their children, Jesuit schools join in movements that promote free educational opportunity for all. "The recovery of genuine equality of opportunity and genuine freedom in the area of education is a concern that falls within the scope of our struggle for promotion of justice."[50]

96/   (88) More basic than the type of student admitted is the type of formation that is given. In Jesuit education, the values which the school community communicates, gives witness to, and makes operative in school policies and structures, the values which flow into the school climate, are those values that promote a special concern for those men and women who are without the means to live in human dignity. In this sense, the poor form the context of Jesuit education: "Our educational planning needs to be made in function of the poor, from the perspective of the poor."[51]

97/   (89) The Jesuit school provides students with opportunities for contact with the poor and for service to them, both in the school and in outside service projects, to enable these students to learn to love all as brothers and sisters in the human community, and also in order to come to a better understanding of the causes of poverty.

98/   (90) To be educational, this contact is joined to reflection. The promotion of justice in the curriculum, described above in (80), has as one concrete objective an analysis of the causes of poverty.

SECTION 6: IN THE CHURCH

99/   (91) *6. For Ignatius, the response to the call of Christ is made in and through the Roman Catholic Church, the instrument through which Christ is sacramentally present in the world. Mary, the Mother of Jesus, is the model of this response. Ignatius and his first companions all were ordained as priests and they put the Society of Jesus at the service of the Vicar of Christ, "to go to any place whatsoever where he judges it expedient to send them for the greater glory of God and the good of souls."*[52]

100/   (92) Jesuit education:

- is an apostolic instrument, in service of the church as it serves human society.
- prepares students for active participation in the church and the local community, for the service of others.

6.1 Characteristic 19: Jesuit Education Is an Apostolic Instrument in Service of the Church as It Serves Human Society.

part of the apostolic mission of the church

Ignatian attitude of loyalty to and service of the church

faithful to the teachings of the church

reflect on culture in the light of church teachings

serve the local civil and religious community

cooperation with other apostolic works

active in the local community

collaboration in ecumenical activities

101/   (93) Jesuit schools are a part of the apostolic mission of the church in building the Kingdom of God. Even though the educational process has changed radically since the time of Ignatius and the ways to express religious concepts are quite different, Jesuit education still remains an instrument to help students know God better and respond to him; the school remains available for use in response to emerging needs of the people of God. The aim of Jesuit education is the formation of principled, value-oriented persons for others after the example of Jesus Christ. Teaching in a Jesuit school, therefore, is a ministry.

102/ (94) Because it is characteristic of all Jesuit works, the Ignatian attitude of <u>loyalty to and service of the church</u>, the people of God, will be communicated to the entire educational community in a Jesuit school. The purposes and ideals of members of other faiths can be in harmony with the goals of the Jesuit school and they can commit themselves to these goals for the development of the students and for the betterment of society.

103/ (95) Jesuit education—while respecting the conscience and the convictions of each student—is <u>faithful to the teachings of the church</u>, especially in moral and religious formation. As far as possible, the school chooses as qualified leaders of the educational community those who can teach and give witness to the teachings of Christ presented by the Catholic Church.

104/ (96) The educational community, based on the example of Christ— and of Mary in her response to Christ[53]—and <u>reflecting on today's culture</u> in the light of the teachings of the church, will promote:[54]

- a spiritual vision of the world in the face of materialism;
- a concern for others in the face of egoism;
- simplicity in the face of consumerism;
- the cause of the poor in the face of social injustice.

105/ (97) As part of its service of the church a Jesuit school will <u>serve the local civil and religious community and cooperate with the local bishop</u>. One example of this is that important decisions about school policy take into account the pastoral orientations of the local church; these same decisions about school policy consider their possible effects on the local church and the local community.

106/ (98) For greater effectiveness in its service of human needs, a Jesuit school works in <u>cooperation with other Jesuit apostolic works</u>, with local parishes and other Catholic and civic agencies, and with centers for the social apostolate.

107/ (99) All members of the educational community are active <u>in service as members of the local community and of their churches</u>. They participate in meetings and other activities, especially those related to education.

108/ (100) The Jesuit school community encourages <u>collaboration in ecumenical activities</u> with other churches and is active in dialogue with all men and women of good will; the community is a witness to the Gospel of Christ, in service to the human community.

6.2 Characteristic 20: Jesuit Education Prepares Students for Active Participation in the Church and the Local Community for the Service of Others.

instruction in the basic truths of the faith

for Catholics, knowledge of and love for the church and the sacraments

concrete experiences of church life

promote Christian Life Communities

109/ (101) Jesuit education is committed to the religious development of all students. They will <u>receive instruction in the basic truths of their faith</u>. For Christian students, this includes a knowledge of the Scriptures, especially the Gospels.

110/ (102) For Catholic students Jesuit education offers a <u>knowledge of and love for the church and the sacraments</u>, as privileged opportunities to encounter Christ.

111/ (103) In ways proper to a school, <u>concrete experiences of church life are available</u> to all students, through participation in church projects and activities. Lay teachers, especially those active in parish activities, can be leaders in promoting this; they can communicate to students the current emphasis on the apostolate of lay people.

112/ (104) Following the example of the early Jesuit schools where the Sodalities of Mary played such an important part in fostering devotion and Christian commitment, opportunities such as the <u>Christian Life Communities</u> are available for those students and adults who want to know Christ more completely and model their lives on his more closely. Similar opportunities are offered to members of other faiths who wish to deepen their faith commitment.

SECTION 7: *MAGIS*

113/ (105) 7.   Repeatedly, Ignatius insisted on the *"Magis"*—the <u>more</u>. His constant concern was for greater service of God through a closer following of Christ and that concern flowed into all the apostolic work of the first companions. The concrete response to God must be "of greater value."[55]

114/ (106) <u>Jesuit education</u>:
  • pursues excellence in its work of formation.
  • witnesses to excellence.

7.1 Characteristic 21: Jesuit Education Pursues Excellence in Its Work of Formation.

"human excellence"

excellence depends on the needs of the region

fullest possible development of individual capacities

leaders in service

excellence in faith

commitment: to do "more"

competition

115/ (107) In Jesuit education, the criterion of excellence is applied to all areas of school life: the aim is the fullest possible development of every dimension of the person, linked to the development of a sense of values and a commitment to the service of others which gives priority to the needs of the poor and is willing to sacrifice self-interest for the promotion of justice.[56] The pursuit of academic excellence is appropriate in a Jesuit school, but only within the larger context of <u>human excellence</u>.[57]

116/ (108) Excellence, like all other Ignatian criteria, is determined by "circumstances of place and persons." "The nature of the institution, its location, the number of students, the formulation of objectives for academic quality or of the publics to be served, etc., are elements which diversify the instrument in order to adapt it to the circumstances in which it is being employed."[58] To seek the *Magis*, therefore, is to provide the type and level of education for the type and age-group of students that best responds to the <u>needs of the region in which the school is located</u>.

117/   (109) "More" does not imply comparison with others or measurement of progress against an absolute standard; rather it is the <u>fullest possible development of each person's individual capacities</u> at each stage of life, <u>joined to the willingness to continue this development</u> throughout life <u>and the motivation to use those developed gifts for others</u>.

118/   (110) A traditional aim of Jesuit education has been to train "leaders": men and women who assume responsible positions in society through which they have a positive influence on others. This objective has, at times, led to excesses which call for correction. Whatever the concept may have meant in the past, the goal of Jesuit education in today's understanding of the Ignatian worldview is not to prepare a socio-economic elite, but rather to educate <u>leaders in service</u>. The Jesuit school, therefore, will help students to develop the qualities of mind and heart that will enable them—in whatever station they assume in life—to work with others for the good of all in the service of the Kingdom of God.

119/   (111) Service is founded on a <u>faith commitment</u> to God; for Christians this is expressed in terms of the following of Christ. The decision to follow Christ, made in love, leads to a desire to always do "more"—enabling us to become multiplying agents.[59] The desire, in turn, is converted into the necessary personal preparation in which a student dedicates himself or herself to study, to personal formation, and ultimately to action.

120/   (112) The *Ratio Studiorum* recommends <u>competition</u>—normally between groups rather than individuals—as an effective stimulus to academic growth. Jesuit education today faces a different reality: a world of excessive competitiveness reflected in individualism, consumerism, and success at all costs. Although a Jesuit school values the stimulus of competitive games, it urges students to distinguish themselves by their ability to work together, to be sensitive to one another, to be committed to the service of others shown in the way they help one another. "A desire for Christian witness . . . cannot thrive in an atmosphere of academic competition, or where one's personal qualities are judged only by comparison to those of others. These things will thrive only in an atmosphere in which we learn how to be available, how to be of service to others."[60]

7.2 Characteristic 22: Jesuit Education Witnesses to Excellence.

excellence in school climate

adult members witness to excellence

cooperation with other schools and educational agencies

121/ (113) The school policies are such that they create an ambience or "climate" which will promote excellence. These policies include ongoing evaluation of goals, programs, services, and teaching methods in an effort to make Jesuit education more effective in achieving its goals.

122/ (114) The adult members of the educational community witness to excellence by joining growth in professional competence to growth in dedication.

123/ (115) The teachers and directors in a Jesuit school cooperate with other schools and educational agencies to discover more effective institutional policies, educational processes, and pedagogical methods.[61]

SECTION 8: THE COMMUNITY

124/ (116) *8. As Ignatius came to know the love of God revealed through Christ and began to respond by giving himself to the service of the Kingdom of God he shared his experience and attracted companions who became "friends in the Lord,"* [62] *for the service of others. The strength of a community working in service of the Kingdom is greater than that of any individual or group of individuals.*

125/ (117) Jesuit education:

- stresses lay-Jesuit collaboration.
- relies on a spirit of community among teaching staff and administrators; the Jesuit community; governing boards; parents; students; former students; benefactors.
- takes place within a structure that promotes community.

8.1 Characteristic 23: A Jesuit Education Stresses Lay-Jesuit Collaboration.

a common mission

willingness to assume responsibilities

the Jesuit attitude

126/ (118) Lay-Jesuit collaboration is a positive goal that a Jesuit school tries to achieve in response to the Second Vatican Council[63] and to recent General Congregations of the Society of Jesus.[64] Because this concept of a common mission is still new, there is a need for growing understanding and for careful planning.

127/ (119) In a Jesuit school, there is a willingness on the part of both lay people and Jesuits to assume appropriate responsibilities: to work together in leadership and in service. Efforts are made to achieve a true union of minds and hearts and to work together as a single apostolic body[65] in the formation of students. There is, therefore, a sharing of vision, purpose, and apostolic effort.

128/ (120) The legal structure of the school allows for the fullest possible collaboration in the direction of the schools.[66]

129/ (121) Jesuits are active in promoting lay-Jesuit collaboration in the school. "Let Jesuits consider the importance for the Society of such collaboration with lay people, who will always be the natural interpreters for us of the modern world and so will always give us effective help in this apostolate."[67] "We must be willing to work with others . . . willing to play a subordinate, supporting, anonymous role; and willing to learn how to serve from those we seek to serve."[68] One of the responsibilities of the Religious superior is to foster this openness in the apostolic work.

8.2 Characteristic 24: A Jesuit Education Relies on a Spirit of Community.

a) Among Teaching Staff and Administrators:

people chosen to join the educational community

common sense of purpose

130/ (122) As far as possible, people chosen to join the educational community in a Jesuit school will be men and women capable of understanding its distinctive nature and of contributing to the implementation of characteristics that result from the Ignatian vision.

131/ (123) In order to promote a <u>common sense of purpose applied to the concrete circumstances of school life</u>, teachers, administrators, and auxiliary staff, Jesuit and lay, communicate with one another regularly on personal, professional, and religious levels. They are willing to discuss vision and hopes, aspirations and experiences, successes and failures.

b) Among the Jesuit Community:

life witness

life within the community

provide knowledge and appreciation of Ignatius

hospitality

priestly activities

relations with school director

132/ (124) The Jesuits working in the school "should be a group of men with a clear identity, who live the true Ignatian charism, closely bound together by union of minds and hearts <u>ad intra</u>, and similarly bound, <u>ad extra</u>, by their generous participation in a common mission. . . . It should be the source of inspiration and stimulation for the other components of the educational community. . . . <u>The witness of our lives is essential</u>."[69]

133/ (125) The Jesuits will be more effective in their service and inspiration of the total educational community if they live in <u>service and inspiration to one another</u>, forming a true community in prayer and in life. This lived witness is one means of making their work in the school a "corporate" apostolate and will help the larger school community be more effectively and affectively united.

134/ (126) At least on special occasions, other members of the educational community are invited to meals and to liturgical and social functions in the Jesuit community. Spending time together informally is a help toward building community, and lay people will come to a better understanding of Jesuit life when they have opportunities to be a part of it.

135/ (127) In addition to their professional responsibilities in the school as teachers, administrators, or pastors, Jesuits are available to <u>provide</u> opportunities such as <u>discussions</u>, <u>workshops</u>, and <u>retreats</u> which can enable others in the school community to come to a better knowledge and appreciation of the worldview of Ignatius.

136/ (128) Education—the work of a teacher or administrator or member of the auxiliary staff—is itself apostolic. In keeping with the nature of the school as an apostolic instrument of the church, however, those Jesuits who are priests are also active in more directly sacerdotal work, including celebration of the Eucharist, being available for the Sacrament of Reconciliation, etc.

137/ (129) The statutes of the school define the responsibilities of the school director and the authority of the Society of Jesus (see Characteristic 25 below). Depending on local circumstances, neither the individual Jesuit nor the group of Jesuits as a community has, as such, any power of decision-making in a Jesuit school not described in these statutes.

c) Among the Governing Boards:

138/ (130) General Congregation XXXI of the Society of Jesus recommended that governing boards be established in Jesuit schools, with membership that includes both lay people and Jesuits.[70] These are a further means of sharing responsibility among both lay people and Jesuits and thus promoting lay-Jesuit collaboration. They take advantage of the professional competencies of a variety of different people. The members of these boards, both Jesuits and lay, are familiar with the purposes of a Jesuit school and with the vision of Ignatius on which these purposes are based.

d) Among Parents:

close cooperation with parents

understanding the school character

consistency between values promoted in the school and those promoted in the home

139/ (131) Teachers and directors in a Jesuit school cooperate closely with parents, who are also members of the educational community. There is frequent communication and on-going dialogue between the home and the school. Parents are kept informed about school activities; they are encouraged to meet with the teachers to discuss the progress of their children. Parents are offered support and opportunities for growth in exercising their role as parents, and they are also offered opportunities to participate in advisory councils. In these and other ways, parents are helped to fulfill their right and responsibility as educators in the home and family and they in turn contribute to the work of education going on in the school.[71]

140/ (132) As far as possible, parents <u>understand</u>, <u>value</u>, and <u>accept the Ignatian worldview</u> that characterizes the Jesuit school. The school community, keeping in mind the different situations in different countries, provides opportunities by which parents can become more familiar with this worldview and its applications to education.

141/ (133) There is <u>consistency between the values promoted in the school and those promoted in the home</u>. At the time their children first enroll in the school, parents are informed about the commitment of Jesuit education to a faith that does justice. Programs of ongoing formation are available to parents so that they can understand this aim better and be strengthened in their own commitment to it.

e) Among Students:

142/ (134) Students form a <u>community of understanding and support</u> among themselves; this is reinforced both informally and through such structures as student government and student councils. Moreover, according to their age and capacity, <u>student participation in the larger school community</u> is encouraged through membership on advisory councils and other school committees.

f) Among Former Students:

143/ (135) Former students are members of the "community working in service of the kingdom"; a Jesuit school has a special responsibility to them. As far as resources permit, the school will offer <u>guidance and ongoing formation</u> so that those who received their basic formation in the school can be more effective in putting this formation into practice in adult life and can continue to deepen their dedication to the service of others.[72] Close bonds of friendship and mutual support exist between the <u>Jesuit school and Alumni (Former Student) Associations</u>.[73]

g) Among Benefactors:

144/ (136) In a similar way, the Jesuit school has a special responsibility toward its benefactors and will offer them the support and guidance that they may need. In particular, benefactors have opportunities to learn more about the distinctive nature of a Jesuit school, the Ignatian vision on which it is based, and its goals, to which they contribute.

8.3 Characteristic 25: Jesuit Education Takes Place within a Structure that Promotes Community.

shared responsibility

mission of the Director

role of the Director

directive team

Jesuit authority and control

structures guarantee rights

145/ (137) A greater degree of shared responsibility has developed in recent years. Increasingly, decisions are made only after receiving advice through informal consultations, formal committees, and other means; all members of the educational community are kept informed about decisions and about important events in the life of the school. In order to be truly effective, a sharing of responsibility must be based on a common vision or common sense of purpose, noted above.

146/ (138) In the past the Rector of the Jesuit community, appointed by the Superior General of the Society of Jesus, was responsible for the direction of the Jesuit school; he reported regularly to the Jesuit Provincial. Today, in many parts of the world, the Rector of the community is not the "Director of the Work": in some cases a governing board works in collaboration with the Society in the appointment of the director; more and more frequently this director is a lay person. Whatever the particular situation and whatever the mode of appointment, the responsibility entrusted to the director of a Jesuit school always includes a <u>mission that comes ultimately from the Society of Jesus</u>. This mission, as it relates to the Jesuit character of the school, is subject to periodic evaluation by the Society (normally through the Jesuit Provincial or his delegate).

147/ (139) The <u>role of the director</u> is that of an <u>apostolic leader</u>. The role is vital in providing inspiration, in the development of a common vision and in preserving unity within the educational community. Since the worldview of Ignatius is the basis on which a common vision is built, the director is guided by this worldview and is the one responsible for ensuring that opportunities are provided through which the other members of the community can come to a greater understanding of this worldview and its applications to education. In addition to his role of inspiration, the director remains <u>ultimately responsible</u> for the <u>execution of the basic educational policy</u> of the school and for the <u>distinctively Jesuit</u> nature of this education. The exact nature of this responsibility is described in the statutes of each school.

148/ (140) In many cases, responsibility for the Jesuit school is shared among several people with distinct roles (Rector, Director, President, Principal, or Headmaster); the final responsibility for policy and practice is often entrusted to governing boards. All those sharing responsibility for the Jesuit school form a <u>directive team</u>. They are aware of and are open to the Ignatian vision as this is applied to education; they are able to work together with mutual support and respect, making use of the talents of each. This type of team structure, which is an application of the principle of subsidiarity, has the advantage of bringing the abilities of more people into the leadership of the school; in addition, it ensures greater stability in carrying forward the policies that implement the basic orientation of the school.

149/ (141) If the school is "Jesuit," then sufficient authority and control remains in the hands of the Society of Jesus to enable that Society to respond to a call of the church through its institutions and to ensure that the Jesuit school continues to be faithful to its traditions. Except for this limitation, effective authority in the school can be exercised by anyone,

Jesuit or lay, who has a knowledge of, sympathy for, identification with, and commitment to the Jesuit character of education.

150/ (142) The structures of the school <u>guarantee</u> the <u>rights</u> of students, directors, teachers, and auxiliary staff, and <u>call each to his or her individual responsibilities</u>. All members of the community work together to create and maintain the conditions most favorable for each one to grow in the responsible use of freedom. Every member of the community is invited to be <u>actively engaged</u> in the growth of the entire community. The school structure reflects the new society that the school, through its education, is trying to construct.

SECTION 9: DISCERNMENT

151/ (143) *9. For Ignatius and for his companions, decisions were made on the basis of an ongoing process of individual and communal "discernment"*[74] *done always in a context of prayer. Through prayerful reflection on the results of their activities, the companions reviewed past decisions and made adaptations in their methods, in a constant search for greater service to God ("Magis").*

152/ (144) Jesuit education:

- adapts means and methods in order to achieve its purposes most effectively.
- is a "system" of schools with a common vision and common goals.
- assists in providing the professional training and ongoing formation that is needed, especially for teachers.

9.1 Characteristic 26: A Jesuit Education Adapts Means and Methods in Order to Achieve its Purposes Most Effectively.

change on the basis of "discernment"

norms for change

adapted to fit the specific needs of the place

153/ (145) The educational community in a Jesuit school studies the needs of present-day society and then reflects on school policies, structures, methods, current pedagogical methods, and all other elements of the school environment, to find those means that will best accomplish the purposes of the school and implement its educational philosophy. On the basis of these reflections changes are made in school structure, methods, curriculum, etc., when these are seen to be necessary or helpful. An educator in the Jesuit tradition is encouraged to exercise great freedom and imagination in the choice of teaching techniques, pedagogical methods, etc. School policies and practices encourage reflection and evaluation; they allow for change when change is necessary.

154/ (146) Though general norms need to be applied to concrete circumstances, principles on which this reflection is based can be found in current documents of the church and of the Society of Jesus.[75] In addition, the Jesuit *Constitutions* provide criteria to guide discernment in order to achieve the *"Magis"*: the more universal good, the more urgent need, the more lasting value, work not being done by others, etc.[76]

155/ (147) The "circumstances of persons and places" require that courses of studies, educational processes, styles of teaching, and the whole life of the school be <u>adapted to fit the specific needs of the place</u> where the school is located, and the people it serves.

9.2 Characteristic 27: Jesuit Education Is a "System" of Schools with a Common Vision and Common Goals.

sharing of ideas and experiences

exchange of teachers and students

experimentation in education for justice

156/ (148) The Jesuits in the first schools of the Society shared ideas and the fruits of their experience, searching for the principles and methods that would be "more" effective in accomplishing the purposes of their educational work. Each institution applied these principles and methods to its own situation; the strength of the Jesuit "system" grew out of this interchange. Jesuit schools still form a network, joined not by unity of administration or uniformity of programs, but by a <u>common vision with common goals</u>; teachers and administrators in Jesuit schools are again <u>sharing ideas and experiences</u> in order to discover the principles and methods that will provide the most effective implementation of this common vision.

157/ (149) The interchange of ideas will be more effective if each school is <u>inserted into the concrete reality</u> of the region in which it is located and is engaged in an <u>ongoing exchange of ideas and experiences with other schools</u> and educational works of the local church and of the country. The broader the interchange on the regional level, the more fruitful the interchange among Jesuit schools can be on an international level.

158/ (150) To aid in promoting this interchange of ideas and experiences, an <u>exchange of teachers and students</u> is encouraged wherever possible.

159/ (151) A wide variety of experimentation to discover more effective ways to make "the faith that does justice" a dimension of educational work is going on in all parts of the world. Because of the importance of this challenge, and the difficulty of achieving it, these experiments need to be evaluated and the results shared with others, so that positive experiences can be incorporated into local school policies, practices, and community. The need for an exchange of ideas and experiences in this area is especially great—not only for the individual schools, but also for the apostolate of education as such.

9.3 Characteristic 28: Jesuit Education Assists in Providing the Professional Training and Ongoing Formation that Is Needed, Especially for Teachers.

opportunities for continuing education

an understanding of Ignatian spirituality

an understanding of lay and Jesuit contributions to the church and the Jesuit school

160/ (152) Rapid change is typical of the modern world. In order to remain effective as educators and in order to "discern" the more concrete response to God's call, all adult members of the educational community need to take advantage of <u>opportunities for continuing education</u> and <u>continued personal development</u>—especially in professional competence, pedagogical techniques, and spiritual formation. The Jesuit school encourages this by providing staff development programs in every school and, as far as possible, providing the necessary time and financial assistance for more extended training and formation.

161/ (153) In order to achieve genuine collaboration and sharing of responsibility, <u>lay people need to have an understanding of Ignatian spirituality</u>, of Jesuit educational history and traditions, and Jesuit life, while <u>Jesuits need</u>

to have an understanding of the lived experience, challenges, and ways in which the Spirit of God also moves lay people, together with the contributions lay people make to the church and to the Jesuit school. The Jesuit school provides special orientation programs to new members of staff; in addition, it provides ongoing programs and processes which encourage a growing awareness and understanding of the aims of Jesuit education, and also give an opportunity for Jesuits to learn from the lay members of the community. Where possible, special programs of professional and spiritual training are available to help lay people prepare themselves to assume directive posts in Jesuit schools.

SOME CHARACTERISTICS OF JESUIT PEDAGOGY

162/ (154) Ignatius insisted that Jesuit schools should adopt the methods of the University of Paris ("modus Parisiensis") because he considered these to be the most effective in achieving the goals he had in mind for these schools. The methods were tested and adapted by Jesuit educators in accordance with their religious experience in the *Spiritual Exercises* and their growing practical experience in education. Many of these principles and methods are still typical of Jesuit education because they are still effective in implementing the characteristics described in the previous sections. Some of the more widely known are listed in this final section by way of example.

From the Experience of the *Spiritual Exercises*[77]

163/ (155) 1. Though there are obvious differences between the two situations, the quality of the relationship between the guide of the *Spiritual Exercises* and the person making them is the model for the relationship between teacher and student. Like the guide of the *Exercises*, the teacher is at the service of the students, alert to detect special gifts or special difficulties, personally concerned, and assisting in the development of the inner potential of each individual student.

164/ (156) 2. The active role of the person making the *Exercises* is the model for the active role of the student in personal study, personal discovery, and creativity.

165/ (157) 3. The progression in the *Exercises* is one source of the practical, disciplined, "means to end" approach that is characteristic of Jesuit education.[78]

166/ (158) 4. The "Presupposition" to the *Exercises*[79] is the norm for establishing personal relations and good rapport—between teachers and students, between teachers and school directors, among teachers, among students, and everywhere in the educational community.

167/ (159) 5. Many of the "Annotations" or "suggestions for the guide to the *Exercises*" are, with appropriate adaptations, suggestions to teachers in a Jesuit school.

168/ (160) 6. There are analogies between methods of the *Exercises* and traditional Jesuit teaching methods, many of which were incorporated into the *Ratio Studiorum*:

169/   a. The "preludes" and "points" for prayer are the prelection of the course material to be covered;

170/   b. The "repetition" of prayer becomes the mastery of course material through frequent and careful repetition of class work;

171/   c. The "application of the senses" ("sentir" for Ignatius) is found in the stress on the creative and the imaginative, in the stress on experience, motivation, appreciation, and joy in learning.

From the *Constitutions* and *Ratio Studiorum*

172/ (161) 1. The curriculum is to be structured carefully: in daily order, in the way that courses build on material covered in previous courses, and in the way courses are related to one another. The curriculum should be so integrated that each individual course contributes toward the overall goal of the school.

173/ (162) 2. The pedagogy is to include analysis, repetition, active reflection, and synthesis; it should combine theoretical ideas with their applications.

174/ (163) 3. It is not the quantity of course material covered that is important but rather a solid, profound, and basic formation. ("Non multa, sed multum.")

CONCLUSION

175/ (164) The introduction refers to a meeting held in Rome in 1980, and to the address that Father Pedro Arrupe gave at the conclusion of that meeting. The address was later published under the title "Our Secondary Schools Today and Tomorrow" and has been quoted several times, both in the characteristics themselves and in the footnotes.

176/ (165) In that address, Father Arrupe described the purpose of a Jesuit school. It is, he said, to assist in the formation of

> "New Persons, transformed by the message of Christ, who will be witnesses to His death and resurrection in their own lives. Those who graduate from our secondary schools should have acquired, in ways proportional to their age and maturity, a way of life that is in itself a proclamation of the charity of Christ, of the faith that comes from Him and leads back to Him, and of the justice which he announced."[80]

177/ (166) More recently the present General of the Society of Jesus, Father Peter-Hans Kolvenbach, expressed the same purpose in very similar words:

> "Our ideal is the well-rounded person who is intellectually competent, open to growth, religious, loving, and committed to doing justice in generous service to the people of God."[81]

178/ (167) The aim of Jesuit education has never been simply the acquisition of a store of information and skills or preparation for a career, though these are important in themselves and useful to emerging Christian leaders. The ultimate aim of Jesuit secondary education is, rather, that full growth of the person which leads to action—action that is suffused with the spirit and presence of Jesus Christ, the Man for Others.

179/ (168) The International Commission on the Apostolate of Jesuit Education has attempted to describe the characteristics of Jesuit education in order to help Jesuit schools to achieve this purpose more effectively. The material is not new; the paper is not complete; the work of renewal is never ended. A description of the characteristics of Jesuit education can never be perfect and can never be final. But a growing understanding of the heritage of these schools, the Ignatian vision applied to education, can be the impetus to renewed dedication to this work and renewed willingness to undertake those tasks which will make it ever more effective.

APPENDIX I: IGNATIUS, THE FIRST JESUIT SCHOOLS, AND THE *RATIO STUDIORUM*

The Spiritual Journey of Ignatius of Loyola: 1491–1540

(This narration of the life of Ignatius is based on *A Pilgrim's Testament*,[82] an autobiography dictated to a fellow Jesuit three years before he died. In speaking, Ignatius consistently referred to himself in the third person.)

Loyola to Montserrat

180/ (169) Ignatius was a minor nobleman, born in 1491 in the family castle of Loyola in Basque country and brought up as a knight in the courts of Spain. In his autobiography he sums up the first twenty-six years of his life in one sentence: "he was a man given to the follies of the world; and what he enjoyed most was warlike sport, with a great and foolish desire to win fame."[83] The desire to win fame brought Ignatius to Pamplona to aid in the defense of that frontier city against French attack. The defense was hopeless; when, on May 20, 1521, he was hit by a cannon ball which shattered one leg and badly injured the other, Ignatius and the city of Pamplona both fell to the French forces.

181/ (170) French doctors cared for the badly-wounded Ignatius and returned him to Loyola, where he spent a long convalescence. In this forced period of inactivity he asked for books to read and, out of boredom, accepted the only ones available—*The Lives of the Saints* and *The Life of Christ*. When not reading, the romantic knight dreamed—at times of imitating the deeds of St. Francis and St. Dominic, at times of knightly deeds of valor in service of "a certain lady."[84] After a time, he came to realize that "there was this difference. When he was thinking of those things of the world, he took much delight in them, but afterwards, when he was tired and put them aside, he found himself dry and dissatisfied. But when he thought of . . . practicing all the rigors that he saw in the saints, not only was he consoled when he had these thoughts, but even after putting them aside he remained satisfied and joyful. . . . His eyes were opened a little, and he began to marvel at the difference and to reflect upon it. Little by little he came to recognize the difference between the spirits that were stirring."[85] Ignatius was discovering God at work in his life; his desire for fame was transformed into a desire to dedicate himself completely to God, although he was still very unsure what this meant. "The one thing he wanted to do was to go to Jerusalem as soon as he recovered . . . with as much of disciplines and fasts as a generous spirit, fired with God, would want to perform."[86]

182/ (171) Ignatius began the journey to Jerusalem as soon as his recovery was complete. The first stop was the famous shrine of Montserrat. On March 24, 1522, he laid his sword and dagger "before the altar of Our Lady of Montserrat, where he had resolved to lay aside his garments and to don the armor of Christ."[87] He spent the whole night in vigil, a pilgrim's staff in his hand. From Montserrat he journeyed to a town named Manresa, intending to remain for only a few days. He remained for nearly a year.

Manresa

183/ (172) Ignatius lived as a pilgrim, begging for his basic needs and spending nearly all of his time in prayer. At first the days were filled with great consolation and joy, but soon prayer became torment and he experienced only severe temptations, scruples, and such great desolation that he wished "with great force to throw himself through a large hole in his room."[88] Finally peace returned. Ignatius reflected in prayer on the "good and evil spirits"[89] at work in experiences such as this, and he began to recognize that his freedom to respond to God was influenced by these feelings of "consolation" and "desolation." "God treated him at this time just as a schoolmaster treats a child whom he is teaching."[90]

184/ (173) The pilgrim gradually became more sensitive to the interior movements of his heart and the exterior influences of the surrounding world. He recognized God revealing His love and inviting a response, but he also recognized that his freedom to respond to that love could be helped or hindered by the way he dealt with these influences. He learned to respond in freedom to God's love by struggling to remove the obstacles to freedom. But "love is expressed in deeds."[91] The fullness of freedom led inevitably to total fidelity; the free response of Ignatius to the love of God took the form of loving service: a total dedication to the service of Christ who, for Ignatius the nobleman, was his "King." Because it was a response in love to God's love, it could never be enough; the logic of love demanded a response that was ever more ("*Magis*").

185/ (174) The conversion to loving service of God was confirmed in an experience that took place as he stopped to rest one day at the side of the river Cardoner. "While he was seated there, the eyes of his understanding began to be opened; not that he saw any vision, but he understood and learned many things, both spiritual matters and matters of faith and of scholarship, and this with so great an enlightenment that everything seemed new to him. . . . He experienced a great clarity in his understanding. This was such that in the whole course of his life, after completing sixty-two years, even if he gathered up all the various helps he may have had from God and all the various things he has known, even adding them all together, he does not think he had got as much as at that one time."[92]

186/ (175) Ignatius recorded his experiences in a little book, a practice begun during his convalescence at Loyola. At first these notes were only for himself, but gradually he saw the possibility of a broader purpose. "When he noticed some things in his soul and found them useful, he thought they might also be useful to others, and so he put them in writing."[93] He had discovered God and thus discovered the meaning of life. He took advantage of every opportunity to guide others through this same experience of discovery. As time went on, the notes took on a more structured form and became the basis for a small book called *The Spiritual Exercises*,[94] published in order to help others guide men and women through the experience of an interior freedom that leads to the faithful service of others in service of God.

187/ (176) *The Spiritual Exercises* is not a book simply to be read; it is the guide to an experience, an active engagement enabling growth in the freedom that leads to faithful service. The experience of Ignatius at Manresa can become a personal lived experience.

188/ In the *Exercises* each person has the possibility of discovering that, though sinful, he or she is uniquely loved by God and invited to respond to His love. This response begins with an acknowledgment of sin and its effects, a realization that God's love overcomes sin, and a desire for this forgiving and redeeming love. The freedom to respond is then made possible through a growing ability, with God's help, to recognize and engage in the struggle to overcome the interior and exterior factors that hinder a free response. This response develops positively through a process of seeking and embracing the will of God the Father, whose love was revealed in the person and life of His Son, Jesus Christ, and of discovering and choosing the specific ways in which this loving service of God is accomplished through active service on behalf of other men and women, within the heart of reality.

Jerusalem to Paris

189/ (177) Leaving Manresa in 1523, Ignatius continued his journey to Jerusalem. His experiences during the months at Manresa completed the break with his past life and confirmed his desire to give himself completely to God's service, but the desire was still not clearly focused. He wanted to stay in Jerusalem, visiting the holy places and serving others, but he was not permitted to remain in that troubled city. "After the pilgrim realized that it was not God's will that he remain in Jerusalem, he continually pondered within himself what he ought to do; and eventually he was rather inclined to study for some time so that he would be able to help souls, and he decided to go to Barcelona."[95] Though he was thirty years old he went to school, sitting in class beside the young boys of the city to learn grammar; two years later, he moved on to university studies at Alcalá. When he was not studying he taught others about the ways of God and shared his *Spiritual Exercises* with them. But the Inquisition would not permit someone without training in theology to speak about spiritual things. Rather than keep silent about the one thing that really mattered to him, and convinced that God was leading him, Ignatius left Alcalá and went to Salamanca. The forces of the Inquisition continued to harass him until finally, in 1528, he left Spain entirely and moved to France and the University of Paris.

190/ (178) Ignatius remained in Paris for seven years. Though his preaching and direction in Barcelona, Alcalá, and Salamanca had attracted companions who stayed with him for a time, it was at the University of Paris that a more lasting group of "friends in the Lord"[96] was formed. Peter Favre and Francis Xavier were his roommates, "whom he later won for God's service by means of the *Spiritual Exercises*."[97] Attracted by the same challenge, four others soon joined them. Each of these men experienced God's love personally, and their desire to respond was so complete that their lives were totally transformed. As each one shared this experience with the others, they formed a bond of community which was to last throughout their lives.

Paris to Rome

191/ (179) In 1534, this small group of seven companions journeyed together to a small monastery chapel in Montmartre, outside of Paris, and the only priest among them—Pierre Favre—celebrated a Mass at which they consecrated their lives to God through vows of poverty and chastity. It was during these days that they "determined what they would do, namely, go to Venice and Jerusalem, and spend their lives for the good of souls."[98] At Venice the six other companions were ordained as priests, Ignatius among them. But their decision to go to Jerusalem was not to become a reality.

192/ (180) Recurring warfare between Christian and Islamic armies made travel to the East impossible. While they waited for the tension to ease and pilgrim journeys to be resumed, the companions spent their days preaching, giving the *Exercises*, working in hospitals and among the poor. Finally, when a year had passed and Jerusalem remained inaccessible, they decided that they would "return to Rome and present themselves to the Vicar of Christ so that he could make use of them wherever he thought it would be more for the glory of God and the good of souls."[99]

193/ (181) Their resolve to put themselves at the service of the Holy Father meant that they might be sent to different parts of the world, wherever the Pope had need of them; the "friends in the Lord" would be dispersed. It was only then that they decided to form a more permanent bond which would keep them united even when they were physically separated. They would add the vow of obedience, thus becoming a religious order.

194/ (182) Toward the end of their journey to Rome, at a small wayside chapel in the village of La Storta, Ignatius "was visited very especially by God. . . . He was at prayer in a church and experienced such a change in his soul and saw so clearly that God the Father placed him with Christ his Son that he would not dare doubt it—that God the Father had placed him with his Son."[100] The companions became Companions of Jesus, to be intimately associated with the risen Christ's work of redemption, carried out in and through the church, working in the world. Service of God in Christ Jesus became service in the church and of the church in its redemptive mission.

195/ (183) In 1539 the companions, now ten, were received favorably by Pope Paul III, and the Society of Jesus was formally approved in 1540; a few months later, Ignatius was elected its first Superior General.

The Society of Jesus Enters Education: 1540–1556

196/ (184) Even though all of these first companions of Ignatius were graduates of the University of Paris, the original purposes of the Society of Jesus did not include educational institutions. As described in the "Formula" presented to Paul III for his approval, the Society of Jesus was founded "to strive especially for the defense and propagation of the faith and for the progress of souls in Christian life and doctrine, by means of public preaching, lectures, and any other ministration whatsoever of the word of God, and further by means of the *Spiritual Exercises*, the education of children and unlettered persons in Christianity, and the spiritual consolation of Christ's faithful through hearing confessions and administering the other sacraments."[101] Ignatius wanted Jesuits to be free to move from place to place wherever the need was greatest; he was convinced that institutions would tie them down and prevent this mobility. But the companions had only one goal: "in all things to love and serve the Divine Majesty";[102] they would adopt whatever means could best accomplish this love and service of God through the service of others.

197/ (185) The positive results to be obtained from the education of young boys soon became apparent, and it was not long before Jesuits became involved in this work. Francis Xavier, writing from Goa, India, in 1542, was enthusiastic in his description of the effect Jesuits there were having when they offered instruction at St. Paul's College; Ignatius responded with encouragement. A college had been established in Gandía, Spain, for the education of those preparing to join the Society of Jesus; at the insistence of parents it began, in 1546, to admit other boys of the city. The first "Jesuit school," in the sense of an institution intended primarily for young lay students, was founded in Messina, Sicily, only two years later. And when it became apparent that education was not only an apt means for human and spiritual development but also an effective instrument for defending a faith under attack by the Reformers, the number of Jesuit schools began to increase very rapidly: before his death in 1556, Ignatius personally approved the foundation of 40 schools. For centuries, religious congregations had contributed to the growth of education in philosophy and theology. For the members of this new order to extend their educational work to the humanities and even to running the schools was something new in the life of the church; it needed formal approval by Papal decree.

198/ (186) Ignatius, meanwhile, remained in Rome and dedicated the last years of his life to writing the *Constitutions*[103] of this new religious order.

199/ (187) Inspired by the same vision embodied in the *Spiritual Exercises*, the *Constitutions* manifest the Ignatian ability to combine exalted ends with the most exact and concrete means for achieving them. The work, divided into ten "Parts," is a formative guidebook for Jesuit life.

200/ In its first draft, Part IV consisted of directives for the education of young men being formed as Jesuits. Since he was approving the establishment of new schools at the same time as he was writing the *Constitutions*, Ignatius partly revised Part IV to include the guiding educational principles work that was to be undertaken in these schools. This section of the *Constitutions* is, therefore, the best source for the explicit and direct thought of Ignatius on the apostolate of education, even though it was largely completed before he realized the extensive role education was to play in the apostolic work of Jesuits.

201/ The preamble to Part IV sets the goal: "The aim which the Society of Jesus directly seeks is to aid its own members and their fellowmen to attain the ultimate end for which they were created . . . . To achieve this purpose, in addition to the example of one's life, learning and a method of expounding it are also necessary."[104]

202/ The priorities in the formation of Jesuits became priorities of Jesuit education: a stress on the humanities, to be followed by philosophy and theology,[105] a careful orderly advance to be observed in pursuing these successive branches of knowledge,[106] repetition of the material, and active involvement of the students in their own education.[107] Much time should be spent in developing good style in writing.[108] The role of the Rector, as the center of authority, inspiration, and unity, is essential.[109] These were not new pedagogical methods; Ignatius was familiar with lack of method and with the methods of many schools, especially the careful methods of the University of Paris. He chose and adapted those which would be most effective in achieving the purposes of Jesuit education.

203/ When speaking explicitly about schools for lay students in Part IV, chapter 7, Ignatius is specific about only a few matters. He insists, for example, that the students (at that time nearly all Christians), be "well-instructed in Christian doctrine."[110] Also, in accordance with the principle that there be no temporal remuneration for any Jesuit ministry, no fees are to be charged.[111] Except for these and a few other details, he is content to apply a basic principle found throughout the *Constitutions*: "Since there must be a great variety in particular cases in accordance with the circumstances of place and persons, this present treatment will not descend further to what is particular, except to say that there should be rules which come down to everything necessary in each college."[112] In a later note, he adds a suggestion: "From the Rules of the Roman College, the part which is suitable to the other colleges can be adapted to them."[113]

204/ (188) In separate correspondence, Ignatius promised further development of the rules, or basic principles, which should govern all the schools. But he insisted that he could not provide these principles until he could derive them from the concrete experiences of those actually engaged in education. Before he could fulfill his promise, Ignatius died. It was the early morning of July 31, 1556.

The *Ratio Studiorum* and More Recent History

205/ (189) In the years following the death of Ignatius, not all Jesuits agreed that involvement in schools was a proper activity for the Society of Jesus; it was a struggle that lasted well into the 17th century. Nevertheless, Jesuit involvement in education continued to grow at a rapid rate. Of the 40 schools that Ignatius had personally approved, at least 35 were in operation when he died, even though the total membership of the Society of Jesuits had not yet reached 1,000. Within forty years, the number of Jesuit schools would reach 245. The promised development of a document describing common principles for all Jesuit schools was becoming a practical necessity.

206/ (190) Successive Jesuit superiors encouraged an exchange of ideas based on concrete experiences so that, without violating the Ignatian principle that "circumstances of place and persons" be taken into account, a basic curriculum and basic pedagogy could be developed which would draw on this experience and be common to all Jesuit schools. A period of intense interchange among the schools of the Society followed.

207/ (191) The first drafts of a common document were, as Ignatius had wished, based on the "Rules of the Roman College." An international committee of six Jesuits was appointed by the Superior General Claudio Acquaviva; they met in Rome to adapt and modify these tentative drafts on the basis of experiences in other parts of the world. In 1586 and again in 1591, this group published more comprehensive drafts which were widely distributed for comments and corrections. Further interchange, commission meetings and editorial work resulted, finally, in the publication of a definitive *Ratio Studiorum*[114] on January 8, 1599.

208/ (192) In its final form the *Ratio Studiorum*, or "Plan of Studies" for Jesuit schools, is a handbook to assist teachers and administrators in the daily operation of the school; it is a series of "rules" or practical directives regarding such matters as the government of the school, the formation and distribution of teachers, the curriculum, and methods of teaching. Like Part IV of the *Constitutions*, it is not so much an original work as a collection of the most effective educational methods of the time, tested and adapted for the purposes of the Jesuit schools.

209/ There is little explicit reference to underlying principles flowing from the experience of Ignatius and his Companions, as these were embodied in the *Spiritual Exercises* and the *Constitutions*; such principles had been stated in earlier versions, but were presupposed in the final edition of 1599. The relationship between teacher and student, to take one example, is to be modelled on the relationship between the director of the *Exercises* and the person making them; since the authors of the *Ratio*, along with nearly all the teachers in the schools, were Jesuits, this could be assumed. Even though it is not stated explicitly, the spirit of the *Ratio*—like the inspiring spirit of the first Jesuit schools—was the vision of Ignatius.

210/ (193) The process leading to and resulting in the publication of the *Ratio* produced a "system" of schools whose strength and influence lay in the common spirit that evolved into common pedagogical principles. The pedagogy was based on experience, then refined and adapted through constant interchange. It was the first such educational system that the world had ever seen.

211/ (194) The system of Jesuit schools developed and expanded for more than two hundred years, and then came to a sudden and tragic end. When the Society of Jesus was suppressed by Papal Order in 1773, a network of 845 educational institutions, spread throughout Europe and the Americas, Asia and Africa, was largely destroyed. Only a few Jesuit schools remained in Russian territories, where the suppression never took effect.

212/ (195) When Pius VII was about to bring the Society of Jesus back into existence in 1814, one of the reasons he gave for his action was "so that the Catholic Church could have, once again, the benefit of their educational experience."[115] Educational work did begin again almost immediately and a short time later, in 1832, an experimental revision of the *Ratio Studiorum* was published. But it was never definitively approved. The turmoil of 19th century Europe, marked by revolutions and frequent expulsions of Jesuits from various countries—and therefore from their schools—prevented any genuine renewal in the philosophy or pedagogy of Jesuit education; often enough the Society itself was divided, and its educational institutions were enlisted in the ideological support of one or the other side of warring nations. Nevertheless, in difficult situations, and especially in the developing nations of the Americas, India, and East Asia, the schools of the Society began once again to flourish.

213/ (196) The 20th century, especially in the years after the Second World War, brought a dramatic increase in the size and number of Jesuit schools. The seeds of a renewed spirit were planted in the decrees of various General Congregations, notably the applications of the Second Vatican Council that were incorporated into decree 28 of General Congregation XXXI. Today, the Jesuit educational apostolate extends to more than 2,000 educational institutions, of a bewildering variety of types and levels. 10,000 Jesuits work in close collaboration with nearly 100,000 lay people, providing education for more than 1,500,000 young people and adults in 56 countries around the world.

214/ (197) Jesuit education today does not and cannot form the unified system of the 17th century and, though many principles of the original

Ratio remain valid today, a uniform curriculum and a structure imposed on all schools throughout the world has been replaced by the distinct needs of different cultures and religious faiths and the refinement of pedagogical methods that vary from culture to culture.

215/ (198) This does not mean that a Jesuit "system" of education is no longer a possibility. It was the common spirit, the vision of Ignatius, that enabled the Jesuit schools of the 16th century to evolve common principles and methods; it was the common spirit joined to a common goal—as much as the more specific principles and methods embodied in the *Ratio*—that created the Jesuit school system of the 17th century. This same common spirit, along with the basic goals, purposes, and policies that follow from it, can be true of "Jesuit" schools of today in all countries throughout the world, even when more concrete applications are very different, or when many of the details of school life are determined by cultural factors or outside agencies.

APPENDIX II: A SCHEMATIC OUTLINE

(This outline puts into schematic form the relationship between the spiritual vision of Ignatius and the characteristics of Jesuit education. The nine points in the first column repeat the Ignatian headings for the first nine sections of the main body of the text; the footnotes relate this material to writings of Ignatius (primarily the *Spiritual Exercises* and the *Constitutions*), and to the paragraphs of the historical summary given in Appendix I. The 28 basic characteristics of Jesuit education are repeated in the second column, placed in a way that is intended to show their foundation in the Ignatian worldview. This is not intended to show an exact parallel: rather than a direct application, it would be more accurate to say that the characteristics are derived from, or find their roots in, the Ignatian vision.)

Ignatian Worldview	Jesuit Education
1. For Ignatius, God is Creator and Lord, Supreme Goodness, the one Reality that is absolute;[116] all other reality comes from God and has value only insofar as it leads us to God.[117] This God is present in our lives, "laboring for us" in all things;	— is an apostolic instrument.
He can be discovered through faith in all natural and human events, in history as a whole,	— includes a religious dimension that permeates the entire education.
and most especially in the lived experience of each individual person.[118]	— is world-affirming.
2. Each man or woman is personally known and loved by God. This love invites a response which, to be authentically human, must be an expression of a radical freedom.[119] Therefore, in order to respond to the love of God, each person is called to be:	— assists in the total formation of each individual within the human community.
	— insists on individual care and concern for each person.
• free to give of oneself, while accepting responsibility for and the consequences of one's actions: free to be faithful;	— encourages life-long openness to growth.
• free to work in faith toward that true happiness which is the purpose of life: free to labor with others in the service of the Kingdom of God for the healing of creation.[120]	— emphasizes activity on the part of the student.

Ignatian Worldview	Jesuit Education
3. Because of sin, and the effects of sin, the freedom to respond to God's love is not automatic. Aided and strengthened by the redeeming love of God, we are engaged in an ongoing struggle to recognize and work against the obstacles that block freedom, including the effects of sinfulness, while developing the capacities that are necessary for the exercise of true freedom.[121]	
• This freedom requires a genuine knowledge, love, and acceptance of self, joined to a determination to be freed from any excessive attachment to wealth, fame, health, power, or even life itself.[122]	—encourages a realistic knowledge, love, and acceptance of self.
• True freedom also requires a realistic knowledge of the various forces present in the surrounding world and includes freedom from distorted perceptions of reality, warped values, rigid attitudes, or surrender to narrow ideologies.[123]	—provides a realistic knowledge of the world in which we live.

Ignatian Worldview	Jesuit Education
• To work toward this true freedom, one must learn to recognize and deal with the influences that can promote or limit freedom: the movements within one's own heart; past experiences of all types; interactions with other people; the dynamics of history, social structures, and culture.[124]	—is value-oriented.
4. The worldview of Ignatius is centered on the historical person of Jesus.[125] He is the model for human life because of his total response to the Father's love, in the service of others.	—proposes Christ as the model of human life.
He shares our human condition and invites us to follow him, under the standard of the cross, in loving response to the Father.[126]	—provides adequate pastoral care.
He is alive in our midst, and remains the Man for others in the service of God.	—celebrates faith in personal and community prayer, worship, and service.

Ignatian Worldview	Jesuit Education
5. A loving and free response to God's love cannot be merely speculative or theoretical. No matter what the cost, speculative principles must lead to decisive action: "love is shown in deeds."[127]	—serves the faith that does justice.
Ignatius asks for the total and active commitment of men and women who, to imitate and be more like Christ, will put their ideals into practice in the real world of ideas, social movements, the family, business, political and legal structures, and religious activities.[128]	—seeks to form "men and women for others." —manifests a particular concern for the poor.
6. For Ignatius the response to the call of Christ is in and through the Roman Catholic Church, the instrument through which Christ is sacramentally present in the world.[129] Mary the Mother of Jesus is the model of this response.[130]	—is an apostolic instrument, in service of the church as it serves human society.
Ignatius and his first companions all were ordained as priests and they put the Society of Jesus at the service of the Vicar of Christ, "to go to any place whatsoever where he judges it expedient to send them for the greater glory of God and the good of souls."[131]	—prepares students for active participation in the church and the local community, for the service of others.

Ignatian Worldview	Jesuit Education
7. Repeatedly, Ignatius insisted on the *"Magis"*—the more. His constant concern was for greater service to God through a closer following of Christ, and that concern flowed into all the apostolic work of the first companions. The concrete response to God must be "of greater value."[132]	—pursues excellence in its work of formation. —witnesses to excellence.
8. As Ignatius came to know the love of God revealed through Christ and began to respond by giving himself to the service of the Kingdom of God he shared his experience and attracted companions who became "friends in the Lord," in the service of others.[133] The strength of a community working in service of the Kingdom is greater than that of any individual or group of individuals.	—stresses collaboration. —relies on spirit of community among teaching staff, administrators, Jesuit community, governing boards, parents, students, former students, and benefactors. —takes place within a structure that promotes community.

Ignatian Worldview	Jesuit Education
9. For Ignatius and for his companions, decisions were made on the basis of an ongoing process of individual and communal "discernment" done always in a context of prayer. Through prayerful reflection on the results of their activities, the companions reviewed past decisions and made adaptations in their methods, in a constant search for greater service to God ("Magis").[134]	—adapts means and methods in order to achieve its purposes most effectively. —is a "system" of schools with a common vision and common goals. —assists in providing the professional training and ongoing formation that is needed, especially for teachers.

1   Pedro Arrupe, S.J., "Our Secondary Schools, Today and Tomorrow," § 10. Given in Rome, September 13, 1980; published in *Acta Romana Societatis Iesu* Volume XVIII (Gregorian University Press, 1981). English text, pp. 257–276. Emphasis added. Hereafter abbreviated OSS.

2   The official document is in Latin: *Apostolicam Actuositatem*; an English translation can be found in *The Documents of Vatican II*, Walter Abbott, S.J., General Editor (The America Press, New York, 1966), pp. 489–521.

3   General Congregation XXXII of the Society of Jesus, Decree 4, "Our Mission Today: The Service of Faith and the Promotion of Justice," no. 2. (Published in English in *Documents of the 31st and 32nd General Congregations of the Society of Jesus*, The Institute of Jesuit Sources, 3700 West Pine Boulevard, St. Louis, Missouri, 63108, U.S.A., 1977.)

4   Ibid., no. 9.

5   *The two* phrases *were* repeatedly *used by Father Pedro* Arrupe *in his* writings *and* talks. *The first use* seems *to have been in an address to the Tenth* International Congress *of Jesuit Alumni of Europe held in* Valencia, Spain, *on July 31,* 1973; *this address has been* published *by* several different *offices* under *the title "Men for* Others," e.g। *by the* International Center *for Jesuit* Education, C.P. 6139, 00195 Rome, Italy.

6   The expression is found in the *Constitutions* and in other writings of Ignatius. Father Pedro Arrupe used the phrase as the theme for one of his last talks: *Our Way of Proceeding*, given on January 18, 1979, during the "Ignatian Course" organized by the Center for Ignatian Spirituality (CIS); published as "Documentation No. 42" by the Information Office of the Society of Jesus, C.P. 6139, 00195 Rome, Italy.

7   *Constitutions of the Society of Jesus*, [351] and *passim*. (An English edition of these *Constitutions*, translated, with an introduction and a commentary by George E. Ganss, S.J., has been published by The Institute of Jesuit Sources, St. Louis, Missouri, U.S.A., 1970.) The sentence in the text is a basic principle and a favorite phrase of Ignatius.

8   "The other things on the face of the earth are created for man to help him in attaining the end for which he is created. Hence, man is to make use of them in so far as they help him in the attainment of his end, and he must rid himself of them in so far as they prove a hindrance to them." (*Spiritual Exercises*, § 23.) This is often referred to as the "tantumquantum," from the words used in the Latin text. (Various translations of the *Spiritual Exercises* are available in English. One common text is that of David L. Fleming, S.J., *The Spiritual Exercises of St. Ignatius: A Literal Translation and a Contemporary Reading*, The Institute of Jesuit Sources, St. Louis, Missouri, U.S.A., 1978.)

9   *Spiritual Exercises*, § 236.

10 From "God's *Grandeur*," a poem by Gerard Manley *Hopkins, S.J.*

11 *Cf.* Genesis 1:27.

12 "Our *ideal is . . . the* unsurpassed model *of the* Greeks, in *its* Christian version: balanced, *serene, and* constant, *open to* whatever *is* human" (OSS § *14).

13 *The* "faith response" *is treated in* greater detail *in* sections *4 and* 6.

14 Pope Paul VI in a letter addressed to the Society of Jesus, *Acta Apostolicae Sedis* 57, 1965, p. 514; the same call was repeated by Pope John Paul II in his homily to the delegates of General Congregation XXIII, September 2, 1983. (Cf. *Documents of the 33rd General Congregation of the Society of Jesus*; The Institute of Jesuit Sources, Saint Louis, Missouri, U.S.A., 1984, p. 81.)

15 *The* characteristic *of* being *an* "apostolic instrument" *is treated in* greater detail *in* section 6.1.

16 *Spiritual Exercises*, § 23.

17 Conversion *is treated in* greater detail *in* section 3.

18 "Inculturation" *is* treated *in* detail *in Decree* 5 of *General Congregation* XXXII of the Society of Jesus. See note 3.

19 "This care for each student individually, as far as this is possible, remains and must remain the characteristic of our vocation. . . . Above all, we need to maintain, in one way or in another, this personal contact with each of the students in our schools and colleges." (Father General Peter-Hans Kolvenbach, S.J., "Informal Remarks on Education" given during a meeting with the Delegates for Education of the Jesuit Provinces of Europe, November 18, 1983. Published in *Education: SJ* 44, January–February, 1984, pp. 3–6.)

20 OSS § 13.

[21]   *See Section* 9.3B. *for* a fuller development *of* ongoing formation.

[22]   Forgiveness *and* conversion *are* religious concepts, treated *in* greater detail *in* section 6.

[23]   Cf. The Meditation on "The Two Standards" in the *Spiritual Exercises*, §§ 136–148.

[24]   "In this sphere, as in so many others, do not be afraid of political involvement! It is, according to the Second Vatican Council, the proper role of the laity. It is inevitable, when you become involved in the struggle for structures that make the world more truly human, that bring into being the new creation that Christ promised." (Father General Peter-Hans Kolvenbach, S.J., at the Opening Session of the World Congress of Alumni, Versailles, France, July 20, 1986. Published in ETC [*Together*] 40, [April—September, nn. 2 and 3, 1986], pp. 7–15.)

[25]   Cf. *Spiritual Exercises*, §§ 143–147.

[26]   "It is very important to note that the consideration of the mission of Jesus is not proposed in order for contemplation, or to understand Jesus better, but precisely in so far as this person is inviting us in a 'call' to which the response is a 'following'; . . . without this disposition, there can be no real understanding. In the logic of Saint Ignatius (more implicitly than explicitly) it is apparent that every consideration of Jesus, including the historical Jesus, is made relevant for today's Christianity from a privileged point of view: the point of view of *following*." (Jon Sobrino, *Cristología desde América Latina*. Colección Teología Latinoamericana, Ediciones CRT, México, 1977; p. 329).

[27]   "Pastoral care" is concerned with spiritual—that is, more than simply human—development. But it is not limited to the relationship between God and the individual; it includes also human relationships as these are an expression of, an extension of, the relationship with God. Therefore, "faith" leads to "commitment;" the *discovery* of God leads to the *service* of God in the service of others in the community.

[28]   "*Those* who graduate *from our* secondary schools *should* have acquired, *in* ways proportional *to their* age *and* maturity, a *way of life that is in* itself a proclamation *of the* charity *of* Christ, *of* the *faith* that comes *from Him and leads back to* Him, *and of the justice* which *He* announced." (OSS § 8).

[29]   See Appendix I for a brief description of the *Spiritual Exercises*.

[30]   This *is* treated *in greater detail in the* next *section* and *in* section 9.

[31]   *Spiritual Exercises*, § 230.

[32]   Ibid., § 167.

[33]   The "Formula of the Institute," which is the original description of the Society of Jesus written by Ignatius, applies this basic principle of the *Spiritual Exercises*: "Whoever desires to serve as a soldier of God beneath the banner of the cross in our Society . . . should . . . keep what follows in mind. He is a member of a Society founded chiefly for this purpose: to strive especially for the defense and propagation of the faith and for the progress of souls in Christian life and doctrine." *(Constitutions, Formula* (pp. 66–68), [3]).

[34]   *Father* General Peter-Hans Kolvenbach speaking *at the* World Congress of *Jesuit Alumni at* Versailles. *See* Note *24.*

[35]   The "faith" is treated in sections 1 and 4; this present section concentrates on "justice." However, it is important not to separate these two concepts:

> "*The* living *out of this* unity *of faith and justice is* made possible through a *close* following *of* the historical Jesus. *As essential* parts *of* this following, *we* propose these points:

> In announcing the Kingdom and in his struggle against sin, Jesus ran into conflict with persons and structures which, because they were objectively sinful, were opposed to the *Kingdom* of God.

> The fundamental basis for the connection between justice and faith has to be seen in their inseparable connection with the new commandment of love. On the one hand, the struggle for justice is the form which love ought to take in an unjust world. On the other hand, the New Testament is quite clear in showing that it is love for men and women which is the royal road which reveals that we are loved by God and which brings us to love for God."

> (*Reunión Latinoamericana de Educación*, Lima, Perú; July, 1976; published by CERPE; Caracas, Venezuela; p. 65.)

[36]   General Congregation XXXII *of the Society of Jesus,* Decree *4,* "Our Mission *Today: The* Service *of Faith and the* Promotion *of* Justice," *no. 4. See note 3.*

[37]   OSS § 11.

[38]   *Cf. the* "Preface" *from the* Roman Catholic *Mass* celebrating *the Feast of* Christ the King.

39 In his address to the Presidents and Rectors of Jesuit Universities at their meeting in Frascati, Italy on November 5, 1985, Father General Peter-Hans Kolvenbach gives several examples of how justice issues can be treated in various academic courses. (Cf. "The Jesuit University Today," published in *Education: SJ* 53, November-December, 1985, pp. 7–8.)

40 Cf. Gabriel Codina, S.J., "Faith and Justice within the Educational Context," (published in *Education: SJ* 56, June-July, 1986, pp. 12–13.)

41 Ibid., p. 11.

42 *Ibid., pp.* 14–15. Emphasis added.

43 *See note 5. The "others" in the* much-repeated phrase *is the "neighbor" in the* parable *of the good Samaritan (Luke 10:29–37). The quotation in the text is Father* Arrupe's development *of this* idea *(see next* Note).

44 "Men for *Others" (see Note 5)*, p. 9.

45 *Concrete examples of a stress on* community values *can be* found *in* nearly every *section of* this *present* description *of* the Characteristics *of* Jesuit Education.

46 *"Outside* of the *influence* of the *home, the* example of the *faculty and the climate* which they create *in the school will* be the *single most influential factor in* any effort *at education for* faith and justice." *("Sowing* Seeds *of Faith* and Justice" *by Robert J. Starratt, S.J. Published* by the Jesuit *Secondary Education Association, Washington, D.C., USA; p. 17.)*

47 *The phrase is common in recent* documents *of the church and of the Society of Jesus. The* exact meaning *is* much discussed; what *it does not* mean *is an* option *for* a single class *of* people *to the* exclusion *of* others. Its meaning *within the* educational context *is* described *in* this section 5.4.

48 "The Society of Jesus has one finality: we are for everyone. Rich and poor, oppressed and oppressors, everyone. No one is excluded from our apostolate. This is true also for the schools." (Pedro Arrupe, S.J., "Reflections During the Meeting on Secondary Education," published in *Education: SJ* 30, October-December, 1980, p. 11.)

49 *The* question *of* admission *of* students varies greatly *from* country. *Where there is no* government aid, the *school exists through* fees *and* gifts. A *concern for* justice includes *just* wages *and good* working conditions *for* everyone *working in the* school, *and this* must *also be* taken *into consideration in* the option for *the* poor.

50 *OSS* § 8.

51 Cf. Codina, *op. cit.* p. 8. A more complete explanation of these points is given in that document.

52 *Constitutions*, [603].

53 Cf. Vatican Council II, The Dogmatic Constitution on the Church (*Lumen Gentium*), nn. 66–69.

54 The "spiritual vision" mentioned here includes the entire faith response of earlier sections. Once again, questions of justice cannot be separated from the faith and evangelical charity on which they are based.

55 The expression is taken from the meditation on "The Kingdom of Christ" in the *Spiritual Exercises*, § 97, where the aim is to lead the person making the *Exercises* to a closer following of Christ.

56 *"The* excellence which *we seek consists in* producing men *and women of* right principles, personally appropriated; men *and* women *open to the* signs *of the* times, *in tune with their* cultural milieu *and its* problems; men *and* women *for others." OSS* § 9.

57 Some *criteria* for excellence *are* given *in section* 9.1; *they are the* same *as the criteria for* discernment.

58 *OSS* § 6.

59 *"The* strange expression which *Father* Pedro Arrupe *used so* frequently—*that we are to* produce 'multiplying agents'—*is, in fact, in* complete accord *with the* apostolic vision *of* Ignatius. *His* correspondence *of* 6,815 letters amply proves *that* Ignatius never *ceased to seek out and* encourage *the* widest possible collaboration, with *all* types *of* people." (Father General Peter-Hans Kolvenbach, *at the* Opening *Session of the* World Congress *of* Jesuit Alumni, Versailles. *See* Note 24.)

60 OSS § 12.

61 *"We need to* learn, *and we have an* obligation *to* share. *There* are *enormous* advantages *to be* gained through collaboration *of* every type. *It would be* foolish *to* pretend *that we have* nothing *to learn. It would be* irresponsible *to* think *only of* ourselves *in our* planning without *considering the need to* cooperate *with other* secondary schools. *This . . .* will *make us* more effective apostolically, *and will at* the same *time increase and* strengthen *our sense of* being a *part of* the church." *(Ibid.*§ 25.) *The* question *of* evaluation *is* taken *up* again *in* greater *detail in section 9.*

[62] Ignatius is the author of this phrase, in a letter written to Juan de Verdolay on July 24, 1537. (*Monumenta Ignatiana Epp. XII*, 321 and 323.)

[63] *Apostolicam Actuositatem*—"On the Apostolate of the Laity"—see note 2.

[64] General Congregation XXXI, *decree 33 ("The* Relationship *of the Society to the Laity and Their* Apostolate"); *decree 28* ("The Apostolate *of* Education") *n. 27.* General Congregation *XXXII, decree 2* ("Jesuits Today") *n. 29.* General Congregation XXXIII, *decree 1* ("Companions of *Jesus Sent into* Today's World"), *n. 47.*

[65] "We used to think of the institution as "ours," with some lay people helping us, even if their number was much greater than the number of Jesuits. Today, some Jesuits seem to think that the number of lay people has so increased and the control has been so radically transferred, that the institution is no longer really Jesuit. . . . I would insist that the [school] itself remains an apostolic instrument: *not of the Jesuits alone, but of Jesuits and lay people working together.*" (Father General Peter-Hans Kolvenbach, "The Jesuit University Today." See note 39.)

[66] See below, sections 8.7 and 9.3.

[67] General Congregation XXXI, *Decree 28, "On the* Apostolate *of* Education," *n. 27.*

[68] General Congregation XXXII, *Decree 1, "Jesuits* Today," 29.

[69] OSS §§ *16,* 18.

[70] "It *will also be* advantageous *to* consider whether *it* would *not be* helpful *to* establish *in* some *of* our institutions *of* higher education a *board of trustees* which *is* composed *partly of Jesuits and partly* of *lay* people." (General Congregation XXXI, *Decree 28, "On the* Apostolate *of* Education," *n. 27.*)

[71] "*We* should cooperate *with* [parents] *in the* work *of* education. . . . I want *to* give *special* praise *to those* organizations—associations, journals, formation *courses*—which promote *the* educational formation *of the parents* of *our* students, *to* prepare them *for* a more effective collaboration *with the* secondary school." (OSS § 22.)

[72] "*The* ongoing formation *of* former students *is an* obligation. . . . *It is* a work *that only we can* do, practically speaking, *because it is* a question *of* redoing *the* formation *that we* gave twenty *or thirty* years ago. *The person* that the world *needs now is* different from *the* persons *we* formed *then! It is an* immense task, *and well* beyond *our* own abilities; *we need to seek the help of lay* people *who can help to* bring *it* about." (*Ibid.*, § 23.)

[73] "*What is the commitment* of *the* Society *of Jesus to its* former students? *It is the* commitment of Ignatius, *repeated by Pedro* Arrupe: *to* make you multiplying *agents, to* make you *capable of* incorporating *the* vision *of* Ignatius *and the* . . . mission *of the* Society *into* your own lives. . . . The formation you *have* received should have given you *the* values *and the commitment that* mark *your* lives, *along with the ability to help one* another *renew this* commitment *and apply these* values *to the* changing circumstances *of* your lives *and the* changing *needs of the* world. *We Jesuits will* not abandon you—*but neither will we* continue *to* direct you! *We will be with* you *to guide and inspire, to* challenge *and to help.* But *we* trust you enough *to carry* forward *in* your lives and *in* the world *the* formation you *have been* given." *(Father* General Peter-Hans Kolvenbach, *address at the Opening Session of the World* Congress *of Jesuit* Alumni, Versailles, 1986; *see note 24. This* entire *address is* a development *of the* relationship between *the Society of Jesus and its* former students.)

[74] The word "discernment" is used in many different contexts. Ignatius has "Rules for the Discernment of Spirits" in the *Spiritual Exercises,* §§ 313–336; in the present context it is rather the "communal apostolic discernment" practiced by the first companions and recommended by General Congregation XXXIII: a review of every work that includes "an attentiveness to the Word of God, an examination and reflection inspired by the Ignatian tradition; a personal and communitarian conversion necessary in order to become 'contemplatives in action'; an effort to live an indifference and availability that will enable us to find God in all things; and a transformation of our habitual patterns of thought through a constant interplay of experience, reflection, and action. We must also always apply those criteria for action found in the *Constitutions,* Part VII, as well as recent and more specific instructions. . . ." (GC XXXIII, Decree 1, n. 40.)

[75] One *of the* most *recent and* most complete *sources is the* letter *on* "Apostolic Discernment *in* Common" published by *Father* General Peter-Hans Kolvenbach *in* November, *1986. It is* a *rich source of* information *on* this topic, *giving an* historical perspective *and also* concrete suggestions.

[76] Cf. *Constitutions,* Part VII, especially [622]–[624].

77 The dependence of Jesuit education on the principles and methods of the *Spiritual Exercises* has been the subject of much study. One of the classic—somewhat outdated, but still valuable—works that treat this matter in great detail is *La Pedagogie des Jesuites*, by François Charmot, S.J., Paris, 1941. More recent treatments of the same subject can be found in "Reflections on the Educational Principles of the *Spiritual Exercises*" by Robert R. Newton (Monograph 1, published in 1977 by the Jesuit Secondary Education Association, 1424 16th Street, NW, Suite 300, Washington, D.C. 20036, U.S.A.), and *Le Secret des Jésuites* (published in 1984 as Number 57 of "Collection Christus" by Desclée de Brouwer, 76 bis, rue des Saints-Pères, 75007 Paris, France).

78 See section 1.

79 Ignatius wrote the "Presupposition" of the Spiritual *Exercises* to indicate the relation between the guide to the *Exercises* and the person making them. It can be the norm for human relations in general and especially within the educational community. What follows is a rather literal translation from the Spanish of Ignatius:

> "To assure better cooperation between the one who is giving the *Exercises* and the exercitant, and more beneficial results for both, it is necessary to suppose that every good Christian is more ready to put a good interpretation on another's statement than to condemn it as false. If an orthodox construction cannot be put on a proposition, the one who made it should be asked how he understands it. If he is in error, he should be corrected with all kindness. If this does not suffice, all appropriate means should be used to bring him to a correct interpretation, and so defend the proposition from error." (*Spiritual Exercises* § 22).

80 OSS § 12.

81 "*Talk of Father* General Peter-Hans Kolvenbach *at St. Paul's* High School, Winnipeg, Canada: *May 14, 1986*"; published *in the* Newsletter of *the* Upper Canadian *Jesuit* Province, *June, 1986,* pp. *7–8.*

82 There are various translations of the Spanish and Italian original of what is often referred to as the "autobiography" of St. Ignatius. The translation used in the text is *A Pilgrim's Testament: The Memoirs of Ignatius of Loyola*, Parmananda R. Divarkar, translator (Gregorian University Press, Piazza della Pilotta 4, 00187 Rome, Italy; 1983). Hereafter abbreviated *Memoirs*.

83 *Memoirs*, § 1.

84 Ibid., § 6.

85 Ibid., § 8.

86 Ibid., § 9.

87 Ibid., § 17.

88 Ibid., § 24.

89 Ibid., § 25.

90 Ibid., § 27.

91 *Spiritual Exercises*, [230]. (See above, note 8.)

92 *Memoirs*, § 30.

93 *Ibid.*, § 99.

94 See note 8.

95 *Memoirs*, § 50.

96 *See* above, *note* 62.

97 *Memoirs*, § 82.

98 *Ibid.*, § 85.

99 *Ibid.*

100 *Ibid*, § 96.

101 *Constitutions, Formula* (pp. 66–68), [3]; see note 7.

102 *Spiritual Exercises*, § 233.

103 See note 7.

104 *Constitutions*, [307].

105 *Ibid.*, [351].

106 *Ibid.*, [366].

107 *Ibid.*, [375] *and* [378].

108 *Ibid.*, [381].

109 *Ibid.*, [421] *to* [439].

110 *Ibid.*, [395].

111 *Ibid.*, [398].

112 *Ibid.*, [395].

113 *Ibid.*, [396]. *The Roman* College *was established by* Ignatius himself *in* 1551; *though its beginnings were very* modest, *he* wished *it to* become *the* model *for all Jesuit* schools throughout *the* world. *It* developed *in* time *into* a University, *whose* name *was changed after* the unification of *Italy into the* Gregorian *University.*

114 The original Latin of the *Ratio Studiorum* of 1599, along with the previous drafts, has been newly published as Volume V of *Monumenta Paedagogica Societatis Iesu*, edited by Ladislaus Lukacs, S.J. (Institutum Historicum Societatis Iesu, Via dei Penitenzieri, 20, 00193 Rome, Italy, 1986). An English translation is available, *The Jesuit Ratio Studiorum of 1599*, translated with an introduction and explanatory notes by Allan P. Farrell, S.J. (The Jesuit Conference, 1424 16th Street, NW, Suite 300, Washington, D.C. 20036, U.S.A.; 1970.)

115 From the Papal Bull *Sollicitudo Omnium Ecclesiarum* of August 7, 1814, by which the Society of Jesus was restored throughout the world.

116 Appendix I (183/); the names that Ignatius uses for God can be found throughout his works; see, for example, *Exercises* §§ 15,16.

117 This is the Principle and Foundation of the *Exercises*, § 23; see note 8, above.

118 God working *for us through creation is basic to Ignatian Spirituality. Two examples in the Exercises are the meditation on the "Incarnation," §§ 101–109, and the "Contemplation for Obtaining Love" §§ 230–237. The quotation is from § 236. Ignatius talked repeatedly about "seeing God in all things" and this was paraphrased by Nadal (one of the first companions of Ignatius) into the famous "contemplatives in action."*

119 Appendix *I (184/).*

120 The purpose of making the *Spiritual Exercises has* been summed up in the expression "Spiritual Freedom." Ignatius himself gives them the title "Spiritual Exercises, which have as their purpose the conquest of self and the regulation of one's life in such a way that no decision is made under the influence of any inordinate attachment." (§ 21).

121 Appendix I (183/); this statement is a summary of the "First Week" of the *Exercises.*

122 Appendix I (184/); *Exercises* § 1; §§ 313–329 ("Rules for the Discernment of Spirits").

123 Appendix I (184/); *Exercises* §§ 142–146 ("The Two Standards").

124 *Exercises* §§ 24–42 ("The Examination of Conscience"), and "The Two Standards," above.

125 Appendix I (184/), (193/); *Exercises* § 53, §§ 95–98 ("The Kingdom of Christ") § 167 ("The Third Degree of Humility"). The 2nd, 3rd, and 4th "Weeks" of the *Exercises are* intended to lead to a commitment to the following of Christ.

126 *Exercises* § 116 ("Contemplation on the Nativity"); see also "The Two Standards" noted above.

127 Appendix I (184/), (190/); *Exercises* § 135, §§ 169–189 ("The Election").

128 Appendix *I (188/),* (184).

129 *Exercises* §§ 352–370 ("Rules for Thinking with the Church"); *Constitutions, Formula (*pp. 66–68), [3], [603], and p*assim* throughout the writings of Ignatius. When he realized that it would not be possible to go to the Holy Land to serve Christ directly, Ignatius chose "the next best thing" by going to Rome to serve the church under the "Vicar of Christ."

130 Devotion to Mary, the Mother of Jesus, is evident throughout the whole life of Ignatius; as noted in Appendix I (171), it was at Montserrat that his pilgrimage began; Mary appears throughout the *Exercises*, for example in §§ 47, 63, 102ff, 111f, 147, 218, 299.

131 Appendix *I (191/), (193/). According to some authors, Ignatius was the originator of the expression "Vicar of Christ"; whether that be true or not, loyalty to the Pope is characteristic both of Ignatius and of the Society of Jesus that he founded.*

132 Appendix I (184/); *Exercises* §§ 97, 155.

133 Appendix *I (189/), (192/).*

134 The "discernment of spirits" is present in the whole life of Ignatius; it is already evident at Manresa (Appendix I, 181/), but it is constantly growing throughout his life. A short document entitled "The Deliberations of the First Fathers" describes the discernment of the first companions of Ignatius that led to the establishment of the Society of Jesus. See also Appendix I (189)–(193) for the process that led to the first R*atio Studiorum* and *Exercises* §§ 313–336 ("Rules for the Discernment of Spirits").

Ignatian Pedagogy: A Practical Approach, 1993

Editor's Introduction: This document, commonly known as the Ignatian Pedagogical Paradigm (IPP), constitutes the third official document on education of the Society. It unpacks the pedagogical style required by *The Characteristics of Jesuit Education* and provides guidelines for the classroom teacher who wants to teach in the Jesuit tradition.

INTRODUCTORY NOTES

1/   1. This document grows out of the 10th part of *The Characteristics of Jesuit Education* in response to many requests for help in formulating a practical pedagogy which is consistent with and effective in communicating the Ignatian worldview and values presented in the *Characteristics* document. It is essential, therefore, that what is said here be understood in conjunction with the substantive Ignatian spirit and apostolic thrust presented in *The Characteristics of Jesuit Education*.

2/   2. The field of Jesuit pedagogy has been discussed in numerous books and scholarly articles over the centuries. In this paper we treat only some aspects of this pedagogy which serve to introduce a practical teaching strategy. The Ignatian Pedagogical Paradigm proposed here can help to unify and incarnate many of the principles enunciated in *The Characteristics of Jesuit Education*.

3/   3. It is obvious that a universal curriculum for Jesuit schools or colleges similar to that proposed in the original *Ratio Studiorum* is impossible today. However, it does seem important and consistent with the Jesuit tradition to have a systematically organized pedagogy whose substance and methods promote the explicit vision of the contemporary Jesuit educational mission. Responsibility for cultural adaptations is best handled at the regional or local level. What seems more appropriate at a more universal level today is an Ignatian Pedagogical Paradigm which can help teachers and students to focus their work in a manner that is academically sound and at the same time formative of persons for others.

4/   4. The pedagogical paradigm proposed here involves a particular style and process of teaching. It calls for infusion of approaches to value learning and growth within existing curricula rather than adding courses. We believe that such an approach is preferable both because it is more realistic in light of already crowded curricula in most educational institutions, and because this approach has been found to be more effective in helping learners to interiorize and act upon the Ignatian values set out in *The Characteristics of Jesuit Education.*

5/   5. We call this document *Ignatian Pedagogy* since it is intended not only for formal education provided in Jesuit schools, colleges, and universities, but it can be helpful in every form of educational service that in one way or other is inspired by the experience of St. Ignatius recorded in the Spiritual Exercises, in Part IV of the Constitutions of the Society of Jesus, and in the Jesuit *Ratio Studiorum.*

6/   6. Ignatian pedagogy is inspired by faith. But even those who do not share this faith can gather valuable experiences from this document because the pedagogy inspired by St. Ignatius is profoundly human and consequently universal.

7/   7. Ignatian pedagogy from its beginnings has been eclectic in selection of methods for teaching and learning. Ignatius Loyola himself adapted the "modus Parisiensis," the ordered pedagogical approach employed at the University of Paris in his day. This was integrated with a number of the methodological principles he had previously developed for use in the Spiritual Exercises. To be sure, the sixteenth century Jesuits lacked the formal, scientifically tested methods proposed, for example, in developmental psychology in recent times. Attention to care for the individual student made these Jesuit teachers attentive to what really helped learning and human growth. And they shared their findings across many parts of the world, verifying more universally effective pedagogical methods. These were specified in the *Ratio Studiorum,* the Jesuit code of liberal education which became normative for all Jesuit schools. (A brief description of some of these methods is presented in Appendix II.)

8/   8. Over the centuries a number of other specific methods more scientifically developed by other educators have been adopted within Jesuit pedagogy insofar as they contribute to the goals of Jesuit education. A perennial characteristic of Ignatian pedagogy is the ongoing systematic incorporation of methods from a variety of sources which better contribute to the integral intellectual, social, moral, and religious formation of the whole person.

9/   9. This document is only one part of a comprehensive, long-term renewal project which has been in progress for several years with such programs as the Colloquium on the Ministry of Teaching, the Curriculum Improvement Process, the Magis Program and the like. Renewal requires a change of heart, an openness of mind and spirit to break new ground for the good of one's students. Thus, building on previous stages of renewal this document aims to move a major step ahead by introducing Ignatian pedagogy through understanding and practice of methods that are appropriate to achieve the goals of Jesuit education. This paper, therefore, must be accompanied by practical staff development programs which enable teachers to learn and to be comfortable with a structure for teaching and learning the Ignatian Pedagogical Paradigm and specific methods to facilitate its use. To assure that this can happen, educators, lay and Jesuit, from all continents are being trained to provide leadership in staff development programs at regional, province, and local school levels.

10/   10. The *Ignatian Pedagogy Project* is addressed in the first instance to teachers. For it is especially in their daily interaction with students in the learning process that the goals and objectives of Jesuit education can be realized. How a teacher relates to students, how a teacher conceives of learning, how a teacher engages students in the quest for truth, what a teacher expects of students, a teacher's own integrity and ideals—all of these have significant formative effects upon student growth. Father Kolvenbach takes note of the fact that "Ignatius appears to place teachers' personal example ahead of learning as an apostolic means to help students grow in values." (cf. Appendix II, #125) It goes without saying that in schools, administrators,

members of governing boards, staff, and other members of the school community also have indispensable and key roles in promoting the environment and learning processes that can contribute to the ends of Ignatian
pedagogy. It is important, therefore, to share this project with them.

IGNATIAN PEDAGOGY

11/   Pedagogy is the way in which teachers accompany learners in their
growth and development. Pedagogy, the art and science of teaching, cannot
simply be reduced to methodology. It must include a world view and a vision
of the ideal human person to be educated. These provide the goal, the end
towards which all aspects of an educational tradition are directed. They also
provide criteria for choices of means to be used in the process of education.
The worldview and ideal of Jesuit education for our time has been expressed
in *The Characteristics of Jesuit Education*. Ignatian Pedagogy assumes that
worldview and moves one step beyond suggesting more explicit ways in
which Ignatian values can be incarnated in the teaching-learning process.

The Goal of Jesuit Education

12/   What is our goal? *The Characteristics of Jesuit Education* offers a
description which has been amplified by Fr. General Kolvenbach:

> The pursuit of each student's intellectual development to the full
> measure of God-given talents rightly remains a prominent goal of
> Jesuit education. Its aim, however, has never been simply to amass a
> store of information or preparation for a profession, though these are
> important in themselves and useful to emerging Christian leaders.
> The ultimate aim of Jesuit education is, rather, that full growth of
> the person which leads to action—action, especially, that is suffused
> with the spirit and presence of Jesus Christ, the Son of God, the
> Man for Others. This goal of action, based on sound understand-
> ing and enlivened by contemplation, urges students to self-discipline
> and initiative, to integrity and accuracy. At the same time, it judges
> slip-shod or superficial ways of thinking unworthy of the individual

and, more important, dangerous to the world he or she is called to serve.[1]

13/   Father Arrupe summarized this by pointing to our educational goal as "forming men and women for others." Father Kolvenbach has described the hoped-for graduate of a Jesuit school as a person who is "well-rounded, intellectually competent, open to growth, religious, loving, and committed to doing justice in generous service to the people of God." Father Kolvenbach also states our goal when he says "We aim to form leaders in service, in imitation of Christ Jesus, men and women of competence, conscience and compassionate commitment."

14/   Such a goal requires a full and deeper formation of the human person, an educational process of formation that calls for excellence—a striving to excel, to achieve one's potential—that encompasses the intellectual, the academic, and more. It calls for a human excellence modelled on Christ of the Gospels, an excellence that reflects the mystery and reality of the Incarnation, an excellence that reveres the dignity of all people as well as the holiness of all creation. There are sufficient examples from history of educational excellence narrowly conceived, of people extraordinarily advanced intellectually who, at the same time, remain emotionally undeveloped and morally immature. We are beginning to realize that education does not inevitably humanize or Christianize people and society. We are losing faith in the naive notion that all education, regardless of its quality or thrust or purpose, will lead to virtue. Increasingly, then, it becomes clear that if we in Jesuit education are to exercise a moral force in society, we must insist that the process of education takes place in a moral as well as an intellectual framework. This is not to suggest a program of indoctrination that suffocates the spirit; neither does it look for the introduction of theoretical courses which are speculative and remote from reality. What is needed is a framework of inquiry for the process of wrestling with significant issues and complex values of life, and teachers capable and willing to guide that inquiry.

Towards a Pedagogy for Faith and Justice

15/   Young men and women should be free to walk a path whereby they are enabled to grow and develop as fully human persons. In today's world, however, there is a tendency to view the aim of education in excessively utilitarian terms. Exaggerated emphasis of financial success can contribute to extreme competitiveness and absorption with selfish concerns. As a result, that which is human in a given subject or discipline may be diminished in students' consciousness. This can easily obscure the true values and aims of humanistic education. To avoid such distortion, teachers in Jesuit schools present academic subjects out of a human centeredness, with stress on uncovering and exploring the patterns, relationships, facts, questions, insights, conclusions, problems, solutions, and implications which a particular discipline brings to light about what it means to be a human being. Education thus becomes a carefully reasoned investigation through which the student forms or reforms his or her habitual attitudes towards other people and the world.

16/   From a Christian standpoint, the model for human life—and therefore the ideal of a humanely educated individual—is the person of Jesus. Jesus teaches us by word and example that the realization of our fullest human potential is achieved ultimately in our union with God, a union that is sought and reached through a loving, just, and compassionate relationship with our brothers and sisters. Love of God, then, finds true expression in our daily love of neighbor, in our compassionate care for the poor and suffering, in our deeply human concern for others as God's people. It is a love that gives witness to faith and speaks out through action on behalf of a new world community of justice, love, and peace.

17/   The mission of the Society of Jesus today as a religious order in the Catholic Church is the service of faith of which the promotion of justice is an essential element. It is a mission rooted in the belief that a new world community of justice, love, and peace needs educated persons of competence, conscience, and compassion, men and women who are ready to embrace and promote all that is fully human, who are committed to working for the freedom and dignity of all peoples, and who are willing to do so in cooperation with others equally dedicated to the reform of society and its structures. Renewal of our social, economic, and political systems so that they nourish and preserve our common humanity and free people to be generous in their love and care for others requires resilient and resourceful persons. It calls for persons, educated in faith and justice, who have a powerful and ever growing sense of how they can be effective advocates, agents, and models of God's justice, love, and peace within as well as beyond the ordinary opportunities of daily life and work.

18/   Accordingly, education in faith and for justice begins with a reverence for the freedom, right and power of individuals and communities to create a different life for themselves. It means assisting young people to enter into the sacrifice and joy of sharing their lives with others. It means helping them to discover that what they most have to offer is who they are rather than what they have. It means helping them to understand and appreciate that other people are their richest treasure. It means walking with them in their own journeys toward greater knowledge, freedom, and love. This is an essential part of the new evangelization to which the Church calls us.

19/   Thus education in Jesuit schools seeks to transform how youth look at themselves and other human beings, at social systems and societal structures, at the global community of humankind and the whole of natural creation. If truly successful, Jesuit education results ultimately in a radical transformation not only of the way in which people habitually think and act, but of the very way in which they live in the world, men and women of competence, conscience, and compassion, seeking the *greater good* in terms of what can be done out of a faith commitment with justice to enhance the quality of peoples' lives, particularly among God's poor, oppressed and neglected.

20/   To achieve our goal as educators in Jesuit schools, we need a pedagogy that endeavors to form men and women for others in a postmodern world where so many forces are at work which are antithetical to that aim.[2] In addition we need an ongoing formation for ourselves as teachers to be able to provide this pedagogy effectively. There are, moreover, many places where governmental entities define the limits of educational programs and where teacher training is counterproductive to a pedagogy which encourages student activity in learning, fosters growth in human excellence, and promotes formation in faith and values along with the transmission of knowledge and skill as integral dimensions of the learning process. This describes the real situation facing many of us who are teachers and administrators in Jesuit schools. It poses a complex apostolic challenge as we embark daily on our mission to win the trust and faith of new generations of youth, to walk with them along the pathway toward truth, to help them work for a just world filled with the compassion of Christ.

21/   How do we do this? Since the publication in 1986 of *The Characteristics of Jesuit Education*, a frequent question of teachers and administrators alike in Jesuit schools has been: "How can we achieve what is proposed in this document, the educational formation of youth to be men and women for others, in the face of present day realities?" The answer necessarily must be relevant to many cultures; it must be usable in different situations; it must be applicable to various disciplines; it must appeal to multiple styles and preferences. Most importantly, it must speak to teachers of the realities as well as the ideals of teaching. All of this must be done, moreover, with particular regard for the preferential love of the poor which characterizes the mission of the Church today. It is a hard challenge and one that we cannot disregard because it goes to the heart of what is the apostolate of Jesuit education. The solution is not simply to exhort our teachers and administrators to greater dedication. What we need, rather, is a model of how to proceed that promotes the goal of Jesuit education, a paradigm that speaks to the teaching-learning process, that addresses the teacher-learner relationship, and that has practical meaning and application for the classroom.

22/   The first decree of the 33rd General Congregation of the Society of Jesus, "Companions of Jesus Sent into Today's World," encourages Jesuits in the regular apostolic discernment of their ministries, both traditional and new. Such a review, it recommends, should be attentive to the Word of God and should be inspired by the Ignatian tradition. In addition, it should allow for a transformation of peoples' habitual patterns of thought through a constant interplay of experience, reflection, and action.[3] It is here that we find the outline of a model for bringing *The Characteristics of Jesuit Education* to life in our schools today, through a way of proceeding that is thoroughly consistent with the goal of Jesuit education and totally in line with the mission of the Society of Jesus. We turn our consideration, then, to an Ignatian paradigm that gives preeminence to the constant interplay of EXPERIENCE, REFLECTION, and ACTION.

Pedagogy of the Spiritual Exercises

23/   A distinctive feature of the Ignatian Pedagogical Paradigm is that, understood in the light of the *Spiritual Exercises of St. Ignatius*, it becomes not only a fitting description of the continual interplay of experience, reflection, and action in the teaching-learning process, but also an ideal portrayal of the dynamic interrelationship of teacher and learner in the latter's journey of growth in knowledge and freedom.

24/   Ignatius' *Spiritual Exercises* is a little book that was never meant to be read, at least as most books are. It was intended, rather, to be used as a way to proceed in guiding others through experiences of prayer wherein they might meet and converse with the living God, come honestly to grips with the truth of their values and beliefs, and make free and deliberate choices about the future course of their lives. The *Spiritual Exercises*, carefully construed and annotated in Ignatius's little manual, are not meant to be merely cognitive activities or devotional practices. They are, instead, rigorous exercises of the spirit wholly engaging the body, mind, heart, and soul of the human person. Thus they offer not only matters to be pondered, but also realities to be contemplated, scenes to be imagined, feelings to be evaluated, possibilities to be explored, options to be considered, alternatives to be weighed, judgments to be reached, and choices of action to be made—all with the expressed aim of helping individuals to seek and find the will of God at work in the radical ordering of their lives.

25/   A fundamental dynamic of the Spiritual Exercises of Ignatius is the continual call to reflect upon the entirety of one's experience in prayer in order to discern where the Spirit of God is leading. Ignatius urges reflection on human experience as an essential means of validating its authenticity because, without prudent reflection, delusion readily becomes possible and, without careful reflection, the significance of one's experience may be neglected or trivialized. Only after adequate reflection on experience and interior appropriation of the meaning and implications of what one studies can one proceed freely and confidently toward choosing appropriate courses of action that foster the integral growth of oneself as a human being. Hence, reflection becomes a pivotal point for Ignatius in the movement from experience to action, so much so that he consigns to the director or guide of persons engaged in the Spiritual Exercises primary responsibility for facilitating their progress in reflection.

26/   For Ignatius, the vital dynamic of the Spiritual Exercises is the individual person's encounter with the Spirit of Truth. It is not surprising, therefore, that we find in his principles and directions for guiding others in the process of the *Spiritual Exercises* a perfect description of the pedagogical role of teacher as one whose job is not merely to inform but to help the student progress in the truth.[4] If they are to use the Ignatian Pedagogical Paradigm successfully, teachers must be sensitive to their own experience, attitudes, and opinions lest they impose their own agenda on their students. (Cf. paragraph #111)

The Teacher-Learner Relationship

27/   Applying, then, the Ignatian paradigm to the teacher-learner relationship in Jesuit education, it is the teacher's primary role to facilitate the growing relationship of the learner with truth, particularly in the matter of the subject being studied under the guiding influence of the teacher. The teacher creates the conditions, lays the foundations, and provides the opportunities for the continual interplay of the student's EXPERIENCE, REFLECTION, and ACTION to occur.

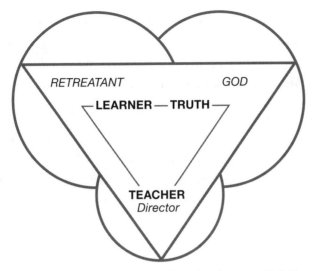

Figure 1. Ignatian Paradigm and the Teacher-Learner Relationship

28/   Starting with EXPERIENCE, the teacher creates the conditions whereby students gather and recollect the material of their own experience in order to distill what they understand already in terms of facts, feelings, values, insights, and intuitions they bring to the subject matter at hand. Later the teacher guides the students in assimilating new information and further experience so that their knowledge will grow in completeness and truth. The teacher lays the foundations for learning how to learn by engaging students in skills and techniques of REFLECTION. Here memory, understanding, imagination, and feelings are used to grasp the essential meaning and value of what is being studied, to discover its relationship to other facets of human knowledge and activity, and to appreciate its implications in the continuing search for truth. Reflection should be a formative and liberating process that so shapes the consciousness of students—their habitual attitudes, values, and beliefs as well as ways of thinking—that they are impelled to move beyond knowing to ACTION. It is then the role of the teacher to see that the opportunities are provided that will challenge the imagination and exercise the will of the students to choose the best possible course of action to flow from and follow up on what they have learned. What they do as a result under the teacher's direction, while it may not immediately transform the world into a global community of justice, peace, and love, should at least be an educational step in that direction and toward that goal even if it merely leads to new experiences, further reflections, and consequent actions within the subject area under consideration.

29/   The continual interplay, then, of EXPERIENCE, REFLECTION, and ACTION in the teaching-learning dynamic of the classroom lies at the heart of an Ignatian pedagogy. It is our way of proceeding in Jesuit schools as we accompany the learner on his or her journey of becoming a fully human person. It is an Ignatian Pedagogical Paradigm which each of us can bring to the subjects we teach and programs we run knowing that it needs to be adapted and applied to our own specific situations.

Ignatian Paradigm

30/   An Ignatian paradigm of experience, reflection, and action suggests a host of ways in which teachers might accompany their students in order to facilitate learning and growth through encounters with truth and explorations of human meaning. It is a paradigm that can provide a more than adequate response to critical educational issues facing us today. It is a paradigm with inherent potential for going beyond mere theory to become a practical tool and effective instrument for making a difference in the way we teach and in the way our students learn. The model of experience, reflection, and action is not solely an interesting idea worthy of considerable discussion, nor is it simply an intriguing proposal calling for lengthy debate. It is rather a fresh yet familiar Ignatian paradigm of Jesuit education, a way of proceeding which all of us can confidently follow in our efforts to help students truly grow as persons of competence, conscience, and compassion.

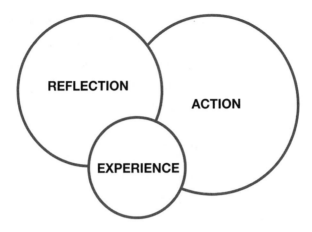

Figure 2. Ignatian Paradigm

31/   A critically important note of the Ignatian paradigm is the introduction of reflection as an essential dynamic. For centuries, education was
assumed to consist primarily of accumulated knowledge gained from lectures and demonstrations.[5] Teaching followed a primitive model of communications in which information is transmitted and knowledge is transferred
from teacher to learner. Students experience a lesson clearly presented and
thoroughly explained and the teacher calls for subsequent action on the
part of students whereby they demonstrate, frequently reciting from memory, that what was communicated has, indeed, been successfully absorbed.
While research over the past two decades has proven time and again, study
after study, that effective learning occurs through the interaction of the
learner with experience, still much of teaching continues to be limited to a
two-step instructional model of EXPERIENCE ➜ ACTION, in which the
teacher plays a far more active role than the student.[6] It is a model often followed where development of memorization skills on the part of students is a
primary pedagogical aim. As a teaching model of Jesuit education, however,
it is seriously deficient for two reasons:

32/   In Jesuit schools the learning <u>experience</u> is expected to move beyond
rote knowledge to the development of the more complex learning skills of
understanding, application, analysis, synthesis, and evaluation.

33/   If learning were to stop there, it would not be Ignatian. For it would lack the component of REFLECTION wherein students are impelled to consider the human meaning and significance of what they study and to integrate that meaning as responsible learners who grow as persons of competence, conscience, and compassion.

Dynamics of the Paradigm

34/   A comprehensive Ignatian Pedagogical Paradigm must consider the context of learning as well as the more explicitly pedagogical process. In addition, it should point to ways to encourage openness to growth even after the student has completed any individual learning cycle. Thus, five steps are involved: CONTEXT; EXPERIENCE; REFLECTION; ACTION; EVALUATION.

35/   1. <u>CONTEXT OF LEARNING:</u> Before Ignatius would begin to direct a person in the Spiritual Exercises, he always wanted to know about their predispositions to prayer, to God. He realized how important it was for a person to be open to the movements of the Spirit, if he or she was to draw any fruit from the journey of the soul to be begun. And based upon this pre-retreat knowledge Ignatius made judgments about readiness to begin, whether a person would profit from the complete *Exercises* or an abbreviated experience.

36/   In the Spiritual Exercises Ignatius makes the point that the experiences of the retreatant should always give shape and context to the exercises that are being used. It is the responsibility of the director, therefore, not only to select those exercises that seem most worthwhile and suitable but to modify and adjust them in order to make them directly applicable to the retreatant. Ignatius encourages the director of the *Spiritual Exercises* to become as familiar as possible beforehand with the life experience of the retreatant so that, during the retreat itself, the director will be better equipped to assist the retreatant in discerning movements of the Spirit.

37/   Similarly, personal care and concern for the individual, which is a hallmark of Jesuit education, requires that the teacher become as conversant as possible with the life experience of the learner. Since human experience, always the starting point in an Ignatian pedagogy, never occurs in a vacuum, we must know as much as we can about the actual context within which teaching and learning take place. As teachers, therefore, we need to understand the world of the student, including the ways in which family, friends, peers, youth culture, and mores as well as social pressures, school life, politics, economics, religion, media, art, music, and other realities impact that world and affect the student for better or worse. Indeed, from time to time we should work seriously with students to reflect on the contextual realities of both our worlds. What are forces at work in them? How do they experience those forces influencing their attitudes, values, and beliefs, and shaping our perceptions, judgments, and choices? How do world experiences affect the very way in which students learn, helping to mold their habitual patterns of thinking and acting? What practical steps can they and are they willing to take to gain greater freedom and control over their destinies?

38/   For such a relationship of authenticity and truth to flourish between teacher and student, mutual trust and respect that grows out of a continuing experience of the other as a genuine companion in learning is required. It means, too, being keenly conscious of and sensitive to the institutional environment of the school or learning center; being alert as teachers and administrators to the complex and often subtle network of norms, expectations, behaviors, and relationships that create an atmosphere for learning.

39/   Praise, reverence, and service should mark the relationship that exists not only between teachers and students but among all members of the school community. Ideally Jesuit schools should be places where people are believed in, honored, and cared for; where the natural talents and creative abilities of persons are recognized and celebrated; where individual contributions and accomplishments are appreciated; where everyone is treated fairly and justly; where sacrifice on behalf of the economically poor, the socially deprived, and the educationally disadvantaged is commonplace; where each of us finds the challenge, encouragement, and support we need to reach our fullest individual potential for excellence; where we help one another and work together with enthusiasm and generosity, attempting to model concretely in word and action the ideals we uphold for our students and ourselves.

40/   Teachers, as well as other members of the school community, therefore, should take account of:

a) the real context of a student's life which includes family, peers, social situations, the educational institution itself, politics, economics, cultural climate, the ecclesial situation, media, music, and other realities. All of these have an impact on the student for better or worse. From time to time it will be useful and important to encourage students to reflect on the contextual factors that they experience, and how they affect their attitudes, perceptions, judgments, choices. This will be especially important when students are dealing with issues that are likely to evoke strong feelings.

41/   b) the socio-economic, political, and cultural context within which a student grows can seriously affect his or her growth as a person for others. For example, a culture of endemic poverty usually negatively affects students' expectations about success in studies; oppressive political regimes discourage open inquiry in favor of their dominating ideologies. These and a host of other factors can restrict the freedom which Ignatian pedagogy encourages.

42/   c) the institutional environment of the school or learning center, i.e., the complex and often subtle network of norms, expectations, and especially relationships that create the atmosphere of school life. Recent study of Catholic schools highlights the importance of a positive school environment. In the past, improvements in religious and value education in our schools have usually been sought in the development of new curricula, visual aids, and suitable textbook materials. All of these developments achieve some results. Most, however, achieve far less than they promised.

The results of recent research suggest that the climate of the school may well be the precondition necessary before value education can even begin, and that much more attention needs to be given to the school environment in which the moral development and religious formation of adolescents takes place. Concretely, concern for quality learning, trust, respect for others despite differences of opinion, caring, forgiveness, and some clear manifestation of the school's belief in the Transcendent distinguish a school environment that assists integral human growth. A Jesuit school is to be a face-to-face faith community of learners in which an authentic personal relationship between teachers and students may flourish. Without such a relationship, much of the unique force of our education would be lost. For an authentic relationship of trust and friendship between teacher and student is an indispensable dispositive condition for any growth in commitment to values. Thus *alumnorum cura personalis*, i.e., a genuine love and personal care for each of our students, is essential for an environment that fosters the Ignatian Pedagogical Paradigm proposed.

43/   d) <u>what previously acquired concepts students bring with them to the start of the learning process</u>. Their points of view and the insights that they may have acquired from earlier study or picked up spontaneously from their cultural environment, as well as their feelings, attitudes, and values regarding the subject matter to be studied form part of the real context for learning.

44/   2. <u>EXPERIENCE</u> for Ignatius meant "to taste something internally." In the first place this calls for knowing facts, concepts, principles. This requires one to probe the connotation and overtones of words and events, to analyze and evaluate ideas, to reason. Only with accurate comprehension of what is being considered can one proceed to valid appreciation of its meaning. But Ignatian experience goes beyond a purely intellectual grasp. Ignatius urges that the whole person—mind, heart, and will—should enter the learning experience. He encourages use of the imagination and the feelings as well as the mind in experience. Thus affective as well as cognitive dimensions of the human person are involved, because without internal feeling joined to intellectual grasp, learning will not move a person to action. For example, it is one thing to assent to the truth that God is Father or Parent. But for this truth to live and become effective, Ignatius would have us feel the tenderness with which the Father of Jesus loves us and cares for us, forgives us. And this fuller experience can move us to realize that God shares this love with all of our brothers and sisters in the human family. In the depths of our being we may be impelled to care for others in their joys and sorrows, their hopes, trials, poverty, unjust situations—and to want to do something for them. For here the heart as well as the head, the human person is involved.

45/   Thus we use the term EXPERIENCE to describe any activity in which in addition to a cognitive grasp of the matter being considered, some sensation of an affective nature is registered by the student. In any experience, data is perceived by the student cognitively. Through questioning, imagining, investigating its elements and relationships, the student organizes this data into a whole or a hypothesis. "What is this?" "Is it like anything I already know?" "How does it work?" And even without deliberate choice there is a concomitant affective reaction, e.g. "I like this"; "I'm threatened by this"; "I never do well in this sort of thing"; "It's interesting"; "Ho hum, I'm bored."

46/   At the beginning of new lessons, teachers often perceive how students' feelings can move them to grow. For it is rare that a student experiences something new in studies without referring it to what he or she already knows. New facts, ideas, viewpoints, theories often present a challenge to what the student understands at that point. This calls for growth—a fuller understanding that may modify or change what had been perceived as adequate knowledge. Confrontation of new knowledge with what one has already learned cannot be limited simply to memorization or passive absorption of additional data, especially if it does not exactly fit what one knows. It disturbs a learner to know that he does not fully comprehend. It impels a student to further probing for understanding—analysis, comparison, contrast, synthesis, evaluation—all sorts of mental and/or psychomotor activities wherein students are alert to grasp reality more fully.

47/   Human experience may be either direct or vicarious:

Direct:

It is one thing to read a newspaper account of a hurricane striking the coastal towns of Puerto Rico. You can know all the facts: wind speed, direction, numbers of persons dead and injured, extent and location of physical damage caused. This cognitive knowing, however, can leave the reader distant and aloof to the human dimensions of the storm. It is quite different to be out where the wind is blowing, where one feels the force of the storm, senses the immediate danger to life, home, and all one's possessions, and feels the fear in the pit of one's stomach for one's life and that of one's neighbors as the shrill wind becomes deafening. It is clear in this example that direct experience usually is fuller, more engaging of the person. Direct experience in an academic setting usually occurs in interpersonal experiences such as conversations or discussions, laboratory investigations, field trips, service projects, participation in sports, and the like.

Vicarious:

But in studies direct experience is not always possible. Learning is often achieved through vicarious experience in reading, or listening to a lecture. In order to involve students in the learning experience more fully at a human level, teachers are challenged to stimulate students' imagination and use of the senses precisely so that students can enter the reality studied more fully. Historical settings, assumptions of the times, cultural, social, political, and economic factors affecting the lives of people at the time of what is being studied need to be filled out. Simulations, role playing, use of audio visual materials, and the like may be helpful.

48/   In the initial phases of experience, whether direct or vicarious, learners perceive data as well as their affective responses to it. But only by organizing this data can the experience be grasped as a whole, responding to the questions: "What is this?" and "How do I react to it"? Thus learners need to be attentive and active in achieving comprehension and understanding of the human reality that confronts them.

49/   3. REFLECTION: Throughout his life Ignatius knew himself to be constantly subjected to different stirrings, invitations, alternatives which were often contradictory. His greatest effort was to try to discover what moved him in each situation: the impulse that leads him to good or the one that inclines him to evil; the desire to serve others or the solicitude for his own egotistical affirmation. He became the master of discernment that he continues to be today because he succeeded in distinguishing this difference. For Ignatius to "discern" was to clarify his internal motivation, the reasons behind his judgments, to probe the causes and implications of what he experienced, to weigh possible options and evaluate them in the light of their likely consequences, to discover what best leads to the desired goal: to be a free person who seeks, finds, and carries out the will of God in each situation.

50/   At this level of REFLECTION, the memory, the understanding, the imagination, and the feelings are used to capture the meaning and the essential value of what is being studied, to discover its relationship with other aspects of knowledge and human activity, and to appreciate its implications in the ongoing search for truth and freedom. This REFLECTION is a formative and liberating process. It forms the conscience of learners (their beliefs, values, attitudes and their entire way of thinking) in such a manner that they are led to move beyond knowing, to undertake action.

51/   **We use the term *reflection* to mean a thoughtful reconsideration of some subject matter, experience, idea, purpose, or spontaneous reaction, in order to grasp its significance more fully. Thus, reflection is the process by which meaning surfaces in human experience:**

52/ • <u>by understanding the truth being studied more clearly</u>. For example, "What are the assumptions in this theory of the atom, in this presentation of the history of native peoples, in this statistical analysis? Are they valid; are they fair? Are other assumptions possible? How would the presentation be different if other assumptions were made?"

53/ • <u>by understanding the sources of the sensations or reactions I experience</u> in this consideration. For example, "In studying this short story, what particularly interests me? Why? . . ." "What do I find troubling in this translation? Why?"

54/ • <u>by deepening my understanding of the implications of what I have grasped for myself and for others</u>. For example, "What likely effects might environmental efforts to check the greenhouse effect have on my life, on that of my family and friends, . . . on the lives of people in poorer countries?"

55/ • <u>by achieving personal insights into events, ideas, truth or the distortion of truth, and the like</u>. For example, "Most people feel that a more equitable sharing of the world's resources is at least desirable, if not a moral imperative. My own life style, the things I take for granted, may contribute to the current imbalance. Am I willing to reconsider what I really need to be happy?"

56/ • <u>by coming to some understanding of who I am</u> ("What moves me, and why?") <u>and who I might be in relation to others</u>. For example, "How does what I have reflected upon make me feel? Why? Am I at peace with that reaction in myself? Why? If not, why not?"

57/ A major challenge to a teacher at this stage of the learning paradigm is to formulate questions that will broaden students' awareness and impel them to consider viewpoints of others, especially of the poor. The temptation here for a teacher may be to impose such viewpoints. If that occurs, the risk of manipulation or indoctrination (thoroughly non-Ignatian) is high, and a teacher should avoid anything that will lead to this kind of risk. But the challenge remains to open students' sensitivity to human implications of what they learn in a way that transcends their prior experiences and thus causes them to grow in human excellence.

58/   As educators we insist that all of this be done with total respect for the student's freedom. It is possible that, even after the reflective process, a student may decide to act selfishly. We recognize that it is possible that due to developmental factors, insecurity or other events currently impacting a student's life, he or she may not be able to grow in directions of greater altruism, justice, etc., at this time. Even Jesus faced such reactions in dealing with the rich young man. We must be respectful of the individual's freedom to reject growth. We are sowers of seeds; in God's Providence, the seeds may germinate in time.

59/   The reflection envisioned can and should be broadened wherever appropriate to enable students and teachers to share their reflections and thereby have the opportunity to grow together. Shared reflection can reinforce, challenge, encourage reconsideration, and ultimately give greater assurance that the action to be taken (individual or corporate) is more comprehensive and consistent with what it means to be a person for others.

60/   (The terms EXPERIENCE and REFLECTION may be defined variously according to different schools of pedagogy, and we agree with the tendency to use these and similar terms to express or to promote teaching that is personalized and learner-active and whose aim is not merely the assimilation of subject-matter but the development of the person. In the Ignatian tradition of education, however, these terms are particularly significant as they express a "way of proceeding" that is more effective in achieving "integral formation" of the student; that is, a way of experiencing and reflecting that leads the student not only to delve deeply into the subject itself but to look for meaning in life, and to make personal options (ACTION) according to a comprehensive world vision. On the other hand, we know that experience and reflection are not separable phenomena. It is not possible to have an experience without some amount of reflection, and all reflection carries with it some intellectual or affective experiences, insights, and enlightenment, a vision of the world, of self, and others.

61/   4. <u>ACTION</u>: For *Ignatius* the acid test of love is what one does, not what one says. "<u>Love is shown in deeds, not words</u>." The thrust of the Spiritual Exercises was precisely to enable the retreatant to know the will of God and to do it freely. So too, Ignatius and the first Jesuits were most concerned with the formation of students' attitudes, values, ideals according to which they would make decisions in a wide variety of situations about what actions were to be done. Ignatius wanted Jesuit schools to form young people who could and would contribute intelligently and effectively to the welfare of society.

62/   • Reflection in Ignatian Pedagogy would be a truncated process if it ended with understanding and affective reactions. Ignatian reflection, just as it begins with the reality of experience, necessarily ends with that same reality in order to effect it. Reflection only develops and matures when it fosters decision and commitment.

63/   • In his pedagogy, Ignatius highlights the affective/evaluative stage of the learning process because he is conscious that in addition to letting one "sense and taste," i.e., deepen one's experience, affective feelings are motivational forces that move one's understanding to action and commitment. And it must be clear that Ignatius does not seek just any action or commitment. Rather, while respecting human freedom, he strives to encourage decision and commitment for the *Magis*, the better service of God and our sisters and brothers.

64/   • The term "Action" here refers to internal human growth based upon experience that has been reflected upon as well as its manifestation externally. It involves two steps:

65/   <u>Interiorized Choices</u>

After reflection, the learner considers the experience from a personal, human point of view. Here in light of cognitive understanding of the experience and the affections involved (positive or negative), the will is moved. Meanings perceived and judged present choices to be made. Such choices may occur when a person decides that a truth is to be his or her personal point of reference, attitude, or predisposition which will affect any number of decisions. It may take the form of gradual clarification of one's priorities. It is at this point that the student chooses to make the truth his or her own while remaining open to where the truth might lead.

66/   Choices Externally Manifested

In time, these meanings, attitudes, values which have been interiorized and made part of the person impel the student to act, to do something consistent with this new conviction. If the meaning was positive, then the student will likely seek to enhance those conditions or circumstances in which the original experience took place. For example, if the goal of physical education has been achieved, the student will be inclined to undertake some regular sport during his free time. If she has acquired a taste for history or literature, she may resolve to make time for reading. If he finds it worthwhile to help his companions in their studies, he may volunteer to collaborate in some remedial program for weaker students. If he or she appreciates better the needs of the poor after service experiences in the ghetto and reflection on those experiences, this might influence his or her career choice or move the student to volunteer to work for the poor. If the meaning was negative, then the student will likely seek to adjust, change, diminish, or avoid the conditions and circumstances in which the original experience took place. For example, if the student now appreciates the reasons for his or her lack of success in school work, the student may decide to improve study habits in order to avoid repeated failure.

67/   5. EVALUATION: All teachers know that from time to time it is important to evaluate a student's progress in academic achievement. Daily quizzes, weekly or monthly tests, and semester examinations are familiar evaluation instruments to assess the degree of mastery of knowledge and skills achieved. Periodic testing alerts the teacher and the student both to intellectual growth and to lacunae where further work is necessary for mastery. This type of feedback can alert the teacher to possible needs for use of alternate methods of teaching; it also offers special opportunities to

individualize encouragement and advice for academic improvement (e.g., review of study habits) for each student.

68/   Ignatian pedagogy, however, aims at formation which includes but goes beyond academic mastery. Here we are concerned about students' well-rounded growth as persons for others. Thus, periodic evaluation of the student's growth in attitudes, priorities, and actions consistent with being a person for others is essential. Comprehensive assessment probably will not occur as frequently as academic testing, but it needs to be planned at intervals, at least once a term. A teacher who is observant will perceive indications of growth or lack of growth in class discussions, students' generosity in response to common needs, etc., much more frequently.

69/   There are a variety of ways in which this fuller human growth can be assessed. All must take into account the age, talents, and developmental levels of each student. Here the relationship of mutual trust and respect which should exist between students and teachers sets a climate for discussion of growth. Useful pedagogical approaches include mentoring, review of student journals, student self-evaluation in light of personal growth profiles, as well as review of leisure time activities and voluntary service to others.

70/   This can be a privileged moment for a teacher both to congratulate and encourage the student for progress made, as well as an opportunity to stimulate further reflection in light of blind spots or lacunae in the student's point of view. The teacher can stimulate needed reconsideration by judicious questioning, proposing additional perspectives, supplying needed information, and suggesting ways to view matters from other points of view.

71/   In time, the student's attitudes, priorities, decisions may be reinvestigated in light of further experience, changes in his or her context, challenges from social and cultural developments and the like. The teacher's gentle questioning may point to the need for more adequate decisions or commitments, what Ignatius Loyola called the *magis*. This newly realized need to grow may serve to launch the learner once again into the cycle of the Ignatian learning paradigm.

An Ongoing Process

72/   This mode of proceeding can thus become an effective ongoing pattern for learning as well as a stimulus to remain open to growth throughout a lifetime.

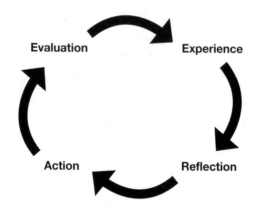

73/   A repetition of the Ignatian paradigm can help the growth of a student:

- who will gradually learn to discriminate and be selective in choosing experiences;
- who is able to draw fullness and richness from the reflection on those experiences; and
- who becomes self-motivated by his or her own integrity and humanity to make conscious, responsible choices.

74/   In addition, perhaps most important, consistent use of the Ignatian paradigm can result in the acquisition of life-long habits of learning which foster attention to experience, reflective understanding beyond self-interest, and criteria for responsible action. Such formative effects were characteristic of Jesuit alumni in the early Society of Jesus. They are perhaps even more necessary for responsible citizens of the third millennium.

Noteworthy Features of the Ignatian Pedagogical Paradigm

75/   We naturally welcome an Ignatian pedagogy that speaks to the characteristics of Jesuit education and to our own goals as teachers. The continual interplay of CONTEXT, EXPERIENCE, REFLECTION, ACTION, and EVALUATION provides us with a pedagogical model that is relevant to our cultures and times. It is a substantial and appealing model that speaks directly to the teaching-learning process. It is a carefully reasoned way of proceeding, cogently and logically argued from principles of Ignatian spirituality and Jesuit education. It consistently maintains the importance and integrity of the interrelationship of teacher, learner, and subject matter within the real context in which they live. It is comprehensive and complete in its approach. Most importantly, it addresses the realities as well as ideals of teaching in practical and systematic ways while, at the same time, offering the radical means we need to meet our educational mission of forming young men and women for others. As we continue to work to make Ignatian pedagogy an essential characteristic of Jesuit education in our schools and classrooms, it may help us to remember the following about the Paradigm itself:

76/ ♦ *The* Ignatian Pedagogical Paradigm *applies to all curricula.* As an attitude, a mentality, and a consistent approach which imbues all our teaching, the Ignatian Pedagogical Paradigm applies to all curricula. It is easily applicable even to curricula prescribed by governments or local educational authorities. It does not demand the addition of a single course, but it does require the infusion of new approaches in the way we teach existing courses.

77/ ♦ *The* Ignatian Pedagogical Paradigm *is fundamental to the teaching-learning process.* It applies not only to the academic disciplines but also to the non-academic areas of schooling, such as extracurricular activities, sports, community service programs, retreat experiences, and the like. Within a specific subject (History, Mathematics, Language, Literature, Physics, Art, etc.), the paradigm can serve as a helpful guide for preparing lessons, planning assignments, and designing instructional activities. The paradigm has considerable potential for helping students to make connections across as well as within disciplines and to integrate their learning with what has gone before. Used consistently throughout a school's program, the paradigm brings coherence to the total educational experience of the student. Regular application of the model in teaching situations contributes to the formation for students of a natural habit of reflecting on experience before acting.

78/ ♦ *The* Ignatian Pedagogical Paradigm *promises to help* teachers *be better teachers.* It enables teachers to enrich the content and structure of what they are teaching. It gives teachers additional means of encouraging student initiative. It allows teachers to expect more of students, to call upon them to take greater responsibility for and be more active in their own learning. It helps teachers to motivate students by providing the occasion and rationale for inviting students to relate what is being studied to their own world experiences.

79/ ♦ *The* Ignatian Pedagogical Paradigm *personalizes learning.* It asks students to reflect upon the meaning and significance of what they are studying. It attempts to motivate students by involving them as critical active participants in the teaching-learning process. It aims for more personal learning by bringing student and teacher experiences closer together. It invites integration of learning experiences in the classroom with those of home, work, peer culture, etc.

80/ ♦ *The* Ignatian Pedagogical Paradigm *stresses the social dimension of both learning and teaching.* It encourages close cooperation and mutual sharing of experiences and reflective dialogue among students. It relates student learning and growth to personal interaction and human relationships. It proposes steady movement and progress toward action that will affect the lives of others for good. Students will gradually learn that their deepest experiences come from their relationship with what is human, relationships with and experiences of persons. Reflection should always move toward greater appreciation of the lives of others and of the actions, policies, or structures that help or hinder mutual growth and development as members of the human family. This assumes, of course, that teachers are aware of and committed to such values.

Challenges to Implementing an Ignatian Pedagogy

81/   Achievement of value-oriented goals like those presented in *The Characteristics of Jesuit Education* is not easy. There are formidable challenges working at cross purposes to our aims. Here are but a few:

1. Limited View of Education

82/   The purpose of education is often presented as cultural transmission, i.e., passing on to new generations the accumulated wisdom of the ages. This is certainly an important function to assure coherence in human endeavors within any society and in the human family at large. Failure to inform and train youth in what we have learned would result in the need for each new generation to reinvent the wheel. In fact, in many places, cultural transmission is the dominant, if not the sole purpose of public education.

83/   But the purpose of education in today's world, marked by rapid changes at every level of human endeavor and competing value systems and ideologies, cannot remain so limited if it is effectively to prepare men and women of competence and conscience capable of making significant contributions to the future of the human family. From a sheerly pragmatic point of view, education which is limited to cultural transmission results in training for obsolescence. This is clear when we consider programs training for technology. Less apparent, however, may be the results of failure to probe human implications of developments that inevitably affect human life such as genetic engineering, the image culture, new forms of energy, the role of emerging economic blocks of nations, and a host of other innovations that promise progress. Many of these offer hope for improved human living, but at what cost? Such matters cannot simply be left to political leaders or the captains of industry; it is the right and responsibility of every citizen to judge and act in appropriate ways for the emerging human community. People need to be educated for responsible citizenship.

84/   In addition, therefore, to cultural transmission, preparation for significant participation in cultural growth is essential. Men and women of the third millennium will require new technological skills, no doubt; but more importantly, they will require skills to lovingly understand and critique all aspects of life in order to make decisions (personal, social, moral, professional, religious) that will impact all of our lives for the better. Criteria for such growth (through study, reflection, analysis, critique, and development of effective alternatives) are inevitably founded on values. This is true whether or not such values are averted to explicitly. All teaching imparts values, and these values can be such as to promote justice, or work partially or entirely at cross purposes to the mission of the Society of Jesus.

85/   Thus, we need a pedagogy that alerts young people to the intricate networks of values that are often subtly disguised in modern life—in advertising, music, political propaganda, etc.—precisely so that students can examine them and make judgments and commitments freely, with real understanding.

2. Prevalence of Pragmatism

86/   In a desire to meet goals of economic advancement, which may be quite legitimate, many governments are stressing the pragmatic elements of education exclusively. The result is that education is reduced to job training. This thrust is often encouraged by business interests, although they pay lip service to broader cultural goals of education. In recent years, in many parts of the world, many academic institutions have acceded to this narrow perspective of what constitutes education. And it is startling to see the enormous shift in student selection of majors in universities away from the humanities, the social and psychological sciences, philosophy and theology, towards an exclusive focus on business, economics, engineering, or the physical and biological sciences.

87/   In Jesuit education we do not simply bemoan these facts of life today. They must be considered and dealt with. We believe that almost every academic discipline, when honest with itself, is well aware that the values it transmits depend upon assumptions about the ideal human person and human society which are used as a starting point. Thus educational programs, teaching and research, and the methodologies they employ in Jesuit schools, colleges, and universities are of the highest importance, for we reject any partial or deformed version of the human person, the image of God. This is in sharp contrast to educational institutions which often unwittingly sidestep the central concern for the human person because of fragmented approaches to specializations.

88/   This means that Jesuit education must insist upon integral formation of its students through such means as required core curricula that include humanities, philosophy, theological perspectives, social questions, and the like, as part of all specialized educational programs. In addition, infusion methods might well be employed within specializations to highlight the deeper human, ethical, and social implications of what is being studied.

3. Desire for Simple Solutions

89/   The tendency to seek simple solutions to complex human questions and problems marks many societies today. The widespread use of slogans as answers does not really help to solve problems. Nor does the tendency we see in many countries around the world toward fundamentalism on one extreme of the spectrum and secularism on the other. For these tend to be reductionist; they do not realistically satisfy the thirst for integral human growth that so many of our brothers and sisters cry out for.

90/   Clearly Jesuit education which aims to form the whole person is challenged to chart a path, to employ a pedagogy, that avoids these extremes by helping our students to grasp more comprehensive truth, the human implications of their learning, precisely so that they can more effectively contribute to healing the human family and building a world that is more human and more divine.

4. Feelings of Insecurity

91/   One of the major reasons contributing to a widespread quest for easy answers is the insecurity many people experience due to the breakdown of essential human institutions that normally provide the context for human growth. Tragically, the family, the most fundamental human society, is disintegrating in countries around the world. In many first world countries, 1 out of 2 marriages end in divorce with devastating effects for the spouses, and especially for the children. Another source of insecurity and confusion is due to the fact that we are experiencing an historic mass migration of peoples across the face of the earth. Millions of men, women, and children are being uprooted from their cultures due to oppression, civil conflicts, or lack of food or means to support themselves. The older emigres may cling to elements of their cultural and religious heritage, but the young are often subject to cultural conflict and feel compelled to adopt the dominant cultural values of their new homelands in order to be accepted. Yet, at heart, they are uncertain about these new values. Insecurity often expresses itself in defensiveness, selfishness, a "me-first" attitude, which blocks consideration of the needs of others. The emphasis that the Ignatian paradigm places upon reflection to achieve meaning can assist students to understand the reasons underlying the insecurities they experience and to seek more constructive ways to deal with them.

5. Government Prescribed Curricula

92/   Cutting across all of these factors is the reality of pluralism in the world today. Unlike Jesuit schools of the sixteenth century, there exists no single universally recognized curriculum like the Trivium or Quadrivium that can be employed as a vehicle for formation in our times. Curricula today justifiably reflect local cultures and local needs that vary considerably. But in a number of countries, governments strictly prescribe the courses that form curricula at the level of elementary and secondary education. This can impede curriculum development according to formational priorities of schools.

93/   Because the Ignatian learning program requires a certain style of teaching, it approaches existing curricular subjects through infusion rather than by changes or additions to course offerings. In this way it avoids further crowding of overburdened school curricula, while at the same time not being seen as a frill tacked on to the "important" subjects. (This does not rule out the possibility that a specific unit concerning ethics or the like may on occasion be advisable in a particular context.)

Theory into Practice: Staff Development Programs

94/   Reflecting on what has been proposed here, some may wonder how it can be implemented. After all, very few teachers really practice such a methodology consistently. And lack of know-how is probably the major obstacle to any effective change in teacher behavior. The members of the International Commission on the Apostolate of Jesuit Education can understand such reservations. Research has shown that many educational innovations have foundered precisely because of such problems.

95/   We are convinced, therefore, that staff development programs involving in-service training are essential in each school, province, or region where this Ignatian Pedagogical Paradigm will be used. Since teaching skills are mastered only through practice, teachers need not only an explanation of methods, but also opportunities to practice them. Over time staff development programs can equip teachers with an array of pedagogical methods appropriate for Ignatian pedagogy from which they can use those more appropriate for the needs of students whom they serve. Staff development programs at the province or local school level, therefore, are an essential, integral part of the Ignatian Pedagogy Project.

96/   Accordingly, we are convinced of the need to identify and train teams of educators who will be prepared to offer staff development programs for province and local groups of teachers in the use of the Ignatian Pedagogical Paradigm. Therefore, training workshops are now being planned. These will, of course, encourage local adaptations of specific methods which are consistent with the Ignatian pedagogy proposed.

Some Concrete Helps to Understand the Paradigm

97/　The appendices to this document provide a further understanding of the roots of Ignatian Pedagogy in Ignatius's own notes (Appendix I) and in Fr. Kolvenbach's address (Appendix II). A brief list of the variety of concrete processes and methods which can be used by teachers in each step of the paradigm is provided (Appendix III). Fuller training protocols, utilizing these pedagogical methods, will form the substance of local or regional staff development programs to assist teachers to understand and use this pedagogy effectively.

An Invitation to Cooperate

98/　Greater understanding of how to adapt and apply the Ignatian Pedagogical Paradigm to the wide variety of educational settings and circumstances which characterize Jesuit schools around the world will come about as we work with the Paradigm in our relationships with students both in and outside the classroom and discover through those efforts concrete, practical ways of using the Paradigm that enhance the teaching-learning process. It can be expected, moreover, that many detailed and helpful treatments of the Ignatian Pedagogical Paradigm will be forthcoming that will be further enriched by the experience of teachers trained and practiced in applying the Paradigm within specific academic fields and disciplines. All of us in the work of Jesuit education look forward to benefiting from the insights and suggestions that other teachers have to offer.

99/　In the Ignatian spirit of cooperation, we hope that teachers who develop their own lessons or brief units in specific subjects of their curriculum utilizing the Ignatian Paradigm will share them with others. Accordingly, from time to time we hope to make brief illustrative materials available. For this reason teachers are invited to send concise presentations of their use of the Ignatian Paradigm in specific subjects to:

The International Center for Jesuit Education

Borgo S. Spirito, 4

C.P. 6139

00195 Rome, ITALY

APPENDICES: TABLE OF CONTENTS

100/ Appendix I: Some Overriding Pedagogical Principles (Ignatian "Annotations")

An adaptation of the introductory notes of St. Ignatius to one who directs another in the *Spiritual Exercises*. Here the more explicit pedagogical implications are highlighted.

101/ Appendix II: Ignatian Pedagogy Today

An Address by Very Rev. Peter-Hans Kolvenbach, S.J., delivered to the Participants at the International Workshop on "Ignatian Pedagogy: A Practical Approach," Villa Cavalletti, April 29, 1993.

102/ Appendix III: A brief list of processes and methods appropriate for each of the steps in the Ignatian Pedagogical Paradigm.

The methods listed derive either from the Jesuit educational tradition (Ignatius, *Ratio Studiorum*, etc.) or from pedagogical methods more recently developed in other circles which are consistent with Ignatian pedagogy.

N.B.: Staff development programs will explain and enable teachers to practice and master these methods.

APPENDIX I

Some Overriding Pedagogical Principles
(Ignatian "Annotations")

103/ There follows a translation of the "Annotations" or guiding notes to the Director of the Spiritual Exercises into Introductory Ignatian Pedagogical statements:

104/ 1. By "learning" is meant every method of experiencing, reflecting, and acting upon the truth; every way of preparing and disposing oneself to be rid of all obstacles to freedom and growth (Annotation 1).

105/ 2. The teacher explains to the student the method and order of the subject and accurately narrates the facts. He/she stays to the point and adds only a short explanation. The reason for this is that when students take the foundation presented, go over it, and reflect on it, they discover what makes the matter clearer and better understood. This comes from their own reasoning and produces greater sense of accomplishment and satisfaction than if the teacher explained and developed the meaning at great length. It is not much knowledge that fills and satisfies students, but the intimate understanding and relish of the truth (Annotation 2).

106/ 3. In all learning, we make use of the acts of intellect in reasoning and acts of the will in demonstrating our love (Annotation 3).

107/ 4. Specific time periods are assigned to learning and generally correspond to the natural divisions of the subject. However, this does not mean that every division must necessarily consist of a set time. For it may happen at times that some are slower in attaining what is sought while some may be more diligent, some more troubled and tired. So it may be necessary at times to shorten the time, at others to lengthen it (Annotation 4).

108/ 5. The student who enters upon learning should do so with a great-heartedness and generosity, freely offering all his or her attention and will to the enterprise (Annotation 5).

109/ 6. When the teacher sees the student is not affected by any experiences, he or she should ply the student with questions, inquire about when and how study takes place, question the understanding of directions, ask what the student's reflection yielded, and ask for an accounting (Annotation 6).

110/ 7. If the teacher observes that the student is having troubles, he or she should deal with the student gently and kindly. The teacher should encourage and strengthen the student for the future by reviewing mistakes kindly and suggesting ways for improvement (Annotation 7).

111/ 8. If during reflection a student experiences joy or discouragement, he or she should reflect further on the causes of such feelings. Sharing such reflection with a teacher can help the student to perceive areas of consolation or challenge that can lead to further growth or that might subtly block growth. (Annotations 8, 9, 10).

112/ 9. The student should set about learning the matter of the present as if he or she were to learn nothing more. The student should not be in haste to cover everything. *"Non multa, sed multum"* ("Treat matter selected in depth; don't try to cover every topic in a given field of inquiry.") (Annotation 11).

113/ 10. The student should give to learning the full time that is expected. It is better to go overtime than to cut the time short, especially when the temptation to "cut corners" is strong, and it is difficult to study. Thus the student will get accustomed to resist giving in and strengthen study in the future (Annotations 12 and 13).

114/ 11. If the student in learning is going along with great success, the teacher will advise more care, less haste (Annotation 14).

115/ 12. While the student learns, it is more suitable that the truth itself is what motivates and disposes the student. The teacher, like a balance of equilibrium, leans to neither side of the matter, but lets the student deal directly with the truth and be influenced by the truth (Annotation 15).

116/   13. In order that the Creator and Lord may work more surely in the creature, it will be most useful for the student to work against any obstacles which prevent an openness to the full truth (Annotation 16).

117/   14. The student should faithfully inform the teacher of any troubles or difficulties he or she is having, so that a learning process might be suited and adapted to personal needs (Annotation 17).

118/   15. Learning should always be adapted to the condition of the student engaged in it (Annotation 18).

119/   16. (The last two annotations allow for creative adaptations to suit persons and circumstances. Such readiness to adapt in the teaching-learning experience is greatly effective.) (Annotations 19 and 20)

APPENDIX II

Ignatian Pedagogy Today

An Address by Very Rev. Peter-Hans Kolvenbach, S.J. Delivered to the Participants at the International Workshop on "Ignatian Pedagogy: A Practical Approach," Villa Cavalletti, April 29, 1993.

Context: Christian Humanism Today

120/ I begin by setting our efforts today within the context of the tradition of Jesuit Education. From its origins in the sixteenth century, Jesuit education has been dedicated to the development and transmission of a genuine Christian humanism. This humanism had two roots: the distinctive spiritual experiences of Ignatius Loyola, and the cultural, social, and religious challenges of Renaissance and Reformation Europe.

121/ The spiritual root of this humanism is indicated in the final contemplation of the Spiritual Exercises. Here Ignatius has the retreatant ask for an intimate knowledge of how God dwells in persons, giving them understanding and making them in God's own image and likeness, and to consider how God works and labors in all created things on behalf of each person. This understanding of God's relation to the world implies that faith in God and affirmation of all that is truly human are inseparable from each other. This spirituality enabled the first Jesuits to appropriate the humanism of the Renaissance and to found a network of educational institutions that were innovative and responsive to the urgent needs of their time. Faith and the enhancement of *humanitas* went hand in hand.

122/ Since the Second Vatican Council we have been recognizing a profound new challenge that calls for a new form of Christian humanism with a distinctively societal emphasis. The Council stated that the "split between the faith that many profess and their daily lives deserves to be counted among the more serious errors of our age" (*Gaudium et Spes* 43). The world appears to us in pieces, chopped up, broken.

123/   The root issue is this: what does faith in God mean in the face of Bosnia and Sudan, Guatemala and Haiti, Auschwitz and Hiroshima, the teeming streets of Calcutta and the broken bodies in Tiananmen Square? What is Christian humanism in the face of starving millions of men, women, and children in Africa? What is Christian humanism as we view millions of people uprooted from their own countries by persecution and terror, and forced to seek a new life in foreign lands? What is Christian humanism when we see the homeless that roam our cities and the growing underclass who are reduced to permanent hopelessness? What is humanistic education in this context? A disciplined sensitivity to human misery and exploitation is not a single political doctrine or a system of economics. It is a humanism, a humane sensibility to be achieved anew within the demands of our own times and as a product of an education whose ideal continues to be motivated by the great commandments—love of God and love of neighbor.

124/   In other words, late twentieth-century Christian humanism necessarily includes social humanism. As such it shares much with the ideals of other faiths in bringing God's love to effective expression in building a just and peaceful kingdom of God on earth. Just as the early Jesuits made distinctive contributions to the humanism of the sixteenth century through their educational innovations, we are called to a similar endeavor today. This calls for creativity in every area of thought, education, and spirituality. It will also be the product of an Ignatian pedagogy that serves faith through reflective inquiry into the full meaning of the Christian message and its exigencies for our time. Such a service of faith, and the promotion of justice which it entails, is the fundament of contemporary Christian humanism. It is at the heart of the enterprise of Catholic and Jesuit education today. This is what *The Characteristics of Jesuit Education* refers to as "human excellence." This is what we mean when we say that the goal of Jesuit education is the formation of men and women for others, people of competence, conscience, and compassionate commitment.

The Society's Reply to This Context

125/ Just a decade ago a request came from many parts of the world for a more contemporary statement of the essential principles of Jesuit pedagogy. The need was felt in light of notable changes and emerging new governmental regulations concerning curriculum, student body composition, and the like; in light of the felt need to share our pedagogy with increasing numbers of lay teachers who were unfamiliar with Jesuit education, in light of the Society's mission in the Church today, and especially in light of the changing, ever more bewildering context in which young people are growing up today. Our response was the document describing *The Characteristics of Jesuit Education* today. But that document which was very well received throughout the world of Jesuit education provoked a more urgent question. How? How do we move from an understanding of the principles guiding Jesuit education today to the practical level of making these principles real in the daily interaction between teachers and students? For it is here in the challenge and the excitement of the teaching-learning process that these principles can have effect. This workshop in which you are participating seeks to provide the practical pedagogical methods that can answer the crucial question: how do we make *The Characteristics of Jesuit Education* real in the classroom? The Ignatian Pedagogical Paradigm presents a framework to incorporate the crucial element of reflection into learning. Reflection can provide the opportunity for students themselves to consider the human meaning and the implications of what they study.

126/ Amid all the conflicting demands on their time and energies, your students are searching for meaning for their lives. They know that nuclear holocaust is more than a madman's dream. Unconsciously at least, they suffer from fear of life in a world held together by a balance of terror more than by bonds of love. Already many young people have been exposed to very cynical interpretations of man: he is a sack of egoistic drives, each demanding instant gratification; he is the innocent victim of inhuman systems over which he has no control. Due to mounting economic pressures in many countries around the world, many students in developed countries seem excessively preoccupied with career training and self-fulfillment to the exclusion of broader human growth. Does this not point to their excessive insecurity? But beneath their fears, often covered over with an air of bravado, and beneath their bewilderment at the differing interpretations of man, is their desire for a unifying vision of the meaning of life and of their own selves. In many developing countries, the young people with whom you work experience the threat of famine and the terrors of war. They struggle to hope that human life has value and a future in the ashes of devastation which is the only world they have ever experienced. In other countries where poverty grinds the human spirit, modern media cynically project the good life in terms of opulence and consumerism. Is it any wonder that our students in all parts of the world are confused, uncertain about life's meaning?

127/   During their years in a secondary school, young men and women are still relatively free to listen and to explore. The world has not yet closed in on them. They are concerned about the deeper questions of the "why" and "wherefore" of life. They can dream impossible dreams and be stirred by the vision of what might be. The Society has committed so much of its personnel and resources to the education of young people precisely because they are questing for the sources of life "beyond academic excellence." Surely every teacher worthy of the name must believe in young people and want to encourage their reaching for the stars. This means that your own unifying vision of life must be tantalizingly attractive to your students, inviting them to dialogue on the things that count. It must encourage them to internalize attitudes of deep and universal compassion for their suffering fellow men and women and to transform themselves into men and women of peace and justice, committed to be agents of change in a world which recognizes how widespread is injustice, how pervasive the forces of oppression, selfishness, and consumerism.

128/   Admittedly, this is not an easy task. Like all of us in our pre-reflective years, your students have unconsciously accepted values which are incompatible with what truly leads to human happiness. More than young people of a previous generation, your students have more "reasons" for walking away in sadness when they see the implications of a Christian vision of life and basic change of worldview which leads to rejection of softness and the distortedly glamorous image of life purveyed in slick magazines and cheap films. They are exposed, as perhaps no generation in history, to the lure of drugs and the flight from painful reality which they promise.

129/ These young men and women need confidence as they look to their future; they need strength as they face their own weakness; they need mature understanding and love in the teachers of all areas of the curriculum with whom they explore the awesome mystery of life. Do they not remind us of that young student of the University of Paris of four and one-half centuries ago whom Inigo befriended and transformed into the Apostle of the Indies?

130/ These are the young men and women whom you are called to lead to be open to the Spirit, willing to accept the seeming defeat of redemptive love; in short, eventually to become principled leaders ready to shoulder society's heavier burdens and to witness to the faith that does justice.

131/ I urge you to have great confidence that your students are called to be leaders in their world; help them to know that they are respected and loveable. Freed from the fetters of ideology and insecurity, introduce them to a more complete vision of the meaning of man and woman, and equip them for service to their brothers and sisters, sensitive to and deeply concerned about using their influence to right social wrongs and to bring wholesome values into each of their professional, social, and private lines. The example of your own social sensitivity and concern will be a major source of inspiration for them.

132/ This apostolic aim needs, however, to be translated into practical programs and appropriate methods in the real world of the school. One of the characteristic Ignatian qualities, revealed in the Spiritual Exercises, the 4th part of the Constitutions, and in many of his letters is Ignatius's insistence simultaneously upon the highest ideals and the most concrete means to achieve them. Vision without appropriate method may be perceived as sterile platitude; while method without unifying vision is frequently passing fashion or gadgetry.

133/   An example of this Ignatian integration in teaching is found in the *Protrepticon* or *Exhortation to the Teachers in the Secondary Schools of the Society of Jesus* written by Fr. Francesco Sacchini, the second official historian of the Society a few years after the publication of the *Ratio* of 1599. In the Preface he remarks: "Among us the education of youth is not limited to imparting the rudiments of grammar but extends simultaneously to Christian formation." The Epitome, adopting the distinction between "instruction" and "education" understood as character formation, lays it down that schoolmasters are to be properly prepared in methods of instruction and in the art of educating. The Jesuit educational tradition has always insisted that the adequate criterion for success in Jesuit schools is not simply mastery of propositions, formulae, philosophies, and the like. The test is in deeds, not words: what will our students do with the empowerment which is their education? Ignatius was interested in getting educated men and women to work for the betterment of others, and erudition is not enough for this purpose. If the effectiveness of one's education is to be employed generously, a person has to be both good and learned. If she is not educated, she cannot help her neighbors as effectively as she might; if not good, she will not help them, or at least she cannot be relied upon to do so consistently. This implies clearly that Jesuit education must go beyond cognitive growth to human growth which involves understanding, motivation, and conviction.

Pedagogical Guidelines

134/   In accord with this goal to educate effectively, St. Ignatius and his successors formulated overriding pedagogical guidelines. Here I mention a few of them:

135/   a) Ignatius conceived of man's stance as being one of awe and wonder in appreciation for God's gifts of creation, the universe, and human existence itself. In his key meditation on God's Presence in creation Ignatius would have us move beyond logical analysis to affective response to God who is active for us in all of reality. By finding God in all things we discover God's loving plan for us. The role of imagination, affection, will, as well as intellect are central to an Ignatian approach. Thus Jesuit education involves formation of the whole person. In our schools we are asked to integrate this fuller dimension precisely to enable students to discover the realm of meaning in life, which can in turn give direction to our understanding of who we are and why we are here. It can provide criteria for our priorities and crucial choices at turning points in our lives. Specific methods in teaching thus are chosen which foster both rigorous investigation, understanding, and reflection.

136/ b) In this adventure of finding God, Ignatius respects human freedom. This rules out any semblance of indoctrination or manipulation in Jesuit education. Jesuit pedagogy should enable students to explore reality with open hearts and minds. And in an effort to be honest, it should alert the learner to possible entrapment by one's assumptions and prejudices, as well as by the intricate networks of popular values that can blind one to the truth. Thus Jesuit education urges students to know and to love the truth. It aims to enable people to be critical of their societies in a positive as well as negative sense, embracing wholesome values proposed, while rejecting specious values and practices.

137/ Our institutions make their essential contribution to society by embodying in our educational process a rigorous, probing study of crucial human problems and concerns. It is for this reason that Jesuit schools must strive for high academic quality. So we are speaking of something far removed from the facile and superficial world of slogans or ideology, of purely emotional and self-centered responses, and of instant, simplistic solutions. Teaching and research and all that goes into the educational process are of the highest importance in our institutions because they reject and refute any partial or deformed vision of the human person. This is in sharp contrast to educational institutions which often unwittingly sidestep the central concern for the human person because of fragmented approaches to specializations.

138/ c) And Ignatius holds out the ideal of the fullest development of the human person. Typically he insists on the "magis," the more, the greater glory of God. Thus in education Loyola demands that our expectations go beyond mastery of the skills and understandings normally found in the well-informed and competent students. *Magis* refers not only to academics, but also to action. In their training, Jesuits are traditionally encouraged by various experiences to explore the dimensions and expressions of Christian service as a means of developing a spirit of generosity. Our schools should develop this thrust of the Ignatian vision into programs of service which would encourage the student to actively experience and test his or her acceptance of the *Magis*. By this service the student can be led to discover the dialectic of action and contemplation.

139/ d) But not every action is truly for God's greater glory. Consequently, Ignatius offers a way to discover and choose God's will. "Discernment" is pivotal. And so in our schools, colleges, and universities, reflection and discernment must be taught and practiced. With all the competing values that bombard us today, making free human choice is never easy. We very rarely find that all of the reasons for a decision are on one side. There is always a pull and tug. This is where discernment becomes crucial. Discernment requires getting the facts and then reflecting, sorting out the motives that impel us, weighing values and priorities, considering how significant decisions will impact on the poor, deciding and living with our decisions.

140/ e) Furthermore, response to the call of Jesus may not be self-centered; it demands that we be and teach our students to be for others. The worldview of Ignatius is centered on the person of Christ. The reality of the Incarnation affects Jesuit education at its core. For the ultimate purpose, the very reason for the existence of schools, is to form men and women for others in imitation of Christ Jesus—the Son of God, the Man for Others par excellence. Thus Jesuit education, faithful to the Incarnational principle, is humanistic. Fr. Arrupe wrote:

141/ "What is it to humanize the world if not to put it at the service of mankind?" But the egoist not only does not humanize the material creation, he dehumanizes people themselves. He changes people into things by dominating them, exploiting them, and taking to himself the fruit of their labor. The tragedy of it all is that by doing this the egoist dehumanizes himself. He surrenders himself to the possessions he covets; he becomes their slave—no longer a person self-possessed but an un-person, a thing driven by his blind desires and their objects.

142/ In our own day, we are beginning to understand that education does not inevitably humanize or Christianize. We are losing faith in the notion that all education, regardless of its quality or thrust or purpose, will lead to virtue. Increasingly, it becomes clear that if we are to exercise a moral force in society, we must insist that the process of education takes place in a moral context. This is not to suggest a program of indoctrination that suffocates the spirit, nor does it mean theory courses that become only speculative and remote. What is called for is a framework of inquiry in which the process of wrestling with big issues and complex values is made fully legitimate.

143/ f) In this whole effort to form men and women of competence, conscience, and compassion, Ignatius never lost sight of the individual human person. He knew that God gives different gifts to each of us. One of the overriding principles of Jesuit pedagogy derives directly from this, namely, *alumnorum cura personalis*, a genuine love and personal care for each of our students.

The Role of the Teacher is Critical

144/ In a Jesuit school, the chief responsibility for moral as well as for intellectual formation rests finally not upon any procedure, or curricular, or extracurricular activity, but upon the teacher, under God. A Jesuit school is to be a face-to-face community in which an authentic personal relationship between teachers and students may flourish. Without such a relation of friendship, in fact, much of the unique force of our education would be lost. For an authentic relationship of trust and friendship between the teacher and pupil is an invaluable dispositive condition for any genuine growth in commitment to values.

145/ And so the *Ratio* of 1591 insists that teachers first need to know their students. It recommends that the masters study their pupils at length and reflect upon their aptitudes, their defects, and the implications of their classroom behavior. And at least some of the teachers, it remarks, ought to be well acquainted with the student's home background. Teachers are always to respect the dignity and personality of the pupils. In the classroom, the *Ratio* advises that teachers should be patient with students and know how to overlook certain mistakes or put off their correction until the apt psychological moment. They should be much readier with praise than blame, and if correction is required it should be made without bitterness. The friendly spirit which is nourished by frequent, casual counselling of the students, perhaps outside class hours, will greatly help this aim along. Even these bits of advice serve only to apply that underlying concept of the very nature of the school as a community and of the teacher's role as crucial within it.

146/ In the Preamble to the Fourth Part of the Constitutions Ignatius appears to place teachers' personal example ahead of learning or rhetoric as an apostolic means to help students grow in values. Within this school community, the teacher will persuasively influence character, for better or for worse, by the example of what he himself is. In our own day, Pope Paul VI observed incisively in *Evangelii Nuntiandi* that "Today students do not listen seriously to teachers but to witnesses; and if they do listen to teachers, it is because they are witnesses."

147/ As teachers in a Jesuit school then, beyond being qualified professionals in education, you are called to be men and women of the Spirit. Whether you like it or not, you are a city resting on a hill. What you are speaks louder than what you do or say. In today's image-culture, young people learn to respond to the living image of those ideals which they dimly sense in their heart. Words about total dedication, service of the poor, a just social order, a non-racist society, openness to the Spirit, and the like may lead them to reflection. A living example will lead them beyond reflection to aspire to live what the words mean. Hence, our continuing growth in the realm of the Spirit of Truth must lead us to a life of such compelling wholeness and goodness that the example we set will challenge our students to grow as men and women of competence, conscience, and compassion.

Methods

148/ His own painful educational experience had proven to Ignatius that enthusiasm was not enough for success in study. How a student was directed and the method of teaching employed were crucial. When we page through the *Ratio*, our first impression is that of a welter of regulations for time schedules; for careful gradation of classes; for the selection of authors to be read; for the diversified methods to be employed at various times of the morning and afternoon; for correction of papers and the assignment of written work; for the precise degree of skill which the students of each class will be expected to possess before moving upward. But all these particulars were designed to create a firm and reassuring framework of order and clarity within which both teacher and student could securely pursue their objectives. Here I mention just a few of the typical methods employed in Jesuit education.

149/ 1) Given this sort of environment of order and care for method, it would be relatively easy to determine precise and limited academic objectives for the individual classes. It was felt that this was the first requirement of any good learning situation—to know just what one sought and how to seek it. The characteristic tool employed here was the Prelection in which the teacher carefully prepared students for their own subsequent immanent activity which alone could generate true learning and firm habits.

150/ 2) But learning objectives needed to be selected and adapted to the students. The first Jesuit teachers believed that even little boys could learn a good deal if they were not overwhelmed with too much at one time. Thus concern for scope and sequence became prominent according to the abilities of each learner. A century after the *Ratio* was published, Jouvancy remarked that youthful talents are like narrow-necked vessels. You cannot fill them by splashing everything in at once. You can, if you pour it in carefully drop-by-drop.

151/ 3) Because he knew human nature well, Ignatius realized that even well-ordered experience in prayer or in academic study could not really help a person to grow unless the individual actively participated. In the Spiritual Exercises Ignatius proposes the importance of self-activity on the part of the exercitant. The second Annotation enjoins the director to be brief in his proposal of matter for each meditation so that by his own activity in prayer the exercitant may discover the truths and practices to which God calls him. This discovery tends to produce delight for the exercitant and greater "understanding and relish of the truth than if one in giving the *Exercises* had explained and developed the meaning at great length." In Annotation fifteen, he writes, "Allow the Creator to deal directly with the creature and the creature directly with His Creator and Lord." Ignatius knew the tendency of all teachers, whether in teaching prayer, history, or science, to discourse at great length about their views of the matter at hand. Ignatius realized that no learning occurs without the learner's own intelligent activity. Thus, in numerous exercises and study, student activities were seen as important.

152/ 4) The principle of self-activity on the part of the learner reinforced the *Ratio*'s detailed instructions for repetitions—daily, weekly, monthly, annually. For these were further devices for stimulating, guiding, and sustaining that student exercise which is aimed at mastery. But repetitions were not meant to be boring re-presentation of memorized material. Rather they were to be occasions when personal reflection and appropriation could occur by reflecting on what troubled or excited the student in the lesson.

153/ 5) If, as we have seen, there is no mastery without action, so too there is no successful action without motivation. Ignatius noted that those who studied should never go beyond two hours without taking a break. He prescribed variety in classroom activities, "for nothing does more to make the energy of youth flag than too much of the same thing." As far as possible, learning should be pleasant both intrinsically and extrinsically. By making an initial effort to orient students to the matter at hand, their interests in the subject may be engaged. In this spirit, plays and pageants were produced by the students, aimed at stimulating the study of literature, since *"Friget enim Poesis sine theatro."* Then too, contests, games, etc., were suggested so that the adolescent's desire to excel might help him to progress in learning. These practices demonstrate a prime concern to make learning interesting and thereby to engage youthful attention and application to study.

154/ All these pedagogical principles are, then, closely linked together. The learning outcome sought is genuine growth which is conceived in terms of abiding habits or skills. Habits are generated not simply by understanding facts or procedures but by mastery and personal appropriation which makes them one's own. Mastery is the product of continual intellectual effort and exercise, but fruitful effort of this sort is impossible without adequate motivation and a reflective, humane milieu. No part of this chain is particularly original, although the strict concatenation had novelty in its day.

155/ Accordingly, to help students develop a commitment to apostolic action, Jesuit schools should offer them opportunities to explore human values critically and to test their own values experientially. Personal integration of ethical and religious values which leads to action is far more important than the ability to memorize facts and opinions of others. It is becoming clear that men and women of the third millennium will require new technological skills, no doubt; but more important, they will require skills to lovingly understand and critique all aspects of life in order to make decisions (personal, social, moral, professional, religious) that will impact all of our lives for the better. Criteria for such growth (through study, reflection, analysis, judgement, and development of effective alternatives) are inevitably founded on values. This is true whether or not such values are made explicit in the learning process. In Jesuit education, Gospel values as focused in the Spiritual Exercises are the guiding norms for integral human development.

156/ The importance of method as well as substance to achieve this purpose is evident. For a value-oriented educational goal like ours—forming men and women for others—will not be realized unless, infused within our educational programs at every level, we challenge our students to reflect upon the value implication of what they study. We have learned to our regret that mere appropriation of knowledge does not inevitably humanize. One would hope that we have also learned that there is no value-free education. But the values imbedded in many areas in life today are presented subtly. So there is need to discover ways that will enable students to form habits of reflection, to assess values and their consequences for human beings in the positive and human sciences they study, the technology being developed, and the whole spectrum of social and political programs suggested by both prophets and politicians. Habits are not formed only by chance occasional happenings. Habits develop only by consistent, planned practice. And so the goal of forming habits of reflection needs to be worked on by all teachers in Jesuit schools, colleges, and universities in all subjects, in ways appropriate to the maturity of students at different levels.

Conclusion

157/ In our contemporary mission the basic pedagogy of Ignatius can be an immense help in winning the minds and hearts of new generations. For Ignatian pedagogy focuses upon formation of the whole person, heart, mind, and will, not just the intellect; it challenges students to discernment of meaning in what they study through reflection rather than rote memory; it encourages adaptation which demands openness to growth in all of us. It demands that we respect the capacities of students at varied levels of their growth; and the entire process is nurtured in a school environment of care, respect, and trust wherein the person can honestly face the often painful challenges to being human with and for others.

158/   To be sure, our success will always fall short of the ideal. But it is the striving for that ideal, the greater glory of God, that has always been the hallmark of the Jesuit enterprise.

159/   If you feel a bit uneasy today about how you can ever measure up to the challenges of your responsibilities as you begin this process of sharing Ignatian Pedagogy with teachers on your continents, know that you do not stand alone! Know, also, that for every doubt there is an affirmation that can be made. For the ironies of Charles Dickens's time are with us even now. "It was the worst of times, the best of times, the spring of hope, the winter of despair." And I am personally greatly encouraged by what I sense as a growing desire on the part of many in countries around the globe to pursue more vigorously the ends of Jesuit education which, if properly understood, will lead our students to unity, not fragmentation; to faith, not cynicism; to respect for life, not the raping of our planet; to responsible action based on moral judgement, not to timorous retreat or reckless attack.

160/   I'm sure you know that the best things about any school are not what is said about it, but what is lived out by its students. The ideal of Jesuit education calls for a life of intellect, a life of integrity, and a life of justice and loving service to our fellow men and women and to our God. This is the call of Christ to us today—a call to growth, a call to life. Who will answer? Who if not you? When if not now?

161/   In concluding, I recall that when Christ left his disciples, He said, "Go and teach!" He gave them a mission. But He also realized that they and we are human beings; and God knows, we often lose confidence in ourselves. So, He continued, "Remember you are not alone! You are never going to be alone because I shall be with you. In your ministry, in difficult times as well as in the times of joy and elation, I shall be with you all days, even to the end of time." Let us not fall into the trap of Pelagianism, putting all the weight on ourselves and not realizing that we are in the hands of God and working hand in hand with God in this, God's Ministry of the Word.

162/   God bless you in this cooperative effort. I look forward to receiving reports on the progress of the *Ignatian Pedagogy Project* throughout the world. Thank you for all you will do!

APPENDIX III

Examples of Methods to Assist Teachers in Using the Ignatian Pedagogical Paradigm

N.B.: These and other pedagogical approaches consistent with Ignatian Pedagogy will be explained and practiced in staff development programs which are an integral part of the Ignatian Pedagogy Project.

163/ *CONTEXT OF LEARNING*

1. The Student: Readiness for Growth
   a) The Student's Situation—Diagnosis of Factors Affecting the a. a. Student's Readiness for Learning and Growth: Physical, academic, psychological, socio-political, economic, spiritual.
   b) Student Learning Styles: How to plan for effective teaching.
   c) Student Growth Profile: A strategy for growth.

2. Society
   a) Reading the Signs of the Times: Some tools for socio-cultural analysis.

3. The School
   a) School Climate: Assessment Instruments
   b) Curriculum
     • Formal/Informal.
     • Scope and Sequence; interdisciplinary possibilities.
     • Assessing values in the curriculum.
   c) Personalized Education
   d) Collegial Relationships among Administrators, Teachers, and Support Staff.

4. The Teacher: Expectations and realities.

164/ *EXPERIENCE*

1. The Prelection
   a) Continuity
   b) Advance Organizers

    c) Clear Objectives

    d) Human Interest Factors

    e) Historical Context of the Matter Being Studied

    f) Point of View/Assumptions of Textbook Authors

    g) A Study Pattern

2. Questioning Skills

3. Student Self-Activity: Notes

4. Problem Solving/Discovery Learning

5. Cooperative Learning

6. Small Group Processes

7. Emulation

8. Ending the Class

9. Peer Tutoring

165/ *REFLECTION*

1. Mentoring

2. Student Journals

3. Ignatian Style "Repetition"

4. Case Studies

5. Dilemmas/Debates/Role Playing

6. Integrating Seminars

166/ *ACTION*

1. Projects/Assignments: Quality Concerns

2. Service Experiences

3. ssays and Essay-Type Questions

4. Planning and Application

5. Career Choices

167/   *EVALUATION*

1. Testing: Alternatives Available

2. Student Self-Evaluation

3. Assessing a Spectrum of Student Behaviors: The Student Portfolio

4. Teachers' Consultative Conferences

5. Questions for Teachers

6. Student Profile Survey

---

¹ (Cf. *Characteristics* #167 and Peter-Hans Kolvenbach, S.J. Address, Georgetown, 1989.)

² Such as secularism, materialism, pragmatism, utilitarianism, fundamentalism, racism, nationalism, sexism, consumerism—to name but a few.

³ Decree 1, #42–43, emphasis added.

⁴ This fundamental insight into the Ignatian Paradigm of the *Spiritual Exercises* and its implications for Jesuit education was explored by François Charmot, S.J., *in La Pédagogie des Jésuites: Ses principes - Son actualité* (Paris: Aux Editions Spes, 1943). "Further convincing information may be found in the first ten chapters of the directory of the *Spiritual Exercises*. Applied to education, they place in relief the pedagogical principle that the teacher is not merely to inform, but to help the student progress in the truth." (A note summarizing a section of the book in which Charmot describes the role of the teacher according to the *Exercises*, taken from an unofficial annotation and translation of sections of Charmot's work by Michael Kurimay, S.J.).

⁵ The methodology of the lecture hall, in which the authority of the teacher (magister) as the dispenser of knowledge reigns supreme, became the predominant instructional model in many schools from the middle ages onward. The reading aloud of the lecture marked the "lectio" or lesson of the class which the student was subsequently expected to recall and defend. Advancements in the technology of printing eventually led to the greater availability of books for private reading and independent study. In more recent times, textbooks and materials written by professionals in the field and commercially published for the mass market of education have had a significant impact on classroom teaching. In many cases, the textbook has replaced the teacher as the primary authority on curriculum and teaching, so much so that textbook selection may be the most important pedagogical decision some teachers make. Coverage of the matter in terms of chapters and pages of text that students need to know to pass a test continues to be the norm in many instances. Often little thought is given to how knowledge and ideas reflected upon within the framework of a discipline might dramatically increase not only students' comprehension of the subject but also their understanding of and appreciation for the world in which they live.

⁶ One only needs to think of discipleship and apprenticeship to appreciate the fact that not all pedagogies have been so passive when it comes to the role of the learner.

PART V: RECENT CONTEMPORARY TEXTS (1995–2015)

The International Apostolate of Jesuit Education: Recent Developments and Contemporary Challenges

José Mesa, S.J., 2013. *International Studies in Catholic Education* 5: 176–189.

INTRODUCTION

1/   The Society of Jesus is well known by its commitment to education. In effect, many people identify Jesuits with education although the Society works in many other apostolic areas. The identification is most surprising if we take into consideration that Saint Ignatius and his companions did not think about funding schools at the beginning. They were more interested in other kind of ministries such as preaching, conversion, spiritual exercises, hearing confessions, or works of mercy (O'Malley 1993). However, the interest for opening schools grew rapidly once Saint Ignatius and other Jesuits like Geronimo Nadal and Juan de Polanco saw the apostolic potential of the schools. In 1548 the first school was opened in Messina, Sicily; by 1773 (when the Society of Jesus was suppressed by Pope Clement XIV),[1] the Jesuits had around 800 schools in Europe, Asia, and Latin America.

2/   When the Jesuits were restored in 1814, opening schools again became a priority and Jesuit schools slowly began to reopen in many of the old places but also in new ones. Today Jesuit education (JE) is offered in many different models that account for around 800 traditional secondary/primary schools and more than 2,000 schools through networks inspired or founded or directed by the Society of Jesus. In addition, there are other schools that share our mission and vision and constitute a growing network of Ignatian schools where the laity is the leading force. There are also 189 Jesuit higher education institutions around the world. In total, JE in one form or another reaches more than 2.5 million students worldwide.

A LIVING TRADITION: FROM THE *RATIO STUDIORUM* TO THE PRESENT DAY

3/   John O'Malley, S.J., argues, "tradition will not make our decisions for us, but it provides, I think, a privileged vantage point from which we can do so" (O'Malley 2000, 144). In this sense, we see JE today as the continuation of a living tradition that began more than 450 years ago. Our understanding of the past allows us to better appreciate the uniqueness of our time and the character of our present challenges and to respond creatively to them.

4/   Saint Ignatius enthusiastically approved the first Jesuit schools; he clearly saw the apostolic significance of a ministry he had not considered before. However, it was under the leadership of Fr. Nadal and Fr. Polanco that the Society undertook the task of shaping the new ministry (O'Malley 1993). In 1599—after 50 years of experimentation as educators—the Jesuits made official the *Ratio Studiorum*, a text that describes the distinct roles and curriculum for the schools (from secondary schools to universities) (Society of Jesus 1970). This document provided unity and guidelines for the ever-growing network of schools. Pedagogically, the *Ratio* adopts the *modus parisiensis* or the University of Paris as the preferred method of the Jesuit schools and the Italian humanism of the sixteenth century—with its primacy of pietas[2]—as the curriculum and philosophy of education guiding them. In addition, the *Ratio* also integrates the best practices of the first 50 years of JE. In this sense JE was the result of an eclectic model (Mesa 2004) in which elements coming from different sources were applied to serve the mission; students "may acquire not only learning but also habits of conduct worthy of a Christian" (*Ratio Studiorum*, Common Rules for the Teacher of the Lower Classes, No. 1). Or as the Rules of the Provincial state:

> It is the principal ministry of the Society of Jesus to educate youth in every branch of knowledge that is in keeping with its Institute. The aim of our educational program is to lead men to the knowledge and love of our Creator and Redeemer. (*Ratio Studiorum*, Rules of the Provincial, No. 1)

5/   The *Ratio Studiorum* was the official document orienting JE for several centuries. At the beginning of the nineteenth century, the Jesuits—just recently restored by Pope Pius VII—tried to update it according to the new educational circumstances that were prevalent in the world after the French Revolution. However, after a first attempt, they decided not to create a new document but rather to adjust the old *Ratio* to the local circumstances of every school, country, and region. Something similar happened at the beginning of the twentieth century (Margenat 2010). The new nationalistic inspiration of many governments made education a cornerstone of state policies and, from then on, the state claimed its right to direct and structure public education according to the political needs of the ruling party.

VATICAN COUNCIL II AND THE RESPONSE OF FATHER PEDRO ARRUPE, S.J.

6/   It was only in recent times that the Society began a serious and systematic renewal of JE worldwide. Fr. Pedro Arrupe, as General of Society appointed in 1965, called for this renewal and he himself helped create the language for it. Fr. Arrupe began a process of "creative fidelity" in response to Vatican Council II, a process to refocus JE on the mission of educating men and women for others; "the prolongation into the modern world of our humanist tradition. Only by being a man-for-others does one become fully human" in the context of a faith that does justice (Arrupe 1973, 8). The following years would become a deep and important moment for JE that served to discover the roots and the original apostolic inspiration of the school ministry. During this time the correlation between one's spiritual experience, as presented in the Spiritual Exercises of Saint Ignatius, and one's education was emphasized. Numerous studies, articles and documents were published analyzing the relationship between the *Spiritual Exercises* as a pedagogical experience and the educational outcomes of the schools. This renewal led to two important documents that have shaped JE in modern times: *The Characteristics of Jesuit Education* (first published 1986, Society of Jesus 2000) and *Ignatian Pedagogy: A Practical Approach* (first published 1993, Society of Jesus 2000). These two documents are the successors of the *Ratio Studiorum* in the sense that they provide unity of language and purpose in a contemporary context in which educational systems are dominated by national standards and requirements that prevent the easy uniformity of the past.

7/   Two other important elements developed during this time and have shaped JE today:

1. Importance of lay-Jesuit collaboration: The Church discovered the importance of the laity in the apostolic works sponsored by religious orders. This has meant a rethinking of the way Jesuits and lay people interact and work together. Today most of the school-teachers and administrators are lay people. We have discovered a new dynamism that comes from this collaboration and it has helped strengthen our identity and mission. It is true that the pace and enthusiasm varies according to the different cultures and regions of the world; but it also constitutes an irreversible and most welcome trend that has allowed for new apostolic energy for the schools. In some regions where Jesuit manpower is scarce, this collaboration has brought vitality to the schools. In a recent visit to Ireland I witnessed the high level of commitment and enthusiasm of our lay partners. A Jesuit even confided to me that this collaboration has allowed for a growing level of identity in our schools despite the shrinking number of Jesuits. However, it is clear that the collaboration should not be the result of fewer Jesuits but the conviction that God has called us to work together as apostles and that the results of this collaboration will be a renewal of the Church and faith.

2. Ignatian pedagogy: Fr. Arrupe argued that any authentic Jesuit school should provide education that gives students "a certain *Ignacianidad*" (Arrupe 1980, #10) or way of proceeding according to the vision that comes from the *Spiritual Exercises*. In this sense, this call to the *Ignacianidad* is a call for renewal in creative fidelity. This term has led to a new concept of Ignatian education/pedagogy as the education that responds to this vision. Ignatian—instead of Jesuit—education is a term now preferred in many documents and

regions of the world; the concept also expresses the fact that many or all aspects of JE can be found in schools run by the laity or other religious communities that share Saint Ignatius's spiritual vision without necessarily being connected to the authority of the Society of Jesus (see Codina 2007).[3]

An important consequence of introducing the concept of Ignatian pedagogy was a broader view of the elements that constitute JE, elements that all need to be renewed in order to attain a real growth and transformation in JE.

IGNATIAN SPIRITUALITY AS THE SOURCE AND BACKGROUND OF JESUIT EDUCATION

8/   The inspiration and background of JE is born out of the spiritual experience that transformed the lives of Saint Ignatius and his first companions and that changed the way they saw the world and understood their relationship to God, to others, and to creation. It is this vision that the concept of *Ignacianidad* expresses. Moreover, this vision truly constitutes the real foundational criterion for our education, the one that determines the mission of the schools at the service of the Gospel and the Kingdom of God. It is clear that our educational mission is faith based, but it is also built on human values that are, for the most part, available to many religious and secular traditions. In this sense, JE is open to students and educators who share these human values regardless of their Christian background.

HUMANISM AS A PHILOSOPHY OF EDUCATION

9/   As previously noted, the first Jesuits adopted the Italian humanism as their preferred philosophy of education and enthusiastically embraced its curriculum and *pietas* as the aim of education. These educators identified so strongly with this humanism that for many they became synonyms. Today we still frame our mission in the humanist tradition in which education centers around the formation of the whole person for the service of faith, justice, and care for the environment. Fr. Arrupe expressed the renovation of the humanist tradition in the well-known expression: "Men and women for others." Fr. Kolvenbach, Fr. Arrupe's successor as Superior General, pointed out the continuity with this tradition and expressed this conviction with the 4 Cs: "educating men and women of conscience, competence, and compassionate commitment" (1993). Fr. Adolfo Nicolás, the current Superior General, has also renewed the humanist conviction of our education by stressing that our present cultural and social context calls all of our schools to educate students in the kind of universality, depth, and imagination that can help solve the difficult and exasperating challenges of a world in need of faith, justice, and reconciliation. In 1986 the International Commission on the Apostolate of Jesuit Education published a document that updated the philosophy of education that underlies our schools, *Characteristics of Jesuit Education*, in which nine dimensions are stressed and connected to the Ignatian vision born of the Spiritual Exercises:

1.1. God is creator and Lord, laboring in all things and can be discovered in natural and human events. Thus, JE is world-affirming.

1.2. God's love invites us to respond in radical freedom. Thus, JE is student-centered (what we usually refer in our tradition as *cura personalis*).

1.3. Because of sin we are engaged in an ongoing struggle for true freedom. Thus, JE is value-oriented and provides a realistic knowledge of the self and the world.

1.4. Ignatius's vision is Christocentric and sees Jesus as the real man for others. Thus, JE proposes Christ as the model of human life.

1.5. For Ignatius, love is shown in actions. Thus, JE is preparation for active life commitment.

1.6. For Ignatius, the response to Christ is made in and through the Church. Thus, JE is an apostolic instrument in service of the Church and prepares students to participate in the Church.

1.7. *Magis*: greater service of God. Thus, JE pursues excellence in formation.

1.8. Ignatius shared his experience with others to create a community at the service of the Kingdom. Thus, JE stresses lay-Jesuit collaboration.

1.9. For Ignatius and his companions, decisions were made by discernment. Thus, JE adapts means and methods; it is a system of schools.

NEW MODELS OF SCHOOLING AND QUALITY EDUCATION FOR THE POOR

10/   This document proved to be important in the process of renewal of JE and inspired many schools to leave the comfort zone of what had become elite centers of education to try new models according to the signs of the times and, at the same time, providing a common language and vision that could replace the timeworn *Ratio Studiorum*. The document also came at an important moment when JE was being criticized by many, inside and outside, for its exclusiveness, its academicism and aloofness from the social concerns better expressed under the concept of social justice. Some Jesuits even questioned whether or not education in general, and schooling in particular, could really be an adequate apostolic tool for the new priorities of faith and justice. Echoes of the anti-schooling movement could be heard here in a time when western cultural discourse was going through turmoil and old principles were questioned.[4] This is not the place to tackle such a complex issue; however, within this context the Jesuit schools began a vigorous process of renovation in which new priorities were conceived and, as a consequence, the schools incorporated new programs to ensure that social justice, lay-religious collaboration, critical thinking, and concern for the poor could be part of our curricula and school ethos. The preferential option of the poor, expressed so well by the Latin American Church at the Conference of Medellin in 1968, made an important impact on the Church at large, just as it shaped the way Jesuits envisioned education. Saint Ignatius conceived JE as free education open to all. For many years Jesuits did not charge tuition for their education and, thus, funds were obtained through donors that kept education available to all regardless of economic means. Today, in the light of the option for the poor, Jesuit schools struggle to make room for all those seeking JE irrespective of their economic situation. Most schools offer scholarships and financial aids to those in need. But, even more important, this option inspired innovative models of JE on different continents. In Latin America, *Fe y Alegria* with more than 1,000 schools—and growing—aims to offer quality education to the poor in a collaborative effort between the laity, the Jesuits, and more than 200 religious congregations. They have developed a successful model for the poor—in more than 20 countries—that combines a strong academic program with the traditional cura personalis of the JE. Among the many awards that *Fe y Alegria* has obtained in recent years, it is important to highlight the 2009 Inter-American Development Bank Juscelino Kubitschek award of merit for regional development in Latin American and the Caribbean since it points the positive macro impact of *Fe y Alegria*.

11/   In the United States new models such as the Cristo Rey and Nativity schools have been developed to creatively offer quality education to the poor. These two models began as a distinctly Jesuit mission but they have expanded to include other religious communities and educational traditions. Cristo Rey has been recognized by:

> the World Innovation Summit for Education (WISE) as one of six groundbreaking projects from around the world to win a 2012 WISE Award . . . The winning projects were selected for their tangible, positive impact upon society and their innovative approach to solving important global problems.[5]

Cristo Rey is now a network of 25 Catholic schools serving 7,400 students nationwide and present in some of the poorest neighborhoods of 24 cities in 17 states and Washington, D.C. Different religious congregations and dioceses sponsor the schools based on a model that combines a strong academic college preparatory program with a whole formation of the person in the Catholic tradition. Cristo Rey has also built a strong network with a central office that coordinates the schools, supports the training of faculty and administrators, and assesses the model of the schools.

12/   Jesuits founded the Nativity school model in New York, which offers quality elementary education to the poor. The model has shown how effective it is to accompany students from very economically deprived neighborhoods to succeed in schools with high academic standards. Its counterpart, *Fe y Alegria*, is now opening new schools in Africa and hoping to develop an African model that brings quality education to the poorest in a continent so needy of new educational models that can respond to its particular challenges and opportunities. It is important to point out that this trend is also present in other continents. India has the largest number of Jesuit schools in any single nation and most of them serve the poor in a context so challenging for social justice and equality (see Toppo 2007); we also have now new schools in the former Soviet Union and Eastern Europe, areas that the Society of Jesus is exploring, discerning what models respond to the particular context of this area. We have just opened the newest Jesuit school in the world in Krakow, Poland, in one of its most socially challenging neighborhoods as a public school run by Jesuit and Ignatian educators. Yet it is in Africa where we have opened most of our newest schools, exploring different models of schooling in the tradition of offering strong academics combined with the education of the whole person. With the help of Jesuit Refugee Service in Africa, we have begun offering basic and higher education classes in the refugee camps as a way to bring hope and dignity to those suffering from one of the most humiliating forms of discrimination in our world.

13/   Today the efforts to redefine the whole concept of humanism in our tradition continue as part of a permanent need to respond to new historical contexts from the perspective of a living tradition.[6]

THE IMPORTANCE OF PEDAGOGY

14/   No real education can be successful without clear pedagogical guidelines about the methods used by students and educators to obtain the knowledge, skills, and values that are deemed important for a flourishing human life. The first Jesuits, as we saw, considered the *modus parisiensis* as the best pedagogy available in the storehouse of pedagogies of their time. Since the restoration of the Society of Jesus in the nineteenth century, Jesuits immersed themselves with other options. During the last decades, as a response to the call for renewal, the schools have "experimented" again and today we find a great variety of pedagogical practices. In Latin America, for example, the so-called personalized education centered in the active partic- ipation of the student according to contemporary criteria has become the rule. This approach has integrated, in recent years, some elements from cognitive pedagogies inspired by Piaget and Vygotsky. In other parts of the world the cognitive movement has also been incorporated along with other pedagogies inspired by the theory of multiple intelligences of Howard Gardner, the smart schools of David Perkins, and many other strategies such as cooperative learning, problem-solving methodologies, peer tutor- ing, and service experiences. All these pedagogies are found in the tradition of active learning since they play better with our own educational history (Vasquez 2006).

15/   In 1993 the document *Ignatian Pedagogy: A Practical Approach* offered a common pedagogical framework that captures some of these new developments and provided a contemporary pedagogical style. This style clearly centers in an active pedagogy and it is expressed in five dimensions of any good pedagogical practice: it promotes acknowledgment and respect for the context of learning; it provides activities that integrate knowledge and emotion in a meaningful experience; it stimulates the process of reflec- tion to grasp the deeper meaning of learning; it fosters decision and com- mitment in a practice transformed in the process; and, finally, the whole process is assessed through an evaluation that reveals the real growth of students not only at the academic level but at all levels of human prog- ress. This common style of active education becomes Ignatian when it is imbued with the spiritual vision of Saint Ignatius. This document, com- monly referred to as the Ignatian Pedagogical Paradigm, does not replace the search for the best pedagogies available in the arena of education, but it provides criteria for selecting them and it also serves as a pedagogical frame- work that orients teachers' planning and interaction with students. The search for contemporary pedagogies compatible with our style has also led the Secretariat for Education to discuss a memorandum of agreement with the International Baccalaureate Organization (IB). The idea is to explore together whether the IB can provide a curricular component to develop the global aspect of JE today. This memorandum expresses the growing interests of some Jesuit schools in Asia, Europe, North America, and Latin America to participate in the academically recognized programs of the IB, especially around sound ways of assessing students' knowledge and development and also to provide faculty with an internationally well-known professional training program. This agreement also signals the Society of Jesus' desire to work with educational networks and organizations that share similar purposes. In our present context, it is not possible or desirable for our education to maintain the kind of self-sufficiency of the past, but we need to work with others in the search for better ways to educate.

REFLECTING ON ITS OWN PRACTICE

16/   JE, from the beginning, put great emphasis in perfecting its education through the reflection on its own practice. This reflection allowed early Jesuits to incorporate elements not present in the educational models of their time, for example, integrating the teaching of Christian doctrine into the schools along with the religious formation through the celebration of the mass, confession, and the establishment of the Marian Congregations. The Jesuits integrated 'Christianitas' (the art of Christian living) into their schools in a way unknown to their contemporaries. The Jesuits also established what historians consider the first international network of schools with a unified curriculum. The practice of reflection made Jesuits aware, in the field of education, of something they had already discovered in their spiritual journey: the importance of responding to the particular circumstances of place, time, and person. Even in the *Ratio Studiorum* there are frequent invitations to respect local customs and develop flexibility according to particular circumstances; for instance, the rules for provincials the *Ratio* state, "in view of differences in places, times, and persons, there are

bound to be certain variations in the order and time schedule of studies . . ."
(*Ratio Studiorum*, Rules of the Provincial No. 39).

17/   It is this tradition of flexibility and respect for the context that Fr.
Arrupe invoked in his invitation to renew JE in the 1970s. It is this sensibility to the contexts that has inspired JE today to adapt to the new educational and social trends that have greatly defined contemporary education.
For example, just to mention four areas of change, many Jesuit schools once
exclusively for boys are now co-educational and open to the new social and
cultural roles of women and men beyond the traditional gendered dichot-
omy of the past. Secondly, JE has been able to integrate, in many parts of
the world, primary education into its school system despite the fact that
the first Jesuits explicitly considered pre-secondary education as not part
of their educational commitment. It is not uncommon for our schools to
offer the whole spectrum of basic education: preschool, primary, and secondary (K–12) education. Thirdly, Jesuit schools have also worked hard
to integrate social justice into their curricula, formation programs, and
ethos. These service programs are now common and many students feel
that this is one of the most significant elements of their educational experience. Fourthly, Jesuit schools have also learned the hard lessons from the
recent sexual abuse crisis that has shaken the Catholic Church in different
countries. Some Jesuit schools have also had to face their own crisis in this
regard. We want to learn from our mistakes and we are now committed to
providing a safe and healthy educational environment based on respect for
diversity and human dignity. Local and national networks have developed
their own comprehensive policies to make sure that our schools will be free
of all forms of abuse: sexual, psychological, physical, and emotional.

CHALLENGES AND OPPORTUNITIES TODAY

18/   The world is changing fast today and there is a clear awareness that
JE should move, at least, at the same speed and in the spirit of creative
fidelity that I have enunciated above. I will explore five of the most important challenges and opportunities that schools are considering or should be

considering. However, it is clear that many other challenges are affecting Catholic education today.

A NEW GLOBAL CONTEXT AND THE OPPORTUNITY OF NETWORKING

19/   Our last General Congregation (GC 35) pointed out that we live in a global world of growing interdependence and that this process:

> has continued at a rapid pace; as a result, our interconnectedness has increased. Its impact has been felt deeply in all areas of our life, and it is sustained by interrelated cultural, social, and political structures that affect the core of our mission of faith, justice, and all aspects of our dialogue with religion and culture. (Society of Jesus 2009, Decree 3, #9)

Decisions that were made before at the local or national level are now made at a global level affecting all people, especially with reference to the environment, economics, and human rights. Of course, GC 35 is well aware that this new interconnectedness has also brought new forms of isolation, exclusion, and marginalization (Decree 3, #11).

20/   In this new context of shadows and hopes, JE can make a difference to diminish the shadows and increase the hopes. Fr. Nicolás challenged Jesuit higher education:

> to promote in creative ways the depth of thought and imagination that are distinguishing marks of the Ignatian tradition . . . to bring our students beyond excellence of professional training to become well-educated "whole person[s] of solidarity." (Nicolás 2010, 3)

We have to strive—and in our case, educate—for a globalization of solidarity, cooperation, and reconciliation. As the GC 35 states, we are called "to bridge the divisions of a fragmented world only if we are united by the love of Christ our Lord" (Decree 3, #17).

21/   One of the possibilities that globalization specifically opens for our schools is networking. Recently the Conference on International Networking in the Society of Jesus—Challenges from a Universal Mission—was held at Boston College in the USA. The final document states "the importance of networking in order to increase the apostolic impact at the regional and global level" (Society of Jesus 2012a, 2). The overall assessment is that we are in a *Kairos*[7] moment that demands imagination, generosity, and a new way of doing things.

22/   The *Ratio Studiorum* created a system of international schools but it did not really establish a network in the way we understand it today because it was based on a model of one school reproduced many times in different places in the world. Today we do not look for this type of organization; we want to keep the tension between being locally rooted, open to international cooperation, and build a global citizenship that can work in solidarity.

INTERNATIONAL COLLOQUIUM ON JESUIT SECONDARY EDUCATION (2012)

23/   In the summer of 2012, for the first time in the history of JE, the leadership of the secondary schools from around the world gathered in Boston, USA, for the International Colloquium on Jesuit Secondary Education, an occasion to explore together the future of JE. At the end of it the participants unanimously approved a final statement that claims:

> The new "signs of the times" warrant a change in our way of proceeding. This new way of proceeding includes on-going communication and collaboration through a continued development of our international network of schools. The goals of our collaboration will be to better serve the faith, justice, and care for the environment, to build bridges between youth and their faith communities, to develop stronger Jesuit/Ignatian Apostolic communities, and to provide our students with opportunities for a truly global education. (Society of Jesus 2012b)

This clear commitment to learn a new way of working together is, at the present time, leading to the exploration of concrete ways in which we can accomplish it; an immediate response has been to strengthen the exchange programs of students and faculty among our schools, the twinning agreements between schools, and the creation of opportunities for common collaborative projects that can develop our apostolic potential. The agreement with the IB is part of this new framework that allows schools, local and regional networks to participate in common projects. The Secretariat of Education is also planning to facilitate a testing ground in our secondary schools for a textbook on ecology that has been created by a pool of Jesuit universities under the auspice of the Secretariat for Higher Education.

24/   We are also working on the development of the new dimension of global education in our schools that can respond to the globalization described before. The idea is that our students and school communities can see themselves as active citizens of the world and can assume their responsibility in shaping the global policies that should make globalization an opportunity for higher levels of solidarity. We are still exploring ways to do this, but one interesting possibility lies in the development of a common global education curricular component in our schools that can give us a sense of a common mission and create a clear unity in our global efforts.

IDENTITY AND MISSION AS AN OPPORTUNITY TO CENTER OUR EDUCATION

25/   Many schools consider today that their main challenge lies in keeping the Ignatian identity of the school vibrant so that it remains faithful to the initial apostolic inspiration that justified it in the first place. In countries with fewer Jesuits, this has become not only a priority but also a matter of survival. Different countries and regions have developed documents dealing with it and trying to answer the question: what makes a Jesuit school Jesuit? For instance, the Jesuit Conference in the USA has created a document to provide criteria for verifying the faithfulness of a school to the mission and Ignatian vision of the institution. Similar documents have been developed in different parts of Europe, Latin America, and Australia. In the USA, many schools have now created a position for a person responsible for the mission and identity of the schools to ensure that this is really central to the whole process.

26/   Fr. Daniel Huang, S.J., rightly argues that "at no time in the past have our schools been so aware of, so insistent on, and so successful in promoting their Jesuit and/or Ignatian identity as today" (Huang 2012, 2). However, as Fr. Huang also points out, there is a common feeling that we still need to do more to clarify the Catholic and Jesuit identity of our schools in:

> light of three factors: the expansion of institutions, the increasing secularization of cultures, and the fact that our institutions are functioning in much more competitive contexts—competition, as you know, that is sometimes based on criteria that are not necessarily those that Jesuit schools should consider most important. (Huang 2012, 4)

As Fr. Nicolás argues:

> If we dream of an educational system that teaches people to decide from inside, from the depths of their hearts, and to serve generously not just a tribe, but as broad a slice of humanity as it can, it is because these were the goals of Jesus, and the only reason Jesuit schools exist is to serve humanity according to the vision and the spirit of the Gospel. (Nicolás 2009, No. 46)

The International Commission on the Apostolate of Jesuit Education is now beginning the work on a third document centered on the identity and mission of the schools; a document that will be a follow up of the two previous ones but that will also update JE to the new challenges and opportunities.

CHALLENGE OF CARING FOR THE ENVIRONMENT AS AN OPPORTUNITY OF ADVANCING THE MINISTRY OF RECONCILIATION

27/   The last General Congregation made care for the environment part of our broader mission of reconciliation. In effect, GC 35 affirms: "care of the environment affects the quality of our relationships with God, with other human beings, and with creation itself. It touches the core of our faith in and love for God." (Decree 3, #32) Our schools are becoming aware of the challenge and some are beginning to respond in different ways: integrating the ecological concern into their curricula, the style of governance, and setting up priorities. In 2010 a new "green" campus was inaugurated in Barranquilla, Colombia. The Colegio San José's new campus was built following the LEED (Leadership in Energy & Environmental Design) certification requirements as part of a desire to seriously respond to the challenges of the environmental crisis and as a way to make the school itself a teaching tool on environmental care. However, our schools in general are just beginning to wonder how to respond to the challenge. One of the opportunities behind this challenge is that this seems to be an area in which the young generations have a special sensitivity and easily engage with the invitation to find ways to overcome the present ecological crisis and become a friendly generation to the environment. The challenge is not small if we consider the implications: to replace our prevalent relationship to the environment as just a provider of raw materials to a relationship of solidarity and reconciliation.

CHALLENGE OF TECHNOLOGY AS AN OPPORTUNITY TO DISCOVER NEW WAYS OF EVANGELIZATION

28/   It is not new to say that technology is changing the world. However, schools in general—and Jesuit schools are no exception—have been slow to respond to it and to understand that the new technologies are changing not only the world but also the way learning and teaching are happening in the new generations. In this case, it is not enough to wire a school, offer Wi-Fi, or provide smartboards. If we take technology seriously we should rethink the way we understand education, schooling, and learning. New models of schooling are developing as I write. For example, there are new models offering online and blended models that promise to open new and unsuspected possibilities. Connections Academy is an example that provides secondary education 100% online,[8] making education available to many with high academic standards. On the other hand, blended models offer different ways of combining online education with the traditional school campus. Some of these models invert the traditional relationship between home and school: "now homework is for the school and instruction (learning/teaching) is for home . . . Students go to school to do their homework through an intense interaction with their peers and teachers."[9]

29/ At the higher education level, something similar and even quicker is happening; many of the leading universities are offering now online courses that can be taken by some; many of them are led by well-known university professors.[10] The Secretariat for Higher Education is beginning to explore the possibility of an online Jesuit University that can respond to this challenge. The Secretariat for Education has also begun to explore models of blended education that can be alternatives to traditional models of education.

30/ As Fr. Lombardi argues: "we note that our mission has been increasingly marked by new communications technologies and by the culture and mentality they have created and diffused" (Lombardi 2012, 7). We cannot ignore this challenge but rather should work creatively so that the new technological context can serve the mission of our schools.

CHALLENGE OF NEW FORMS OF ATHEISM AND AGNOSTICISM AS AN OPPORTUNITY TO RENEW OUR SPIRITUAL FORMATION

31/ Fr. Adolfo Nicolás explains:

> I have heard that a recent survey in Britain showed that the majority of the people surveyed felt religion did more harm than good in the world. This is obviously not the same everywhere, but this kind of attitude is more and more prevalent, in many parts of the world, not just in the West, and it weakens the ability of the Church to gain a listening for the message of life and hope of the Gospel. We have been seeking to understand the causes of this apparent weakening of the credibility of the Church, hoping to see how the Society of Jesus,

as servant of the Church, can help. The causes are complex, and this is not the place to discuss them. But, one thing that emerged very clearly when we discussed this problem from the perspective of various continents is that there are two groups who especially feel this alienation: intellectuals and the youth. (Nicolás 2009, Nos 34–35)

Our schools are not isolated islands in the ocean of the world, although sometimes they can appear as such. Rather, they have made important progress to respond to the call for a new evangelization in recent years: new ways of teaching religion, the renovation of the campus ministry offices, the creation and strengthening of apostolic groups (in the tradition of the Marian Congregations of the past) in which students learn about faith by doing service and engaging in spiritual practices. These new and creative ways of expressing faith, however, are still an area in need of study, serious research, and innovative practice that can allow the younger generations and their parents to experience the transforming power of faith and Church. As Fr. Nicolás claims: "Yes, we plan, coordinate, organize—but only so that we can preach the good news to the poor, heal the sick, liberate the enslaved, raise the dead!" (Nicolás 2009, No. 47); in other words, we educate to share our experience of the Gospel that brings hope and light to the world.

CONCLUDING THOUGHTS

32/   The Society of Jesus has engaged in the apostolate of education since its earliest times despite the fact that it did not contemplate it at the moment of its foundation. The Jesuits embraced the new ministry with enthusiasm and professionalism because they saw it as conducive to the Society's mission of helping people find God in their lives. The schools rapidly multiplied and an international system of schools was established, with the *Ratio Studiorum* providing the curriculum and pedagogy needed for this. In recent times, especially as a response to the Vatican II Council and inspired by Fr. Arrupe, the schools began a long process of renovation that has centered around preparing students as men and women for others in the framework of a faith that promotes justice without abandoning the traditional academic excellence for which schools are known. Today the process of renovation must continue in the face of the new challenges and opportunities that our historical context offers. There is no option different than a creative fidelity that can maintain our education as a meaningful apostolic instrument in the service of the mission.

Notes on Contributor

José Mesa S.J. is the Worldwide Secretary for Secondary and Pre-secondary Education of the Society of Jesus. He is also a visiting Professor at Loyola University—School of Education in Chicago, teaching in the areas of Philosophy of Education and Jesuit Education/Pedagogy.

References
Arrupe, P. 1973. "Men for Others." http://www.sjweb.info/education/doclist.cfm
Arrupe, P. 1980. "Our Secondary Schools Today and Tomorrow." http://www.sjweb.info/education/doclist.cfm
Codina, G. 2007. "Pedagogía Ignaciana." In Diccionario de Espiritualidad Ignaciana. Bilbao-Santander: Mensajero-Sal Terrae.
Huang, C. 2012. "Report from Nairobi: Reflections on Jesuit Identity from the 70th Congregation of Procurators." Paper presented at the International colloquium on Jesuit secondary education, Boston, MA, August.
Kolvenbach, P. 1993, July 31. Letter to all Major Superiors. http://www.sjweb.info/curiafrgren/curia_secretariats.cfm
Lombardi, F. 2012. "Staying Faithful to the Jesuit Mission in Our Schools." Paper presented at the international colloquium on Jesuit secondary education, Boston, MA, August.
Margenat, J. 2010. Competentes, conscientes, compasivos, y comprometidos, la educación de los Jesuitas. Madrid: PPC.
Mesa, J. 2004. "La pedagogía ignaciana: una pedagogía ecléctica al servicio de una visión espiritual." Paper presented at the Encuentro Internacional de Investigadores y Archiveros de la Compañía de Jesús: Nuevo Reino de Granada y Quito, s. XVI, XVII y XVIII, Universidad Javeriana. Bogota,′ Colombia, March.
Modras, R. 2004. Ignatian Humanism. Chicago: Loyola Press.
Montes, F. 2010. "La Universidad Jesuita como nuevo Proyecto Humanista." Paper presented at the Conference on Networking Jesuit Higher Education: Shaping the Future for a Humane, Just, Sustainable Globe, Mexico City, April.
Nicolás, A. 2009. "Challenges and Issues in Jesuit Education." Paper presented

at the Ateneo de Manila on the occasion of the 150th Anniversary of Jesuit Education in the Philippines. Manila, Philippines, July.

Nicolás, A. 2010. "Depth, Universality, and Learned Ministry: Challenges to Jesuit Higher Education Today." Paper presented at the Conference on Networking Jesuit Higher Education: Shaping the Future for a Humane, Just, Sustainable Globe, Mexico City, April.

O'Malley, J. 1993. The First Jesuits. Cambridge, MA: Harvard University Press.

O'Malley, J. 2000. "From the 1599 *Ratio Studiorum* to the Present: A Humanistic Tradition?" In The Jesuit *Ratio Studiorum*: 400th Anniversary Perspectives, edited by J. Duminuco, 127–144. New York: Fordham University Press.

Society of Jesus. 1970. The Jesuit *Ratio Studiorum* of 1599. Translated into English by Allan P. Farrell, S.J. Washington, DC: Conference of Major Superiors of Jesuits.

Society of Jesus. 2000. *The Characteristics of Jesuit Education.* In The Jesuit *Ratio Studiorum*: 400th Anniversary Perspectives, edited by V. Duminuco, 161–230. New York: Fordham University.

Society of Jesus. 2000. "Ignatian Pedagogy: A Practical Approach." In The Jesuit *Ratio Studiorum*: 400th Anniversary Perspectives, edited by V. Duminuco, 231–293. New York: Fordham University.

Society of Jesus. 2009. "General Congregation 35." In Jesuit Life & Mission Today, edited by J. Padberg. Saint Louis, MO: The Institute of Jesuit Sources.

Society of Jesus. 2012a. "Final Document." International Networking in the Society of Jesus: Challenges from a Universal Mission, April. http://historial. pastoralsj.org/jesuitnetworking/docs/2012_Conference_International_Jesuit_ Networking.pdf

Society of Jesus. 2012b. "Vision Statement." International Colloquium on Jesuit Secondary Education, Boston, MA, August. http://www.icjse.org/

Toppo, T. 2007. "Catholic Education and the Church's Concern for the Marginalized: A View from India." International Handbook of Catholic Education 2: 653–663.

Vasquez, C. 2006. Propuesta educativa de la compañía de Jesús: Fundamentos y práctica. Bogota, DC: Asociación de Colegios Jesuitas de Colombia, ACODESI.

Worcester, T., ed. 2008. The Cambridge Companion to the Jesuits. Cambridge: Cambridge University Press.

---

[1] The Society of Jesus was suppressed by the brief *Dominus ac Redemptor* signed by Pope Clement XIV on 8 June 1773. This suppression was preceded by the expulsion of the Jesuits in Portugal (1759), France (1764) and Spain (1767). Even today there are different interpretations of the reasons why all this happened. The Jansenists accused the Jesuits of moral relaxation and being willing to negotiate the faith to accommodate to other cultures, especially in China; the Gallicans saw the Jesuits as the agents of a foreign authority since they were too close to the Papacy; the anti-clerical Enlightenment saw the Jesuits as defending the culture they wanted to overcome. However, the Society survived thanks to a provision in the brief that required it to be promulgated by the civil authorities. The Czars in Russia never allowed such promulgation

in their territories and the Society kept a few numbers and institutions there. On 7 August 1814, Pope Pius VII universally restored the Society of Jesus by the bull *Sollicitudo omnium Eclesiarum*. See Worcester (2008).

[2] *Pietas* was the concept used by the humanist to express the goal of education as forming an upright character. See O'Malley (1993, 212).

[3] The idea behind the concept of Ignatian Education/Pedagogy is that the *Spiritual Exercises* constitute the ultimate source and inspiration for the education the Society of Jesus offers. This intuition, in many ways, advanced by Fr. Arrupe became the source of a profound renewal in JE and has changed the way training educators is conceived today since it brings to the front the need for sharing the foundational experience of the Jesuits and of any follower of Saint Ignatius. During the last decades, the renewal of JE has centered in the studies and practices around the connection between education and Ignatian spirituality in a way that the Society had not witnessed before.

[4] See the de-schooling movement, so strong in the 1970s and 1980s, inspired by Ivan Illich and Everett Reimer among others.

[5] See http://www.cristoreynetwork.org/page.cfm?p_359

[6] See, for example, Montes (2010) and Modras (2004).

[7] *Kairos*: a special time that brings new opportunities.

[8] See http://www.connectionsacademy.com

[9] Nexus Academy Schools: http://www.nexusacademyschool.com

[10] See https://www.coursera.org

From *The Constitutions of the Society of Jesus and
Their Complementary Norms.* Edited by John W. Padberg, S.J.

5. EDUCATIONAL APOSTOLATE

a. General remarks about the educational apostolate

1/ 277. The educational apostolate in all its ramifications, recommended in a special way by the Church in our day, is to be valued as of great importance among the ministries of the Society for promoting today's mission in the service of faith from which justice arises. For this work, when carried out in the light of our mission, contributes greatly to "the total and integral liberation of the human person, leading to participation in the life of God himself."[89]

2/ Our members can exercise this apostolate in various ways either in our own institutions or by collaborating with other institutions. The Society should have its own educational institutions where resources and circumstances permit this and where there is well-grounded hope for the greater service of God and the Church.[90]

3/ Those who work in schools of whatever kind or level or who are engaged in nonformal or popular education can exercise a deep and lasting influence on individuals and on society.[91]

4/ All educational initiatives of the Society must look to the plurality of cultures, religions, and ideologies as well as to local socioeconomic needs.

5/ 278. Keeping intact our preferential option for the poor, we must not neglect students expected to make greater progress and to exercise greater influence on society in the service of the neighbor, no matter to what social class they belong.[92]

6/ 279. We must in a special way help prepare all our students effectively to devote themselves to building a more just world and to understand how to labor with and for others.[93]

7/   When dealing with Christian students, we should take particular care that along with letters and sciences they acquire that knowledge and character which are worthy of Christians and that, animated by a mature faith and personally devoted to Jesus Christ, learn to find and serve him in others.[94] For this, it will help to establish groups of Christian Life Communities in our schools.

8/   Regarding all other students of other religions, we must take care throughout the whole course of studies and especially in the teaching of ethics courses to form men and women who are endowed with a sound moral judgment and solid virtues.[95]

9/   In our educational work we must sensitize our students to the value of interreligious collaboration and instill in them a basic understanding of and respect for the faith vision of those belonging to diverse local religious communities.[96]

10/   280. In this new communications-media culture, it is of great importance to educate our students to a critical understanding of the news transmitted by the media, so that they can learn to be selective in personally assimilating such news. Therefore, our educators should be among the best-trained people in media.[97]

11/   281. Young people who travel abroad for their education, as is common nowadays, should be attentively helped.[98]

12/   282. For its part, the Society should help those many children of the Church who are being educated in non-Catholic schools, collaborating insofar as we are able, in directing Catholic centers for students, serving as chaplains, and also teaching in these schools.[99]

13/   283. We should continue to relate to and advise our former students so that, imbued with gospel values, they may take their place in society and help one another in their respective tasks to work for its good.[100]

14/   284. To foster a close collaboration with the laity in the work of education, we should hand over to them, as far as is possible, the roles they are prepared to assume, whether these are in teaching, in academic and financial administration, or even on the board of directors.[101]

b. Educational institutions of the Society

15/   285. Documents on our educational apostolate, elaborated by the Central Secretariat for Education and approved by Father General,[102] allowing for different local and cultural differences and adapted to the nature of different institutions, should inspire school mission statements, policies, teaching programs, and the entire academic milieu of the educational institutions of the Society.

16/   In order to ensure the proper character of our schools and a fruitful Jesuit-lay cooperation, it is altogether necessary to carefully select administrators and teachers, both Jesuits and others, and to form them adequately in Ignatian spirituality and pedagogy, especially those who will assume positions of major responsibility.[103]

17/   286. In many places, primary schools can be one of the most effective services we offer to people, especially the poor, because they can provide a solid academic and religious foundation during the formative early years.[104]

18/   287. So-called nonformal education, by which both youths and adults are educated outside the traditional school system in both rural and urban areas of developing countries, is a very apt means to promote justice; hence, it is fully in accord with the mission of the Society and has greatly enriched it.[105]

19/   Cooperation is to be fostered between centers for nonformal education conducted by schools, universities, and social centers of the Society, since such cooperation is beneficial to all.[106]

20/   288. Secondary schools should improve continually both as educational institutions and as centers of culture and faith for lay collaborators, for families of students and former students, and through them for the

whole community of a region. Our members should also foster close cooperation with parents of students, who bear the primary responsibility for
education.[107]

21/   Where need or great utility suggests it, other schools, such as technical and agricultural schools, may well be opened.[108]

22/   In establishing coeducation in our secondary schools for the greater
good of souls, ecclesiastical and civil norms existing in various places are to
be observed.[109]

23/   289. Universities and institutions of higher learning play an increasingly important role in the formation of the whole human community, for
in them our culture is shaped by debates about ethics, future directions
for economics and politics, and the very meaning of human existence.[110]
Accordingly, we must see to it that the Society is present in such institutions, whether directed by itself or by others, insofar as we are able to do
so.[111] It is crucial for the Church, therefore, that dedicated Jesuits continue
to engage in university work.[112]

24/   We must continue to work strenuously, with imagination and faith
and often under very difficult circumstances, to maintain and even to
strengthen the specific character of each of our institutions of higher education both as Jesuit and as university, and bring it about that both of these
aspects always remain fully operative.[113]

25/   Universities of the Society, participating in its mission, must discover in their own proper institutional forms and authentic purposes a specific and appropriate arena, consonant with their nature, for fostering the
faith that does justice.[114]

26/   The complexity of a Jesuit university today can require new structures of government and control in order to preserve its identity and at
the same time allow it to relate effectively to the academic world and the
society of which it is a part, including the Society of Jesus and the Church.
Periodic evaluation and accountability are necessary to judge whether or

not its dynamics are being developed in line with the mission of the Society. Jesuits who work in these universities should actively involve themselves in directing them toward the objectives desired for them by the Society.[115]

27/   A Jesuit university must be outstanding in its human, social, spiritual, and moral formation, as well as in its pastoral attention to its students and to the different groups of people who work in it or are related to it.[116]

28/   Among the faculties of our institutions of higher learning, theology and philosophy should especially exercise their proper role to the extent that they contribute to the greater service of God according to local circumstances.[117] Interdisciplinary work should also be promoted, which implies a spirit of cooperation and dialogue among specialists within the university itself and with those of other universities.[118]

29/   290. The education of priests, as a work of the highest value, is to be considered one of the chief ministries of the Society. Therefore, seminarians who attend our universities are to be cared for with special attention, and directors and teachers chosen from among our best men are to be assigned to those clerical seminaries whose direction the Society has accepted. But if there is question of accepting diocesan seminaries, a definite agreement should be made with the bishop with the approval of Father General.[119]

30/   291. Not only youth but adults also are to be educated both in advancements made in their professions and in steps that can be taken to make their conjugal, family, and social life more human and, where appropriate, more Christian and therefore just; they are to be educated also in what will serve to develop a better understanding of their own religious life.[120]

31/   292. Our colleges and universities may have protectors, that is, friends who undertake to protect the work; however, names connoting jurisdiction should be avoided when and where these have no place.[121]

6. INTELLECTUAL APOSTOLATE

32/   293. Research in philosophy and theology, in the other sciences, and in every branch of human culture is extremely necessary to fulfill our mission today and to help the Church to understand the contemporary world and speak to it the Word of salvation.[122]

33/   Ours whom superiors assign to this scholarly work are to give themselves to it entirely and with a strong and self-denying spirit, for in one way or another such work makes demands upon the whole person. They should know that they are making an invaluable contribution to the contemporary mission of the Society. At the same time, they should do this in such a way that they do not lose touch with other apostolic activities of the Society and should cooperate with our members who are engaged in more direct social and pastoral ministries.[123]

34/   294. Among all the ways of being engaged in the intellectual apostolate in the service of the Kingdom of God, theological research and reflection, when undertaken with the seriousness of research and the creativity of imagination that they merit, within the broad spectrum of Catholic theology and in the midst of the varied circumstances in which Jesuits live and work, have a special place because of their unique value to discern, illuminate, and interpret the opportunities and problems of contemporary life and thus to respond to the broadest questions of the human mind and the deepest yearnings of the human heart.[124]

35/   295. In the elaboration and expression of our theological views and in our choice of pastoral options, we must always actively seek to understand the mind of the hierarchical Church, having as our goal the Society's objective to help souls. At the same time, we must try to articulate the *sensus fidelium* and help the magisterium discern in it the movements of the Spirit in accord with the teaching of Vatican II.[125]

36/   296. The office of writer should be regarded as a ministry that is most profitable to souls and altogether appropriate to the Society; therefore, it is to be diligently encouraged by superiors.[126] Regulations enacted both by the common law of the Church and our own Institute with regard to the publishing of books should be exactly and fairly put into practice.[127]

37/   297. We must never forget the distinctive importance of the intellectual quality of all our ministries.[128] Therefore we must all insist on the ongoing development of our capacity to analyze and evaluate our mission, which is indispensable if we wish to integrate the promotion of justice with the proclamation of faith, and if we hope to be effective in our work for peace, in our concern to protect life and the environment, in our defense of the rights of individual men and women and of entire peoples.[129]

---

[89] *General Congregation* (GC) 33, d. 1, no. 44: see GC 32, d. 2, no. 11; d. 4, no. 60; GC 31, d. 28, no. 6.

[90] GC 31, d. 28, no. 5.

[91] GC 33, d.1, no. 44.

[92] See GC 31, d. 28, no. 10, a.

[93] GC 32, d. 4, no. 60.

[94] GC 31, d. 28, no. 12, a; GC 32, d. 4, no. 60; see P. IV, c. 7, nos. 1, 2 [392, 395].

[95] See GC 31, d. 28, no. 12f.

[96] GC 34, d. 5, no. 9.8.

[97] See GC 34, d. 15, no. 6.

[98] *Collectio Decretorum Congregationum Generalium Societatis* Iesu (*CollDecr*) d. [418] (GC 30, d. 51, §2); GC 31, d. 28, no. 15, a.

[99] GC 31, d. 28, no. 14.

[100] See GC 31, d. 28, no. 15, b.

[101] GC 31, d. 28, no. 27.

[102] See "The Characteristics of *Jesuit Education*," Dec. 8, 1986 (Acta Romana Societatis Iesu [ActRSJ] 19:767ff.); "Ignatian Pedagogy Project," July 31, 1993 (ActRSJ 20:911ff.).

[103] GC 34, d. 18, no. 2.

[104] GC 34, d. 18, no. 3; see *CollDecr* d. 132 (GC 31, d. 28, no. 16).

[105] See GC 34, d. 18, no. 4.

[106] See GC 34, d. 18, no. 4.

[107] GC 31, d. 28, no. 18.

[108] GC 31, d. 28, no. 19, c.

[109] See GC 31, d. 28, no. 23.

[110] See GC 34, d. 17, no. 2.

[111] See GC 31, d. 28, no. 24, a.

[112] See GC 34, d. 17, no. 12.

[113] See GC 34, d. 17, nos. 5–6.

[114] See GC 34, d. 17, no. 7; see d. 3, no. 21.

[115] See GC 34, d. 17, no. 9.

[116] GC 34, d. 17, no. 11.

[117] See GC 31, d. 28, no. 24, a, b; CollDecr d. [417] (GC 30, d. 51, §1); P. IV, c. 12, no. 1 [446].

[118] GC 34, d. 17, no. 10.

[119] GC 31, d. 28, no. 25; see CIC 681, §2.

[120] See GC 31, d. 28, no. 26.

[121] See *CollDecr* d. 216 (GC 1, d. 112).

[122] GC 33, d. 1, no. 44; see GC 31, d. 29; GC 32, d. 4, nos. 59–60; GC 34, d. 16, nos. 1–3.

[123] See GC 31, d. 29, no. 2; GC 33, d. 1, no. 44; GC 34, d. 16, no. 5.

[124] See GC 34, d. 16, nos. 7–9; d. 4, nos. 19–24; d. 6, no. 12; d. 11, no. 27.

[125] GC 34, d. 11, no. 20; see Vat. Council II, Dogmatic constitution *Lumen gentium*, no. 12.

[126]See *CollDecr* d. 230 (GC 5, d. 9); GC 22, d. 20.
[127]See "An Ordination on Writings and other Works Intended for Publication," *ActRSJ* 19:1016ff.
[128]See GC 34, d. 6, no. 21; ibid., d. 16, no. 1.
[129]See GC 34, d 16, no. 3.

General Congregation 34, 1995

Jesuit Life & Mission Today: The Decrees & Accompanying Documents of the 31st–35th General Congregations of the Society of Jesus.
Edited by John W. Padberg, S.J.

Editor's Introduction: General Congregation 34 was convoked by Fr. General Peter-Hans Kolvenbach in order to provide an orientation on the mission of the Society. This Congregation ratified the mission of the Society as the service of faith and the promotion of justice and added the need to engage in interreligious dialogue. This Congregation also produced the three decrees dealing with education presented in this book.

Decree 16

THE INTELLECTUAL DIMENSION OF JESUIT MINISTRIES

1/ Since its foundation, the Society has held intellectual labour in high esteem, as a significant contribution to the discovery of the creative work of God and to the recognition of the legitimate autonomy of human inquiry. This tradition of the Society is particularly relevant today within the context of urgent issues confronting us in our mission. For this reason, General Congregation 34 (GC 34) strongly reaffirms the distinctive importance of the intellectual quality of each of our apostolic works. The value of this aspect of our ministry is fundamental in contemporary circumstances, characterized as they are by changes which are as rapid as they are radical.

2/ Where pietism and fundamentalism join forces to disparage human abilities *human reason* will be ignored or held of little account. Contrariwise, especially in countries where secularism holds sway or which have recently emerged from Marxist atheism, some seem to regard *faith* as little more than a "superstition" which will gradually disappear in the face of ever more rapid human progress. But freedom and the ability to reason are attributes which characterize human beings as created in the likeness of God and are closely tied to genuine faith. Therefore, everywhere and in all circumstances an intellectual tradition continues to be of critical importance for the Church's vitality as well as for the understanding of cultures which deeply affect each person's way of thinking and living. All of us experience the need to "explain" the hope that dwells in us (cf. 1Pt 3:15) and the concern to acknowledge "everything that is true, everything that is honourable, everything that is upright and pure, everything that we love and admire, whatever is good and praiseworthy" (Phil 4:8).

3/   For this reason, GC 34 resolutely encourages a vigorous spiritual and intellectual formation for young Jesuits and ongoing spiritual and intellectual formation for every Jesuit. The Society, sensitive to present needs and challenges, must insist on the necessity not only for each one's ongoing acquisition of knowledge but also on the ongoing development of each one's personal capacity to analyze and evaluate, in our circumstances of rapid change, the mission which he has received. There can be no substitute for individual, painstaking, and, quite frequently, solitary work. Such capacity is indispensable if we wish to integrate the promotion of justice with the proclamation of faith, and if we hope to be effective in our work for peace, in our concern to protect life and the environment, in our defence of the rights of individual men and women and of entire peoples. Serious and active intellectual inquiry must also characterize our commitment to integral evangelization. This assumes a basic knowledge of the economic, social, and political structures in which our contemporaries find themselves immersed, and it cannot be ignorant of the development of traditional and modern cultures, nor of the effects of the emerging culture of communication. For evangelization to be effective, accuracy in knowledge, respect for the other in intercultural dialogue, and critical analysis are all imperative.

4/   In apostolic works which are more directly intellectual, professional formation and competence are to be accompanied by that legitimate responsible autonomy and freedom which are requisites for progress in scholarly teaching and research. Furthermore, today more than ever before, it is essential that we recognize the specific characteristics of each of the various scholarly disciplines, including science and technology. We must help our contemporaries to respect this autonomy and freedom, and to recognize these specific characteristics. For those with faith to deny "the rightful autonomy of science"[1] can lead to tragedies well-known in the history of recent centuries. We who have learned to pray before the "Eternal Lord of all things,"[2] must, therefore, be especially careful to avoid the same mistakes under new forms.

5/   The intellectual dimension of every apostolic work also supposes that each Jesuit knows how to be active in companionship with others. Those engaged in an intellectual life experience periods of exaltation and of doubt, of recognition and of being ignored, of intense satisfaction and of bitter trial. More than in other areas, an intellectual mission calls for a humble ability to accept praise and also to face rejection and controversy; this mission is constantly exposed to the judgement of others in conversations, in scholarly publications, and in the media. To accept this reality simply and directly is one way of being "Servants of Christ's Mission"—the Christ who continues his paschal mystery through us.

6/   These characteristic challenges of the intellectual apostolate require that each of us acquire the ability to live the creative tension between profound insertion into all the details of our work and an open and critical attitude towards other points of view and other cultural or confessional positions. However, acceptance of such tension must not lessen our witness or personal commitment to the service of the Church in its journey towards the Kingdom of God.

7/   Among the ways of being engaged in the intellectual apostolate in the service of the Kingdom of God, theological research and reflection has a special place and merits specific mention. Father Pedro Arrupe named theological reflection as one of the four priority apostolates of the Society of Jesus.[3] Among the urgent contemporary issues needing theological reflection, he listed humanism, freedom, mass culture, economic development, and violence. GC 32 cited and confirmed Father Arrupe's emphasis on theological reflection, and also called for a social analysis of the structural causes of contemporary injustices[4] and for Ignatian discernment regarding the appropriate apostolic response to these injustices. GC 34 reconfirms the need for this theological reflection and, to the issues it must address, adds the contemporary understanding of the promotion of justice, including enculturation and interreligious dialogue.

8/   Theological reflection, social analysis, and discernment are phases of a process which Pope John XXIII and Vatican II called "reading the signs of the times"[5] the effort to discern the presence and activity of God in the events of contemporary history in order to decide what to do as servants of the Word. This will bring the perennial sources of Catholic theology to bear upon the lived experiences, individual and communal, of the members of the faith community that is the Church, especially their experience of poverty and oppression; it relates Catholic theology to the secular disciplines, especially philosophy and the social and natural sciences, in order to discern, illuminate, and interpret the opportunities and problems of contemporary life.

9/   When theological reflection is undertaken with the seriousness of research and the creativity of imagination that it merits, within the broad spectrum of Catholic theology and in the midst of the varied circumstances in which Jesuits live and work, it can give rise to specific theologies which, in diverse times and places, incarnate the Gospel message. Theological research and reflection in service of the Gospel can thus help to respond to the broadest questions of the human mind and the deepest yearnings of the human heart.

10/   Not only in our ministries, but also in our personal way of seeing and interpreting individual, social, cultural, and political situations, and even in our spiritual life, we can be guided by such reflection. It will be more productive to the extent that it roots itself in a personal faith lived and expressed in the Christian community. It must be attentive to the questions which reality poses to believing men and women. And the Jesuit engaged in such reflection must know how to join awareness of contemporary circumstances with a careful listening to the voice of God in personal prayer.

[1]   Vatican Council II, *Gaudium et Spes,* n. 36.
[2]   *Spiritual Exercises (SpEx.)* [98].
[3]   Pedro Arrupe, Address to the Congregation of Procurators 65, 10 May 1970, AR 15 (1970); pp. 908–909.
[4]   GC 32, D 4, nn. 59f; cf. nn. 44, 71–74.
[5]   Cf. Vatican Council II, *Gaudium et Spes,* nn. 4, 11, 44.

Decree 17

JESUITS AND UNIVERSITY LIFE

11/   Jesuits have been engaged in university teaching, research, and scholarly publication almost since the foundation of the Society. From astronomy to classical ballet, from the humanities to theology, Jesuits try to enter into the languages and discourses of their inherited or emerging cultures. They attempt to discover, shape, renew, or promote human wisdom, while at the same time respecting the integrity of disciplined scholarship. They also seek to accompany in faith the men and women molded by the potent cultural forces inherent in the university as an institution. St. Ignatius was aware of the wide cultural impact of universities and chose to send Jesuits there, as places where a more universal good might be achieved. Throughout our history we have continued to affirm this basic Ignatian intuition.

12/   Today, approximately three thousand Jesuits work in nearly two hundred of our own institutions of higher learning, touching the lives of more than half a million students; other Jesuits exercise this mission in other universities. This apostolic activity not only has an influence on the lives of students; it goes beyond the immediate university milieu. We recognize that universities remain crucial institutional settings in society. For the poor, they serve as major channels for social advancement. In and through universities, important debates take place—about ethics, future directions for economics and politics, and the very meaning of human existence— that shape our culture. Neither the university as an institution and as a value for humanity, nor the still-urgent imperative for an unflagging Jesuit commitment to our tradition of fostering university life, stand in need of any fresh defence.

13/   Moreover, many excellent documents already exist which treat the role and future of Jesuit universities.[1] General Congregation 34 wishes only to encourage Jesuits engaged in this important and traditional Jesuit work and to consider two relatively fresh challenges to Jesuit universities.

A Challenge from the Structure of Universities

14/   During the past thirty years, Jesuit higher education has undergone very rapid development in size, complexity, and the evolution of more participative governance structures. During this same period, the number of Jesuits engaged in a university, or at least the proportion of Jesuits within the entire university community, has greatly diminished; lay and religious colleagues join with us in a common enterprise. In some places, Jesuits no longer "own" our universities in any real sense. In others, government regulations create a situation in which we no longer fully "control" them. In places, some ecclesiastical superiors may be distrustful of the freedom necessary for a university truly to function in accord with its specific aims.

15/   In response to this challenge, Jesuits must continue to work hard, with imagination and faith and often under very difficult circumstances, to maintain and even to strengthen the specific character of each of our institutions both as *Jesuit* and as a *university*. As we look to the future, we need consciously to be on guard that both the noun "university" and the adjective "Jesuit" always remain fully honoured.

16/   The noun guarantees a commitment to the fundamental autonomy, integrity, and honesty of a university, precisely as a university: a place of serene and open search for and discussion of the truth. It also points to the mission proper to every university—its dedication to research, teaching, and the various forms of service that correspond to its cultural mission[2]—as the indispensable horizon and context for a genuine preservation, renewal, and communication of knowledge and human values. As Jesuits, we seek knowledge for its own sake and at the same time must regularly ask "knowledge for what?"

A Challenge from Faith and Justice

17/   We affirm the adjective, "Jesuit," no less strongly. This presupposes the authentic participation in our basic Jesuit identity and mission of any university calling itself Jesuit, or any university which operates ultimately under our responsibility. While we want to avoid any distortion of the nature of a university or any reduction of its mission to only one legitimate goal, the adjective Jesuit nevertheless requires that the university act in harmony with the demands of the service of faith and promotion of justice found in Decree 4 of GC 32. A Jesuit university can and must discover in its own proper institutional forms and authentic purposes a specific and appropriate arena for the encounter with the faith which does justice.

18/   We applaud the many ways in which Jesuit universities have tried to apply this decree, both in the lives of students through outreach programmes of mutual contact and service with the poor, and in the central teaching, research, and publication aims of the university. If it remains true that most Jesuit universities must, in various ways, strive to do even more in order to embody this mission of service to the faith and its concomitant promotion of justice, this only reflects the challenge all Jesuits face to find concrete and effective ways in which large and complex institutions can be guided by and to that justice which God himself so insistently calls for and enables. The task is possible; it has produced martyrs who have testified "that an institution of higher learning and research can become an instrument of justice in the name of the Gospel."[3]

19/   The complexity of a Jesuit university can call for new structures of government and control on the part of the Society in order to preserve its identity and at the same time allow it to relate effectively to the academic world and the society of which it is part, including the Church and the Society of Jesus. More specifically, in order for an institution to call itself Jesuit, periodic evaluation and accountability to the Society are necessary in order to judge whether or not its dynamics are being developed in line with the Jesuit mission. The Jesuits who work in these universities, both as a community and as individuals, must actively commit themselves to the institution, assisting in its orientation, so that it can achieve the objectives desired for it by the Society.

20/   Jesuit universities will promote interdisciplinary work; this implies a spirit of cooperation and dialogue among specialists within the university itself and with those of other universities. As a means toward serving the faith and promoting justice in accord with their proper nature as universities, they can discover new perspectives and new areas for research, teaching, and university extension services, by means of which they can contribute to the transformation of society towards more profound levels of justice and freedom. Thus our universities have a clear opportunity to promote inter-university collaboration and, in particular, to undertake common projects between Jesuit universities of developed and developing countries.

21/   A Jesuit university must be outstanding in its human, social, spiritual, and moral formation, as well as for its pastoral attention to its students and to the different groups of people who work in it or are related to it.

22/   Finally, we recall how crucial it is for the whole Church to continue to have dedicated Jesuits engaged in university work. They are committed, in the most profound sense, to the search for the fullness of truth. We are assured that, despite occasional appearances to the contrary, the truth we seek will ultimately be one. That truth, rooted as it is in God, will make us free. GC 34 sends a warm word of greeting and encouragement to all those Jesuits dedicated to make authentic and currently fresh this long-standing but sometimes challenged Jesuit commitment to the university apostolate.

---

[1]   Cf. - GC 31 DD 28, 29, 30; GC 32, D 4; GC 33, D 1, n. 44;
    - Pedro Arrupe, "Discourse at the Universidad de Deusto," Bilbao, May, 1970. (Rome, C.I.S. 1971, pp. 102–116); "Apostolic Priorities," Address to the Congregation of Procurators, Rome, 5 October 1978, (AR 17 [1980], pp. 518–581); "The Intellectual Apostolate as a Mission of the Society Today," (AR. 16, [1976]), p. 76;
    - Peter-Hans Kolvenbach, "The Jesuit University Today," 5 November 1985 (AR 19[1985], pp. 394–403); "Address at the Centenary Celebration of the Universidad de Deusto," Bilbao, 5 June 1987 (Selección de escritos del Padre Peter-Hans Kolvenbach, Provincia de España, 1992, pp. 377–384); "Address to the U. S. Jesuit Higher Education Assembly," 7 June 1989. (S.J. Documentation 64; August 1989, pp. 1–11); "La Universidad: espacio para la unidad de las ciencias," Universidad Javeriana, Bogota, 26 February 1990; "Educación y valores: a la Universidad Iberoamericana sobre un nuevo modelo de Universidad," Mexico City, 23 August, 1990; "Apostolado educativo, familia y sociedad nueva," Guadalajara; Mexico, 29 August 1990; "En el centenario de la Universidad Pontificia Comillas," October 1992.
    - John Paul II, Apostolic Constitution Ex Corde Ecclesiae.
[2]   John Paul II, Apostolic Constitution Ex Corde Ecclesiae, Art. 2.1.
[3]   Peter-Hans Kolvenbach, Address to the Congregation of Provincials 1, 20 September 1990, AR 20 (1990) p. 452.

Decree 18

SECONDARY, PRIMARY, AND NON-FORMAL EDUCATION

23/   In the past twenty years, in response to General Congregations 32 and 33, significant apostolic renewal has been initiated and carried forward by the large number of Jesuits and lay people working in the apostolate of secondary education. In increasing numbers, our educational institutions are accessible to students from economically disadvantaged groups. The quality of the education has improved in line with the principles enunciated in recent educational documents of the Society.[1] Jesuit-lay cooperation has developed significantly, with each party contributing in a distinctive way towards the total formation of the students. Our schools have become platforms, reaching out into the community, not only to the extended school community of parents, former students, and friends, but also to the poor and the socially disadvantaged in the neighbourhood. Furthermore, we have willingly shared our educational heritage with others when asked to do so.

24/   GC 34 gratefully acknowledges these developments and urges that they be continued. Allowing for diverse situations throughout the world, the ideas and practices drawn from the documents mentioned above must inspire school mission statements, policies, programmes, and the entire school milieu. The Jesuit identity of our schools and Jesuit-lay cooperation can be ensured only by careful selection of administrators and teachers, both Jesuits and others and—especially for those who will assume positions of major responsibility—adequate formation in the Ignatian charism and pedagogy. In some regions well-designed formation programmes are already being offered to Jesuit and lay teachers and administrators; the Society's Secretary for Education should encourage such programmes elsewhere; they can yield great dividends for the ends that we desire.[2]

25/   In response to different situations and for a variety of apostolic reasons, Jesuits in many areas are engaged in the apostolate of primary and pre-primary education. We confirm that such schools "are very important and not contrary to our Institute"[3] and also declare that, because they can provide a solid academic and religious foundation during the formative early years, they can be one of the most effective services we offer to people, especially the poor.

26/   The educational apostolate of the Society has been greatly enriched by the contributions made by centres of nonformal education, established in both rural and urban areas of developing countries. These centres provide education outside the traditional school system for both youth and adults among the poor. With the help of a participative pedagogy, they organize programmes to eradicate illiteracy and supply training in technical and social skills as well as offering a religious and ethical formation geared to the analysis and transformation of the society in which the students live. They educate their students as "men and women for others" who can assume leadership roles in their own communities and organizations. The number of persons whom we serve through these centres is very large; as a means towards the promotion of justice, this ministry of nonformal education is fully in accord with our Jesuit mission. Especially in the light of the Decree "Servants of Christ's Mission," GC 34 encourages Jesuits, religious, and lay persons to continue their dedicated work in this important but difficult apostolate and recommends cooperation between Jesuit centres for nonformal education and our Jesuit schools, universities, and social centres.

---

[1] *The Characteristics of Jesuit Education* (1987) and *Ignatian Pedagogy: A Practical Approach* (1993).

[2] Cf. Pedro Arrupe, "Our Secondary Schools Today and Tomorrow," 13 September 1980, n. 21, AR 18 (1980), pp. 268–270.

[3] GC 31, D 28, n.16.

Current Characteristics of Education in the Society of Jesus

Peter-Hans Kolvenbach, S.J., 1998. Speech given on the occasion of the 75th Anniversary of the San Ignacio School, Caracas.

Editor's Introduction: Fr. Peter-Hans Kolvenbach (1928–2016) was elected as the 29th Superior General of the Society by General Congregation 33 in 1983. He resigned in 2008. Fr. Kolvenbach wrote extensively about Jesuit education and made an everlasting impression in the way we understand Jesuit education today. In the four discourses presented in this book, Fr. Kolvenbach states some of his most important contributions to Jesuit education. In his discourse in Caracas in 1998, Fr. Kolvenbach recognized the serious questions and debate within the Society surrounding the capacity of Jesuit education to really educate for justice and transform society. Schools have adapted to the new challenges, and Fr. Kolvenbach argues that a Jesuit school "remains irreplaceable for individual and social growth of people, communities, and community advancement." In his 2000 address at Santa Clara University (*The Service of Faith and the Promotion of Justice in American Jesuit Higher Education*, p. 477), Fr. Kolvenbach calls for Jesuit universities to embrace the Jesuit commitment to faith and justice. In *The Jesuit University in the Light of the Ignatian Charism* (p. 496), Fr. Kolvenbach addresses Jesuits and laity working for higher education, stressing the relationship between education and Ignatius's spiritual experience. He uses Ledesma's reasons for education to explain the goals of Jesuit education today. In 2007, Fr. Kolvenbach addressed the board of directors of Georgetown University (p. 516) and further developed Ledesma's vision to explain the meaning of Jesuit education.

1/ May my first words be of greeting and gratitude to all the members of the Educational Community of the San Ignacio School: to the Father Rector, to the directors and the Jesuits; to the teachers and the staff; to the parents and representatives, and to the students. I join you during these days of joy and with you I thank God for these 75 years of service to the Church and the society of Venezuela.

2/   The 8th of January, 1923, sets a milestone in the apostolate of the Society of Jesus in Venezuela. From this moment on, the educational task of the Jesuits is reinstated in this country after having been interrupted in 1767 by the expulsion decree of Carlos III.

3/   With the opening of the San Ignacio school, the Society tried to respond, from the educational field, to the demands of the Church at that moment in history. In a society that was marked by libertarian and positivist ideas, there was a need for well-instructed Catholic leaders. These leaders had to be loyal to their Church and their doctrinal and moral orthodoxy and be able to give support to an extremely weak establishment with a lack of religious institutions and with little significance in the educational and cultural spheres.

4/   The recount of the results shows that the San Ignacio school was able to respond to the expectations of the time. The 75-year path of the San Ignacio school gives me the opportunity to share with you some reflections on the characteristics of education of the Society now and then, and on the ways in which the schools of the Society and of this school in particular respond to the future challenges.

THE SCHOOLS THEN AND NOW

5/   About 30 years ago, the institutions suffered a strong external attack and deep internal questioning. May of 1968 was not in vain in history. But the foreign anti-scholar and anti-institutional movements were not the only ones to move the foundations of the schools. The Second Vatican Council had suggested a new kind of Church-world relationship, which lead to healthy reviewing and an update of the structures and institutions of the Church, amongst which was the Catholic school.

6/   Within the Society, in 1975 the General Congregation 32 asked the Jesuits to take part in a process of reflection and reviewing of all their apostolic works to better adapt them to the requirements of the moment according to the new reformulation of the Society: service of the faith and the promotion of justice.

7/   The fact is that schools—traditionally seen as successful—became the focus of serious questions, especially from the point of view of their capacity to educate for justice and social transformation. The indifference of many Jesuits towards schools and scathing criticism that was often slightly Manichean created a generalized situation of crisis and a decrease in the number of Jesuit replacements, which nowadays still has a negative impact on many schools.

8/   In the midst of this discussion, the idea that it was better to leave the traditional educational institutions to work on other kinds of direct ministry, social or pastoral, arose. The arrival of new educational alternatives brought some people to believe that there was no future for the traditional schools and that the best idea would be to abandon them to their own devices.

9/   The vast majority of Jesuit educational institutions were brave when facing the challenge and knew how to react. The **process of self-evaluation and transformation** that they started by redefining their aims and procedures bore fruit. In the province of Venezuela, it is important to highlight the role of CERPE for its support to the educational institutions in the province during this process of institutional evaluation and reshaping.

10/   Now, after some time, we must admit that the balance of this period of desolation has been, in general, positive. To renew or to die, that seemed to be the motto. Those who chose change transformed the institutions and found once more a new sense of the traditional educational apostolate of the Society. Others did not know how to survive.

11/   In 1980, Father Pedro Arrupe had already warned schools about the need to "speed up" so as to conform to a world, a Church, and a Society that had already arrived at a new pace. "A community that thinks its schools do not need any transformation leads to a set period of agony of the school; it is a matter of one generation. Even if it is painful, the tree must be pruned in order to be stronger," he stated (*Our Schools Then and Now*).

12/   *The Characteristics of a Jesuit Education* was published in 1986. This document was decisive in the process of recovery and transformation of the schools. And not only of the schools; higher education institutions in the Society, in Latin America, and in other regions considered the Characteristics a source of inspiration towards infusing their educational task with the Ignatian nature. Some years later, in 1993, the *Ignatian Pedagogic Paradigm* was published, a practical application of the *Characteristics* in class.

13/   Today, the situation has reversed, and the educational institutions in the Society have found **a new meaning to their being and their work**. Maybe some of the *Jesuit* nature has been lost since the Society parted with the immediate or ultimate responsibility of some institutions. **However, the Ignatian side—meaning the** spiritual **part which arises from Saint Ignatius's** Exercises **and which has been the inspiration for a secular** pedagogical **tradition and which could be translated as "our procedures in education"—grew stronger.**

14/   If school as an institution was once able to be questioned, nowadays it is universally accepted that—without omitting the growing importance of non-scholarly modes of education—**school remains irreplaceable for individual and social growth of people, communities, and community advancement**. With all its limitations, school stands in a key position in the configuration of 21st century society.

15/   From an apostolic point of view, there is no need to highlight the importance that the Society renders to education. "Help the souls" was the permanent motto of Ignatius's apostolic spirit. This was the reason why Ignatius favored schools for "external people"—even if he did not consider it at the beginning—when he realized the enormous apostolic fruit that could be borne through the schools.

16/   Nowadays, over a fourth of the Jesuits work in the educational apostolate, in different areas, levels, and modalities (primary, secondary, high school, nonformal, informal, radio, people-centered) constituting the **apostolic sector that includes the greatest number of Jesuits**. With its highs and lows, its weaknesses, shortcomings, and its real achievements, educational institutions of the Society remain a **privileged means to** *"help the souls."* Today it would be completely irresponsible for the Society to leave the field of education.

17/   The challenges to educational institutions have not disappeared, and it is good that schools and other educational works keep alive a healthy sense of self-criticism and openness to change; conversion is a never-ending process. However, reflection and experience have taught us not to fall into the trap of exclusive dilemmas: being exclusively social, or educational, or pastoral. The solution is not in the choice but in the conception of evangelization as a whole. Each apostolate in the Society has, in one way or another, all three of these dimensions: pastoral, educational, and social.

THE SCHOOLS OF TOMORROW: A NEW EDUCATIONAL MODEL

18/   Nevertheless, to continue in the educational field does not mean that educational institutions have to remain as they were in the past. Change for the sake of changing is not what we intend. We seek **a way to serve more and better** while adapting to the circumstances of the time and place according to a truly Ignatian principle. It is almost a cliché to state that we are not only going through an era of change but also a change of era.

19/   This forces the school and the rest of educational institutions in the Province to develop an educational proposal that, on the one hand, means a contribution to Venezuelan education and to social transformation in this time of transition; and that, on the other hand, is consistent with the principles and educational practice of the Society.

20/   To this end, we should **re-read the educational documents of the Company** (the *Characteristics* and the *Ignatian Pedagogy*) within the context of the reality in Venezuela. Moreover, we should also read the country to learn how it is projecting itself into the future and to combine our educational proposal with that of the state.

21/   The Society of Jesus serves education and the country from various fields. In the mosaic of the educational apostolate in the Province, there is a profusion of educational institutions and works. Each of them has a specific role, they are all necessary, and they depend on each other. **Our apostolate is not a conglomerate of works but a body**. And the educational apostolate must particularly act like a body in which each member is relevant and fulfills a role from its own location. Any exclusive behavior, regardless of where it comes from, would be an error.

22/   Some time ago, the Provincial Father of Venezuela appeared to erase any misunderstanding, stating that within the educational task of the Society of Jesus, the San Ignacio school is an inalienable work. I am enormously pleased by the will of the Province of Venezuela in devoting all their available means towards a better performance of the school while reflecting the educational proposal of the Society for today's Venezuela.

23/   Within a context of transition like the one that the country is currently experiencing, it is reasonable for the school to accelerate in order to answer to the demands of the moment. Not with immediate or short-term perspectives, but with those with a medium or long-term reach.

24/   The aim is clear. In the same way that the San Ignacio school had once faced the challenges posed by conjunctures of the moment, today it must give an answer to the challenges posed by Venezuelan society. Carrying the glory and the weight of its own history, faithful to the past, and open to the demands of the present, the San Ignacio school should play a role of paramount importance for the future from its own identity as part of the Society of Jesus, by providing the Venezuelan education with a valid educational model, precisely from the concrete reality in which the action unfolds.

25/   It is true that the social location of an individual and the environment in which one works will greatly determine their way of thinking and acting, as well as their willingness to change. Living in the inner city is not the same as living in a neighborhood. To teach or study in a school like this one is not the same as doing it in a school in the suburbs. However, **transforming the education and the country, and all the education across the country, is everyone's duty, and it reaches everyone, each from his own place and all acting together as a body.**

26/   For this reason, because God's mandate tells us to spread the Gospel, because we believe in the human person and the power of the Gospel, and because the Society in Venezuela is committed to this project for the country, the Society will keep working on San Ignacio school and in other educational works in the Province.

FEATURES

27/   Once more, I will refer to the document *Characteristics* to clearly state the framework that defines the education of the Society. I would just like to highlight some of the isolated aspects that I believe should be especially taken into consideration in the educational model that this school should adopt.

28/   1. One of the features of the Company's education is **academic quality and** excellence. This quality is understood functionally: to serve more and better, using Ignatius's terms. In a world of individualism, wild competitiveness and growing lack of solidarity, this feature is not negotiable. This attitude must be shown in very specific ways, particularly in serving those who are in need in our society.

29/   2. Likewise, the **leadership** taught to our students must be applied as part of the service to the common welfare. If knowledge is power and if the "society of knowledge" is more powerful every day, then our students, their families, and the whole educational community must be aware that we consider power a way of service. "From everyone who has been given much, much will be demanded" (Luke 12:48). In the context of corruption, violence, abuses of power, and exclusion, democratic education in ethics, values, and citizenship are absolutely fundamental.

30/   3. **Options for the** poor sounds almost like an overused slogan because it has been repeated so many times. However, this is another of those indispensable points. It is true that the school has evolved regarding social balance and that today its audience is not as it was years ago. Nevertheless, we cannot state that the social segment served by the school is exponent of the majority of this country.

31/   No one should discredit this school because of its students; but neither should anyone seek for a consolidation of their privilege in this school. We cannot be more demanding than Jesus, who does not evict anyone, but neither can we be less demanding than Him.

32/   We are all aware of the limitations on private education. If we do not work with the poor, or among them, let's at least make clear that we work from their perspective and for them. The poor, not as the object of our compassion nor the beneficiaries of our social actions, but as an essential reference of our education, searching for a fair and equal society.

33/   4. **The role of the** teachers in this process is crucial. Without committed teachers who are truly imbued with Ignatian identity none of this would be possible. I would like to thank all the educators for their generous dedication to the mission of the school with all their competence and responsibility. At the same time, I would like to ask the Jesuits that they try their best to share with them our spiritual and apostolic heritage, offering them the possibility of receiving a specific formation in Ignatian values so they can properly carry out their mission and eventually assume leadership responsibilities.

34/   5. Finally, a school must be a meeting place and point of convergence for **all the members of the community** to achieve a common mission. Parents and guardians should participate actively and continuously in the life of the school, particularly in this process of renewal. Our educational offer includes values that very often contradict the "market" values. Home and school must be in harmony so that the goals and criteria of the school will be assumed and strengthened by the family.

35/   These are, broadly speaking, yesterday's lessons and the horizons of today and tomorrow. These are some of the characteristics of Ignatian education for you today. The challenge of the future cannot be more exciting. This is a task that cannot be accomplished autonomously by the school. The collaboration, reflection, and joint action by other entities in the Province will be needed—other schools, *Fe y Alegría*, the University, other spheres of social and educational research—while searching for a common vision for the country and its education.

36/   The task of San Ignacio school has not come to an end. After 75 years, the mission continues. May Saint Ignatius, the man of **MORE**, help you contribute in the development of the Society of Jesus' educational proposal for Venezuela, for the greater glory of God.

The Service of Faith and the Promotion of Justice in American Jesuit Higher Education

Peter-Hans Kolvenbach, S.J., 2000. Santa Clara University.

INTRODUCTION

1/   This conference on the commitment to justice in American Jesuit higher education comes at an important moment in the rich history of the twenty-eight colleges and universities represented here this evening. We also join Santa Clara University in celebrating the 150th anniversary of its founding.

2/   Just as significant as this moment in history, is our location. Santa Clara Valley, named after the mission at the heart of this campus, is known worldwide as "Silicon Valley," the home of the microchip. Surely when Father Nobili, the founder of this University, saw the dilapidated church and compound of the former Franciscan mission, he could never have imagined this valley as the center of a global technological revolution.

3/   This juxtaposition of mission and microchip is emblematic of all the Jesuit schools. Originally founded to serve the educational and religious needs of poor immigrant populations, they have become highly sophisticated institutions of learning in the midst of global wealth, power, and culture. The turn of the millennium finds them in all their diversity: they are larger, better equipped, more complex and professional than ever before and also more concerned about their Catholic, Jesuit identity.

4/   In the history of American Jesuit higher education, there is much to be grateful for, first to God and the Church and surely to the many faculty, students, administrators, and benefactors who have made it what it is today. But this conference brings you together from across the United States, with guests from Jesuit universities elsewhere, not to congratulate one another but for a strategic purpose. On behalf of the complex, professional, and pluralistic institutions you represent, you are here to face a question as difficult

477

as it is central: How can the Jesuit colleges and universities in the United States express faith-filled concern for justice in what they are as Christian academies of higher learning, in what their faculty do, and in what their students become?

5/   As a contribution to your response, I would like to (I.) reflect with you on what faith and justice have meant for Jesuits since 1975, and then (II.) consider some concrete circumstances of today, (III.) to suggest what justice rooted in faith could mean in American Jesuit higher education, and (IV.) conclude with an agenda for the first decade of the years 2000.

I. THE JESUIT COMMITMENT TO FAITH AND JUSTICE, NEW IN 1975

6/   I begin by recalling another anniversary, which this conference commemorates. Twenty-five years ago, ten years after the closing of the Second Vatican Council, Jesuit delegates from around the world gathered at the 32nd General Congregation (GC), to consider how the Society of Jesus was responding to the deep transformation of all Church life that was called for and launched by Vatican II.

7/   After much prayer and deliberation, the Congregation slowly realized that the entire Society of Jesus in all its many works was being invited by the Spirit of God to set out on a new direction. The overriding purpose of the Society of Jesus, namely "the service of faith," must also include "the promotion of justice." This new direction was not confined to those already working with the poor and marginalized in what was called "the social apostolate." Rather, this commitment was to be "a concern of our whole life and a dimension of all our apostolic endeavors."[i] So central to the mission of the entire Society was this union of faith and justice that it was to become the "integrating factor" of all the Society's works,[ii] and in this light "great attention" was to be paid in evaluating every work, including educational institutions.[iii]

8/ I myself attended GC 32, representing the Province of the Near East where, for centuries, the apostolic activity of the Jesuits has concentrated on education in a famous university and some outstanding high schools. Of course, some Jesuits worked in very poor villages, refugee camps, or prisons, and some fought for the rights of workers, immigrants, and foreigners; but this was not always considered authentic, mainstream Jesuit work. In Beirut we were well aware that our medical school, staffed by very holy Jesuits, was producing, at least at that time, some of the most corrupt citizens in the city, but this was taken for granted. The social mood of the explosive Near East did not favor a struggle against sinful, unjust structures. The liberation of Palestine was the most important social issue. The Christian churches had committed themselves to many works of charity, but involvement in the promotion of justice would have tainted them by association with leftist movements and political turmoil.

9/ The situation I describe in the Near East was not exceptional in the worldwide Society at that time. I was not the only delegate who was ignorant of matters pertaining to justice and injustice. The 1971 Synod of Bishops had prophetically declared, "Action on behalf of justice and participation in the transformation of the world fully appear to us as a constitutive dimension of the preaching of the gospel, or, in other words, of the church's mission for the redemption of the human race and its liberation from every oppressive situation,"[iv] but few of us knew what this meant in our concrete circumstances.

10/ Earlier, in 1966, Father Arrupe had pointed out to the Latin American Provincials how the socio-economic situation throughout the continent contradicted the Gospel, and "from this situation rises the moral obligation of the Society to rethink all its ministries and every form of its apostolates to see if they really offer a response to the urgent priorities which justice and social equity call for."[v] Many of us failed to see the relevance of his message to our situation. But please note that Father Arrupe did not ask for the suppression of the apostolate of education in favor of social activity. On the contrary, he affirmed that "even an apostolate like education—at all levels—which is so sincerely wanted by the Society and whose importance is clear to the entire world, in its concrete forms today must be the object of reflection in the light of the demands of the social problem."[vi]

11/   Perhaps the incomprehension or reluctance of some of us delegates was one reason why GC 32 finally took a radical stand. With a passion both inspiring and disconcerting, the General Congregation coined the formula "the service of faith and the promotion of justice," and used it adroitly to push every Jesuit work and every individual Jesuit to make a choice, providing little leeway for the fainthearted. Many inside and outside the Society were outraged by the "promotion of justice." As Father Arrupe rightly perceived, his Jesuits were collectively entering upon a more severe way of the cross, which would surely entail misunderstandings and even opposition on the part of civil and ecclesiastical authorities, many good friends, and some of our own members. Today, twenty-five years later, this option has become integral to our Jesuit identity, to the awareness of our mission, and to our public image in both Church and society.[vii]

12/   The summary expression "the service of faith and the promotion of justice" has all the characteristics of a world-conquering slogan using a minimum of words to inspire a maximum of dynamic vision, but at the risk of ambiguity. Let us examine, first the service of faith, then the promotion of justice.

A. The Service of Faith

13/   From our origins in 1540 the Society has been officially and solemnly charged with "the defense and the propagation of the faith." In 1995, the Congregation reaffirmed that, for us Jesuits, the defense and propagation of the faith is a matter of to be or not to be, even if the words themselves can change. Faithful to the Vatican Council, the Congregation wanted our preaching and teaching not to proselytize, not to impose our religion on others, but rather to propose Jesus and his message of God's Kingdom in a spirit of love to everyone.

14/   Just as the Vatican had abandoned the name *Propaganda Fidei*, GC 32 passed from propagation to <u>service</u> of faith. In Decree 4, the Congregation did use the expression "the proclamation of faith," which I prefer.[viii] In the context of centuries of Jesuit spirituality, however, "the service of faith" cannot mean anything other than to bring the counter-cultural gift of Christ to our world.[ix]

15/   But why "the service of faith"? The Congregation itself answers this question by using the Greek expression *diakonia fidei*.[x] It refers to Christ the suffering Servant carrying out his "diakonia" in total service of his Father by laying down his life for the salvation of all. Thus, for a Jesuit, "not just any response to the needs of the men and women of today will do. The initiative must come from the Lord laboring in events and people here and now. God invites us to follow Christ in his labors, on his terms and in his way."[xi]

16/   I do not think we delegates at the 32nd Congregation were aware of the theological and ethical dimensions of Christ's mission of service. Greater attention to the *diakonia fidei* may have prevented some of the misunderstandings provoked by the phrase "the promotion of justice."

B. The Promotion of Justice

17/   This expression is difficult to translate in many languages. We delegates were familiar with sales promotions in a department store or the promotion of friends or enemies to a higher rank or position; we were not familiar with the promotion of justice. To be fair, let us remember that a general congregation is not a scientific academy equipped to distinguish and to define, to clarify, and to classify. In the face of radically new apostolic needs, it chose to inspire, to teach, and even to prophesy. In its desire to be more incisive in the promotion of justice, the Congregation avoided traditional words like charity, mercy, or love: unfashionable words in 1975. Neither philanthropy nor even development would do. The Congregation instead used the word "promotion" with its connotation of a well-planned strategy to make the world just.

18/   Since Saint Ignatius wanted love to be expressed not only in words but also in deeds, the Congregation committed the Society to the promotion of justice as a concrete, radical but proportionate response to an unjustly suffering world. Fostering the virtue of justice in people was not enough. Only a substantive justice can bring about the kinds of structural and attitudinal changes that are needed to uproot those sinful oppressive injustices that are a scandal against humanity and God.

19/   This sort of justice requires an action-oriented commitment to the poor with a courageous personal option. In some ears the relatively mild expression, "promotion of justice," echoed revolutionary, subversive, and even violent language. For example, the American State Department recently accused some Colombian Jesuits of being Marxist-inspired founders of a guerilla organization. When challenged, the U.S. government apologized for this mistake, which shows that some message did get through.

20/   Just as in *diakonia fidei* the term *faith* is not specified, so in the "promotion of justice," the term *justice* also remains ambiguous. The 32nd Congregation would not have voted for Decree 4 if, on the one hand, socio-economic justice had been excluded or if, on the other hand, the justice of the Gospel had not been included. A stand in favor of social justice that was almost ideological and, simultaneously, a strong option for "that justice of the Gospel which embodies God's love and saving mercy"[xii] were both indispensable. Refusing to clarify the relationship between the two, GC 32 maintained its radicality by simply juxtaposing *diakonia fidei* and "promotion of justice."

21/   In other decrees of the same Congregation, when the two dimensions of the one mission of the Society were placed together, some delegates sought to achieve a more integrated expression by proposing amendments such as the service of faith <u>through</u> or <u>in</u> the promotion of justice. Such expressions might better render the 1971 Synod's identification of "action on behalf of justice and participation in the transformation of the world [as] a constitutive dimension of the preaching of the gospel."[xiii] But one can understand the Congregation's fear that too neat or integrated an approach might weaken the prophetic appeal and water down the radical change in our mission.

22/   In retrospect, this simple juxtaposition sometimes led to an "incomplete, slanted and unbalanced reading" of Decree 4,[xiv] unilaterally emphasizing "one aspect of this mission to the detriment of the other,"[xv] treating faith and justice as alternative or even rival tracks of ministry. "Dogmatism or ideology sometimes led us to treat each other more as adversaries than as companions. The promotion of justice has sometimes been separated from its wellspring of faith."[xvi]

23/   On the one side, the faith dimension was too often presumed and left implicit, as if our identity as Jesuits were enough. Some rushed headlong towards the promotion of justice without much analysis or reflection and with only occasional reference to the justice of the Gospel. They seemed to consign the service of faith to a dying past.

24/   Those on the other side clung to a certain style of faith and Church. They gave the impression that God's grace had to do only with the next life and that divine reconciliation entailed no practical obligation to set things right here on earth.

25/   In this frank assessment I have used, not so much my own words but rather those of subsequent Congregations, so as to share with you the whole Society's remorse for whatever distortions or excesses occurred and to demonstrate how, over the last twenty-five years, the Lord has patiently been teaching us to serve the faith that does justice in a more integral way.

C. The Ministry of Education

26/   In the midst of radical statements and unilateral interpretations associated with Decree 4, many raised doubts about our maintaining large educational institutions. They insinuated, if they did not insist, that direct social work among the poor and involvement with their movements should take priority. Today, however, the value of the educational apostolate is generally recognized, being the sector occupying the greatest Jesuit manpower and resources, but only on condition that it transform its goals, contents, and methods.

27/ Even before GC 32, Father Arrupe had already fleshed out the meaning of *diakonia fidei* for educational ministries when he told the 1973 International Congress of Jesuit Alumni of Europe: "Today our prime educational objective must be to form men for others; men who will live not for themselves but for God and his Christ—for the God-man who lived and died for all the world; men who cannot even conceive of love of God which does not include love for the least of their neighbors; men completely convinced that love of God which does not issue in justice for men is a farce."[xvii] My predecessor's address was not well received by many alumni at the Valencia meeting, but the expression, "men and women for others," really helped the educational institutions of the Society to ask serious questions that led to their transformation.[xviii]

28/ Father Ignacio Ellacuría, in his 1982 convocation address here at Santa Clara University, eloquently expressed his conviction in favor of the promotion of justice in the educational apostolate: "A Christian university must take into account the Gospel preference for the poor. This does not mean that only the poor study at the university; it does not mean that the university should abdicate its mission of academic excellence—excellence needed in order to solve complex social problems. It does mean that the university should be present intellectually where it is needed: to provide science for those who have no science; to provide skills for the unskilled; to be a voice for those who do not possess the academic qualifications to promote and legitimate their rights."[xix]

29/ In these two statements, we discover the same concern to go beyond a disincarnate spiritualism or a secular social activism, so as to renew the educational apostolate in word and in action at the service of the Church in a world of unbelief and of injustice. We should be very grateful for all that has been achieved in this apostolate, both faithful to the characteristics of 400 years of Ignatian education and open to the changing signs of the times. Today, one or two generations after Decree 4, we face a world that has an even greater need for the faith that does justice.

II. A "COMPOSITION" OF OUR TIME AND PLACE

Let us turn now to a mention of some of the changing signs of the times.

30/   Meeting in Silicon Valley brings to mind not only the intersection of the mission and the microchip, but also the dynamism and even dominance that are characteristics of the United States at this time. Enormous talent and unprecedented prosperity are concentrated in this country, which spawns 64 new millionaires every day. This is the headquarters of the new economy that reaches around the globe and is transforming the basic fabric of business, work, and communications. Thousands of immigrants arrive from everywhere: entrepreneurs from Europe, high-tech professionals from South Asia who staff the service industries as well as workers from Latin America and Southeast Asia who do the physical labor—thus, a remarkable ethnic, cultural, and class diversity.

31/   At the same time the United States struggles with new social divisions aggravated by "the digital divide" between those with access to the world of technology and those left out. This rift, with its causes in class, racial, and economic differences, has its root cause in chronic discrepancies in the quality of education. Here in Silicon Valley, for example, some of the world's premier research universities flourish alongside struggling public schools where Afro-American and immigrant students drop out in droves. Nationwide, one child in every six is condemned to ignorance and poverty.

32/   This valley, this nation and the whole world look very different from the way they looked twenty-five years ago. With the collapse of Communism and the end of the Cold War, national and even international politics have been eclipsed by a resurgent capitalism that faces no ideological rival. The European Union slowly pulls the continent's age-old rivals together into a community but also a fortress. The former "Second World" struggles to repair the human and environmental damage left behind by so-called socialist regimes. Industries are re-locating to poorer nations, not to distribute wealth and opportunity, but to exploit the relative advantage of low wages and lax environmental regulations. Many countries become yet poorer, especially where corruption and exploitation prevail over civil society and where violent conflict keeps erupting.

33/   This composition of our time and place embraces six billion people with their faces young and old, some being born and others dying, some white and many brown and yellow and black.[xx] Each one a unique individual, they all aspire to live life, to use their talents, to support their families and care for their children and elders, to enjoy peace and security, and to make tomorrow better.

34/   Thanks to science and technology, human society is able to solve problems such as feeding the hungry, sheltering the homeless, or developing more just conditions of life, but remains stubbornly unable to accomplish this. How can a booming economy, the most prosperous and global ever, still leave over half of humanity in poverty? GC 32 makes its own sober analysis and moral assessment: "We can no longer pretend that the inequalities and injustices of our world must be borne as part of the inevitable order of things. It is now quite apparent that they are the result of what man himself, man in his selfishness, has done . . . . Despite the opportunities offered by an ever more serviceable technology, we are simply not willing to pay the price of a more just and more humane society."[xxi]

35/   Injustice is rooted in a spiritual problem, and its solution requires a spiritual conversion of each one's heart and a cultural conversion of our global society so that humankind, with all the powerful means at its disposal, might exercise the will to change the sinful structures afflicting our world. The yearly *Human Development Report* of the United Nations is a haunting challenge to look critically at basic conditions of life in the United States and the 175 other nations that share our one planet.[xxii]

36/   Such is the world in all its complexity, with great global promises and countless tragic betrayals. Such is the world in which Jesuit institutions of higher education are called to serve faith and promote justice.

III. AMERICAN JESUIT HIGHER EDUCATION FOR FAITH AND JUSTICE

37/   Within the complex time and place we are in, and in the light of the recent General Congregations, I want to spell out several ideal charac-teristics as manifest in three complementary dimensions of Jesuit higher education: in who our students become, in what our faculty do, and in how our universities proceed. When I speak of ideals, some are easy to meet, others remain persistently challenging, but together they serve to orient our schools and, in the long run, to identify them. At the same time, the U.S. Provincials have recently established an important Higher Education Committee to propose criteria on the staffing, leadership, and Jesuit spon-sorship of our colleges and universities.[xxiii] May these criteria help to imple-ment the ideal characteristics we now meditate on together.

A. Formation and Learning

38/   Today's predominant ideology reduces the human world to a global jungle whose primordial law is the survival of the fittest. Students who subscribe to this view want to be equipped with well-honed professional and technical skills in order to compete in the market and secure one of the relatively scarce fulfilling and lucrative jobs available. This is the success which many students (and parents!) expect.

39/   All American universities, ours included, are under tremendous pressure to opt entirely for success in this sense. But what our students want—and deserve—includes but transcends this "worldly success" based on marketable skills. The real measure of our Jesuit universities lies in who our students become.

40/   For four hundred and fifty years, Jesuit education has sought to educate "the whole person" intellectually and professionally, psychologically, morally, and spiritually. But in the emerging global reality, with its great possibilities and deep contradictions, the whole person is different from the whole person of the Counter-Reformation, the Industrial Revolution, or the 20th century. Tomorrow's "whole person" cannot be whole without an educated awareness of society and culture with which to contribute socially, generously, in the real world. Tomorrow's whole person must have, in brief, a <u>well-educated solidarity</u>.

41/   We must therefore raise our Jesuit educational standard to "educate the whole person of solidarity for the real world." Solidarity is learned through "contact" rather than through "concepts," as the Holy Father said recently at an Italian university conference.[xxiv] When the heart is touched by direct experience, the mind may be challenged to change. Personal involvement with innocent suffering, with the injustice others suffer, is the catalyst for solidarity which then gives rise to intellectual inquiry and moral reflection.

42/   Students, in the course of their formation, must let the gritty reality of this world into their lives, so they can learn to feel it, think about it critically, respond to its suffering and engage it constructively. They should learn to perceive, think, judge, choose, and act for the rights of others, especially the disadvantaged and the oppressed. Campus ministry does much to foment such intelligent, responsible, and active compassion, compassion that deserves the name solidarity.

43/   Our universities also boast a splendid variety of in-service programs, outreach programs, insertion programs, off-campus contacts, and hands-on courses. These should not be too optional or peripheral, but at the core of every Jesuit university's program of studies.

44/   Our students are involved in every sort of social action—tutoring drop-outs, demonstrating in Seattle, serving in soup kitchens, promoting pro-life, protesting against the School of the Americas—and we are proud of them for it. But the measure of Jesuit universities is not what our students do but who they become and the adult Christian responsibility they will exercise in the future towards their neighbor and their world. For now, the activities they engage in, even with much good effect, are for their formation. This does not make the university a training camp for social activists. Rather, the students need close involvement with the poor and the marginal now, in order to learn about reality and become adults of solidarity in the future.

B. Research and Teaching

45/   If the measure and purpose of our universities lies in what the students become, then the faculty are at the heart of our universities. Their mission is tirelessly to seek the truth and to form each student into a whole person of solidarity who will take responsibility for the real world. What do they need in order to fulfill this essential vocation?

46/   The faculty's "research, which must be rationally rigorous, firmly rooted in faith and open to dialogue with all people of good will,"[xxv] not only obeys the canons of each discipline, but ultimately embraces human reality in order to help make the world a more fitting place for six billion of us to inhabit. I want to affirm that university knowledge is valuable for its own sake and at the same time is knowledge that must ask itself, "For whom? For what?"[xxvi]

47/   Usually we speak of professors in the plural, but what is at stake is more than the sum of so many individual commitments and efforts. It is a sustained interdisciplinary dialogue of research and reflection, a continuous pooling of expertise. The purpose is to assimilate experiences and insights according to their different disciplines in "a vision of knowledge which, well aware of its limitations, is not satisfied with fragments but tries to integrate them into a true and wise synthesis"[xxvii] about the real world. Unfortunately many faculty still feel academically, humanly, and—I would say—spiritually unprepared for such an exchange.

48/   In some disciplines such as the life sciences, the social sciences, law, business, or medicine, the connections with "our time and place" may seem more obvious. These professors apply their disciplinary specialties to issues of justice and injustice in their research and teaching about health care, legal aid, public policy, and international relations. But every field or branch of knowledge has values to defend, with repercussions on the ethical level. Every discipline, beyond its necessary specialization, must engage with human society, human life, and the environment in appropriate ways, cultivating moral concern about how people ought to live together.

49/   All professors, in spite of the cliché of the ivory tower, are in contact with the world. But no point of view is ever neutral or value-free. By preference, by option, our Jesuit point of view is that of the poor. So our professors' commitment to faith and justice entails a most significant shift in viewpoint and choice of values. Adopting the point of view of those who suffer injustice, our professors seek the truth and share their search and its results with our students. A legitimate question, even if it does not sound academic, is for each professor to ask, "When researching and teaching, where and with whom is my heart?" To expect our professors to make such an explicit option and speak about it is obviously not easy; it entails risks. But I do believe that this is what Jesuit educators have publicly stated, in Church and in society, to be our defining commitment.

50/   To make sure that the real concerns of the poor find their place in research, faculty members need an organic collaboration with those in the Church and in society who work among and for the poor and actively seek justice. They should be involved together in all aspects: presence among the poor, designing the research, gathering the data, thinking through problems, planning and action, doing evaluation, and theological reflection. In each Jesuit Province where our universities are found, the faculty's privileged working relationships should be with projects of the Jesuit social apostolate—on issues such as poverty and exclusion, housing, AIDS, ecology, and Third World debt—and with the Jesuit Refugee Service helping refugees and forcibly displaced people.

51/ Just as the students need the poor in order to learn, so the professors need partnerships with the social apostolate in order to research and teach and form. Such partnerships do not turn Jesuit universities into branch plants of social ministries or agencies of social change, as certain rhetoric of the past may have led some to fear, but are a verifiable pledge of the faculty's option and really help, as the colloquial expression goes, "to keep your feet to the fire!"

52/ If the professors choose viewpoints incompatible with the justice of the Gospel and consider researching, teaching, and learning to be separable from moral responsibility for their social repercussions, they are sending a message to their students. They are telling them that they can pursue their careers and self-interest without reference to anyone "other" than themselves.

53/ By contrast, when faculty do take up inter-disciplinary dialogue and socially-engaged research in partnership with social ministries, they are exemplifying and modeling knowledge which is service, and the students learn by imitating them as "masters of life and of moral commitment,"[xxviii] as the Holy Father said.

C. Our Way of Proceeding

54/ If the measure of our universities is who the students become, and if the faculty are the heart of it all, then what is there left to say? It is perhaps the third topic, the character of our universities—how they proceed internally and how they impact on society—which is the most difficult.

55/ We have already dwelt on the importance of formation and learning, of research and teaching. The social action that the students undertake, and the socially-relevant work that the professors do, are vitally important and necessary, but these do not add up to the full character of a Jesuit university; they neither exhaust its faith-justice commitment nor really fulfill its responsibilities to society.

56/   What, then, constitutes this ideal character? And what contributes to the public's perception of it? In the case of a Jesuit university, this character must surely be the mission, which is defined by GC 32 and reaffirmed by GC 34: the *diakonia fidei* and the promotion of justice as the characteristic Jesuit university way of proceeding and of serving socially.

57/   In the words of GC 34, a Jesuit university must be faithful to both the noun "university" and to the adjective "Jesuit." To be a university requires dedication "to research, teaching, and the various forms of service that correspond to its cultural mission." To be Jesuit "requires that the university act in harmony with the demands of the service of faith and promotion of justice found in Decree 4 of GC 32."[xxix]

58/   The first way, historically, that our universities began living out their faith-justice commitment was through their admissions policies, affirmative action for minorities, and scholarships for disadvantaged students,[xxx] and these continue to be effective means. An even more telling expression of the Jesuit university's nature is found in policies concerning hiring and tenure. As a <u>university</u> it is necessary to respect the established academic, professional, and labor norms, but as <u>Jesuit</u> it is essential to go beyond them and find ways of attracting, hiring, and promoting those who actively share the mission.

59/   I believe that we have made considerable and laudable <u>Jesuit</u> efforts to go deeper and further: we have brought our Ignatian spirituality, our reflective capacities, some of our international resources, to bear. Good results are evident, for example, in the Decree "Jesuits and University Life" of the last General Congregation and in this very Conference on "Commitment to Justice in Jesuit Higher Education," and good results are hoped for from the Higher Education Committee working on Jesuit criteria.

60/   Paraphrasing Ignacio Ellacuría, it is the nature of every University to be a social force, and it is the calling of a Jesuit university to take conscious responsibility for being such a force for faith and justice. Every Jesuit academy of higher learning is called to live <u>in</u> a social reality (as we saw in the "composition" of our time and place) and to live <u>for</u> that social reality, to shed university intelligence upon it and to use university influence to transform it.[xxxi] Thus Jesuit universities have stronger and different reasons than many other academic and research institutions for addressing the actual world as it unjustly exists and for helping to reshape it in the light of the Gospel.

IV. IN CONCLUSION, AN AGENDA

The twenty-fifth anniversary of GC 32 is a motive for great thanksgiving.

61/ We give thanks for our Jesuit university awareness of the world in its entirety and in its ultimate depth, created yet abused, sinful yet redeemed, and we take up our Jesuit university responsibility for human society that is so scandalously unjust, so complex to understand, and so hard to change. With the help of others and especially the poor, we want to play our role as students, as teachers and researchers, and as Jesuit university in society.

62/ As Jesuit higher education, we embrace new ways of learning and being formed in the pursuit of adult solidarity; new methods of researching and teaching in an academic community of dialogue; and a new university way of practicing faith-justice in society.

63/ As we assume our Jesuit university characteristics in the new century, we do so with seriousness and hope. For this very mission has produced martyrs who prove that "an institution of higher learning and research can become an instrument of justice in the name of the Gospel."[xxxii] But implementing Decree 4 is not something a Jesuit university accomplishes once and for all. It is rather an ideal to keep taking up and working at, a cluster of characteristics to keep exploring and implementing, a conversion to keep praying for.

64/ In *Ex Corde Ecclesiae*, Pope John Paul II charges Catholic universities with a challenging agenda for teaching, research, and service: "The dignity of human life, the promotion of justice for all, the quality of personal and family life, the protection of nature, the search for peace and political stability, a more just sharing in the world's resources, and a new economic and political order that will better serve the human community at a national and international level."[xxxiii] These are both high ideals and concrete tasks. I encourage our Jesuit colleges and universities to take them up with critical understanding and deep conviction, with buoyant faith, and much hope in the early years of the new century.

65/   The beautiful words of GC 32 show us a long path to follow: "The way to faith and the way to justice are inseparable ways. It is up this undivided road, this steep road, that the pilgrim Church"—the Society of Jesus, the Jesuit College and University—"must travel and toil. Faith and justice are undivided in the Gospel which teaches that 'faith makes its power felt through love.'[xxxiv] They cannot therefore be divided in our purpose, our action, our life."[xxxv] For the greater glory of God.

Thank you very much.

---

[i]   GC 32, D.4, n.47.

[ii]   GC 32, D.2, n.9.

[iii]   See GC 32, D.2, n.9 and D.4, n.76.

[iv]   1971 Synod of Bishops, "Justice in the World."

[v]   Pedro Arrupe, S.J., "On the Social Apostolate in Latin America," December 1966 (*AR* XIV, 791).

[vi]   Ibid.

[vii]   Cf. Peter-Hans Kolvenbach, S.J., "On the Social Apostolate," January 2000, n.3.

[viii]   "Since evangelization is proclamation of that faith which is made operative in love of others (see Galatians 5:6; Ephesians 4:15), the promotion of justice is indispensable to it," (GC32, D.4, n.28).

[ix]   Cf. GC 34, D.26, n.5.

[x]   For example, GC32, D.11.

[xi]   n.13.GC 34, D. 26, n.8.

[xii]   GC 33, D.1, n.32.

[xiii]   1971 Synod of Bishops, "Justice in the World."

[xiv]   Pedro Arrupe, *Rooted and Grounded in Love*, 67 (AR XVIII, 500).

[xv]   GC33, D.1, n.33.

[xvi]   GC34, D.3, n.2.

[xvii.]   Pedro Arrupe, S.J., Address to the European Jesuit Alumni Congress, Valencia, August 1973, in *Hombres para los demás*, Barcelona: Diafora, 1983, p. 161.

[xviii]   Cf. *The Characteristics of Jesuit Education,* Washington, D.C.: Jesuit Secondary Education Association, 1987.

[xix]   Ignacio Ellacuría, S.J., "The Task of a Christian University," Convocation address at the University of Santa Clara, June 12, 1982; "Una universidad para el pueblo," *Diakonía* 6:23 (1982), 41–57.

[xx]   See "Contemplation on the Incarnation," Ignatius of Loyola, *Spiritual Exercises*, nos. 101–109.

[xxi]   GC 32, D.4, nn.27, 20.

[xxii]   United Nations Development Program, *Human Development Report*, 1990–present (annual).

[xxiii]   In February 2000, the Jesuit Conference established a five-man Committee on Higher Education to prepare recommendations regarding 1) sponsorship by the Society of U.S. Jesuit colleges and universities; 2) assignment of personnel to these institutions; 3) selection of

Presidents (particularly non-Jesuit Presidents) for these institutions.

xxiv John Paul II, Address to Catholic University of the Sacred Heart, Milan, May 5, 2000, n.9.

xxv Ibid. n.7.

xxvi Cf. GC 34, D.17, n.6.

xxvii John Paul II, *op.cit.*, n.5.

xxviii John Paul II, Address to the Faculty of Medicine, Catholic University of the Sacred Heart, 26 June 1984.

xxix GC 34, D.17, nn.6,7.

xxx "For the poor [the universities] serve as major channels for social advancement" (GC 34, D.17, n.2).

xxxi Ellacuría, *op.cit.*

xxxii Peter-Hans Kolvenbach, S.J., Address to the Congregation of Provincials (20/09/90), *AR* 20 (1990), p. 452.

xxxiii John Paul II, *Ex Corde Ecclesiae*, August 1990, n. 32.

xxxiv Galatians 5:6.

xxxv GC 32, D.2, n.8.

The Jesuit University in the Light of the Ignatian Charism

Peter-Hans Kolvenbach, S.J., 2001.
Address to the International Meeting of Jesuit Higher Education, Rome.

INTRODUCTION

1/   It gives me great pleasure to greet all of you—Jesuits, lay men and women—responsible for higher education for the Society throughout the world and to welcome you to Rome. I thank you for finding time, amid all your activities and responsibilities, to come to this meeting. I very much appreciate your commitment and devotion to the service of the mission of the Society in the field of education in your various countries.

2/   The last time I addressed an assembly such as this was in Frascati in 1985. In barely sixteen years, events have occurred which have changed the world. To respond to the challenges of the new times, the universities of the Society have undertaken during this period a profound reflection and have taken action. At this meeting, the body and the head of the Society have a wonderful opportunity for contact, in order to discern the signs of the times and try to discover together what it is that the Lord wants of us.

3/   I would like in this address to comment upon the topics you have chosen for this Conference, from the perspective of the founding charism of Ignatius of Loyola, and contribute some elements which may help in the process of your reflection. I realize that you represent very diverse institutions. Thus, when I refer without distinction to the universities or to higher education, in your reflections and discussions you will have to make the necessary adjustments to your particular situation.

1. A LEARNED MINISTRY
The Society's Option for Education

4/   The ties that unite the Society of Jesus with the university world date from the time when Ignatius and the first companions met at the University of Paris. This was where Ignatius recruited his first followers, for the most part lay students. Nevertheless, at first Jesuits did not consider the university as a special instrument of the apostolate. The active involvement of the Society with education, in particular with higher education and the education of externs, came later, but still within the lifetime of Ignatius.

5/   We need to go back to the founding charism of Ignatius to understand fully the evolution of the Society's involvement in education, and to recover the meaning of Jesuit education today. We would look in vain, however, for this charism in the person of Ignatius himself. His education takes place outside the university. He is a gentleman of the sword, not of the pen. After the military defeat at Pamplona, the Lord enters into his life of sickness as a school teacher treats a child—as St. Ignatius would say much later—that is to say, teaching him.[1] After this mystical experience, there follow three years of human counter-culture, leading to a new defeat: his apostolic plan to follow the steps of Jesus in Palestine fell through, even though he was convinced that the Lord wanted him in the Holy Land. Not knowing what to do, he lets himself be guided in Barcelona by his inclination to "study for some time."[2] Prayerfully considering options, he acts "according to the greater motion arising from reason, and not according to some motion arising from sensitive human nature."[3] He starts to frequent universities—Alcalá, Salamanca, and Paris—in order to obtain a university diploma, also to protect himself from the Inquisition, suspicious of charismatic movements without proper credentials.

6/   The Society was born in a university environment, but not for the purpose of founding universities and colleges. The Constitutions of 1541 would still impose a prohibition: "no studies or lectures in the Society."[4] Initially the Society was content to take advantage passively of existing university structures, such as in Coimbra and in Padua, in Louvain and in Cologne, for the formation and education of the Jesuits. But by 1548, eight years before the death of Ignatius, the involvement in the educational apostolate moved from being passive to being active, even ultra-active. At the rate sometimes of four or five new colleges per year, often without the necessary academic, professional, and financial preparation, the Society founded educational institutions both for the formation of Jesuit students, and, significantly, for the education of "externs."

7/   The "priests of Christ who have chosen to be poor," as the first companions were recognized,[5] had opted for a "learned" ministry. The reason why the Society had embraced colleges and universities was to "provide for the edifice of learning, and of skill in employing it so as to help make God our Creator and Lord better known and served."[6] Ignatius realized the formidable apostolic potential to be found in education, and did not hesitate to give it pride of place above the other "usual ministries." The Society of the last years of Ignatius underwent a new radical change. At the death of Ignatius, the "colleges" of the Society exceeded 30 in number, while the professed houses, conceived as the classic residence of the itinerant Society, were no more than two. Clearly, the Society had taken "another path."[7]

8/   Changing course so many times in a few years, had it not disfigured the initial image of a Society pilgrim and poor? Once again, it is essential to recall the founding charism. If Ignatius introduced the new ministry of teaching into his apostolic plan, he was "moved by the desire of serving" his Divine Majesty,[8] as a new "offering of greater worth and moment."[9] The involvement of the Society with what we today call the "intellectual apostolate" was a consequence of the MAGIS, the result of the search for a greater apostolic service through an insertion into the world of culture.

9/   The option for a learned ministry and the involvement in the field of education had, in fact, changed the face of the early Society. Poverty, the gratuity of ministries, apostolic mobility, the assignment of personnel, the governance of the Society itself, all this was affected by the entry of the Society into education and by the entry of education into the Society.

For some, the Society had gotten itself into a minefield. The Rector of the German College in Rome from 1564 until 1569, Gioseffo Cortesono, wrote bluntly: "The Society of Jesus is being ruined by taking on so many schools."[10] But the "greater glory and service of God our Lord and the universal good, which is the only end sought in this matter,"[11] as the reason for the Society's initial involvement and for its persistence in the field of education. For the Society there is no such thing as an either-or approach between God *or* the world, however dangerous the latter may look. The meeting with God always takes place *in* the world so that the world may come to be fully *in* God.[12]

The Objectives of Higher Education

10/   If we now ask ourselves why the Society entered into higher education, we cannot find the answer in Ignatius himself but in his mission; that is, his eagerness to be available apostolically to assume any ministry whatever that the mission requires. We have to wait until late in the 16th century when the Spanish Jesuit Diego Ledesma was finally able, after long inquiry, to list four reasons for promoting the Jesuit involvement in higher education.[13] It is quite astonishing to read in many mission statements or charters of Jesuit universities today—400 years after Ledesma—these same characteristics updated according to the needs and feelings of our times, translated into modern language. Let us look at Ledesma's reasons and compare them with the statement of a college in the United States, published in November 1998.

11/   The first motivation given by Ledesma is "to give students advantages for practical living." Four centuries later it is expressed this way: "Jesuit education is eminently practical, focused on providing students with the knowledge and skills to excel in whatever field they choose." That demands academic excellence. The second reason Ledesma proposes is "to contribute to the right government of public affairs." This short sentence becomes in 1998: "Jesuit education is not merely practical, but concerns itself also with questions of values, with educating men and women to be good citizens and good leaders, concerned with the common good, and able to use their education for the service of faith and promotion of justice."

12/   Ledesma formulates with baroque words a third dimension of Jesuit higher education: "to give ornament, splendor and perfection to the rational nature of humanity." More sober, but to the point, is the U.S.A. college: "The Jesuit education celebrates the full range of human intellectual power and achievement, confidently affirming reason, not as antithetical to faith, but as its necessary complement." Finally, Ledesma's God-centered view of higher education: "to be a bulwark of religion, and to guide man most surely and easily to the achievement of his last end." In more inclusive language, and in a broader dialogue approach, our modern charter states: "The Jesuit education places all that it does firmly within a Christian understanding of the human person as a creature of God whose ultimate destiny is beyond the human."

13/   Ignatius and the first Jesuits saw in letters and science a way to serve souls. Within the modern mentality, in which science and faith seem to run on parallel tracks, this approach may seem to many today as a threat to the essence of a university and to the methodology proper to academic research. Far be it for us to try to convert the university into a mere instrument for evangelization or, worse still, for proselytizing. The university has its own purposes that cannot be subordinated to other objectives. It is essential to respect institutional autonomy, academic freedom, and to safeguard personal and community rights within the requirements of truth and the common good.[14] Still, a Jesuit university pursues other objectives beyond the obvious objectives of that institution. In a Catholic university, or one of Christian inspiration, under the responsibility of the Society of Jesus, there does not exist—nor can there exist—incompatibility between the goals proper to the university and the Christian and Ignatian inspiration that should characterize any apostolic institution of the Society. To believe the contrary, or to act in practice as if it were necessary to choose between being a university or being of the Society, would be to fall into a regrettable reductionism.

14/ More now than ever, the Christian identity of our universities and the public witnessing to that identity are crucial issues because of increased secularization and de-Christianization in some areas and the total marginalization of Christianity in other regions. I could say that never as in these last years have the universities of the Society shown such concern about deepening and manifesting their Catholic, Christian, Jesuit, or Ignatian identity, as the case may be. According to the specific cultural and ecclesial context, this concern has been experienced in some places without special difficulty, while in others there have been tensions and misunderstandings. With "creative fidelity" to the charism of Ignatius and to the mission of the Society, I am sure that Jesuit higher education will know how to find ways to overcome the tensions and continue to "distinguish itself" in its service to the Church and to the world.

15/ We would fall into a historical anachronism if we understood today "study" and the "help of souls" literally as Ignatius and the first companions understood them. Nevertheless, in continuity with the Ignatian charism, we must ask ourselves how we can make present this reality today and maintain the balance between the academic dimension and the apostolic dimension in Jesuit higher education. In a modern transposition of the problematic of times past, today we ask ourselves how we can respect the noun "university" and the adjective "Catholic," "Christian," or "Ignatian" of our institutions; how to recognize the autonomy of earthly realities and, at the same time, the referral of all things to the Creator; how to reconcile the "service of faith" with the "promotion of justice;" how to fly in the search for truth with the two wings of faith and reason.

The Involvement of the Society with Intellectual Work

16/ Let us highlight now some specific aspects of the Ignatian understanding of higher learning. Ignatius very quickly saw the need for learning and teaching. Progressively the Jesuits felt called to learned ministry with the creative tension of a total reliance on divine grace and of the use of all human means, science and art, research and intellectual life.

17/   With its lights and its shadows, the history of the Society has a long trajectory in the intellectual field through teaching and research. This tradition would appear, according to some, to be on the wane. Several of the preparatory documents for this Conference call for the taking of a more determined position and the adoption of a clear policy on the part of the Society with respect to the intellectual apostolate. The 34th General Congregation (GC) proved to be elusive and deceptive for many, who think that intellectual apostolate was brushed aside and that the General Congregation limited itself to generalities regarding the "intellectual dimension of Jesuit ministries."[15]

18/   It will not be documents that will invigorate intellectual work. Nevertheless, it will not be out of place to recall that already the 31st General Congregation (1965) emphasized the importance of this apostolate, insisted upon the need to prepare competent personnel and asked that facilities be given to those who work in institutions of the Society, or in other universities and scientific institutions not attached to the Society.[16]

19/   The 32nd General Congregation (1975), which seems to some to have signified a questioning of the university apostolate for the sake of social activism, in reality insisted on scientific rigor in social research and upon the need to dedicate oneself to the hard and in-depth study required to understand contemporary problems.[17] The 33rd General Congregation once again stressed the importance of the social apostolate and of research, recommending a closer link between the intellectual, pastoral, and social fields.[18] The tension and uneasiness lasted for several years, aggravated by a disaffection of the young with respect to education. This situation, in general, appears to have now reversed itself, although the decline in the recruitment of Jesuits and the rising age of the Jesuits in some countries present a serious problem for the foreseeable future.

20/   After my address at the University of Santa Clara last October, I hope it has become clear that it is not legitimate to make an incomplete, slanted, and unbalanced reading of the Decree on faith and justice. The theme should be part of a comprehensive vision of the mission of the Society, such as the 34th General Congregation proposes in its Decrees on the mission.[19] The unique character of a university of the Society is given by the mission: "the *diakonia fidei* and the promotion of justice, as the characteristic Jesuit university way of proceeding and of servicing socially."[20]

21/ Periodically, in the history of the Society, there have been phases of increased intellectualism or of strident anti-intellectualism, which keep springing up in our times as well. Perhaps in our days, the temptation to short-term efficiency and the search for rapid results are threatening more than in other times the commitment of the Society to a deep intellectual effort.

22/ The quality of the apostolic service which the Society renders will depend in large measure on its academic rigor and the level of its intellectual research. Not all Jesuits are called to work in the intellectual apostolate, but each one is called to competent and serious work in whatever field he is involved, including the pastoral and social areas. The availability to render this type of service is becoming a criterion of a vocation to the Society.[21] The work of a Jesuit scholar, often hard and solitary, is already a form of apostolate for Ignatius.[22] Plainly speaking, a vigorous spiritual and intellectual formation is necessary for our young people, as is necessary the on-going formation for every Jesuit.[23]

23/ The Society, then, still considers the intellectual apostolate along the lines of its mission to be of the highest importance. In a world at once globalized and diversified, one cannot expect the Society to give universal norms valid for all contexts. The fundamental criterion will always be the greater divine service and the good of souls and the wise Ignatian principle of "adapting to places, times, and persons."[24] It will be up to each Province or Region to discern what their involvement with the intellectual apostolate should be, and the means to put it seriously into practice.

2. UNIVERSITY AND SOCIETY

Academia and Society

24/   Earlier when we referred to the four reasons why the Society actively took up university education, we listed the link between academic life and human society. It is already a cliché to repeat that the university is not an ivory tower and that it does not exist for itself but for society. Other than theory, the profound meaning of this affirmation was given by the witness of Ignacio Ellacuría and his companions, assassinated in the UCA of El Salvador, who demonstrated with their lives the seriousness of their commitment and that of their university to society. Few other events have had such an impact and led to so much reflection in our universities these past years.

25/   I do not think that any of our universities today run the risk of academic isolation in a tower. The danger could be considering that what happens in a distant university of a small country is felt to be detached from one's own reality. It is true that the surrounding reality varies from one country to another and from one continent to another. Nevertheless, whatever may be the context, the university should see itself as challenged by society, and the university should challenge society. Within an unequal interaction of mutual influences, the local and global context influences the university, and the university is called to influence society, locally and globally.

26/   Pure science and research still maintain their purpose, although apparently they are no longer always linked to the practical sphere. According to John Henry Newman—perhaps more often quoted than read, now 200 years since his birth—"knowledge is capable of being its own end, [. . .] an end sufficient to rest in and to pursue for its own sake, surely."[25] This was not exactly Ignatius's way of thinking. While Cardinal Newman defended knowledge for its own sake, Ignatius stressed the education of future "doctores" as the practical end of a Jesuit university. Because if higher education as both means and medium has intrinsic value, it must still always ask itself: "For whom? For what?"[26] The answer to these questions will always be related to the common good and the progress of human society.

27/   Let us not delude ourselves: knowledge is not neutral, because it always implies values and a specific conception of the human person. Teaching and research cannot turn their backs on the surrounding society. It was in and through the colleges that the early Society interacted with culture. The university remains the place where fundamental questions that touch the person and community can be aired: in the areas of economics, politics, culture, science, theology, the search for meaning. The university should be a bearer of human and ethical values; it should be the critical conscience of the society; it should illuminate with its reflection those who are addressing the problematic of the modern or postmodern society; it should be the crucible where the diverse tendencies in human thought are debated and solutions proposed.

University and Globalization

28/   We have to keep in mind that Ignatius inaugurated the commitment to higher learning because the good that could be accomplished was more "universal." To come back for a moment to Cardinal Newman: for him the university comprises the universality of knowledge; for Ignatius a university accomplishes the function of education and scholarly investigation more universally. The originality of the Society of Jesus in creating its own universities in the 16th century was that of proposing a new model of higher education in response to the needs of the new culture and the new society that was being born. The Jesuit universities sprung up as a critique of the model of the university closed in upon itself, the heirs of the "cathedral schools," incapable of finding answers to the new times. Although at first with reticence, the Jesuits made a clear option for Christian humanism and, by means of education, contributed to the shaping of the new society.

29/   Likewise Jesuit higher education is called upon in our day to give creative responses to the changing times. Ignatius would be fascinated by the phenomenon of globalization, with its incredible opportunities and threats, and would not run from the challenges that it involves. To the universities corresponds an indispensable role in the critical analysis of globalization, with its positive and negative connotations, to orient the thought and the action of society. In Ignatian language, it is a matter of an authentic process of discernment, in order to discover what is coming from the good spirit and what is coming from the bad.

30/   We will discover at a glance that making the market and the economic interest the only driving force in society cannot come from God. The frightful results of economic globalization that have been introduced, against all ethics, are obvious: dehumanization, individualism, lack of solidarity, social fragmentation, a widening of the already existing gap between rich and poor, exclusion, lack of respect for human rights, economic and cultural neo-colonialism, exploitation, deterioration of the environment, violence, frustration. Not to speak of the "perverse connection" with the globalization of crime: traffic in human beings and arms, drugs, exploitation of women and sex, child labor, manipulation of the media, mafia of all types, terrorism, war, and the debasement of the value of human life. How can we not in this moment think of Africa, the paradigm for all the negative faces that the globalization of the market can offer?

31/   The university as a university has its word to say on these topics, which touch on fundamental aspects of the person and society. I know of the efforts that our universities are making, depending on their contexts, to address questions such as ethnic minorities, cultural pluralism, diversity, interreligious dialogue, migrants, refugees, injustice, poverty, exclusion, unemployment, the crisis of democracy. It is not enough to denounce; it is necessary to also pronounce and propose. Committing oneself in this field is one consequence of the service that the university should render to society. And for Jesuit universities, it is also a consequence of the vision of Ignatius in the contemplation of the Kingdom and of the mission of the Society to strive for the service of faith and the promotion of justice.

32/   Although closely tied to economic processes, it must be recognized that globalization also includes other dimensions which offer unique possibilities for the construction of a world more fraternal and solidary. Never before have there been so many opportunities for communication, for integration, for interdependence and unity of the human race. The growing awareness of the dimensions of globalization, the tension between the global and the local, the emergency of civil society, the forces of resistance from different sides which have entered the scene—such as the "Seattle people"—constitute opportunities and threats which the university cannot overlook.

33/ The universities have the duty to orient, to stand at the convergence between the diverse currents, to bring to bear their thought to the deep study and the search for solutions to burning issues. In the words of John Paul II, it is necessary to contribute to the "globalization of solidarity."[27] The "complete person," the ideal of Jesuit education for more than four centuries, will, in the future, be a competent, conscious person, capable of compassion and "well educated in solidarity."[28]

34/ Ignatius's vision of the world was clearly global. Although he wanted Jesuits to adapt to the place where they were working and learning the local language and culture—"enculturation" we would say today—he wanted them to be available to "travel through the world and live in any part of it,"[29] always open to the Magis. This is the way he experienced the tension between the local and the global; that is, thinking on a global level, but acting on the local.

Academia and the Market

35/ One last word on the university and the market economy. Whether we like it or not, the academy cannot evade from the forces of the market. The financial limitations faced by universities not subsidized with public funds force them to depend ever more on the financial support of their students and to make recourse to various systems for raising funds to secure the necessary resources to operate. Ignatius knew this, concerned as he was with foundations and always so grateful to the founders, such that in 1551 he would open the doors of the Roman College with the title of "gratis." In spite of efforts to create funds that would permit the granting of scholarships to those who needed them, the danger of elitism is real.

36/   It may happen that a university has to redesign its degree programs and offer courses according to the demands of the market and thereby yield to the pressures of its clients in an ever-competitive environment. Let us not deceive ourselves: how many of our students come to our universities simply in search of the excellence we offer and the preparation that permits them to obtain a good position and earn more money. Some can spend years in our institutions of higher education without ever taking notice that this is a Catholic institution directed by the Society of Jesus.

37/   The growing costs of education and the trend to privatization imply a progressive dependence on financial subsidies, which can turn into a veritable social mortgage. It may happen that not all the sponsors or trustees are always disinterested, nor identify with the mission statements and the orientation of the university. The autonomy itself of the university and the freedom of research and instruction are at stake. The institution may end up moderating the tone of its voice, or refrain from speaking about certain issues. There are faculties which are "for sale" and others that "are not for sale," according to economic swings, or the interests of industry, commerce, and tourism; there are profitable professions and non-profitable ones; there is money for some schools, faculties, laboratories, research, topics, while there is none for others. The quality of the teachers who can be hired and their stay in the institution are conditional in large part on economic factors and by what similar institutions may offer.

38/   The challenge could not be greater. It is necessary at all costs to not lose sight of the raison d'être of the university as a center of integration of knowledge which proposes the search, not for the "narrow truth," but for the "whole truth" of which Newman spoke,[30] with an "accurate vision and comprehension of all things."[31] It is necessary to discern and to make a choice for the kind of greater service, which we intend to give to Church and society through our universities. More than knowledge and science, it is wisdom which our academies should offer. "For what fills and satisfies the soul consists, not in knowing much, but in our understanding the realities profoundly and in savoring them interiorly."[32] The Ignatian seal is what can and should make the difference.

3. JESUIT-LAY PARTNERSHIP

A Change of Accent

39/   The few references in the Constitutions to the participation of lay people in the educational process are not very heartening for a modern reader. The only role especially conferred upon lay people is no more than the *corrector*; that is to say, the person who should "keep in fear and should punish" those who have deserved correction. Ignatius and the Jesuits were scrupulous about applying physical punishment on the students with their own hands, according to the usage of the time. The ingenious solution was to give those who were guilty to the secular arm, engaging a lay person to give the culprit a proper thrashing. One can suppose there was "much to be done," because such a person was to "receive a good salary."[33] Times have changed, and today the Society depends upon lay men and women for more noble tasks.

40/   We should recognize that, in fact, it has been the decrease in the number of Jesuits which has made us to turn our eyes to lay people and to develop a theological reflection and practice of Jesuit-lay collaboration. The figures are eloquent: it is estimated that the proportion for education at large in the Society is 95% lay and 5% Jesuits. For simple realism and by the Ignatian principle of accommodation to persons and times, the Society considers today the "partnership with others" to be one of the characteristics of our way of proceeding.[34]

41/   The change of accent came a mere six years ago with the two Decrees of the General Congregation on "Cooperation with the Laity in Mission" and on "Jesuits and the Situation of Women in Church and Civil Society."[35] Both documents were considered at the time of their appearance to be innovative, although sometimes our practice does not always respond everywhere to the ideal we have set.

The Practice of Collaboration

42/   On the part of the Jesuits, at times a certain hesitation and doubt is detected as far as collaboration with lay people is concerned, when it is not rejected outright. On the part of lay people, the desire for more information and formation. It pleases me to know of the efforts that Jesuit higher education has made to explore this new ground. In the last few years there has been undeniable progress, but in the venture that Jesuits and lay people have jointly undertaken there still remains much road to cover. This meeting is a good opportunity to share the best practices as well as deficiencies and push forward together.

43/   I will not repeat what is already in the official documents and what you yourselves have prepared in your regional reports. I would like only to highlight some aspects, which I consider to be greater challenges for our higher education. Whether we like it or not, the identity of Jesuit higher education is at stake for the short term, especially in the West and in the industrialized countries. The problem of the "next generation" is not an imaginary one. At the pace that the physical presence of the Jesuits is disappearing, the ethos of the institution, its Ignatian, Catholic, Christian culture, may also disappear if no attention is paid to the preparation of the generation that is to take over. This responsibility falls above all on Jesuits themselves. Preparation in the vision and the shared mission between Jesuits and collaborators is a priority of the first order in our higher education. (I am aware of the negative connotations that the word "mission" can have in some countries. In that case, you will have to make the necessary adaptations.)

44/   There exist various levels of collaboration, according to the vocation and level of commitment of each person—human, professional, Christian. Not all collaboration with the laity is in keeping with the mission. We have the right to assume that the Jesuits identify with their mission, but we cannot assume that all the lay people identify themselves with the specific mission of the Jesuits. Lay people are not called to be mini-Jesuits, but rather to live their own lay vocation. Respecting the way in which the Lord leads each person is fundamental to Ignatian spirituality. This having been said, a collaborator of an institution of higher education in the Society should identify in some manner with the institutional mission.

45/   On the other hand, it would be odious to catalogue and discriminate among personnel according to their supposed level of commitment with the mission. In the mission of the Society, as in the house of the Lord, there are many mansions. For Ignatius, there is no worse error in spiritual life than trying to lead all by the same road. The mission of a Jesuit institution of higher education—as with the faith—is not imposed, rather it is proposed. In an "interface" of mutual respect and sincerity, collaborators are invited to share this mission and make it their own, to different degrees.

46/   The level of partnership in mission and identity will depend upon the dynamics of the institution and the options that each person takes. There are minimum limits of commitment that, for reasons of honesty and coherence, should be respected. The only limit on the top is imposed by the capacity for response of a human being to the call of God. We are touching upon the Ignatian "Magis," the "ALL"—another Ignatian word which embraces the totality of the human person: "Loving and serving in all things." I would like to emphasize only some concrete practices, which without a doubt are helping to share the mission and deepen the identity:

47/   a) *The courses for orientation or induction for new professors and board members, to share the ethos of our education:* It may happen that not all the lay persons will choose to commit themselves wholeheartedly to the Jesuit mission of the work. But the Society expects of all, including people of others faiths, that they recognize and accept the values contained in the Ignatian spirituality and apostolic mission that animate the work.[36]

48/   b) *The programs of on-going formation, as much for lay people as for Jesuits:* The goal is to form an apostolic team of Jesuits and colleagues for the purpose of realizing the Jesuit identity and mission of the work.[37] This would be the way to create the "critical mass"—as is said now—indispensable to insure the identity of the institution.

49/   c) *The priority given to the identity and the mission in the hiring of personnel:* "Hiring for mission" is a delicate point, and can result in a veiled form of apartheid. A university cannot discriminate in its personnel, but—if it is still possible—one does have the right to choose men and women capable of sharing its identity. Other non-confessional corporations know how to do this very well for their own aims.

50/   d) *The offering of the* Spiritual Exercises *to our personnel, in their various modalities, particularly through the practice of the Exercises in daily life.*

51/   e) *Finally, the decisive role corresponding to the Jesuits*: Even while responsibilities are shared more and more or are transferred to non-Jesuit collaborators, the Jesuits, both as a community and as individuals, should see ways of still being present, now no longer exercising power but still exercising influence in the institution.

The topic of Jesuit-lay collaboration is far from being exhausted.

4. INTERNATIONAL COOPERATION

52/   By definition, universality and the possibility of exchanges at all levels belong to the very nature of the university. Nevertheless, it must be admitted that universities, including those of the Society, are extremely jealous of their autonomy and independence and more easily lend themselves to scientific exchange than to concrete forms of joint cooperation among equals. This being said, the need for coordination, often more than the concern for the universal, has brought Jesuit higher education to come together in various ways, as is demonstrated by the regional associations represented here. I am pleased to know that Europe, the only region which up until now has not had an instance of common coordination, is also planning to form an association, which will include the Near East and Africa. These associations are limited by general rule to lending services to their members and have no more attributions than those, which their members have conferred. But they are absolutely indispensable if we hope to see the Society act as a body.

53/   There are several other groups and platforms for scientific encounters for those working in Jesuit higher education, by disciplines, specialties, or interests: theology, philosophy, spirituality, social sciences, positive sciences, communication, research centers, journals, and surely many others. All of these accomplish their role in the universal apostolic service of the Society. By its universal vocation, and even more in times of globalization, the Society encourages the creation of these national and international networks. This is the way in which Jesuit higher education can face common global problems, by means of mutual assistance, information, planning and shared evaluation, or the putting into action of projects which are beyond the capacity of each individual institution. Obviously, the institutions of higher education participate in many networks other than Jesuit. But this does not substitute for the coordination and cooperation of Jesuit institutions among themselves.

54/   Successful experiences of international cooperation are now underway within the Society which can serve as an inspiration. Permit me to mention the MBA Program in Beijing, under the responsibility of the AJCU, and the consortium effort in The Beijing Center for Language and Culture; the collaboration of various universities of the AJCU-EAO in the training of professors in Cambodia, and in the reconstruction of the University of East Timor; the coordination between AJCU and AUSJAL and the exchanges of universities of Latin America with universities in Spain and in the United States; the programs of distance education, with their enormous possibilities of mutual exchange.

55/   Although each university has a particular responsibility in a concrete and limited place in the vineyard of the Lord, the Ignatian MAGIS and the "more universal" impel us not to enclose ourselves in this particularity but to open out to a greater service in the Lord's vineyard.

56/   As we consider more deeply the international dimension of the Society, it becomes clearer how much more we can accomplish by cooperation, not competition, as we venture abroad. This is especially true in developing countries. I am thinking of consortium efforts, which can reach out eventually to Vietnam, Laos, East Timor, Cambodia, as well as to Africa and developing countries around the world. I think also of the examples of fraternal collaboration and concrete gestures of solidarity, which can arise in a meeting such as this, between Jesuits and lay people from different continents. The important thing is to cooperate together for the sake of our brothers and sisters around the world as we seek to put a human face on the process of globalization.

CONCLUSION

57/   In 1551, the Roman College opened its doors, an emblematic figure of what would become the Society's venture in the university field. Four and a half centuries later, the Society remains intensely dedicated to the work of higher education, with numberless universities and other institutions throughout the world. The times in which we happen to live are radically different from those lived by Ignatius of Loyola. But the "help of souls," the "greater glory of God and the universal good" remain the fundamental motivation for the Society's commitment to education. The "for whom" and the "for what" of our universities, the profound importance of the work that Jesuits and lay people accomplish in them, and the reason for the presence of all of you here, are anchored in this vision of Ignatius.

58/   May the creative fidelity to the founding charism of Ignatius of Loyola inspire all of you to make real in your institutions the greater divine service and the help of men and women of our age.

---

[1] Autobiography. 27.
[2] Autobio. 50.
[3] Spiritual Exercises. 182.
[4] MI Const. I, 47.
[5] Cf. The Bull of Approbation, 1540.
[6] Constitutions. [307].
[7] Const. [308].
[8] Const. [540].
[9] Sp.Ex. 97.
[10] Monumenta paedagogica Societatis Jesu. (M Paed) II, 870. Cf. John W. O'Malley, The First Jesuits, Harvard Univ. Press, Cambridge Mass, 1993, p. 227.
[11] Const. [508].
[12] GC34, D.4, n.7.
[13] M Paed. II, 528–529.

[14] John Paul II, Ex Corde Ecclesiae, Rome,1990, n.12.

[15] GC34, D.16.

[16] GC31, D.29.

[17] GC32, D.4, nn.35,44.

[18] GC33, D.1, n.44.

[19] GC34, DD.3,4,5.

[20] Peter-Hans Kolvenbach, S.J., The Service of Faith and the Promotion of Justice in Higher Education of the Society of Jesus in the United States, Santa Clara, 6 October 2000. This address in included in Part 5 of this book.

[21] Peter-Hans Kolvenbach, S.J., Address to the Congregation of Procurators 3 September 1987, AR XX, 1987, pp.1076–1077.

[22] Const. [361].

[23] GC34, D.16, n.3.

[24] Const. [455].

[25] John Henry Newman, The Idea of a University, Discourse V, 2.

[26] GC34, D.17, n.6.

[27] John Paul II, Address to the Secretary General and the Administrative Committee on Coordination of the United Nations, April 7, 2000.

[28] Peter-Hans Kolvenbach, S.J., The Service of Faith and the Promotion of Justice in University Education of the Society of Jesus in the United States, Santa Clara, 6 October 2000. This address in included in Part 5 of this book.

[29] Const. [304].

[30] John Henry Newman, Op.cit., Discourse IV, 12.

[31] John Henry Newman, Op.cit., Discourse VI, 6.

[32] Sp.Ex. 2.

[33] Const. [397,488,500], as well as other similar quotations in the Ratio Studiorum.

[34] GC34, D.26, n.15.

[35] GC34, DD.13 & 14.

[36] Guidelines for the Relationship between the Superior and the Director of the Work, Rome, Curia of the Society of Jesus, 1998, n.16.

[37] Ibid.

Address to the Georgetown University Board of Directors

Peter-Hans Kolvenbach, S.J., 2007. Pontifical Gregorian University.

1/ First, let me extend to you a warm welcome to Rome on the occasion of your first Board meeting here. I am most grateful for this opportunity to speak with you, and I am especially pleased to meet with you here at the Pontifical Gregorian University, which St. Ignatius of Loyola originally inaugurated as the Roman College in 1551, as Dr. DeGioia mentioned. Although Georgetown was founded a few years later (238 years later to be exact!), both institutions share the same mission and identity described by Saint Ignatius when he envisioned "a university of all nations, for the defence and propagation of the faith and for the training of wise and qualified leaders of the Church and society."[1]

2/ As members of the Board of Directors, the ultimate academic authority of Georgetown University, you have yourselves chosen to use the word Jesuit in your mission statement. You have pledged to adapt the characteristics of Jesuit education to your unique circumstances as Americans at the beginning of the 21st century. Many contemporary charters of Jesuit universities and colleges in the United States and around the world find the original description of these Jesuit characteristics in a strange document composed by Father Diego de Ledesma, a Jesuit professor and principal of the Roman College. Born in Spain in 1524, Ledesma died here in Rome the 10th of November 1575 and was known as a "trouble shooter." His field of training and expertise was theology, and some of his fellow Jesuits who criticised his ideas about Jesuit education would have preferred that he limit himself to theological speculation, which was his field. Nevertheless, his idea of what a Jesuit institution should be has been repeated in many editions of the famous *Ratio Studiorum* since the version of 1586.

3/ Addressing the criticism of those who thought Jesuits should only work in explicitly spiritual ministries, Father Ledesma answered the question why the Society of Jesus should conduct educational institutions in these words:

> First, because they supply people with many advantages for practical living; secondly, because they contribute to the right *government* of public affairs and to the proper making of laws; third, because they give ornament, splendour, and perfection to our rational nature, and fourth, in what is most important, because they are the bulwark of religion and guide us most surely and easily in the achievement of our last end.[2]

4/   This quite baroque language was reworked by The Middle States Working Group on Jesuit and Catholic Identity in November 1998, which tried to rephrase and update Ledesma's expression this way, using American terminology in our times to describe Jesuit education:

> 1) it is eminently practical, focused on providing students with the knowledge and skills to excel in whatever field they choose; 2) it is not merely practical, but concerns itself also with questions of values, with educating men and women to be good citizens and good leaders, concerned with the common good, and able to use their education for the service of faith and promotion of justice; 3) it celebrates the full range of human intellectual power and achievement, confidently affirming reason, not as opposed to faith, but as its necessary complement; 4) it places all that it does firmly within a Christian understanding of the human person as a creature of God whose ultimate destiny is beyond the human.[3]

5/   This short version was not simple enough for Father Padberg who has simplified all these phrases into four key words: a Jesuit education should develop four purposes: practical and social, humanistic and religious.[4] But because of where we gather today, perhaps it would be best to use four Latin words dear to the Gregorian: *Utilitas, Justitia, Humanitas, et Fides.*

6/   How is the Jesuit university today still moved by the four characteristics originally articulated by Father Ledesma almost five centuries ago? I want to invite you to take time for a kind of evaluation recommended by

Saint Ignatius for the purpose of discovering how one has responded to the Lord's presence and how one might respond in the future to the invitation of the Lord to act in this world. This evaluation cannot be made in general by a Superior General, who suddenly descends from the lofty heights of the ideal into the complexities of a local situation. Rather, it is something that those most intimately and specifically involved with an institution— you yourselves—must undertake. My remarks about these characteristics of Jesuit education are merely intended to help frame a conversation and discussion for you to have among yourselves and with those most knowledgeable about Georgetown University. It is also important to keep in mind throughout this talk that according to the paradigm of Jesuit education, the purpose of evaluation is not only to detect mistakes and errors made in decision-making, but also to reach out for the magis, the more, in order to face new challenges and to welcome new opportunities.

7/   The first of Ledesma's purposes is not in danger of disappearing. On the contrary, the practical purpose of the university, the *Utilitas,* sometimes threatens to overwhelm everything else. To focus <u>exclusively</u> on the pragmatic elements of education, <u>only</u> on economic advancement, <u>merely</u> on scientific technological progress, <u>solely</u> on business interests, can easily isolate the practical purpose of a university to a narrow academic perspective that turns the three other purposes of university life into mere abstractions. Rather, a Jesuit university will be eminently practical when it continues to insist upon an integral formation and a holistic approach to education as you are doing so well. It has *Utilitas* because it addresses the obvious need for human society to consider technological progress and all the scientific specialities in the light of deeper human, ethical, and social implications, so that science and technology serve humanity and do not lead to its destruction. It is the university that has to take the lead in promoting this holistic approach in the service of mankind and Georgetown, thanks to your efforts, is doing that.

8/   The term *Justitia* expresses Ledesma's stress on the need to educate women and men so they can embrace and promote readily and willingly all that must be done to build up just social, economic, and political structures that preserve our common humanity. In spite of the strong individualistic impulses in us, a Jesuit university should succeed in transforming its students into women and men for others as Father Arrupe so often repeated, but also and even more these days into women and men with others. Indeed, impelled by the positive effects of globalization, the accent now falls heavily and happily on the preposition "with"—on fruitful partnership—not only from the side of the individual person but also from the side of the university itself. More than ever, the university cannot be just an isolated island or an ivory tower: it has to reach out and make its specific academic ways of doing things available to enrich educational systems locally, nationally, and internationally, quite aware that all these initiatives will ultimately enhance the institution itself. Georgetown, because of its location in the capital city of the United States, has particular international responsibilities. And I am grateful to Georgetown for reaching out to more and more countries in need.

9/   Much more complex is Father Ledesma's third purpose: to give ornament, splendor, and perfection to our rational nature. With this grandiose expression Father Ledesma tells us that he believed passionately that Jesuit education was and is about the formation of more fully human persons and that this humanistic creed and tradition should have impact on every aspect and every discipline of the Jesuit educational enterprise. This humanistic tradition does not limit itself to a *mens sana in corpore sano*, a healthy mind in a healthy body. Instead, right from its beginning, Jesuit education has consisted in a struggle for human dignity and human rights, enlightened freedom of conscience and responsible freedom of speech, respectful dialogue and patient promotion of justice.

10/   The best way to achieve this purpose in the 16th century was through the broadly humanising potential of the humanities. Father John O'Malley, in one of his many interesting writings, recalls that during his own Jesuit training, superiors stated with conviction that the intensive study of the classics was the best means for training the human mind. In the late

16th century, in spite of the official backing of the Jesuit *Ratio Studiorum*, the *Studia Humanitatis*—humanities studies—in actual fact were quickly shrinking as they were absorbed by other faculties or as they became one speciality among many other specialities. They were more or less saved by a compulsory *studium generale* and this still exists in many of our universities. Already in the 16th century, in this holy building, the Jesuit Christopher Clavius (1537–1612) fought against the philosophers who taught, and they were Jesuits, that "mathematical sciences are not sciences." Clavius insisted that science and technology should be seen in the same humanistic tradition, stating that since "the mathematical disciplines in fact require truth, delight in truth, and honour truth . . . there can be no doubt that they must be conceded the first place among all the other sciences."[5] Today, when the scholar committed to solving speculative intellectual problems through study and research encounters on the same campus the skilled professional who has mastered all the technicalities of his or her speciality including technical jargon, both should give thanks to their *alma mater* for the ornament, splendor, and perfection to their rational nature, the *Humanitas* of Ledesma's vision.

11/   This openness and willingness to explore scientifically all that is human leads logically to the fourth purpose of a university: the religious dimension. In the most profound sense, *Fides* is commitment to the search for the fullness of truth. In the wording of Ledesma, the rigorous intellectual activity it presupposes shines beyond the mere presence of a university chapel, a department of religious sciences, or even a faculty of theology. The university as university should propose and defend the Christian faith as a bulwark of religion, and it should shine as a beacon that helps every human being encounter The Lord who stands at the beginning of every human life and who will be there to welcome us at the end. In the case of a Jesuit university that seeks to be faithful to its name, this ultimate purpose of the university's activities should be explicitly present in all its options and choices, all its projects and plans.

12/   For, when all is said and done, the cornerstone of Jesuit education is finally not a manual or a charter, but a Person, a Person who taught, by word and by lifestyle, God's vision and values, in order to build up and to save humanity in all things. In this sense, Jesuit universities remain crucial institutional settings in human society. After centuries of unflagging commitment from the Society of Jesus, a Jesuit university does not stand in need of any fresh defence; however, the way a university's Jesuit identity will be lived out does need, always, ever new structures and expressions in research and in teaching, in academic organization, and in the many forms of science, all situated in a particular socio-political place and cultural mission.

13/   In the never-ending process of discerning how to make better the practical, social, humanistic, and religious dimensions of a Jesuit university, leadership plays a decisive role. Your leadership as members of the Board of Directors is clearly crucial as you ask yourselves again and again, "How effectively does Georgetown incarnate Father Ledesma's four characteristics? What programs and policies does it have in place to support, promote, and extend the commitment to its Catholic and Jesuit character? What resources need to be available to accomplish the mission? What obstacles must be removed in order to free the energies required to enable Georgetown to become more and more what it claims to be? As you ask these questions, I hope and pray you are particularly demanding of your Jesuit Board Members in insisting that they help you use the Ignatian *Examen* as a tool for your governance.

14/   As you know, in addition to decisive leadership, personnel play a crucial role in Jesuit education. We all know that there is simply no substitute for good teachers, good staff members, and good administrators at a good university. You as Board Members make sure that the pieces are in place for the selection, training, and retention of the finest possible faculty, staff, and administration. When the Roman College, the mother of the Gregoriana, started, the staff was exclusively Jesuit. In the four handbooks and charters—the *Ratios* produced by the Jesuits between 1565 and 1599— only Jesuits are mentioned, except in the method of punishment. The Jesuit professor "should not himself [use the] whip[,] for the disciplinarian ought to take care of that."[6] Thus we can see that the first instance of Jesuit-Lay partnership was born out of a need to have the laity do the dirty work. Later, there was a need to ask non-Jesuits to join the faculty in order to address governmental regulations and to cover specialisations for which no Jesuit was trained. Later still, the starkly decreasing numbers of competent Jesuits led to the inclusion of non-Jesuits in order to assure the survival of many contemporary universities.

15/ It took us some time, but <u>eventually</u> we hard-headed Jesuits began to realize that the hand of the Lord might be directing us to realize that selecting the finest possible faculty, staff, and administration might involve people outside the Society of Jesus. Just as the instinct that Jesuits should not administer corporal punishment grew into the conviction that no one should use corporal punishment in a Jesuit school, so too the instinct grew that Jesuit education was considerably better if Jesuits and non-Jesuits worked together as partners, as colleagues in a common enterprise. There is no doubt that Vatican II led the whole Church to recognize that the needs of our world required increasing participation and contribution by the laity in real partnership. The Council's graced insights and our own lived experience have led us to recognize the innate richness of collaboration, of partnership in ministry. Providing access to Ignatian spirituality for everyone involved in Jesuit education presents important opportunities to those willing to respond generously to its promptings.

16/ The characteristics of Jesuit education flourish as never before on the level of higher learning. Our experience reveals that Jesuit institutions around the world have been revitalised as they have worked to make Ignatian spirituality and the insights of Jesuit education available to more and more people in new and exciting ways and also to learn from our partners in these enterprises. In the process, the identities and vocations appropriate to each, and Jesuit, have been enhanced. The General Congregation coming up in January 2008 will look again at the issue of how Jesuits can support the laity in our common mission in a partnership that is essential for the future and how we can really learn from one another in our own charisms.

17/   A preliminary report in anticipation of General Congregation 35, based on responses from throughout the world, showed clearly that laypersons and Jesuits have been learning to cooperate with each other in a common task, a common mission. At the same time, mutual enrichment as real partners has taken place so that each person understands and appreciates his or her unique vocation in a deeper way. This process of growth in partnership is still going on; hence, its future developments may have even more surprises for us. In any case, what is already clear is the impossibility of using only one monolithic paradigm of Jesuit-lay partnership, because the wide diversity of works and ministries, tasks and challenges, contextualised by quite different civil statutes and cultural traditions, makes this impossible. The motivation to work together can be very different, from sharing a common faith to solidarity in a common cause. The mode of involvement is different as well: counsellor, advisor, director, volunteer, paid employee, and part-time worker only begin to suggest the variety of partnership that is possible. Different religious convictions or different humanistic outlooks are not necessarily reasons to be excluded from this partnership. What is central is mutual respect of each person's unique identity. In addition, the distinctiveness of the religious and the lay vocation has to be preserved. In a genuine Ignatian partnership of laity and Jesuits, each of the two partner groups must act according to its proper vocation.

18/   I am grateful for all that is being done to foster more and more of this partnership. It presupposes a clear charter, a clear mission-statement, as the basis and foundation for a common venture. At the same time, it requires carefully conceived programs that empower all those involved in Jesuit education to acquire greater knowledge about the profound meaning of the university and its commitment to Ignatian values. However, real partnerships will only grow through shared discernment in bodies like the Board of Directors, the Board of Trustees and through participative decision-making in the school's governing bodies. It is a sense of co-responsibility for the university that in a large variety of ways transforms the desired partnership into a reality.

19/   I now quote from ten years ago,

Georgetown seeks to be a place where understanding is joined to commitment; where the search for truth is informed by a sense of responsibility for the life of society; where academic excellence in teaching and research is joined with the cultivation of virtue; and where a community is formed which sustains men and women in their education and their conviction that life is only lived when it is lived generously in the service of others.[7]

20/   This quotation does not contain the word "partnership," but without the reality this term signifies, Georgetown would not be able to make this idea-statement a reality that motivates staff—the teaching one and the administrative one—to join in partnership with the Jesuits who have a specific responsibility to guarantee what Jesuit education means at Georgetown in solidarity with all their lay partners. For that reason the next General Congregation will, I hope, explore all that still has to be fostered and promoted so that Jesuits can be more effectively with others in mission; your input will be most welcomed. In our initial Jesuit formation and in our ongoing formation, in offering more generously the experience of the Spiritual Exercises to lay persons, in cooperating more collegially in mission, in investing more in the formation of lay leadership through new proposals and new initiatives, we Jesuits want to do whatever we can to share our Ignatian heritage and tradition, our educational and spiritual birthright, in the interests of promoting the common mission we share with you, our colleagues.

21/   In the history of American Jesuit higher education, there is much to be grateful for; first to the Lord and to the Church and surely to you, to the many teachers, students, administrators, benefactors, and board members who have made it what it is today. We Jesuits thank you, our partners in mission. We are grateful for your ongoing work to deepen your knowledge of and commitment to the charisms of the Ignatian heritage. This is a life-long journey. And as Ignatius said himself, it is only one among many ways to the Lord, but it is a way that many have walked before us. We Jesuits thank you for the tremendous skills and talents you bring to our work together. We owe you our deepest gratitude and support. Today, the Society of Jesus renews its pledge to walk with you Board members along what will no doubt frequently be a difficult and challenging path. But we will not walk alone. The Lord who calls us, the Lord for whom the Society of Jesus is named, will be walking with us as our Companion. Thank you so much for your patience.

---

[1] See Philip Caraman, S.J., *University of the Nations,* (New York: Paulist Press, 1981).

[2] *Monumenta Historica Societatis Iesu,* (Roma: Institutum Historicum Societatis Iesu, 1974), vol. 107, pp. 528–9.

[3] *Middle States Working Group on Jesuit and Catholic Identity,* (Loyola College, Baltimore: 20 November 1998). See William J. Byron, S.J., *Jesuit Saturdays: Sharing the Ignatian Spirit with Lay Colleagues and Friends,* (Chicago: Loyola Press, 2000).

[4] Vincent J. Duminuco, S.J. (ed.), The *Jesuit Ratio Studiorum,* 400th Anniversary Perspectives, p. 98, (New York: Fordham University Press, 2000).

[5] Christopher Clavius, *Opera Mathematica,* (Roma: Reinhard Eltz, 1612), vol. I, p. 5.

[6] Claude Pavur, S.J. (trans.), *The Ratio Studiorum: The Official Plan for Jesuit Education,* (St. Louis: The Institute of Jesuit Sources, 2005), n. 364.

[7] August 1992 Discussion Paper drafted by Georgetown Faculty and Administrators. Quoted in *Living Generously in the Service of Others,* Keynote Address to Jesuit Alumni/ae delivered by Rev. William J. Byron, S.J., Sidney, Australia, 9 July 1997.

General Congregation 35, 2010

Jesuit Life & Mission Today: The Decrees & Accompanying Documents of the 31st–35th General Congregations of the Society of Jesus. Edited by John W. Padberg, S.J.

Editor's Introduction: General Congregation 35 elected Fr. Adolfo Nicolás as Superior General. It also reaffirmed the mission of the Society in terms of the service of faith and the promotion of justice. However, the Congregation was aware of the context for mission and highlighted several new aspects: the global context of our world, new technologies, the call for reconciliation with creation, and the extraordinary potential if we act as an international body.

Decree 3

CHALLENGES TO OUR MISSION TODAY—SENT TO THE FRONTIERS

I. Re-affirming Our Mission

1/   1. As servants of Christ's mission, we recall with gratitude the graces received from the Lord during the past years. In our lives together as Jesuits, we have experienced an ongoing process of renewal and adaptation of our mission and way of proceeding as called for by the Second Vatican Council.[1]

2/   2. Since the Council, the Spirit has led the whole Society gathered in General Congregations to the firm conviction that

> The aim of our mission received from Christ, as presented in the Formula of the Institute, is the service of faith. The integrating principle of our mission is the inseparable link between faith and the promotion of the justice of the Kingdom.[2]

3/   3. Reflecting on our experience during General Congregation (GC) 34, we discerned that the service of faith in Jesus Christ and the promotion of the justice of the Kingdom preached by him can best be achieved in the contemporary world if enculturation and dialogue become essential elements of our way of proceeding in mission.[3] We experience this mission as being part of the Church's overall mission of evangelization, "a single but complex reality" containing all these essential elements.[4] We want to re-affirm this mission which gives meaning to our religious apostolic life in the Church:

> Thus the aim of our mission (the service of faith) and its integrating principle (faith directed toward the justice of the Kingdom) are dynamically related to the enculturated proclamation of the Gospel and dialogue with other religious traditions as integral dimensions of evangelization.[5]

4/   4. During the past years, the fruitful engagement of the Society in the dialogue with people belonging to different cultures and religious traditions has enriched our service of faith and promotion of justice and confirmed that faith and justice cannot be simply one ministry among others; they are integral to all ministries and to our lives together as individuals, communities, and a worldwide brotherhood.[6]

5/   5. Our pastoral, educational, social, communication, and spiritual ministries have increasingly found creative ways of implementing this mission in the challenging circumstances of the modern world. Different ministries carry out the mission in ways that are appropriate to them. However, all have experienced mission as the grace of being "placed with the Son." We remember with gratitude so many of our brothers and collaborators who have offered their lives generously in response to the call of the Lord to labor with him.

6/   6. In our desire to continue "serving the Lord alone and his spouse, the Church, under the Roman Pontiff,"[7] we find confirmation in the words the Holy Father addressed to the members of this Congregation:

> Today I want to encourage you and your brothers to go on in the fulfillment of your mission, in full fidelity to your original charism, in the ecclesial and social context that characterizes the beginning of this millennium. As my predecessors have often told you, the Church needs you, counts on you, and continues to turn to you with confidence . . .[8]

7/   7. In response to the challenging new contexts we face, we want to reflect further on our mission in the light of our experience.

II. A New Context for Mission

8/   8. The new context in which we live our mission today is marked by profound changes, acute conflicts, and new possibilities. In the words of the Holy Father:

> Your Congregation takes place in a period of great social, economic, and political changes; sharp ethical, cultural, and environmental problems, conflicts of all kinds, but also of more intense communication among peoples, of new possibilities of acquaintance and dialogue, of a deep longing for peace. All these are situations that challenge the Catholic Church and its ability to announce to our contemporaries the Word of hope and salvation.[9]

9/   9. We live in a global world. GC 34 already noted the "growing consciousness of the interdependence of all people in one common heritage."[10] This process has continued at a rapid pace; as a result, our interconnectedness has increased. Its impact has been felt deeply in all areas of our life, and it is sustained by interrelated cultural, social, and political structures that affect the core of our mission of faith, justice, and all aspects of our dialogue with religion and culture.

10/   10. Globalization has also given birth to a world culture affecting all cultures; often this has resulted in a process of homogenization and in policies of assimilation that deny the right of individuals and groups to live and develop their own cultures. In the midst of this upheaval, post-modernism, mentioned also by GC 34,[11] has continued to shape the way the contemporary world and we Jesuits think and behave.

11/   11. In this new world of instant communication and digital technology, of worldwide markets, and of a universal aspiration for peace and wellbeing, we are faced with growing tensions and paradoxes: we live in a culture that shows partiality to autonomy and the present, and yet we have a world so much in need of building a future in solidarity; we have better ways of communication but often experience isolation and exclusion; some have greatly benefited, while others have been marginalized and excluded; our world is increasingly transnational, and yet it needs to affirm and protect local and particular identities; our scientific knowledge has reached the deepest mysteries of life, and yet the very dignity of life itself and the world we live in are threatened.

III. Call to Establish Right Relationships: A Mission of Reconciliation

12/   12. In this global world marked by such profound changes, we now want to deepen our understanding of the call to serve faith, promote justice, and dialogue with culture and other religions in the light of the apostolic mandate to establish right relationships with God, with one another, and with creation.[12]

[13–14] (These sections have been omitted.)

13/   15. Ignatius and his first companions understood the importance of reaching out to people on the frontiers and at the center of society, of reconciling those who were estranged in any way.[16] From the center in Rome, Ignatius sent Jesuits to the frontiers, to the new world, "to announce the Lord to peoples and cultures that did not know him as yet."[17] He sent Xavier to the Indies. Thousands of Jesuits followed, preaching the Gospel to many cultures, sharing knowledge with and learning from others. He also wanted Jesuits to cross other types of frontiers between rich and poor, between educated and unlearned. He wrote a letter to the Jesuits at the Council of Trent on how to behave and insisted that they should minister to the sick. Jesuits opened colleges in Rome and in the great cities of Europe, and they taught children in villages across the world.

[16.] (This section has been omitted.)

14/   17. This tradition of Jesuits building bridges across barriers becomes crucial in the context of today's world. We become able to bridge the divisions of a fragmented world only if we are united by the love of Christ our Lord, by personal bonds like those that linked Francis Xavier and Ignatius across the seas, and by the obedience that sends each one of us in mission to any part of this world.[19]

IV. Our Apostolic Response

15/   18. As servants of Christ's mission, we are invited to assist him as he sets right our relationships with God, with other human beings, and with creation. "Our world is the theatre of a battle between good and evil," the Holy Father reminded us:[20] and so we again place ourselves before the Lord in the meditation on the Two Standards. There are powerful negative forces in the world, but we are also aware of God's presence permeating this world, inspiring persons of all cultures and religions to promote reconciliation and peace. The world where we work is one of sin and of grace.

Reconciliation with God

16/   19. The Spiritual Exercises invite us to a renewed and deepened experience of reconciliation with God in Christ. We are called to share, with joy and respect, the grace of this experience that we have received and that nourishes our hope. Globalization and new communication technologies have opened up our world and offer us new opportunities to announce with enthusiasm the Good News of Jesus Christ and the Kingdom he proclaimed. Our ministries of the proclamation of the Word and the celebration of the life of Christ in the sacraments continue to be fundamental for our mission and our lives together as Jesuits. They must be seen as part of the three-fold responsibility that lies at the heart of the deepest nature of the Church: proclamation of the word of God (*kerygma-martyria*), celebrating the sacraments (*leitourgia*), and exercising the ministry of charity (*diakonia*).[21] In fulfilling this responsibility, we search for new forms of integral evangelization to "reach the geographical and spiritual places others do not reach or find it difficult to reach,"[22] always attentive to the demands of the cultural context within which we carry out our mission.

[20–24] (These sections have been omitted.)

Reconciliation with One Another

17/   25. In this global world, there are social, economic, and political forces that have facilitated the creation of new relationships among people, but there are other forces which have broken the bonds of love and solidarity within the human family. While many poor people have been lifted from poverty, the gap between rich and poor within nations and across national boundaries has increased. From the perspective of those living at the margins, globalization appears to be a massive force that excludes and exploits the weak and the poor, which intensifies exclusion on the basis of religion, race, caste, and gender.

[26–30] (These sections have been omitted.)

Reconciliation with Creation

18/   31. Following the directive[30] of GC 34, Fr. Peter-Hans Kolvenbach commissioned a study and invited all "Jesuits and those who share our mission to show ever more effective ecological solidarity in our spiritual, communal, and apostolic lives."[31] This invitation calls us to move beyond doubts and indifference to take responsibility for our home, the earth.

19/   32. Care of the environment affects the quality of our relationships with God, with other human beings, and with creation itself. It touches the core of our faith in and love for God, "from whom we come and 'towards whom we are journeying."[32] It might be said that St. Ignatius teaches us this care of the environment in the Principle and Foundation[33] when speaking of the goodness of creation, as well as in the Contemplatio ad Amorem when describing the active presence of God within creation.[34]

[33–35] (These sections have been omitted.)

20/   36. In our preaching, teaching, and retreat direction, we should invite all people to appreciate more deeply our covenant[36] with creation as central to right relationships with God and one another, and to act accordingly in terms of political responsibility, employment, family life, and personal lifestyle.

V. Global Preferences

21/   37. In continuity with the recommendations[37] made by GC 34 and to respond effectively to the global challenges described above, this Congregation has emphasized the importance of structures for apostolic planning, implementation, and accountability at all levels of the Society's government.[38]

[38] (This section has been omitted.)

22/   39. While respecting provincial or regional priorities, these "preferences" indicate apostolic areas requiring "special or privileged attention."[40] In our present context, we may confidently say that they offer areas for the realization of the mission orientations provided by this decree. In consultation with the Conferences of Major Superiors, Fr. Peter-Hans Kolvenbach decided on the following apostolic preferences:

[39i–39ii] (These sections have been omitted.)

(iii) The intellectual apostolate has been a defining characteristic of the Society of Jesus from its beginning. Given the complex yet interrelated challenges that Jesuits face in every apostolic sector, GC 35 calls for a strengthening and renewal of this apostolate as a privileged means for the Society to respond adequately to the important intellectual contribution to which the Church calls us. Advanced studies for Jesuits must be encouraged and supported throughout formation.

[39iv–39v] (These sections have been omitted.)

[40–42] (These sections have been omitted.)

23/   43. In this global context, it is important to highlight the extraordinary potential we possess as an international and multicultural body.

Acting consistently with this character can not only enhance the apostolic effectiveness of our work but in a fragmented and divided world it can witness to the reconciliation in solidarity of all the children of God.

1   Vatican II, *Peifectae Caritatis*, 2.
2   General Congregation (GC) 34, D. 2, n. 14.
3   GC 34, D. 2, nn. 14–21.
4   Cf. JOHN PAUL II, *Redemptoris Missio*, 41: "Mission is a single but complex reality, and it develops in a variety of ways." Cf. nn. 52–54; 55–57.
5   GC 34, D. 2, n. 15.
6   GC 32, D. 2, n. 9.
7   *Exposcit debitum (1550)*, § 3 (MHSI 63, 375).
8   BENEDICT XVI, *Allocution to the 35th General Congregation of the Society of Jesus (21 February 2008)*, § 2 (Allocution).
9   *Allocution*, § 2.
10 GC 34, D. 3, n. 7.
11 GC 34, D. 4, nn. 19–24.
12 *Compendium of the Social Doctrine of the Church*, § 575.
16 *Exposcit debit11m (1550)*, § 3 (MHSI 63, 376).
17 *Allocution*, § 3.
19 *Constitutions*, 655–659.
20 *Allocution*, § 6.
21 BENEDICT XVI, *Deus Caritas Est (2005)*, 25.
22 *Allocution*, § 2.
30 GC 34, D. 20, n. 2.
31 Peter-Hans KOLVENBACH, S.J., *We Live in a Broken World. Introduction*, Promotio Iustitiae 70, April 1999.
32 BENEDICT XVI, *Message of Peace (1 January 2008)*, § 7.
33 *Spiritual Exercises*, 23.
34 *Spiritual Exercises*, 230–237.
36 Peter-Hans KOLVENBACH, S.J., *"Souhaits de Noel et de Nouvel An: Nos preferences apostoliques" (1 January 2003)*, AR 23,1 (2003) 31–36: "[The choice of apostolic priorities] has been accomplished in prayerful discernment, identifying some of the most important and urgent needs, those that are more universal, or those to which the Society is being called to respond more generously."
37 GC 34, D. 2 n. 1.
38 GC 35, D. 5, nn. 12, 18–21.
40 Peter-Hans KOLVENBACH, S.J., *"Souhaits de Noel et de Nouvel An: Nos preferences apostoliques" (1 January 2003)*, AR 23,1 (2003) 31–36: "[The choice of apostolic priorities] has been accomplished in prayerful discernment, identifying some of the most important and urgent needs, those that are more universal, or those to which the Society is being called to respond more generously."

Depth, Universality, and Learned Ministry: Challenges to Jesuit Higher Education Today

Adolfo Nicolás, S.J., 2010. Remarks for "Networking Jesuit Higher Education: Shaping the Future for a Humane, Just, Sustainable Globe," Mexico City.

Editor's Introduction: Fr. Adolfo Nicolás (1936–) was elected the 30th Superior General of the Society of Jesus by General Congregation 35, in 2008. Fr. Nicolás continued the call to renewal of Jesuit education and highlighted the extraordinary apostolic potential of networking for our schools. He called Jesuit education to embrace the challenges of our era with creativity and imagination. Fr. Nicolás also enthusiastically called Jesuit schools and universities to fight the contemporary culture of superficiality with the promotion of depth of thought. His two most important speeches in education are presented in this book: his speech to the Jesuit universities in Mexico in 2010 and to the World Congress of the Alumni in Medellin in 2013 (p. 555).

1/ I AM VERY HAPPY TO BE WITH YOU THIS MORNING, ON THIS REMARKABLE OCCASION, AS COLLEAGUES OF NEARLY ALL OF THE ROUGHLY 200 INSTITUTIONS OF HIGHER EDUCATION OPERATING UNDER THE BANNER OF THE SOCIETY OF JESUS GATHER TO CONSIDER THE IMPORTANCE OF JESUIT EDUCATION AND ITS FUTURE. I am happy to greet all of you—collaborators in the mission and ministry of the Society, Jesuits, friends of the Society and of Jesuit higher education, and any students who might be present. I thank Father José Morales, President of the *Iberoamericana*, and the staff of the *Iberoamericana* for their hospitality and extraordinary efforts in ensuring all the arrangements for this conference. Finally, I thank all of you for your participation in Jesuit higher education and in this conference, which some of you began before arriving here by authoring the excellent papers that served to stimulate our discussions.

2/ For the sake of simplifying language, I will use "universities" when referring to the wide range of higher education institutions represented in this assembly, ranging from specialized research centers to technical institutes, to colleges, and to large, complex universities.

3/   In the past two years in my present service, I have traveled to many parts of the world to encounter Jesuits and our collaborators, and I have always emphasized that I am as eager—in fact, *more* eager—to listen and to learn, rather than to speak from the lofty—and mythical—heights of Borgo Santo Spirito 4. I bring this same dialogical spirit to this meeting of Jesuit higher education. As I listened yesterday to your discussion of regional challenges and the three frontier challenges that you selected to address, I could see that you already tackle many of the "serious contemporary problems" that Pope John Paul II identified for us in his apostolic constitution, *Ex Corde Ecclesiae*, and that you are doing so with the depth of thought, imagination, moral passion, and spiritual conviction that characterize Catholic and Jesuit education at its best.

4/   What I wish to share this morning, therefore, should be taken as adding my perspective to what I hope will be an ongoing and ever deeper conversation on the future of Jesuit higher education. My own experience is that university people, especially university presidents, are not shy about sharing their points of view, so I am confident as you continue your consideration of important issues that your conversations will, at the very least, be spirited and insightful!

5/   The theme of our conference—*Networking Jesuit Higher Education: Shaping the Future for a Humane, Just, Sustainable Globe*—involves a bold proposal. It suggests that we have today an extraordinary opportunity to have a hand in helping to shape the future, not only of our own institutions, but of the world, and that the way we can do that is through "networking." That word, "networking," so often used these days, is, in fact, typical of the "new world" in which we live—a world which has as its "principal new feature," what Pope Benedict XVI calls "the explosion of worldwide interdependence, commonly known as globalization."[1]

6/   The 35th General Congregation (GC) also saw our interconnectedness as the new context for understanding the world and discerning our mission. I am aware that the word "globalization" carries different meanings and evokes different reactions for people of diverse cultures. There has been much discussion on both the positive features and the negative effects of globalization, and I need not review them here. Rather, what I wish to invite us to reflect on together is this: How does this new context challenge us to re-direct, in some sense, the mission of Jesuit higher education?

7/   You represent very different kinds of institutions from every part of the world, serving students, regions, and countries with widely divergent cultures, religions, resources, and having distinctive regional and local roles to play. Clearly, the question of the challenge of globalization for the mission of Jesuit higher education needs to be answered by each institution in its unique social, cultural, and religious circumstances. But I wish to emphasize that it is also a question that calls for a common and universal response, drawn of course from your diverse cultural perspectives, from Jesuit higher education as a whole, as an apostolic sector.

8/   How then does this new context of globalization, with the exciting possibilities and serious problems it has brought to our world, challenge Jesuit higher education to re-define, or at least, re-direct its mission? I would like to invite you to consider three distinct but related challenges to our shared mission that this new "explosion of interdependence" poses to us: First, promoting depth of thought and imagination. Second, re-discovering and implementing our "universality" in the Jesuit higher education sector. Third, renewing the Jesuit commitment to learned ministry.

I. PROMOTING DEPTH OF THOUGHT AND IMAGINATION

9/   I will begin quite forthrightly with what I see as a negative effect of globalization, what I will call the globalization of superficiality. I am told that I am the first Jesuit General to use e-mail and to surf the Web, so I trust that what I will say will not be mistaken as a lack of appreciation of the new information and communication technologies and their many positive contributions and possibilities.

10/   However, I think that all of you have experienced what I am calling the globalization of superficiality and how it affects so profoundly the thousands of young people entrusted to us in our institutions. When one can access so much information so quickly and so painlessly; when one can express and publish to the world one's reactions so immediately and so unthinkingly in one's blogs or micro-blogs; when the latest opinion column from the *New York Times* or *El Pais*, or the newest viral video can be spread so quickly to people half a world away, shaping their perceptions and feelings, then the laborious, painstaking work of serious, critical thinking often gets short-circuited.

11/   One can "cut-and-paste" without the need to think critically or write accurately or come to one's own careful conclusions. When beautiful images from the merchants of consumer dreams flood one's computer screens, or when the ugly or unpleasant sounds of the world can be shut out by one's MP3 music player, then one's vision, one's perception of reality, one's desiring can also remain shallow. When one can become "friends" so quickly and so painlessly with mere acquaintances or total strangers on one's social networks—and if one can so easily "unfriend" another without the hard work of encounter or, if need be, confrontation and then reconciliation—then relationships can also become superficial.

12/   When one is overwhelmed with such a dizzying pluralism of choices and values and beliefs and visions of life, then one can so easily slip into the lazy superficiality of relativism or mere tolerance of others and their views, rather than engaging in the hard work of forming communities of dialogue in the search of truth and understanding. It is easier to do as one is told than to study, to pray, to risk, or to discern a choice.

13/   I think the challenges posed by the globalization of superficiality—superficiality of thought, vision, dreams, relationships, convictions—to Jesuit higher education need deeper analysis, reflection, and discernment than we have time for this morning. All I wish to signal here is my concern that our new technologies, together with the underlying values such as moral relativism and consumerism, are shaping the interior worlds of so many, especially the young people we are educating, limiting the fullness of their flourishing as human persons and limiting their responses to a world in need of healing intellectually, morally, and spiritually.

14/   We need to understand this complex new interior world created by globalization more deeply and intelligently so that we can respond more adequately and decisively as educators to counter the deleterious effects of such superficiality. For a world of globalized superficiality of thought means the unchallenged reign of fundamentalism, fanaticism, ideology, and all those escapes from thinking that cause suffering for so many. Shallow, self-absorbed perceptions of reality make it almost impossible to feel compassion for the suffering of others; and a contentment with the satisfaction of immediate desires or the laziness to engage competing claims on one's deepest loyalty results in the inability to commit one's life to what is truly worthwhile. I'm convinced that these kinds of processes bring the sort of dehumanization that we are already beginning to experience. People lose the ability to engage with reality; that is a process of dehumanization that may be gradual and silent, but very real. People are losing their mental home, their culture, their points of reference.

15/   The globalization of superficiality challenges Jesuit higher education to promote in creative new ways the depth of thought and imagination that are distinguishing marks of the Ignatian tradition.

16/   I have no doubt that all our universities are characterized by the striving towards excellence in teaching and learning and research. I want to put this in the context of the Ignatian tradition of "depth of thought and imagination." This means that we aim to bring our students beyond excellence of professional training to become well-educated "whole person[s] of solidarity," as Father Kolvenbach noted.[2] Perhaps what I mean can be best explained by reflecting a bit on the "pedagogy" in the contemplations on the mysteries of the life of Jesus in the Spiritual Exercises—which pedagogy Ignatius later applied to Jesuit education.

17/   One might call this "pedagogy" of Ignatian contemplation the exercise of the creative imagination. The imagination works in cooperation with Memory, as we know from the Exercises. The English term used for the acts of the faculty of memory—*to remember*—is very apropos.

18/   Imagine a big jigsaw puzzle with your face in the middle. Now Ignatius asks us to break it into small pieces, that is, to DIS-member before we can remember. And this is why Ignatius separates seeing from hearing, from touching, from tasting, from smelling, and so on. We begin to RE-member—through the active, creative imagination—to rebuild ourselves as we rebuild the scenes of Bethlehem, the scenes of Galilee, the scenes of Jerusalem. We begin the process of RE-creating. And in this process, we are RE-membering. It is an exercise. At the end of the process—when the jigsaw puzzle is formed again—the face is no longer ours but the face of Christ, because we are rebuilding something different, something new. This process results in our personal transformation as the deepest reality of God's love in Christ is encountered.

19/   The Ignatian imagination is a creative process that goes to the depth of reality and begins recreating it. Ignatian contemplation is a very powerful tool, and it is a shifting from the left side of the brain to the right. But it is essential to understand that *imagination* is not the same as *fantasy*. Fantasy is a flight from reality, to a world where we create images for the sake of a diversity of images. Imagination *grasps* reality.

20/   In other words, depth of thought and imagination in the Ignatian tradition involves a profound engagement with the real, a refusal to let go until one goes beneath the surface. It is a careful analysis (dismembering) for the sake of an integration (remembering) around what is deepest: God, Christ, the Gospel. The starting point, then, will always be what is real: what is materially, concretely thought to be there; the world as we encounter it; the world of the senses so vividly described in the Gospels themselves;

a world of suffering and need, a broken world with many broken people in need of healing. We start there. We don't run away from there. And then Ignatius guides us and students of Jesuit education, as he did his retreatants, to enter into the depths of that reality. Beyond what can be perceived most immediately, he leads one to see the hidden presence and action of God in what is seen, touched, smelt, felt. And that encounter with what is deepest changes the person.

21/   A number of years ago, the Ministry of Education of Japan conducted a study in which they found that modern Japanese education had made great advances in science and technology, mathematics, and memory work. But, in their honest assessment, they saw that the educational system had become weaker in teaching imagination, creativity, and critical analysis. These, notably, are three points that are essential to Jesuit education.

22/   Creativity might be one of the most needed things in present times—real creativity, not merely following slogans or repeating what we have heard or what we have seen in Wikipedia. Real creativity is an active, dynamic process of finding responses to real questions, finding alternatives to an unhappy world that seems to go in directions that nobody can control.

23/   When I was teaching theology in Japan, I thought it was important to begin with pastoral theology—the basic experience—because we cannot ask a community that has been educated and raised in a different tradition to begin with speculative theology. But in approaching pastoral theology, I was particularly puzzled by creativity: What makes a pastor creative? I wondered. I came to realize that very often we accept dilemmas where there are no dilemmas. Now and then, we face a true dilemma: We don't know what to choose, and whatever we choose is going to be wrong. But those situations are very, very rare. More often, situations appear to be dilemmas because we don't want to think creatively, and we give up. Most of the time, there is a way out, but it requires an effort of the imagination. It requires the ability to see other models, to see other patterns.

24/ In studying that issue, I found one concept developed by psychologists particularly helpful: floating awareness. Psychologists study Sigmund Freud, Erich Fromm, and others from different schools of psychology to develop what they call "floating awareness." When psychologists encounter a patient and diagnose the person, they choose from different methods of helping people, deciding on the process that is going to help most. I think this is exactly what a Spiritual Father should do. And I wish we had this floating awareness when we celebrate the liturgy: the ability to see the community and grasp what it needs now. It's a very useful concept when it comes to education as well.

25/ It strikes me that we have problems in the Society with formation because, perhaps, our floating awareness is not so well developed. For about 20 years or so, we have been receiving vocations to the Society from groups that we didn't have before: tribal groups, Dalit in India, and other marginal communities. We have received them with joy because we have moved to the poor and then the poor have joined us. This is a wonderful form of dialogue.

26/ But we have also felt a bit handicapped: How do you train these people? We think they don't have enough educational background, so we give them an extra year or two of studies. I don't think this is the right answer. The right answer is to ask: From where do they come? What is their cultural background? What kind of awareness of reality do they bring to us? How do they understand human relationships? We must accompany them in a different way. But for this we need tremendous imagination and creativity—an openness to other ways of being, feeling, relating.

27/ I accept that the dictatorship of relativism is not good. But many things are relative. If there is one thing I learned in Japan, it is that the human person is such a mystery that we can never grasp the person fully. We have to move with agility, with openness, around different models so that we can help them. For education, I would consider this a central challenge.

28/   Our universities are now teaching a population that is not only diverse in itself; it's totally unlike the former generation. With the generational and cultural change, the mentality, questions, and concerns are so different. So we cannot just offer one model of education.

29/   As I said, the starting point will always be the real. Within that reality, we are looking for change and transformation, because this is what Ignatius wanted from the retreatant and what he wanted through education, through ministry: that retreatants and others could be transformed.

30/   Likewise, Jesuit education should change us and our students. We educators are in a process of change. There is no real, deep encounter that doesn't alter us. What kind of encounter do we have with our students if we are not changed? And the meaning of change for our institutions is "who our students become," what they value, and what they do later in life and work. To put it another way, in Jesuit education, the depth of learning and imagination encompasses and integrates intellectual rigor with reflection on the experience of reality together with the creative imagination to work toward constructing a more humane, just, sustainable, and faith-filled world. The experience of reality includes the broken world, especially the world of the poor, waiting for healing. With this depth, we are also able to recognize God as already at work in our world.

31/   Picture in your mind the thousands of graduates we send forth from our Jesuit universities every year. How many of those who leave our institutions do so with both professional competence *and* the experience of having, in some way during their time with us, a depth of engagement with reality that transforms them at their deepest core? What more do we need to do to ensure that we are not simply populating the world with bright and skilled superficialities?

II. RE-DISCOVERING UNIVERSALITY

32/   I would now like to turn to a second challenge of the new globalized world to Jesuit higher education. One of the most positive aspects of globalization is that it has, in fact, made communication and cooperation possible with an ease and at a scale that was unimaginable even just a decade ago. The Holy Father, in his address to the 35th General Congregation (GC), described our world as one "of more intense communication among peoples, of new possibilities for acquaintance and dialogue, of a deep longing for peace." As traditional boundaries have been challenged by globalization, our narrower understandings of identity, belonging, and responsibility have been re-defined and broadened. Now, more than ever, we see that, in all our diversity, we are, in fact, a single humanity, facing common challenges and problems, and, as GC 35 put it, we "bear a common responsibility for the welfare of the entire world and its development in a sustainable and life-giving way."[3] And the positive realities of globalization bring us, along with this sense of common belonging and responsibility, numerous means of working together if we are creative and courageous enough to use them.

33/   In today's university world, I know that many of you experience this breakdown of traditional boundaries in the contemporary demand that you internationalize in order to be recognized as universities of quality—and rightly so. Already many of you have successfully opened offshore or branch campuses, or entered into twinning or cross-border programs that allow your students or faculty members to study or work abroad, to engage and appreciate other cultures, and to learn from and with people of diverse cultures.

34/   When I travel, I am often asked why the number of Jesuits fully involved in social centers or social apostolate has come down; we are far less than we were before. This is true. But also in our schools we have far fewer Jesuits. And yet, at the same time, in our universities and our schools, we have many more programs than before with a social relevance. When I visited California last year—my first visit to the United States—I was greatly encouraged to see that in every one of our schools there was an outreach program, a broadening of horizons: bringing students to other countries, to other continents, to heighten their awareness and concern.

35/   You have also been able to welcome more international students into your own universities, and all of these cross-cultural encounters and experiences surely enrich the quality of scholarship and learning in your institutions, as well as help you to clarify your own identity and mission as Catholic, Jesuit universities. Internationalization is helping your universities become better.

36/   It is not this, however, that I wish to emphasize at this point. What I wish to highlight flows from your discussions yesterday. I will break down my argument into three points.

37/   First, I am sure that all of you will agree with Pope John Paul II who, in *Ex Corde Ecclesiae*, observed that in addition to quality teaching and research, every Catholic university is also called on to become an effective, responsible instrument of progress—for individuals as well as for society.[4] For Ignatius, every ministry is growth, transformation. We are not talking about progress in material terms but about progress that supposes the person goes through a number of experiences, learning and growing from each of them. I know that, in different ways, every Jesuit university is striving to become what Ignacio Ellacuría, the Jesuit rector of the Universidad Centroamericana Simeon Cañas, who was martyred 20 years ago, called a *proyecto social*. A university becomes a social project. Each institution represented here, with its rich resources of intelligence, knowledge, talent, vision, and energy, moved by its commitment to the service of faith and promotion of justice, seeks to insert itself into a society, not just to train professionals, but in order to become a cultural force advocating and promoting truth, virtue, development, and peace in that society. We could say every university is committed to *caritas in veritate*—to promote love and truth—truth that comes out in justice, in new relationships, and so forth. We would be here all day if I were to list all that you do for your regions or countries, all the programs and initiatives in public education, health, housing, human rights, peace and reconciliation, environmental protection, micro-finance, disaster response, governance, inter-religious dialogue, and the like.

38/   Second: however, thus far, largely what we see is each university, each institution working as a *proyecto social* by itself, or at best with a national or regional network. And this, I believe, does not take sufficient advantage of what our new globalized world offers us as a possibility for greater service. People speak of the Jesuit university or higher education system. They recognize the "family resemblances" between Comillas in Madrid and Sanata Dharma in Yogyakarta, between Javieriana in Bogota and Loyola College in Chennai, between St. Peter's in Jersey City and St. Joseph in Beirut. But, as a matter of fact, there is only a commonality of Ignatian inspiration rather than a coherent "Jesuit university network": Each of our institutions operates relatively autonomously of each other, and as a result, the impact of each as a *proyecto social* is limited. The 35th General Congregation observed that "in this global context, it is important to highlight the extraordinary potential we possess as an international and multicultural body."[5] It seems to me that, until now, we have *not* fully made use of this "extraordinary potential" for "universal" service as institutions of higher education. I think this is precisely the focus of many of your presentations and your concerns here.

39/   This brings me to my third and main point: Can we not go beyond the loose family relationships we now have as institutions and re-imagine and re-organize ourselves so that, in this globalized world, we can more effectively realize the universality which has always been part of Ignatius's vision of the Society? Isn't this the moment to move like this? Surely the words used by the 35th General Congregation to describe the Society of Jesus as a whole apply as well to Jesuit universities around the world:

> "The new context of globalization requires us to act as a universal body with a universal mission, realizing at the same time the radical diversity of our situations. It is as a worldwide community—and, simultaneously, as a network of local communities—that we seek to serve others across the world."[6]

40/   To be concrete, while regional organizations of cooperation in mission exist among Jesuit universities, I believe the challenge is to expand them and build more universal, more effective international networks of Jesuit higher education. If each university, working by itself as a *proyecto social*, is able to accomplish so much good in society, how much more can we increase the scope of our service to the world if all the Jesuit institutions of higher education become, as it were, a single global proyecto social? So it is expanding already the awareness that you and we all have.

41/   Before coming here, I met with the Provincials of Africa in Rome; some other Provincials from Latin America were passing through as well. A couple of them mentioned, "Since you are going to Mexico for this meeting, can you tell the directors and the deans and the universities to *share* the resources they have? We who have only beginning institutions—if we could access the libraries and resources that are offered in universities with tradition and know-how and resources that we cannot afford, that would be a great, great help."

42/   As you know, the Society of Jesus is moving from having a historical institute in Rome to having branches or small historical institutes around the world. I hope that these branches can network, because this is the time that every culture, every group can have its own voice about its own history—and not have Europeans interpreting the history of everybody else. In Rome, we are going to work in our own archives to copy, digitalize, and do whatever we can so that this can be shared with other centers. Likewise, it would be a tremendous service if the universities possessing tremendous resources of materials, libraries, etc., could open these to universities that could not hope to build a library in 10 years.

43/   Your presence at this conference indicates your openness to a more universal dimension to your life and service as universities. My hope, however, is that we can move from conferences and discussions like those we had yesterday to the establishment of operational consortia among our universities focused on responding together to some of the "frontier challenges" of our world which have a supra-national or supra-continental character. The three discussion groups you participated in yesterday could serve as the start of three such consortia.

44/   First, a consortium to confront creatively the challenge of the emergence of aggressive "new atheisms." In Europe they don't use this term. They use "new aggressive secularism" and it is very anti-Church. Interestingly, Japan has been secular for 300 or 400 years, with total separation of church and state, but they have a secularism that is peaceful and respectful of religions. In Europe, I have found a very aggressive secularism, not peaceful. Secularism without peace has to be anti-something or against somebody. Why have we come to that? We see it particularly in countries that have been most Catholic: Spain, Italy, Ireland. There, secularism goes against the historical presence of a church that was very powerful and influential. These new atheisms are not confined to the industrialized North and West, however; they affect other cultures and foster a more generalized alienation from religion, often generated by false dichotomies drawn between science and religion.

45/   Second, a consortium focused on more adequate analyses and more effective and lasting solutions to the world's poverty, inequality, and other forms of injustice. In my travels, a question that comes up over and over again is: What are the challenges of the Society? The only answer is: the challenges of the world. There are no other challenges. The challenge is looking for meaning: Is life worth living? And the challenges of poverty, death, suffering, violence, and war. These are our challenges. So what can we do?

46/   And third, a consortium focused on our shared concerns about global environmental degradation, which affects more directly and painfully the lives of the poor, with a view to enabling a more sustainable future for our world.

47/   This third consortium could further network the already existing ecology network currently under the direction of the Secretariat for Social Justice and Ecology of the *Curia Generalizia*. We have been very blessed with a very imaginative and active Secretary, who is here. And we are now developing a section on social justice and ecology. So this would also be a point of reference in this networking.

48/   Let me end this section by reminding you that universities as such came very late into Ignatius's understanding of how the Society of Jesus was to fulfill its mission in the Church. What is striking is that, in the Constitutions, Ignatius makes clear why he is won over to the idea of what he calls "Universities of the Society": the Society of Jesus accepts "charge of universities" so that the "benefits" of "improvement in learning and in living . . . be spread more universally."[7] The more *universal good* is what prompts Ignatius to accept responsibility for universities. With all the means globalization makes possible, then, surely more effective networking in the manner I have described will allow us to spread the benefits of Jesuit higher education more universally in today's world.

III. LEARNED MINISTRY

49/   In a sense, what I have described thus far as challenges to Jesuit higher education in this globalized world correspond to two of the three classic functions of the university. Insofar as universities are places of instruction, I have stressed the need to promote depth of thought and imagination. Insofar as universities are centers of service, I have invited us to move more decisively towards international networks focused on important supranational concerns. This leaves us with the function of research—the genuine search for truth and knowledge—but what is often called today "the production of knowledge"—a theme that, in today's university world, has generated much discussion on questions like the modes of research and its communication, the centers of knowledge production, areas of study, and the purposes of research.

50/   I am sure you will agree that, if we are true to our Ignatian heritage, research in our universities must always ultimately be conceived of in terms of what the 34th General Congregation calls "learned ministry" or the "intellectual apostolate." (This is Jesuit jargon. And a tangential but important point to note is that the intellectual apostolate, sometimes a confusing term, applies to all Jesuit works and apostolates.)

51/ All the virtues of the rigorous exercise of the intellect are required: "learning and intelligence, imagination and ingenuity, solid studies and rigorous analysis."[8] And yet, it is always "ministry" or "apostolate": in the service of the faith, of the Church, of the human family, and the created world that God wants to draw more and more into the realm of his Kingdom of life and love. It is always research that is aimed at making a difference in people's lives, rather than simply a recondite conversation among members of a closed elite group. Again, I am sure that if I were to enumerate all the serious scholarly work and discussion being done in Jesuit universities to address "the serious contemporary problems" Pope John Paul II enumerates in *Ex Corde Ecclesiae*—that is, "the dignity of human life, the promotion of justice for all, the quality of personal and family life, the protection of nature, the search for peace and political stability, a more just sharing in the world's resources, and a new economic and political order that will better serve the human community at a national and international level"[9]—if I were to enumerate all that is being done, my allotted time would not be enough, and both you and I would faint in the process!

52/ In keeping with my approach throughout this reflection, I would now like to ask what challenges globalization poses to the "learned ministry" of research in Jesuit universities? I propose two.

53/ First, an important challenge to the learned ministry of our universities today comes from the fact that globalization has created "knowledge societies," in which development of persons, cultures, and societies is tremendously dependent on access to knowledge in order to grow. Globalization has created new inequalities between those who enjoy the power given to them by knowledge and those who are excluded from its benefits because they have no access to that knowledge. Thus, we need to ask: who benefits from the knowledge produced in our institutions and who does not? Who needs the knowledge we can share, and how can we share it more effectively with those for whom that knowledge can truly make a difference, especially the poor and excluded? We also need to ask some specific questions of faculty and students: How have they become voices for the voiceless, sources of human rights for those denied such rights, resources for protection of the environment, persons of solidarity for the poor? And the list could go on.

54/   In this connection, the work-in-progress of the "Jesuit Commons," which you will discuss tomorrow, is extremely important, and it will require a more serious support and commitment from our universities if it is to succeed in its ambitious dream of promoting greater equality in access to knowledge for the sake of the development of persons and communities.

55/   Second, our globalized world has seen the spread of two rival "-ism's:" on the one hand, a dominant "world culture"[10] marked by an aggressive secularism that claims that faith has nothing to say to the world and its great problems (and which often claims that religion, in fact, is one of the world's great problems); on the other hand, the resurgence of various fundamentalisms, often fearful or angry reactions to postmodern world culture, which escape complexity by taking refuge in a certain "faith" divorced from or unregulated by human reason. And, as Pope Benedict points out, both "secularism and fundamentalism exclude the possibility of fruitful dialogue and effective cooperation between reason and religious faith."[11]

56/   The Jesuit tradition of learned ministry, by way of contrast, has always combined a healthy appreciation for human reason, thought, and culture, on the one hand, and a profound commitment to faith, the Gospel, the Church, on the other. And this commitment includes the integration of faith and justice in dialogue among religions and cultures. The training of the early Jesuits, for example, included the study of pagan authors of antiquity, the creative arts, science, and mathematics, as well as a rigorous theological course of study. One only need consider the life and achievements of Matteo Ricci, whose 400th death anniversary we celebrate this year, to see how this training that harmoniously integrated faith and reason, Gospel and culture, bore such creative fruit.

57/   Many people respond, "Please, don't compare me to Matteo Ricci. He was a genius." I take the point. But at the same time, the formation he received gave him the tools to develop his genius. So the question is: The formation that we give today—does it offer such tools? Are we that integrated? Are we that open in our training?

58/ As secularism and fundamentalism spread globally, I believe that our universities are called to find new ways of creatively renewing this commitment to a dialogue between faith and culture that has always been a distinguishing mark of Jesuit learned ministry. This has been the mission entrusted to us by the Papacy in the name of the Church. In 1983, at the 33rd General Congregation, Pope John Paul II asked the Society for a "deepening of research in the sacred sciences and in general even of secular culture, especially in the literary and scientific fields." More recently, this was the call of Pope Benedict XVI to the Society of Jesus, its collaborators, and its institutions during the 35th General Congregation. The Holy Father affirmed the special mission of the Society of Jesus in the Church to be "at the frontiers," "those geographical and spiritual places where others do not reach or find it difficult to reach," and identified particularly as frontiers those places where "faith and human knowledge, faith and modern science, faith and the fight for justice" meet. As Pope Benedict observed, "this is not a simple undertaking" (Letter, No. 5), but one that calls for "courage and intelligence," and a deep sense of being "rooted at the very heart of the Church."[12]

59/ I am convinced that the Church asks this intellectual commitment of the Society because the world today needs such a service. The unreasoning stance of fundamentalism distorts faith and promotes violence in the world, as many of you know from experience. The dismissive voice of secularism blocks the Church from offering to the world the wisdom and resources that the rich theological, historical, cultural heritage of Catholicism can offer to the world. Can Jesuit universities today, with energy and creativity, continue the legacy of Jesuit learned ministry and forge intellectual bridges between Gospel and culture, faith and reason, for the sake of the world and its great questions and problems?

CONCLUSION

60/   According to good Jesuit tradition, the time has now come for a *repetitio!*—a summing up. I have sought to reflect with you on the challenges of globalization to Jesuit universities as institutions of learning, service, and research. First, in response to the globalization of superficiality, I suggest that we need to study the emerging cultural world of our students more deeply and find creative ways of promoting depth of thought and imagination, a depth that is transformative of the person. Second, in order to maximize the potentials of new possibilities of communication and cooperation, I urge the Jesuit universities to work towards operational international networks that will address important issues touching faith, justice, and ecology that challenge us across countries and continents. Finally, to counter the inequality of knowledge distribution, I encourage a search for creative ways of sharing the fruits of research with the excluded; and in response to the global spread of secularism and fundamentalism, I invite Jesuit universities to a renewed commitment to the Jesuit tradition of learned ministry which mediates between faith and culture.

61/   From one point of view, I think you can take everything I have said and show that the directions I shared are already being attempted or even successfully accomplished in your universities. Then, one can take what I have said as a kind of invitation to the *"magis"* of Ignatius for the shaping of a new world, calling for some fine-tuning, at it were, of existing initiatives, asking that we do better or more of what we are already doing or trying to do. I think that is a valid way of accepting these challenges.

62/   I would like to end, however, by inviting you to step back for a moment to consider a perhaps more fundamental question that I have been asking myself and others over the past two years: If Ignatius and his first companions were to start the Society of Jesus again today, would they still take on universities as a ministry of the Society?

63/   Already in 1995, General Congregation 34 saw that the universities were growing in size and complexity, and at the same time, the Jesuits were diminishing in number within the universities. In 1995, when GC 34 spoke about the diminishing number of Jesuits in universities, there were about 22,850 Jesuits in the world. Today, in 2010, there are about 18,250— about 4,600 fewer Jesuits. I need not go into further statistics to indicate the extent of this challenge. I am very aware of and grateful for the fact that, in the past 15 years, there has been much creative and effective work aimed at strengthening the Catholic and Ignatian identity of our institutions, at creating participative structures of governance, and at sharing our spiritual heritage, mission, and leadership with our collaborators. I am also very aware of and delighted to see how our colleagues have become true collaborators—real partners—in the higher education mission and ministry of the Society. These are wonderful developments the universities can be proud of and need to continue as the number of Jesuits continues to decline.

64/   I believe we need to continue and even increase these laudable efforts of better educating, preparing, and engaging lay collaborators in leading and working in Jesuit institutions. I can honestly say that this is one of the sources of my hope in the service of the Society and of the Church. If we Jesuits were alone, we might look to the future with a heavy heart. But with the professionalism, commitment, and depth that we have in our lay collaborators, we can continue dreaming, beginning new enterprises, and moving forward together. We need to continue and even increase these laudable efforts.

65/   I think one of the most, perhaps *the most*, fundamental ways of dealing with this is to place ourselves in the spiritual space of Ignatius and the first companions and—with their energy, creativity, and freedom—ask their basic question afresh: What are the needs of the Church and our world, where are we needed most, and where and how can we serve best? We are in this together, and that is what we must remember rather than worrying about Jesuit survival. I would invite you, for a few moments, to think of yourselves, not as presidents or CEOs of large institutions, or administrators or academics, but as co-founders of a new religious group, discerning God's call to you as an apostolic body in the Church. In this globalized world, with all its lights and shadows, would—or how would—running all these universities still be the best way we can respond to the mission of the Church and the needs of the world? Or perhaps, the question should be: What kind of universities, with what emphases and what directions, would we run, if we were re-founding the Society of Jesus in today's world? I am inviting, in all my visits to all Jesuits, to re-create the Society of Jesus, because I think every generation has to re-create the faith, they have to re-create the journey, they have to re-create the institutions. This is not only a good desire. If we lose the ability to re-create, we have lost the spirit.

66/   In the Gospels, we often find "unfinished endings": the original ending of the Gospel of Mark, with the women not saying a word about the message of the angel at the tomb; the ending of the parable of the prodigal Son, which ends with an unanswered question from the Father to the older brother. These ambiguous endings may be unsettling and precisely meant to provoke deeper, more fundamental questioning and responses. I therefore have good precedents to conclude my talk in this open-ended way. I hope I leave you reflecting to what extent the challenges I have offered this morning are about improving our institutions and the mission and ministry to help shape a more humane, just, faith-filled, sustainable world or are calls to, in some sense, re-found what Ignatius called "the universities of the Society."

---

[1] *Caritas in Veritate*, n. 33.

[2] Rev. Peter-Hans Kolvenbach, S.J., "The Service of Faith and the Promotion of Justice in American Jesuit Higher Education," lecture at Santa Clara University, Oct. 6, 2000. See also Kolvenbach, "The Jesuit University in the Light of the Ignatian Charism," unpublished lecture from the International Meeting of Jesuit Higher Education, Rome, May 27, 2001. This address is included in Part 5 of this book.

[3] GC 35. Decree 2, n. 20.

[4] *Ex Corde Ecclesiae*, n 32.

[5] GC35, Decree 3, n. 43.

[6] GC35, Decree 2, n. 20.

[7] *Constitutions of the Society of Jesus*, n. 440.

[8] GC 34, Decree 26, n. 20.

[9] *Ex Corde*, ibid.

[10] Cf. GC 35, Decree 3, n. 10, n.20.

[11] *Caritas in Veritate*, n. 56.

[12] GC 35, Decree 1, n. 13.

Jesuit Alumni and Their Social Responsibility: The Quest for a Better Future for Humanity. What Does It Mean to Be a Believer Today?

Adolfo Nicolás, S.J., 2013. Eighth Congress World Union of
Jesuit Alumni, Medellín.

INTRODUCTION

1/   I would like to give everyone here a warm greeting. First, to those coming from other countries to this friendly country of Colombia and the city of Medellín; my greeting also extends to the alumni who have gathered here at the Colegio San Ignacio from all corners of Colombia. And of course, in particular, to the alumni of this school who have joyfully hosted this meeting.

2/   My feelings of gratitude to the organizing committee of this 8th Congress. I know that for many months they have been working very hard to prepare for this event. A special tribute of admiration and gratitude for Fabio Londono Tobon and Tom Bausch. Sadly, both died almost simultaneously a month before the Congress. Fabio, alumnus of San Bartolomé La Merced in Bogotá, and ex-president of the World Union of Jesuit Alumni and President of the organizing committee, left us on July 17, after a heroic struggle with illness. Tom Bausch, President of the World Union, died quite unexpectedly the next day, on July 18. Many thanks to both, for their testimony to life and for their leadership that gave life to the World Union of Jesuit Alumni. Truly, we are grateful for their efforts.

3/   My thanks also go to the Colegio San Ignacio de Medellín, to the Fr. Provincial and Fr. Rector, as well as the Directors and members of ASIA Ignaciana for their gracious hospitality, and all they have done to welcome us and make us feel at home.

I. FROM "RESPONSIBILITY" TO "GRATITUDE"

4/   The theme of "social responsibility" chosen for the conference is very appropriate. It takes us out of ourselves and makes us think about what we are doing and what we can do for the good of others and the world. I hope that this reflection will bring many benefits in our personal, familial, professional, and social development, as well as to the alumni associations represented here.

5/ The purpose of this subject plays an important role in the experience of faith and, consequently, the educational purpose of the Society of Jesus. As I have been given the delicate task of starting this discussion, I intend with my words to achieve three objectives: first, to offer a Christian perspective in the approach to this subject, second, to frame it in our Ignatian approach to education, and third, to project it towards a collective commitment on the global horizon.

6/   "Responsibility" in the Spanish language has two meanings: in the first, "responsible" is one who is bound to himself or to others to do something in their favor and therefore accountable to others in a task or mission assigned, whether immediately or in the future. In the second meaning, "responsible" is one who cares for others and pays them attention. In the English language, "responsibility" has to do only with the first meaning and is within the scope of what has been called "accountability."

7/   Ignatian tradition, meanwhile, has intended to put the human being not in the orbit of "responsibility" but in that of "gratefulness." In his Spiritual Exercises, Ignatius of Loyola proposes to the exerciser the possibility of "bringing to mind the benefits received" (Spiritual Exercises, 234), to arouse in him feelings of gratitude and generosity in response. Indeed, a person who shares this value would respond to generosity with like expressions of the kindness from which he had benefited, and thus give reason to the wise dictum "Love is repaid with love," exactly what St. Ignatius meant by "love should be put more in deeds than in words" (Spiritual Exercises, 230).

8/   Only those who have had an **"internal understanding of every-thing well-received"** and a full recognition of them, can feel the desire to direct their life so they can "love and serve above all" (Spiritual Exercises, 233). In this way, Ignatian spirituality offers a strong motivation to take action or—more accurately—to guide our lives toward service of others.

9/   In this perspective I invite you to consider our responsibility to other human beings (those similar and different) and to creation. I propose that we place the subject of our social responsibility more in the **logic of love and gratitude** than the logic that comes from duty, obligation, or "accountability."

10/   This is not to undermine the concept of "accountability" as less important. To be "responsible" it is essential to account for and assume the consequences of actions and decisions; in fact, in our educational institutions we are making great efforts so that all—the Rector, the Directors, the different partners, and even students—realize their responsibilities and feel capable of entering into a process of accountability. . . . What I propose is that, in addition to having as a base this dynamic that asks us to respond to those who have been entrusted to us and to maintain full transparency as we exercise our approach, we place ourselves in the dynamics of gratitude and, finally, the recognition of what we have received. Like St. Ignatius, I consider this perspective moves us powerfully toward service, given that it raises a dynamic of loving harmony.

11/   To conclude this initial consideration, I might point out that the experience of gratitude, or thankfulness, is one of the characteristics of one who is animated by Faith. It is the experience of those who know that everything in life is a present or undeserved gift, who know nothing belongs to him, and that everything has been given to him: his life, family, abilities, education, friendships, property, health, etc.

II. RECOGNIZE THE GIFT RECEIVED: "BE MEN AND WOMEN FOR OTHERS AND WITH OTHERS"

12/   The force that moved the work of Ignatius of Loyola after his conversion was gratitude for all he had received. From there was born his desire to serve. The very purpose of the Society of Jesus, structured with a group of similarly-motivated university classmates, was precisely that of "helping neighbors," in the same way that he and his companions had been helped to find the purpose and meaning of their lives. With the founding of the Society, Ignatius wanted to institutionally structure the ideal of service as a way of living, working, and serving God, not just as isolated individuals but with a group of companions.

13/   And, if "love and serve" is the purpose of the Society of Jesus, what else could be expected from their institutions and in particular the schools? That was the reason that moved Ignatius to accept the founding of the schools. He wanted them to be privileged instruments for forming youth, so that they could desire "all in love and service" thanks to knowledge and exercising the virtues acquired there.

14/   Thus, as Jesuits, recognizing what we have received, we yearn to be followers and companions of Jesus, to help others to adopt that same wisdom of life. This explains why, no matter what our ministry, we will always be educators who try to show, with our lives and words, the face of God that Jesus has shown us, manifesting as a source of life, love, and goodness.

15/   This wisdom of life was expressed clearly, in 1973, by Father Pedro Arrupe, addressing the Society's Alumni in his famous speech in Valencia[1], Spain, entitled "Educating for the Promotion of Justice." There, Father Arrupe noted that since its inception, the mission of the Society was to form "agents of change," in society and in the Church, to renew and transform the structures of society that were expressions of sin and embodied unjust relationships.

16/   Arrupe stressed that the promotion of justice was a constitutive element of the Jesuit mission, because for Jesus the genuine love for God is always linked to love of neighbor and from this stems just relationships. Therefore, it follows that our students would train as **"men and women for others,"** i.e., not focused on their "own love, desire or interest" (Spiritual Exercises, 189) but open to others and ready to serve their brothers in need, as part of the promotion of justice.

17/ Since Fr. Arrupe made that call, our schools and our Alumni, through their associations, have changed positively in this regard. Today, 40 years later, education for justice, and its implied social responsibility, has become a hallmark of Jesuit education. Although much has been done in this area, we still need to do more and continue the endeavor; although, indeed, we have come a long way from the resistance to social justice education that we had in the '70s.

18/ At present, most of our schools in the world have serious programs, innovative and creative, to educate for social commitment. Educational institutions of other religious congregations, or even public institutions, benefit from these achievements and often ask for assistance in this area. To cite examples nearby, in Colombia, schools have successfully implemented the program "Training and Social Action" (FAS); *Fe y Alegría*, in Latin America, is implementing the program "Skills for Life"; FLACSI, the Jesuit school network in Latin America, is promoting "Ignatians for Haiti"; all programs that have enabled our students to come into contact with social reality and injustice in a way that was unthinkable before. In other parts of the world they have similar programs and the emphasis on groups and social service experiences have become an essential part of "our way of proceeding" in education. It is interesting to note that as a result, many of our former students have linked with social volunteer programs or NGOs that serve the poor, migrants, displaced persons, and refugees. In this regard, the response of many alumni has been extraordinarily generous.

19/ Deepening the call of Fr. Arrupe, his successor Fr. Peter-Hans Kolvenbach pointed out that our educational tradition urges the formation of men and women who are **competent, conscious,** and **committed** with compassion.[2] That is what in the English Ignatian pedagogy has been called the "3Cs." In Spanish it has been translated as "4Cs": **competent, conscious, compassionate,** and **committed**.[3] Personally I prefer the Spanish version that offers more emphasis on the latter two features.

20/   These four adjectives express the "human excellence" that the Society of Jesus wants for the youth who society has entrusted to us: **competent**, professionally speaking, because they have an academic background that exposes them to advances in science and technology; conscious, because in addition to knowing themselves, thanks to developing their ability to internalize and cultivate a spiritual life, they have a consistent knowledge and experience of society and its imbalances; **compassionate**, because they are able to open their hearts to be in solidarity with and assume the suffering of others; and **committed**, because, being compassionate, they honestly strive toward faith, and through peaceful means, work for social and political transformation of their countries and social structures to achieve justice.

21/   Two years before, Fr. Kolvenbach, explaining who the Jesuits were, correctly added to the assertion of P. Arrupe "for others," the words "**with others**," pointing more fully to the purposes of our spirituality and our education[4]. It is evident that our educational efforts intend not to form students in solitary leadership but in recognition of the other, in the spirit of healthy cohabitation, in teamwork, in collaboration, and in our common labors.

22/   No wonder, then, that in the current global culture in which dominant economic forces emphasize educational models that chiefly favor utilitarianism, the Jesuits continue faithfully their purpose of forming "**men and women for others and with others**."

23/   This approach to education enables young people to access another characteristic of faith. This is that hidden treasure that Jesus showed us: the deep and lasting joy of discovering that by putting life in service to others, or giving it to others, giving up personal or group benefits in order to seek the greater good is not to lose life, but to find it in its fullest sense.

III. THE ISSUES WITH "GLOBALIZATION": THE RESPONSIBILITY FOR GREATER SERVICE

24/   The most recent (35th) General Congregation, as the highest organ of Jesuit government and orientation and aware of the social, cultural, and technological changes we are experiencing globally, emphasized certain aspects of our mission and called for more effective forms of service, consistent with current times. Because of our greater awareness of and deeper appreciation for the benefits and possibilities that exist in today's world, the General Congregation encouraged us to enter into greater communion with humanity and all of God's creation; to keep offering him life in abundance and fullness.

25/   In order to achieve greater effectiveness and impact in international terms, the GC challenged us to take better advantage of the global **potential that exists in our numerous apostolic institutions for building networks**. The expectation is that they can promote projects beyond provincial, national, and continental boundaries. Clearly, besides convenient technologies, this endeavor requires a new thinking and the use of imagination and creativity. We hope that alumni can help us make this possible, as many of you have significant experience in the world of networks and global affairs.

26/   Looking at the complexity of the challenges currently facing humanity, the Society feels called to exercise **greater advocacy in favor of the society's neediest** at key points in economic, political, cultural, and religious life. This, in order to provide a contribution to the process of reconciliation between individuals and communities, as well as in the search for a more harmonious relationship between humanity and the environment.

27/   Our service to reconciliation between human beings corresponds not only to Gospel mandate but to the existence, at the beginning of the third millennium, of a new vision of mankind, with clear awareness of the equal dignity of all human beings, clamoring for **overcoming existing prejudices and exclusions**. Surely the international community still has broad work to do in this area, to establish legal instruments to ensure just and peaceful coexistence among peoples. This vision, however, in our view, remains an unattainable ideal if not formed by minds and hearts capable of understanding the fundamental unity of human beings in their diversity, in close interdependence, and the need to welcome and affirm the other, respecting their diversity.

28/   Today we also feel clearly that humanity is indebted to the **ecological balance of our planet.** We are more aware of the delicate interdependence between humans and nature. The environmental crisis that we perceive affects us all, but certainly affects the poor more severely. Our institutions are aware of the importance of this dimension in educational processes and see the need to act decisively to encourage respect and solidarity with creation. We hope for institutions that are truly "green" because they live in and are in harmony with the environment.

29/   On the other hand, we realize that until now we have educated our students in a local vision of belonging to the school where they have been taught and consequently they have much affection for "their" school and their peers. Nevertheless, in a context like the present in which social networks are multiplying across geographical borders, if we long to offer a better service within the international community, it is necessary to create global citizenship. With it, we want our students to feel capable of intervening in the international arena and to assume the new reality of a world that is built beyond narrow frontiers, where we are all citizens and stewards; a path that provides for the achievement of this proposal belongs in the educational and social networks of the Company or those of alumni working for many humanitarian causes. In this paradigm shift, which our educational institutions are beginning to assume, the World Union of Jesuit Alumni can contribute greatly.

IV. THE VOCATION AND RESPONSIBILITY TO GUARD AND MAKE LIFE GROW

30/   In today's globalized society intelligent and critical information management plays a central role. In such a context, participating or having received a quality education is of incalculable benefit. This is our case. The education that we received has helped us to constructively harness the imagination and develop a mental structure for analysis and discernment to become lifelong learners. **Education has allowed us to develop valuable human capabilities and, whether we want it or not, grants us a certain amount of power and social recognition.**

31/ If this is our case, the experience of gratitude for gifts received thanks to the educational processes requires a look beyond ourselves. We cannot forget that our condition on this planet that is our common home is privileged, for in it there are more than one billion men, women, and children who go to bed hungry every night and have no access to drinking water; that more still have not received primary and secondary or university education and that, unfortunately, we are promoting unbalanced economic growth and competition among nations that stimulates the rapacious exploitation of the planet's resources with a severe deterioration of the environment, generation of violent conflict, and inequitable enjoyment of the goods of creation that benefit very few.

32/ These immense challenges show that something must be done; those who are believers recognize from their faith that this reality does not reflect the will of God, but rather rejects it, and that there exist situations of personal and social sin. Their longing, consequently, will not peacefully transform such situations. They know that for this task men and women of compassion and generosity are required, men and women who use their intelligence, social influence, and creativity to create a community that is international more than dissimilar, more economically stable and environmentally sustainable; that is, they assume with passion this vocation to guard and protect the gift of life in all its amazing diversity.

33/ Before these challenges, on March 19, comes Pope Francis beginning his ministry as successor of St. Peter. On this day, when the Church celebrated the feast of St. Joseph the Father of Jesus and husband of Mary, Pope Francis pointed out to the whole Church and the many world leaders who were present in Rome that the "vocation of caring" for life is a mission that concerns not only believers but "is a dimension that precedes" the option of faith because "it is simply human" because life "belongs to everyone," in particular to those who exercise the power of nations. Indeed, when talking about his new responsibility, Pope Francis said that Jesus granted Peter with a certain power, but said that the **true power is, above all, service,** and this culminated on the cross, that is, the gift of Himself.

34/   According to these words, **the honest vocation and legitimate source of all power,** whatever it may be, **is to preserve, protect, and serve life.** It is the call present in every conscience to always be "careful of and attentive to" human life, starting with those who are most threatened or fragile, but also other forms of life present in nature.

35/   This task, according to Pope's thought, requires above all self-care, i.e., feelings that inhabit one's heart where "good and bad intentions emerge; those that build and destroy."[5] But, above all, it requires kindness, even tenderness, which is defined not as a virtue of the weak, but rather as a sign of fortitude, compassion, openness to the other and to love.

V. QUALITY EDUCATION FOR ALL: PATH TO JUSTICE AND PEACE IN THE WORLD

36/   In line with the call of Pope Francis to everyone who possesses a bit of power and therefore has the opportunity to contribute to the growth of humanity, this past July 12, before the UN Assembly full of world leaders, Malala Yousafzai, a 16-year-old Pakistani woman who in October 2012 was the victim of an attack by a Taliban group opposed to education, delivered a rousing speech. She concluded, solemnly, "a child, a teacher, a book, a pencil, can change the world. *Education is the only solution*"[6] against the many discriminations, exclusions, and wars that affect millions of human beings. In her view, "books and pencils are our most powerful weapons." By that she asks all leaders of great nations to invest in schools, books, and teachers to ensure universal primary education, so that by 2015, she proposes, this Millennial Goal can be achieved.

37/   It is probable, in working for this goal, that many countries will come forward with efforts to extend educational coverage. We, as a Society, have given support to this dynamic that invites governments to allocate more in their budgets for education, but it is equally true that we Jesuits feel called to work not only by extension but by offering a quality education for the poor.

38/   Thus, Jesuit education has intensified its work with the poor and marginalized throughout the world to provide quality education. Networks such as *Fe y Alegría* in Latin America, schools for Adivasis (indigenous) and Dalits in India, the education offered by the Jesuit Refugee Service and the network of Cristo Rey and Nativity schools in the United States, along with many other efforts, are creative responses to the challenge of providing quality education to the poor, as offered in our traditional schools. We can say today that the number of disadvantaged students who are educated in the Society exceeds that of those from our more traditional schools. Even many alumni of these schools have contributed significantly so that these new ventures are successful, or they themselves, through their associations, have sought to contribute to these processes of education for the poor.

39/   This contribution, however, is but a "drop" in the ocean. There are hundreds of million children and young people in the world who require more years of schooling. This means extending the educational network, but above all it requires a quality education, from the most diverse inspirations and pedagogies to make them competent, conscientious, committed, and compassionate, so that they can be "men and women with others and for others" in the various social, cultural, and religious contexts of our world. Indeed, the road to justice, solidarity, reconciliation, and peace in the world will be passable only to the extent that all can be offered this opportunity.

VI. RESPONDING TO THE GIFT: AN EFFORT TOWARD QUALITY EDUCATION FOR ALL

40/   Knowing that this 8th World Congress of alumni will offer a clear understanding of the gift received through the educational process, I invite you to make it bear fruit, not just as an exclusive benefit for achieving personal interests, but as a gift that transforms into work and commitment to youth around the world suffering the humiliation of exclusion.

41/   St. Ignatius sent a letter to Philip II, king of Spain, in favor of education in which he said that "**all the well-being of Christianity and of the whole world depends on the proper education of youth.**"[7] At that time only a small minority received education. Today, on the contrary, as we have seen, all of humanity requires education and one who is excluded from it is condemned to poverty and discrimination and often pushed to crime.

42/   So today we are all part of "the Ignatian family" because we are beneficiaries of that spirituality and pedagogy; we feel called to deepen and continue to offer quality education in our schools, colleges, and universities. But, given that in a global context our institutions will always be a numerically small minority, we are called to strengthen international awareness of the need for quality education for all, since it is a right of all human beings and, therefore, a requirement for public policy regarding education.

43/   For this reason, the Society of Jesus is encouraging among its colleagues, benefactors, and friends, the development of an international network for **the right of all people to a quality education**. In this vein, the network has developed a document which I invite you to get to know and reflect on to assist in its action, as it requires the combined efforts of all society.[8]

44/   I am convinced that you, as Jesuit Alumni, not just as individuals but as associations in each of the countries where you are present, are likely to influence such policies for states, each for their own or allied with each other, to give priority to the implementation of this fundamental right, thereby achieving a fundamental step for the exercise and respect of others' rights.

45/   Since quality education provides not only knowledge but values, it can achieve the ideas that Malala, the brave young Pakistani, has proposed to the UN leaders, but also go far beyond, advancing toward overcoming any exclusion and discrimination based on gender, nation, race, religion, or socioeconomic status.

46/ You are at the heart of the world, working in various social institutions, private or public, who daily exercise social responsibility in decisions and analysis at home, in the professional world, or on the ground with public tasks or policies. I propose, therefore, that one of the conclusions of the 8th Congress is the conviction expressed by St. Ignatius that the good of the world and the meaning of the message and Christian experience "depends on the proper education of youth" and, as a result, that **along with the Society of Jesus, you also assume the** purpose **of generating a broad global awareness for quality education for all.**

VII. CONCLUSION: BELIEVERS ARE RESPONSIBLE FOR THEMSELVES, FOR THE HUMAN COMMUNITY, AND CREATION

47/ The deaths of Fabio Tobon and Tom Bausch remind us of the simple fact of our lives: our existence in this world is temporary. Their departures, which we too will experience, make us wonder about our origins, about our destiny, and the path we take during this movement in space and time that makes up our lives. No doubt there are many questions and concerns that are placed on our intelligence. According to the recent encyclical *Lumen Fidei*, issued by Pope Francis, "The light of faith doesn't dispel all our darkness, but as a lamp, it guides our steps in the night, and that is good enough for walking" (n. 57).

48/ Who owns this "lamp" knows he is on the road and moves towards a fullness that awaits him and that is his future. He also knows that all he has received is an undeserved gift: life, health or sickness, wealth or poverty, triumphs or failures. All of this comes from the loving grace of God, who is near, present, and active in the world. To know and experience God's call, in the deepest conscience of every human being, believer or not, moving him toward compassion and goodness; know that this drives all of us to be "responsible" for life, to become "neighbors" or "guardians" of our brothers and creation. To be full of gratitude for this kind and discreet presence of God in our lives and in the life of the world, a God who doesn't interfere with free will, but desires that we not be deaf to his call and that we answer with generosity.

49/   On the other hand, far from the longing for a past that was better and looking upon this culture with pessimism and distrust for changes being made, we examine the changes to discern how the presence of God is in them. The desire is to encounter the signs of such life-giving presence and join with them. Therefore one cannot be indifferent to the reality that surrounds him. One feels the responsibility to discern what is inside himself, in society and the world, to grow human beings with inalienable human dignity and communion among themselves. Such was the vision, for example, of many Jesuit missionaries and educators, such as Matteo Ricci in China, who understood that God was already working in that ancient culture and that God had come here before Ricci and the Church.

50/   It is reasonable then that faith is understood and lived as double experience of encounter. Above all, with Him who is the source and destination of life, who assumed human form in Jesus of Nazareth, the personal dialogue with this "inner teacher" that respectfully guides the sacred precincts of consciousness, provides the light that helps us understand "the way, truth and life." And this deep experience to become a disciple, far from leading to individualism or spiritual solipsism, leads to another experience of encounter, or communion, with others living the same experience in the Church. In this ecclesial community, despite the limitations and institutional opacities that come from entire human condition, through the faith handed down from generation to generation, signs and symbols give the possibility of renewing and nourishing the evangelical experience.

51/   Finally, whoever directs his way toward the light of faith is inhabited by the challenging longing and unattainable utopia of ensuring the full sovereignty of God and his goodness, above all, in himself, but also in other human beings and their communities, so that, day by day, he renews his personal willingness to take responsibility for others and therefore to serve and to work towards the dream that animated Jesus to reach a new earth and a new heaven where "there will be no more death, nor sorrow, nor complaint, nor pain" (Revelation 21:4).

Thank you very much.

Adolfo Nicolás, S.J.
Superior General of the Society of Jesus
Medellín, August 15, 2013
On the Feast of the Assumption of Mary,
Educator of Jesus and the Church

---

[1] Arrupe, Pedro, *Education for the Promotion of Justice*. To the Jesuit Alumni of Europe. Valencia. 1973, in "La Iglesia de hoy y del futuro." Ediciones Mensajero y Sal Terrae. España, pp. 347–359. This document is included in Part 4 of this book.

[2] English version at http://www.sjweb.info/documents/education/PHK_pedagogy_en.pdf, Kolvenbach, PH., Letter presenting the document, "Ignatian Pedagogy: A Practical Approach" 1993.

[3] Cf. Spanish version http://www.sjweb.info/documents/education/pedagogy_sp.pdf, in particular, #19: "If truly successful, Jesuit education results ultimately in a radical transformation not only of the way in which people habitually think and act, but of the very way in which they live in the world, men and women of competence, conscience and compassion, seeking the greater good in terms of what can be done out of a faith commitment with justice to enhance the quality of peoples' lives, particularly among God's poor, oppressed, and neglected."

[4] Cf. Kolvenbach, P.H., *To friends and colleagues of the Society of Jesus*, 1991.

[5] March 19, 2013: Holy Mass of the Inauguration of the Pontificate, http://www.vatican.va/holy_father/francesco/homilies/2013/index_en.htm.

[6] "Malala Yousafzai Addresses United Nations Youth Assembly" You Tube video, 17.42, Education activist Malala Yousafzai marks her 16th birthday, on Friday, 12 July 2013 at the United Nations by giving her first high-level public appearance and statement on the importance of education. Posted by United Nations, July 12, 2013, http://www.youtube.com/watch?v=QRh_30C8I6Y

[7] Cf. Kolvenbach, P.H. "Selected Writings, 1983–1990." Edited, Spanish Province of the Society of Jesus. Arts Press, 1992. Page 453. Regardless, John W. O'Malley in his book "The First Jesuits" (Harvard University Press, 1993, p. 209) reports this letter was written by Pedro de Ribadeneira, S.J., on behalf of St. Ignatius, which would make him the author of this famous phrase.

[8] *Promotio Iustitiae*, n. 110, published by the Secretariat of Social Justice and Ecology, in the Curia General of the Society of Jesus. http://www.sjweb.info/sjs/documents/PJ_110_ENG.pdf

Jesuit Education—Our Commitment
to Global Networking, 2012

Vision Statement of the International Colloquium
on Jesuit Secondary Education. 2012. Boston.

Editor's Introduction: More than 450 participants from all the Jesuit regions of the world came together for the International Colloquium on Jesuit Secondary Education (ICJSE), organized by Boston College High School. The vision statement presented here captures very well the significance and importance of this meeting. It triggered a renewed interest in Jesuit education and presented a path to answer General Congregation 35 and Fr. Nicolás's calls for a "universal body with a universal mission."

1/ From July 29 through August 2, 2012, for the first time in the history of the Society of Jesus, with the encouragement of Father General, and under the guidance of the International Commission on the Apostolate of Jesuit Education, the leaders of our secondary schools from around the world assembled in Boston, Massachusetts, U.S.A. Their goal was to strengthen our global network by providing a venue to share ideas and resources and to discuss their strengths and challenges in the light of our Jesuit mission and identity as expressed in the documents from the Thirty-fifth General Congregation of the Society of Jesus.

2/ At the conclusion of the meeting, the delegates are convinced that the new "signs of the times" warrant a change in our way of proceeding. This new way of proceeding includes on-going communication and collaboration through a continued development of our international network of schools. The goals of our collaboration will be to better serve the faith, justice, and care for the environment, to build bridges between youth and their faith communities, to develop stronger Jesuit/Ignatian Apostolic communities, and to provide our students with opportunities for a truly global education.

3/ Our international network of schools is uniquely suited to educate global citizens who will be able to participate in a globalization of solidarity, cooperation, and reconciliation that fully respects human life and dignity and all of God's creation. Our commitment to networking as a universal body, and our call to the frontiers, comes from our awareness of the world and our desire to effectively help students face global challenges.

4/   We are committed to:

1. Developing our truly unique global community and network: Our ability to respect and participate in our own situation, and yet be mindful of our universal identity and mission as Jesuit schools, is one of our greatest resources and unparalleled in the world.

2. Working with our established local and regional networks: While remaining committed to our regional priorities, we will at the same time focus on the importance of nurturing global relationships within the Jesuit network and other networks of secondary schools.

3. Using technology as a way to create, develop, and foster our global relationships: We recognize that the physical distance that has historically formed significant obstacles to our communication still exists, but that it should no longer prohibit global communication and collaboration. We will provide opportunities for our students and staff to experience the world from a vantage point made possible by the vast reach of our network.

4. Developing twinning relationships, service outreach programs, virtual classroom experiences, and more, to provide students with experiences that truly prepare them to become leaders in the transformation of the world.

5. Providing a safe educational environment based on respect and dignity. This environment, conducive to learning, growing, and developing, will be free of all forms of abuse.

5/   Derived from our commitments, we leave this meeting with the following suggested actions:

1. The momentum of the International Colloquium on Jesuit Secondary Education impels us to develop new and creative collaborative efforts amongst the global network of Jesuit secondary schools. These new

efforts will fall under the leadership of the Secretariat of Secondary and Pre-Secondary Education and the International Commission on the Apostolate of Jesuit Education (ICJSE).

2. The Jesuit secondary schools represented at the ICJSE recognize the importance of assigning a member of its leadership team the responsibility of facilitating global collaboration and outreach to the global network. These representatives will work with already existing networks and structures to ensure that the efforts started at the ICJSE continue.

3. We recommend that the ICJSE newsletter and web page continue as a forum for global communication, collaboration, and networking. This newsletter will ensure that our global network has a specific avenue to regularly communicate, share network initiatives, express desires for collaboration, and engage in conversation and share resources.

4. We recommend that this Colloquium experience should be continued in the future, and that plans should be made for the next colloquium to take place in 2016 or 2017 at a time and place to be determined.

International Seminar on Ignatian Pedagogy and Spirituality (SIPEI)

Vision Statement. 2014. Manresa, Spain.

Editor's Introduction: The Seminar on Ignatian Pedagogy and Spirituality (**SIPEI**) gathered in Manresa, Spain, in 2014. The seminar was a fruitful discussion of the interaction of Ignatian pedagogy and spirituality and deepened the understanding of Jesuit education through the discussion of the "4 Cs"—competence, conscience, compassion, and commitment—first used by Fr. Kolvenbach and then explained by Fr. Nicolás. The SIPEI made clear the conviction that a "deep change is required in our schools" at the pedagogical level, which has not followed the necessary path of renewal that other aspects of the schools have enjoyed since Fr. Arrupe's strong call for renewal. The SIPEI also made clear that networking, at all levels, is now the ordinary way of proceeding for our schools.

"What New Kind of Life Is This Upon Which I Am Entering?" —Ignatius of Loyola, Manresa

1/ From November 2–8, 2014, 80 participants from the six Jesuit regions of the world came together in Manresa, convened by the Secretary of Education of the Society of Jesus. They were joined by over 4,000 participants via social networks and live streaming, representing all corners of our vast Jesuit network of schools.

2/ They met with the following objectives in mind:

3/ **I. To facilitate dialogue between those dedicated to the educational apostolate and those dedicated to Ignatian** Spirituality **within the tradition of the Society of Jesus.**

4/ **II. To encourage dialogue among some of the most significant contemporary educational trends, Ignatian** pedagogy, **and spirituality.**

5/   III. To contribute to the pedagogical renewal of Jesuit Education within the framework of the construction of a global network of Jesuit secondary **and pre-secondary educational institutions.**

6/   Throughout the world, education is at a crossroads as a result of the extraordinary societal changes stemming from globalization, the widening gap between the rich and the poor, technological developments, changes in families, and new quests for peace and equality.

7/   During five days of deep conversation around the meaning of forming a person of conscience, competence, compassion, and commitment as the general framework for our education, we feel the power of our challenges and the need to continue the path of renewal that gets us closer to our dream of being persons for others and with others. We are aware of the immensity of our task and the many tensions that this implies for our schools and for us as educators. We feel humbled by a work that seems greater than our capacities and filled with insurmountable obstacles because of their complexities and our limitations. However, inspired by our spiritual experience, deepened during these days in a place that speaks about Ignatius's own struggles to trust God as his ultimate strength and inspiration, we hear again the words of the Gospel: DO NOT FEAR. Trusting in God we renew our commitment to provide an educational experience that can transform our students, ourselves, and our school communities as places where the dream of the Gospel can be seen and experienced.

8/   Thus we are convinced that a deep change is required in our schools. Genuine discernment, at the core of our spirituality, will guide us through it. We have also experienced the immense possibilities that thinking, working, and dreaming together as a global network open for us. We want to take seriously the General Congregation (GC) 35, D.2 N.20, call to *"serv[e] Christ's mission today means paying special attention to its global context. This context requires us to act as a universal body with a universal mission, realizing at the same time the radical diversity of our situations. It is as a worldwide* *community—and, simultaneously, as a network of local communities—that we seek to serve others across the world."*

9/   In 1993, Fr. General Peter-Hans Kolvenbach summarized our goal as educators to be the formation of "men and women of competence, conscience, and compassionate commitment." We believe this formation must be understood within the framework of the creativity, flexibility, and network-wide action that define our times. We are convinced that human growth and spiritual growth are inseparably intertwined. The following summaries were produced at SIPEI:

10/   **I. The Person of Conscience**—The formation of the conscience to distinguish and discern between good and bad, right and wrong is necessary for the welfare of the individual and society. This formation of conscience is influenced and affected by the totality of a person's surrounding. Jesuit Education aims to form free persons of conscience who utilize their personal consciences to make a difference in the world.

11/   **II. The Person of Competence**—The person of competence is capable of creating, understanding, and using knowledge and skills to live in his/her own context and transform it; is able to be part of the changing and diverse world creating a life project for others and with others; and is able to develop the intellectual, academic, emotional, and social skills required for professional and human achievement. We are committed to renewing our pedagogical practices, curriculum, and school environments according to the new pedagogical developments that allow our schools to be closer to our Ignatian vision and to our eclectic tradition of combining the best practices to serve our mission.

12/   **III. The Person of Compassion**—Compassion does not imply simply feeling sorry for someone or a group of people. Anyone can feel sympathetic but do nothing. Compassion is a prerequisite to positive action; it recognizes human dignity, a person's worth that stems simply and profoundly from being loved by God. Compassion, leading to solidarity, should compel us to address the structures of any institution so that we and our students can become agents of change in order to go on dreaming God's dream.

13/   IV. The Person of Commitment—A person of commitment is one of courageous action. Through our openness to the guidance of the Spirit and companionship with Jesus, he or she will be able to discern the urgent needs of our time, so that our ways of serving will be as rich and deep as our ways of loving. We realize that an ecological commitment to the reconciliation and healing of the earth, hand in hand with the commitment for social justice are urgent needs as they affect all persons everywhere on the earth.

14/   SIPEI members were fully aware that the major challenges to educational transformation in our century demand a systemic point of view; they also require that we act in all areas of our school environment: our methodology, the organization of our schools and classrooms, and the academic curriculum.

15/   The deliberations of SIPEI members concluded that our schools should commit to:

16/   I. Profound transformation and change in order to answer the challenges of the 21st century in the spirit of "ever searching for the magis" (GC 34).

17/   II. Connecting the objectives of the formation of the Ignatian individual (a person of conscience, competence, and compassionate commitment) with the changing and challenging characteristics of our century: globalization, diversity, inclusiveness, personal autonomy, and networking.

18/   III. Continuing to examine, expand, and understand, in new, vibrant ways, the relationship between Ignatian spirituality and the new pedagogy we consider to be necessary for our schools.

19/   IV. Refusing to allow fear to hinder or detour important, necessary change.

20/   V. Promoting and fostering experiences and activities of growth in spirituality for students, educators, and families as part of the foundation of our schools.

21/   VI. Strengthening our commitment to justice through specific gestures and actions in order to enter into solidarity with the less fortunate in our local, regional, and global communities.

22/   VIII. Taking firm steps toward collaborating as a worldwide network of Jesuit schools, in keeping with the commitments of the ICJSE in Boston.

23/   With these commitments in mind, we recommend the following actions, which will help us drive pedagogical renovation as a global network:

24/   I. Commit, as schools, to the local and global network in order to encourage a process of diagnosis and reflection that will bring on profound, global changes to our learning and teaching environments.

25/   II. Incorporate a social action program, focusing on solidarity with others, into the pedagogical programs and the foundations of our schools.

26/   III. Support, embrace, and become members of the Educate Magis community as a global platform for connecting, collaborating, and transforming our worldwide network of schools.

27/   IV. Continue the initiatives of the SIPEI through the continued creation of new regional and worldwide events, in the vein of the ICJSE (International Colloquium on Jesuit Secondary Education, Boston 2012), which assume the commitments of both events.

28/   "Love is shown more in deeds than in words."

Manresa, November 7, 2014

Jesuit Education Aims to Human Excellence: Men and Women of Conscience, Competence, Compassion, and Commitment

Secretariat for Education, Society of Jesus. 2015. Rome.

1/ In 1973 Fr. Arrupe wrote that "today our prime educational objective must be to form *men-for-others*: men who will live not for themselves but for God and his Christ" (Men for Others, Valencia, 1973). "**Men and women for others and with others**" is considered a contemporary expression of the humanism that Jesuit education has embraced from the beginning. It captures, in a nutshell, the ultimate goal of our educational efforts and our current emphasis in a faith *that does justice.*

2/ Twenty years later, in 1993 Fr. Kolvenbach, commenting on the publication of the document *Ignatian Pedagogy: A Practical Approach,* ratified Arrupe's formulation and expanded its meaning, stating that "our goal as educators [is] to form *men and women of competence, conscience, and compassionate commitment*" (*Letter Regarding the Ignatian Pedagogical Paradigm,* Rome, 1993). These four Cs have also inspired the renewal of Jesuit education in the last two decades. Many of our schools have used the four Cs as a way to explain our vision of educating the whole person. The four Cs capture the true meaning of excellence as explained by Fr. Kolvenbach: "maximum development of the gifts and capacities with which each person is endowed . . . for the deployment of [them] in the best possible service of others." (*Contemporary Education in the Spirit of Saint Ignatius,* Toulouse-Purpan, November 26, 1996)

3/ Lately, Fr. Nicolás has unpacked the meaning of the four Cs and their contribution to the vision of the human excellence we offer to our students: "These four adjectives express the '**human excellence**' that the Society of Jesus wants for the youth who society has entrusted to us:

4/ **Conscience,** because in addition to knowing themselves thanks to developing their ability to internalize and cultivate a spiritual life, they have a consistent knowledge and experience of society and its imbalances.

5/ **Competent**, professionally speaking, because they have an academic background that exposes them to advances in science and technology.

6/ **Compassionate**, because they are able to open their hearts to be in solidarity with and assume the suffering of others.

7/ **Committed**, because, being compassionate, they honestly strive toward faith and, through peaceful means, work for social and political transformation of their countries and social structures to achieve justice." (*Jesuit Alumni and Their Social Responsibility: The Quest for a Better Future for Humanity. What Does It Mean to Be a Believer Today?* Medellín, 2013.)

8/ The **SIPEI** (International Seminar on Ignatian Pedagogy and Spirituality)—celebrated in Manresa, Spain, in 2014—**focused on the four Cs as the pillars and background for Jesuit Education**, thus the seminar provided a unique opportunity to discuss, in depth, the meaning of each one of the four Cs and their implications for defining Jesuit/Ignatian education/pedagogy today. The Secretariat for Education wants to offer a short reflection on each of the four Cs, based on the discussions during SIPEI, with the hope that our schools can find them useful in their ongoing efforts to renew and, at the same time, they can help them maintain **our tradition of creative fidelity.**

THE PERSON OF CONSCIENCE

9/ In his speech to the *Congress World Union of Jesuit Alumni(ae)* in Medellín, Colombia, on August 15th, 2013, Father Adolfo Nicolás defined the person of conscience we want to form in our schools as "**an individual who, besides knowing himself**, thanks to the development of his capacity for internalization and his cultivation of spirituality, **has a significant knowledge and experience of society and its imbalances.**"

10/ At the SIPEI (International Seminar on Ignatian Pedagogy and Spirituality)—held in Manresa in the Sanctuary of the Manresa Cave from November 3rd to 7th, 2014—Jesuit representatives of the entire Society of Jesus reflected on this trait and its importance in this moment in history.

11/   From its beginning, the Society has participated in education, striving to ensure that all students were exposed to

a) eruditio: the acquisition of knowledge (not erudition!)

b) **pietas**: the formation of an individual's moral and personal character in the service of the common good (not pity!)

12/   Within this task of forming a good character, the formation of a conscience is of great importance. Keeping in mind that a **conscience is "an individual's intrinsic ability to discern the rightness and goodness of their own actions"** (George Nedumattam, S.J., in *The Conscious Person;* SIPEI, Manresa, March 2014), we affirm that this conscience can be educated.

13/   In this education, **profound work on our spirituality will be extremely useful.** We should feel inhabited and accompanied by God the Father, who sends us his Spirit to help us discover and discern our life's paths, following the example of Jesus of Nazareth.

14/   The Ignatian Examen (Spiritual Exercises; Ignatius of Loyola, #43) is a great tool for rediscovery and exercise and it offers us clues to choose what most helps to make this world the kind of world God wants: a world of fellowship, where no one is in need. We'll learn that each of us has the possibility of doing our part for this objective every day.

15/   The person of conscience will feel called to look at the world, at reality, with the eyes of God; to discover the goodness and beauty of creation and individuals but also places of pain, misery, and injustice. From this contemplation will come thankfulness for all the goodness received, and from this thankfulness, the desire to dedicate oneself to being an agent of change.

16/   In this age we've been chosen to live in, **we need to take care of the time in our curricula allocated to looking at the world and helping to move affections;** the time we dedicate to accompanying actions that might arise in our students and the proposal of models that, from our position of educators, we can make them witness and present to them.

17/   All of this will help our students develop their life projects; it will help them have a life horizon; it will illuminate their choices in study, work, family, social commitment . . .

18/   In order to achieve all of this, **in our educational task we have to promote the creativity we need in order to propose new learning models**, which can lead us to a greater and better understanding of reality, to analyze it and look for ways to contribute to the generation of new personal habits, new forms of organization, and happiness and justice for all. These are models that will generate a better society, according to God's dream.

19/   By doing so, we will remain loyal to our mission, and the existence of the Jesuit schools will be justified and will have a purpose.

THE COMPETENT PERSON

20/   "**Competent**, professionally speaking, because they have an academic background that exposes them to advances in science and technology." (Fr. Nicolás, Medellín, 2013)

21/   As Fr. General Nicolás points out, the four Cs manifest the **human excellence** we want to share with our students. All of the four Cs must be considered together although each one refers to a specific dimension of our educational vision. In the case of the **competent person,** it refers to the traditional academic dimension that leads to solid knowledge, to an adequate development of skills and abilities to reach an effective/satisfactory professional performance that can contribute to human fulfillment. "**Competent students are able to interact with reality;** they are the ones who have learned to be amazed, to ask questions and to be able to understand and resolve problems . . . so they are the ones who learn for life." (Montserrat del Pozo, *The Competent Person*, SIPEI, 2014). Thus, in the Ignatian vision it is not possible to be a person of competence without interacting with the world as it is and as it should be . . . a competent person must engage the world to learn from it and, at the same time, transform it.

22/   The SIPEI vision statement defines the **competent person as someone who is "capable of creating, understanding and using knowledge and skills to live in his/her own context and transform it**; able to be part of the changing and diverse world creating a life project for others and with others; and able to develop the intellectual, academic, emotional, and social skills required for professional and human achievement." (SIPEI Vision Statement)

23/   As the SIPEI vision statement points out, preparing competent students means that **Ignatian education commits to a process of continuing pedagogical renewal** that helps students to reach a satisfactory command of knowledge and skills. This is certainly a **student-centered approach**. This ongoing process of renewal, faithful to our tradition, must be able to incorporate new pedagogical practices that suit our vision better. Certainly, preparing competent persons today also requires not only the renewal of our pedagogies but the renewal of our classroom environments, school organization, and the curriculum (to the point each nation's legislation allows) so that **the manner we educate can be consistent with our vision,** the 21st century requirements, and **our eclectic tradition of combining the best practices to serve our mission.** The **IPP** (Ignatian Pedagogical Paradigm) provides the *style* for any such change, but the IPP requires, instead of replacing, the incorporation of current pedagogies and methodologies that can implement the sort of renewal we need in our schools.

24/   Thus, in today's educational context, educating competent students requires a school that is able to adapt to the students' individual-cultural-social differences and find the best ways to accompany them in their development. Of course, this entails, on the part of students, **their willingness and commitment to their education.** It also requires **an educator conceived as a facilitator-guide-tutor-coach** and not the teacher-centered education of the past.

25/ It is important to stress that a competent student, in the context of the human excellence, is well aware that **being competent means being able to work and flourish with others** and that the competitive character of some of the contemporary pedagogical styles is actually a hindrance to the competence we have been describing.

THE COMPASSIONATE PERSON

26/ "**Compassionate,** because they're capable of opening their hearts in solidarity and taking on the suffering others experience" (F. Nicolás, Medellín, 2013).

27/ **The compassionate person is capable of evolving from feelings of charity and compassion towards a sense of justice and solidarity,** which favors their contribution to changing the unjust social structures of the world they live in.

28/ **Ignatian pedagogy combines processes of reflection and an active stance against injustice and the pain of others** through the classical curriculum presented in the IPP (Ignatian Pedagogical Paradigm), made up of Experience, Reflection, and Action. Compassion doesn't just mean feeling sorry for an individual or group of individuals. **Compassion is a prerequisite for positive action. It involves recognizing human dignity and the value of the person** who, just for having been born, is deeply loved by God.

29/ Jesuit education promotes experiences that encourage students to put themselves in their fellows' shoes, of the marginalized. **Our educational reference for the compassionate person is the figure of Jesus in his most human form: understanding of our weaknesses, but steadfast in denouncing injustice.**

30/ Father Peter-Hans Kolvenbach (*La Pedagogía Ignaciana: un planteamiento práctico,* Villa Cavalletti, 1993) and Father Adolfo Nicolás have encouraged, in numerous texts, reflection on Jesuit education in order to promote compassionate individuals in the context of the globalization that has dominated the world since the end of the 20th century. It becomes necessary for Ignatian pedagogy to update the education of an individual "capable of compassion," because the **globalization of solidarity certainly needs us not only to be on the bounds of universality, but also to live on the bounds of profoundness**" (Margenat, J., *Competentes, conscientes, compasivos y comprometidos*, PPC, 2010). It's not enough to be conscious of the reality of injustice and violence in the world; **we need to educate in commitment to collaborate in the transformation of these realities.** It's the Social Humanism P. Kolvenbach describes as **the specific translation of Jesuit humanism, challenging Christian humanism in our time**.

31/   In the words of Father Peter McVerry (*The Compassionate Person*, SIPEI, 2014), "first, we have to offer our students the opportunity for an intensive experience of being with the poor." He adds that "experience on its own is a necessary, but not sufficient, condition for creating students who are compassionate. That experience must be reflected upon within the school context. A structured reflection, supported by the school, is critical." The challenge of Jesuit education is centered on the creation of a compassionate school context.

32/   Compassion that leads to solidarity should move us to shake the structures of our schools, so that our educators and students can become agents of change and collaborate with God's dream.

THE COMMITTED PERSON

33/   "Committed, because, being compassionate, they honestly strive toward faith and, through peaceful means, work for social and political transformation** of their countries and social structures to achieve justice" (Fr. Nicolás, Medellín, 2013).

34/   As Fr. General clearly illustrates, being committed is inseparably tied to being compassionate.

35/   The **SIPEI vision statement** defines the committed person as, *"A person of commitment is one of courageous action.* Through our openness to the guidance of the Spirit and companionship with Jesus, he or she will be *able to discern the urgent needs of our time, so that our ways of serving will be as rich and deep as our ways of loving. We realize that an Ecological commitment to the reconciliation and healing of the earth, hand in hand with the commitment for social justice, are urgent needs as they affect all persons everywhere on the earth.*"

36/   Fr. Carver identified our need for a substantive commitment to the environment as an **"urgent need of our time"** (*Committed Person*, SIPEI, Manresa, 2014). The SIPEI appropriately reminded that as a global network, Jesuit schools have yet to fully embrace this particular call of past General Congregations with a response that reflects the attention it so deserves; **a call that requires our schools to work more and more as a global network to respond to a challenge that is really global in its roots, impact, and solution**. Caring for the environment will compel our school communities to work closely and globally.

37/   This essential commitment to ecology cannot be seen as weakening or replacing the **service of a faith that does justice**, but, on the contrary, it has to be seen as an integral part of this service.

38/   The education of the committed person according to the Ignatian perspective will require our schools to provide students with **transformative experiences to help them form expansive hearts and minds, real persons of** solidarity with all those in suffering, disadvantage, or oppression. These experiences, informed by the values of the Gospels, should call Jesuit/Ignatian schools to a deep reflection on how we educate, why we educate, and the importance of creating and sustaining educational structures, curricula, and environments that embody the kind of commitment we want to see in our alumni/ae: **we need to educate by example . . .**

BIBLIOGRAPHY

Arrupe, Pedro. *Our Secondary Schools: Today and Tomorrow.* Rome: IHSI, 1980.

————. *Promotion of Justice and Education for Justice.* Rome: IHSI, 1973.

Biblioteca Instituti Historicum Societatis Iesu. *The Characteristics of Jesuit Education.* Rome, 1986.

————. *Ignatian Pedagogy: A Practical Approach.* Rome, 1993.

Codina, Gabriel. "'Our way of Proceeding' in Education: The *Ratio Studiorum.*" *Educatio S.J.* 1 (May 1999): 1–15.

Codina, Gabriel. "Pedagogia Ignaciana [Ignatian Pedagogy]." In *Diccionario de Espiritualidad Ignaciana,* Edited by José García de Castro, 2 vols. [Original in Spanish.] Bilbao: Ediciones Mensajero, 2007.

Coll, Miguel, S.J. "The Beginnings of the New Society." *Jesuits: Yearbook of the Society of Jesus,* 2014: 65–68.

International Colloquium on Jesuit Secondary Education. *Jesuit Education—Our Commitment to Global Networking.* Boston, 2012.

International Seminar on Ignatian Pedagogy and Spirituality (SIPEI). Vision Statement, 2014.

Kolvenbach, Peter Hans. "Características Actuales de la Educación de la Compañía de Jesús." ["Current Characteristics of Education in the Society of Jesus"] Speech given on the occasion of the 75th Anniversary of the San Ignacio School. [Original in Spanish.]

————. "The Service of Faith and the Promotion of Justice in American Jesuit Higher Education." The Santa Clara Lecture. Santa Clara: Santa Clara University, 6 Oct. 2000.

————. "The Jesuit University in the Light of the Ignatian Charism." Address to the International Meeting of Jesuit Higher Education, Rome (Monte Cucco), May 27, 2001.

————. Address to the Georgetown University Board of Directors. Given at the Pontifical Gregorian University, Rome, May 10, 2007.

Ledesma, Diego. "Constitutio seu disposition et ordo septem classium grammatices, humanitatis et rhetorices" ["Constitution or Arrangement

and Order of the Seven Classes of Grammar, Humanities and Rhetoric"].
In *Monumenta paedagogica Societatis Jesu,* vol. 2, edited by Lazlo Lukács
[original in Latin], Rome: IHSI, 1974.

Nadal, Jerónimo. *Pláticas Espirituales del P. Jerónimo Nadal S.I. en Coimbra.*
Edited by Miguel Nicolau, S.J. [original in Spanish]. Granada: Facultad
Teológica de la Compañía de Jesús, 1945.

Nicolás, Adlofo. "Depth, Universality, and Learned Ministry: Challenges
to Jesuit Higher Education Today." Remarks for "Networking Jesuit
Higher Education: Shaping the Future for a Humane, Just, Sustainable
Globe," Mexico City, April 23, 2010.

———. Jesuit Alumni and Their Social Responsibility: The Quest for
a Better Future for Humanity. What Does It Mean to Be a Believer
Today? Address in Medellin, 2013.

O'Malley, John, S.J. "The Schools." Chapter 6 in *The First Jesuits.*
Cambridge, MA: Harvard University Press, 1993.

Mesa, José. "The International Apostolate of Jesuit Education: Recent
Developments and Contemporary Challenges." *International Studies in
Catholic Education* 5, no. 2 (2013): 176–189. http://www.tandfonline.
com/doi/full/10.1080/19422539.2013.821339

Padberg, John W., S.J., ed. *For Matters of Greater Moment: The First Thirty
Jesuit General Congregations: A Brief History and a Translation of the
Decrees.* Boston: Institute for Advanced Jesuit Studies, 1994.

———. *Jesuit Life & Mission Today: The Decrees & Accompanying
Documents of the 31st–35th General Congregations of the Society of Jesus.*
Boston: Institute for Advanced Jesuit Studies, 2009.

———. "Perpetually Abolished, Entirely Extinguished: The Society of
Jesus Suppressed," *Conversations on Jesuit Higher Education* 45 (Spring
2014): 2–4.

———. *The Constitutions of the Society of Jesus and Their Complementary
Norms: A Complete English Translation of Official Latin Texts,* especially
Part IV and Part VII. Boston: Institute for Advanced Jesuit Studies,
1996.

Pavur, Claude, S.J., trans. *The Ratio Studiorum: The Official Plan for Jesuit Education.* Boston: Institute for Advanced Jesuit Studies, 2005.

Polanco, Juan de. Letters and instructions, December 1, 1551. In *Monumenta Ignatiana. Sancti Ignatti de Loyola Societatis Jesu fundatoris epistolae et instuctiones,* vol. 4 [original in Spanish], S.J. Madrid: Society of Jesus, 1906.

Ribadeneira, Petrus de. Letter to King Philip II of Spain. In Monumenta paedagogica Societatis Jesu, vol. 1, edited by Lazlo Lukács [original in Spanish], S.J. Rome: IHSI, 1965.

Roothaan, Jan. Cover Letter to the *Ratio Studiorum* of 1832. Translated by Claude Pavur, S.J. Rome: IHSI.

Secretariat for Education Society of Jesus. *Jesuit Education Aims to Human Education: Men and Women of Conscience, Competence, Compassion, and Commitment.* Rome, 2015.

Index